# SSAT* & ISEE†

## For Private and Independent School Admissions

## 2015

Kaplan offers resources and options to help you prepare for the PSAT, SAT, ACT, AP exams, and other high-stakes exams. Go to www.kaptest.com or scan this code below with your phone (you will need to download a QR code reader) for free events and promotions.

snap.vu/m87n

# SSAT* & ISEE†

## For Private and Independent School Admissions

## 2015

by Joanna Cohen, EdM; Darcy L. Galane, JD;
Simone Zamore Curbelo, EdM; and the Staff of
Kaplan Publishing

PUBLISHING

New York

# Table of Contents

# A NOTE TO STUDENTS: GETTING STARTED

Kaplan's experience shows that the best SSAT scores result from active and thorough preparation. We'll give you direction and focus for your training. We'll teach you the specific skills that the test demands as well as how to use the most effective Kaplan test-taking strategies. We'll train you to achieve peak performance on Test Day, but your effort is crucial to your success. The more time and effort you spend in preparing for the SSAT, the higher the score you'll earn. In your hands, you have the best test prep available for the SSAT and ISEE, the admissions tests for private and independent schools.

This book covers *all levels* of these tests (grades 3–11).

---

**SSAT**

- *Upper Level* (for students currently in grades 8–11)
- *Middle Level* (for students currently in grades 5–7)
- *Elementary Level* (for students currently in grades 3–4)

**ISEE**

- *Upper-level* (for students currently in grades 8–11)
- *Middle-level* (for students currently in grades 6 and 7)
- *Lower-level* (for students currently in grades 4 and 5)

---

Since this book covers all levels of the SSAT and ISEE, you will understandably find certain questions too difficult. While you should try your best to solve all of the questions, do not be discouraged if you cannot. Other students in your age group will find these hard to solve as well. Keeping in mind that your test will be scored in relation to other students your age should help relieve some pressure.

Not every topic covered in this book appears on every test level. Quantitative Comparisons questions, for instance, do not appear on the Lower-level ISEE, though they do appear on the Upper and Middle levels. (They do not appear at all on the SSAT.) At the beginning of each chapter, there is a note indicating what level or test applies to that topic. Keep an eye out for these notes to guide you in your preparation and skip those chapters that are not relevant.

Ideally, you should take a couple of months to work through this book. That gives you enough time before test day to absorb the strategies thoroughly so that they become second nature during practice and on Test Day. Do just two or three chapters a week and let the material sink in slowly.

If you don't have a few months for review, however, don't freak out: By working through a chapter or two every day, you can finish this book in a couple of weeks.

Here's how you should approach the review:

1. Read through each chapter completely, learning from the examples and trying the practice questions. Don't just read them: Work through them first as much as you can, before reading the explanation. Remember: Know the context, the strategies, and the test's structure.

2. Read the stress management section in chapter 6 to set the stage for your training and testing success.

3. Take the practice tests for your level under strictly timed conditions. Score your test, find out where you need help, and then review the appropriate chapters.

4. Give yourself a day of rest right before the real exam.

Don't hesitate to take some time off from your SSAT/ISEE preparation when you need to.

**Q. It's two days before the SSAT/ISEE and I'm clueless. What I do?**

**A.** First of all, don't panic. If you have only a day or two to prepare, then you won't be able to prepare thoroughly. But that doesn't mean you should give up. There's a lot you can do. First and foremost, get familiar with the test. And if you don't do anything else, take a full-length practice test under reasonably testlike conditions. When you have finished that, check your answers to see what you didn't get right.

**Q: The test is tomorrow. Should I stay up all night studying geometry formulas?**

**A:** The best thing to do now is to stay calm. Read chapter 15 to find out the best way to survive—and thrive—on Test Day.

**Q: I don't feel confident. Should I just guess?**

**A:** That depends on whether you're taking the SSAT or the ISEE. The SSAT does penalize you for wrong answers (one-quarter of a point), so you want to be careful, but that doesn't mean you should never guess. If you can rule out at least one answer choice, preferably two, you should guess because you have better odds at guessing correctly. Also, on questions that appear early in a section, more obvious answers will tend to be correct, so you can guess more confidently on those questions. If you're taking the ISEE, you should ALWAYS guess since there's no wrong-answer penalty.

**Q: What's the most important thing I can do to get ready quickly?**

In addition to basic math and verbal skills, the SSAT/ISEE mainly tests your ability to take the test. So the most important thing you can do is to familiarize yourself with the directions, the question types, the answer grid, and the overall structure. Read everything carefully—many mistakes are the result of simply not reading thoroughly.

**Q. So it's okay to panic, right?**

**A.** No! No matter how prepared you are for the test, stress will hurt your performance, and it's really no fun. Stay confident and don't cram. So…breathe, stay calm, and remember: It's just a test.

# A NOTE TO PARENTS

Congratulations! By purchasing this book, you have taken the first step toward helping your son or daughter prepare for the SSAT or ISEE, the required admissions tests for independent schools. Each school has a different requirement policy for admission exams, so check with your schools of interest to find out which test your child should take. These days, many schools accept either test.

## How can I help my child prepare for the exam?

This book covers all levels of the SSAT and ISEE: Upper, Middle, and Lower/Elementary. If your son or daughter is applying to private high school, chances are that he or she already studies well alone. Check on progress regularly by proctoring practice tests as the test date nears.

If your child is at the Middle or Lower level, you may need to get more involved. Sit down together and write out a study plan. To start, your child should take a practice exam under timed conditions as a diagnostic.

Then, once you have identified the areas that need focus, set up specific study activities.

## What do the scores mean?

Scores are designed to measure a student's potential performance in private school—not to measure intelligence.

Each level of the test encompasses more than one grade level, but students are graded only against others in their own grade.

## What should I know about Test Day?

A few things you will want to know about Test Day:

- During the test, your child must remember to mark his or her current grade level on the answer sheet, not the grade he or she will be entering next year.
- No calculators, cell phones, electronic alarm watches, or books will be permitted in the test room.
- Testing normally begins at 9:00 A.M., so students should arrive at the test center by 8:15–8:30 A.M.
- It is possible to get a good score even if some questions are left blank. Many students leave a few questions unanswered.

# HOW DO I USE THIS BOOK?

| | SSAT | ISEE |
|---|---|---|
| **All Levels** **(Grades 4–11)** | • Chapters 1– 2<br>• Chapters 6–15<br>• Chapters 24–26 | • Chapters 3–5<br>• Chapters 6–15<br>• Chapters 24–26 |
| **Lower/Elementary Level** **(Grades 4–7)** | • Chapter 18/Practice Test<br><br>• Page 423: Scoring the Elementary-Level SSAT Practice Test | • Chapter 22/Practice Test<br><br>• Page 575: Scoring Your ISEE Practice Test |
| **Middle Level** **(Grades 6–7)** | • Chapter 16/Practice Test<br>• Chapter 17/Practice Test | • Chapter 20/Practice Test<br>• Chapter 21/Practice Test |
| **Upper Level** **(Grades 8–11)** | • Page 422: Scoring Upper- and Middle-Level SSAT Practice Tests | • Page 575: Scoring Your ISEE Practice Test |

# ABOUT THE AUTHORS

**Joanna Cohen** received her BS in Human Development and Family Studies from Cornell University and her EdM from Harvard University. As an educator, she has taught, conducted research, and written educational materials for students and teachers. Until recently, Ms. Cohen was manager of Kaplan's Pre-College Curriculum.

**Darcy L. Galane** is the Associate Director of Pre-College Curriculum at Kaplan's Corporate Office. She received a BA from UCLA and began teaching SAT and LSAT classes for Kaplan while earning her JD at the University of Connecticut School of Law. Having taught and written curriculum for most of Kaplan's courses, Ms. Galane has helped thousands of students to raise their scores on standardized tests.

**Simone Zamore Curbelo** is a Kaplan Instructor who scored in the 99th percentile on the SAT, ACT, and GRE. She holds a bachelor's degree in English from Princeton University, with certificates in Theater and Dance, and a master's degree in education from Harvard University. For nearly 15 years, she has worked as a teacher and tutor for Kaplan, instructing students on the SAT, ACT, SSAT, ISEE, and SHSAT; providing academic subject tutoring; and assisting with the college application process. She has guided students to achieve admission to the nation's best private schools and most prestigious colleges, including Ivy Leagues and top international universities. Over the years, Simone has also created training curriculum, professionally trained new tutors, and managed their professional development. As a curriculum designer for Kaplan, she managed product development for the Pre-College national team for several years. She is honored to continue working with students to achieve their goals toward higher education.

# AVAILABLE ONLINE

## FOR ANY TEST CHANGES OR LATE-BREAKING DEVELOPMENTS

### kaptest.com/publishing

The material in this book is up-to-date at the time of publication. However, the test makers may have instituted changes in the test after this book was published. Be sure to carefully read the materials you receive when you register for the test. If there are any important late-breaking developments—or any changes or corrections to the Kaplan test preparation materials in this book—we will post that information online at **kaptest.com/publishing**.

For customer service, please contact us at **booksupport@kaplan.com**.

# Part One

# SSAT WORKSHOP

# CHAPTER 1: INSIDE THE SSAT

## THE SSAT EXAM

The SSAT (Secondary School Admission Test) is a required entrance exam at many independent schools throughout the United States. The test, created and administered by the Secondary School Admission Test Board in Princeton, New Jersey, is a multiple-choice exam that consists of Verbal, Reading Comprehension, and Quantitative (Math) sections. In addition, there is a writing sample in which you respond to a topic sentence. This essay is not graded but is submitted along with your multiple-choice score report to the schools to which you have applied. The Middle and Upper Level exams will also contain an experimental section of problems that will not be scored.

There are three levels of the SSAT, one for Upper Level students, one for Middle Level students, and one for Elementary Level students.

- Upper Level (for students currently in grades 8–11)
- Middle Level (for students currently in grades 5–7)
- Elementary Level (for all students currently in grades 3–4)

Following is a breakdown of the tests.

| Section | Elementary Level | Time Allowed |
|---|---|---|
| Math I | 30 questions | 30 minutes |
| Verbal | 30 questions | 20 minutes |
| Break | | 15 minutes |
| Reading | 28 questions | 30 minutes |
| Essay* | One writing prompt | 15 minutes |
| Total | 89 questions | 110 minutes |

| Section | Middle Level | Upper Level | Time Allowed |
|---|---|---|---|
| Essay* | One writing prompt | | 25 minutes |
| Break | | | 5 minutes |
| Math I | 25 questions | 25 questions | 30 minutes |
| Reading | 40 questions | 40 questions | 40 minutes |
| Break | | | 10 minutes |
| Verbal | 60 questions | 60 questions | 30 minutes |
| Math II | 25 questions | 25 questions | 30 minutes |
| Experimental | 16 questions | 16 questions | 15 minutes |
| Total | 167 questions | 167 questions | 3 hours, 5 minutes |

\* The essay will not be scored, nor will it be included with your home report. It will be sent to the schools to which you are applying.

- All questions have five answer choices, (A) through (E).

- You are not permitted to use calculators, dictionaries, tablets, or rulers. Cell phones and electronic watches are not allowed.

- Bring your own pencils and erasers; they will not be provided. Neither mechanical pencils nor pens will be allowed.

## SCORING

The first thing you might notice with respect to grades is that students from other class years are taking the same test as you. Not to worry! You are graded according to your age. In other words, if you're in 9th grade, you aren't expected to get as many questions right as someone in 11th grade, even though you take the same test. One note of caution: You are scored according to the grade level you report on the answer sheet on Test Day. Be sure to indicate your current grade level, not the grade for which you are applying.

Given this fact, you can expect to see questions on the test that may be too hard for you. Just remember, you don't need to get every question right to get a great score.

**Keep moving.** Timing is extremely tight on the SSAT, so it's critical that you spend your time working on questions that you know you can solve without too much difficulty. Give yourself a time limit for each question, and move on once you reach that limit, even if you haven't answered the question.

**Be flexible.** You don't have to answer the questions in the order they're presented to you. If a particular question type is your strength, get points under your belt by tackling those questions first. For the same reason, don't panic when you encounter a tough question. If it's too hard, skip it. You may be able to return to it later, if you reach the end of the section before time is called.

**Be careful how you bubble.** Don't lose points on Test Day by bubbling in your correct answers in the wrong place! Here are some tips:

- Circle your chosen answer in the test booklet.
- Enter your answers on the grid five at a time.
- At the end of each section, check your gridded answers against the circled answers in your test booklet.

Your score report will include the following:

**Raw scores,** which is the number that results from a calculation of your right, wrong, and omitted answers. To calculate your Middle/Upper Level raw score, the formula is:

$$\# \text{ Correct} - \frac{1}{4} \# \text{ Incorrect}$$

Each correct answer increases your raw score by 1 point. Each incorrect answer decreases your raw score by a fraction of a point. An easier question is worth the same as a difficult question. Don't waste precious test time agonizing over a difficult question (that you may still not get right) when you could be answering five easier questions correctly.

To calculate your Elementary Level raw score, simply add the number of correct answers. There is no wrong answer penalty for wrong or omitted answers.

Depending on the test you take, the same raw score from one test administration can be converted to different scaled scores and different corresponding percentiles.

Scaled scores are provided for three sections: Verbal, Quantitative (Math), and Reading.

Upper Level Score Range: 500–800

Middle Level Score Range: 440–710

Elementary Level Score Range: 300–600

In addition to **scaled scores** for Verbal, Math, and Reading, there is a total scaled score.

There are **percentile ranks** for each category. These compare your scores to those of others who have taken the SSAT in the past three years. You are also provided an Estimated National Percentile, which describes how many students received a lower score than you did.

**Personal Score Ranges** are spectrums of measurement for each subject area. A student's score can usually be located within the center of this range.

Regarding points for each question, each correct answer earns one point. For every wrong answer, one-fourth of a point is deducted, though for questions left blank, nothing is deducted.

**How the Wrong Answer Penalty Works**

1. ● Ⓑ Ⓒ Ⓓ Ⓔ ✗ $-\frac{1}{4}$
2. ● Ⓑ Ⓒ Ⓓ Ⓔ ✗ $-\frac{1}{4}$
3. ● Ⓑ Ⓒ Ⓓ Ⓔ ✗ $-\frac{1}{4}$
4. ● Ⓑ Ⓒ Ⓓ Ⓔ ✗ $-\frac{1}{4}$
5. ● Ⓑ Ⓒ Ⓓ Ⓔ ✓ $+1$
$= 0$

If you guess randomly, the points you lose for incorrect answers will likely cancel out the points you get for correct answers. However, if you can eliminate at least one wrong answer, your odds of guessing correctly increase.

*Bottom line: If you can eliminate at least one answer choice, it is in your best interest to guess.*

**When should you guess?** Guess when (and only when) you can eliminate at least one of the wrong answer choices. Random guessing won't increase your score, but strategic guessing when you can eliminate wrong answer choices can be very helpful.

In the Lower and Upper Level SSAT tests, there will be one additional 25-minute section that will contain either critical reading, mathematics or writing multiple-choice questions. This section does not count towards your score; however, you will not know which section is unscored. Therefore, treat every section as if it counts. This experimental section is an opportunity for the exam creators to try out new questions that function as content for future tests.

Scores are mailed to you and your school two to three weeks after you take the test. Make sure you test early enough in the year that schools will receive your scores by application deadlines. If you feel that you have not tested well after you leave the test, you have the option of canceling your score. To do so, you must send your request to SSAT by mail, fax, or email. This request must be received no later than the Tuesday after Test Day. If you cancel them, your canceled scores will not be sent to any of your designated score recipients.

# HOW TO REGISTER

There are two different administrations of the SSAT: Standard and Flex test. Flex tests are proctored by educational consultants or schools at times that can be more convenient for busy students' schedules and are subject to an administration fee. Standard tests are given eight times during the academic year: October, November, December, January, February, March, April, and June. While most students choose a Standard test option, a Flex test is helpful for students who are unable to meet the eight scheduled Standard times. However, a student can only take one Flex test between August and July. You may register online, by fax, or by mail. For more information, go to the official test site at **ssat.org**.

| | |
|---|---|
| Phone: | (609) 683-4440 |
| Email: | info@ssat.org |
| Fax: | 800-442-7728 (Domestic) or (609) 683-4507 (International) |
| Mail: | SSATB |
| | CN 5339 |
| | Princeton, NJ 08543 |

# CHAPTER 2: SSAT-SPECIFIC VERBAL WORKOUT: ANALOGIES

Analogies appear *only on the SSAT*. If you are not taking the SSAT, you should skip this section.

Analogies may seem frightening because they look pretty weird at first glance. You'll feel better about them as soon as you realize that you speak and think in analogies all the time. Anytime you say, "My sister is like a slug," you're drawing an analogy between your sister and slugs—perhaps your sister is as gross as a slug, or maybe she's as slow as a slug getting out of bed in the morning. That may not be the kind of relationship that will appear on your test, but the thinking is the same.

Once you become familiar with their format, you'll find that Analogy questions are pretty straightforward and very predictable. In fact, prepping often gains you more points on Analogies than on any other Verbal question type. With practice, you can learn to get them right even when you don't know all of the vocabulary words involved.

## WORKBOOK ACTIVITY

Fill in the blanks, choosing the words from the list that best complete each sentence. You'll use each word exactly once.

modesty
singer
novice
raft
chorus
glide

1. Kite is to _____ as _____ is to float.

2. _____ is to experience as braggart is to _____.

3. Instrumentalist is to orchestra as _____ is to _____.

## THE FORMAT

The instructions will tell you to select the pair of words that is *related in the same way* as the two words in the beginning of the question. Those two words are called the *stem words*. SSAT Analogies test your ability to determine relationships between words. These relationships are called *bridges*. The SSAT tests certain specific relationships time and time again. These are called *classic bridges*.

Consider the example from the Workbook Activity:

Instrumentalist is to orchestra as _____*singer*_____ is to _____*chorus*_____ .

How are these things similar? How would you describe the relationship between the words in each pair?

One classic bridge is **group**: one word is a part or element of the other word. Try to use this classic bridge on a test-like question.

1. Flake is to snow as
    (A) storm is to hail.
    (B) drop is to rain.
    (C) field is to wheat.
    (D) stack is to hay.
    (E) cloud is to fog.

In this example, the answer is (B). A flake is a small unit of snow, just as a drop is a small unit of rain.

Another classic bridge is **characteristic**: one word describes what the other word is, has, uses, causes, or does. You saw an example of this in the Workbook Activity:

Kite is to _____*glide*_____ as _____*raft*_____ is to float.

Let's look at one final relationship, again using a sentence from the Workbook Activity:

_____*Novice*_____ is to experience as braggart is to _____*modesty*_____ .

In this example, the classic bridge is **lack**: one word describes what the other word lacks, cannot be, or does not do.

On Test Day, you can find the correct answer by putting relationships, like these classic ones, in your own words. This crucial skill is the first step in the Kaplan 3-Step Method, which will help you handle Analogy questions, even the toughest ones. This way, you can approach every question systematically rather than just using instinct. Let's see how it works.

# KAPLAN 3-STEP METHOD FOR ANALOGIES

**Step 1.** Build a bridge.

**Step 2.** Plug in the answer choices.

**Step 3.** Adjust your bridge if necessary.

Remember, a bridge expresses the relationship between the words in the stem pair, so you can find the correct answer quickly and avoid wrong-answer traps. Let's take a closer look to see how it works.

## STEP 1: BUILD A BRIDGE

In every Analogy question, there's a strong, definite connection between the two stem words. Your task is to identify this relationship and then look for a similar relationship among the answer pairs.

What's a strong, definite relationship?

- The words *library* and *book* have a strong, definite connection. A library is defined as a place where books are kept. *Library is to book as* could be a question stem.

- The words *library* and *child* do not have a strong, definite connection. A child may or may not have anything to do with a library, and vice versa. *Library is to child* would never be a question stem.

A bridge is a short sentence that relates the two words in the stem, and every pair of stem words will have a strong bridge that links them.

## STEP 2: PLUG IN THE ANSWER CHOICES

You figured out how the words *flake* and *snow* are related. Now you need to determine which answer choice relates words in the same way. Don't just rely on your feeling about the words unless you don't know the vocabulary (more on that later). Go through the choices systematically, building bridges between each word pair as you go. Here's how it would work:

If a *flake* is a small unit of *snow*, then . . .
(A) a *storm* is a small unit of *hail*
(B) a *drop* is a small unit of *rain*
(C) a *field* is a small unit of *wheat*
(D) a *stack* is a small unit of *hay*
(E) a *cloud* is a small unit of *fog*

Going through the choices, you can see that only one of them makes sense, (B). At this point, you would be done.

## STEP 3: ADJUST YOUR BRIDGE IF NECESSARY

If your bridge is very specific, you won't need to go to step 3, but sometimes you will. For example, if you had the question:

Fish is to gill as
(A) oyster is to shell
(B) penguin is to wing
(C) whale is to flipper
(D) mammal is to lung
(E) dolphin is to flipper

Let's say you made the bridge "A fish has a gill." Then you went to the choices and plugged in that bridge:

(A) An oyster has a shell.
(B) A penguin has a wing.
(C) A whale has a tail.
(D) A mammal has a lung.
(E) A dolphin has a flipper.

Every choice fits! In this case, the bridge was too general, so you'll need to adjust your bridge.

What would a good adjustment be? Try to articulate to yourself the most specific relationship between the words, because the more specific your bridge is, the fewer choices will match it. A good bridge for this pair might be: "A fish uses a gill to breathe." Now try plugging the bridge into the answer choices.

(A) An oyster uses a shell to breathe.
(B) A penguin uses a wing to breathe.
(C) A whale uses a tail to breathe.
(D) A mammal uses a lung to breathe.
(E) A dolphin uses a flipper to breathe.

It should now be easier to see the correct answer, (D), a mammal uses a lung to breathe.

# STRONG BRIDGES AND WEAK BRIDGES

Just to make sure you have your strong and weak bridges straight, try the following exercise. For each phrase, decide whether there is a strong relationship or a weak one.

1. Dog is to canine _____

2. Dog is to friendly _____

3. Dog is to kennel _____

4. Dog is to mammal _____

5. Dog is to cat _____

6. Dog is to paw _____

7. Dog is to puppy _____

8. Dog is to hound _____

9. Dog is to bark _____

10. Dog is to biscuit _____

## ANSWERS TO STRONG/WEAK BRIDGES

| | |
|---|---|
| 1. strong | 6. strong |
| 2. weak | 7. strong |
| 3. strong | 8. strong |
| 4. strong | 9. strong |
| 5. weak | 10. weak |

# SIX CLASSIC BRIDGES

There are six classic bridges that appear on the SSAT over and over again. By getting to know these bridges, you'll be able to identify them quickly, saving yourself a lot of time as you go through Analogy questions.

## BRIDGE TYPE 1: CHARACTER

**One word characterizes the other.**
Quarrelsome is to argue (Someone quarrelsome tends to argue.)

## BRIDGE TYPE 2: LACK

**One word describes what someone or something is *not*.**
Coward is to bravery (A coward lacks bravery.)

## BRIDGE TYPE 3: FUNCTION

**One word names an object; the other word defines its function.**
Scissors is to cut (Scissors are used to cut.)

## BRIDGE TYPE 4: DEGREE

**One word is a greater or lesser degree of the other word.**
Deafening is to loud (Something deafening is extremely loud.)

## BRIDGE TYPE 5: EXAMPLE

**One word is an example of the other word.**
Measles is to disease (Measles is a type of disease.)

## BRIDGE TYPE 6: GROUP

**One word is made up of several of the other word.**
Forest is to trees (A forest is made up of many trees.)

---

**I AM, BY DEFINITION, CONFUSED**

“ When making a bridge, a good rule of thumb is to relate the words in such a way that you'd be able to insert the phrase *by definition* and the relationship would hold true. A poodle, by definition, is a type of dog. However, a poodle does not, by definition, have a collar. If you can't use *by definition* in the sentence to relate the stem words, your bridge isn't strong and it needs to be reworked. ”

# PREDICTING ON THREE-TERM ANALOGIES

Some Analogies will have three terms in the stem and only one word in each answer choice. For example:

Delight is to grin as dismay is to
(A) frown
(B) smile
(C) shrug
(D) stare
(E) giggle

Three-term Analogies aren't very different from two-term Analogies. The key difference is that you need to predict your answer *before* you look at the answer choices. Otherwise, the choices won't make much sense to you! Here's how it works.

First, make your bridge:

A grin shows delight and a —— shows dismay.

Now predict your answer. What might show *dismay*? *Tears,* perhaps, or a *frown.* Look at the answer choices. At this point, the question should be easier than a two-term Analogy, because you already have one of the two words in the answer.

Does a *frown* show dismay?
Does a *smile* show dismay?
Does a *shrug* show dismay?
Does a *stare* show dismay?
Does a *giggle* show dismay?

As you'll see, (A) is the answer: A frown shows dismay. That makes a lot of sense. Can you see how much harder this would have been if you hadn't gone through the steps of building a bridge and predicting the answer? You would likely be staring blankly at five words. Always predict your answer on three-term Analogies, and you'll whiz through them in no time.

Practice your skills of prediction on these stems:

1. Thicket is to bush as grove is to _____.

2. Mason is to brick as carpenter is to _____.

3. Enthusiast is to apathy as miser is to _____.

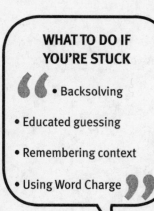

**WHAT TO DO IF YOU'RE STUCK**

" • Backsolving

• Educated guessing

• Remembering context

• Using Word Charge "

Now let's see how well you did on predicting:

1. Thicket is to bush as grove is to *tree*.

2. Mason is to brick as carpenter is to *wood*.

3. Enthusiast is to apathy as miser is to *generosity*.

Even with your arsenal of tools, you may run into Analogy questions where you don't know what to do. Perhaps you won't know what a word in the question stem means or how the words relate to one another. What should you do?

There are a few strategies that will really up your chances of getting the question right, even if you're stuck. How cool is that?

## BACKSOLVING

What is Backsolving? It may sound like an obscure form of chiropractic medicine, but it's actually just a nifty way of approaching Analogies when you can't answer them directly. So how does it work?

Basically, you skip right past the question stem and head straight for the answer choices. You may be wondering, "How you can figure out the answer without knowing what the question is asking?" Well, you can't necessarily figure out the answer right away, but you can start to eliminate *clearly* wrong answer choices, leaving fewer options. When you rule out choices that you know can't be right, the odds are better that you'll pick the right choice from what's left.

**BOTH ARE . . . WRONG!**

" Watch out for the *Both Are* trap, seen in choice (A) in the screwdriver example: Both *animal* and *plant* are part of a larger group, but there's no connection, by definition, between the words themselves. Bread and bananas are both types of food, but what exactly is their relationship? Bananas aren't a type of bread, a lack of bread, or a function of bread. Watch out for this trap, particularly on harder Analogy questions. "

Screwdriver is to tool as
(A)  animal is to plant
(B)  garden is to bed
(C)  banana is to bread
(D)  tree is to leaf
(E)  rose is to flower

Even if you didn't know that a screwdriver is a type of tool, what could you rule out? Well, in (A), there's no logical connection between animal and plant, except that they're both living things. Choice (B), garden is to bed, also sounds somewhat off. You could make the argument that a garden has a bed, but does it have to? What about a hanging garden or a rock garden? You could rule out (B) since it has a weak bridge.

By eliminating even one illogical answer choice, you'll narrow down your choices and have a better chance of getting the question right. Always keep your eye out for *Both Are* traps and *Weak Bridges* as you work through the Analogy section, and you'll rack up lots of points on even the toughest questions.

# GUESSING

What if you reach the point where you can't figure out the bridge for the stem words, you can't rule out wrong answer choices, and you want to cry? Well, first of all, don't cry. It's a waste of time and it makes it difficult to read the questions. You have a few options.

## TECHNIQUE 1: MAKE AN EDUCATED GUESS

You know the six classic bridges. You know they show up often on Analogy questions.
So even if you don't know the exact definition of one (or both!) words, you could make an educated guess about the bridge. For example, say you saw this stem:

> Word is to philologist as
>
> (A) ————
> (B) ————
> (C) ————
> (D) ————
> (E) ————

What might the bridge be? Well, a *philologist* sounds like a type of person (since it ends in *-ologist*), and a *word* is a thing, so maybe a philologist does something with words. Philologist is a tricky word, but you could make a great guess by saying that a philologist studies words, which is exactly right!

## TECHNIQUE 2: REMEMBER THE CONTEXT

Sometimes a word sounds familiar, but you can't remember why. If that happens, try to think of a place where you may have heard it before. Putting words into context makes it easier to determine their meaning. For example:

> Vote is to suffrage as
>
> (A) ————
> (B) ————
> (C) ————
> (D) ————
> (E) ————

What does *suffrage* mean? Have you heard of the suffrage movement? Or the suffragists? Think about the word *suffrage* in the context of *voting*. What could the words have to do with each other? Well, suffrage is the right to vote, and the movement to give women the right to vote at the beginning of the 20th century was commonly known as the Suffrage Movement. Just looking at the word *suffrage* in isolation might have left you scratching your head, but putting it in context with the concept of voting could get you back on track and help you home in on the right answer.

## TECHNIQUE 3: USE WORD CHARGE

Some words give you the feeling that they're either positive or negative. Use this sense to help you figure out the bridge between words in the stem when you don't actually know what one of them means—or both!

Decide whether the following words are positive or negative:

1.  Cruel (+, –) is to clemency (+, –) as
2.  Boorish (+, –) is to polite (+, –) as
3.  Animated (+, –) is to ecstatic (+, –) as
4.  Annoyed (+, –) is to enraged (+, –) as

So how does Word Charge help you find the right answer? Once you determine the charge of the words in the stem pair, you can look for words in the answer choices that have the same charge relationship. When both words in the stem are either positive or negative, both words in the correct answer choice will have the same charge, too, though it may be the opposite charge from the words in the stem. If one stem word is positive and the other is negative, chances are that the right answer will have the same relationship.

So what charge does each word above have?

1.  (–, +)
2.  (–, +)
3.  (+, +)
4.  (–, –)

# PRACTICE QUESTIONS

1. Circumference is to circle as
   (A) diameter is to sphere
   (B) height is to width
   (C) side is to hexagon
   (D) perimeter is to square
   (E) round is to oval

2. Write is to paper as paint is to
   (A) board
   (B) canvas
   (C) brush
   (D) palette
   (E) can

3. Collar is to shirt as
   (A) toe is to shoe
   (B) cuff is to trousers
   (C) waist is to belt
   (D) hat is to head
   (E) zipper is to button

4. Hysteria is to control as
   (A) joke is to laughter
   (B) feeling is to emotion
   (C) absurdity is to sense
   (D) calm is to serenity
   (E) passion is to insanity

5. Square is to cube as
   (A) dot is to point
   (B) angle is to triangle
   (C) rectangle is to parallelogram
   (D) hexagon is to octagon
   (E) circle is to sphere

6. Shark is to aquatic as
   (A) world is to hungry
   (B) camel is to terrestrial
   (C) bird is to winged
   (D) bat is to blind
   (E) pig is to hairless

7. Admonish is to mild as castigate is to
   (A) tepid
   (B) sweet
   (C) unbeatable
   (D) uncertain
   (E) harsh

8. Abrupt is to gradual as
   (A) corrupt is to virtuous
   (B) stirring is to sudden
   (C) sneaky is to criminal
   (D) remarkable is to alarming
   (E) conspicuous is to extreme

9. Stanza is to poem as
   (A) rhythm is to beat
   (B) verse is to word
   (C) movement is to symphony
   (D) play is to theater
   (E) column is to journal

10. Violin is to string as
    (A) harp is to angelic
    (B) drum is to stick
    (C) score is to music
    (D) oboe is to reed
    (E) bass is to large

11. Canter is to horse as
    (A) hop is to rabbit
    (B) halt is to pony
    (C) hunt is to lion
    (D) beg is to dog
    (E) chew is to cow

12. Baseball is to game as
    (A) hurricane is to storm
    (B) overcast is to cloud
    (C) stadium is to sport
    (D) wind is to tornado
    (E) conflict is to violence

13. Rigid is to bend as
    (A) tremulous is to sway
    (B) incomprehensible is to think
    (C) immortal is to die
    (D) lazy is to perspire
    (E) stiff is to divide

14. Canine is to wolf as feline is to
    (A) panther
    (B) pig
    (C) monkey
    (D) rat
    (E) vulture

15. Rind is to melon as
    (A) skin is to mammal
    (B) armor is to shield
    (C) shell is to claw
    (D) peel is to core
    (E) pod is to vine

16. Mile is to length as
    (A) acre is to land
    (B) inch is to foot
    (C) kilometer is to race
    (D) yard is to fabric
    (E) fathom is to depth

17. Truthful is to dishonest as arid is to
    (A) sublime
    (B) aloof
    (C) innocent
    (D) moist
    (E) clear

18. Tarnish is to silver as
    (A) break is to glass
    (B) dirt is to car
    (C) rust is to iron
    (D) dull is to wax
    (E) dust is to wood

19. Delay is to hasten as
    (A) misunderstand is to dislike
    (B) undermine is to improve
    (C) sink is to descend
    (D) remove is to indict
    (E) facilitate is to impede

20. Think is to daydream as walk is to
    (A) stagger
    (B) crawl
    (C) meander
    (D) run
    (E) prance

21. Gram is to ounce as
    (A) Celsius is to temperature
    (B) minute is to year
    (C) meter is to yard
    (D) ton is to pound
    (E) dollar is to cent

22. Veil is to bride as
    (A) hat is to pitcher
    (B) helmet is to soldier
    (C) crown is to monarch
    (D) apron is to gourmet
    (E) goggles is to scientist

23. Anomalous is to standard as
    (A) rude is to kind
    (B) demonstrative is to impassive
    (C) profound is to brief
    (D) taxing is to exhausting
    (E) stoic is to urbane

24. Wing is to bird as
    (A) scale is to fish
    (B) rudder is to canoe
    (C) foot is to human
    (D) talon is to raptor
    (E) shell is to tortoise

25. Fight is to surrender as resist is to
    (A) affect
    (B) triumph
    (C) evade
    (D) submit
    (E) deny

26. Defilement is to shrine as
    (A) disrespect is to fool
    (B) vilification is to traitor
    (C) execution is to dungeon
    (D) breech is to contract
    (E) ostracism is to politician

27. Restaurant is to pasture as
    (A) fountain is to trough
    (B) meal is to feed
    (C) cafeteria is to lavatory
    (D) kitchen is to dining room
    (E) stable is to barracks

28. Necessity is to luxury as oxygen is to
    (A) water
    (B) food
    (C) sleep
    (D) shelter
    (E) wine

29. Idealistic is to quixotic as
    (A) crazy is to insane
    (B) smart is to intelligent
    (C) jaded is to cynical
    (D) resolute is to stubborn
    (E) weak is to forceful

30. Water is to froth as
    (A) broth is to vegetables
    (B) shower is to steam
    (C) juice is to blender
    (D) oil is to gasoline
    (E) cream is to butter

31. Fish is to school as
    (A) cow is to cattle
    (B) crop is to farm
    (C) gaggle is to geese
    (D) lion is to pride
    (E) general is to army

32. Silo is to grain as
    (A) ramp is to boat
    (B) arsenal is to munitions
    (C) gate is to horse
    (D) student is to school
    (E) meat is to ice

33. Aquarium is to fish as arboretum is to
    (A) elephant
    (B) horse
    (C) flower
    (D) tree
    (E) dog

34. Cadet is to soldier as
    (A) apprentice is to craftsman
    (B) private is to army
    (C) yeoman is to sailor
    (D) rookie is to athlete
    (E) lawyer is to judge

35. Passive is to aggressive as
    (A) simple is to complex
    (B) meek is to overbearing
    (C) shy is to garrulous
    (D) bellicose is to amiable
    (E) terrified is to composed

36. Dime is to coin as almond is to
    (A) fruit
    (B) delicacy
    (C) food
    (D) bush
    (E) nut

37. Ice is to skating as
    (A) highway is to driving
    (B) ballroom is to dancing
    (C) ring is to boxing
    (D) felt is to billiards
    (E) water is to diving

38. Paranoid is to suspicious as
    (A) distraught is to perturbed
    (B) urban is to rural
    (C) wealthy is to affluent
    (D) jubilant is to ecstatic
    (E) melancholy is to aloof

39. Fireman is to extinguish as
    (A) principal is to teach
    (B) vendor is to sell
    (C) policeman is to warn
    (D) worker is to retire
    (E) accountant is to save

40. Pearl is to oyster as
    (A) silk is to thread
    (B) marble is to statue
    (C) web is to spider
    (D) ivory is to elephant
    (E) calcium is to bone

41. Chandler is to wax as
    (A) cooper is to barrel
    (B) wheelwright is to wheel
    (C) baker is to bread
    (D) carpenter is to wood
    (E) blacksmith is to horseshoe

42. Gathering is to mob as
    (A) frenzy is to shark
    (B) stray is to cat
    (C) fire is to inferno
    (D) storm is to tempest
    (E) filibuster is to speech

43. Acre is to land as
    (A) luminosity is to space
    (B) piquant is to dish
    (C) fathom is to water
    (D) millimeter is to fluid
    (E) second is to velocity

44. Bison is to plains as kangaroo is to
    (A) savanna
    (B) desert
    (C) tundra
    (D) outback
    (E) forest

45. Grape is to vineyard as
    (A) pumpkin is to patch
    (B) cherry is to blossom
    (C) cabbage is to vine
    (D) milk is to dairy
    (E) potato is to orchard

46. Head is to neck as
    (A) arm is to leg
    (B) hand is to glove
    (C) foot is to ankle
    (D) finger is to toe
    (E) ear is to eye

47. Liquid is to gas as condensation is to
    (A) precipitation
    (B) evaporation
    (C) sublimation
    (D) freezing
    (E) crystallization

48. Authenticity is to verify as
    (A) skill is to jump
    (B) competence is to test
    (C) science is to reason
    (D) soundtrack is to compose
    (E) bliss is to uphold

49. Gap is to continuity as
    (A) intermission is to film
    (B) prosperity is to happiness
    (C) native is to tribal
    (D) mannequin is to display
    (E) destruction is to design

50. Wrist is to watch as
    (A) remote control is to button
    (B) wallet is to money
    (C) camper is to tent
    (D) skin is to muscle
    (E) torso is to shirt

51. Watt is to energy as
    (A) joule is to distance
    (B) crime is to civil unrest
    (C) string is to guitar
    (D) grade is to quality
    (E) stock market is to money

52. Mongoose is to mammal as
    (A) bush is to crustacean
    (B) sycamore is to tree
    (C) reptile is to flora
    (D) venom is to snake
    (E) fool is to human

53. Vassal is to king as
    (A) employee is to manager
    (B) financier is to accountant
    (C) stranger is to outsider
    (D) journeyman is to neophyte
    (E) infielder is to outfielder

54. Turtle is to shell as
    (A) lion is to roar
    (B) human is to house
    (C) letter is to mailbox
    (D) cola is to bottle
    (E) disk is to computer

55. Earth is to sun as
    (A) sun is to galaxy
    (B) wheel is to car
    (C) glove is to boot
    (D) fire is to inferno
    (E) moon is to Earth

56. Knife is to dull as
    (A) conceptualization is to execution
    (B) tire is to flat
    (C) hammer is to weak
    (D) torch is to burn
    (E) microphone is to static

57. Time is to control as
    (A) tiger is to cage
    (B) strength is to increase
    (C) falsehood is to substantiate
    (D) product is to import
    (E) fool is to follow

58. Shadow is to substantial as
    (A) book is to clever
    (B) forest is to wild
    (C) fire is to raging
    (D) machine is to alive
    (E) currency is to wealth

59. Fervent is to nonchalant as
    (A) crippled is to puissant
    (B) furnace is to heat
    (C) anger is to aggression
    (D) balmy is to torpid
    (E) rancid is to spoiled

60. Ship is to port as
    (A) card is to deck
    (B) leviathan is to ocean
    (C) turn is to game
    (D) flight is to destination
    (E) traveler is to hotel

61. Sketch is to painting as
    (A) dream is to reality
    (B) note is to symphony
    (C) design is to prototype
    (D) amoeba is to dog
    (E) birth is to death

62. Ornamented is to plain as
    (A) shovel is to spade
    (B) mural is to wall
    (C) philosophy is to questions
    (D) automobile is to bicycle
    (E) strong is to simple

63. Iron is to steel as
    (A) apathy is to interest
    (B) love is to silence
    (C) wheat is to bread
    (D) structure is to high-rise
    (E) truck is to van

64. Medicine is to illness as
    (A) might is to weakness
    (B) affliction is to malady
    (C) evidence is to vindication
    (D) food is to hunger
    (E) sail is to wind

65. Matriarch is to patriarch as
    (A) daughter is to father
    (B) girl is to boy
    (C) right is to wrong
    (D) male is to female
    (E) clan is to family

66. Hope is to optimism as despair is to
    (A) sadness
    (B) pessimism
    (C) desolation
    (D) skepticism
    (E) ostracism

67. Fireman is to fire as editor is to
    (A) newspaper
    (B) style
    (C) error
    (D) story
    (E) book

68. Glory is to accomplishment as obscurity is to
    (A) underachievement
    (B) pain
    (C) confusion
    (D) misanthropy
    (E) happiness

69. Conflict is to peace as
    (A) calm is to quiet
    (B) mobile is to stationary
    (C) chaos is to order
    (D) wave is to ripple
    (E) hurricane is to storm

70. Piano is to pianist as
    (A) flute is to flautist
    (B) piccolo is to percussionist
    (C) harpsichord is to harpist
    (D) rhythm is to guitarist
    (E) tenor is to vocalist

71. Punchline is to joke as
    (A) bookend is to shelf
    (B) word is to dictionary
    (C) moral is to fable
    (D) line is to play
    (E) equation is to math

72. Trust is to strut as
    (A) pompous is to bearing
    (B) rely is to liar
    (C) believe is to false
    (D) true is to brace
    (E) faith is to swagger

73. Quartz is to mineral as
    (A) grape is to vine
    (B) quadruped is to mammal
    (C) player is to team
    (D) squash is to vegetable
    (E) heat is to fire

74. Cow is to bull as
    (A) fox is to pup
    (B) gander is to duck
    (C) doe is to buck
    (D) nanny is to goat
    (E) lion is to lioness

75. Cleat is to skate as soccer is to
    (A) tennis
    (B) hockey
    (C) baseball
    (D) skiing
    (E) squash

76. Perimeter is to square as
    (A) chord is to cylinder
    (B) side is to polygon
    (C) degree is to angle
    (D) height is to pyramid
    (E) circumference is to circle

77. Brick is to wall as
    (A) house is to roof
    (B) mortar is to stone
    (C) pixel is to picture
    (D) car is to road
    (E) sand is to beach

78. Incensed is to calm as
    (A) hasty is to lenient
    (B) enraged is to sedate
    (C) tragic is to relaxed
    (D) fussy is to picky
    (E) furious is to angry

79. Speaker is to sound as
    (A) ocean is to water
    (B) projector is to light
    (C) speech is to voice
    (D) orator is to volume
    (E) spray is to geyser

80. Cheese is to milk as
    (A) churn is to butter
    (B) juice is to squeeze
    (C) bread is to grain
    (D) bake is to oven
    (E) apple is to pie

81. City is to sport as Chicago is to
    (A) game
    (B) exercise
    (C) ball
    (D) athlete
    (E) tennis

82. Flower is to sour as
    (A) fable is to table
    (B) morrow is to sorrow
    (C) anemone is to lemony
    (D) flavor is to quaver
    (E) rose is to sweet

83. Raise is to lower as
    (A) port is to starboard
    (B) upward is to onward
    (C) sprint is to dash
    (D) advance is to retreat
    (E) ascend is to descend

84. Year is to month as
    (A) foot is to inch
    (B) cloth is to thread
    (C) yard is to foot
    (D) juror is to jury
    (E) hour is to minute

85. Stately is to mean as
    (A) noble is to gas
    (B) metal is to base
    (C) capable is to cruel
    (D) august is to ignoble
    (E) condition is to intend

86. Script is to movie as blueprint is to
    (A) building
    (B) carpenter
    (C) plan
    (D) city
    (E) actor

87. Drizzle is to downpour as breeze is to
    (A) hail
    (B) torrent
    (C) gust
    (D) thunder
    (E) flood

88. Spray is to skunk as
    (A) beaver is to dam
    (B) quill is to porcupine
    (C) wool is to sheep
    (D) bee is to sting
    (E) aerie is to eagle

89. Flock is to sheep as
    (A) ship is to fleet
    (B) lion is to pride
    (C) herd is to cattle
    (D) fork is to road
    (E) jam is to traffic

90. Dehydrate is to water as
    (A) drought is to dry
    (B) dark is to shine
    (C) draft is to fan
    (D) smother is to air
    (E) heat is to sun

91. Experience is to naive as
    (A) obedience is to order
    (B) expose is to mask
    (C) width is to depth
    (D) field is to stream
    (E) caution is to reckless

92. Cow is to milk as bee is to
    (A) comb
    (B) queen
    (C) hive
    (D) sting
    (E) honey

93. Miller is to flour as
    (A) connoisseur is to wine
    (B) librarian is to newspaper
    (C) soldier is to firearm
    (D) baker is to bread
    (E) spectator is to binoculars

94. Conductor is to symphony as foreman is to
    (A) client
    (B) worker
    (C) welder
    (D) architect
    (E) project

95. Helicopter is to aircraft as
   (A) hammer is to tool
   (B) jet is to blimp
   (C) blimp is to glider
   (D) plier is to wrench
   (E) blowtorch is to fire

96. Oak is to maple as
   (A) poplar is to tree
   (B) moss is to fern
   (C) hedge is to vine
   (D) dandelion is to mushroom
   (E) daffodil is to violet

97. Ounce is to gram as
   (A) scale is to kilogram
   (B) acre is to fathom
   (C) inch is to centimeter
   (D) millimeter is to mile
   (E) Celsius is to degree

98. Dash is to race as
   (A) marathon is to triathlon
   (B) skirmish is to battle
   (C) sprint is to hurdle
   (D) hour is to day
   (E) set is to match

99. Balloon is to inflate as tank is to
   (A) fill
   (B) drive
   (C) ignite
   (D) gasoline
   (E) hold

100. Telegraph is to communication as abacus is to
   (A) decoration
   (B) arrangement
   (C) navigation
   (D) calculation
   (E) design

101. Piercing is to sound as
   (A) illusory is to sight
   (B) lukewarm is sensation
   (C) piquant is to flavor
   (D) shocking is to sight
   (E) odorless is to smell

102. Cafeteria is to students as
   (A) trough is to horses
   (B) feed is to livestock
   (C) kitchen is to families
   (D) mess hall is to soldiers
   (E) restaurant is to waiters

103. Ungulate is to donkey as amphibian is to
   (A) alligator
   (B) frog
   (C) reptile
   (D) turtle
   (E) fish

104. Lace is to shoe as
   (A) cuff is to pants
   (B) hand is to watch
   (C) bridge is to spectacles
   (D) brim is to hat
   (E) catch is to necklace

105. Strait is to sea as
   (A) exit is to roadway
   (B) isthmus is to landmass
   (C) island is to archipelago
   (D) ridge is to mountain
   (E) port is to harbor

106. Conscription is to enlistment as tax is to
   (A) payment
   (B) collection
   (C) adherence
   (D) refund
   (E) revenue

107. Stoic is to reaction as spontaneous is to
   (A) randomness
   (B) intelligence
   (C) remorse
   (D) forethought
   (E) shallowness

108. Crow is to murder as
   (A) dog is to kennel
   (B) whale is to pod
   (C) bird is to nest
   (D) elephant is to gaggle
   (E) lion is to pack

109. Arc is to circumference as
   (A) radius is to circle
   (B) speed is to distance
   (C) segment is to line
   (D) diagonal is to square
   (E) degree is to triangle

110. Ammunition is to magazine as
   (A) money is to vault
   (B) car is to lot
   (C) water is to faucet
   (D) chemical is to test tube
   (E) guard is to prison

111. Pasture is to pastor as
   (A) sensor is to censor
   (B) creature is to censor
   (C) censure is to censor
   (D) cinch is to censor
   (E) simple is to censor

112. Equivocal is to indecisiveness as boorish is to
   (A) cruelty
   (B) rudeness
   (C) ineptitude
   (D) stubbornness
   (E) rashness

113. Scalding is to tepid as
   (A) hot is to boiling
   (B) frigid is to freezing
   (C) ecstatic is to piqued
   (D) demure is to shy
   (E) loud is to deafening

114. Helpful is to patronizing as witty is to
   (A) humorous
   (B) condescending
   (C) vulgar
   (D) fake
   (E) smug

115. Adore is to loathe as
   (A) honor is to defame
   (B) worship is to revere
   (C) cherish is to salvage
   (D) encourage is to coach
   (E) despise is to condemn

116. Arm is to shoulder as leg is to
   (A) knee
   (B) joint
   (C) foot
   (D) hip
   (E) neck

117. Thrifty is to miser as
   (A) charitable is to benefactor
   (B) cheap is to pauper
   (C) frugal is to accountant
   (D) frivolous is to youth
   (E) violent is to convict

118. Delectable is to dish as
   (A) prosaic is to artwork
   (B) simple is to costume
   (C) eloquent is to speech
   (D) phlegmatic is to match
   (E) profound is to novel

119. Sunday is to Wednesday as
    (A) Thursday is to Saturday
    (B) Monday is to Friday
    (C) Saturday is to Sunday
    (D) Tuesday is to Saturday
    (E) Friday is to Monday

120. Needle is to sewing as
    (A) memories is to scrapbook
    (B) hammer is to carpenter
    (C) pen is to calligraphy
    (D) bat is to hitter
    (E) canvas is to painting

121. Erratic is to consistency as
    (A) absurd is to foolishness
    (B) unique is to commonness
    (C) runner is to track
    (D) appropriate is to choice
    (E) unusual is to helpfulness

122. Former is to future as previous is to
    (A) prior
    (B) present
    (C) bygone
    (D) next
    (E) current

123. Belief is to discredited as
    (A) authority is to obeyed
    (B) task is to completed
    (C) responsibility is to denied
    (D) claim is to challenged
    (E) personality is to assuaged

124. Rose is to granite as
    (A) poppy is to slate
    (B) oat is to grain
    (C) bread is to sandwich
    (D) calorie is to nutrient
    (E) decanter is to farmer

125. Inevitable is to possible as will is to
    (A) must
    (B) won't
    (C) do
    (D) shall
    (E) might

126. Wheat is to apple as
    (A) barley is to ale
    (B) leaf is to root
    (C) coarse is to smooth
    (D) acorn is to sapling
    (E) flour is to cider

127. Arboretum is to tree as greenhouse is to
    (A) seed
    (B) bud
    (C) dirt
    (D) plant
    (E) sapling

128. Amateur is to champion as
    (A) matriculant is to graduate
    (B) intern is to volunteer
    (C) teacher is to principal
    (D) prodigy is to professional
    (E) student is to subject

129. Active is to passive as
    (A) joyful is to pleasant
    (B) tranquil is to bored
    (C) placid is to pleased
    (D) sorrowful is to cry
    (E) frenetic is to apathetic

130. Concerned is to apprehensive as
    (A) appealing is to attractive
    (B) objective is to subjective
    (C) untenable is to intrigued
    (D) dissuaded is to convinced
    (E) interested is to eager

131. Meteorologist is to forecast as
    (A) zoologist is to animal
    (B) scientist is to hypothesis
    (C) psychologist is to disease
    (D) internist is to nurse
    (E) obstetrician is to maternity

132. Steep is to tea as
    (A) percolate is to coffee
    (B) stir is to ingredients
    (C) steam is to broil
    (D) baste is to gravy
    (E) simmer is to broth

133. Cartographer is to map as
    (A) photographer is to camera
    (B) biographer is to author
    (C) navigator is to ship
    (D) stenographer is to transcription
    (E) sculptor is to chisel

134. Frond is to palm as
    (A) petal is to daisy
    (B) leaf is to branch
    (C) school is to fish
    (D) coach is to team
    (E) letter is to vowel

135. Midpoint is to line as
    (A) hypotenuse is to triangle
    (B) volume is to solid
    (C) diameter is to circle
    (D) gallon is to milk
    (E) length is to depth

136. Bison is to plain as cougar is to
    (A) desert
    (B) valley
    (C) crest
    (D) mountain
    (E) bay

137. Finale is to musical as
    (A) intermission is to play
    (B) stanza is to poem
    (C) epilogue is to novel
    (D) lyric is to sing
    (E) overture is to orchestra

# PRACTICE QUESTION ANSWERS

| | | |
|---|---|---|
| 1. D | 32. B | 63. C |
| 2. B | 33. D | 64. D |
| 3. B | 34. A | 65. B |
| 4. C | 35. B | 66. B |
| 5. E | 36. E | 67. C |
| 6. B | 37. D | 68. A |
| 7. E | 38. A | 69. C |
| 8. A | 39. B | 70. A |
| 9. C | 40. D | 71. C |
| 10. D | 41. D | 72. E |
| 11. A | 42. C | 73. D |
| 12. A | 43. C | 74. C |
| 13. C | 44. D | 75. B |
| 14. A | 45. A | 76. E |
| 15. A | 46. C | 77. C |
| 16. E | 47. B | 78. B |
| 17. D | 48. B | 79. B |
| 18. C | 49. A | 80. C |
| 19. E | 50. E | 81. E |
| 20. C | 51. D | 82. C |
| 21. C | 52. B | 83. E |
| 22. C | 53. A | 84. A |
| 23. B | 54. B | 85. D |
| 24. C | 55. E | 86. A |
| 25. D | 56. B | 87. C |
| 26. D | 57. C | 88. B |
| 27. A | 58. D | 89. C |
| 28. E | 59. A | 90. D |
| 29. D | 60. E | 91. E |
| 30. E | 61. C | 92. E |
| 31. D | 62. B | 93. D |

| | |
|---|---|
| 94. E | 116. D |
| 95. A | 117. A |
| 96. E | 118. C |
| 97. C | 119. E |
| 98. B | 120. C |
| 99. A | 121. B |
| 100. D | 122. D |
| 101. C | 123. D |
| 102. D | 124. A |
| 103. B | 125. E |
| 104. E | 126. E |
| 105. B | 127. D |
| 106. A | 128. A |
| 107. D | 129. E |
| 108. B | 130. E |
| 109. C | 131. B |
| 110. A | 132. A |
| 111. C | 133. D |
| 112. B | 134. A |
| 113. C | 135. C |
| 114. E | 136. D |
| 115. A | 137. C |

# Part Two

# ISEE WORKSHOP

# CHAPTER 3: INSIDE THE ISEE

## THE ISEE EXAM

The ISEE (Independent School Entrance Exam) has three tests: Upper Level, Middle Level, and Lower Level.

* Upper Level     (for students currently in grades 8–11)
* Middle Level    (for students currently in grades 6 or 7)
* Lower Level     (for students currently in grades 4 or 5)
* Primary Level   (for students currently in grades 1–3)

The ISEE Primary Level exam is an online test that consists of a Mathematics section, a Reading section, and a Writing prompt.

There are some differences between each of the Primary Level exams. For example, both the Primary Level 2 and 3 exams (for students currently in 1st and 2nd grades) contain a picture with the Writing Prompt, which offers students the opportunity to be creative and self-expressive with their individual writing styles. In Primary Level 2 Reading Comprehension, there is a short Auditory Comprehension section that tests how students listen to a passage, which contains no text. Students then answer questions that relate to the passage.

Each ISEE Primary Level exam is one hour long and is only available at some schools. For all Primary Level tests, the Writing section is untimed, allowing all students to type at their own pace. Following is a breakdown of the Primary Level tests.

|  | Primary 2 for current 1st grade students | Primary 3 for current 2nd grade students | Primary 4 for current 3rd grade students |
|---|---|---|---|
| Auditory Comprehension | 6 questions (7 min.) | 24 questions (28 min.) | 28 questions (30 min.) |
| Reading Comprehension | 18 questions (20 min.) | | |
| Mathematics | 24 questions (26 min.) | 24 questions (26 min.) | 28 questions (30 min.) |
| Essay* | one writing prompt, with a picture | one writing prompt, with a picture | one writing prompt |
| Total Time | 53 minutes (+ writing time) | 1 hour (+ writing time) | 1 hour (+ writing time) |

Following is a breakdown of the paper-based tests.

|  | Lower Level | Middle Level | Upper Level |
|---|---|---|---|
| Verbal Reasoning | 34 questions (20 min.) | 40 questions (20 min.) | 40 questions (20 min.) |
| Quantitative Reasoning | 38 questions (35 min.) | 37 questions (35 min.) | 37 questions (35 min.) |
| Reading Comprehension | 25 questions (25 min.) | 36 questions (35 min.) | 36 questions (35 min.) |
| Mathematics Achievement | 30 questions (30 min.) | 47 questions (40 min.) | 47 questions (40 min.) |
| Essay* | one writing prompt (30 min.) | | |
| Total Time | 2 hours 20 minutes | 2 hours 40 minutes | 2 hours 40 minutes |

* The essay will not be scored, nor will it be included with your home report, but it will be sent to the schools to which you are applying.

- All questions have four answer choices, (A) through (D).
- You are not permitted to use calculators, dictionaries, or rulers.
- You must bring your own pencils and erasers, as well as black or blue pens for your essay.

## SCORING

Scores on the ISEE work similarly to those on the SSAT in that you will be compared against national and local averages. Your score report for the ISEE will include test scores and diagnostic information. It will also indicate whether your scores are at the expected level given your performance on the Verbal Reasoning and Quantitative Reasoning sections.

An ISEE score report will include a stanine score, which indicates a student's percentile range. Percentile ranks range from 1–99, while stanines range from 1–9. Think of stanines in groups of three: a score of 1–3 is below average, 4–6 is an average score, and 7–9 indicates an above average performance.

| Percentile | Stanine |
| --- | --- |
| 1–3 | 1 |
| 4 –10 | 2 |
| 11–22 | 3 |
| 23–39 | 4 |
| 40–59 | 5 |
| 60–76 | 6 |
| 77–88 | 7 |
| 89–95 | 8 |
| 96–99 | 9 |

As on the SSAT, you are not expected to answer every question. Your test performance is compared only to others in your grade. Unlike with the SSAT, you are not penalized for wrong answers. You will be graded only on the number of correct answers you get.

## HOW TO REGISTER

ISEE accepts registration by mail, phone, fax, or online. For more information, go to the official site at **erblearn.org**.

Phone: 800-446-0320
Fax: (919) 682-5775
Mail: ISEE Operations
423 Morris Street
Durham, NC 27701
Email: ISEE@measinc.com

## HOW THE ISEE DIFFERS FROM THE SSAT

- On the ISEE, the Verbal section contains Synonym and Sentence Completion questions. On the SSAT, the Verbal section contains Synonym and Analogy questions.

- On the ISEE, there are Quantitative Comparisons in the Quantitative Reasoning section (Upper and Middle Levels only).

- On the ISEE, there is no penalty for a wrong answer. That means it is always in your favor to guess if you're not sure of the answer.

- On the ISEE, there are four answer choices, (A) through (D). On the SSAT, there are five answer choices, (A) through (E).

# CHAPTER 4: ISEE-SPECIFIC VERBAL WORKOUT: SENTENCE COMPLETIONS

Sentence Completions appear **on every level of the ISEE.** If you are not taking the ISEE, you should skip this section.

## THE FORMAT

Of all the questions in the Verbal Reasoning section, approximately half are Sentence Completions. They're arranged in order of increasing difficulty.

Sentence Completions are fill-in-the-blank questions. Each question will have one or two blanks, and you must select the best fit from the four choices provided.

These are probably the easiest of all the Verbal Reasoning question types. Unlike Analogies, they give you some context in which to think about vocabulary words, and unlike Reading Comprehension questions, they require you to focus on only a single sentence at a time.

Sentence Completions are about the sentence much more than they are about the answer choices. To answer these questions correctly on Test Day, look for clues in each sentence and predict the answer before approaching the choices. This way, you will answer Sentence Completions more quickly, reliably, and accurately than you would by rushing to the answer choices.

First, familiarize yourself with the directions before you take the official test:

Select the word(s) that best fits the meaning of each sentence.

**EXAMPLE**

Although the tomato looked sweet and ___, it tasted more like a very sour, dried-out old sponge.

(A) arid

(B) juicy

(C) enormous

(D) cloying

A contrast is presented between the way the tomato looked and the way it tasted. It tasted sour and had the texture of dry sponge. Since we were previously told that it looked *sweet* (the opposite of *sour*), we can infer that we need to find the opposite of *dry*. Therefore the tomato must have looked juicy, so (B) is the answer.

# KAPLAN 4-STEP METHOD FOR SENTENCE COMPLETIONS

**Step 1:** Read the sentence carefully, looking for clues.

**Step 2:** Predict the answer.

**Step 3:** Pick the best match.

**Step 4:** Plug in your selection.

To check your answers, always read the selected choice back into the sentence. Sometimes, a selected choice may feel right at first, but does not actually make sense in the context of the sentence. Let's take a closer look at each step.

## 1. READ THE SENTENCE CAREFULLY, LOOKING FOR CLUES

Think carefully about the sentence before looking at the answer choices. What does the sentence mean? Are there any clue words?

## 2. PREDICT THE ANSWER

Take a look at the following examples:

"They say that M&M's do not melt in your hands, but last summer . . ."

"Despite the fact that it was 50 degrees below zero, we were . . . "

"I am so hungry I could . . . "

> **KAPLAN EXCLUSIVE TIP**
>
> " The meaning of each missing word in a Sentence Completion question is provided by the clues in the sentence. "

You could probably fill in the rest of these sentences using words similar to the speaker's own. It's often easy to see the direction in which a sentence is going; that's because the structure and the tone of a sentence can clue you in to its meaning.

Your job for the ISEE Sentence Completion questions is to fill in the missing piece. One way to do this is to anticipate the answer before looking at the answer choices. Clue words and sentence structure (construction and punctuation) can help you determine where a sentence is headed.

Making an exact prediction isn't necessary. If you can even identify the missing word as being positive or negative, that will often be sufficient.

## 3. PICK THE BEST MATCH

Make sure to scan every choice before deciding.

## 4. PLUG IN YOUR SELECTION

Only one of the four possible answer choices will make sense. However, if you've gone through the four steps and more than one choice still seems possible, don't dwell on it. Try to eliminate at least one choice, guess, and move on. Remember, on the ISEE, a wrong answer will not affect your score.

Using some examples, let's see how Kaplan's 4-Step Method works.

### EXAMPLE

The _____ pace of life in the crowded city became so upsetting to Amy that she decided to move to the country.

(A) hectic
(B) agreeable
(C) accidental
(D) confused

**Step 1.** Think about marking clues. What kind of "pace of life" would be "upsetting"?

**Step 2.** Predict an answer.

PREDICTION: *frantic, hectic*

**Step 3.** Find the fit—select the answer choice that best fits your prediction. Which choice is the best match?

**Step 4.** Plug in your selection—read your answer choice back into the sentence to check it.

(A) is the correct answer.

**EXAMPLE**

Most North American marsupials are ___; at night they forage for food, and during the day they sleep.

(A) fastidious

(B) amiable

(C) monolithic

(D) nocturnal

Read the sentence carefully, looking for clues. The semicolon (;) is a big clue. It tells you that what comes after the semicolon follows the direction of what comes before it. In other words, you're looking for a word that means nighttime activity and daytime rest.

Predict which word should go into the blank.

Compare the answer choices with your prediction. Pick the best match. (A), *fastidious*, has nothing to do with being active at night. Neither does (B), *amiable*, or for that matter (C), *monolithic*. (D), *nocturnal*, however, means to be active at night, so that seems correct.

Check your choice by plugging it into the sentence. "Most North American marsupials are nocturnal; at night they forage for food, and during the day they sleep." Sounds pretty good. Finally, scan the other choices to make sure that (D) is indeed the best choice. No other choice works in the sentence, so (D) is right.

**EXAMPLE**

Juniper skated with such ___ that no one could ___ her talent any longer.

(A) speed . . ascertain

(B) melancholy . . deny

(C) agility . . question

(D) grace . . affirm

Read the sentence carefully, looking for clue words. A major clue here is *such ... that*. You know that Juniper's skating ability, whether good or bad, has led to everybody agreeing about her talent. So whatever words go into the two blanks, they must agree.

Predict the words that go into the blanks, making sure that whatever goes in the second blank supports the meaning of the first. If Juniper skated well, no one would deny that she has a lot of talent. If she skated terribly, everyone would agree that she had no talent. Don't let the negative structure of the second part of the sentence fool you: It's written as "no one could ——," as opposed to "everyone could ——." Make some predictions about the two missing pieces.

Compare your predictions with each answer choice and pick the best fit. Which two words, when in context, will agree and support each other?

In (A), *speed* and *ascertain* don't make sense together. In (B), *melancholy* and *deny* don't support one another. It doesn't make sense that "no one could *deny* her talent" because she skated sadly, or with *melancholy*. In (C), *agility* and *question* do fit together well. Juniper skates with *agility*, so who could question her ability? In (D), *grace* and *affirm* initially seem to support one another. But remember the negative in the second part of the sentence: " . . . *no one* could —— her talent." It's illogical to say that she skated with such *grace* that "no one could *affirm* her talent." (C) must be the answer.

## PICKING UP ON CLUES

In order to do well on Sentence Completions, you need to show how a sentence fits together. Clue words will help you do that. The more clues you can find, the clearer the sentence will become. The clearer the sentence, the better your prediction.

What are clue words? There are a variety of clue words. Some will indicate **cause and effect** and others a **contrast,** and some others will **define the missing word.**

### EXAMPLES

- Clues that indicate cause and effect:

  <u>Because</u> he was so scared of the dark, we were —— to find him sleeping without a night light.

  <u>As a result</u> of her constant lying, Sheila was —— to trust anyone else.

- Clues that indicate contrast:

  Rita is funny and light hearted; her twin, Wendy, <u>however</u> is —— and ——.

  <u>Following</u> the wonderful news, Harry's visage changed <u>from</u> an expression of —— to one of ——.

- Clues that define the missing word:

  A <u>loud and tiresome child</u>, he acted particularly —— during the long car trip.

  <u>Smart and witty</u>, Roger was the most —— student in the class.

### EXAMPLE

Fiona's bedroom still looks like ___, despite her efforts to keep it tidy.

In this example, whatever goes into the blank must complete the contrast implied by the word *despite*. You know then that it must describe the *opposite of tidy*. *Messy* or *disorganized* would be good predictions.

> **KAPLAN EXCLUSIVE TIP**
>
> " Clue words like *and, but, such as, however,* and *although* can indicate where a sentence is heading. Keep your eyes open for these kinds of helpful words. "

> **BE CAREFUL**
>
> " A single word can change the meaning of the entire sentence, so make sure to read the sentence carefully. "

# EXERCISE I

**Practice making predictions on the following examples. Begin by circling the clue words in each sentence, then fill in your prediction.**

I like baseball and other _____.

With clothes and empty soda cans all over the floor, Sam's apartment was very _____.

Mary's _____ expression was a clear indication that something great had happened.

She was very _____ and had never hesitated to say what she thought.

The sergeant used _____ language to show his contempt for the recruits.

Even more _____ in person than in her photos, the actress dazzled us.

The violin is a _____ instrument that many people find hard to play.

Some problems are unexpected, but others are _____.

Turning the corner, the car _____ on the slippery road.

Even the musician's critics _____ his fundraising efforts.

# ANSWERS

I like baseball (and other) _____ *sports* _____ .

(With) clothes and empty soda cans all over the floor, Sam's apartment was very _____ *messy* _____ .

Mary's _____ *joyous* _____ expression (was a clear indication) that something great had happened.

She was very _____ *outspoken* _____ (and) had never hesitated to say what she thought.

The sergeant used _____ *condescending* _____ language (to show) his contempt for the recruits.

(Even more) _____ *beautiful* _____ in person than in her photos, the actress dazzled us.

The violin (is) a _____ *difficult* _____ instrument (that) many people find hard to play.

Some problems are unexpected, (but others) are _____ *foreseeable* _____ .

Turning the corner, the car _____ *skidded* _____ on the slippery road.

(Even) the musician's critics _____ *applauded* _____ his fundraising efforts.

Try the predictions for the following questions on your own:

## EXERCISE II

Practice Steps 1 and 2 on the following examples.

1. The funds projected for next year's budget are so _____ that the library will barely be able to maintain its regular hours.

   **CLUES:** _____

   **PREDICTION:** _____

2. Despite a stern and forbidding demeanor in class, the professor was _____ to students who approached him in his office.

   **CLUES:** _____

   **PREDICTION:** _____

3. Certain types of spiders are poisonous, while others are relatively _____.

   **CLUES:** _____

   **PREDICTION:** _____

Now find the fit among the answer choices.

1. The funds projected for next year's budget are so _____ that the library will barely be able to maintain its regular hours.

   (A) generous
   (B) meager
   (C) expansive
   (D) extravagant

2. Despite a stern and forbidding demeanor in class, the professor was _____ to students who approached him in his office.

   (A) insensitive
   (B) inhospitable
   (C) remote
   (D) receptive

3. Certain types of spiders are poisonous, while others are relatively _____.

   (A) social
   (B) adventurous
   (C) harmless
   (D) energetic

# ANSWERS

Practice Steps 1 and 2 on the following examples.

1.  The funds projected for next year's budget are so _____ that the library will barely be able to maintain its regular hours.

    **CLUES:** _____*so...that (cause and effect)*_____

    **PREDICTION:** _____*limited*_____

2.  Despite a stern and forbidding demeanor in class, the professor was _____ to students who approached him in his office.

    **CLUES:** _____*despite (contrast)*_____

    **PREDICTION:** _____*friendly*_____

3.  Certain types of spiders are poisonous, while others are relatively _____.

    **CLUES:** _____*while others (contrast)*_____

    **PREDICTION:** _____*benign*_____

Now find the fit among the answer Choices.

1.  The funds projected for next year's budget are so _____ that the library will barely be able to maintain its regular hours.

    (A)  generous
    (B)  meager
    (C)  expansive
    (D)  extravagant

2.  Despite a stern and forbidding demeanor in class, the professor was _____ to students who approached him in his office.

    (A)  insensitive
    (B)  inhospitable
    (C)  remote
    (D)  receptive

3.  Certain types of spiders are poisonous, while others are relatively _____.

    (A)  social
    (B)  adventurous
    (C)  harmless
    (D)  energetic

<u>Transition</u>: "Now you've learned the method that you'll use for every Sentence Completion on Test Day.  We'll revisit this in greater detail in Lesson 6B.  For homework, be sure to do the Session 2 Review and all "The Same, But Different" questions that we didn't do in class. Also complete the Session 3 Preview for next time."

# TACKLING HARD QUESTIONS

Sentence Completions will get more difficult as you go through them, so the last few will be the most difficult. If you get stuck, here are a few tips to help you through:

- Avoid tricky wrong answers.
- Take apart tough sentences.
- Work around tough vocabulary.

## AVOID TRICKY WRONG ANSWERS

Toward the end of a set, keep your eyes open for tricky answer choices. Avoid these:

- Opposites of the correct answer
- Words that may sound right because they are tough
- Questions with two missing pieces, where one word sounds right but the other doesn't. Note: Lower-Level ISEE Sentence Completion questions will have only one blank.

The following would be the 12th question out of a 15-problem set.

## EXAMPLE

At first, the house seemed frightening with all its cobwebs and creaking shutters, but we soon realized that it was quite ___.

(A) benign
(B) deceptive
(C) affluent
(D) haunted

Read this sentence carefully. If you read it too quickly, it may sound like "The house was really scary with all of those cobwebs and creaking shutters, and we soon realized ... it was!" So you would pick (D), *haunted,* or maybe (B), *deceptive*, when in fact the correct answer is (A), *benign*.

## PICK UP THE CLUES

There are two major clues here, and you should have picked them up right away. The first one, *At first*, indicate that the author perceived something to be one way in the beginning—but after taking a second look realized it was different. That leads us to the second clue word, *but*. Just as we predicted, the author thought the house was creepy at first *but* then felt differently. We know, therefore, that the word in the blank must be the *opposit* of *creepy* or *haunted*.

### DON'T PICK AN ANSWER JUST BECAUSE IT SOUNDS HARD

*Affluent* means wealthy. You might be tempted to choose it because it looks or sounds impressive. But it's thrown in there just to tempt you. Don't choose a word without good reason.

Let's look at a two-blank sentence. The following example is the 15th of a 15-problem set.

### EXAMPLE

Screaming and laughing, the students were ___ by their ___ experience on the white-water raft.

(A) amused . . tepid

(B) irritated . . continued

(C) exhilarated . . first

(D) frightened . . secure

### LOOK AT ALL THE CHOICES

Check out the first blank first. Sometimes you can eliminate one or more answer choices right away if some possibilities don't fit. *Irritated* and/or *frightened* students do not scream and laugh, so eliminate (B) and (D).

Now check the second blank. A *tepid* (or half-hearted) experience wouldn't make a bunch of students scream and laugh, either, so (A) is out. Only (C) fits both of the blanks: The students would laugh and scream due to *exhilaration* on their *first* white-water rafting experience.

### TAKE APART TOUGH SENTENCES

Look at the following example, the last question in a 15-question set.

### EXAMPLE

The ___ agreement had never been written down but was understood and upheld by the governments of both countries.

(A) tacit

(B) public

(C) distinguished

(D) illegal

> **TWO-BLANK SENTENCES**
>
> " Sentences with two blanks can be easier than those with one blank.
>
> • Try the easier blank first.
> • Save time by eliminating all choices that won't work for that blank. "

What if you were stumped? What if you had no idea which word to pick? Try this method:

*Tacit*—Hmm, sounds familiar.

*Public*—Nope. It doesn't sound right in this context.

*Distinguished*—If it was so distinguished, why was it never written down?

*Illegal*—Nope. Do governments uphold illegal agreements? That doesn't sound right.

Choice (A) sounds the best. As it turns out, it's also correct. *Tacit* agreements are unspoken or silent ones; they're not expressed or declared openly but instead are implied.

Let's try a complex sentence with two blanks. Remember the rules:

- Try the easier blank first.

- Save time by eliminating all choices that won't work for that blank.

## EXAMPLE

The old ___ hated parties and refused to ___ in the festivities.

- (A)  actor . . direct
- (B)  curmudgeon . . partake
- (C)  mediator . . take
- (D)  surgeon . . place

For the first blank, it's impossible to rule out any choices because an actor, a curmudgeon (especially), a mediator, and a surgeon all have the potential to be old and to hate parties.

Try the second blank and see what can be ruled out. (A) doesn't make any sense; what does *direct* in the festivities mean? It's nonsensical. (B), *partake* makes sense. (C), *take* in the festivities doesn't sound right, and neither does (D), *place* in the festivities. That leaves (B) as the best and only fit. A *curmudgeon* is, by definition, an ornery or grumpy person, so it makes sense that he wouldn't want to *partake* in the festivities.

Here are a few final strategies to help you on Test Day:

- On tough Sentence Completions, remember that you can eliminate answer choices that you know are wrong. Make an educated guess among the remaining answer choices.

- When eliminating, look for a word charge—is your prediction strongly positive or negative? Eliminate any choices with an opposite or neutral charge.

- Trust your ear! Sometimes the correct answer sounds like it fits the situation. Many phrases on the ISEE will be familiar terms you have heard or seen before.

- Finally, remember to use structural clues in the sentence to predict the missing word(s).

# PRACTICE QUESTIONS

## LL Only

1. At his funeral, Malcolm X was ___ by admirers such as Ossie Davis.

    (A) praised

    (B) rescued

    (C) delighted

    (D) forgotten

2. The art collector must have very ___ tastes; he owns pieces from all over the world.

    (A) crude

    (B) broad

    (C) good

    (D) old-fashioned

3. The water in the pond was ___ enough to allow one to see objects on the bottom.

    (A) deep

    (B) clear

    (C) salty

    (D) cold

4. Since moisture hastens decay, ___ vegetation can often last a long time.

    (A) rare

    (B) dead

    (C) tasty

    (D) dried

5. Because Joel did not ___ his homework assignment on time, the teacher ___ his grade.

    (A) submit . . accepted

    (B) notify . . ignored

    (C) understand . . contradicted

    (D) complete . . lowered

## LL-ML

6. Because of ___ in the temperature of the region, it is difficult to know whether to dress for hot weather or cold.

    (A) rainfalls

    (B) changes

    (C) heat waves

    (D) cold snaps

7. The two houses do not ___ each other; there is a narrow alleyway ___ them.

    (A) neighbor . . separating

    (B) resemble . . under

    (C) face . . above

    (D) touch . . between

8. The athlete was so ___ by the heat that he could barely walk.

    (A) annoyed

    (B) strengthened

    (C) pleased

    (D) exhausted

9. Only the most ___ soldiers volunteered to be in the platoon, since that was where they were in greatest danger of being wounded or ___.

    (A) cheerful . . promoted

    (B) clever . . scratched

    (C) polite . . maimed

    (D) courageous . . killed

10. The new senator was ___ , so he only proposed legislation that stood a reasonable chance of passing.

    (A) confident

    (B) realistic

    (C) ambitious

    (D) inexperienced

11. She didn't like her birthday present, but she ___ to like it to avoid ___ her grandfather's feelings.

    (A) hid .. showing
    (B) suppressed .. displaying
    (C) pretended .. hurting
    (D) felt .. creating

12. Rats mature very quickly and ___ prolifically, facilitating the ___ of disease.

    (A) run .. control
    (B) hide .. prevention
    (C) breed .. spread
    (D) mutate .. obstruction

13. A public official who accepts ___ is guilty of ___.

    (A) aid .. abuse
    (B) awards .. dishonesty
    (C) bribes .. corruption
    (D) advice .. misbehavior

14. Though Elena had received the company's ___ possible service award, her supervisor felt it necessary to ___ her for arriving ten minutes late.

    (A) highest .. admonish
    (B) poorest .. vex
    (C) best .. commend
    (D) finest .. extol

15. As the supply of fresh water ___ , the castaways were forced to ___ the remainder.

    (A) dwindled .. ration
    (B) stabilized .. waste
    (C) grew .. preserve
    (D) drained .. distribute

16. He was an ___ art collector and had ___ several fine paintings by such artists as Picasso and Matisse.

    (A) unsuccessful .. bought
    (B) active .. released
    (C) avid .. acquired
    (D) enthusiastic .. destroyed

17. Most of those polled seemed ___ a change and ___ that they would vote to re-elect the mayor.

    (A) wary of .. stated
    (B) cautious about .. denied
    (C) afraid of .. disputed
    (D) open to .. asserted

18. Before rolling out the pie crust, the chef ___ the counter with flour to ___ the dough from sticking.

    (A) drenched .. halt
    (B) baked .. banish
    (C) kneaded .. alleviate
    (D) dusted .. prevent

19. Despite the ___ price of the car, Jose's parents were ___ to permit him to buy it.

    (A) affordable .. willing
    (B) outrageous .. hesitant
    (C) usual .. afraid
    (D) reasonable .. reluctant

20. The speaker ___ on for hours, repeating herself at length and ___ her audience to tears.

    (A) prated .. frightening
    (B) simpered .. forcing
    (C) whined .. provoking
    (D) droned .. boring

## ML-UL

21. He was ___ enough by the affront to ___ the person who had insulted him.

    (A) incensed . . strike
    (B) sad . . congratulate
    (C) glad . . thank
    (D) scared . . frighten

22. Although they were intelligent people, they were ___ by the advertiser's false ___ .

    (A) addressed . . messages
    (B) displeased . . speech
    (C) amused . . budget
    (D) deceived . . claims

23. Newcastle in northern England is an important source of coal, so "carrying coals to Newcastle" means doing something ___ .

    (A) appropriate
    (B) normal
    (C) unnecessary
    (D) dirty

24. George concealed his true ___ under a guise of ___ .

    (A) passions . . instability
    (B) humility . . modesty
    (C) concern . . indifference
    (D) generosity . . altruism

25. Though normally quite ___ , the grizzly can become ___ when disturbed by a human.

    (A) enormous . . frightened
    (B) affectionate . . happy
    (C) harmless . . ferocious
    (D) voracious . . appeased

26. Many people ___ that owls are intelligent, but this claim is nothing more than a ___ .

    (A) assume . . fact
    (B) agree . . rebuttal
    (C) refute . . tale
    (D) believe . . myth

27. Roberta was ___ for cheating, though she believed that her ___ use of encyclopedia entries was not deceitful.

    (A) censured . . fraudulent
    (B) reprimanded . . paltry
    (C) honored . . primitive
    (D) chastised . . treacherous

28. The newspaper editorial argued that allowing violence to pass without ___ gives the appearance of ___ it.

    (A) comment . . condoning
    (B) incident . . provoking
    (C) activity . . soothing
    (D) agitation . . pacifying

29. Investigators believe that the rash of fires was not the work of ___ but a ___ of unfortunate accidents.

    (A) a pyromaniac . . factor
    (B) an accomplice . . consequence
    (C) a criminal . . premonition
    (D) an arsonist . . series

30. Archaeologists ___ the documents while ___ the remains of a 1,000-year-old Roman fort in what is now northern England.

    (A) attached . . marring
    (B) unearthed . . excavating
    (C) diverted . . mourning
    (D) construed . . surmising

31. At his concert debut, the young violinist tossed off the most difficult passages without any apparent effort, ___ the audience with his ___ .

    (A) enraging . . timorousness

    (B) impressing . . prestige

    (C) enthralling . . stolidity

    (D) dazzling . . virtuosity

32. Except for a few ___ shrubs, the frozen, windswept tundra provides little ___ for the herds of caribou that migrate across it seasonally.

    (A) stunted . . nourishment

    (B) harmful . . credit

    (C) formless . . refuge

    (D) premature . . privacy

33. The writing process is ___ for most, but she is able to compose poems without much ___ .

    (A) repugnant . . skill

    (B) amusing . . pain

    (C) tedious . . excitement

    (D) arduous . . effort

34. Despite the ___ predictions of noted meteorologists, the damage caused by the storm was ___ .

    (A) accurate . . foreseen

    (B) ominous . . minimal

    (C) dire . . terrible

    (D) encouraging . . slight

35. Tony and Marcia spent an ___ afternoon ___ hand in hand through the sun-dappled park.

    (A) untimely . . traipsing

    (B) ebullient . . recurring

    (C) exhaustive . . persevering

    (D) idyllic . . strolling

36. Since Ricky's college interview had gone well, his counselor was ___ to learn that he was ___ about applying for college.

    (A) relieved . . ambivalent

    (B) troubled . . decisive

    (C) disappointed . . unenthusiastic

    (D) delighted . . aghast

37. Deirdre was ___ as a leader in student government, even though she would have been just as happy to play a(n) ___ role.

    (A) questioned . . minor

    (B) applauded . . pivotal

    (C) hailed . . integral

    (D) recognized . . supporting

38. Later that evening, the snow ___ in huge drifts, making driving ___ difficult and finally impossible.

    (A) melted . . continually

    (B) accumulated . . increasingly

    (C) amassed . . conversely

    (D) evaporated . . starkly

39. Because the astronomy textbook was so difficult to ___ , she had to rely on the physics professor's lectures to explain the more ___ concepts.

    (A) consider . . intricate

    (B) orbit . . essential

    (C) repudiate . . basic

    (D) follow . . complicated

40. The 16th-century chateau is ___ decorated with delicately wrought tapestries, hand-crafted ___ , and leaded stained glass windows.

   (A) sumptuously . . furnishings

   (B) artistically . . accompaniments

   (C) concisely . . cadences

   (D) imprudently . . trappings

41. At the mercy of his ___ appetite, Henry was ___ to stay on his diet.

   (A) light . . unwilling

   (B) moderate . . free

   (C) massive . . sure

   (D) healthy . . unable

42. Weighted down with heavy armor, medieval knights ___ their broadswords too ___ to fight for more than a few minutes at a time.

   (A) wielded . . awkwardly

   (B) parried . . perversely

   (C) hoisted . . obdurately

   (D) swung . . actively

43. To his admirers, the Prime Minister was ___ ; to his ___ , merely stubborn.

   (A) eminent . . imitators

   (B) remarkable . . adherents

   (C) tenacious . . detractors

   (D) complimentary . . endorsers

44. In his ___ to eliminate clutter, Terry discarded old files and documents ___ , heedless of their potential future importance.

   (A) zeal . . indiscriminately

   (B) agitation . . persuasively

   (C) bravado . . competitively

   (D) insomnia . . tactfully

## UL Only

45. The author's first novel was critically acclaimed for its originality and ___ , but its ___ appeal was limited.

   (A) repartee . . individual

   (B) suspensefulness . . vital

   (C) obscurity . . lasting

   (D) sophistication . . popular

46. Given the ___ in today's market, our sale predictions may have been a little ___ .

   (A) upturn . . inexact

   (B) boom . . audacious

   (C) instability . . reckless

   (D) stagnation . . optimistic

47. Tory painted a(n) ___ view of the city, starting at the lakefront and ___ inland for several miles.

   (A) impressionistic . . burnishing

   (B) ascetic . . eddying

   (C) intrinsic . . embellishing

   (D) panoramic . . ranging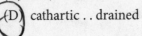

48. The film has a ___ effect on viewers, leaving them emotionally ___ and physically spent.

   (A) flippant . . relaxed

   (B) normal . . intact

   (C) stern . . laconic

   (D) cathartic . . drained

## All Levels

49. She was a(n) ___ , living by herself and avoiding other people.

    (A) adventurer
    (B) socialite
    (C) hermit
    (D) fool

50. As a strict vegetarian, she ___ meat, eggs, and dairy products.

    (A) sells
    (B) ignores
    (C) avoids
    (D) grades

51. The professor's students ___ him so much that they would ___ his mannerisms and style of dress.

    (A) admired . . imitate
    (B) feared . . plan
    (C) ignored . . notice
    (D) fought . . see

52. The utter failure in which the project ended is evidence of the ___ of the people who planned it.

    (A) lack of ability
    (B) strength of character
    (C) careful planning
    (D) wild imagination

53. The hummingbird is a voracious eater, ___ many times its own weight in food each day.

    (A) finding
    (B) rejecting
    (C) making
    (D) consuming

54. The witness had always shown great ___ in the past, so it seemed reasonable to believe her account now.

    (A) honesty
    (B) kindness
    (C) cowardice
    (D) care

55. Some animals will ___ themselves when presented with a(n) ___ amount of food.

    (A) control . . absent
    (B) deceive . . plentiful
    (C) starve . . eaten
    (D) gorge . . unlimited

56. He was too ___ to compromise even with people whose views were relatively close to his own.

    (A) loyal to his friends
    (B) strongly opinionated
    (C) quick to action
    (D) friendly to strangers

57. The child was obedient and well-behaved at home, but at school her teachers found her ___ .

    (A) small and weak
    (B) hard to control
    (C) eager to learn
    (D) slow and careful

58. The theory of evolution is probably true, since scientists have found a lot of ___ for it.

    (A) supporting evidence
    (B) other names
    (C) public scorn
    (D) popular support

59. Because the instructor was so ___ , the explanation took much longer than necessary.

(A) serious
(B) intelligent
(C) wordy
(D) experienced

60. On an assembly line, each step in the production process is ___ in exactly the same way every time, ensuring that the finished items are ___ .

(A) costly . . cheap
(B) repeated . . identical
(C) complicated . . efficient
(D) strange . . unique

61. It was once common for younger people to show ___ by standing up when an elder entered the room.

(A) respect
(B) bravery
(C) fear
(D) intelligence

62. Because leather is so ___ , it is used in clothing to ___ fabric from cuts and scrapes.

(A) tough . . protect
(B) warm . . cool
(C) smelly . . prevent
(D) attractive . . design

63. Widely reported incidents of crime in a city tend to ___ fear and suspicion among the residents.

(A) create
(B) reduce
(C) confuse
(D) condemn

64. In the film *Citizen Kane*, a reporter tries and fails to make sense of the title character's ___ last word, "Rosebud."

(A) clever
(B) mysterious
(C) sarcastic
(D) dying

65. The governor's opponents looked for evidence of past wrongdoing on her part, but her record was ___ .

(A) unbroken
(B) conclusive
(C) popular
(D) spotless

66. The teacher tried to ___ the student's ___ use of grammar and vocabulary.

(A) replace . . remarkable
(B) distort . . uncomplimentary
(C) approve . . perfect
(D) correct . . faulty

67. After its engine ___ , the boat drifted ___ for days.

(A) started . . swiftly
(B) raced . . slowly
(C) died . . aimlessly
(D) broke . . briefly

68. Cowbirds ___ their eggs in the nests of other birds, who ___ raise the chicks as their own.

(A) deposit . . unwittingly
(B) steal . . enthusiastically
(C) exchange . . debatably
(D) ignore . . unanimously

69. The politician's thoughtful ___ helped to ___ the skeptical public.

    (A) beliefs . . warn
    (B) service . . justify
    (C) presence . . betray
    (D) argument . . convince

70. The lake was in serious jeopardy; it was being contaminated and ___ by human beings faster than nature could ___ and replenish it.

    (A) endangered . . flow
    (B) drained . . purify
    (C) modified . . improve
    (D) impelled . . filter

71. Because it features many ___ actors, the new film is ___ to be a major box office success.

    (A) important . . doomed
    (B) prominent . . expected
    (C) unknown . . certain
    (D) talented . . unlikely

72. The shrewd private investigator noticed several ___ clues that the police had failed to ___ .

    (A) significant . . detect
    (B) irrelevant . . pursue
    (C) crucial . . scan
    (D) spurious . . find

73. After being unfairly ___ by the chairperson, Luis ___ out of the meeting room.

    (A) upbraided . . stormed
    (B) burdened . . sauntered
    (C) scrutinized . . strolled
    (D) heckled . . strutted

74. Through years of ___ , the once ___ cathedral was allowed to become shabby, dirty, and increasingly unappealing.

    (A) renovation . . impressive
    (B) adornment . . decrepit
    (C) neglect . . majestic
    (D) improvement . . towering

75. Although the game was ___ in its early stages, it later turned into a ___ .

    (A) unfair . . debacle
    (B) close . . rout
    (C) uneven . . trouncing
    (D) uncontested . . stalemate

76. The news wire service ___ information so ___ that events are reported all over the world shortly after they happen.

    (A) records . . precisely
    (B) falsifies . . deliberately
    (C) verifies . . painstakingly
    (D) disseminates . . rapidly

77. Nearly everyone has seen photographs of the Grand Canyon, but its ___ topography cannot be fully ___ through two-dimensional images.

    (A) spectacular . . appreciated
    (B) copious . . decorated
    (C) dingy . . screened
    (D) peripheral . . saturated

78. The farmers continued to work long hours throughout the fall and winter, ___ their ___ and repairing buildings and equipment.

    (A) clearing . . crop
    (B) reaping . . fauna
    (C) securing . . debris
    (D) tending . . livestock

79. The ancient stone carvings are wonderfully ___ , depicting in intricate detail the ___ in battle of thousands of soldiers.

    (A) fragmentary . . succumbing
    (B) beautiful . . lunging
    (C) worn . . enacting
    (D) ornate . . clashing

80. Faced with such a paucity of ___ information about the millionaire's new husband, the newspaper has ___ printing unsubstantiated rumors.

    (A) paramount . . balked at
    (B) reliable . . resorted to
    (C) wealthy . . refrained from
    (D) immediate . . wavered about

81. Once ___ across the continent, wolves had been ___ almost to extinction by the 1950s.

    (A) nonexistent . . propelled
    (B) numerous . . hunted
    (C) garrulous . . abducted
    (D) captive . . secured

82. The hostess invited relatively ___ guests, making the party seem less ___ than it had last year.

    (A) eccentric . . unique
    (B) talkative . . lengthy
    (C) ordinary . . banal
    (D) undistinguished . . exclusive

83. The best archaeological evidence ___ that the gigantic structures were ___ by an extinct aboriginal people.

    (A) indicates . . erected
    (B) specifies . . registered
    (C) replies . . built
    (D) imagines . . drafted

84. Cockroaches are one of the most ___ of all creatures because they can ___ in almost any situation.

    (A) adaptable . . thrive
    (B) disgusting . . reside
    (C) frail . . survive
    (D) versatile . . die

85. The violinist gave an ___ performance in the final movement and left the audience ___ .

    (A) extended . . early
    (B) accomplished . . astounded
    (C) exquisite . . afflicted
    (D) absorbing . . distracted

86. Somehow, in spite of her ___ study habits, Mary always received ___ grades on her history exams.

    (A) atrocious . . failing
    (B) lackadaisical . . mediocre
    (C) careful . . outstanding
    (D) excellent . . poor

87. Having seen the film before, Mark was ___ to be as ___ as we who were viewing it for the first time.

    (A) prone . . bewildered
    (B) predicted . . critical
    (C) flagrant . . blissful
    (D) unlikely . . shocked

88. A born pessimist, Lisa was ___ when her favorite team ___ in the final quarter of the last regular season game.

    (A) impartial . . tied
    (B) forgiven . . forfeited
    (C) depressed . . conceded
    (D) stunned . . triumphed

89. Having procrastinated far too long, he attacked the project so ___ that he made many ___ errors.

    (A) hastily . . inadvertent
    (B) learnedly . . noticeable
    (C) methodically . . fundamental
    (D) weakly . . trivial

90. Most of the opinions expressed in her book are ___ , but it does contain a few ___ insights.

    (A) sensible . . intelligent
    (B) absurd . . brilliant
    (C) useless . . ambitious
    (D) sound . . practical

91. The politician ___ his position and ___ a proposal he had previously opposed.

    (A) changed . . criticized
    (B) reversed . . supported
    (C) modified . . blocked
    (D) upheld . . defended

92. Moviegoers were thrilled by the hero's daring ___ and amused by his sidekicks madcap ___ .

    (A) feats . . tribulations
    (B) escapades . . ordeals
    (C) tedium . . zaniness
    (D) exploits . . antics

93. Some claim that the new educational project ___ to gifted pupils while ___ the needs of average students, who constitute a clear majority.

    (A) adapts . . emulating
    (B) salutes . . effecting
    (C) objects . . implying
    (D) caters . . ignoring

94. The bears that frequent the campground are bold and occasionally ___ in their ___ for food.

    (A) abundant . . capacity
    (B) emphatic . . inclination
    (C) aggressive . . quest
    (D) unbalanced . . pressure

95. Brett brought Vicky's horse back to the stable by improvising a harness that ___ the mare to his own ___ .

    (A) hitched . . zenith
    (B) motivated . . goal
    (C) spurred . . steed
    (D) yoked . . mount

96. The whale shark is ___ encountered by divers because of its low numbers and ___ habits.

    (A) successfully . . congenial
    (B) anxiously . . unfortunate
    (C) constantly. . . indifferent
    (D) rarely . . solitary

97. The ___ deposited tons of mineral-rich volcanic ash, restoring to the soil nutrients ___ decades of farming.

    (A) eruption . . depleted by
    (B) abyss . . harvested during
    (C) tumult . . alien to
    (D) barrier . . entrenched in

98. Members of the sect ___ from before sun-up until long after dusk, ___ the sin of sloth.

    (A) fasted . . savoring
    (B) sanctified . . tainting
    (C) concealed . . deploring
    (D) toiled . . avoiding

99. Meteorologists ___ storm systems in order to give shoreline residents adequate ___ of hurricanes, floods, and other disasters.

    (A) track . . forewarning

    (B) study . . almanacs

    (C) record . . barometers

    (D) design . . pretense

100. The firm employed many lackadaisical employees, who had a(n) ___ approach to their work.

    (A) creative

    (B) independent

    (C) unproductive

    (D) discontented

101. Due to ___ weather, the school closed and ___ all classes.

    (A) cold . . continued

    (B) severe . . cancelled

    (C) humid . . relieved

    (D) frosty . . alleviated

102. Many paleontologists believe that modern birds and crocodiles are the ___ of the ancient dinosaurs.

    (A) descendants

    (B) ancestors

    (C) neologisms

    (D) reptiles

103. Her eyes were wide with ___ as the ship ___ with gold, jewels, and precious metals sailed into port.

    (A) amazement . . arrived

    (B) reason . . purged

    (C) wonder . . laden

    (D) purpose . . meandered

104. It was Mount Vesuvius that erupted and ___ the city of Pompeii in the year 79 C.E.

    (A) desiccated

    (B) decimated

    (C) erected

    (D) detected

105. The determined young cadet ___ every character trait that the ideal soldier should have.

    (A) embodied

    (B) created

    (C) secluded

    (D) vaporized

# PRACTICE QUESTION ANSWERS

## LL Only

### 1. A

Using the clue word "admirers," we realize that the blank must be correspondingly positive. When you admire someone, you offer "praise," so (A) is the correct choice.

### 2. B

The key phrase here is "owns pieces from all over the world," since it tells us the blank should indicate a wide range of tastes, or choice (B), "broad."

### 3. B

A Logic Sentence Completion: if the water was ___ enough to see things on the bottom of the pond, the water must be fairly "clear."

### 4. D

The structural clue word "Since" tells us that the blank must be opposite in meaning to the first portion of the sentence and the key phrase "last a long time" tells us that the blank must mean without moisture, or "dried," (D).

### 5. D

Cause and effect again—if Joel did not "complete" his homework on time, you would expect his teacher to "lower" his grade.

## LL-ML

### 6. B

The key phrase "difficult to know whether to dress for hot or cold" tells us the blank must be a word indicating variability, hence (B), "changes," is correct.

### 7. D

The clue "narrow alleyway" indicates that the buildings are separate, making (D) correct.

### 8. D

Excessive heat rendered the athlete barely able to walk, so the blank must mean something close to "weakened." Choice (D), "exhausted," is correct.

### 9. D

To "volunteer" for a spot in which soldiers are in great danger, the soldiers must be "courageous," so (D) fits the first blank. (D) also fits the second blank best. (C), "maimed," would be redundant.

### 10. B

The key phrase here is "stood a reasonable chance of passing," so "realistic" is the most consistent adjective to describe the senator.

### 11. C

The second word must be "hurting," (C), since the second words in the other choices don't make sense.

### 12. C

"Mature quickly and breed prolifically" (meaning a lot) describes why rats contribute to the "spread" of disease.

### 13. C

This is a clear cause and effect statement: A public official who accepts "bribes" is by definition guilty of "corruption."

### 14. A

Elena was "ten minutes late," so we can assume her supervisor would "admonish," or scold, her. This stands in direct opposition to the fact that she received the "highest" service award.

**15. A**

We are looking for a logical connection here. Because ___ happened to the water, the castaways had to ___ the water. Only (A), "dwindled" and "rationed," makes sense.

**16. C**

What kind of an art collector would have paintings by Picasso and Matisse? Someone either (C), "avid," or (D), "enthusiastic." However, only (C), "acquired," makes any sense in the second blank.

**17. A**

Voters who say they would "vote to re-elect the mayor" are not in favor of change. They are "wary of" change, and this is what they "stated."

**18. D**

What would the chef do to the counter? Would he want the pie crust to stick? He'd probably want to "prevent" it from sticking, and he'd do this by making sure that he'd "dusted" the counter.

**19. D**

"Despite" tells us that the cost of the car and Jose's parents response to his buying it stood in opposition to each other. While the cost was "reasonable," his parents were "reluctant."

**20. D**

The speaker repeated herself at length—in other words, she "droned" on for hours, consequently "boring" her audience to tears.

## ML-UL

**21. A**

The clue word here is "affront," meaning offense. This would inspire a negative reaction, which is only offered by choice (A).

**22. D**

The clue word "Although" indicates a contrast between the intelligence of the people described and their behavior. (D) supplies the right contrast—they were "deceived" by false "claims."

**23. C**

If there is coal in Newcastle already, then bringing more is "unnecessary," choice (C).

**24. C**

The clue words "true" and "guise" indicate a contrast between the two words—George concealed his "concern" under a guise of "indifference."

**25. C**

Again, the clues indicate a contrast—the grizzly is normally "harmless" but can become "ferocious."

**26. D**

"But this claim" suggests that what people ___ about owls is false—"believe" and "myth" fit the assumption-reality structure here.

**27. A**

The second blank should suggest cheating—it's her "fraudulent" use of encyclopedia entries that gets Roberta in trouble. "Censured" means scolded or reprimanded.

**28. A**

Tricky vocabulary here. "Condoning" means approving, so if a newspaper editorial didn't offer any "comment" on a violent incident, it might seem like they were "condoning" violence, (A).

**29. D**

"Arsonist" and "pyromaniac" are both words for people who start fires—but "series" is the only word that fits the second half of the sentence.

**30. B**

When archeologists dig things up, they "excavate," sometimes "unearthing" treasures.

**31. D**

"Virtuosity" is the word that best describes "dazzling" musical ability here.

**32. A**

The clue words "except for" indicate a contrast here—except for "stunted" shrubs, the tundra provides little "nourishment" for the caribou.

**33. D**

Contrast between most people's experience and that of the poet is what you're looking for here. Most people find writing "arduous" (hard work), but she does it without "effort."

**34. B**

"Despite" indicates that the predictions of the meteorologists were the opposite of the damage the storm actually caused. "Ominous" and "minimal" are the opposites that we are looking for.

**35. D**

The phrases "hand in hand" and "sun-dappled" suggest that Tony and Marcia's walk was pleasant or "idyllic." Also, only "strolling" fits in with the kind of meandering action we are looking for.

**36. C**

"Since" is the key word here. Ricky's interview went well, but his counselor was "disappointed" to learn Ricky was "unenthusiastic" about going to college.

**37. D**

"Even though" tells us that we have a contrast. While Deidre was a clear leader, or "recognized" as a leader, she was just as happy to play a secondary, or "supporting," role.

**38. B**

Driving must go from one state of difficulty to being "finally impossible." Logically, only "increasingly" difficult fits here. Also, the fact that the snow "accumulated" in big drifts accounts for the worsening driving conditions.

**39. D**

The textbook was difficult it logically follows that the professor's lectures would have to help her with the more "intricate," (A), or "complicated," (D), concepts. However, only "follow" logically fits in the first blank.

**40. A**

What would be hand-crafted? A strong case can be made for "furnishings," and a weaker case made for "trappings." Looking at the first blank, however, only "sumptuously," (A), makes sense.

**41. D**

"At the mercy of" is the clue here. Henry has a "healthy" appetite, which renders him "unable" to stay on his diet.

**42. A**

The knights are "Weighted down with heavy armor." It follows logically that fighting, or "wielding," a sword with all that armor would be very uncomfortably, or "awkwardly," performed.

### 43. C

The semicolon and the key word "merely" indicate that we need words that are opposites. His admirers found the Prime Minister tough, or "tenacious," but his enemies, or "detractors," found him merely stubborn.

### 44. A

"Heedless" tells us that Terry was a little careless and overeager to clean up his mess. In other words, he had too much "zeal" and carelessly, or "indiscriminately," discarded the files.

## UL Only

### 45. D

Positive word for the first blank—originality and "sophistication." Limited in "popular" appeal is another way of saying the book did not appeal to a broad range of people.

### 46. D

"Given" and "may have been" tell us that whatever the market is doing, the "predictions" were the opposite. Given the "stagnation" or slowness of the market, predictions were too "optimistic," or positive.

### 47. D

Tory's painting depicts the "lakefront" and "inland." Such a broad view is summed up in the word "panoramic" for the first blank. "Ranging" is also the only word to fit logically into the second blank.

### 48. D

"And physically spent" clues us that the viewers were also emotionally spent, or "drained." Something "cathartic" would accomplish this.

## All Levels

### 49. C

The key phrase here is "living by herself," which tells us that the woman may be reclusive and a "hermit," choice (C).

### 50. C

A logic Sentence Completion: if she is a vegetarian, she must not eat meat. In other words, she "avoids" it, choice (C).

### 51. A

This two-blank cause-and-effect Sentence Completion must have a second blank that logically follows the implication of the first blank. Using word charge, you'll find that (A) is the only positive-positive pair.

### 52. A

"Utter failure" are the strong clue words here—they show that the project planners had a "lack of ability," (A). All the other choices are too positive.

### 53. D

"Voracious eater" is the key phrase here. You're looking for a word that means eating—(D), "consuming," fits the bill.

### 54. A

"Reasonable to believe her" is the key phrase in this question, indicating that "honesty," (A), is the word you're looking for.

### 55. D

There's a strong connection between the two blanks here, so plug each choice in to see which one fits. (D) has the most logical connection.

**56. B**

"Too ___ to compromise" is the key phrase in this question, indicating that "strongly opinionated," (B), is the phrase you're looking for.

**57. B**

The structural clue "but" indicates a contrast—that the child was "obedient and well-behaved" at home, but "hard to control" at school.

**58. A**

What phrase would support the assertion that a theory was "probably true"? "Supporting evidence" is the best answer.

**59. C**

Explanations taking longer than necessary? Couldn't have been a Kaplan teacher. Might have been an excessively "wordy" teacher from another test-prep service.

**60. B**

The key phrase is "exactly the same way," which tells you to look for a word that means the same in the second blank. Choice (B) is the only option.

**61. A**

By standing up when an elder enters, one shows "respect," choice (A).

**62. A**

The key phrase is "from cuts and scrapes," which tells us that the second blank should indicate that leather "protects" against cuts and scrapes. Choice (A) is the correct answer.

**63. A**

Increases in crime lead to fear, so "create," choice (A), is the most logical choice.

**64. B**

The key phrase is "make sense of," which leads us to "mysterious," or hard to explain.

**65. D**

The structural clue word "but" tells us that if opponents searched for wrongdoing, the blank should indicate that they didn't find any. "Spotless," choice (D), is correct.

**66. D**

What's a likely scenario between a teacher and student here? "Correct" and "faulty" make the best sense in this sentence.

**67. C**

"Drifted" is the clue word here—a boat would drift "aimlessly" if its engine "died."

**68. A**

Here, it's hard to predict the blanks; you have to plug in each answer choice. Only (A) makes sense—other birds would "unwittingly" (without realizing it) raise cowbird chicks as their own if the eggs were "deposited" in their nests.

**69. D**

The clue words "thoughtful" and "helped" indicate positive words for both blanks here. With a thoughtful "argument," a politician might "convince" a skeptical public.

**70. B**

Only "purify" fits the second blank here; "purify" describes the natural process by which a lake replenishes itself.

**71. B**

A typical cause-and-effect sentence here—because *x*, then *y*. (B) fits the structure of the sentence; a film with "prominent," or famous, actors would be "expected" to be successful.

**72. A**

The clues are obviously either (A), "significant," or (C), "crucial," here. Only "detect" fits the second blank, however.

**73. A**

"After" indicates cause and effect. "Unfairly" tells us that Luis was not treated kindly—he was either (A), "upbraided," or (D), "heckled." But only (A), "stormed," shows the effect we are looking for.

**74. C**

Cause and effect again. The cathedral has become "shabby, dirty, and increasingly unappealing," so the cathedral was once either (A), "impressive," or (C), "majestic." But only (C), "neglect," fits the first blank.

**75. B**

You are looking for opposites. The game was "close" but became a "rout."

**76. D**

Events are reported "shortly," or "rapidly," after they happen, because the news wire service is able to "disseminate," or spread, information.

**77. A**

"But" tells us that "photographs" and "two-dimensional images" don't give us the full impact of the real Grand Canyon. Its "spectacular" topography cannot be fully "appreciated" through pictures alone.

**78. D**

Only (D) makes sense here. While "repairing buildings and equipment," farmers are also "tending" their "livestock."

**79. D**

The stone carvings depict a battle scene "in intricate detail." While both (B), "beautiful," and (D), "ornate," seem like possibilities for the first blank, the answer clearly must be (D), because "clashing" is the only appropriate word to describe a battle scene.

**80. B**

"Paucity" means scarcity. "Unsubstantiated" means unproven. So we can assume that the newspaper has very little proven, or "reliable," information and has relied on, or "resorted to," rumors.

**81. B**

The word "Once" tells us that while wolves are now extinct, they were "numerous" at one point. The only word to logically fit into the second blank is "hunted."

**82. D**

The hostess has done something to make this year's guests less ____ than last year's. In other words, we want opposites. "Undistinguished" and "exclusive" fit the bill.

**83. A**

What would "an extinct aboriginal people" have done with a "gigantic structure"? Either (A), "erected" it, or (C), "built" it. But only (A), "indicates," fits into the first blank.

**84. A**

The two words we are looking for relate closely to each other. Cockroaches are ___ and consequently can ___. "Adaptable" and "thrive" are the only words that relate to each other in this way.

**85. B**

The audience reacted in a particular way as a direct result of how the violinist played. Again, we need words that relate to each other strongly. Only "accomplished" and "astounded" fit the bill.

**86. D**

"Somehow" tells us that Mary's study habits and grades are in opposition to each other. The answer must be (D), since "excellent" and "poor" are opposites.

**87. D**

Mark has already seen the film, while everyone else is seeing it for the first time. Both parties' reactions will be opposite each other. Mark is "unlikely" to be as "shocked" as everyone else.

**88. D**

The sentence sets up a contrast. While Lisa is a "pessimist," or someone who looks at the down side of things, her team did well. So she was "stunned" when her team "triumphed."

**89. A**

He "procrastinated," or waited until the last minute to do his work. It follows that he would have to attack the project in a big hurry, or "hastily." As a result of this haste, it follows that he would make careless or "inadvertent" errors.

**90. B**

"But" tells us that most of her "opinions" stand in contrast to a "few ___ insights." "Absurd" and "brilliant" oppose each other in the way that we want.

**91. B**

"Previously" tells us that what the politician is now doing with the proposal stands in opposition to what he did formerly. In other words, he "reversed" his position on a proposal that he had "supported" earlier.

**92. D**

A hero would perform either daring (B), "escapades," or (D), "exploits." However, only "antics" would amuse an audience.

**93. D**

"While" tells us that the "new educational project" appears one way to some and another way to others. In other words, it "caters" to some people while "ignoring" others.

**94. C**

If the bears are "bold," it follows logically that they would be "aggressive" in their search, or "quest," for food.

**95. D**

If Brett "improvised" a harness, he had to make one up. (A), "hitched," or (D), "yoked," makes sense for the first blank, but only (D), "mount," fits the second blank.

### 96. D

"Low numbers" tells us that there aren't many sharks. In other words, they are "rarely" encountered by divers due to their lonely, or "solitary," habits.

### 97. A

We know that soil nutrients were restored. This must mean that the soil nutrients were at one time taken away, or "depleted," from the Earth. Volcanic ash is deposited by a volcano's "eruption."

### 98. D

What would a sect do from "sun-up until long after dark"? Logically, they would work or "toil," thus "avoiding" laziness or the "sin of sloth."

### 99. A

Meteorologists would either (A), "track," or (B), "study," storm systems. But only (A), "forewarning," fits logically into the second blank.

### 100. C

"Lackadaisical" means showing a lack of interest or spirit, being listless or languid. If the firm employed lackadaisical workers, these workers probably had an "unproductive" approach to their work.

### 101. B

If you tried each of the choices in the first blank, you'd see that they all fit. As for the second blank, only one choice makes sense: Because of "severe" weather, all classes were "cancelled."

### 102. A

This question is filled with elements that the test makers hope to fool you with. Both the answer choices and the question itself contain difficult vocabulary (i.e., "neologisms" and "paleontologists").

In addition, the antonym for the correct answer is thrown in as a curve ball. However, the only choice that makes sense is (A), "descendants." Many paleontologists believe that birds and crocodiles are descended from dinosaurs.

### 103. C

Her eyes could well have been wide with "amazement," "reason," "wonder," or "purpose" as the ship sailed in. But the only choice that makes sense when you try to fill in the second blank is that "her eyes were wide with *wonder* as the ship *laden* with gold, jewels, and precious metals sailed into port." The other combinations just don't make sense.

### 104. B

It's possible to infer from the information in the sentence that Mount Vesuvius is a volcano. Regular hills and mountains don't erupt; only volcanoes do. And volcanoes don't "erect" cities, nor do they "detect" or "desiccate" cities. Indeed, volcanoes are very dangerous because they have the potential to "decimate" cities.

### 105. A

To "embody" means to personify. (A) is the only choice that works here. The cadet doesn't "create" the characters of an ideal soldier, nor does he "seclude" or for that matter "vaporize" those character traits.

# CHAPTER 5: ISEE-SPECIFIC MATH WORKOUT: QUANTITATIVE COMPARISONS

Quantitative Comparisons, or QCs, appear **on only the Upper- and Middle-Level ISEE**. If you are not taking one of those tests, you may skip this section.

## THE FORMAT

Of the approximately 37 math questions in the Quantitative Reasoning section, about 15 are QCs. In a QC, instead of solving for a particular value, you need to compare two quantities. You'll see two mathematical expressions: one in Column A, the other in Column B. Your job is to compare them.

Some questions include additional information about one or both quantities. This information is centered, unboxed, and essential to making the comparison.

The directions will look something like this:

---

In questions 1–10, note the given information, if any, and then compare the quantity in Column A to the quantity in Column B. Next to the number of each question, select

(A) if the quantity in Column A is greater

(B) if the quantity in Column B is greater

(C) if the two quantities are equal

(D) if the relationship cannot be determined from the information given

---

### THREE RULES FOR CHOICE (D)

Choice (D) is the only choice that represents a relationship that cannot be determined. (A), (B), and (C) all mean that a definite relationship can be found between the quantities in Columns A and B.

There are three things to remember about choice (D):

**Rule 1:** (D) is rarely correct for the first few QC questions.

**Rule 2:** (D) is never correct if the two columns contain only numbers.

**Rule 3:** (D) is correct if there's more than one possible relationship between the two columns.

### EXAMPLE

Column A                    Column B

| $3x$ | | $2x$ |

(A)  If the quantity in Column A is greater
(B)  If the quantity in Column B is greater
(C)  If the two quantities are equal
(D)  If the relationship cannot be determined from the information given

If $x$ is a positive number, then Column A is larger. If $x$ is equal to zero, then the quantities in Columns A and B are equal. If $x$ is a negative number, then Column B is larger.

There is more than one possible relationship between Columns A and B here, so according to rule 3, (D) is the correct choice. As soon as you realize that there is *more than one* possible relationship, choose (D) and move on.

## KAPLAN'S 5 STRATEGIES FOR QCS

The following five strategies will help you to make quick comparisons. The key is to *compare* the values rather than *calculate* them.

**Strategy 1:** Compare piece by piece.

**Strategy 2:** Make one column look like the other.

**Strategy 3:** Do the same thing to both columns.

**Strategy 4:** Pick numbers.

**Strategy 5:** Avoid QC traps.

**KAPLAN EXCLUSIVE TIPS**

" Compare, don't calculate. There's usually an easier way to solve a QC than to calculate it out. "

Let's look at each strategy in detail.

## STRATEGY 1: COMPARE PIECE BY PIECE

This applies to QCs that compare two sums or two products.

**EXAMPLE**

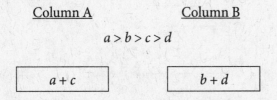

Column A      Column B

$$a > b > c > d$$

$a + c$        $b + d$

We're given four variables, or "pieces," in the above example, as well as the relationship between these pieces. We're told that $a$ is greater than all of the other pieces, while $c$ is greater than only $d$, etc. The next step is to compare the value of each piece in each column. If every piece in one column is greater than the corresponding piece in the other column, and if addition is the only mathematical operation involved, the column with the greater individual values ($a > b$ and $c > d$) will have the greater total value ($a + c > b + d$).

In other words, we know from the information given that $a > b$, and $c > d$. Therefore, the first term in Column A, $a$, is greater than its corresponding term in Column B, $b$. Likewise, the second term in Column A, $c$, is greater than $d$, its corresponding term in Column B. Since each individual "piece" in Column A is greater than its corresponding "piece" in Column B, the total value of Column A must be greater. The answer is (A).

## STRATEGY 2: MAKE ONE COLUMN LOOK LIKE THE OTHER

Use this strategy when the quantities in the two columns look so different that a direct comparison would be impossible.

If the quantities in Column A and B are expressed differently, or if one looks more complicated than the other, try to make a direct comparison easier by changing one column to look more like the other.

Let's try an example in which the quantities in Column A and Column B are expressed differently.

**EXAMPLE**

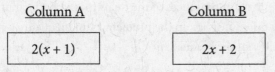

Column A      Column B

$2(x + 1)$        $2x + 2$

In the example above, it's difficult to make a direct comparison as the quantities are written. However, if you get rid of the parentheses in Column A so that the quantity more closely resembles that in Column B, you should see the relationship right away. If you multiply to get rid of the parentheses in Column A, you'll end up with $2x + 2$ in both columns. Therefore, the columns are equal in value, and the answer is (C).

This strategy is also useful when one column looks more complicated than the other.

**EXAMPLE**

Column A                    Column B

Try simplifying Column A, since it is the more complicated-looking quantity.

1) $\dfrac{2\sqrt{3}}{\sqrt{6}} = \dfrac{2\sqrt{3}}{\sqrt{2}\sqrt{3}}$

2) $\dfrac{2\sqrt{3}}{\sqrt{2}\sqrt{3}} = \dfrac{2}{\sqrt{2}}$

3) $\dfrac{2}{\sqrt{2}} = \dfrac{2}{\sqrt{2}} \times \dfrac{\sqrt{2}}{\sqrt{2}} = \dfrac{2\sqrt{2}}{2}$

4) $\dfrac{2\sqrt{2}}{2} = \sqrt{2}$

By simplifying Column A, we are able to make a direct and easy comparison between the two columns. Column A, when simplified, is equivalent to $\sqrt{2}$, which is the quantity in Column B. Therefore, (C) is the correct answer.

## STRATEGY 3: DO THE SAME THING TO BOTH COLUMNS

By adding or subtracting the same amount from both columns, you can often unclutter a comparison and make the relationship more apparent. You can also multiply or divide both columns by the same positive number. This keeps the relationship between the columns the same. If the quantities in both columns are positive, you can square both columns. This also keeps the relationship between the columns the same.

Changing the values, and not just the appearances of the quantities in both columns, is often helpful in tackling QC questions. Set up the problem as an inequality with the two columns as opposing sides of the inequality.

To change the values of the columns, add or subtract the same amount from both columns and multiply or divide by a positive number without changing the absolute relationship. But **be careful.** Remember that the direction of an inequality sign will

**KAPLAN EXCLUSIVE TIPS**

" Do not multiply or divide both QC columns by a negative number. "

be reversed if you multiply or divide by a negative number. Since this reversal will alter the relationship between the two columns, avoid multiplying or dividing by a negative number.

You can also square the quantities in both columns when both columns are positive. But **be careful.** Do not square both columns unless you know for certain that both columns are positive. Remember these two things when squaring the quantities in both columns: (1) the direction of an inequality sign can be reversed if one or both quantities are negative, and (2) the inequality sign can be changed to an equals sign if one quantity is positive and the other quantity is negative, with one quantity being the negative of the other. For example, $4 > -5$, yet $4^2 < (-5)^2$, since $16 < 25$. Likewise, $2 > -2$, yet $2^2 = (-2)^2$, since $2^2 = (-2)^2 = 4$.

In the QC below, what could you do to both columns?

## EXAMPLE

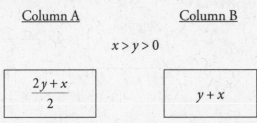

Column A       Column B

$$x > y > 0$$

| $\dfrac{2y + x}{2}$ | $y + x$ |

Try multiplying both columns by 2 to get rid of that fraction in Column A. You're left with $2y + x$ in Column A and $2y + 2x$ in Column B. We know that $2y = 2y$. But what about the relationship between $x$ and $2x$? The centered information tells us that $x > 0$. Therefore, $2x > x$, and Column B is greater than Column A. Choice (B) is the right answer.

In the next QC, what could you do to both columns?

## EXAMPLE

Column A       Column B

| $\dfrac{1}{4} + \dfrac{1}{5} - \dfrac{1}{3}$ | $\dfrac{1}{2} - \dfrac{1}{3} + \dfrac{1}{20}$ |

Try adding $\dfrac{1}{3}$ to both sides.

If you do this, you'll be left with $\dfrac{1}{4} + \dfrac{1}{5}$ in Column A and $\dfrac{1}{2} + \dfrac{1}{20}$ in Column B. Now treat this QC like a standard fraction problem. To find the sums in each column, you

---

**KAPLAN EXCLUSIVE TIPS**

When you plug in negative numbers and fractions, remember the following:

- When you square a positive fraction less than 1, the result is a smaller fraction than the original.
- When you square a negative number, the result is a positive number.
- When you square 0 and 1, they remain the same.

must find the lowest common denominator. Upon adding, you get $\frac{9}{20}$ in Column A and $\frac{11}{20}$ in Column B. Column B is greater than Column A, so the answer is (B).

## STRATEGY 4: PICK NUMBERS

Substitute numbers into those abstract algebra QCs. Try using a positive, a negative, and zero. A fraction can also be a handy choice for high difficulty problems.

If a QC involves variables, Pick Numbers to clarify the relationship. Here's what to do:

1. Pick Numbers that are easy to work with: positive, negative, zero, and fraction.

2. Plug in the numbers and calculate the values. What's the relationship between the columns?

3. Pick a different number for each variable and recalculate. See if you get a different relationship.

> **KAPLAN EXCLUSIVE TIPS**
>
> " Try setting up a chart when you Pick Numbers. "

| Column A | Column B |
|----------|----------|

$$x > 0$$

| $x$ | $\frac{1}{x}$ |
|-----|---------------|

It often helps to show the numbers you pick in a chart. When in doubt, sketch it out! This example has a restriction: $x > 0$. This means that the number you pick should be positive. Let's try to pick different types of numbers: 1, 100, and $\frac{1}{2}$. Notice that these numbers are examples of a wide spectrum of positive numbers.

| Number | Column A | Column B | Answer Choice |
|--------|----------|----------|---------------|
| 1 | 1 | $\frac{1}{1} = 1$ | C |
| 100 | 100 | $\frac{1}{100} = 0.01$ | A |
| $\frac{1}{2}$ | $\frac{1}{2}$ | **2** | B |

You could probably select (D) immediately after trying 1 and 100. Both (C) and (A) are correct answer choices. When you try $\frac{1}{2}$, the answer is (B). There are three different possible answers; therefore, the relationship cannot be determined from the information given, and (D) is the correct answer.

### PICK DIFFERENT KINDS OF NUMBERS

Never assume that all variables represent positive integers. Unless you're told otherwise, as in the case above, variables can be positive or negative, and they can be zero or fractions. Because different kinds of numbers behave differently, you should always choose a different kind of number the second time around. In the previous example, we knew that $x$ wasn't a negative number, nor was it zero, so we tried a fraction and discovered that the relationship between the columns did not remain the same.

In the next three examples, we'll choose different kinds of numbers and observe the results. Remember that if there's more than one possible relationship between the two columns, the answer is (D).

> **KAPLAN EXCLUSIVE TIPS**
>
> " Not all numbers are positive. Not all numbers are integers. "

### EXAMPLE

| Column A | Column B |
|----------|----------|
| $-b$ | $b$ |

| Number | Column A | Column B | Answer Choice |
|--------|----------|----------|---------------|
|  |  |  |  |
|  |  |  |  |
|  |  |  |  |
|  |  |  |  |

### EXAMPLE

| Column A | Column B |
|----------|----------|

$$m > 0$$

| Column A | Column B |
|----------|----------|
| $m + \dfrac{1}{m}$ | $2$ |

| Number | Column A | Column B | Answer Choice |
|--------|----------|----------|---------------|
|  |  |  |  |
|  |  |  |  |
|  |  |  |  |
|  |  |  |  |

## EXAMPLE

Column A          Column B

$$y \neq 0$$

| $y^3$ | | $y^2$ |

| Number | Column A | Column B | Answer Choice |
|---|---|---|---|
| | | | |
| | | | |
| | | | |
| | | | |

## EXAMPLE

Column A          Column B

| $-b$ | | $b$ |

Selected numbers were 0, 2, –2, and $\frac{1}{2}$.

| Number | Column A | Column B | Answer Choice |
|---|---|---|---|
| 0 | 0 | 0 | C |
| 2 | –2 | 2 | B |
| –2 | 2 | –2 | A |
| $\frac{1}{2}$ | $-\frac{1}{2}$ | $\frac{1}{2}$ | B |

Since (A), (B), and (C) are all possible choices, (D) is the correct choice.

## EXAMPLE

Column A          Column B

| $m + \dfrac{1}{m}$ | | 2 |

Selected numbers were 0, 2, –2, and $\frac{1}{2}$.

| Number | Column A | Column B | Answer Choice |
|--------|----------|----------|---------------|
| 1 | 2 | 2 | C |
| 2 | $\frac{5}{2} = 2.5$ | 2 | A |
| 100 | 100.01 | 2 | A |
| $\frac{1}{2}$ | $\frac{5}{2} = 2.5$ | 2 | A |

Since (A) and (C) are both possible choices, (D) is the correct choice.

**EXAMPLE**

Column A

$$\frac{1}{y^5}$$

Column B

$$\frac{1}{y^4}$$

Selected numbers were 2, –2, and $\frac{1}{2}$.

| Number | Column A | Column B | Answer Choice |
|--------|----------|----------|---------------|
| 2 | $\frac{1}{32}$ | $\frac{1}{16}$ | B |
| –2 | $-\frac{1}{32}$ | $\frac{1}{16}$ | B |
| $\frac{1}{2}$ | 32 | 16 | A |

Since (A) and (B) are both possible choices, (D) is the correct choice.

## STRATEGY 5: AVOID QC TRAPS

Keep your eyes open for those trick questions designed to fool you into the obvious but wrong answer. Questions are arranged in order of increasing difficulty, so chances are you'll see traps toward the end of the set.

To avoid these nasty traps, always be on your toes. Never assume anything. Be particularly careful toward the end of a QC set.

## DON'T BE TRICKED BY MISLEADING INFORMATION

### EXAMPLE

<u>Column A</u>                          <u>Column B</u>

Frank weighs more
than Hector.

| Frank's height in meters | Hector's height in meters |
|---|---|

The test makers are hoping that you'll follow some faulty logic and think, "If Frank is heavier, he must be taller." But that's not necessarily so. The answer in this case would be (D). If you keep your eyes open for these kinds of things, you'll spot them immediately.

## DON'T ASSUME

### EXAMPLE

<u>Column A</u>                          <u>Column B</u>

$$1 + x^2 = 10$$

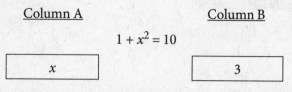

| $x$ | 3 |
|---|---|

A common mistake on QC questions is to assume that variables represent positive integers. We already dealt with these kinds of problems in the Picking Numbers strategy. Remember that positive and negative numbers, as well as fractions and zeros, behave differently.

In the example above, the test makers are hoping you'll assume that $x = 3$, since the square of 3 = 9. But $x$ could also be equal to –3. Because $x$ could be 3 or –3, (D) is the correct answer.

## DON'T FALL FOR LOOK-ALIKES

### EXAMPLE

<u>Column A</u>                          <u>Column B</u>

| $\sqrt{4} + \sqrt{4}$ | $\sqrt{8}$ |
|---|---|

Now, 4 + 4 = 8, *but* $\sqrt{4} + \sqrt{4} > \sqrt{8}$! Don't forget the rules of radicals. The test makers are counting on you to rush and look for the obvious choice, (C), that the two quantities are equal. Don't let them fool you. If $a > 0$ and $b > 0$, then $\sqrt{a+b} \neq \sqrt{a} + \sqrt{b}$.

Remember the convention that if $x$ is positive, $\sqrt{x}$ means the positive square root. So $\sqrt{4} + \sqrt{4} = 2 + 2 = 4$. Now we have 4 in Column A and $\sqrt{8}$ in Column B. Since $\sqrt{8} < \sqrt{9}$ and $\sqrt{9} = 3$, $\sqrt{8} < 3 < 4$. Thus, $4 > \sqrt{8}$ and Column A is greater. Because 4 and $\sqrt{8}$ are both positive, you could also show that $4 > \sqrt{8}$ by squaring both 4 and $\sqrt{8}$: $4^2 = 16$ and $(\sqrt{8})^2 = 8$; 16 > 8, so $4 > \sqrt{8}$. Choice (A) is correct.

# PRACTICE QUESTIONS

Directions: In the following questions, note the given information, if any, and then compare the quantity in Column A to the quantity in Column B. Next to the number of each question, select

(A) if the quantity in Column A is greater

(B) if the quantity in Column B is greater

(C) if the two quantities are equal

(D) if the relationship cannot be determined from the information given

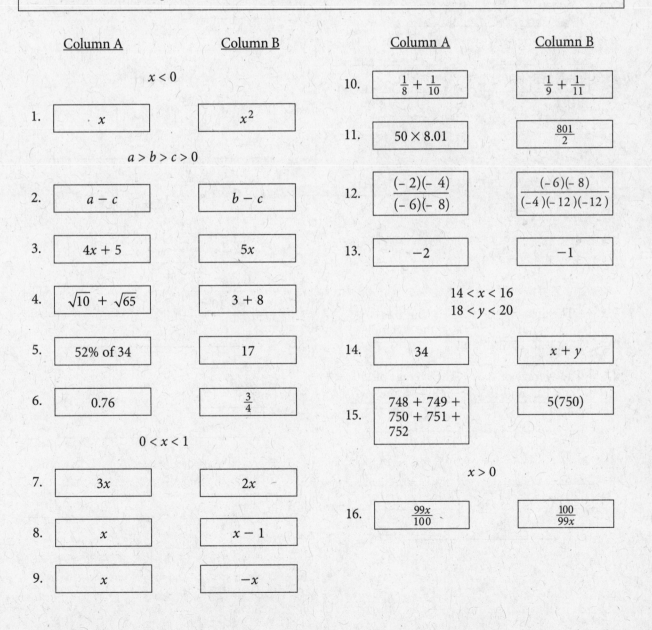

| | Column A | Column B |
|---|---|---|
| | $x < 0$ | |
| 1. | $x$ | $x^2$ |
| | $a > b > c > 0$ | |
| 2. | $a - c$ | $b - c$ |
| 3. | $4x + 5$ | $5x$ |
| 4. | $\sqrt{10} + \sqrt{65}$ | $3 + 8$ |
| 5. | 52% of 34 | 17 |
| 6. | 0.76 | $\frac{3}{4}$ |
| | $0 < x < 1$ | |
| 7. | $3x$ | $2x$ |
| 8. | $x$ | $x - 1$ |
| 9. | $x$ | $-x$ |

| | Column A | Column B |
|---|---|---|
| 10. | $\frac{1}{8} + \frac{1}{10}$ | $\frac{1}{9} + \frac{1}{11}$ |
| 11. | $50 \times 8.01$ | $\frac{801}{2}$ |
| 12. | $\frac{(-2)(-4)}{(-6)(-8)}$ | $\frac{(-6)(-8)}{(-4)(-12)(-12)}$ |
| 13. | $-2$ | $-1$ |
| | $14 < x < 16$ | |
| | $18 < y < 20$ | |
| 14. | 34 | $x + y$ |
| 15. | $748 + 749 + 750 + 751 + 752$ | $5(750)$ |
| | $x > 0$ | |
| 16. | $\frac{99x}{100}$ | $\frac{100}{99x}$ |

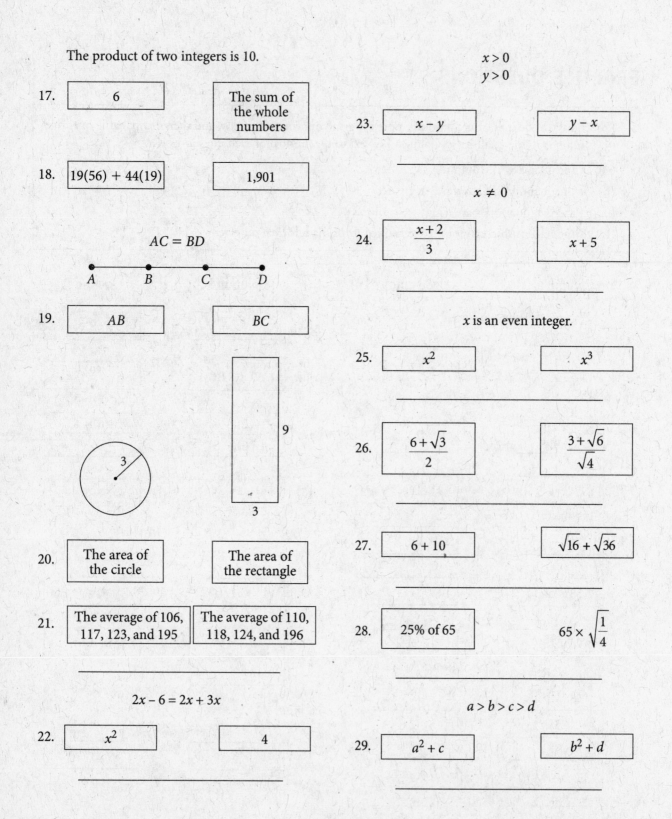

The product of two integers is 10.

17. | 6 | | The sum of the whole numbers |

18. | $19(56) + 44(19)$ | | 1,901 |

$AC = BD$

A    B    C    D

19. | $AB$ | | $BC$ |

20. | The area of the circle | | The area of the rectangle |

9

3

21. | The average of 106, 117, 123, and 195 | | The average of 110, 118, 124, and 196 |

$2x - 6 = 2x + 3x$

22. | $x^2$ | | 4 |

$x > 0$
$y > 0$

23. | $x - y$ | | $y - x$ |

$x \neq 0$

24. | $\dfrac{x+2}{3}$ | | $x + 5$ |

$x$ is an even integer.

25. | $x^2$ | | $x^3$ |

26. | $\dfrac{6 + \sqrt{3}}{2}$ | | $\dfrac{3 + \sqrt{6}}{\sqrt{4}}$ |

27. | $6 + 10$ | | $\sqrt{16} + \sqrt{36}$ |

28. | 25% of 65 | | $65 \times \sqrt{\dfrac{1}{4}}$ |

$a > b > c > d$

29. | $a^2 + c$ | | $b^2 + d$ |

# PRACTICE QUESTION ANSWERS

## 1. B

Since $x$ is negative, Column A is negative. But because a negative number squared is positive, Column B is positive and therefore greater than Column A.

## 2. A

Add $c$ to both columns and you end up comparing $a$ and $b$. The centered information tells you straight out that $a$ is greater.

## 3. D

If you tried to do this one by Picking Numbers and all you picked were small integers like 1, 2, or 3, you'd think the answer was (A). Try taking a value for $x$ that's greater than 5. When $x = 6$, for example, Column A is 29 and Column B is 30. More than one relationship is possible, so the answer is (D).

## 4. A

Compare piece by piece. You know that $\sqrt{9}$ is 3, so $\sqrt{10}$ is more than 3. By similar reasoning, you know that $\sqrt{65}$ is more than 8. Each piece of Column A is greater than the corresponding piece of Column B, so the sum of the pieces in Column A will be greater than the sum of the pieces in Column B.

## 5. A

Don't calculate. Compare Column A to a percent of 34 that's easy to find. Think of 52% as just a bit more than 50%, or $\frac{1}{2}$. 52% of 34, then, is just a bit more than half of 34, so it's more than 17.

## 6. A

If you know your standard fraction-decimal equivalents, you know that $\frac{3}{4}$ is the same as 0.75, which is less than 0.76.

## 7. A

Tripling $x$ doesn't necessarily give you more than doubling $x$, but it does when $x$ is positive, as is the case here.

## 8. A

Subtract $x$ from both columns to get 0 in Column A and $-1$ in Column B. Column A is greater.

## 9. D

At first glance, you might think that $x$ is greater than $-x$ because a positive is greater than a negative, but nothing says that $x$ has to be positive or that $-x$ has to be negative. If $x$ is negative to start with, then $-x$ is positive, and the relationship is reversed. And if $x = 0$, the columns are equal, so the answer is (D).

## 10. A

Don't calculate; compare piece by piece. The first fraction in Column A is greater than the first fraction in Column B, and the second fraction in Column A is greater than the second fraction in Column B. Therefore, the sum in Column A is also greater.

## 11. C

Multiply both columns by 2 and you end up with $100 \times 8.01$, or 801, in Column A, and you also end up with 801 in Column B.

## 12. A

Just look at the number of negative signs in each column, use what you know about numbers, and you won't have to evaluate the two expressions. In Column A, you have a positive over a positive, which is positive, and in Column B you have a positive over a negative, which is negative. There's no need to calculate to see that Column A is greater.

**13. B**

−1 is further to the right on the number line than −2, so −1 is greater.

**14. D**

Use what you know about $x$ and $y$ to figure out the greatest and least possible values of $x + y$. Don't assume that $x$ and $y$ are integers. That would make $x = 15$ and $y = 19$, and then the columns would be equal. But $x$ might be less than 15, perhaps 14.5, and $y$ might less than 19, perhaps 18.5. In that case, Column A would be greater. (It's also possible for $x + y$ to be *greater* than 34.) More than one relationship is possible, so the answer is (D).

**15. C**

There's no need to calculate. The sum of the five consecutive integers in Column A will be simply 5 times the middle number, exactly what you have in Column B.

**16. D**

These two quantities are reciprocals, so when Column A is greater than 1, Column B is less than 1, and vice versa. Column A will be greater than 1, and consequently greater than Column B, when $99x$ is greater than 100—in other words, when $x$ is greater than $\frac{100}{99}$. On the other hand, Column A will be less than 1, and consequently less than Column B, when $x$ is *less* than $\frac{100}{99}$. And, of course, the columns will be equal when $x = \frac{100}{99}$. More than one relationship is possible, so the answer is (D).

**17. D**

There are several pairs of integers that have a product of 10. You don't need to find every pair. Just try to find a pair that has a sum greater than 6 (like 5 and 2) and another pair that has a sum less than 6 (like −5 and −2). Since more than one relationship is possible, the answer is (D).

**18. B**

Note that if you factor 19 out of Column A, you end up with 19 times 100, which is 1 less than 1,901. $19(56) + 44(19) = 19(56 + 44) = 19(100) = 1,900$. Column B is larger.

**19. D**

It looks at first glance like $B$ and $C$ divide the segment into three equal pieces. But check the mathematics of the situation to be sure. You're given that $AC = BD$:

What can you deduce from that? You can subtract $BC$ from both equal lengths, and you'll end up with another equality: $AB = CD$. But what about $BC$? Does it have to be the same as $AB$ and $CD$? No. The diagram could be resketched like this:

Now you can see that it's possible for $AC$ and $BD$ to be equal but for $BC$ to be longer than $AB$. It's also possible for $BC$ to be shorter:

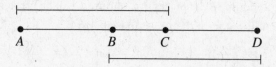

More than one relationship is possible, so the answer is (D).

**20. A**

The area of the circle is $\pi r^2 = \pi(3)^2 = 9\pi$. The area of the rectangle is $9 \times 3$. Don't think of it as 27; it's easier to compare in the form $9 \times 3$. $\pi$ is more than 3, so $9\pi$ is more than $9 \times 3$.

### 21. B

Compare piece by piece. The corresponding numbers in Column B are greater than those in Column A. Therefore, the average in Column B must be greater.

### 22. C

Solve for $x$ in the centered equation. First, subtract $2x$ from both sides. This will leave you with $-6 = 3x$. Divide both sides by 3. Now, $x = -2$. Plug in $-2$ for $x$ to find the value of $x^2$ in Column A: $x^2 = (-2)^2 = 4$. The quantities in both columns are equal.

### 23. D

From the centered information, you know only that the variables $x$ and $y$ must be positive. So plug in some positive integers. If $x = 5$ and $y = 3$, then Column A is $x - y = 5 - 3 = 2$ and Column B is $y - x = 3 - 5 = -2$. In this case, Column A is greater. Now plug in some different numbers. Notice that you have not been given any information about the relationship between $x$ and $y$. If you were to switch the values that you used on the first try, so that $x = 3$ and $y = 5$, then Column A is $x - y = 3 - 5 = -2$ and Column B is $y - x = 5 - 3 = 2$. Column B is greater. Since more than one relationship between the columns is possible, choice (D) is correct.

### 24. D

This problem appears to be an obvious candidate for the Picking Numbers strategy. But be careful with the numbers you choose. Let's plug in 2 for $x$. Column A is $\dfrac{2+2}{3}$, or $\dfrac{4}{3}$, and Column B is $2 + 5$, or 7. Column B is greater. Your next likely step would be to switch your plug-in number from a positive to a negative. Here's where the test makers will mislead you if you aren't careful. By letting $x = -2$, you find that Column A is $\dfrac{-2+2}{3}$, or 0, while

Column B is $-2 + 5$, or 3. Once again, Column B is greater. But what happens if you plug in a negative number considerably farther away from 0? If $x = -100$, then Column A is $\dfrac{-100+2}{3} = \dfrac{-98}{3}$, or $-32\dfrac{2}{3}$, and Column B is $-100 + 5$, or $-95$. In this case, Column A is greater. More than one relationship between the columns is possible.

### 25. D

This is another Picking Numbers type of problem. Let's begin by plugging in a positive value for $x$ that is consistent with the centered information. Let $x = 2$. So Column A is $2^2 = 2 \times 2$, or 4, and Column B is $2^3 = 2 \times 2 \times 2$, or 8. In this case, Column B is greater. Now pick a negative value for $x$ that is consistent with the centered information. Let $x = -2$. Now, Column A is $(-2)^2 = (-2) \times (-2) = 4$ and Column B is $(-2)^3 = (-2) \times (-2) \times (-2) = -8$. Column A is greater. Since more than one relationship between the columns is possible, (D) is correct.

### 26. A

While it is true that every positive number has two square roots—a positive and a negative square root—the convention with the symbol $\sqrt{\phantom{x}}$ is that if $x$ is positive, $\sqrt{x}$ means the positive square root of $x$. For example, 16 has the two square roots, 4 and $-4$, while $\sqrt{16}$ means the positive square root of 16, which is 4. Thus, $\sqrt{16} = 4$.

First, notice that the denominator $\sqrt{4}$ of Column B is equal to 2. So we're comparing $\dfrac{6 + \sqrt{3}}{2}$ in Column A with $\dfrac{3 + \sqrt{6}}{2}$ in Column B. Now try doing the same thing to both columns. Multiplying both columns by 2 leaves us with $6 + \sqrt{3}$ for Column A and $3 + \sqrt{6}$ for Column B. Next, subtracting 3 from both columns leaves us with $3 + \sqrt{3}$ for Column A and $\sqrt{6}$ for Column B. Now $3 = \sqrt{9}$ and $\sqrt{9}$ is greater than $\sqrt{6}$. So 3 is greater than $\sqrt{6}$. Surely $3 + \sqrt{3}$ (which is what we now have for Column A) is greater than 3. Also, 3 is greater than $\sqrt{6}$, with $\sqrt{6}$ being what we have for Column B. So $3 + \sqrt{3}$ for Column A must be greater than $\sqrt{6}$ for Column B. Choice (A) is correct.

## 27. A

Just as we saw in the previous question, if $x$ is positive, that means $\sqrt{x}$ is the positive square root of $x$. In Column A, $6 + 10 = 16$. In Column B, we have $\sqrt{16} + \sqrt{36}$. By convention, $\sqrt{16} = 4$ and $\sqrt{36} = 6$. So $\sqrt{16} + \sqrt{36} = 4 + 6 = 10$. Column A is greater.

## 28. B

Change one of the columns so you can make a direct comparison. A percentage can be written as a fraction and vice versa. It's generally easier to work with fractions, so convert 25% in Column A to a fraction. The fractional equivalent of 25% is $\frac{1}{4}$. (You convert a percent to a fraction (or decimal) by dividing the percent by 100%, so $25\% = \frac{25\%}{100\%} = \frac{25}{100} = \frac{1}{4}$.)

Therefore, Column A is $\frac{1}{4}$ of 65, or $\frac{65}{4}$. Column B is $65 \times \sqrt{\frac{1}{4}}$. Let's first simplify $\sqrt{\frac{1}{4}}$. $\sqrt{\frac{1}{4}} = \frac{\sqrt{1}}{\sqrt{4}} =$

$\frac{1}{2}$. So Column B is $65 \times \frac{1}{2}$, or $\frac{65}{2}$. Since $\frac{65}{2}$ is greater than $\frac{65}{4}$, Column B is greater.

## 29. D

Since the variables could be positive or negative, pick different kinds of numbers for the variables to see if different relationships between the columns are possible. Remember that the values you pick must be consistent with the centered information, which is that $a > b > c > d$.

If $a = 4$, $b = 3$, $c = 2$, and $d = 1$, then the value of Column A is $a^2 + c = 4^2 + 2 = 16 + 2 = 18$, and the value of Column B is $b^2 + d = 3^2 + 1 = 9 + 1 = 10$. Column A is greater. If you pick only positive numbers, then it will always be true that $a^2 + c > b^2 + d$. You could fall for the trap here of thinking that $a^2 + c$ is always greater than $b^2 + d$ if you don't let some or all of the variables be negative. Let $a = -1$, $b = -2$, $c = -3$, and $d = -4$. These values are consistent with the centered information. This time the value of Column A is $a^2 + c = (-1)^2 + (-3) = 1 - 3 = -2$, and the value of Column B is $b^2 + d = (-2)^2 + (-4) = 4 - 4 = 0$. So in this case, Column B is greater. More than one relationship between the columns is possible.

| Part Three |

# COMMON CONTENT FOR THE SSAT AND ISEE

# CHAPTER 6: SSAT AND ISEE MASTERY

Every year, close to 100,000 students take either the SSAT or ISEE for admission to nearly 2,000 independent (private) schools. Although the components of the two tests are remarkably similar, there are some critical differences.

To get a great score on a private school admissions test, you need to to know some key things that have nothing to do with vocabulary words or isosceles triangles. Namely, you need to know how to be a good test taker.

- You need to have a basic understanding of the nature of the test.
- You need to hone your math and verbal skills.
- You need to develop test-taking strategies and techniques.

Having a solid grasp of the content on the test is obviously important. You can't do well if you don't know the material. But it's also just as important to know how the test is set up, what kinds of questions it has, and what kinds of traps it commonly sets. If you don't know these things, you will be at a severe disadvantage on Test Day.

## USING THE TEST STRUCTURE TO YOUR ADVANTAGE

Whether you're taking the SSAT (Secondary School Admission Test) or the ISEE (Independent School Entrance Exam), you'll notice pretty quickly that it is very different from the tests you're used to taking in school. On a school test, you're often told to show your work, spend more time on tough questions (since they're worth more points), and work thoroughly, even if it means taking extra time.

None of these things apply in the world of standardized testing. On your private school admissions test, it won't matter how you answer a question; it only matters what your final answer is. Also, all questions are worth the same number of points, so it's always to your advantage to answer easier questions first to get them out of the way.

The SSAT and ISEE are each given to students in a range of grades, so if you're in 9th grade, for example, you're not expected to get as many questions right on the Upper Level test as someone in 11th grade. Keep that in mind as you take the test so you won't get discouraged if you find a lot of questions that you can't answer!

To succeed in this unique testing environment, you need to know some fundamentals. The SSAT and ISEE have differences, so read carefully.

Because the format and directions of the SSAT and ISEE remain relatively unchanged from year to year, you can learn the setup in advance. Then on Test Day, all you'll have to worry about will be answering each question, not learning how a Synonym question works.

One of the easiest and most useful things you can do to boost your performance is to learn and understand the directions before Test Day. Since the instructions are always exactly the same, there's no reason to waste your time on the day of the test reading them. Get them straight in your head beforehand, while you go through this book, and you'll be able to skip them during the test.

## SKIPPING AROUND

You're allowed to skip around as much as you'd like within each section of the SSAT or ISEE. High scorers know this and use it to their advantage. They move through the test efficiently, quickly marking and leaving questions they can't answer immediately, racking up points on questions they do know, then coming back to the tough ones later. They don't dwell on any question, even a hard one, until they've tried every question at least once.

When you see questions that look tough, circle them in your test booklet and skip them for later. Gather points on easy questions first. On a second look, some tricky-looking questions can turn out to be much easier than they initially looked. And remember, if you're on the younger side of the testing group within your level, expect to see several questions that you won't be able to answer. The test is intentionally set up this way, so don't let it discourage you.

## GUESSING—KNOW YOUR TEST

When should you guess? That's a question we hear from students all the time. It depends on which test you're taking. Read the following information and follow the instructions for your test. Guessing is one of the few areas in which the SSAT and ISEE operate differently, so read carefully!

**SSAT:** There is a *wrong-answer penalty*. For each answer you get right, you get one point. For each answer you get wrong, one-quarter of a point is deducted from your total score. Does this mean you shouldn't guess? No, not at all. What it means is that you need to be smart about it. Essentially, if you can eliminate at least one—and preferably two—answer choices, it's to your advantage to guess, because you've tipped the odds of guessing correctly in your favor. If you can't eliminate anything, however, you're better off leaving the question blank.

**ISEE:** There is *no* wrong-answer penalty. That means you should answer every single question on the test, even if you have no idea what it's asking you. The ISEE calculates your score simply by adding up your right answers, so you might as well fill in all those ovals completely. You never know what you might get right by luck!

## GRIDDING—THE ANSWER GRID HAS NO HEART

Misgridding. It sounds so basic, but it happens all the time: When time is short, it's easy to get confused going back and forth between your test booklet and your answer grid. If you know the answer but misgrid, you won't get any points, so be careful. Don't let it happen to you. Here are some tips to help you avoid making mistakes on the answer grid:

### CIRCLE THE QUESTIONS YOU SKIP

Put a big circle in your test booklet around any question numbers you skip. When you go back, these questions will be easy to locate. Also, if you accidentally skip a box on the grid, you can check your grid against your booklet to see where you went wrong.

### ALWAYS CIRCLE THE ANSWERS YOU CHOOSE

Circling your answers in the test booklet, as well as clearly marking your answers in the answer grid as you work on each question, makes it easier to check your grid against your booklet.

### GRID FIVE OR MORE ANSWERS AT ONCE

Don't transfer your answers to the grid after every question. Do it after every five questions or at the end of each reading passage. That way, you won't keep breaking your concentration. You'll save time and you'll gain accuracy.

Be careful at the end of a section, when time may be running out. You don't want to have your answers in the test booklet and not be able to transfer them to your answer grid because you have run out of time. Make sure to transfer your answers after every five questions or so.

# APPROACHING SSAT OR ISEE QUESTIONS

Apart from knowing the setup of the SSAT or ISEE, you need to have a system for attacking the questions. You wouldn't travel around a foreign city without a map, and you shouldn't approach your private school admissions test without a plan, either. Once you know the basics about how each test is set up, you can approach each section more strategically. We recommend the following method for approaching test questions systematically.

## THINK ABOUT THE QUESTION BEFORE YOU LOOK AT THE ANSWER

The people who make the tests love to put distracters among the answer choices. Distracters are answer choices that look like the right answer, but aren't. If you jump right into the answer choices without thinking first about what you're looking for, you're more likely to fall for one of these traps.

## USE BACKDOOR STRATEGIES IF NECESSARY

There are usually a number of ways to get to the right answer on an SSAT or ISEE question. Most of the questions are multiple-choice. That means the answer is right in front of you—you just have to find it. But if you can't figure out the answer in a straightforward way, try other techniques. We'll talk about specific Kaplan Methods such as Backsolving, Picking Numbers, and eliminating wrong answers in later chapters.

## PACE YOURSELF

The SSAT and ISEE give you a lot of questions in a short period of time. In order to get through an entire section, you can't spend too much time on any one question. Keep moving through the test at a good speed; if you run into a hard question, circle it, skip it, and go back later if there's time.

Typically, the questions get harder as you move through a problem set. Ideally, you can work through the easy problems at a brisk, steady clip and use a little more of your time for the harder ones that come at the end of the set.

One caution: Don't completely rush through the easy problems just to save time for the harder ones. These early problems are points in your pocket, and you don't want to work through them with such haste that you end up making careless mistakes.

## LOCATE QUICK POINTS IF YOU'RE RUNNING OUT OF TIME

Some questions can be done quickly; for instance, some reading questions will ask you to identify the meaning of a particular word in the passage. These can be done at the last minute, even if you haven't read the passage. When you start to run out of time, locate and answer any of the quick points that remain.

When you take the SSAT or ISEE, you have one clear objective in mind: to score as many points as you can. It's that simple. The rest of this book will help you do that.

# MANAGING STRESS

The countdown has begun. Your date with the test is looming on the horizon. Anxiety is on the rise. The butterflies in your stomach have gone ballistic. Your thinking is getting cloudy. Maybe you think you won't be ready. Maybe you already know your stuff, but you're going into panic mode anyway. Don't freak! It's possible to tame that anxiety and stress—*before* and *during* the test.

Remember, a little stress is good.  Anxiety is a motivation to study. The adrenaline that gets pumped into your bloodstream when you're stressed helps you stay alert and think more clearly. But if you feel that the tension is so great that it's preventing you from using your study time effectively, here are some things you can do to get it under control.

## TAKE CONTROL

Lack of control is a prime cause of stress. Research shows that if you don't have a sense of control over what's happening in your life, you can easily end up feeling helpless and hopeless. Try to identify the sources of the stress you feel. Which sources can you do something about? Can you find ways to reduce the stress you're feeling about any of these sources?

## FOCUS ON YOUR STRENGTHS

Make a list of areas of strength you have that will help you do well on the test. We all have strengths, and recognizing your own is like having reserves of solid gold at Fort Knox. You'll be able to draw on your reserves as you need them, helping you solve difficult questions, maintain confidence, and keep test stress and anxiety at a distance. And every time you recognize a new area of strength, solve a challenging problem, or score well on a practice test, you'll increase your reserves.

## IMAGINE YOURSELF SUCCEEDING

Close your eyes and imagine yourself in a relaxing situation. Breathe easily and naturally. Now, think of a real-life situation in which you scored well on a test or did well on an assignment. Focus on this success. Now turn your thoughts to the SSAT or ISEE and keep your thoughts and feelings in line with that successful experience. Don't make comparisons between them; just imagine yourself taking the upcoming test with the same feelings of confidence and relaxed control.

## SET REALISTIC GOALS

Facing your problem areas gives you some distinct advantages. What can you accomplish in the time remaining? Make a list of realistic goals. You can't help but feel more confident when you know you're actively improving your chances of earning a higher test score.

## MASTER YOUR PHYSICAL WELL-BEING

How well you do on Test Day doesn't only have to do with how prepared you are. It also has to do with what kind of condition you are in physically.

### EXERCISE YOUR FRUSTRATIONS AWAY

Whether it's jogging, biking, push-ups, or a pickup basketball game, physical exercise will stimulate your mind and body and improve your ability to think and concentrate. A surprising number of students fall out of the habit of regular exercise, ironically because they're spending so much time prepping for exams. A little physical exertion will help to keep your mind and body in sync and help you sleep better at night.

### AVOID DRUGS

Using drugs (prescription or recreational) specifically to prepare for and take a big test is definitely self-defeating. (And if they're illegal drugs, you may end up with a bigger problem than the SSAT or ISEE on your hands.) Mild stimulants, such as coffee or cola, can sometimes help as you study, since they keep you alert. On the downside, too much of these can also lead to agitation, restlessness, and insomnia. It all depends on your tolerance for caffeine.

### EAT WELL

Good nutrition will help you focus and think clearly. Eat plenty of fruits and vegetables; low-fat protein such as fish, skinless poultry, beans, and legumes; and whole grains such as brown rice, whole-wheat bread, and pastas. Don't eat a lot of sugar and high-fat snacks or salty foods.

### KEEP BREATHING

Conscious attention to breathing is an excellent way to manage stress while you're taking the test. Most of the people who get into trouble during tests take shallow breaths: They breathe using only their upper chests and shoulder muscles, and they may even hold their breath for long periods of time. Conversely, those test takers who breathe deeply in a slow, relaxed manner are likely to be in better control during the session.

### STRETCH

If you find yourself getting spaced out or burned out as you study or take the test, stop for a brief moment and stretch. Flex your feet and arms. Even though you'll be pausing on the test for a moment, it's a moment well spent. Stretching will help to refresh you and refocus your thoughts.

# CHAPTER 7: SYNONYMS

Synonyms appear on all levels of the SSAT and ISEE. At its most basic level, a synonym is a word that is similar in meaning to another defined word. *Fast* is a synonym for *quick*. OK, that makes sense. Unfortunately, if synonyms were that easy on the SSAT or ISEE, the tests wouldn't tell admissions officers very much.

## THE FORMAT

The synonyms you'll see on your actual test will be much more challenging than the sample above, but they'll all follow the same logic. You'll see a word in capital letters (we call this the *stem word*), and it will be followed by five other words on the SSAT or four on the ISEE). One of them will be the synonym of the given word, and the others will not.

**EXAMPLE**

AUTHENTIC:

(A) genuine
(B) valuable
(C) ancient
(D) damaged
(E) historical

Which of these words means "authentic"? Maybe you "just knew" that the answer was (A), *genuine,* and maybe you didn't. Either way, you need a method that will work for you on both the easy and the hard Synonym questions. What you need is the . . .

# KAPLAN 3-STEP METHOD FOR SYNONYMS

**Step 1.** Define the stem word.

**Step 2.** Find the answer choice that best fits your definition.

**Step 3.** If no choice fits, think of other definitions for the stem word and go through the choices again.

Let's take another look at the previous example, using the 3-Step Method.

## STEP 1: DEFINE THE STEM WORD

What does *authentic* mean? Something authentic is something *real,* such as an authentic signature, rather than a forgery. Your definition might look like this: Something authentic can be *proven* to be what it *claims* to be.

## STEP 2: FIND THE ANSWER CHOICE THAT BEST FITS YOUR DEFINITION

Go through the answer choices one by one to see which one fits best. Your options are: *genuine, valuable, ancient, damaged,* and *historical.* Something "authentic" could be worth a lot or not much at all, old or new, in good shape or bad, or even recent or historical. The only word that really means the same thing as authentic is (A) genuine.

## STEP 3: IF NO CHOICE FITS, THINK OF OTHER DEFINITIONS FOR THE STEM WORD AND GO THROUGH THE CHOICES AGAIN

In the previous example, one choice fit, but take a look at another one:

**EXAMPLE**

GRAVE:

(A) regrettable

(B) unpleasant

(C) serious

(D) careful

(E) lengthy

Say you defined "grave" as *a burial location.* You looked at the choices and didn't see any words like *tomb* or *coffin.* What to do? Move to step 3 and go back to the stem word, thinking about other definitions. Have you ever heard of a "grave situation"? Grave can also mean *serious* or *solemn,* and you can see that (C), *serious,* now fits the bill perfectly. If none of the answer choices seem to work with your definition, there may be a secondary definition you haven't yet considered.

---

**WALK THE WALK**

" What if WALK were your stem word. What part of speech is it? It could be the *act of* walking (a verb), or *to take* a walk (the noun). Just look at the answer choices. They'll always be the same part of speech as the stem word. So you'll always know whether to WAVE to Mom or ride the WAVE . . . though she'd probably prefer you do both at once! "

# AVOIDING PITFALLS

OK, so we lied just a little bit. The 3-Step Method should always be the basis for tackling every question, but there are a few other things you need to know to perform your best on Synonyms. Fortunately, there are only two big pitfalls to watch out for.

## PITFALL 1: RUNNING OUT OF TIME

Pace yourself. You have a limited amount of time, so make sure you use it wisely. Never waste time on a question you don't know—circle it and come back to it later. Synonyms get harder as they go, so move through the early questions quickly, leaving more time for the tougher ones at the end.

## PITFALL 2: CHOOSING TEMPTING WRONG ANSWERS

The test makers choose their wrong answer choices very carefully. Sometimes that means throwing in answers that will tempt you but that aren't right. Be a savvy test taker: Don't fall for these distracters!

What kinds of wrong answers are we talking about here? There are two types of wrong answers to watch out for: answers that are *almost right* and answers that *sound like the stem word*. Let's illustrate both types to make it concrete.

**EXAMPLE**

REPUTE:

(A) renewal
(B) renown
(C) priority
(D) mutability
(E) reaction

FAVOR:

(A) award
(B) recognize
(C) respect
(D) improve
(E) prefer

> **ARDUOUS, OR JUST HARD?**
>
> " One other trap to watch out for is answer choices that sound hard. Particularly if the stem word is pretty tough, you might be tempted to pick an answer choice that sounds similarly difficult. Often, the correct answer is straightforward. When you see a tough word, keep your cool and ask yourself, is this arduous, or just hard? "

In the first example, choices (A), (B), and (E) might be tempting, because they all start with the prefix *re-*, just like the stem word, repute. It's important that you examine all the answer choices, because otherwise you might choose (A) and never get to the correct answer, (B).

In the second example, you might look at the word favor and think, oh, that's something positive. It's something you do for someone else. It sounds a lot like choice (A), *award*. Maybe you pick (A) and move on. If you do that, you would fall for a trap. The correct answer is (E) *prefer*, since favor is being used as a verb, and to favor someone or something is to like it better than something else, in other words, to prefer it. As in the first example, if you don't read through all of the choices, you might be tricked into choosing a wrong answer.

At this point, you have a great set of tools for answering most Synonym questions. You know how to approach them, and you know some traps to avoid. But what happens if you look at the word in capitals and you don't know what it means? Should you just give up and move on, fill out the rest of your test in crayon, or start waving your arms around saying, "They're after us!"? Well, probably not.

## VOCABULARY TECHNIQUES

There are several things you can do to figure out the meaning of a tough vocabulary word and, thus, to answer a hard Synonym question. Here are four techniques that will help you when you don't know a stem word.

**Technique 1.** Look for familiar roots and prefixes.

**Technique 2.** Use your knowledge of foreign languages.

**Technique 3.** Remember the context.

**Technique 4.** Use Word Charge.

Let's examine each technique more closely.

### TECHNIQUE 1: LOOK FOR FAMILIAR ROOTS AND PREFIXES

Remember how we told you in chapter 6 to start working on your vocabulary skills? Well, having a good grasp of how words are put together will help you tremendously on Synonyms, particularly when you don't know a vocabulary word. If you can break a word into pieces that you *do* understand, you'll be able to answer questions that you might have thought too difficult to tackle.

Look at the words below. Circle any prefixes or roots that you know.

- BENEVOLENCE
- INSOMNIA
- INSCRIBE
- CONSPIRE
- VERITY

"Bene" means *good*; "somn" has to do with *sleep*; "scrib" has to do with *writing*; "con" means doing something *together*; and "ver" has to do with *truth*.

## TECHNIQUE 2: USE YOUR KNOWLEDGE OF FOREIGN LANGUAGES

Do you study a foreign language? If so, it can help you decode lots of vocabulary words on the SSAT or ISEE, particularly if it's one of the Romance languages (French, Spanish, Italian, Portuguese). Look at the example words below. Do you recognize any foreign language words in them?

- FACILITATE
- DORMANT
- EXPLICATE

*Facile* means "easy" in French and Italian; *dormir* means "to sleep" in French and Spanish; and *expliquer* means "to explain" in French.

## TECHNIQUE 3: REMEMBER THE CONTEXT

Sometimes a word might look strange sitting on the page by itself, but if you think about it, you realize you've heard it before in other phrases. If you can put the word into context, such as in a cliché, you're well on your way to deciphering its meaning.

**EXAMPLE**

GNARLED:

(A) fruitful
(B) dead
(C) twisted
(D) flowering
(E) drooping

What kind of plant have you heard described as *gnarled*? *Trees* are often described as gnarled, particularly old ones. They are knotty and twisted, the kind you think would appear in fairy tales. The answer is (C).

**EXAMPLE**

ALLEGATION:

(A) evidence

(B) accusation

(C) conservation

(D) foundation

(E) fabrication

What does "making an allegation" mean? *Making an allegation* is accusing someone of committing a crime, a phrase you might have seen on the news or on a police-related TV show. The answer is (B).

**EXAMPLE**

LAURELS:

(A) vine

(B) honor

(C) lavender

(D) cushion

(E) work

Have you heard the expression *Don't rest on your laurels*? What do you think it might mean? *Don't rest on your laurels* originated in ancient Greece, where heroes were given wreaths of laurel branches to signify their accomplishments. Saying you shouldn't rest on your laurels is the same thing as saying you shouldn't get too comfortable or smug, just enjoying your accomplishment rather than striving for improvement.

## Technique 4: Use Word Charge

Even if you know nothing about the word, have never seen it before, don't recognize any prefixes or roots, and can't think of any word it resembles in another language, you can still make a stab at a Synonym question. One useful strategy when you're stumped is Word Charge.

What do we mean by Word Charge? Are some words electric? Or do they spend too much money on credit cards? No, and no. Word charge refers to the *sense* that a word gives you as to whether it's a positive word or a negative one.

VILIFY: This sounds like *villain*, a word most people would say is bad.

GLORIFY: This sounds like *glorious*, a word most people would say is good.

Let's say that "vilify" has a negative charge (–) and "glorify" has a positive charge (+). On all Synonym questions, the correct answer will have *the same charge as the stem word*, so use your instincts about word charge to help you when you're stuck on a tough word.

Decide whether each of the following words has a positive (+) or negative (–) charge.

AUSPICIOUS       _____

MALADY           _____

NOXIOUS          _____

AMIABLE          _____

BOORISH          _____

MELANCHOLY       _____

HUMANE           _____

Often words that sound harsh have a negative meaning, while smooth-sounding words tend to have positive meanings. If *cantankerous* sounds negative to you, you would be right. It means difficult to handle.

You can also use prefixes and roots to help determine a word's charge. *Mal, de, dis, un, in, im, a,* and *mis* often indicate a negative, while *pro, ben,* and *magn* are often positives.

Not all words sound positive; some sound neutral. But if you can define the charge, you can probably eliminate some answer choices on that basis alone.

Now let's see how you did on identifying the charge of the words listed above.

*Auspicious* (+) means favorable; a *malady* (–) means an illness; *noxious* (–) means harmful; *amiable* (+) means agreeable; *boorish* (–) means rude; *melancholy* (–) means sadness; and *humane* (+) means kind.

## PRACTICE MAKES PERFECT

Now that you've been through all of the techniques to succeed on Synonym questions, it's time for some practice. Work through the following 20 questions, using the Kaplan 3-Step Method, avoiding pitfalls, and employing vocabulary techniques when you get stuck.

# PRACTICE QUESTIONS

1. DISMAL:

   (A) bleak
   (B) crowded
   (C) comfortable
   (D) temporary
   (E) typical

2. HUMID:

   (A) damp
   (B) windy
   (C) hot
   (D) stormy
   (E) hazy

3. DEPORT:

   (A) punish
   (B) banish
   (C) censor
   (D) jail
   (E) praise

4. PEDDLE:

   (A) assemble
   (B) steal
   (C) edit
   (D) deliver
   (E) sell

5. TERMINATE:

   (A) extend
   (B) renew
   (C) end
   (D) sell
   (E) finalize

6. DEARTH:

   (A) explosion
   (B) increase
   (C) shortage
   (D) change
   (E) surplus

7. OBSCURE:

   (A) tragic
   (B) dark
   (C) obligatory
   (D) ignored
   (E) legendary

8. MOURN:

   (A) inaugurate
   (B) celebrate
   (C) greet
   (D) oppose
   (E) grieve

9. RECLUSE:

   (A) artist
   (B) beggar
   (C) lunatic
   (D) scavenger
   (E) hermit

10. HOMAGE:

   (A) youth
   (B) wreath
   (C) respect
   (D) affection
   (E) household

11. HERBIVOROUS:

   (A) huge
   (B) warm-blooded
   (C) endangered
   (D) plant-eating
   (E) intelligent

12. SYNOPSIS:

   (A) summary
   (B) satire
   (C) paragraph
   (D) update
   (E) rebuttal

13. WANTON:

   (A) fantastic
   (B) repeated
   (C) lustful
   (D) careful
   (E) needy

14. IMPERIOUS:

   (A) royal
   (B) friendly
   (C) gusty
   (D) arrogant
   (E) insightful

15. HALLOW:

   (A) revere
   (B) dig
   (C) inhabit
   (D) discover
   (E) release

16. BLISS:

   (A) ecstasy
   (B) escape
   (C) prayer
   (D) terror
   (E) fun

17. INDECENT:

   (A) centralized
   (B) immortal
   (C) improper
   (D) incessant
   (E) recent

18. TANGIBLE:

   (A) unrelated
   (B) glib
   (C) touchable
   (D) tanned
   (E) incapable

19. FEROCITY:

   (A) hardness
   (B) humility
   (C) narrowness
   (D) scarcity
   (E) fierceness

20. TENACIOUS:

   (A) tender
   (B) determined
   (C) temporary
   (D) talkative
   (E) discouraged

# PRACTICE QUESTION ANSWERS

1. A
2. A
3. B
4. E
5. C
6. C
7. B
8. E
9. E
10. C

11. D
12. A
13. C
14. D
15. A
16. A
17. C
18. C
19. E
20. B

# CHAPTER 8: READING COMPREHENSION

Critical Reading questions appear on all levels of the SSAT and ISEE. The Reading section presents you with five to seven passages (depending on the test and level) and questions that follow. The passages will generally cover topics such as history, science, or literature. For each passage, you'll be asked about the main idea and details presented. You'll only get points for answering questions correctly, not for reading the text thoroughly, so keep your attention on reading as quickly as possible and answering as many questions as you can.

However, remember that if you are in the lower grade within your level, you DON'T need to answer all of the questions—in fact, you don't even need to read all of the passages. You can get a great score even if you don't answer all the questions, so don't sweat it.

## READING STRATEGIES

On the one hand, it's a good thing that you're inherently prepared for this section because you already know how to read. On the other hand, your previous reading experience has the potential to get you into a bit of trouble on this section of the test. Reading habits that may serve you well in school can get in the way on the test.

There are three traps that students commonly fall into on the test.

> **Trap 1:** Reading too slowly
>
> **Trap 2:** Continually rereading things you do not understand
>
> **Trap 3:** Spending more time on the passages than on the questions

It is a mistake to approach the reading passages with the intention of understanding them thoroughly. You need to focus on answering the questions, not on getting to know the text.

---

**READ, DON'T LEARN**

" On the SSAT or ISEE, you'll have to read quickly and efficiently. Your goal is not to learn the information presented, or even to think about it very much. Rather, you need to figure out the main point and where to look for any details you might be asked about. "

# SSAT AND ISEE READING IS DIFFERENT FROM EVERYDAY READING

This is an important point. You already know how to read, but the way that you read normally may not help you maximize your points on the test. There are three main skills you'll need to employ to ace the Reading Comprehension section:

1. **Summarize:** You'll need to be able to sum up what the passage is all about.

2. **Research:** You'll need to be able to find facts, figures, and names in the passage.

3. **Make inferences:** You'll need to be able to figure out information that isn't directly stated.

How can you make sure you do all of these very official-sounding things? Here are some solid strategies.

## 1. LOOK FOR THE BIG IDEA

Don't read as if you're memorizing everything. Aim to pick up just the gist of the passage—the author's main idea.

## 2. PAY ATTENTION TO LANGUAGE

The author's choice of words can tell you everything about his or her point of view, attitude, and style.

## 3. BE A CRITICAL READER

As you read, ask yourself critical questions: "What's the author's main point? What message is the author trying to get across?"

## 4. MAKE IT SIMPLE

Despite the fancy language, Reading passages are usually about pretty simple topics. Don't get bogged down by technical language; translate the author's ideas into your *own words.*

## 5. KEEP MOVING

Aim to spend no more than one minute reading each passage; remember, just reading the passage won't score you points.

## 6. DON'T SWEAT THE DETAILS

Don't waste time reading and rereading parts you don't understand. Move swiftly through the passage to answer the questions, which is what really counts.

You've probably realized by now that Kaplan has a multistep method for all the question types on the SSAT and ISEE. It's in your best interest to approach the test as a whole and the individual sections systematically. If you approach every passage the same way, you'll work your way through the Reading Comprehension section efficiently.

# KAPLAN 4-STEP METHOD FOR READING COMPREHENSION

**Step 1.** Read the passage.

**Step 2.** Decode the question.

**Step 3.** Research the details.

**Step 4.** Predict the answer and check the answer choices.

Like the other multistep methods, the Kaplan 4-Step Method for Reading Comprehension requires you to do most of your work before you attempt to answer the questions. It's very tempting to read the questions and immediately jump to the answer choices. Don't do this. The work you do up front will not only save you time in the long run, it will increase your chances of avoiding the tempting wrong answers.

## STEP 1: READ THE PASSAGE

The first thing to do is to read the passage. This shouldn't come as a big surprise. And although you don't want to memorize or dissect the passage, you *do* need to read it. If you try to answer the questions without doing so, you're likely to make mistakes. Although you'll learn more about *how* to read the passages later, keep in mind that the main things you want to look for are the **Big Idea** and the **paragraph topics.** Additionally, you'll want to note where the passage seems to be going.

For example, if you saw the following passage (which, admittedly, is a little shorter than the average SSAT or ISEE passage), these are some of the thing you might want to note . . .

|  |  |
|---|---|
| The first detective stories, written by Edgar Allan Poe and Sir Arthur Conan Doyle, emerged in the mid-nineteenth century, at a time when there was an *Line* enormous public interest in scientific progress. The (5) newspapers of the day continually publicized the latest scientific discoveries, and scientists were acclaimed as the heroes of the age. Poe and Conan Doyle shared this fascination with the step-by-step, logical approach used by scientists in their experiments, and instilled in (10) their detective heroes outstanding powers of scientific reasoning. | **This passage is basically about detective stories . . . and science.** |
| | **Poe and Conan Doyle seem to be important.** |
| The character of Sherlock Holmes, for example, illustrates Conan Doyle's admiration for the scientific mind. In each case that Holmes investigates, he is able (15) to use the most insubstantial evidence to track down his opponent. Using only his restless eye and ingenious reasoning powers, Holmes pieces together the identity of the villain from such unremarkable details as the type of cigar ashes left at the crime scene, | **Holmes is an <u>example</u> of a detective hero with a brilliant scientific mind . . .** |

*(20)* or the kind of ink used in a handwritten letter. In fact, Holmes's painstaking attention to detail often reminds the reader of Charles Darwin's *On the Origin of Species*, published some twenty years earlier.

**Comparison between Holmes and Darwin.**

Again, you'll spend more time later learning how to read the passage. The point here is that the first thing you want to do is read through the entire passage noting the major themes and a few details.

## STEP 2: DECODE THE QUESTION

Several questions will follow the passage. And *before* you can answer each question, you'll have to figure out exactly what's being asked. You need to make the question make sense to you.

> Which of the following is implied by the statement that Holmes was able to identify the villain based on "unremarkable details"?
>
> (A) Holmes's enemies left no traces at the crime scene.
>
> (B) The character of Holmes was based on Charles Darwin.
>
> (C) Few real detectives would have been capable of solving Holmes's cases.
>
> (D) Holmes was particularly brilliant in powers of detection.
>
> (E) Criminal investigation often involves tedious, time-consuming tasks.

Remember to predict before you peek at the answer choices. First, let's determine what the question is asking. The word "implied" means that you need to understand how the phrase "unremarkable details" relates to Holmes's ability to identify the villain.

## STEP 3: RESEARCH THE DETAILS

This does *not* mean that you should start rereading the entire passage from the beginning to find the reference to "unremarkable details." Focus your research. Where does the author mention Holmes? You should have noted when you read the passage that the author discusses Holmes in the second paragraph. So scan that paragraph for the reference to "unremarkable details." (Hint: The reference can be found in lines 18–19.)

Additionally, don't answer questions based on your memory. Go back and do the research. In other words, if you can answer questions based on your memory, you have spent too much time on the passage.

## STEP 4: PREDICT THE ANSWER AND CHECK THE ANSWER CHOICES

When you find the detail in the passage, think about the *purpose* that it serves. Why does the author mention the "unremarkable details"? If you read the lines

**KAPLAN EXCLUSIVE TIPS**

❝ Don't try to answer questions just from your memory. ❞

surrounding the phrase, you'll see that the author talks about how amazing it is that Holmes can solve mysteries based on such little evidence. Therefore, the *reason* the author mentions "unremarkable details" is to show how impressive Holmes is. Now scan your answer choices.

(A)  Holmes's enemies left no traces at the crime scene.

(B)  The character of Holmes was based on Charles Darwin.

(C)  Few real detectives would have been capable of solving Holmes's cases.

(D)  Holmes was particularly brilliant in powers of detection.

(E)  Criminal investigation often involves tedious, time-consuming tasks.

Answer (D) should leap out at you.

# READING SKILLS IN ACTION

Remember earlier in the lesson when we discussed the three key reading skills: summarizing, researching, and making inferences? Let's look at how these skills can help you not only to read the passage but also to answer the questions.

## SUMMARIZING

For the purposes of the SSAT and ISEE, *summarizing* means capturing in a single phrase what the *entire* passage is about. Most passages will be followed by a question that deals with the passage as a whole. Wrong answers will include choices that cover only one paragraph or some other subset of the passage. You'll need to recognize the answer choice that deals with the passage as a whole. If you've thought about the Big Idea ahead of time, you're more likely to determine the correct answer.

      The four brightest moons of Jupiter were the first objects in the solar system discovered with the use of the telescope. Their proven existence played a central
*Line* role in Galileo's famous argument in support of the
(5) Copernican model of the solar system, in which the planets are described as revolving around the Sun.

      For several hundred years after their discovery by Galileo in 1610, scientific understanding of these moons increased fairly slowly. Observers on Earth
(10) succeeded in measuring their approximate diameters, their relative densities, and eventually some of their light-reflecting characteristics. However, the spectacular close-up photographs sent back by the 1979 *Voyager* missions forever changed our
(15) impressions of these bodies.

**EXAMPLE**

Which of the following best tells what this passage is about?

(A)  Galileo's invention of the telescope

(B)  The discovery of the Galilean moons

(C)  Scientific knowledge about Jupiter's four brightest moons

(D)  The Copernican model of the solar system

(E)  The early history of astronomy

Decode the question first. This question is global, which focuses on the main idea of the entire passage. Try to summarize the paragraphs as a whole entity.

Only one answer choice here sums up the contents of both paragraphs. (B) is just a detail. (A) cannot be correct because Galileo's telescope is not even mentioned. (D) is mentioned only in the first paragraph and is a distortion of the author's point. (E) is too broad in scope.

Only (C) summarizes the entire passage. The passage deals with scientific knowledge about Jupiter's four brightest moons. The four moons are the first things mentioned in the first paragraph, and the rest of the first paragraph discusses the role they played for Galileo. The second paragraph deals with how the moons were perceived by scientists throughout history. In sum, both paragraphs deal with scientific knowledge about these moons.

## RESEARCHING

Researching essentially means knowing *where* to look for the details. Generally, if you note your paragraph topics, you should be in pretty good shape to find the details. Once you know where to look, just scan for key phrases found in the question.

A human body can survive without water for several days and without food for as much as several weeks. If breathing stops for as little as three to six
*Line* minutes, however, death is likely. All animals require a
(5)  constant supply of oxygen to the body tissues, and especially to the heart or brain. In the human body, the respiratory system performs this function by delivering air containing oxygen to the blood.

**Breathing is the most urgent human bodily function.**

But respiration in large animals possessing lungs
(10)  involves more than just breathing. It is a complex process that delivers oxygen to internal tissues while eliminating waste carbon dioxide produced by cells. More specifically, respiration involves two processes known as bulk flow and diffusion. Oxygen and carbon
(15)  dioxide are moved in bulk through the respiratory and circulatory systems; gaseous diffusion occurs at different points across thin tissue membranes.

**Respiration in large animals is a complex process.**

Take a look at the previous passage and paragraph topics. The paragraph topics are very general; they just note the gist of the paragraphs. If you saw the following questions, would you know where to find the answers?

## EXAMPLE

Which bodily function, according to the passage, is least essential to the survival of the average human being?

(A)  Eating

(B)  Drinking

(C)  Breathing

(D)  Blood circulation

(E)  The oxygen supply

**The first paragraph deals with bodily functions. Lines 2–3 note that food is most expendable.**

Now that you have researched the passage in the correct location, find the choice that has the correct answer. Since food is most expendable, it is therefore least essential. The correct answer, (A), should be the clearest choice.

## EXAMPLE

Which part of an animal's body is responsible for producing waste carbon dioxide?

(A)  The internal tissues

(B)  The circulatory systems

(C)  The tissue membranes

(D)  The bloodstream

(E)  The cells

**The second paragraph deals with the complex details of respiration. Carbon dioxide is mentioned in lines 14–15.**

According to lines 14–15, waste carbon dioxide is "produced by cells." Therefore, (E) is correct.

## MAKING INFERENCES

Making an inference means looking for something that is strongly implied but not stated explicitly. In other words, making an inference means *reading between the lines*. What did the author *almost* say, but not say exactly?

Inferences will not stray too far from the language of the text. Wrong answers on Inference questions will often fall beyond the subject matter of the passage.

Children have an amazing talent for learning
vocabulary. Between the ages of one and seventeen,
the average person learns the meaning of about 80,000

*Line* words—about 14 per day. Dictionaries and traditional
(5)    classroom vocabulary lessons only account for part of
this spectacular knowledge growth. More influential
are individuals' reading habits and their interaction
with people whose vocabularies are larger than their
own. Reading shows students how words are used in
(10)    sentences. Conversation offers several extra benefits
that make vocabulary learning engaging—it supplies
visual information, offers frequent repetition of new
words, and gives students the chance to ask questions.

**EXAMPLE**

The author of the passage most likely believes that a child is most receptive to learning the
meaning of new words at which time?

(A)  When the child reaches high school age

(B)  When the child is talking to other students

(C)  When the child is assigned vocabulary exercises

(D)  When the child is regularly told that he or she needs to improve

(E)  When vocabulary learning is made interesting

This short passage discusses how children learn vocabulary. The question asks when children are *most* receptive to learning new words. No sentence in the passage states that "children are *most* receptive to learning new words . . ." However, in lines 6–9, the author mentions that reading and conversation are particularly helpful. Lines 10–13 note how conversation makes vocabulary engaging. This is consistent with (E). Nothing in the passage suggests that children learn more at high school age, (A). (B) might be tempting, but it is too specific: There's no reason to believe that talking to students is more helpful than talking to anyone else. (C) contradicts the passage, and (D) is never mentioned at all.

At this point, you have a lot of tools to help you read passages and approach questions. It's a good idea to have a solid understanding of what the questions are, what types of questions you'll see, and how to best approach each one. There are three basic question types in the Reading Comprehension section: **Main Idea, Detail,** and **Inference** questions.

Since you can't exactly deal with questions unless you have an accompanying passage, take one or two minutes to read the following passage. As usual, mark it up. Read it with the goal of answering questions afterwards.

Line The first truly American art movement was formed
by a group of landscape painters that emerged in the
early nineteenth century called the Hudson River
School. The first works in this style were created by
(5) Thomas Cole, Thomas Doughty, and Asher Durand, a
trio of painters who worked during the 1820s in the
Hudson River Valley and surrounding locations.
Heavily influenced by European Romanticism, these
painters set out to convey the remoteness and splendor
(10) of the American wilderness. The strongly nationalistic
tone of their paintings caught the spirit of the times, and
within a generation the movement had mushroomed to
include landscape painters from all over the United
States. Canvases celebrating such typically American
(15) scenes as Niagara Falls, Boston Harbor, and the
expansion of the railroad into rural Pennsylvania were
greeted with enormous popular acclaim.

One factor contributing to the success of the
Hudson River School was the rapid growth of
(20) American nationalism in the early nineteenth century.
The War of 1812 had given the United States a new
sense of pride in its identity, and as the nation continued
to grow, there was a desire to compete with Europe on
both economic and cultural grounds. The vast
(25) panoramas of the Hudson River School fit the bill

perfectly by providing a new movement in art that was
unmistakably American in origin. The Hudson River
School also arrived at a time when writers in the United
States were turning their attention to the wilderness as a
(30) unique aspect of their nationality. The Hudson River
School profited from this nostalgia because they
effectively represented the continent the way it used to
be. The view that the American character was formed
by the frontier experience was widely held, and many
(35) writers were concerned about the future of a country
that was becoming increasingly urbanized.

In keeping with this nationalistic spirit, even the
painting style of the Hudson River School exhibited a
strong sense of American identity. Although many of
(40) the artists studied in Europe, their paintings show a
desire to be free of European artistic rules. Regarding
the natural landscape as a direct manifestation of God,
the Hudson River School painters attempted to record
what they saw as accurately as possible. Unlike
(45) European painters who brought to their canvases the
styles and techniques of centuries, they sought neither
to embellish nor to idealize their scenes, portraying
nature with the care and attention to detail of
naturalists.

Hopefully, you understood that this passage was about why the Hudson River School became so successful.
You should have also noted that the second paragraph addresses how American nationalism contributed to the
success of the Hudson River School and the third paragraph discusses how nationalist sentiment was evident in
the Hudson River School painting style.

## Main Idea Questions

A **Main Idea** question asks you to summarize the topic of the passage.

**EXAMPLE**

Which of the following best tells what this passage is about?

(A) The history of American landscape painting

(B) Why an art movement caught the public imagination

(C) How European painters influenced the Hudson River School

(D) Why writers began to romanticize the American wilderness

(E) The origins of nationalism in the United States

> Main Idea questions are pretty easy to recognize. They will always ask something general about the passage.
>
> Look for the answer choice that summarizes the entire passage. Rule out choices that are too broad or too narrow.

Do you see which one of these answers describes the entire passage without being too broad or too narrow?

(A) is too broad, as is (E). The passage is not about all American landscape painting; it's about the Hudson River School. Nationalism in the United States is much larger than the role of nationalism in a particular art movement. (C) and (D) are too narrow. European painters did influence the Hudson River School painters, but that wasn't the point of the whole passage. Similarly, writers are mentioned in paragraph 2, but the passage is about an art movement. Only (B) captures the essence of the passage—it's about an art movement that caught the public imagination.

## Detail Questions

Detail questions are straightforward—all you've got to do is locate the relevant information in the passage. The key strategy is to **research** the details by relating facts, figures, and names in the question to a *specific* paragraph.

**EXAMPLE**

Which of the following is not mentioned as one of the reasons for the success of the Hudson River School?

(A) American nationalism increased after the War of 1812.

(B) Americans were nostalgic about the frontier.

(C) Writers began to focus on the wilderness.

(D) The United States wanted to compete with Europe.

(E) City dwellers became concerned about environmental pollution.

> Note how the Detail question asks about what is specifically mentioned—or not mentioned.
>
> Scan the passage words or phrases in the answer choices. When you find the references, cross out the answer choices that do appear in the passage. The one left over will be the correct answer.

Four of the five answer choices are mentioned explicitly in the passage. (A) is mentioned in lines 18–22. (B) appears in line 31. (C) shows up in lines 28–29. (D) is mentioned in line 23. Only (E) does not appear in the passage.

## INFERENCE QUESTIONS

An **Inference** question, like a **Detail** question, asks you to find relevant information in the passage. But once you've located the details, you have to go one step farther: You have to figure out the underlying point of a particular phrase or example. Use your inference skills to figure out the author's point. The answer will not be stated, but it will be *strongly implied*.

### EXAMPLE

Which of the following best describes what is suggested by the statement that the Hudson River School paintings "fit the bill perfectly" (lines 25–26)?

(A) The paintings depicted famous battle scenes.

(B) The paintings were very successful commercially.

(C) The paintings reflected a new pride in the United States.

(D) The paintings were favorably received in Europe.

(E) The paintings were accurate in their portrayal of nature.

> "Suggested" is a classic Inference clue. If something is "suggested," it is not stated outright.
>
> Read the lines surrounding the quote. Summarize the author's point in your mind before you check the answer choices.

First, read the lines surrounding the quote to put the quote in context. Paragraph 2 talks about American pride; that's why Hudson River School paintings "fit the bill." Hudson River School paintings were about America. (C) summarizes the point nicely. Note how this question revolves around the interplay between main idea and details. This detail strengthens the topic of the paragraph, the growing sense of nationalism in America. (A) superficially relates to the War of 1812 but doesn't answer the question. (B), (D), and (E) are way off base.

**A WORD ABOUT SCIENCE PASSAGES**

" At least one reading passage may deal with a scientific or technical topic. You will NOT be tested on any outside science knowledge, so do not answer the questions based on anything other than the information contained in the passage. "

## A Reminder about Timing

Plan to spend approximately one minute reading the passage and roughly a minute to a minute and a half on each question. When you first start practicing, you'll probably find yourself spending more time than that on the passages. That's OK. However, you need to pay attention to your timing and cut the time down to around a minute. If you don't, it will hurt you in the long run.

# PRACTICE QUESTIONS—GENERAL

Almost everyone enjoys hearing some kind of live music. But few of us realize the complex process that goes into designing the acoustics of concert and
Line lecture halls. In the design of any building where
(5) audibility of sound is a major consideration, architects have to carefully match the space and materials they use to the intended purpose of the venue. One problem is that the intensity of sound may build too quickly in an enclosed space. Another problem is that only part
(10) of the sound we hear in any large room or auditorium comes directly from the source. Much of it reaches us a fraction of a second later after it has been reflected off the walls, ceiling, and floor as reverberated sound. How much each room reverberates depends upon both
(15) its size and the ability of its contents to absorb sound. Too little reverberation can make music sound thin and weak; too much can blur the listener's sense of where one note stops and the next begins.

Consequently, the most important factor
(20) in acoustic design is the time it takes for these reverberations to die down altogether, called the reverberation time.

1. Which of the following is the main topic of this passage?

   (A) The challenges of an architect's job

   (B) The differences between speech and music

   (C) The experience of hearing live music

   (D) The role of reverberation in acoustic design

   (E) The construction of large buildings

2. The passage suggests that the "complex process" of acoustic design (line 2) is

   (A) not widely appreciated by the public

   (B) really a matter of listener sensitivity

   (C) wholly dependent on the choice of construction materials

   (D) an engineer's problem, not an architect's

   (E) most difficult in concert hall construction

3. According to the passage, audibility of sound is influenced by which of the following factors?

   I. The type of materials used to construct a building

   II. The reflection of sound off a room's ceiling or walls

   III. The size and purpose of a particular room or space

   (A) I only

   (B) II only

   (C) I and II only

   (D) II and III only

   (E) I, II, and III

4. According to the passage, too little reverberation in a concert hall can result in

   (A) a rapid increase in the volume of sound

   (B) the blurring of details in a piece of music

   (C) a quiet and insubstantial quality of sound

   (D) confusion among a listening audience

   (E) an inaccurate estimate of its reverberation time

5. Which of the following does the author regard as the most significant consideration in the design of a concert hall?

   (A) An appreciation for music

   (B) An understanding of reverberation time

   (C) The choice of building materials

   (D) The purpose of the venue

   (E) The audience capacity

# PRACTICE QUESTIONS—BY LEVEL

## ELEMENTARY, LOWER, AND PRIMARY LEVELS

The environment of the coral reef is formed over thousands of years by the life cycle of vast numbers of coral animals. The main architect of the
Line reef is the stony coral, a relative of the sea anemone
(5) that lives in tropical climates and secretes a skeleton of almost pure calcium carbonate. Its partner is the green alga, a tiny unicellular plant, which lives within the tissues of the coral. The two organisms coexist in a mutually beneficial relationship, with
(10) the algae consuming carbon dioxide given off by the corals and the corals thriving in the abundant oxygen produced photosynthetically by the algae. When the coral dies, its skeleton is left, and other organisms grow on top of it. Over the years, the
(15) sheer mass of coral skeletons, together with those of associated organisms, combine to form the petrified underwater forest that divers find so fascinating.

6. According to the passage, the skeleton of the stony coral is mostly composed of

   (A) cartilage
   (B) stone
   (C) calcium carbonate
   (D) carbon dioxide
   (E) sediment

7. This passage primarily deals with

   (A) different forms of marine life
   (B) the contribution of the stony coral to reef formation
   (C) the interaction between two inhabitants of coral reefs
   (D) the physical beauty of coral reefs
   (E) the geological origins of reef islands

8. It can be inferred from the passage that divers are primarily interested in which aspect of reefs?

   (A) The biological cycles of reef animals
   (B) The visual appeal of a mass of coral skeletons
   (C) The fertile growing environment that reefs provide
   (D) The historical implications of reef development
   (E) The actual number of dead animals required to form a reef

9. The relationship between the coral and the algae is best described as

   (A) unfriendly
   (B) competitive
   (C) predatory
   (D) collaborative
   (E) mysterious

10. All of the following are mentioned in the passage as part of the life cycle of reef organisms EXCEPT

    (A) the coral lives within the tissues of the algae
    (B) algae consumes carbon dioxide emitted by corals
    (C) the skeleton of the coral provides an environment for other organisms
    (D) corals secrete a calcium carbonate skeleton
    (E) corals consume oxygen produced by algae

Tunnel construction is costly and dangerous, but new technologies are allowing tunnelers to work more quickly and safely than ever before.
Line Today's rock tunnels are being drilled by modern
(5) full-face tunnel-boring machines (TBMs). The drilling end of a TBM consists of a rotating cutterhead whose diameter covers the entire face of a tunnel. As the cutterhead turns, hard-steel blades cut steadily through the rock. The first successful
(10) hard-rock TBM was built in 1957, and many improvements have been made in TBM design in subsequent years.

Developments in TBM technology have helped spur ambitious new projects. Most notable
(15) is the 50-kilometer Eurotunnel (also known as the Chunnel), which has been bored by modern TBMs beneath the English Channel. The tunneling was done by British and French teams that started on opposite sides of the Channel and eventually met
(20) underground, in the middle. Thus, TBMs have contributed to building a technological and cultural milestone. Trains can now travel between England and France in less than an hour, and for the first time in history, Britain and continental
(25) Europe are linked by land.

11. The passage suggests that, despite three decades' worth of technological improvement, tunnel construction is

(A) rarely worth the risks involved

(B) still expensive and dangerous

(C) possible only with international cooperation

(D) heavily reliant on geological guesswork

(E) not as efficient as it should be

12. Which of the following best describes what this passage is about?

(A) Why tunnel construction is expensive

(B) The significance of the Eurotunnel

(C) How TBMs operate

(D) Tunnel construction with TBMs

(E) Why the Eurotunnel was difficult to dig

13. As it is used in line 14, the word "notable" most nearly means

(A) popular

(B) legendary

(C) remarkable

(D) weighty

(E) memorable

14. The author most likely describes the Eurotunnel as a "cultural milestone" (line 22) because it

(A) lifts travel restrictions among all European countries

(B) connects Europe and Britain by land for the first time

(C) harms the relationship between Britain and France

(D) affects the way all future tunnels will be dug

(E) changes the political climate in Europe

15. The attitude of the writer towards the subject is best described as

(A) enthusiastic

(B) uncertain

(C) cautious

(D) bitter

(E) jubilant

Usually regarded as pests, the termites of South Florida provide an excellent illustration of nature at work. In the natural world, when two or more *Line* different organisms coexist to each other's benefit, (5) it's called a symbiotic relationship. The dominant member of the symbiotic pair or group is known as the "host," while a smaller, less dominant member is a "parasite." A classic symbiotic relationship of this kind takes place in the digestive tract of Florida (10) wood-eating termites. We think of a termite as being able to digest wood, but it really cannot. The termite plays host to parasitic protozoans, single-celled organisms that live in the termite's gut. The protozoans provide the termite with a service (15) necessary to its survival: they digest the cellulose in the wood that it consumes.

16. Which of the following is suggested in the passage about the protozoans?

   (A) They are essential to the continued existence of termites.

   (B) They are both a parasitic and a host organism.

   (C) They are roughly equal in size to bacteria.

   (D) They attach themselves to the membranes of termites.

   (E) They can survive on their own when necessary.

17. Which of the following best describes what this passage is about?

   (A) Why most parasites perform a useful function

   (B) Why a termite cannot digest food

   (C) How symbiotic relationships have evolved

   (D) Why protozoans digest wood

   (E) How two organisms cooperate to survive

18. According to the passage, a "host" organism is generally

   (A) found in South Florida

   (B) the dominant partner in a symbiotic relationship

   (C) unable to digest cellulose

   (D) able to survive on its own

   (E) associated with single-celled organisms

19. With which of the following statements about a symbiotic relationship would the author most likely agree?

   (A) It involves organisms that are alike.

   (B) It often involves harmful parasites.

   (C) It mostly involves tiny organisms.

   (D) It usually involves organisms that are similar.

   (E) It may be beneficial to both organisms.

20. The relationship between termites and protozoans is best described as

   (A) cooperative

   (B) occasional

   (C) friendly

   (D) violent

   (E) improbable

The ozone layer of the atmosphere protects
Earth from harmful solar radiation. But the
ozonosphere is fragile, and evidence indicates
*Line* that it is thinning: since 1975, the amount of
(5) radiation reaching Earth has increased steadily. The
implications of this are not good. Solar radiation
causes cancer and contributes to other serious
illnesses. Also, as radiation increases, more and
more warm air gets trapped near Earth, and hot,
(10) humid conditions like those in a greenhouse begin
to prevail. Some scientists warn that, within 50
years, people could be facing major climatic changes
and sea levels far above what they are now. Public
outcry about the issue has led to international
(15) efforts to stop the release of CFCs and other
pollutants harmful to the ozonosphere. Thanks
to a global pact to eliminate the production of
CFCs by 1996, the ozone layer should stop losing
ozone around the turn of the century. Total ozone
(20) recovery, however, is predicted to take more than a
century beyond that.

21. Which of the following is directly mentioned
    as evidence of ozone depletion?

    (A) An increase in unusual disturbances on
        the sun's surface
    (B) A decrease in the amount of sunlight
        reaching the Earth
    (C) A decline in skin cancers among people
    (D) An increase in solar radiation reaching
        the Earth's surface
    (E) Gaps in the ozonosphere over North
        America

22. This passage deals primarily with

    (A) the reasons why solar radiation is
        damaging
    (B) the atmosphere over Antarctica
    (C) how pollutants are destroying the
        environment
    (D) the discovery of the hole in the ozone layer
    (E) the loss of ozone from the ozone layer

23. Which of the following explains why ozone
    depletion has occurred?

    (A) Oxygen is disappearing from the
        atmosphere.
    (B) Temperatures on Earth are rising.
    (C) The ozone layer is being broken down by
        pollutants.
    (D) The sun's rays are becoming stronger.
    (E) Sea levels are falling.

24. The author most likely mentions a greenhouse
    (line 10) in order to

    (A) suggest a way to protect plants from
        harmful radiation
    (B) describe an effect of increasing solar
        radiation
    (C) explain how ozone forms in the
        atmosphere
    (D) explain that heat and humidity are
        destroying the ozonosphere
    (E) describe a climate that would be
        healthier for people

25. The passage suggests that a full restoration of
    the ozonosphere

    (A) is the only way to save Antarctica from
        destruction
    (B) will probably occur by the year 2000
    (C) depends on the frequency of future
        volcanic eruptions
    (D) remains an impossibility despite
        international efforts
    (E) is highly unlikely in the near future

For thousands of years, smallpox was one of the world's most dreaded diseases. An acutely infectious disease spread by a virus, smallpox
*Line* was the scourge of medieval Europe, where it
(5) was known by its symptoms of extreme fever and disfiguring rash as "the invisible fire." In many outbreaks, mortality rates were higher than 25 percent. Ancient Chinese medical texts show that the disease was known as long ago as 1122 B.C.E.
(10) But as recently as 1967, more than 2 million people died from the disease annually.

A method of conferring immunity from smallpox was discovered in 1796 by an English doctor named Edward Jenner. It was not until
(15) 1966, however, that the World Health Organization was able to marshal the resources to launch a worldwide campaign to wipe out the disease. In an immense project involving thousands of health workers, WHO teams moved from country to
(20) country, locating every case of active smallpox and vaccinating all potential contacts. In 1977, the last active case of smallpox was found and eliminated. Since there are no animal carriers of smallpox, the WHO was able to declare in 1980 that the dreaded
(25) killer had been conquered. For the first time in the history of medicine, a disease had been completely destroyed.

26. Which of the following best tells what this passage is about?

    (A) How to treat viral diseases

    (B) The purpose of the World Health Organization

    (C) The tragic symptoms of smallpox

    (D) The history of the fight against smallpox

    (E) Early efforts at controlling infectious diseases

27. In line 2, the word "acutely" most nearly means

    (A) painfully

    (B) extremely

    (C) unnaturally

    (D) sensitively

    (E) partly

28. It can be inferred from the passage that the earliest recorded cases of smallpox were located in

    (A) China

    (B) Europe

    (C) The Middle East

    (D) North America

    (E) Africa

29. The passage implies that smallpox was not eliminated before 1966 because

    (A) vaccination did not prevent all forms of the disease

    (B) not enough was known about immunity to disease

    (C) there was no effective protection against animal carriers

    (D) there had never been a coordinated worldwide vaccination campaign

    (E) the disease would lie dormant for many years and then reappear

30. According to the passage, the WHO's fight against smallpox was a unique event because

    (A) it involved a worldwide campaign of vaccination

    (B) a disease had never before been utterly wiped out

    (C) animals carriers had to be isolated and vaccinated

    (D) doctors were uncertain as to whether Jenner's methods would work

    (E) it was more expensive than any other single vaccination campaign

# MIDDLE AND UPPER LEVELS

Animals that use coloring to safeguard themselves from predators are said to have "protective coloration." One common type of
Line protective coloration is called cryptic resemblance,
(5) in which an animal adapts in color, shape, and behavior in order to blend into its environment. The camouflage of the pale green tree frog is a good example of cryptic resemblance. The tree frog blends so perfectly into its surroundings that, when
(10) it sits motionless, it is all but invisible against a background of leaves.

Many animals change their protective pigmentation with the seasons. The caribou sheds its brown coat in winter, replacing it with white fur.
(15) The stoat, a member of the weasel family, is known as the ermine in winter, when its brown fur changes to the white fur prized by royalty. The chameleon, even more versatile, changes color in just a few minutes to match whatever surface it happens to be
(20) lying on or clinging to. Some animals use protective coloration not for camouflage but to stand out against their surroundings. The skunk's brilliant white stripe is meant to be seen, as a warning to predators to avoid the animal's stink. Similarly,
(25) the hedgehog uses its "salt and pepper" look to loudly announce its identity, since it depends on its evil stench and unpleasant texture to make it unpalatable to the predators around it.

31. The author uses the caribou and the stoat as examples of animals that

    (A) change their color according to the time of year
    (B) are protected by disruptive coloring
    (C) possess valuable white fur
    (D) have prominent markings to warn predators
    (E) protect themselves by constantly changing their coloring

32. Which of the following best describes what the passage is about?

    (A) How animals blend into their surroundings
    (B) Several types of protective coloration
    (C) A contrast between the tree frog, the zebra, the caribou, and the skunk
    (D) A description of predators in the animal kingdom
    (E) The difference between cryptic resemblance and disruptive coloring

33. The feature of the chameleon discussed in this passage is its ability to

    (A) camouflage itself despite frequent changes in location
    (B) cling to surfaces that are hidden from attackers
    (C) adapt easily to seasonal changes
    (D) use disruptive coloring to confuse predators
    (E) change the colors of surfaces it is resting on

34. It can be inferred from the passage that which of the following animals employ cryptic resemblance?

    I.  The green tree frog
    II. The chameleon
    III. The skunk

    (A) I only
    (B) II only
    (C) I and II
    (D) I and III
    (E) I, II, and III

35. The passage suggests that the hedgehog is different from the chameleon primarily in that

    (A) it changes its skin color less frequently
    (B) it makes its presence known to potential predators
    (C) it has fewer predators to avoid
    (D) its predators find it unpleasant to eat
    (E) its skin is almost devoid of color

Being out of heart with government
I took a broken root to fling
Where the proud, wayward squirrel went,
Line Taking delight that he could spring;
(5) And he, with that low whinnying sound
That is like laughter, sprang again
And so to the other tree at a bound.
Nor the tame will, nor timid brain,
Nor heavy knitting of the brow
(10) Bred that fierce tooth and cleanly limb
And threw him to laugh on the bough;
No government appointed him.

(From "An Appointment," *Responsibilities,*
W.B. Yeats, 1914)

36. The author's attitude toward the government
in this poem would best be described as

    (A) amused

    (B) disenchanted

    (C) furious

    (D) melancholy

    (E) neutral

37. Which of the following does the author
admire about the squirrel?

    I.   His independence
    II.  His faith in systems of government
    III. His ability to spring from tree to tree

    (A) I only

    (B) III only

    (C) I and II

    (D) I and III

    (E) I, II, and III

38. The passage implies that the squirrel most
resembles humans in

    (A) the timidity of his intellect

    (B) the sounds that he makes

    (C) the fierce expression on his face

    (D) his contempt for the world of politics

    (E) his concentration in moving from tree
to tree

39. The author most likely regards the squirrel's
laugh as

    (A) a warning about the future

    (B) a reflection of his own happiness

    (C) a symbol of his freedom

    (D) a sign of friendliness toward the poet

    (E) an unexplained natural phenomenon

40. In line 9, the phrase "heavy knitting of the
brow" most likely refers to

    (A) the movement toward political reform

    (B) the seriousness of government officials

    (C) the expression on the squirrel's face

    (D) the poet's attitude toward politicians

    (E) the beauty of the natural world

The American Revolution is more notable for
the absence of major American victories in set-piece
battles than for their occurrence. While it is widely
Line known that George Washington was an American
(5) hero in the nascent United States' successful bid to
win independence, a cursory examination reveals
that Washington was soundly defeated in almost
every pitched battle he fought against the British. Two
principal American cities, New York and Philadelphia,
(10) were captured by the British, and Washington could do
nothing to prevent their capture or to take back either
city. In a classic example of Colonial military futility,
Washington deployed his troops on Brooklyn Heights
to repel the British invasion of New York. After his
(15) troops were thoroughly routed, Washington regrouped
in Manhattan, only to be chased from the island with
the humiliating sound of foxhunt bugles in his ears.
The retreat would not stop until he and his troops
safely crossed the Delaware River into Pennsylvania.
(20)     Unfortunately for the British, however,
America was not a land of Old World conventions.
The Colonial soldier did not fight for wealth, for
territory, or out of service to a nobleman. He fought
for his home, and his war required a different level
(25) of commitment. George Washington is remembered
as an American hero not because he was able to
win battles against the British by their own rules of
engagement, but because he was able to outlast their
resolve, defiantly keep an army in the field, and await
(30) foreign aid. While Washington had little to do with
the long awaited set-piece victory at Saratoga,* his
principal success was in his tenacity and daring to
keep fighting. Washington's victories at Trenton and
Princeton were over minuscule forces, but they kept
(35) his army together and resurrected the American
cause in the minds of his countrymen, at an hour
when the Colonies seemed certain of its failure. It is
only fitting that when the final vise-grip was applied
to Cornwallis at Yorktown, George Washington was
(40) there to preside over the culmination of his uniquely
American war.

*Major Colonial win in upstate New York in 1777 that
earned the Colonies the recognition and aid of the
French

41. According to the passage, George Washington
is regarded as successful because

(A) he waged war according to
unconventional rules

(B) he triumphed over the British at
Saratoga

(C) he was able to defend American cities

(D) he was able to find a way to win pitched
battles

(E) he was able to cross the Delaware into
Pennsylvania

42. The author mentions which of the following
about the victories at Trenton and Princeton?

I. They had a significant impact on
Colonial morale.
II. They were achieved over sizeable forces.
III. They earned French aid in the
Revolution.

(A) I only

(B) II only

(C) III only

(D) I and II

(E) II and III

43. According to the passage, which of the
following was a "classic example of Colonial
military futility"?

(A) Washington's failure to win a pitched
battle

(B) Washington's inability to keep an army in
the field

(C) The American failure to attract foreign
aid

(D) Washington's inability to repel the attack
on New York

(E) The deployment of Washington's troops
on Brooklyn Heights

44. Why does the author state in line 20 that "America was not a land of Old World conventions"?

    (A) To indicate why the Colonial troops were unable to imitate British victories in pitched battle

    (B) To illustrate how Washington's successes did not follow the British model for victory

    (C) To praise Washington's indifference to failure in pitched battle

    (D) To give the Americans credit for their defiance of British customs

    (E) To excuse the Colonial defeats at New York and Philadelphia

45. Which of the following does the author suggest is the reason for the American triumph in the Revolution?

    (A) The American victory in a pitched battle at Saratoga

    (B) The lack of British commitment to winning as compared to the Americans

    (C) The better morale and supplies of the American troops

    (D) The inherent superiority of George Washington's military strategy

    (E) The American victories at Trenton and Princeton

On one of the ridges of that wintry waste
stood the low log house in which John Bergson was
dying. The Bergson homestead was easier to find
*Line* than many others, because it overlooked Norway
(5) Creek, a shallow, muddy stream that sometimes
flowed, and sometimes stood still, at the bottom of
a winding ravine with steep, shelving sides which
were overgrown with brush and cottonwoods and
dwarf ash. This creek gave a sort of identity to
(10) the farms that bordered it. Of all the bewildering
things about a new country, the absence of human
landmarks is one of the most depressing and
disheartening. The houses on the Divide were small
and were usually tucked away in low places; you did
(15) not see them until you came directly upon them.
Most of them were built of the sod itself, and were
only the inescapable ground in another form. The
roads were but faint tracks in the grass, and the
fields were scarcely noticeable. The record of the
(20) plow was insignificant, like the feeble scratches on
stone left by prehistoric races, so indeterminate that
they may, after all, be only the markings of glaciers,
and not a record of human strivings.

In eleven long years John Bergson had made little
(25) impression upon the wild land he had come to tame.
It was still a wild thing that had its ugly moods; and
no one knew when they were likely to come, or why.
Mischance hung over it. Its genius was unfriendly to
man. The sick man was feeling this as he lay looking
(30) out of the window, after the doctor had left him, on
the day following Alexandra's trip to town. There it
lay outside his door, the same land, the same lead-
colored miles. He knew every ridge and draw and
gully between him and the horizon. To the south, his
(35) plowed fields; to the east, the sod stables, the cattle
corral, the pond—and then the grass.

(Adapted from Willa Cather's *O Pioneers!*, 1913)

46. According to the passage, most houses on the
Divide were made of

(A) earth
(B) planks
(C) bricks
(D) stone
(E) logs

47. The Bergson homestead was more distinctive
than others because it was

(A) a large farmstead
(B) on Norway Creek
(C) made of sod
(D) in the new country
(E) surrounded by plowed fields

48. According to the author, the settler's plowed
fields were

(A) carved out by glaciers
(B) bordered by cottonwood trees
(C) planted with corn
(D) slight compared to the plains
(E) west of Norway Creek

49. As used in line 33, "draw" is most likely a type of

(A) quick sketch
(B) terrain feature
(C) homestead
(D) building
(E) plant

50. According to the passage, John Bergson's life
on the frontier has

(A) been directed by his mother Alexandra
(B) not given him freedom to express his
genius
(C) been characterized by illness
(D) transformed the town of Norway Creek
(E) had little impact on the plains

51. The tone of the passage could best be
described as

(A) bleak
(B) informative
(C) objective
(D) sunny
(E) comic

The Trans-Alaska Pipeline System is a
799-mile long pipe that carries oil from the Arctic
Ocean to a port in Valdez, on the southern coast of
*Line* Alaska. Before construction of the pipeline began in
(5) 1975, scientists undertook environmental impact
studies to predict how the pipeline might affect the
migration of Alaska's North Slope caribou. These
caribou travel hundreds of miles between their winter
feeding grounds and their spring calving grounds, and
(10) there was concern that the four-foot-diameter elevated
pipeline might hamper this migration. Scientists
worried that any delays might cause caribou cows to
give birth in transit and abandon their newborn calves
as they instinctually continued north. To avoid this,
(15) special pipeline crossings were built, including sections
of buried pipe and sections that were elevated so high
that caribou could pass underneath without being
aware of the pipe overhead. After the completion of the
pipeline, however, scientists found that caribou would
(20) cross it at any point, not just at the crossings. While the
design precautions were ultimately unnecessary, the
pipeline planners were wise not to run risks that could
have harmed the region's wildlife.

52. What did scientists worry might happen if
caribou migrations were disrupted?

(A) Migrating herds would interfere with oil
production.

(B) Caribou would not be able to feed in the
winter.

(C) Births during migration would cause
caribou to orphan their calves.

(D) Subsistence hunters would lose their
supply of meat.

(E) The caribou would find a route farther
away from humans.

53. It can be inferred that the author thinks the
special pipeline crossings

(A) were a waste of state resources

(B) were essential to protecting the caribou

(C) were worthwhile, though ultimately
unnecessary

(D) were not well designed to do the job

(E) caused an increase in the price of oil

54. Why did planners expect the pipeline might
disrupt migrations?

(A) Construction was planned during the
migration season.

(B) Frequent oil spills created a toxic
environment.

(C) Caribou avoid objects that bear human
scent.

(D) The pipe was physically bulky and built
aboveground.

(E) The machinery associated with the pipe
made a lot of noise.

55. As used in line 11, the word "hamper" most
nearly means

(A) accelerate

(B) depose

(C) obstruct

(D) contain

(E) direct

56. The passage answers which of the following questions?

    (A) Exactly how high is the pipeline elevated above the ground?

    (B) How many caribou live on Alaska's North Slope?

    (C) Migration disruptions cause how many caribou deaths per year?

    (D) What was the cost of the special caribou crossings?

    (E) What is the purpose of the Trans-Alaska Pipeline?

57. Which of the following best summarizes the main idea of the passage?

    (A) Human development has harmed northern caribou populations.

    (B) Planners took steps to protect caribou along the pipeline.

    (C) Scientists have mapped caribou migration routes.

    (D) Most Alaskans are concerned about the ecosystem.

    (E) The pipeline had unforeseen financial and environmental costs.

Five months ago the stream did flow,
The lilies bloomed within the sedge,
And we were lingering to and fro
*Line* Where none will track thee in this snow,
(5) Along the stream, beside the hedge.
Ah, sweet, be free to love and go!
For, if I do not hear thy foot,
The frozen river is as mute,
The flowers have dried down to the root:
(10) And why, since these be changed since May,
Shouldst *thou* change less than *they*?
And slow, slow as the winter snow,
The tears have drifted to mine eyes;
And my poor cheeks, five months ago
(15) Set blushing at thy praises so,
Put paleness on for a disguise.
Ah, sweet, be free to praise and go!
For, if my face is turned too pale,
It was thine oath that first did fail;
(20) It was thy love proved false and frail:
And why, since these be changed enow,
Should *I* change less than *thou*?

(From "Change upon Change," Elizabeth Barrett
Browning, 1846)

58. In this poem, the changing emotions of the
writer's beloved are compared to which of the
following?

    I. Flowers that have died and shriveled
   II. The drifting winter snow
  III. Lilies blooming along a stream

(A) I only
(B) II only
(C) III only
(D) I and III only
(E) I, II, and III

59. The writer's lament that she "Put paleness on
for a disguise" (line 16) suggests that

(A  she powdered her face
(B) the falling snow covered her face
(C) she put on a mask to hide her
    unhappiness
(D) her sadness has changed how her face
    looks
(E) winter made her cheeks cold

60. The flowing stream and the frozen river most
likely represent

(A) the passing of time
(B) warmth and cold
(C) love and hate
(D) the writer's attitude toward nature
(E) waning love

61. The writer would most likely agree with which
of the following statements about love?

(A) Love is immutable and everlasting, just
    like a river.
(B) Changes in emotion are unusual and
    unexpected when you're in love.
(C) People may not always feel as strongly
    about their beloved as they do at the
    beginning of a relationship.
(D) People in love are seldom affected by any
    emotional changes in their beloved.
(E) Love is full of difficult obstacles and
    should be avoided.

Over the past two decades, the field of information technology has become one of the most popular career destinations for new graduates in the United
*Line* States. High pay, strong benefits, and the allure of
(5) working in a cutting-edge field have made IT* the most explosive industry in the world. Despite the much-publicized failed investments that have hurt the tech sector's "Wall Street Cred," the IT industry continues to grow at a staggering pace. In 2004,
(10) the U.S. Department of Labor reported that more than 2.5 million Americans worked in a "computer occupation." Considering that the Department of Labor did not even have a "computer occupation" category in the 1970s, that number is astounding.
(15) It only continues to increase with the proliferation of (and dependence on) computer technology in twenty-first century America.

The independence of the computer industry from outside influences makes it unique among
(20) historical "boom industries." Unlike wartime manufacturing or disaster reconstruction, for example, the computer industry is mostly free from political and environmental constraints. Because of the industry's independence and steady growth,
(25) a new graduate with a computer degree should have strong earning potential until retirement. This long-term career track remains attractive to young professionals willing to look past the media hype regarding the "collapse of the dot-com bubble,"
(30) especially considering the high median salary and strong benefits common in the field. Health and dental plans are expected in the industry, as are the enticing investment opportunities that have created so many thirty-year-old millionaires.
(35) The considerable advantages that come with a job in information technology are not without costs to the worker, however. Frequent training and retraining is necessary due to the ever-changing and highly technical nature of the field. Computer
(40) programmers must occasionally learn newer, more robust programming languages, in addition to conforming to the style guidelines of each individual workplace. Network technicians must continuously adapt their highly technical work
(45) to a field that sees new systems and technology

introduced every four to six months. In addition to the perpetual training, many in the IT field, particularly programmers, complain of long hours during the "crunch time" required when a deadline
(50) is looming.

On the whole, though, tech workers are generally more pleased with their jobs than are other laborers. A recent study conducted by the Department of Labor found that the majority of IT
(55) professionals described themselves as "satisfied" to "very satisfied" with their employment. This trend has contributed to the unusually high workforce retention in the tech sector and is one of many factors that combine to project steady growth for
(60) IT in the future. As one analyst for Merrill-Lynch commented, "The more complex the machines get, the more of these guys are needed to fix them."

*A common abbreviation for information technology

62. As used in line 9, the word "staggering" most nearly means

(A) unsteady

(B) astonishing

(C) alternating

(D) tottering

(E) wavering

63. Information technology can best be described as

(A) a relatively new industry populated by skilled computer workers

(B) a consortium of major tech-sector employers

(C) a field with limited investment opportunities

(D) a new workforce for the twenty-first century

(E) a developing method of propulsion to be used in future space travel

64. The computer industry is different from previous boom industries because

   (A) it is a hot topic in American politics

   (B) computers did not exist in the time of other boom industries

   (C) computer jobs require significantly more education than those of previous boom industries

   (D) it has no immediately obvious outside constraints

   (E) it is a direct result of wide-scale devastation

65. The author of this passage would most likely agree with which of the following statements?

   I. Tomorrow's workplace will be dependent on computers.
   II. A career in information technology is a hassle due to the frequent training.
   III. There is a direct relationship between salary and job satisfaction.

   (A) I only

   (B) II only

   (C) III only

   (D) I and II only

   (E) I and III only

66. The best assumption that can be made from the passage is that

   (A) the market for IT workers will never collapse

   (B) the Department of Labor considers "computer occupations" the best new career track for university graduates

   (C) "crunch time" is a new problem that is unique to the IT industry

   (D) information technology is usually chosen as a career because of the strong financial benefits

   (E) investment firms (such as Merrill-Lynch) believe that computers are a great investment opportunity

67. The overall tone of the passage is

   (A) promotional

   (B) critical

   (C) informative

   (D) conciliatory

   (E) acerbic

68. As used in line 59, the word "project" most nearly means

   (A) display

   (B) propose

   (C) undertake

   (D) throw

   (E) predict

69. The purpose of the passage is to

   (A) discuss the popularity and long-term potential of "computer occupations"

   (B) encourage university freshmen to major in computer science

   (C) weigh the financial benefits of information technology against other careers

   (D) point out the disparity between working in the computer field and investing in it

   (E) explain how IT is different from previous boom industries

Life is a stream
On which we strew
Petal by petal the flower of our heart;
*Line* The end lost in dream,
(5) They float past our view,
We only watch their glad, early start.
Freighted with hope,
Crimsoned with joy,
We scatter the leaves of our opening rose;
(10) Their widening scope,
Their distant employ,
We never shall know. And the stream as it flows
Sweeps them away,
Each one is gone
(15) Ever beyond into infinite ways.
We alone stay
While years hurry on,
The flower fared forth, though its fragrance still stays.

(From "Petals," Amy Lowell, 1916)

70. In the poem, our lives are compared with which of the following?

   I. A stream
  II. A ship
 III. A perfume

(A) I only
(B) II only
(C) III only
(D) I and II only
(E) I, II, and III

71. "The end lost in dream" (line 4) suggests that

(A) the flower petals sink after some distance
(B) the flower petals become trapped in eddy currents
(C) the flower petals do not lose their red color
(D) the destination of the flower petals can only be imagined
(E) the narrator is asleep

72. In this poem, the rose most probably represents

(A) employment opportunities
(B) love
(C) death
(D) happiness
(E) life

73. With which of the following statements about life is the speaker most likely to agree?

(A) The future can be determined through careful planning.
(B) The course of life is determined equally in old age as in youth.
(C) Follow your heart and have few regrets.
(D) Nothing lasts from life's early experiences.
(E) There are only a few true friends but many acquaintances.

In Central Europe, the confluence of nations and cultures can be staggering. Vienna, the city of Mozart, Beethoven, and Freud, the seat of the
Line former Austro-Hungarian Empire and Habsburg
(5) dynasties, lies on the Danube River, called the *Donau* in German. This grand city lies a scant 30 miles from Bratislava, the capital of Slovakia, whose inhabitants refer to the river in the Slavic tongue as the *Dunaj*. Ninety miles further up the
(10) river lies the magnificent city of Budapest, where Hungarians call the river the *Duna*. The rising spires of her parliament and august grandeur of the Chain Bridge present Hungary's proudest and most exquisite face. The three languages spoken
(15) in this short stretch of the broad Danube are most striking in their total dissimilarity to one another. Their cultures likewise could not be more disparate, and yet throughout a long, volatile history, they have been unified under common empires,
(20) fought common enemies, and suffered common privations.

74. The passage is mainly focused on

   (A) the difficulty of navigating a river that lies in so many different countries
   (B) the grandeur of Central European cities
   (C) the juxtaposition of different cultures in Central Europe
   (D) the difficult history endured by the people of Vienna, Bratislava, and Budapest
   (E) the notable challenges for linguists who study Central European languages

75. Which of the following is true, according to the passage?

   (A) The people of Bratislava call the Danube a different name in Slavic.
   (B) The Chain Bridge and Parliament can be found in Austria.
   (C) The people of Vienna, Bratislava, and Budapest have a common ancestry.
   (D) The three cities mentioned in the passage are unified in their reliance on the Danube.
   (E) The people of Vienna, Bratislava, and Budapest cannot understand one another.

76. The author of this passage implies which of the following?

   (A) The people of Vienna, Bratislava, and Budapest share common history, cultures, and languages.
   (B) The city of Budapest is more exquisite than either Bratislava or Vienna.
   (C) The disparity between the three cultures in such a small area is overwhelming to outsiders.
   (D) The history of the people of Vienna, Bratislava, and Budapest is marked by an absence of privation and strife.
   (E) All three cities have at one time or another been under the possession of foreign powers.

77. The author most likely mentions the different words for the Danube River in order to

   (A) emphasize the river's length
   (B) illustrate specific linguistic differences in the three cities
   (C) highlight the differences in language and culture in such a small area
   (D) demonstrate the need for a unified translation of the word
   (E) discuss the differences created by repeated wars in Central Europe

78. The passage suggests which of the following about languages in the three cities?

   (A) They are difficult for visitors to the region to master.
   (B) Among their most noticeable characteristics is how different they are from one another.
   (C) They are exquisite sounding to anyone who hears them.
   (D) They have taken on many similarities because of the unification of the region under past empires.
   (E) They represent a cultural distinctness found nowhere else in the world.

During peak travel hours, as many as 5,000 airplanes fly in the continental United States. How can each airplane be sure to take off and land safely,
*Line* avoiding the others? Air traffic control coordinates
(5) all air travel, directing takeoffs and landings, ensuring safe distances between airplanes, and keeping routes away from bad weather. The air traffic control system forms a seamless web across all private commercial airline flight. As an airplane
(10) travels, a well-defined authority, or responsibility for the flight, is passed from one air traffic controller to the next. Smooth transfer of authority ensures safe travel; this authority passes from the most local level, at airport control towers, to the
(15) most national level, at centralized national facilities, and back again during flight.

Prior to takeoff, the airplane's path is guided by local air traffic controllers located in towers near the airport. These controllers make a record of each
(20) departing flight, direct all ground traffic on the airport runways, and determine when it is safe for airplanes to take off. Once an airplane is cleared for takeoff, the pilot is in control, but authority for the flight is transferred to the TRACON facility nearby.
(25) After this transfer, the pilot of the flight speaks with a newly assigned controller.

The TRACON (Terminal Radar Approach CONtrol) area covers a fifty-mile radius around a control tower. This area may include several
(30) airports. A controller in this facility dictates to the pilot what path to follow on ascent, making sure that the corridor is clear and a safe distance is maintained between this and other departing aircraft.

(35) When the flight departs TRACON airspace, authority is transferred to an Air Route Traffic Control Center (ARTCC). These regional control centers, of which 21 exist in the continental US, cover zones roughly equal in area and centered
(40) around major airports. ARTCC controllers communicate with national level controllers, who direct flights around bad weather, turbulence, and inactive runways.

Given the enormous volume of air travel and
(45) its ongoing growth, improved information systems are needed to assist air traffic controllers. TRACON controllers direct an aircraft's final approach, before transferring authority back to local airport air traffic controllers. They coordinate several planes
(50) approaching from different directions into a closely spaced, single-file line. This task, like much of air-traffic control, requires superb three-dimensional visualization skills and split-second decision-making abilities. Only computer-controlled direction systems
(60) can help lighten the difficult burden placed on the TRACON staff.

79. In air traffic control, the purpose of transfer of authority for a flight is to

(A) delegate powers in the event of an emergency

(B) designate a control center that can direct the pilot at a given time

(C) allow computer control

(D) complete the sale of excess seating

(E) inspect worn parts

80. According to the passage, all are true about TRACON areas EXCEPT

(A) TRACON areas must include only one or two airports

(B) TRACON controllers direct takeoff and landing

(C) TRACON areas are smaller than ARTCC areas

(D) TRACON controls flights in airspace near airports

(E) TRACON controllers supervise two of the most critical phases of flight

81. The author apparently believes that

    I.  ARTCC control rooms are generously staffed
    II. air traffic controllers must be highly capable to handle the demands of routing air traffic
    III. improved computer systems can aid air traffic control

    (A) I only
    (B) II only
    (C) II and III
    (D) III and I
    (E) I and II

82. According to the passage, it is reasonable to assume that

    (A) the transfer of authority for a flight is automatic
    (B) wages for ARTCC controllers are too low
    (C) airports have insignificant responsibility for air traffic control
    (D) once an airplane lands, authority is transferred to the airport control tower
    (E) pilots never have authority for a flight

83. This passage would likely appear in

    (A) a novel
    (B) an aircraft technical manual
    (C) a textbook
    (D) a policy briefing
    (E) a history of aviation

84. As used in line 60, "lighten" most nearly means

    (A) brighten
    (B) clarify
    (C) reduce
    (D) calcify
    (E) compound

85. The main purpose of the passage is to

    (A) describe the air traffic control system and its needs as the volume of air traffic increases
    (B) argue against the system of transfer of authority
    (C) compare and contrast airplane travel with other modes of transportation
    (D) add to the long-running debate between ARTCC and TRACON authority systems
    (E) allow the reader to understand the need for fuel economy in air travel

The quest for glory consumed Howard
Hughes. In July of 1946, his test flight of a prototype
XF-11 spy plane over Los Angeles ended in disaster.
*Line* Hughes, the self-proclaimed "fastest man in the
(5) world," was forced to crash land in Beverly Hills.
After tearing the roofs from three houses, the plane
smashed into the ground, leaving Hughes all but
dead. His brush with death changed him, speeding
him into the madness that would consume the
(10) twilight of his life. The eccentric entrepreneur and
adventurer became a recluse. In the decades that
followed the crash, Hughes gradually became more
myth than man, the subject of a thousand folk tales
and outrageous stories. His death in 1976 became
(15) public spectacle; even after two decades of complete
isolation, he was still perhaps the most popular,
romanticized, and genuinely interesting celebrity of
the twentieth century.

86. As a result of his crash landing in Beverly
Hills, Howard Hughes

    (A) paid damages to the three homeowners
who suffered property damage

    (B) was romanticized in modern myth

    (C) began to behave in an even more
eccentric manner

    (D) had to abandon the XF-11 project

    (E) became known as the "fastest man in the
world"

87. The author would most likely describe
Howard Hughes as

    (A) arrogant and ambitious

    (B) both tragic and intriguing

    (C) completely insane

    (D) underappreciated in his time

    (E) a myth

88. The passage was most likely written as part of

    (A) an argument detailing the psychological
causes of Hughes's madness

    (B) a drastic reinterpretation of the life of a
famous individual

    (C) a clinical study of mental illness in America

    (D) a discussion about the most prominent
figures of the modern era

    (E) the dramatized account of a fictional
character

89. The author's attitude toward Howard Hughes
can best be described as

    (A) condescending

    (B) sympathetic

    (C) spiteful

    (D) awestruck

    (E) amused

90. The passage deals primarily with the subject of

    (A) fame

    (B) aviation

    (C) isolation

    (D) madness

    (E) wealth

On May 24, 1844, Samuel Morse sent the first telegram from Baltimore to Washington, D.C. His simple message "What hath God wrought?" marked
Line the beginning of modern telecommunications.
(5) Within two decades, telegraph cables crisscrossed the United States. The telegraph allowed real-time communication between troops during the American Civil War. With the laying of the transatlantic cable in 1866, such communication became possible the world
(10) over. For the first time, the instantaneous transmission of information around the globe was possible.

More than a century and half after Morse's coded message, the telegraph has been rendered completely obsolete, first by the telephone, then
(15) by the fax machine and Internet. In January 2006, Western Union brought the telegraph era to a close by discontinuing their telegraph service. Even though the dots and dashes of Morse code are now a thing of the past, the telecommunications industry
(20) and indeed, modern journalism, owe a considerable amount of their development to the telegraph.

91. Which of the following best describes the author's main idea in this passage?

(A) The development of modern telecommunications

(B) The disappearance of the telegram as a form of communication

(C) The invention, use, and obsolescence of telegraph technology

(D) The difficulty of using Morse code for telecommunication

(E) The story of the last telegram transmitted by Western Union

92. The author's tone in this passage can best be described as

(A) discouraged

(B) respectful

(C) warning

(D) descriptive

(E) nostalgic

93. According to the passage, which of the following statements is NOT true of the telegraph?

(A) Samuel Morse sent the first telegram from Baltimore to Washington, D.C.

(B) The invention of the telegraph was made possible by the laying of the transatlantic cable.

(C) The telegraph had an impact on the conduct of warfare.

(D) Journalism benefited greatly from the telecommunications possibilities offered by the telegraph.

(E) The subsequent development of other telecommunications systems rendered the telegraph obsolete.

94. Which of the following would be the most appropriate title for this passage?

(A) Cell Phones, the Internet, and the Demise of the Telegraph

(B) The Telegraph and the Dawn of Modern Communications

(C) Samuel Morse and Invention of the Telegraph

(D) The Development of Telecommunications Prior to the Telegraph

(E) The Telegraph and the Evolution of Modern Journalism

95. The passage suggests which of the following?

(A) Information transmitted by telegraph is less likely to be accurate than that transmitted by telephone, fax, or Internet communication.

(B) The development of the telegraph system was slowed by the American Civil War.

(C) Western Union stopped telegraph service because of the Internet.

(D) The difficulty of Morse code prevented most people from learning how to use the telegraph.

(E) Gathering and reporting the news before the invention of the telegraph was more difficult.

On April 12 at 4:30 A.M. in Charleston Harbor, the strongest blow against the institution of slavery was struck—by its very defenders. After U.S. Army
*Line* Major Robert Anderson gallantly refused the rebel
(5) General Beauregard's demands to surrender the fortress, Beauregard gave the order to open fire. Despite President Lincoln's best efforts to assure the suspicious southerners of his and the Federal government's desire for peace, the secessionists
(10) have brought civil war upon themselves. Reportedly, Secretary of State Robert Toombs of the newly formed Confederate States of America has himself decried the attack, stating "(it) will lose us every friend at the North. You will wantonly strike
(15) a hornet's nest…Legions now quiet will swarm out and sting us to death. It is unnecessary; it puts us in the wrong; it is fatal."

In accordance with Secretary Toombs's prophetic words, President Lincoln, upon
(20) hearing of the surrender of Fort Sumter, has called for 75,000 volunteers to recapture all Federal forts ceded to the Confederacy and to preserve the Union by any and all means necessary. The response to the President's call has been
(25) overwhelming throughout states still loyal to the Union. Throughout the North, the strains of the *Star Spangled Banner* can be heard as an unparalleled surge of patriotism sweeps the nation. With the advantages of men and material that
(30) the North possesses and this newly galvanized determination, it should be a short war indeed!

96. The author's primary purpose in writing this passage is to

(A) chronicle a major historic event

(B) justify a particular side in a conflict

(C) call for volunteers in a military struggle

(D) deplore the institution of slavery

(E) ensure a Confederate victory

97. The author suggests that the coming civil war

(A) was instigated by Major Robert Anderson's refusal to surrender Fort Sumter

(B) was spurred by the words of Secretary of State Robert Toombs

(C) was initiated against President Abraham Lincoln's explicit orders

(D) was begun to end slavery in the Confederate States of America

(E) was not the aim of the Federal government before the attack

98. In line 2, the phrase "strongest blow" most probably refers to

(A) the author's belief that, by starting a war that they will most likely lose, the Southerners have ensured slavery's destruction

(B) Robert Toombs's statement that the attack on Fort Sumter alienated all Northern supporters of slavery

(C) the fact that the Southerners had finally found the means to bring slavery to an end

(D) the strength of the attack ordered by General Beauregard against the garrison at Fort Sumter

(E) the orders of President Lincoln for 75,000 volunteers and to preserve the Union by any available means

99. The author would most likely characterize the Southerners as

(A) treacherous

(B) distrustful

(C) belligerent

(D) comical

(E) patriotic

100. The characterization of Secretary Toombs's words as "prophetic" in line 19 most likely refers to

(A) the author's knowledge that the Union won the Civil War

(B) Toombs's expert knowledge of military and political conflicts

(C) the author's confidence that the Northerners will prevail in the impending conflict

(D) Lincoln's immediate response to the attack

(E) the patriotism immediately stirred by the attack throughout the states loyal to the Union

101. As used in line 26, "strains" most nearly means

(A) difficulties

(B) sounds

(C) exclamations

(D) outbursts

(E) feelings

102. Each of the following is mentioned as a response to the attack on Fort Sumter EXCEPT

(A) the fall of the fort's garrison

(B) the raising of volunteer troops

(C) a changing of federal policy

(D) an incredible decline in patriotism

(E) mass mobilization for war

"I stand before you today not to voice a complaint, but to plead for justice. I implore the council to reconsider the recent decision to rebuild Line my neighborhood, the area surrounding the North (5) Freeway.

In recent legislation, our friends on the city council described this area as dilapidated and, therefore, a threat to the local economy. Council members determined that these homes should be (10) replaced with newer construction simply because the area is unattractive to tourists.

In response to this decision, I would like to point out that the houses in this neighborhood are homes to several families. These families—these citizens—do (15) not wish to leave the homes they cherish. Though one house may be more attractive than another, no home that houses a comfortable, tax-paying family should be deemed a threat to the economy. This is not *Animal Farm*, in which George Orwell wrote "All (20) animals are equal, but some animals are more equal than others." I remind the council that the citizens of this neighborhood are already equal. Replacing older houses with newer ones will not make the area "more equal" than it currently is.

(25) Today, I request that the council reconsider the justification of rebuilding the North Freeway community. This project will prove a great injustice to the citizens of this neighborhood. The families who live in these homes have the same rights as (30) other citizens in this city and do not deserve to be forced out of their homes."

103. In paragraph 2, the speaker's reference to "our friends" is ironic because

(A) the council members were opposed to the speaker's neighborhood.

(B) the speaker did not personally know the members of the council.

(C) most of the audience knew him very well.

(D) those in the audience who were his friends were not city council members.

(E) the speaker did not have permission to speak on this topic.

104. This speech mentions an idea presented in the novel *Animal Farm*, in order to show that

(A) no neighborhood or group of citizens is more important than another

(B) educated people can solve the construction problems in the city

(C) certain citizens can only have a small interest in city government

(D) the speaker was violating his rights as a citizen

(E) any action that violates the U.S. Constitution will not be voted into action

105. Why does the speaker claim that the reconstruction project would be "a great injustice"?

(A) The U.S. Constitution explicitly prohibits the city's actions.

(B) The city is blessed by beautiful neighborhoods.

(C) The people of this neighborhood would be happy to leave the dilapidated area.

(D) Tourists only want to see the most attractive neighborhoods.

(E) The people in this neighborhood are equal to other citizens and do not deserve to lose their homes.

106. Which of the following is the purpose of this speech?

(A) To influence the citizens of a particular area

(B) To prove that the city council promotes tourism

(C) To convince the audience that a project is unfair

(D) To present a new plan to the city council

(E) To convince people of the need for social justice

She trudged through the remnants of the
once swirling storm. Her only landmarks were
the colored plastic stakes and occasional cairn the
*Line* others had left behind. Every so often, through
(5) the haze, the amorphous shape of a snow-covered
boulder rose into sight. The trees were gone. She
had left those behind long ago. Though she knew
this to be true, she thought she caught a glimpse of
the tree line from the corner of her eye. At times,
(10) severe bursts of wind penetrated her specialized,
technical coverings and made her feel as if she were
fighting to take each step forward as she continued
to traverse the landscape.

As she began to ascend the final peak, she
(15) witnessed what appeared to be a glittering ice
wall. When at last the sun retreated behind the
occasional cloud she realized the vision had been
an illusion. Her limbs felt numb, though she was, in
fact, stronger than ever.
(20) She had been climbing for two days now, but
time had succumbed to force of will. Suddenly she
heard a distant rumble. She feared the worst. An
avalanche now would be the end. Sweating with
fear and anticipation despite the frigid cold, she
(25) had no choice but to continue her trek, so on she
ventured, into the blank landscape. She relied on
her vast well of experience, her senses, and the aura
of footsteps that had come before to lead the way.
Finally, she started to make out the vague outline
(30) of a structure. First, a mere dot, then, quickly the
cottage came into view. She pounded on the door.
"It's me, I found you!" the desperate relief spilled
from her mouth. The door opened to a warm,
familiar scene. She was gratefully welcomed.

107. The protagonist must battle

(A) an active avalanche
(B) severe wind
(C) thick cloud cover
(D) scorching heat
(E) an ice wall

108. It can be inferred that the story takes place

(A) on the beach
(B) in a swampy area
(C) on a mountaintop
(D) in a rain forest
(E) in the desert

109. According to the passage, the main character
relies on all of the following to persevere
EXCEPT

(A) physical strength
(B) her senses
(C) prior knowledge
(D) navigation instruments
(E) technical coverings

110. As used in line 5, the word "amorphous" most
nearly means

(A) baggy
(B) distinct
(C) rugged
(D) triangular
(E) formless

Nuclear fallout, radioactive material left behind after a nuclear explosion, is known to be hazardous to humans. While many people realize

*Line* that direct contact with contaminated objects is
(5) harmful to the human body, many do not realize that the fallout can enter the human body in a variety of other ways. Years after a nuclear incident, various carriers can deliver fallout material to humans.

(10) When radioactive material enters the atmosphere of an explosion site, it becomes a danger to plants. Just as the air is immediately affected, the soil absorbs the material. Unfortunately, the radioactive material dusted

(15) across the soil remains toxic and eventually poisons local plant life. Plants absorbing radioactive materials present in the soil can be detrimental to the health of humans, because the human diet often consists of vegetables and fruits produced by these

(20) plants.

Just as the radioactive material can affect the plants eaten by humans, it can contaminate animals and milk. As cows eat grass from a contaminated site, the milk and beef become poisonous as well.

(25) Then, when humans drink the milk or eat the beef, they absorb the same harmful material that the cows ingested.

111. Which of the following states the main purpose of the passage?

(A) To report the effects of nuclear fallout on cows

(B) To discuss the changes an environment may experience after a nuclear explosion

(C) To show that radioactive material can enter humans in various ways

(D) To examine the effect of nuclear fallout on the environment

(E) To show how nuclear explosions contaminate the air

112. According to the passage, nuclear fallout enters plants primarily through

(A) contaminated soil

(B) contaminated cow's milk

(C) contaminated air

(D) contaminated humans

(E) contaminated fertilizer

113. The author most likely mentions contaminated cow's milk in order to show

(A) the potential harm to certain animal species

(B) the food chain of an explosion site

(C) the changes in an ecosystem

(D) how nuclear fallout affects plants and animals

(E) the role of animals in the human contamination process

114. The tone of the passage is best described as

(A) excited

(B) fearful

(C) threatening

(D) informative

(E) argumentative

115. The author would most likely follow this passage with a paragraph that includes which of the following?

    (A) A detailed list of plants most susceptible to nuclear contamination

    (B) More details about the many ways humans can be contaminated

    (C) A comparison of different fallout scenes across the world

    (D) A list of the various causes of nuclear explosions

    (E) An argument that humans should work together to prevent nuclear explosions

116. The passage mentions the contamination of each of the following EXCEPT

    (A) cows

    (B) humans

    (C) plants

    (D) dust

    (E) soil

Wintry boughs against a wintry sky;
Yet the sky is partly blue
And the clouds are partly bright—
Line Who can tell but sap is mounting high
(5) Out of sight,
Ready to burst through?
Winter is the mother-nurse of Spring,
Lovely for her daughter's sake,
Not unlovely for her own:
(10) For a future buds in everything;
Grown, or blown,
Or about to break.

(From "There Is a Budding Morrow in Midnight,"
Christina Rossetti, 1888)

117. In this poem, which of the following is
presented to symbolize a distinct season?

   I. Buds about to bloom
   II. Bare branches on the trees
   III. Mothers and their children

   (A) I only
   (B) II only
   (C) III only
   (D) I and II only
   (E) I, II, and III

118. "Who can tell but sap is mounting high" (line 4)
suggests that

   (A) sap from the trees is ready to collect
   (B) winter trees don't produce any sap
   (C) the cloudy sky doesn't prevent the trees
       from producing sap
   (D) sap is produced only in the warmer
       weather
   (E) some natural cycles may not be visible in
       winter

119. In this poem, the wintry sky and the partly
blue sky most likely represent

   (A) different weather conditions
   (B) an approaching snow storm
   (C) sorrow and joy
   (D) present and future
   (E) winter and spring

120. The author would most likely agree with
which of the following statements about the
seasons?

   (A) Spring doesn't last long enough.
   (B) People should prefer spring to winter.
   (C) Winter is enjoyable even if it seems
       bleak.
   (D) People only enjoy winter because they
       know it leads to spring.
   (E) Broken branches in winter turn into new
       growth in spring.

Much attention and envy is always directed toward the unusual genius. Countless biographies and biographical films chronicle a modern world shaped
*Line* by the blinding innovations of restless mavericks.
(5) For example, Alexander Fleming discovered the antibacterial agent in penicillin by accidentally allowing a culture plate to be contaminated by mold, but he is hailed for his insight and originality. For every Fleming, however, there is always a Jonas
(10) Salk. Salk was ridiculed by much of the scientific community for his use of other scientists' research and mundane scientific procedure in his successful quest to cure polio. Nevertheless, Salk did develop the cure for a twentieth-century plague. While the restless
(15) genius may sometimes catch lightning in a bottle, it is the unheralded and methodical scholar who often carries the bulk of the scientific workload.

121. According to the passage, what is the principal reason Salk's discovery was ridiculed by other scientists?

(A) Salk borrowed heavily from the work of Alexander Fleming.

(B) Salk was unable to master mundane scientific procedure.

(C) The cure for polio was found to be the work of other scientists.

(D) Salk's work did not rely principally on independent innovation.

(E) Salk was incapable of blinding innovation.

122. The author discusses biographies and biographical films in the second sentence in order to

(A) demonstrate the layperson's total lack of interest in scientific discovery

(B) illustrate the degree to which people are curious about individualistic thinkers

(C) describe the controversy surrounding the discovery of penicillin

(D) demonstrate the need for a biography detailing the life and discoveries of Jonas Salk

(E) emphasize a need for greater research into the lives of modern innovators

123. The author suggests that other scientists initially viewed Salk's work as

(A) brilliant

(B) innovative

(C) prosaic

(D) complex

(E) minor

124. Which of the following best describes the author's main purpose in writing this passage?

(A) To show that not all scientific discovery is made by unconventional geniuses

(B) To relate the superiority of one method of scientific discovery over another

(C) To describe the dramatic discovery of penicillin by Alexander Fleming

(D) To give examples of discoveries that were not made by maverick innovators

(E) To recommend greater scientific funding for scientists whose work mirrors Salk's

# PRACTICE QUESTION ANSWERS—GENERAL

## 1. D

Lines 14–22 focus on reverberation, which the author describes as the "most important factor in acoustic design" at the end of the passage.

## 2. A

Choice (A) is the correct answer because the author says that "few of us realize the complex process that goes into designing the acoustics of concert and lecture halls."

## 3. E

All three options are mentioned in the passage as factors that affect the acoustics of a building, so (E) is the right answer.

## 4. C

According to the passage, too little reverberation can make sound thin and weak.

## 5. B

The final sentence of the passage says that the most important factor in acoustic design is the reverberation time, which makes (B) correct.

# PRACTICE QUESTION ANSWERS—BY LEVEL

## ELEMENTARY, LOWER, AND PRIMARY LEVELS

### 6. C

The stony coral secretes a skeleton of calcium carbonate, as stated in lines 5–6.

### 7. C

(B) may look tempting but it's too narrow—the passage is about how *both* the stony coral and the green algae interact to help form coral reefs.

### 8. B

You can infer from the final sentence that divers are primarily interested in the visual appeal of the coral reef.

### 9. D

(D) is correct because the passage states that the coral and the algae have a "mutually beneficial relationship."

### 10. A

(A) has things backwards; the algae live within the tissues of the coral.

**11. B**

In the very first sentence, the author says that tunnel construction is costly and dangerous, and nowhere does he say that TBMs have made tunnel construction less expensive or less dangerous, so (B) is correct.

**12. D**

(D) is a better answer than (C) because (D) covers the entire passage, while (C) is only discussed in the first paragraph.

**13. C**

In this context, "notable" means "remarkable."

**14. B**

(B) echoes the final sentence of the passage.

**15. A**

The author certainly thinks highly of TBMs, so "enthusiastic" is correct. "Jubilant" (E) is too strong a word, however.

**16. A**

The last sentence of the passage says that the protozoans provide the termite with a service necessary to its survival, so (A) is correct.

**17. E**

The passage is about the symbiotic relationship between termites and protozoans, two organisms that cooperate to survive. (E) is the correct answer.

**18. B**

According to the passage, the host organism is the dominant member of the symbiotic pair or group, (B).

**19. E**

The author defines a symbiotic relationship as one in which two organisms coexist to each other's benefit, so (E) is correct.

**20. A**

"Cooperative" is the proper word here. "Friendly" (C) would imply that termites and protozoans have feelings, which is going a little bit too far.

**21. D**

The second sentence of the passage supports (D) as the correct answer.

**22. E**

(E) is the one that captures the central focus of the passage without being too narrow or too broad.

**23. C**

One way the international community responded to the ozone problem was to ban CFCs and other pollutants; this is supposed stop ozone loss by the turn of the century. From this, you can infer that ozone loss was due to pollutants, (C).

**24. B**

The author uses the greenhouse image to describe the effect of increased radiation on the climate of the Earth.

**25. E**

(E) is correct because the last sentence of the passage says that "total ozone recovery" will not occur for more than 100 years.

**26. D**

(D) is better than (C) because (C) only covers the first paragraph, whereas (D) is broad enough to cover the whole passage.

**27. B**

In the context of the second sentence, "acutely" means "extremely."

**28. A**

"China" is the correct answer, judging from the fourth sentence of the first paragraph.

**29. D**

The problem before 1966 was not that there was no smallpox immunization; the problem was that no worldwide campaign had been launched to wipe out the disease.

**30. B**

(B) paraphrases the final sentence of the passage and is correct.

## MIDDLE AND UPPER LEVELS

**31. A**

The caribou and the stoat are examples of animals that change their color with the change of seasons, so (A) is correct.

**32. B**

As mentioned in the passage summary, this passage is a discussion of different types of protective coloration.

**33. A**

(A), the correct answer, is just another way of saying, as the author does, that the chameleon changes colors rapidly to match whatever surface it happens to be on.

**34. C**

Cryptic resemblance is the process by which an animal adapts in color, shape, and behavior in order to blend into its environment. The green tree frog (I) and the chameleon (II) blend into their environment, but the skunk (III) definitely does not.

**35. B**

The hedgehog, unlike the chameleon, "loudly announce[s] its identity" to predators, so (B) is correct.

**36. B**

"Disenchanted" expresses the poet's sentiment well; "furious" (C) is too strong to be correct.

**37. D**

Option II you can omit right away because the poet dislikes government. Option III is taken right from the poem. Option I is also correct but is not as evident as Option III; you have to infer that the poet likes the squirrel's independence from the overall description of the squirrel and its movement.

**38. B**

(B) is correct because the most human aspect of the squirrel the poet mentions is its low whinnying sound "That is like laughter."

**39. C**

The squirrel's laughter is an expression, in the poet's eyes, of its freedom. None of the other choices matches the overall message of the poem.

**40. B**

"Heavy knitting of the brow" is an expression a serious government official would have, not a squirrel.

**41. A**

Detail questions are a great place to rack up points. Make sure that you read the question carefully so that you don't miss the opportunity. The passage discusses the fact that George Washington was a hero not because he was able to win major battles over the British, but because he was able to keep the Colonial war effort together. The passage credits Washington with (A), winning a "uniquely American war."

(B) Opposite; line 29 states that Washington had "little to do" with the victory at Saratoga.

(C) Opposite; lines 9–11 state that Washington could not protect or take back New York or Philadelphia.

(D) Out of Scope; the passage never states that Washington was able to find a way to win pitched battles.

(E) Misused Detail; the passage does state that Washington crossed the Delaware, but it does not give this as a reason for Washington's success.

### 42. A

Roman numeral questions are a great place to be strategic in your approach. Test the most common numerals first so that you have a chance to eliminate the greatest number of answer choices. First, try II because it appears in the most choices. Line 32 states that the victories at Trenton and Princeton "were over minuscule forces," so you can eliminate (B), (D), and (E). I states that the victories had a significant impact on morale, which can be found in line 34, which states that they "kept his army together and resurrected the American cause in the minds of his countrymen." Since I is true, you can eliminate (C).

### 43. D

Watch out for certain verbal cues that indicate what question type you are reading. The words "according to the passage" indicate a Detail question. Lines 15–19 discuss Washington's defeats in both Brooklyn Heights and Manhattan, as well as the retreat across the Delaware, as details of the British invasion of New York. (D) matches this prediction.

(A) Misused Detail; while the passage does cite this failure, it is not the "classic example" referred to by the question.

(B) Opposite; the passage states that Washington was able to keep an army in the field.

(C) Opposite; the passage does state that the Colonies were able to secure the aid of the French.

(E) Misused Detail; while Washington's deployment of troops on Brooklyn Heights did result in defeat, ultimately, the futility referred to is the total failure to defend New York.

### 44. B

In Tone questions, you need to consider how the details or cited lines support the author's overall point. The cited lines serve as an introduction to paragraph 2, which shows that Washington was not a conventional hero. The line beginning "Unfortunately for the British" indicates that their strategy for success was different from Washington's and ultimately foreshadows Washington's victory. (B) agrees with this prediction.

(A) Distortion; while the passage does state that Washington was unable to win pitched battles, the cited lines refer to Washington's unconventional battle tactics, not his inability to imitate the British.

(C) Extreme; the passage does not state that Washington was indifferent to his losses.

(D) Out of Scope; the passage never discusses the American defiance of British customs.

(E) Extreme; the author never attempts to excuse the defeats at New York and Philadelphia.

### 45. B

When a question asks what the author "suggests," the answer must be supported by information in the passage. Paragraph 2 discusses the reasons for Washington's reputation as a hero and the American success in the Revolution. The passage states that Washington was able to "outlast" the British "resolve." In addition, lines 22–24 states that the level of commitment was different for the American soldier. (B) agrees with this information.

(A) Misused Detail; the passage does cite Saratoga as an important victory, but Saratoga is not credited with the ultimate triumph in the war.

(C) Out of Scope; the passage does not compare the morale or supplies of the American and British troops.

(D) Extreme; the passage does not state that Washington's strategy was "inherently superior," only that it worked.

(E) Misused Detail; the passage does not state that Trenton and Princeton were responsible for American victory.

## 46. A

Detail questions occasionally test your ability to define a word. When you research "houses" or "Divide" in the passage, you'll find that they were "built of the sod itself." If you identify "sod" as blocks of dirt with grass on top, you can choose (A). There are also context clues that connect "sod" to the "inescapable ground."

(B) Out of Scope; this detail does not appear in the passage.

(C) Out of Scope; this detail does not appear in the passage.

(D) Out of Scope; this detail does not appear in the passage.

(E) Misused Detail; the Bergson house was log, but the other houses were predominantly sod.

## 47. B

When Detail questions offer five choices from the passage, don't rely on your memory to eliminate choices; go back and research. Research will tell you that the Bergson homestead was easier to find than others "because it overlooked Norway Creek." This is a good match for (B).

(A) Out of Scope; the passage suggests the opposite, as it mentions how little impression John Bergson had made on the land.

(C) Misused Detail; other houses on the Divide were sod, but the Bergson house was made of logs.

(D) Misused Detail; while the Bergson house was in the new country, so were all of the other houses on the Divide.

(E) Misused Detail; the ground was plowed only to the south.

## 48. D

Your understanding of the scope and tone of a passage can often give insight on Detail questions. The passage mentions plowed earth twice, first noting that the marks of the plow were insignificant, then mentioning the fields south of Bergson's house. Of these, "insignificant" is a good match for (D). You can also get a clue from the fact that the passage stresses the insignificance of people on the Great Plains, or you can use elimination strategies.

(A) Misused Detail; glaciers are mentioned only as a metaphor, to show how little impact people have had on the land.

(B) Misused Detail; cottonwood trees are mentioned, but they surround the ravine, not the fields.

(C) Out of Scope; this detail does not appear in the passage.

(E) Misused Detail; the placement of the fields is given in relation to the house, not the creek.

## 49. B

The most common meaning of a word may not be the correct meaning in context. A "draw" is a slight depression in the land, similar to a gully. Even without this precise definition, the context clues of "ridge" and "gully" should suggest that a "draw" is feature of the landscape, (B).

(A) Out of Scope; a "drawing" can be a "quick sketch," but that does not fit this context.

(C) Misused Detail; a "homestead" is a piece of land earned through use and habitation and is not related to a draw.

(D) Misused Detail; the discussion of buildings is not related to the mention of the draw.

(E) Misused Detail; the passage discusses various plants, but not in the context of the draw.

## 50. E

You will frequently see deceptive answers that misuse details from the passage. Lines 24–25 states that "Bergson had made little impression upon the wild land," so it is a short jump to predict (E). It is also possible to eliminate your way to the answer or to notice the phrase "in eleven long years" in your research.

(A) Out of Scope; the name "Alexandra" is mentioned, but her relationship to John is unknown.

(B) Out of Scope; the "genius" mentioned in the passage is a reference to nature's indifference to man, not to John himself.

(C) Extreme; while John is ill in the passage, there is no reason to suspect his entire life has been defined by illness.

(D) Misused Detail; Norway Creek is a waterway, not a town.

## 51. A

Your first read-through of a passage should provide a broad picture of both content and tone. The passage repeats the idea that human strivings are insignificant compared to nature. The author credits the environment with "ugly moods" and unfriendly genius, and describes it as "lead-colored." This is a grim and gloomy tone, (A).

(B) While this passage contains information, an informative tone is more like the voice of a textbook writer or a journalist.

(C) An objective tone conveys information without bias or opinion. This writer clearly had a point of view.

(D) "Sunny" is bright and cheery, whereas this passage is more dark and gloomy.

(E) "Comic" is funny, which is the opposite of the tone of this passage.

## 52. C

Detail questions will often test your vocabulary as well as your critical reading skills. You may have to look for synonyms when you research a question.

When you research, you can look for words meaning either "worry" or "disrupt." You'll find "worry" in the fourth sentence, which mentions how caribou might abandon their young, a good match for (C).

(A) Out of Scope; the passage says nothing about how the migration would affect oil production.

(B) Misused Detail; while the passage mentions winter feeding grounds, it does so in another context.

(D) Out of Scope; subsistence hunters do not appear in the passage.

(E) Out of Scope; the passage does not discuss how the migration would be disrupted.

## 53. C

A thorough critical read, including an understanding of key points, will prepare you for broad Inference questions.

The last line calls the crossing planners "wise" for avoiding risks. While the crossings were ultimately unnecessary, they were still a good idea, which best matches (C).

(A) Out of Scope; the passage does not discuss the cost of the crossings.

(B) Misused Detail; while the crossings were not needed to protect the caribou, this was not known before construction began.

(D) Distortion; the passage says the crossings were not needed, not that they were badly designed.

(E) Out of Scope; the passage makes no mention of how the crossings affected oil prices.

## 54. D

Remember to eliminate Out-of-Scope choices to improve your odds.

The sentence that mentions how the migration might be hampered also contains a discussion of the dimensions of the pipe and the fact that it is elevated, which provides a match for (D). In this question, it is also possible to eliminate all four incorrect answers.

(A) Out of Scope; seasons are mentioned, but the precise timing of the construction was not.

(B) Out of Scope; the passage discusses the possible impact of the pipeline, but not of the oil it carries.

(C) Out of Scope; the passage does not discuss how caribou react to people.

(E) Out of Scope; the passage makes no mention of this.

## 55. C

Some words have multiple definitions. Always read for context clues. The sentences around the word "hamper" contain words like "delay" and a discussion of the size of the pipe. These clues might lead you to predict a synonym like "block," "impede," or "interfere with," which are a good match with (C).

(A) "Accelerate" is to speed up, which is the opposite of "hamper."

(B) "Depose" is to overthrow or dethrone, which does not fit the context of the sentence.

(D) A hamper could be a type of basket or container, but, in this context, it has a different meaning.

(E) While the pipeline might cause caribou to redirect their migration, the meaning of "hamper" is closer to "block" or "impede."

## 56. E

Never rely on memory to answer a Detail question. Always refer directly to the passage. A question like this must be handled by process of elimination. As you test each choice, you'll find that only (E) appears in the passage, in the first sentence.

(A) Out of Scope; the passage tells you the pipe is elevated, but never how high.

(B) Out of Scope; the passage discusses North Slope caribou, but never gives their number.

(C) Out of Scope; the passage speculates that migration disruption could orphan calves, but it never provides a number of deaths.

(D) Out of Scope; the passage does not discuss costs.

## 57. B

For questions, like this one, think about which choice would make the best headline for the passage. Global questions can best be solved with a prediction based on your critical read. For this passage, you might predict something like "How scientists tried to protect migrating caribou," which is a good match for (B). It is also possible to eliminate four wrong answers.

(A) Opposite; the passage claims that the pipeline has not disrupted caribou migrations.

(C) Distortion; migration routes appear in the passage, but they are not the main idea.

(D) Out of Scope; the passage does not speak on behalf of most Alaskans; instead, it discusses one issue surrounding pipeline planning and construction.

(E) Out of Scope; the passage makes no mention of the costs of the pipeline.

## 58. A

Use your notes to locate the stanza that the question stem refers to, and then evaluate one statement at a time, beginning with the statement that appears in the most answer choices. With this strategy, you'll usually be able to eliminate enough wrong answers to find the right answer without needing to evaluate all three statements, which will save you time on Test Day. I and III both appear in three answer choices, so begin with I. The question stem refers to the changing emotions of the writer's beloved, and this is the theme of the end of the first stanza, so reread until you find something that helps to determine whether I is true or false. Line 9 ("The flowers have dried down to the root") provides a paraphrase for I, so you know that this statement is true, and you can eliminate (B) and (C) because they don't include I. Then move on to III. Line 2 ("The lilies bloomed within the sedge") is the only line that refers to lilies, but the first half of this stanza does not refer to any changes in the beloved's emotions, so III is false. This

means you can eliminate (D) and (E), leaving you
with the correct answer, (A).

(B) Eliminate; doesn't include I.

(C) Eliminate; III is false.

(D) Eliminate; doesn't include I, and III is false.

(E) Eliminate; III is false.

## 59. D

Many Detail questions on poetry passages require
you to use some of your critical thinking skills, just
like Inference questions do, because you need to be
able to interpret language that doesn't explicitly say
what it means. If you reread line 16, you can see from
the period at the end that this line forms the final part
of an idea that begins two lines earlier. Reread lines
14–15 ("And my poor cheeks, five months ago / Set
blushing at thy praises so") to understand the context
of the line quoted in the question stem. You can then
understand that the writer has become sad because
of some change in her beloved, and this sadness has
caused her face to turn pale, which matches (D).

(A) Nothing in the poem suggests that the writer
actively tried to make her face white or paler by
putting on makeup.

(B) Distortion; the beginning of the second stanza
refers to snow in the context of how long it took the
writer to become sad, so the comparison to snow is
not directly related to the writer's face.

(C) The writer never mentions or suggests that she
has physically put on a mask to hide herself.

(E) Distortion; the writer doesn't blame winter
for her paleness, and, as the explanation for (B)
points out, the comparison to snow and winter
is not directly related to the appearance of the
writer's face.

## 60. E

Sometimes you'll need to reread several lines of a
poem to fully understand the meaning of a specific
detail. Do so if the question stems direct you to

particularly difficult lines. The first stanza contains
the references in the question stem. Line 1 ("Five
months ago the stream did flow") and line 8 ("The
frozen river is as mute") demonstrate the contrast
and change that have occurred in the writer's beloved
as the latter begins to lose interest, (E).

(A) Misused Detail; although the poem does refer to
passing time ("Five months ago"), the references to
the stream are used figuratively to represent changing
emotions rather than as proof of the changing seasons.

(B) Distortion; again, the change in the river reflects the
emotional change in the writer's beloved and doesn't
refer to the tangible sensations of warmth and cold.

(C) Extreme; nothing in the poem suggests that the
writer's beloved has changed so drastically as to
hate her.

(D) Distortion; the writer doesn't express her feelings
about nature but rather uses examples from nature to
illustrate the changing emotions of her beloved.

## 61. C

Sometimes you can use your understanding of the
writer's tone and attitude to answer an Inference
question, just like you would a Global question.
Remember to always look for familiar themes in
poetry passages to help you stay focused on the
writer's central idea. The overall theme of this
poem is that the emotions of the writer's beloved
have changed as some time has passed. The writer
compares these changes to the changes that occur in
nature with the passing of the seasons and concludes
that it's equally natural for people to change as well
(lines 10–11, "And why, since these be changed
since May, / Shouldst *thou* change less than *they*?"
and lines 21–22, "And why, since these be changed
now, / Should I change less than *thou*?"). Although
the writer is sad that her beloved has changed, she
implies through these lines that she can understand
this as a natural part of the relationship, (C).

(A) Opposite; the entire poem focuses on changes in love.

(B) Opposite; the writer suggests that changes are common and can be expected.

(D) Opposite; the writer describes her sadness at the change in her beloved's emotions.

(E) Distortion/Extreme; although the writer acknowledges that love may be difficult if one person starts to lost interest, she never recommends avoiding love entirely.

## 62. B

To answer Inference questions about particular words, focus on the cited text and how the word is used in that sentence and in the larger context of the passage. The word "staggering" is describing the growth of the "booming" IT industry. (B) best fits this.

(A) Opposite; the IT industry is booming despite recent fluctuations.

(C) Opposite; the IT industry continues to grow despite market shifts.

(D) Distortion; the IT industry is not on the verge of collapse.

(E) Distortion; the IT industry's growth is sustained, not intermittent.

## 63. A

To answer a Detail question effectively, look for more information on the detail being presented. Information technology is a "field" or "sector." (A) best matches this prediction. (B) Out of Scope; IT employers are never discussed directly in the passage. (C) Misused Detail; the industry's "Wall Street Cred" is not applicable here. (D) Misused Detail; this is a projection regarding the industry, not a definition of it. (E) Out of Scope; space travel is completely irrelevant to the passage.

## 64. D

To answer Detail questions, focus directly on what is being asked. Ignore irrelevant and unrelated facts.

What would make one boom industry temporary, while another lasts? The passage states that outside constraints, such as politics, are responsible. This best matches (D).

(A) Out of Scope; information technology in American politics is never discussed.

(B) Distortion; the question is contrasting industries, not technologies.

(C) Misused Detail; the education required for IT jobs is never compared to the education required in collapsed boom industries.

(E) Opposite; the passage states that the computer industry is specifically *not* the result of devastation.

## 65. E

The answer to an Inference question always follows from what is in the passage. Don't stray too far from what is on the page. Relate each of the three statements to the author's overall assessment of information technology. Since the author refers to the "escalation of (and dependence on) computer technology," I seems a logical conclusion. Although the author does mention frequent training, he does not imply that it is bothersome, so you can eliminate choices that include II. The author discusses both the fact that technology jobs have a higher salary and the fact that IT workers are more sastified with their jobs, so III is a logical conclusion. (E) is the only answer that includes I and III.

## 66. D

Inference questions will always be related to an idea addressed in some fashion within the passage. The author states that the career is attractive because of a "high median salary" and "strong benefits," (D).

(A) Distortion; the author states that it is only *unlikely* that the market will collapse.

(B) Distortion; this is implied by the author, not by the Department of Labor.

(C) Distortion; "crunch time" is never stated to be new or unique to the IT industry.

(E) Opposite; the passage indicates that the computer industry provides good careers for workers but questionable investment opportunities.

## 67. C

Answer Tone questions by getting a feel for the entirety of the passage. Don't focus on small details. The author tells us that the IT industry is booming and then touches on some of the pros and cons of the field. He explains both the positive and negative aspects of a career in information technology and then lists reasons why it is likely to remain a strong industry in the future. This best matches (C).

(A) Distortion; the author discusses the benefits of a career in IT but devotes just as much time to explaining the drawbacks.

(B) Distortion; the author does point out some of the common problems with information technology but also states that it is a strong career option.

(D) Distortion; the author is not apologizing to the reader.

(E) Distortion; the author is not overly critical of IT careers, nor is the commentary vicious.

## 68. E

Answer Inference questions about the meanings of words in context by focusing on the sentence and the area immediately surrounding the word in question. "Strong growth" is being projected for the future, which best fits (E).

(A) Distortion; nothing is being displayed in this sentence.

(B) Distortion; growth is not being proposed but predicted.

(C) Distortion; to "project" here means to predict or forecast, not to undertake a project.

(D) Distortion; "strong growth" is not being thrown into the future.

## 69. A

To answer Global questions, look at the passage as a whole, rather than focusing on specific details. The author makes his purpose clear at the start of the passage. He gives us reasons why IT is a popular field and also discusses long-term career potential, (A).

(B) Out of Scope; computer science is never mentioned, nor is the tone of the passage promotional.

(C) Misused Detail; although it is noted that information technology pays well, this is not the focus of the passage.

(D) Misused Detail; the author does mention that investing in the field has not been as attractive as working in it, but this is not the primary intent of the passage.

(E) Misused Detail; the author compares IT to other boom industries to discuss its long-term career potential, not simply for the sake of comparison.

## 70. A

Remember to look for relevant details directly in the text. "Life is a stream" is the opening line of the poem; the correct choice will contain only statement I. (A) is correct.

(B) and (D) contain statement II, which is incorrect.

(C) and (E) contain statement III, which is incorrect.

## 71. D

Inferences need to be supported by the text. In the poem, the writer stands on the bank of a stream (of life) and tosses flower petals in, after which they drift out of view: "Their distant employ / we shall never know." (D) describes the writer's comfortable uncertainty regarding the path of the rose petals.

(A) Out of Scope; sinking or floating is not mentioned in the poem.

(B) Out of Scope; eddy currents are not mentioned in the poem.

(C) Misused Detail; the roses' color is not relevant.

(E) Distortion; the narrator is not asleep.

## 72. B

This question asks about the broader sense of the poem. Look carefully for specific words in the poem to support a particular interpretation. In the symbolism of the poem, the rose ("flower of our heart") is tossed petal by petal into the stream of life; the petals "widening scope...we never shall know." The emphasis on the heart and the lingering fragrance of the flower suggests that love is symbolized in the poem, (B).

(A) Misused Detail; "employ" is not the same as employment.

(C) Out of Scope; death is not a subject of the poem.

(D) Misused Detail; "joy" does not describe the petals at all points on their drift.

(E) Opposite; life is symbolized by the stream; the petals are carried on by life.

## 73. C

Poetry questions requiring Inference need to be answered carefully, finding specific words to support each claim. The representation of life as a stream, unknowable in destination, communicates unpredictability. The author comfortably states that once petals are launched, "each one is gone," (C).

(A) Opposite; life as a stream does not allow for predicted consequences.

(B) Extreme; "We only watch their glad, early start" communicates greater influence over the beginning of life experiences.

(D) Extreme; "its fragrance still stays," so something remains of early experiences.

(E) Out of Scope; the poem does not address friendship.

## 74. C

The correct answer to a Global question must take into account information found throughout the passage. The author focuses on how very different cultures live in close proximity in Central Europe, (C).

(A) Out of Scope; the author never discusses the difficulty of navigating the Danube.

(B) Misused Detail; while the grandeur of these cities is certainly described, this is not the focus of the passage.

(D) Misused Detail; the history endured by Central European people is only mentioned at the end of the passage.

(E) Out of Scope; the challenges to linguists are not discussed in this passage.

## 75. A

The key to correctly answering Detail questions is to research the passage carefully. The passage mentions people from each of three cites calling the Danube a different name, (A).

(B) Opposite; these landmarks can be found in Budapest, not Vienna.

(C) Out of Scope; while the passage does state that these three peoples have common history, the passage never states that they have a common origin.

(D) Out of Scope; reliance on the river is never discussed in the passage.

(E) Extreme; the passage states that the languages are dissimilar, not necessarily that the people cannot understand each other.

## 76. E

When a Detail question does not offer specific line references, you must research each answer choice to find evidence to support or eliminate it. The passage, in the discussion of history found at the end, mentions that the three cities have been united under common empires, which means that they had been the territories of other powers, (E).

(A) Opposite; the passage clearly states that their cultures and languages are very different.

(B) Extreme; the passage never states which city is the most beautiful.

(C) Extreme; the passage does not state that it is overwhelming, merely that the disparity can be staggering.

(D) Opposite; the passage states that the people of the three cities have privation and strife in common.

## 77. C

The answer to an Inference question will not be stated in the passage, but it will be supported by the text. The passage is most concerned with the differences in culture in cities that are in close proximity to each other. Mentioning different words for the Danube emphasizes this, (C).

(A) Out of Scope; the passage never discusses the length of the river.

(B) Misused Detail; the author is not focused on the differences between the three languages, but rather on how many linguistic and cultural differences there are in such a small geographic area.

(D) Out of Scope; the need for a unified translation is never discussed.

(E) Distortion; the difference between the languages is never linked to the wars in this passage.

## 78. B

Wrong answers will often employ language from the passage. Forming a good prediction will help you avoid confusion. The passage discusses languages in the Danube region to emphasize their dissimilarity, (B).

(A) Out of Scope; the passage never states how difficult these languages are to master.

(C) Out of Scope; the passage never mentions how these languages sound to observers.

(D) Distortion; the passage does not state that the languages of the three cities have taken on any similarities because of forced unification.

(E) Extreme; the passage does not state that such distinctness cannot be found elsewhere.

## 79. B

Detail questions ask for you to find specific information in the text. Supporting details can be found only in the text; do not use your prior knowledge or jump to conclusions. Only (B) is contained in the text.

(A) Out of Scope; the author does not mention emergencies.

(C) Misused Detail; while computer assistance may be helpful for controllers, according to the author, it is not enabled by transfer of authority.

(D) Out of Scope; the author does not mention seat sales.

(E) Out of Scope; the author does not mention maintenance.

## 80. A

Detail questions ask you to find specific details in the text. This is an EXCEPT question, so you are looking for the detail that is not in the passage. This is (A).

(B) Mentioned in paragraph 2.

(C) Mentioned in paragraph 4.

(D) Mentioned in paragraph 3.

(E) Mentioned in paragraph 1.

## 81. C

Inference questions ask you to draw conclusions based on evidence in the passage. In the last paragraph, the author states that air traffic controllers need more modern equipment. For I, no mention is made of staffing needs at ARTCC, though the author does state that TRACON centers have a heavy burden. So you can eliminate (A), (D), and (E). II must be true, because it appears in both of the remaining answer choices. III is stated in the final paragraph. (C) is therefore correct.

## 82. D

Inference questions ask you to draw conclusions based on the text. The inference that authority for an airplane, once landed, is transferred to the airport control tower can be based on the statement at the end of paragraph 1.

The airport tower's responsibility during takeoff is detailed in paragraph 1; the responsibility on landing is shown indirectly ("and back again," end of paragraph 1), which is (D).

(A) Extreme; transfer of authority is never automatic and always involves human decisions.

(B) Out of Scope; the author does not address wages.

(C) Extreme; airports are responsible during taxiing on takeoff and landing.

(E) Extreme; pilots have some responsibility during takeoff.

## 83. D

Tone questions concern the point of view of the author. While the four nonfiction options are all plausible, only one describes the persuasive writing in the final paragraph. A policy briefing would provide an opportunity for the author to argue for increased resources for air traffic control, (D).

(A) Distortion; the tone of the passage is factual and not similar to what would be found in a novel.

(B) Distortion; too little technical detail is provided for the passage to be appropriate for an aircraft technical manual.

(C) Distortion; the persuasive writing in the final paragraph is inappropriate for a textbook.

(E) Distortion; too little historical detail is provided for the piece to be useful as a history.

## 84. C

Remember that context is your biggest advantage on Inference questions that ask for the meaning of a specific word. Several words that are similar at first glance are not fitting when considered carefully.

Only "reduced," (C), fits in the sentence, describing the reduction of a burden.

(A) Distortion; "brighten" sounds similar to the chosen word but does not have a similar meaning in the context of the sentence.

(B) Distortion; "clarify" may lighten in appearance but does not lighten a burden.

(D) Distortion; "calcify" is placed here to tempt you, since it's spelled similarly to "clarify."

(E) Opposite; "compound" would imply a desire to make the situation yet more difficult.

## 85. A

This question requires your overall comprehension of the passage. Several tempting answers are given, but (A) is the only choice that describes the real sense of the section, which presents no debate and has no broader content.

(B) Opposite; the author presents no such argument.

(C) Distortion; the author does not compare this with other modes.

(D) Out of Scope; the author presents no conflict between the two control centers, which are part of the same system.

(E) Out of Scope; the author does not mention fuel economy.

## 86. C

Answers to Detail questions will always be found in the passage. The passage states that the crash nearly killed Hughes and that the "brush with death" changed the man. Predict that after the crash, Hughes's behavior was different, (C).

(A) Out of Scope; although Hughes probably did compensate the homeowners, this is never stated in the passage.

(B) Misused Detail; although the passage states that Hughes was romanticized, this is not necessarily linked to the crash.

(D) Out of Scope; the continuation of the XF-11 project is not mentioned.

(E) Distortion; Hughes did not become known as the "fastest man in the world" because of the crash—that is what he called himself before the crash.

### 87. B

Make sure to keep the author's tone and overall point in mind when answering an Inference question. The author uses the words "interesting" and "adventurer" to describe Hughes, who became increasingly disturbed after a flying accident. Predict that Hughes is not only an interesting figure, but also a tragic one, (B).

(A) Distortion; although his "quest for glory" indicates that Hughes was ambitious, consider the overall tone of the passage. (A) is too harsh on Hughes, who is never described as arrogant.

(C) Extreme; although the passage deals with Hughes's madness in his later years, the author counters this by mentioning his other qualities as well.

(D) Opposite; Hughes was quite a celebrity.

(E) Distortion; the statement that Hughes became "more myth than man" is a metaphor referring to Hughes's fame and seclusion.

### 88. D

Global questions will encompass the entire passage. The passage discusses Howard Hughes and how his life changed after a plane crash. The author seems particularly interested in Hughes's fame and legacy and how his behavior affected public perception of him. Predict that the passage source would be concerned mostly with famous people, (D).

(A) Distortion; although the passage indicates that Hughes's madness was worsened by the crash, this is not the focal point of the passage.

(B) Out of Scope; there is nothing in the passage to suggest that this is a new or revolutionary analysis of Hughes's life.

(C) Distortion; Hughes's mental illness is discussed, but the tone and scope of the passage are not at all indicative of a clinical study.

(E) Opposite; the passage is biographical in tone and scope.

### 89. B

Tone questions require an understanding of the author's position. The author states that, despite the way Hughes lived out his later years, he remained "genuinely interesting." Predict that the author viewed Hughes as a compelling and tragic figure, rather than a larger-than-life hero or a tyrant. (B) matches best.

(A) Distortion; the author states that Hughes was a mad recluse but does not ridicule or attempt to debase him.

(C) Out of Scope; the author never displays any anger or hostility toward Hughes or his legacy.

(D) Distortion; the author does not gush over Hughes or seem intimidated by him.

(E) Out of Scope; the tone of the passage is not humorous.

### 90. A

To answer Global questions, focus on the author's main theme and predict carefully. The passage deals with Howard Hughes, his "quest for glory," his eventual madness, and his public legacy. The best prediction here is that the passage deals with celebrity, (A).

(B) Misused Detail; Hughes was a pilot and aircraft designer, but this is not the focus of the passage. The plane crash is a detail used to explain his worsening mental condition.

(C) Misused Detail; Hughes was a recluse later in his life, but this is mostly mentioned to show how his ambition affected his life and his reputation.

(D) Distortion; although Hughes's ambition and eccentricities contributed to his fame, it is his fame that is the focus of the passage.

(E) Out of Scope; Hughes's personal fortune is outside the scope of the passage; it is never mentioned.

### 91. C

When answering a Global question, you must consider the passage as a whole, not merely isolated ideas or details. The passage focuses in paragraph 1 on the invention of the telegraph and the growth of its use. Paragraph 2 discusses how the telegraph became obsolete. The correct answer will encompass this information. (C) does so.

(A) Out of Scope; the passage is not focused on telecommunications in general, but specifically on the telegraph.

(B) Misused Detail; the disappearance of the telegraph is solely the focus of paragraph 2.

(D) Out of Scope; the difficulty of Morse code is never discussed in the passage.

(E) Misused Detail; while this difficulty is mentioned, the passage is not focused on it.

### 92. D

Tone questions ask you to assess the overall feel of the passage. The passage discusses the telegraph in fairly neutral to positive terms. The author's purpose is to describe, not to make recommendations or warnings, (D).

(A) Opposite; the author is never negative in his description.

(B) Extreme; while there is a positive tone in the passage, the author never focuses his effort on specifically praising the telegraph.

(C) Opposite; there is no warning or negative statement in the passage.

(E) Extreme; while the author does state that the telegraph is obsolete, the passage never focuses negatively or positively on this.

### 93. B

Pay close attention to the exact wording of questions. Reading too quickly can result in missing critical words like EXCEPT or NOT. The author states that the transatlantic cable was laid because of the telegraph's invention, not the other way around, (B).

(A) Mentioned in line 1.

(C) Mentioned in lines 6–8; the author discusses the telegraph and the Civil War.

(D) Mentioned in lines 19–21.

(E) Mentioned in paragraph 2; telephone, fax, and email have rendered the telegraph "completely obsolete."

### 94. B

Title questions are Global questions. Look for a title that encapsulates the entire passage. The passage is focused on the telegraph, its invention, importance, and ultimate demise. (B) best captures this focus.

(A) Misused Detail; the passage only focuses on the end of telegraphy in paragraph 2.

(C) Misused Detail; Morse and the invention of the telegraph are discussed only in the first part of the passage.

(D) Out of Scope; telecommunications before the telegraph are not discussed in this passage.

(E) Misused Detail; journalism is mentioned but is not the focus of the entire passage.

### 95. E

Remember, the correct answer to an Inference question MUST be true based on the passage. The question is too open-ended to predict, so evaluate each answer choice in turn; the passage suggests that the telegraph was a major innovation which improved communications. (E) follows logically.

(A) Out of Scope; the passage never states that the telegraph is less accurate.

(B) Distortion; the passage never discusses how the telegraph was affected by the war.

(C) Distortion; Despite the Internet, Western Union would likely have continued telegraph service had there been a demand for it.

(D) Out of Scope; the difficulty of Morse code is never discussed in the passage.

## 96. B

Questions that ask about the author's purpose for writing a passage are concerned with the passage as a whole. You should consider the author's tone throughout the passage as well as what the author is trying to accomplish. There are several instances in which the author praises the Northern cause in this passage. While the author does describe the events of Fort Sumter's surrender, there is a distinct indication of support toward the Northern cause. This partiality is best reflected in (B).

(A) Distortion; the writer doesn't know at the point he writes how significant this act will be.

(C) Misused Detail; the passage discusses Lincoln's call to arms, but that is not the purpose of the passage.

(D) Misused Detail; slavery is only mentioned in the first sentence.

(E) Opposite; the last sentence of the passage indicates that the North possesses the advantage in the coming war.

## 97. E

The correct answer to an Inference question must be supported by information in the passage. The passage states in lines 7–9 that both the Federal government and President Lincoln desired peace, (E).

(A) Extreme; the author states that Anderson did refuse to surrender, but the author never implies that this instigated the war.

(B) Opposite; lines 11–13 make it clear that Toombs did not support the attack.

(C) Out of Scope; the passage never discusses Lincoln's explicit orders.

(D) Distortion; the passage does mention slavery but states that the Southerners, the "defenders of slavery," brought the war on themselves.

## 98. A

The correct answer to an Inference question must follow logically from the passage. This is a tricky question. After researching the citation, it is clear that the Southerners are the defenders of slavery, and they started the war by attacking Fort Sumter. The author further suggests in lines 26–28 that, because of its advantages, the North will win the war. From this information, you can infer that, because they started the war and will probably lose, the Southerners have doomed slavery, (A).

(B) Out of Scope; the author does not mention any Northern supporters of slavery.

(C) Opposite; the passage states that the Southerners were defenders of slavery.

(D) Misused Detail; the "blow" mentioned refers to a threat to slavery, not the strength of Beauregard's attack.

(E) Misused Detail; the "blow" referred to in line 2 was struck by the Southerners, not Lincoln.

## 99. B

Be on the lookout for clues that reveal the author's views. The author states in line 8 that the Southerners are "suspicious," which best matches (B).

(A) Extreme; while the author does state that the Northerners are loyal, the Southerners are never explicitly referred to as traitors.

(C) Distortion; while the Southerners do attack the fort, the author never explicitly states that they are "belligerent."

(D) Out of Scope; this choice is not supported by the passage.

(E) Opposite; the author states that the Northerners are patriotic.

## 100. C

Always keep track of whose opinion is whose in a Reading Comprehension passage. The author describes Toombs's words as "prophetic," thus stating his opinion that Toombs will, indeed, be correct and the North will win the war.

(A) Out of Scope; the victor of the Civil War can't be known by the author at this time.

(B) Out of Scope; the author never discusses Toombs's expert knowledge of anything.

(D) Distortion; while the author does correlate Toombs's words with Lincoln's response, he never actually states that this single action of Lincoln's will win the war.

(E) Misused Detail; the author does not state that the immediate patriotic response will alone prove Toombs's words prophetic.

## 101. B

When answering an Inference question that asks about a word's meaning in context, beware of the most common definition of the cited word. A secondary definition will likely be correct on Test Day. In line 26, "strains" refers to the playing of the *Star Spangled Banner*. In this case, "strains" can be predicted to mean "tones" or "playing." (B) is closest to your prediction.

(A) is the primary definition of "strains" and does not fit your prediction.

(C) "Exclamations" is close but too literal.

(D) Again, close, but "outburts" is too literal an answer choice.

(E) "Strains" refers to the playing of the *Star Spangled Banner*, not feelings.

## 102. D

Always be sure to read each question stem and answer choice carefully! There is no need to lose points on Detail questions from careless errors. The response to the attack is discussed in paragraph 2. The author states that there was an intense upsurge of patriotism, not a "decline," (D).

(A) Line 20 states that Fort Sumter was surrendered.

(B) Lines 20–21 states that Lincoln called for 75,000 volunteers.

(C) Lines 21–23 state that Lincoln called for troops and authorization of any means to preserve the Union, which is a change from his desire for peace.

(E) The raising of troops and subsequent response in the states constitutes mobilization.

## 103. A

Consider the context of this quote. The speaker does not use this term in its literal sense. He refers to the council as "friends" to show the unfriendliness or injustice of their actions. (A) shows this contrast between the designation of "friends" and the actions of the city council.

(B) This is not the meaning of the word in context.

(C) This is not the meaning of the word in context.

(D) This speech solely addresses the city council—the passage makes no mention of the speaker's actual friends.

(E) The passage does not state whether the speaker received any sort of permission to address the council.

## 104. A

You will need to dettermine the content of the quotation. By using this quotation, the speaker sets up a comparison. He shows that the people in his neighborhood are already "equal." The council's plan is a flawed attempt to make it "more equal."

(B) Opposite; this quote reminds the council that citizens are equal; it doesn't claim that educated people have more rights to the government.

(C) Opposite; this quote reminds the council that citizens are equal.

(D) Distortion; the speaker was not in violation. In fact, he claims that the city's actions were a violation of equality.

(E) Out of Scope; the passage does not discuss the Constitution or voting.

## 105. E

Answers to Detail questions are always found in the passage. Be careful with the wrong answers here. The author mentions several facts and opinions about the North Freeway neighborhood. You'll have to sort through the answers to determine which piece of evidence is presented to support his opinion: that the people of the neighborhood have equal right to their homes. (E) does just that.

(A) Out of Scope; the passage does not discuss the Constitution.

(B) Out of Scope; the passage does not mention the other beautiful neighborhoods in the city.

(C) Opposite; the speech makes clear that the citizens should *not* be forced to leave the area.

(D) Misused Detail; while the area is described as "unattractive to tourists," this statement is not used to support the speaker's claim that the project is an injustice.

## 106. C

Take the entire passage into consideration when answering Global questions. The speaker is concerned with the reconstruction project. His speech is meant to point out the injustice of this venture, (C).

(A) Distortion; the speaker wants to influence the city council members, not "citizens of a particular area."

(B) Misused Detail; the speaker does mention tourism in his speech. However, this reference is only a detail; his purpose is to discuss the reconstruction project, not tourism.

(D) Out of Scope; the speaker argues that one plan is unjust, but he does not present an alternative plan.

(E) Misused Detail; the speaker uses a reference to social justice and equality. However, this reference is only a detail; his purpose is more focused on the reconstruction project.

## 107. B

Remember to look for details directly in the passage. The answer to this Detail question is in the final sentence of paragraph 1: "At times, severe bursts of wind penetrated her specialized, technical coverings and made her feel as if she were fighting to take each step forward."

(B) is correct.

(A) Misused Detail; the climber worries about the possibility of an avalanche, but it does not occur.

(C) Opposite; paragraph 1 mentions only an occasional cloud.

(D) Opposite; the passage describes a cold setting.

(E) Misused Detail; the ice wall is a hallucination.

## 108. C

Look for supporting details when making an Inference. The passage mentions several details describing a mountain setting: tree line, final peak, avalanche. (C) is correct.

(A) Opposite; the setting describes cold, snow, and wind, rather than warmth, sand, and sun.

(B) Opposite; there is no mention of the heat and humidity characteristic of a swamp.

(D) Opposite.

(E) Opposite; heat and dehydration are not on the protagonist's mind.

### 109. D

Look for specific information in the text to help answer Inference questions. "She relied on her vast well of experience, her senses, and the aura of footsteps that had come before to lead the way." (D), technical instruments, are not described in the text.
(A) Opposite; "She was, in fact, stronger than ever"; her strength aids her climb.
(B) Opposite; "senses" are mentioned specifically.
(C) Opposite; the protagonist is familiar with the cottage she enters at the end.
(E) Opposite; her technical coverings are mentioned in line 11.

### 110. E

Use context to determine the meaning of an unknown word. The meaning of the word "amorphous" is described best by (E).
(A) The shapes of rocks in the snow may be described loosely as baggy, but "amorphous" is not a close match for the meaning of "baggy."
(B) Amorphous shapes are not distinct shapes.
(C) Mountaineering is rugged, but "amorphous" does not mean rugged.
(D) "Triangular" describes a well-defined shape; "amorphous" does not.

### 111. C

Many Global questions will ask you to identify the purpose of the passage. To answer this type of question, ask yourself why the author presented this information and what the author wanted the reader to learn from this passage. Paragraph 1 reveals the purpose. The introduction states that nuclear fallout may contaminate humans in many ways. The next paragraphs show ways in which humans come into contact with the toxic material, so you can predict that the author is primarily concerned with human contamination.

(A) Misused Detail; this answer focuses on only the last paragraph. You want an answer that takes into account the entire passage.
(B) and (D) Distortion; the passage is primarily concerned with how humans absorb nuclear material. The environmental changes are only details used in support of this purpose.
(E) Misused Detail; this answer focuses on one sentence in paragraph 1. You need an answer that takes into account the entire passage.

### 112. A

This is a Detail question, so you only need to look at a small portion of the information given. Paragraph 2 discusses how plants become toxic. Look to paragraph 2 for this answer. The author writes, "The soil remains toxic and eventually poisons local plant life," so you'll need an answer that states that the soil contaminates the plants.
(B) Misused Detail; the author states that cow's meat and milk are contaminated but claims that it is the soil that directly affects the plants.
(C) Misused Detail; the author states that the air is contaminated but claims that it is the soil that directly affects the plants.
(D) Distortion; humans are contaminated through the plants, not vice versa.
(E) Out of Scope; the passage does not mention fertilizer.

### 113. E

Answers to Inference questions will follow logically from the text. Paragraph 3 uses cow's milk as an example of animal products passing radioactive contamination to humans. Look for an answer that uses the cows as an illustration of the main point. (E) is the only answer that includes the example as part of the purpose of the passage.

(A) Distortion; the example is used to show how cows help to contaminate humans, not to show the effect on the cows themselves.

(B) Out of Scope; while the author does show the cows being part of the food chain, this is not the purpose of this detail. The contaminated cows are examples of how nuclear fallout is passed on through affected milk.

(C) Distortion; the example is used to show how cows can contaminate humans. The phrase "changes in an ecosystem" is too broad for the author's purpose.

(D) Misused Detail; the plants are discussed in the previous paragraph.

## 114. D

On Test Day, you will be asked to identify the tone of some passages. To answer these questions, think about the author's purpose. The author uses a very straightforward tone and does not use persuasive or emotional language. You can predict that the passage is simply meant to present information, (D).

(A) Out of Scope; there is no emotional language to show excitement in this passage.

(B) Distortion; the passage presents the information in an objective manner. The author does not express any feelings of fear.

(C) Distortion; the passage presents the information without any warning or threat.

(E) Distortion; the author does not attempt to persuade the reader in any way.

## 115. B

To predict what the author would write about next, you must consider the outline of the passage so far. Consider the structure of the passage so far. First, the author claims that there are many ways that humans can become contaminated. Then you see an example of plants carrying fallout to humans. The passage ends with a discussion of animals' role in human contamination. Logically, the next paragraph would

discuss another method of human contamination, (B).

(A) Distortion; the contamination of plants appears in paragraph 2; a further discussion of plants would not logically follow the paragraph about animals.

(C) Out of Scope; the passage never discusses any particular scenes; the author is only concerned with how humans are exposed to fallout through various carriers.

(D) Out of Scope; the passage does not mention the causes of explosions; the author is only concerned with how humans are exposed to fallout through various carriers.

(E) Out of Scope; the passage does not present an argument and does not allude to preventing explosions.

## 116. D

When dealing with an EXCEPT question, you must rule out the wrong answers. Each of these items is mentioned in the passage. The key here is identifying which one is not a contamination source. While paragraph 2 does use the word "dust," the author is not using the word to show that the dust is contaminated. (D) accounts for this.

(A) The last paragraph discusses the milk and meat of cows being contaminated.

(B) The entire passage focuses on how humans are contaminated through plant and animal sources.

(C) Paragraph 2 discusses plants absorbing nuclear fallout through the soil.

(E) This one also appears in paragraph 2: the plants absorb nuclear contamination through the soil.

## 117. B

Whenever you see a Roman numeral question on the SSAT, look at the answer choices to see which statement appears in the most answers. Then evaluate that statement first, eliminating answers based on whether that statement is true or false. In this question, both I and II appear an equal number of times. If you start with I, you can see that the second stanza includes the line "For a future buds in everything," but this doesn't refer literally to flower buds in spring, so I is false, meaning you can eliminate answers (A), (D), and (E). Looking at II, you can see that the first line of the poem mentions "Wintry boughs against a wintry sky." Since most trees lose their leaves in winter, this statement paraphrases that line, meaning that statement II is true, which leaves you with (B).

(A) Eliminate; I is false.

(C) Eliminate; III distorts lines 7–8 and doesn't describe a seasonal symbol.

(D) Eliminate; I is false.

(E) Eliminate; I and III are false.

## 118. E

When you see a line reference in a question stem, that's a strong indication that you're looking at a Detail question, which will ask about a specific piece of information in the passage. Read a line or two before and after the quoted phrase to understand the context of the detail, especially in a poetry passage. Here, the clues come in the following lines: "Out of sight, / Ready to burst through?" Based on these lines, you can predict that the quoted line refers to some sort of natural activity that isn't visible to human eyes, which matches (E).

(A) Distortion; nothing in the poem suggests that the sap is ready for harvest.

(B) Extreme; the poem suggests that the trees may actually be producing sap even if the end product is not yet visible.

(C) Out of Scope; the poem doesn't try to create any direct link between the sky and the trees.

(D) Extreme; line 4 suggests that the production of sap begins during the colder weather.

## 119. D

Even if the question stem doesn't give you a line reference, you can scan the passage to find clues and then reread the relevant lines. The first two lines of the poem describe different aspects of the sky. "Wintry" sky suggests cold and bleak conditions, but the "partly blue" sky suggests that some warmth may be coming soon. For these reasons, the "wintry" sky refers to the present conditions, and the "partly blue" sky refers to the near future, which matches (D).

(A) This is too literal, since the poem uses weather to figuratively represent the seasons.

(B) Again, this is too literal an interpretation of the lines, and nothing in the rest of the poem refers to any kind of storm.

(C) The poem doesn't mention feelings associated with each type of sky.

(E) The second stanza personifies winter and spring by comparing them to a mother and daughter, so the references to the sky in the first stanza are not directly related to this symbolism.

## 120. C

The phrase "would most likely agree" in a question stem indicates an Inference question. Predicting answers for Inference questions can be challenging, so go directly to the answer choices and determine whether each is true or false, based on the passage. The writer of this poem has an overall positive tone toward both seasons. She doesn't state a strong preference or suggest that either season is better than the other, rather that both have positive characteristics, including winter, as suggested in lines 7–9: "Winter is the mother-nurse of Spring, / Lovely for her daughter's sake, / Not unlovely for her own."

(C) expresses this idea.

(A) Out of Scope; the poem doesn't discuss the duration of spring.

(B) Distortion; the author doesn't make any recommendations.

(D) Opposite; lines 7–9 suggest that the author enjoys winter for its own sake, not simply because it leads to spring.

(E) Distortion; no connection is made between the "wintry boughs" in the first stanza and the "future buds" in the second stanza.

### 121. D

For a Detail question, always refer directly back to the passage. The author uses the work of Jonas Salk to contrast the work of innovative geniuses such as Fleming. The author states that Salk's work was based on the work of others and scientific principle, rather than independent innovation, (D).

(A) Distortion; the passage states that Salk borrowed from other scientists but does not specifically state that he borrowed from Fleming.

(B) Opposite; the passage states that Salk based his work on mundane procedure.

(C) Extreme; while the passage states that Salk did base much of his work on that of others, the author never gives credit to other scientists for curing polio.

(E) Extreme; the passage states that Salk did not rely on innovation, not that he was incapable of such discoveries.

### 122. B

Inference questions ask you to make a logical assumption based on details in the passage. You should always be able to support your answer with facts from the passage. The passage is focused on the disproportionate credit given to maverick innovators for scientific discovery. The author mentions biographies and biographical films to illustrate this tendency, (B).

(A) Opposite; the passage states that people are interested.

(C) Out of Scope; the passage never discusses a controversy surrounding penicillin.

(D) Misused Detail; the passage does not discuss the need for biographies of Salk.

(E) Extreme; the passage is describing the curiosity of others, not a need for more information.

### 123. C

The word "suggests" should be your clue that this is an Inference question. The correct answer will be something not directly stated but clearly implied. The passage discusses Salk's work in comparison with the highly respected, unorthodox techniques of Alexander Fleming. The passage states that other scientists ridiculed Salk's work as "mundane" because it was based on other people's work and basic scientific procedure rather than dramatic innovation, (C).

(A) Opposite; while the author gives credit to Salk, other scientists ridiculed his work.

(B) Opposite; again the author states this, but other scientists do not.

(D) Out of Scope; the passage does not discuss the complexity of Salk's work.

(E) Opposite; the passage states that Salk discovered a major cure.

### 124. A

The correct answer to a Global question will reference the entire passage, not just isolated details. The author argues in this passage that discoveries are made not only by maverick geniuses, but also by methodical workers like Jonas Salk, (A).

(B) Extreme; the author never recommends a particular method.

(C) Misused Detail; the passage does not focus on Fleming.

(D) Misused Detail; while Salk is a non-dramatic example, this is not the author's overall purpose.

(E) Out of Scope; the author never makes funding recommendations.

# CHAPTER 9: THE ESSAY

Both the SSAT and ISEE (all levels) require an essay, though neither one is graded. So why do you need to write it? Well, the essay is a great way for schools to see how you express yourself. The rest of the test tells them how well you perform on a series of standard tasks, but the essay is the one part of the exam where you get to shine as an individual. Schools look closely at your essay, so think of it as part of your application and take it seriously.

So, what do you need to know to write an essay that will stand out? Really, only a few key things. First and most important, stick to the topic. Second, write clearly and logically. And finally, proofread your essay before you finish. Even if you think you have been very careful, you'll undoubtedly find things that you'll want to fix or change.

## INTRODUCTION TO THE ESSAY

There are five important things to know about the essay:

1. You'll need to organize your thoughts quickly (you'll have 25 minutes on the SSAT and 30 minutes on the ISEE to write a complete essay).
2. Your essay is limited to two pages.
3. Essay topics will be easy to grasp.
4. What you say is more important than using perfect grammar.
5. Your essay will not be graded.

### WHAT'S WRONG WITH THIS PICTURE?

Writing a good essay means following a few key rules about writing. Take a look at the following paragraph and think about what's wrong with it. Use the space that follows to jot down the problems you notice.

**Sample Topic:** <u>Do you agree that no good deed goes unpunished?</u>

> It always bothers me when people talk about punishment. It's not fair.
> I mean, there are some kids out there who do really good things, even
> though people don't notice them. In my opinion, everyone spends too
> much time talking about whether or not there is enough punishment
> in the world. We should really be talking about more important things
> like the environment . . .

_____

_____

_____

_____

_____

## COMMON PITFALLS IN ESSAY WRITING

What's wrong with the paragraph you just read? The biggest problem is that it goes off topic. Granted, you're only seeing the beginning of the essay, but you can tell from the way it ends that the author is about to go off on a tangent about the environment instead of discussing the topic. Remember, *always* stay on course.

What else is wrong with the sample paragraph? You might have noticed that it sounds very casual, almost like a conversation. Phrases such as "I mean" and "In my opinion" give the essay a tone that's too familiar and too emotional. While you always want to present your opinion, you should do it in a detached, formal way, as if writing a newspaper article. Try to avoid "I" statements in your essay writing.

How can you avoid making these types of mistakes? How can you make sure you don't get sidetracked while you write or repeat yourself? Kaplan has an easy method that you should follow when you write your essay. By following each and every step, you'll be guaranteed to create an organized, clear essay.

## KAPLAN 4-STEP METHOD FOR WRITING

**Step 1.** Brainstorm.

**Step 2.** Make an outline.

**Step 3.** Write your essay.

**Step 4.** Proofread.

> ## PLEASE JUST ANSWER THE QUESTION, MA'AM
>
> " The Golden Rule of essay writing is to stick to the topic. All you need to do is stay on course and write clearly, giving examples to support your points. Whether a question is academic or creative, there should always be a beginning or introduction, a middle (body paragraphs), and a conclusion. "

The Kaplan Method might sound pretty general, a lot like the essays you've written for school. In fact, the essay is the part of the test that most closely resembles the work you do in school. However, the essay follows a much more specific format than most essays assigned in school, and you don't have a lot of time to do it, so it's very important that you follow all four steps. Let's break them down.

## STEP 1: BRAINSTORM

When you start to brainstorm for ideas, first think about the topic. With the sample topic, your thinking might go like this: I believe that people are rewarded for good deeds, not punished. Okay, what examples can I use to support this point of view?

It's important that you're clear in your head about what your stance is *before* you start to organize your essay. Once you start to put your examples together, you don't want to have to go back and figure out what you're trying to show.

## STEP 2: MAKE AN OUTLINE

Once you've decided on your topic or opinion, the next step is to write an outline. Come up with three examples to support your points or opinion.

Next, decide the best order in which to present your examples. Is there a logical order to lay out your ideas? How do you want to start your essay? How do you want to end it? Make some notes on your scratch paper so when you start to write, you can glance at them to keep you on track and writing quickly.

## STEP 3: WRITE YOUR ESSAY

Now you have to write the essay. Follow your outline carefully, but be flexible. Maybe you'll think of another great idea midway through your writing. Should you ignore it, or should you substitute it for the third example you had planned to include? If you think it's better than what you originally came up with, go ahead and write about it instead. Just make sure that any deviation you make from your outline is in fact an improvement over the original idea.

**WHAT WAS I THINKING?**

" Even if you're feeling rushed, don't skip the Outlining step. Planning your essay will make the entire writing process easier and faster, and it will ensure that your writing is well organized. Remember, wear a watch on Test Day so you can keep a handle on your pacing. "

## STEP 4: PROOFREAD

Wrap up your writing five minutes before the end of your allotted time. Give your essay a good read-through, making sure you haven't made any spelling mistakes, written any run-on sentences, or forgotten to capitalize a proper name. You won't be able to make any huge changes at this point—after all, you only have a few minutes left—but you do want to make sure that you haven't made any egregious errors.

# PACING

How much time should you spend on each step? Use your watch and this guideline as you write. You want to give yourself sufficient time for each step, because planning and proofreading will make your essay much stronger. Use the following guidelines for timing:

|  | SSAT | ISEE |
|---|---|---|
| Outlining/ Planning | 5 minutes | 5 minutes |
| Writing | 15 minutes | 20 minutes |
| Proofreading | 5 minutes | 5 minutes |
| Total time: | 25 minutes | 30 minutes |

# BRAINSTORMING IN ACTION

When you get to the essay section, the last thing you want to happen is a *brain freeze*. You know the feeling: You look at the page, you see the words, your brain doesn't register, you stare into space . . . you can't think of a thing to write about.

How do you avoid such a situation? One of the best ways to make sure your brain is in gear and ready to brainstorm on the spot is to practice doing it. Take a look at the following statements. If it is an "agree or disagree" prompt, decide what position you would take and think of three examples you would present in support of your opinion. If it is a "describe" or "explain" prompt, pick your topic and think of three examples you would use to explain or describe your topic. Give yourself about five minutes to do each one.

**Sample Topic 1:** Should free speech on the Internet be protected? Why or why not?

_____

_____

_____

_____

_____

_____

_____

**Sample Topic 2:** Do we learn more from our mistakes than our successes? Why?

_____

_____

_____

_____

_____

_____

_____

**Sample Topic 3:** My fondest memory is.,.

_____

_____

_____

_____

_____

_____

## SHOW, DON'T TELL

You've probably heard the saying that good writing *shows* rather than *tells*. What does that mean, and what do examples have to do with it?

Take the statement "You can't teach an old dog new tricks." Say you wanted to disagree with it. You could explain why you believe the statement isn't true, what you think about teaching and age, and so forth. Or, you could use examples that *illustrate* the same point. You could discuss the fact that retired people now use the Internet on a regular basis. The fact that people generally considered *old* by society are adapting to a *new* technology in large numbers serves to show that you can, in fact, teach an old dog new tricks.

What makes a good example? A good example illustrates the point you want to make. In addition, it comes from the world at large rather than from your personal life. While it may be true that your grandmother emails you, it's more powerful to say that many retirees use the Internet every day.

If you're not doing so already, try reading the newspaper on a regular basis. Not only will you know more about what's going on in the world and be ready with great examples for your essays, you'll also improve your vocabulary, which will improve your performance on the Verbal section of your test.

## JUST THE FACTS

What do you need to do as you write your essay?

- Develop and organize your ideas.
- Use three paragraphs.
- Use appropriate examples.
- Write in standard English.
- Stick to the topic.
- Use proper spelling, grammar, and punctuation.

---

**READING TIPS**

" When you read the newspaper, look at the editorial page. You'll see how writers argue their opinions on a variety of topics and what kinds of examples they use. And you might learn something interesting in the process, too. "

# PRACTICE ESSAY

Work through this topic as though it were the real thing. Brainstorm your ideas, make an outline, write, and proofread. Time yourself (25 minutes if you're taking the SSAT and 30 minutes if you're taking the ISEE).

**Essay Topic:** <u>Voting is such an important responsibility that all citizens should be required to vote in every election.</u>

**Step 1. Brainstorm.**

Brainstorm in the space provided below. Do you agree or disagree? What examples might you use to support your argument? (Remember, give yourself only a few minutes to do this!)

_____

_____

_____

_____

_____

_____

_____

**Step 2. Make an outline.**

Write your outline here. Keep your essay to three paragraphs. Paragraph 1 gives your introduction and an example. Paragraph 2 gives another example, and paragraph 3 gives your final example and/or your conclusion.

Paragraph 1

_____

_____

Paragraph 2

_____

_____

Paragraph 3

_____

_____

**Step 3. Write your essay.**

Write your essay below. Give yourself 15 minutes if you're taking the SSAT and 20 minutes if you're taking the ISEE.

_____

_____

_____

_____

_____

_____

_____

_____

_____

_____

_____

**Step 4. Proofread.**

Go back to your essay and read through it again. Does it make sense? Have you made any spelling or grammar errors? Fix them. Get used to making corrections clearly on your page, since that's what you will do the day of the test.

# CHAPTER 10: INTRODUCTION TO SSAT AND ISEE MATH

Before we dive into the actual math, let's take a step back and think about how to approach math problems in general. You've done math in school already. In all likelihood, you've already been exposed to most of the math concepts you'll see on your private school admissions test. So, why do you need to approach SSAT or ISEE math differently than you approach any other math?

The answer is, it's not that you have to do the math *differently*; it's just that you have to do it *deliberately*. You'll be under a lot of time pressure when you take your test, so you need to use your time well.

## HOW TO APPROACH SSAT OR ISEE MATH

Ultimately, the best way to take control of your testing experience is to approach every math question the same way. This doesn't mean you'll *solve* every problem the same way. Rather, it means that you'll use the same process to *decide* how to solve, or even whether to solve, each problem.

### READ THROUGH THE QUESTION

Okay, this may seem a little too obvious. Of course, you're going to read the question. How else can you solve the problem? In reality, this isn't quite as obvious as it seems. The point here is that you need to read the entire question before you start solving. When you don't read carefully, it's incredibly easy to make careless mistakes. Consider the following problem:

**EXAMPLE**

For what positive value of $x$ does $\frac{4}{3} = \frac{x^2}{27}$?

(A) 3
(B) 6
(C) 12
(D) 18
(E) 36

It's crucial that you pay close attention to precisely what the question is asking. The question contains a classic trap that's very easy to fall into if you don't read it carefully. Did you notice how easy it would be to solve for $x^2$ instead of $x$? Yes, this would be careless, but it's easy to be careless when you're working quickly. Therefore, don't select the trap answer (E)! The correct answer is (B).

There are other reasons to read the whole question before you start solving the problem. One is that you may save yourself some work. If you start to answer too quickly, you may assume that a problem is more difficult than it actually is. Or you might assume that it is *less* difficult than it actually is and skip a necessary step or two.

Another reason to read carefully before answering is that you probably shouldn't solve *every* question on your first pass. Taking control of your test experience means deciding which questions to answer, which to save for later, and which to skip (unless you're taking the ISEE, in which case you should NEVER skip a question).

## Decide Whether to Do the Question or Skip It for Now

Each time you approach a new math problem, you have the option of answering it immediately or putting it aside. You have to make a decision each time about how best to use your time. You have three options.

1. **If you can solve the question relatively quickly and efficiently, do it!** This is the best option.

2. **If you think you can solve it but that it will take you a long time, circle the number in your test booklet and go back to it later.** Remember that when you go back to the problems you have skipped the first time, you'll want to try your best to fill in an answer. Don't underestimate your ability to eliminate wrong answers even when you don't know how to solve. Every time you rule out a wrong answer choice, you increase your chances of guessing correctly.

3. **If you have no idea what to do, skip the question and circle it.** Save your time for the questions you *can* do.

### EXAMPLE

Tamika, Becky, and Kym were investors in a new restaurant. Tamika and Becky each invested one-half as much as Kym invested. If the total investment made was $5,200, how much did Kym invest?

(A)   $900
(B)   $1,300
(C)   $1,800
(D)   $2,100
(E)   $2,600

Different test takers will have different reactions to this question. Some students may quickly see the algebra—or the backdoor method for solving this problem—and do the math. Others may see a word problem and run screaming from the room. This approach is not recommended. However, if you know that you habitually have difficulty with algebra word problems, you may choose to save this problem for later or make an educated guess.

Here's the algebra, by the way. Kym, Tamika, and Becky contributed a total of $5,200. You can represent this algebraically as $K + T + B = \$5,200$. Since Tamika and Becky each contributed half as much as Kym, you can represent these relationships as follows:

$$T = \frac{1}{2}K$$
$$B = \frac{1}{2}K$$

Now, substitute variables so that you can solve the equation.

$$K + T + B = 5,200$$
$$K + \frac{1}{2}K + \frac{1}{2}K = 5,200$$
$$2K = 5,200$$
$$K = 2,600, \textbf{(E)}$$

Alternatively, you can use the Backsolving strategy. Start with (C). If Kym invested $1,800, and Tamika and Becky each invested half of that, or $900 each, then the total investment would have been $1,800 + $900 + $900 = $3,600. But the total investment was $5,200, so our answer isn't large enough. We can rule out (C)—and (A) and (B).

Now try (D): $2,100 + $1,050 + $1,050 = $4,200. This is still not enough money. Therefore, the answer must be (E).

If you want to check, $2,600 + $1,300 + $1,300 = $5,200, which is the correct total investment. (E) works and is the correct answer.

If you choose to tackle the problem, look for the fastest method.

## EXAMPLE

Jenna is now $x$ years old, and Amy is 3 years younger than Jenna. In terms of $x$, how old will Amy be in 4 years?

(A)  $x - 1$

(B)  $x$

(C)  $x + 1$

(D)  $x + 4$

(E)  $2x + 1$

Here is the algebraic solution. If Jenna is $x$ years old, then Amy is $x - 3$ years old, since Amy is 3 years younger than Jenna. So, in 4 years, Amy will be $(x - 3) + 4$, or $x + 1$. The correct answer is (C).

Here is the Picking Numbers solution. Suppose that $x = 10$. Then Jenna is now 10 years old. Amy is now 7 years old because Amy is 3 years younger than Jenna. In 4 years, Amy will be 11. Now plug 10 for $x$ into all of the answer choices and see which one equals 11. You can eliminate any answer choice that does not equal 11. Since only (C), $x + 1$, equals 11, it must be correct.

With the method of Picking Numbers, it sometimes happens that more than one answer choice gives you the correct result for the particular number or numbers that you choose. When that happens, go back and pick another number(s) to eliminate the remaining incorrect answer choices.

The lesson here is that you have to know your own strengths. Again, in case you missed the point, *know your strengths and use them to your advantage.*

Some people intuitively understand algebra. Others have a harder time with it. The same is true for geometry, word problems, etc. There's often more than one way to solve a question. The *best* method is the method that will get you the correct answer accurately and quickly.

Remember, only guess on the SSAT if you can eliminate at least one answer choice. But on the ISEE, don't leave any answers blank. Since there's no penalty for wrong answers, there is no harm in guessing. Of course, the fact that random guessing won't hurt you does not mean that you shouldn't be strategic about guessing. Remember, every answer choice you rule out increases your odds of guessing correctly.

**EXAMPLE**

What is the greatest common factor of 95 and 114?

   (A)   1
   (B)   5
   (C)   6
   (D)  19
   (E)  38

If you couldn't remember how to find the greatest common factor or were running out of time and wanted to save your time for other questions, you should be able to eliminate at least one answer choice pretty easily. Do you see which one?

**HELPFUL HINT**

When you skip a question, circle it in your test booklet so that it will be easy to spot if you have time to go back.

Since all multiples of 5 end in 5 or zero, 5 cannot be a factor of 114. Therefore, (B) must be incorrect. Eliminate it and then guess, starting with the largest answer choice. 38 divides evenly into 114, but $95 \div 38 = 2.5$. We can eliminate (E). 19 divides evenly into both numbers, so it must be correct. Therefore, (D) is the right answer.

## PICKING NUMBERS

Sometimes a math problem can appear more difficult than it actually is because it's general or abstract. You can make it more concrete—and easier—by temporarily substituting numbers for the variables. Kaplan's Picking Numbers strategy can help make the math easier.

### EXAMPLE

$3a(2b + 2) =$

(A) $2b + 3a$

(B) $5ab + 2b$

(C) $5ab + 2a + 1$

(D) $6ab + 2a$

(E) $6ab + 6a$

The algebra in this question is pretty straightforward. According to the distributive property, $3a(2b + 2) = (3a)(2b) + (3a)(2) = 6ab + 6a$, or choice (E). Most test takers will probably use algebra to solve the question.

However, if you have trouble with algebra or simply find that it takes you a long time, you can approach the problem another way. Pick simple numbers for $a$ and $b$ and plug them into the expression $3a(2b + 2)$. If $a = 2$ and $b = 3$, then $3a(2b + 2) = (3)(2)[2(3) + 2] = 6(6 + 2) = 48$. Now you know that if $a = 2$ and $b = 3$, the expression equals 48.

Once you know this, simply plug 2 in for $a$ and 3 in for $b$ in each of the answer choices. Any answer choice that does not equal 48 can be eliminated. Since only (E) equals 48, (E) is the answer.

(A) $2b + 3a = 2(3) + 3(2) = 12$

(B) $5ab + 2b = 5(2)(3) + 2(3) = 36$

(C) $5ab + 2a + 1 = 5(2)(3) + 2(2) + 1 = 35$

(D) $6ab + 2a = 6(2)(3) + 2(2) = 40$

(E) $6ab + 6a = 6(2)(3) + 6(2) = 48$

If two or more answer choices had come out to 48, you would have had to do a little more work. You would have had to pick new numbers for $a$ and $b$, come up with a new value, and then plug those numbers into the answer choices that came out the same the first time.

In other words, if (B) and (E) had both equaled 48, you could have made $a = 3$ and $b = 4$, discovered that the expression $3a(2b + 2)$ equals 90, and then plugged 3 and 4 into only choices (B) and (E) to determine which one equaled 90.

## WORD PROBLEMS

Picking Numbers can be extremely helpful when the answer choices to a word problem contain variables. Remember this problem?

### EXAMPLE

Jenna is now $x$ years old, and Amy is 3 years younger than Jenna. In terms of $x$, how old will Amy be in 4 years?

(A) $x - 1$

(B) $x$

(C) $x + 1$

(D) $x + 4$

(E) $2x + 1$

> ### BE WARY OF PICKING ZERO OR 1
>
> " Pick small numbers that are easy to use, but not zero or 1. Even though they're small, easy numbers, they often give several "possibly correct" answers. "

As you saw earlier, there's more than one way to solve this problem. Some test takers will find it easier to solve this question by working with algebraic expressions. Others may feel that this will slow them down. Picking a number for $x$ may be faster and easier.

If you say that $x = 10$, then Jenna is 10 years old and Amy is 7, since she's three years younger. In four years, Amy will be 11. Once you have this value, plug in 10 for $x$ in each of the answer choices to see which ones equal 11. Those answer choices that don't equal 11 can be eliminated.

(A) $10 - 1 = 9$

(B) $10$

(C) $10 + 1 = 11$

(D) $10 + 4 = 14$

(E) $2(10) + 1 = 21$

Only (C) equals 11, so (C) must be correct.

## PERCENT INCREASE/DECREASE PROBLEMS

If you see a problem that deals with percents, picking 100 is the easiest and quickest way to solve.

## EXAMPLE

If the price of a stock decreases by 20 percent, and then by an additional 25 percent, by what percent has the price decreased from its original value?

(A) 40%

(B) 45%

(C) 50%

(D) 55%

(E) 60%

Make the original price of the stock $100. The initial 20 percent decrease brings the price down to $80. (Twenty percent of 100 is 20.) Twenty-five percent of 80 or one-quarter of $80 is $20, so the stock price is decreased by an additional $20, bringing the final price down to $60. Since the price dropped from $100 to $60, the total decrease is $40 or 40 percent of the original price. (A) is the correct answer.

You may have been able to solve this problem by setting up algebraic equations, but picking 100 is easier and faster here.

## BACKSOLVING

Backsolving is another tool to help you get a math answer more quickly. What this means is that you can work backward from the answer choices. Backsolving will work only if your answer choices are all numbers (and they don't include variables).

Here's how it works. When answer choices are numbers—i.e., not variables—you can expect them to be arranged from *small to large* or *large to small*. The test maker does not get creative with the order of the answer choices. What you do is to start with the *middle* answer choice and plug it directly into the problem. If it works, you're set. If it doesn't, you can usually determine whether to try a larger or smaller answer choice. Look at the following problem and explanation.

## EXAMPLE

Three consecutive multiples of 20 have a sum of 300. What is the middle of these numbers?

(A) 60

(B) 80

(C) 100

(D) 120

(E) 140

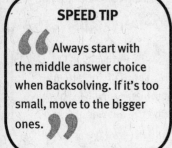

**SPEED TIP**

Always start with the middle answer choice when Backsolving. If it's too small, move to the bigger ones.

Begin with the middle answer choice. If 100 is the middle of the three numbers, the three numbers must be 120, 100, and 80, and $120 + 100 + 80 = 300$. Choice (C) is correct.

It's worth noting that if (D) had given you a sum less than 300, you would not have had to check choice (E). Think about it. If the numbers are arranged from small to large and the second-largest number gives you an answer that is too small, you know that the largest number has to be correct.

# A WORD ABOUT CALCULATORS

This is an easy one. You *cannot* use a calculator on the SSAT or ISEE. Leave your calculator home. End of story.

The rest of the Math chapters in this book deal with Math Content review. Some of this will be familiar; some may be less familiar. Take a look at all of it, but spend more time with the subjects that are less familiar. Even if you don't need to review a particular subject, however, make sure you do the practice set. There's no harm in practicing extra problems.

# CHAPTER 11: ARITHMETIC

On the SSAT and ISEE, **arithmetic** means more than addition and subtraction. Arithmetic is the umbrella term for a wide range of math concepts, including **number properties, factors, divisibility, fractions, decimals, exponents, radicals, percents, averages, ratios, proportions, rates,** and **probability.** These concepts are summarized in your Math Reference at the end of the book. This section will go over these important concepts and give you a chance to practice problems dealing with these subjects.

## DEFINITIONS

| Number Type | Definition | Examples |
|---|---|---|
| Integers | *Whole numbers including 0 and their opposites (negative whole numbers)* | $-900, -3, 0, 1, 54$ |
| Fractions | *A **fraction** is a number that is written in the form $\frac{A}{B}$ where A is the numerator and B is the denominator.* | $-\frac{5}{6}, -\frac{3}{17}, \frac{1}{2}, \frac{899}{901}$ |
| Improper fractions | *An **improper fraction** is a fraction whose value is greater than 1 (or less than −1).* | $-\frac{65}{64}, \frac{9}{8}, \frac{57}{10}$ |
| Mixed numbers | *An improper fraction can be converted into a **mixed number**. A mixed number has an integer part and a fraction part.* | $-1\frac{1}{64}, 1\frac{1}{8}, 5\frac{7}{10}$ |
| Positive/Negative | *Numbers greater than 0 are **positive numbers**; numbers less than 0 are **negative**. 0 is neither positive nor negative.* | Positive: $\frac{7}{8}, 1, 5, 900$  Negative: $-64, -40, -11, -\frac{6}{13}$ |

| Number Type | Definition | Examples |
|---|---|---|
| Even/Odd | An **even number** is an integer that is a multiple of 2. Even numbers end in 0, 2, 4, 6, or 8. | Even numbers: −8, −2, 0, 4, 12, 188 |
| | An **odd number** is an integer that is not a multiple of 2. Odd numbers end in 1, 3, 5, 7, or 9. | Odd numbers: −17, −1, 3, 9, 457 |
| Prime numbers | A **prime number** is an integer greater than 1 that has exactly two factors: 1 and itself. 2 is the only even prime number. | 2, 3, 5, 7, 11, 59, 83 |
| Composite numbers | A **composite number** is an integer greater than 1 that has more than two factors. | 12, 35, 84 |
| Consecutive numbers | Numbers that follow one after another, in order, without skipping any. | Consecutive integers: 3, 4, 5, 6 Consecutive even integers: 2, 4, 6, 8, 10 Consecutive multiples of 9: 9, 18, 27, 36 |
| Factors | A positive integer that divides evenly into a given number with no remainder. | The complete list of factors of 12: 1, 2, 3, 4, 6, 12 |
| Multiples | A number that a given number will divide into with no remainder. | Some multiples of 12: 0, 12, 24, 60 |

## ODDS AND EVENS

There are a few things to remember when you're dealing with odd and even numbers:

Even ± Even = Even

Even ± Odd = Odd

Odd ± Odd = Even

Even × Even = Even

Even × Odd = Even

Odd × Odd = Odd

## POSITIVES AND NEGATIVES

You will not see many problems that focus specifically on positives and negatives, but you must know the basics because these concepts will show up as part of harder problems.

To **add** any two integers with the **same sign,** keep the sign and add the integers.

**EXAMPLES**

$$(-3) + (-8) = -11$$
$$9 + 12 = 21$$

To **add** any two integers with **opposite signs,** keep the sign of the integer farther from zero, then subtract the integers, ignoring the signs.

**EXAMPLES**

$$3 + (-8) = -(8 - 3)$$
$$= -5$$

$$-9 + 12 = +(12 - 9)$$
$$= 3$$

To **subtract** two integers, change the subtraction sign to addition, then change the sign of the number being subtracted to its opposite.

**EXAMPLES**

$$(3) - (-8) = 3 + (+8)$$
$$= 11$$
$$-9 - 12 = -9 + (-12)$$
$$= -21$$

**Multiplying** and **dividing** positives and negatives is like all other multiplication and division, with one catch. To figure out whether your answer is positive or negative, count the number of negatives you had to start. If you had an odd number of negatives, the answer is negative. If you had an even number of negatives, the answer is positive.

$$6 \times (-4) = -24 \text{ (1 negative} \rightarrow \text{negative product)}$$
$$(-6) \times (-4) = 24 \text{ (2 negatives} \rightarrow \text{positive product)}$$
$$(-1) \times (-6) \times (-4) = -24 \text{ (3 negatives} \rightarrow \text{negative product)}$$

Similarly,

$$-24 \div 6 = -4 \text{ (1 negative} \rightarrow \text{negative quotient)}$$
$$-24 \div (-4) = 6 \text{ (2 negatives} \rightarrow \text{positive quotient)}$$

> **REMEMBER**
>
> " Negative × or ÷ Negative = Positive
> Positive × or ÷ Negative = Negative "

## ABSOLUTE VALUE

To find the **absolute value** of a number, simply find the number's distance from zero on a number line. Because distance cannot be negative, the absolute value of a number will always be greater than or equal to zero.

$$|4| = 4 \text{ (because 4 is four units from zero)}$$

$$|-4| = 4 \text{ (because } -4 \text{ is four units from zero)}$$

When absolute value expressions contain different arithmetic operations, perform the operation inside the bars first and then find the absolute value of the result.

$$|-6 + 4| = |-2|$$

$$= 2$$

$$|(-6) \times 4| = |-24|$$

$$= 24$$

## FACTORS AND MULTIPLES

To find the **prime factorization** of a number, keep factoring it until you are left with only prime numbers. To find the prime factorization of 168:

$$168 = 4 \times 42$$

$$= 4 \times 6 \times 7$$

$$= 2 \times 2 \times 2 \times 3 \times 7$$

To find the **greatest common factor (GCF)** of two integers, break down both integers into their prime factorizations and multiply all prime factors they have in common. If you're looking for the GCF of 40 and 140, first identify the prime factors of each integer.

$$40 = 4 \times 10$$

$$= 2 \times 2 \times 2 \times 5$$

$$140 = 10 \times 14$$

$$= 2 \times 5 \times 2 \times 7$$

$$= 2 \times 2 \times 5 \times 7$$

Next, see what prime factors the two numbers have in common and then multiply these common factors. Both integers share two 2s and one 5, so the GCF is $2 \times 2 \times 5$, or 20.

If you need to find a **common multiple** of two integers, you can always multiply them. However, you can use prime factors to find the **least common multiple (LCM)**. To do this, multiply all of the prime factors of each integer the most amount of times as they appear. This may sound confusing, but it becomes clear once it's demonstrated. Take a look at the example to see how it works.

Common multiple of 20 and 16:    $20 \times 16 = 320$

Although 320 is a common multiple of 20 and 16, it is not the least common multiple.

LCM of 20 and 16:
$$20 = 2 \times 2 \times 5$$
$$16 = 2 \times 2 \times 2 \times 2$$
$$= 2 \times 2 \times 2 \times 2 \times 5 = 80$$

Note that there are four factors of 2 in the LCM because there were four factors of 2 in 16, and that's the largest number of 2s present in either number.

## THE ORDER OF OPERATIONS

There is a specific order in which arithmetic operations must be performed.

1. **Parentheses:** Simplify all operations inside parentheses first.

2. **Exponents:** Simplify any exponential expressions.

3. **Multiplication and Division:** Perform all multiplications and divisions as they occur in the problem from left to right.

4. **Addition and Subtraction:** Perform all additions and subtractions as they occur in the problem from left to right.

An easy way to help you remember this order is to use the mnemonic "Please Excuse My Dear Aunt Sally" (or **PEMDAS**). This phrase uses the first letter of each operation in the order in which it is to be performed.

$$(3 + 5)^2 - 7 + 4 = (8)^2 - 7 + 4$$
$$= 64 - 7 + 4$$
$$= 57 + 4$$
$$= 61$$

# RULES FOR DIVISIBILITY

If you've forgotten—or never learned—divisibility rules, spend a little time with this chart. Even if you remember the rules, take a moment to refresh your memory. Remember, there are no easy divisibility rules for 7 and 8.

| Divisible by | The Rule | EXAMPLE: 558 |
| --- | --- | --- |
| 2 | The last digit is even. | a multiple of 2 because 8 is even |
| 3 | The sum of the digits is a multiple of 3. | a multiple of 3 because 5 + 5 + 8 = 18, which is a multiple of 3 |
| 4 | The last two digits comprise a two-digit multiple of 4. | NOT a multiple of 4 because 58 is not a multiple of 4 |
| 5 | The last digit is 5 or 0. | NOT a multiple of 5 because it doesn't end in 5 or 0 |
| 6 | The last digit is even AND the sum of the digits is a multiple of 3. | a multiple of 6 because it's a multiple of both 2 and 3 |
| 9 | The sum of the digits is a multiple of 9. | a multiple of 9 because 5 + 5 + 8 = 18, which is a multiple of 9 |
| 10 | The last digit is 0. | NOT a multiple of 10 because it doesn't end in 0 |

**Hint:** To test for 2, 4, 5, or 10, look at the last digit or two. To test for 3, 6, or 9, add all the digits.

# FRACTIONS AND DECIMALS

Generally, there are eight operations you should feel comfortable performing with fractions:

1. Simplifying fractions

2. Converting a fraction to one with a different denominator

3. Adding fractions

4. Subtracting fractions

5. Multiplying fractions

6. Dividing fractions

7. Comparing fractions

8. Converting fractions to decimals and vice versa

To **simplify a fraction,** find the GCF of the numerator and denominator of the fraction, then divide both numerator and denominator by this quantity.

**EXAMPLE**

Simplify $\dfrac{18}{30}$.

The GCF of 18 and 30 is 6, so divide both 18 and 30 by 6:

$$\frac{18}{30} = \frac{18 \div 6}{30 \div 6}$$

$$= \frac{3}{5}$$

To **convert a fraction to one with a different denominator,** multiply both numerator and denominator by the same quantity.

**EXAMPLE**

Convert $\dfrac{3}{7}$ into a fraction with a denominator of 28.

Since $7 \times 4 = 28$, multiply the 3 and the 7 each by 4:

$$\frac{3}{7} = \frac{3 \times 4}{7 \times 4}$$

$$= \frac{12}{28}$$

To **add and subtract fractions with the same denominator,** keep the denominator the same and add or subtract the numerators. Simplify the result if possible.

**EXAMPLE**

Add.

$$\frac{1}{8} + \frac{3}{8} = \frac{4}{8}$$

$$= \frac{1}{2}$$

To **add and subtract fractions with the different denominators,** find the least common multiple (LCM) of the denominators, convert the fractions so they have this denominator, and then add or subtract and simplify.

**EXAMPLE**

Subtract.

$$\frac{7}{8} - \frac{5}{12} = \frac{21}{24} - \frac{10}{24}$$

$$= \frac{11}{24}$$

To **multiply fractions,** multiply the numerators and multiply the denominators, then simplify the result. It is also possible to simplify the fractions before multiplying by canceling like factors from the numerators and denominators of the fractions:

**EXAMPLE**

Multiply.

$$\frac{11}{12} \times \frac{9}{22} = \frac{99}{264} \text{ OR } \frac{\overset{1}{\cancel{11}}}{\underset{4}{\cancel{12}}} \times \frac{\overset{3}{\cancel{9}}}{\underset{2}{\cancel{22}}} = \frac{3}{8}$$

$$= \frac{99 \div 3}{264 \div 3}$$

$$= \frac{33 \div 11}{88 \div 11}$$

$$= \frac{3}{8}$$

To **divide fractions,** multiply the dividend (the first fraction) by the reciprocal of the divisor (the second fraction).

**EXAMPLE**

Divide.

$$\frac{8}{15} \div \frac{2}{3} = \frac{\overset{4}{\cancel{8}}}{\underset{5}{\cancel{15}}} \times \frac{\overset{1}{\cancel{3}}}{\underset{1}{\cancel{2}}}$$

$$= \frac{4}{5}$$

To **compare fractions,** convert both fractions to the same denominator and compare the numerators. Or find the cross-products and compare as follows.

**EXAMPLE:** Which is larger, $\frac{3}{4}$ or $\frac{10}{13}$?

Find the cross-products by multiplying the numerator of the first fraction by the denominator of the second, then multiplying the denominator of the first by the numerator of the second:

$$
\begin{array}{cc}
3 \times 13 & 4 \times 10 \\
39 & 40
\end{array}
$$

Because 39 is less than 40, the first fraction is less than the second. The second fraction is the larger fraction.

To **convert a fraction to a decimal**, divide the denominator into the numerator.

To convert $\frac{8}{25}$ to a decimal, divide 25 into 8.00.

$$
\begin{array}{r}
.32 \\
25\overline{)8.00} \\
\underline{-7\,5} \\
50 \\
\underline{-50} \\
0
\end{array}
$$

To **convert a decimal to a fraction,** use the place value of the digits in the decimal. Recall that beginning at the decimal point, the first place to the right is the tenths place, followed by the hundredths place, the thousandths place, the ten-thousandths place, the hundred-thousandths place, etc.

### EXAMPLES

Convert the decimal 0.4 into a fraction.

Because the last decimal place is the tenths place, the decimal is four-tenths, so the fraction is as well:

$$0.4 = \frac{4}{10}$$
$$= \frac{2}{5}$$

Convert the decimal 0.825 into a fraction.

Because the last decimal place is the thousandths place, the decimal is eight hundred twenty-five thousandths, so the fraction is as well:

$$0.825 = \frac{825}{1,000}$$
$$= \frac{165}{200}$$
$$= \frac{33}{40}$$

## COMMON PERCENT EQUIVALENCIES

Familiarity with the relationships among percents, decimals, and fractions can save you time on Test Day. Don't worry about memorizing the following chart. Simply use it to refresh your recollection of relationships you already know (e.g., $50\% = 0.50 = \frac{1}{2}$) and to familiarize yourself with some that you might not already know. To convert a decimal to a percent, multiply by 100 and add a % sign. To convert a percent to a decimal, divide by 100% (drop the percent sign and move the decimal point two spaces to the left).

| Fraction | Decimal | Percent |
|---|---|---|
| $\frac{1}{20}$ | 0.05 | 5% |
| $\frac{1}{10}$ | 0.10 | 10% |
| $\frac{1}{8}$ | 0.125 | 12.5% |

**KAPLAN EXCLUSIVE TIPS**

" To change a fraction to a percent, multiply by 100%. "

**KAPLAN EXCLUSIVE TIPS**

" A handy shortcut: $x\%$ of $y = y\%$ of $x$. "

| Fraction | Decimal | Percent |
|----------|---------|---------|
| $\frac{1}{6}$ | $0.16\overline{6}$ | $16\frac{2}{3}\%$ |
| $\frac{1}{5}$ | $0.20$ | $20\%$ |
| $\frac{1}{4}$ | $0.25$ | $25\%$ |
| $\frac{1}{3}$ | $0.33\overline{3}$ | $33\frac{1}{3}\%$ |
| $\frac{3}{8}$ | $0.375$ | $37.5\%$ |
| $\frac{2}{5}$ | $0.40$ | $40\%$ |
| $\frac{1}{2}$ | $0.50$ | $50\%$ |
| $\frac{3}{5}$ | $0.60$ | $60\%$ |
| $\frac{2}{3}$ | $0.66\overline{6}$ | $66\frac{2}{3}\%$ |
| $\frac{3}{4}$ | $0.75$ | $75\%$ |
| $\frac{4}{5}$ | $0.80$ | $80\%$ |
| $\frac{5}{6}$ | $0.83\overline{3}$ | $83\frac{1}{3}\%$ |
| $\frac{7}{8}$ | $0.875$ | $87.5\%$ |

# EXPONENTS AND ROOTS

Exponents are the small raised numbers written to the right of a variable or number. They indicate the number of times that variable or number is to be used as a factor. On the SSAT or ISEE, you'll usually deal with numbers or variables that are squared, but you could see a few other concepts involving exponents.

## EXAMPLES

$$2^3 = 2 \times 2 \times 2$$
$$= 8$$
$$-(3^2) = -(3 \times 3)$$
$$= -9$$
$$3(-2)^2 = 3[(-2)(-2)]$$
$$= 3(4)$$
$$= 12$$

A **square root** of a nonnegative number is a number that, when multiplied by itself, produces the given quantity. The radical sign $\sqrt{\phantom{x}}$ is used to represent the positive square root of a number, so $\sqrt{25} = 5$, since $5 \times 5 = 25$.

To **add** or **subtract** radicals, make sure the numbers under the radical sign are the same. If they are, you can add or subtract the coefficients outside the radical signs.

**EXAMPLE**

$$2\sqrt{2} + 3\sqrt{2} = 5\sqrt{2}$$

$\sqrt{2} + \sqrt{3}$ cannot be combined because the quantities inside the radical signs are not the same.

To **simplify** a radical, factor out the perfect square factor(s) from under the radical, simplify them, and put the result in front of the radical sign.

**EXAMPLE**

$$\sqrt{32} = \sqrt{16 \times 2} = \sqrt{16}\sqrt{2} = 4\sqrt{2}$$

To **multiply** or **divide** radicals, multiply (or divide) the coefficients outside the radical. Then, multiply (or divide) the numbers inside the radicals.

**EXAMPLE**

$$\sqrt{x} \times \sqrt{y} = \sqrt{xy}$$
$$3\sqrt{2} \times 4\sqrt{5} = 12\sqrt{10}$$
$$\frac{\sqrt{x}}{\sqrt{y}} = \sqrt{\frac{x}{y}}$$
$$\frac{12\sqrt{10}}{3\sqrt{2}} = 4\sqrt{5}$$

To **take the square root of a fraction,** break the fraction into two separate roots and take the square root of the numerator and the denominator.

**EXAMPLE**

$$\sqrt{\frac{16}{25}} = \frac{\sqrt{16}}{\sqrt{25}} = \frac{4}{5}$$

# POWERS OF 10 AND SCIENTIFIC NOTATION

The exponent of a power of 10 indicates how many zeros the number would contain if it were written out. For example, $10^4 = 10,000$ (4 zeros) since the product of 4 factors of 10 is equal to 10,000.

When multiplying a number by a power of 10, move the decimal point to the right the same number of places as the number of zeros in that power of 10.

**EXAMPLE**

$0.0123 \times 10^4 = 123$ (four places to the right)

When dividing by a power of 10, move the decimal point to the left.

**EXAMPLE**

$43.21 \div 10^3 = 0.04321$ (three places to the left)

Multiplying by a power with a negative exponent is the same as dividing by a power with a positive exponent. Therefore, when you multiply by a number with a positive exponent, move the decimal to the right. When you multiply by a number with a negative exponent, move the decimal to the left.

**EXAMPLE**

$$28.5 \times 10^{-2} = 28.5 \div 10^2$$
$$= 0.285$$
$$0.36 \div 10^{-4} = 0.36 \times 10^4$$
$$= 3,600$$

Scientific notation is commonly used in science and mathematics as a shorthand method for writing very large or very small numbers. A number is in scientific notation if it is in the form $a \times 10^n$ where $a < 10$ and $n$ is an integer.

To convert a number from **standard notation to scientific notation,** simply move the decimal point in the number to the right if the exponent on 10 is a positive number and to the left if the exponent is negative.

**EXAMPLE**

$4.23 \times 10^6 = 4,230,000$     The decimal point is moved to the right six places.

$9.6 \times 10^{-2} = 0.096$     The decimal point is moved to the left two places.

To convert a number from **scientific notation to standard notation,** find the decimal point in the number. If there is no decimal point, put one at the end of the number. Now move the decimal point to the right or to the left until the resulting quantity is a number between 1 and 10. The number of places the decimal point moved indicates the exponent to be placed on the 10. The direction indicates the sign of the exponent; if the decimal point was moved to the left, the exponent will be positive, if the decimal point was moved to the right, the exponent will be negative.

**EXAMPLE**

$82,000,000,000 = 8.2 \times 10^{10}$     The decimal point moved from the end of 82,000,000,000 to the left 10 places.

$0.00004138 = 4.138 \times 10^{-5}$     The decimal point moved from the front of 0.00004138 to the right five places.

# PERCENTS

The key to solving most fractions and percents word problems is to identify the part and the whole. Usually you'll find the **part** associated with the verb *is/are* and the **whole** associated with the word *of*. In the sentence "Half of the boys are soccer players," the whole is the boys ("*of* the boys"), and the part is the soccer players ("*are* soccer players").

Whether you need to find the part, the whole, or the percent, use the same formula:

**Part = Percent × Whole**

OR

$$\text{Percent} = \frac{\text{Part}}{\text{Whole}}$$

Let's look at some examples.

**EXAMPLE**

What is 12% of 25?     **Setup:**  $0.12 = \dfrac{\text{Part}}{25}$

$$\text{Part} = 0.12 \times 25$$
$$\text{Part} = 3$$

**EXAMPLE**

15 is 3% of what number?     **Setup:**  $0.03 = \dfrac{15}{\text{Whole}}$

$$\frac{15}{0.03} = \frac{0.03 \times \text{Whole}}{0.03}$$
$$500 = \text{Whole}$$

**EXAMPLE**

45 is what percent of 9?     **Setup:**  $\text{Percent} = \dfrac{45}{9} = 5$

$$500 = \text{Percent}$$

Move the decimal point two places to the right to convert to a percent: 5.00 = 500%.

To increase or decrease a number by a given percent, **take that percent of the original number and add it to or subtract it from the original number.**

To increase 25 by 60%, first find 60% of 25.

$$25 \times 0.6 = 15$$

Then, add the result to the original number:

$$25 + 15 = 40$$

To decrease 25 by 60%, subtract the 15:

$$25 - 15 = 10$$

To find the **original whole before a percent increase or decrease,** set up an equation. Think of a 15% increase over $x$ as being $1.15x$, since it's really 115% of $x$.

### EXAMPLE

A country's population after a 5% increase was 59,346. What was the population *before* the increase?

**Setup:**
$$\frac{1.05x}{1.05} = \frac{59,346}{1.05}$$
$$x = 56,520$$

To determine the combined effect of multiple percent increases and/or decreases, **start with 100 and see what happens.**

### EXAMPLE

A price went up 10% one year, and the new price went up 20% the next year. What was the combined percent increase?

**Setup:**      First year: 100 + (10% of 100) = 110

Second year: 110 + (20% of 110) = 132

Combined increase = 32%

## AVERAGE, MEDIAN, AND MODE

The **average,** or mean, of a group of terms is the sum of the terms divided by the number of terms.

The average of 15, 18, 15, 32, and 20 is $\dfrac{15 + 18 + 15 + 32 + 20}{5} = \dfrac{100}{5} = 20$

The **median** is the value of the middle term, with the terms arranged in increasing or decreasing order. Suppose you want to find the median of the terms 15, 18, 15, 32, and 20. First, put the terms in order from small to large. 15, 15, 18, 20, 32. Then, identify the middle term. The middle term is 18. If there is an even number of terms, the median is the average of the two middle terms with the terms arranged in order.

The **mode** is the value of the term that occurs most. Of the terms 15, 18, 15, 32, and 20, the number 15 occurs twice, so it is the mode. If every number occurs only once, there is no mode. If more than one number occurs the most, then both numbers would be the modes.

## RATIOS, PROPORTIONS, AND RATES

**Ratios** can be expressed in two forms. The first form is $\dfrac{a}{b}$.

If you have 15 dogs and 5 cats, the ratio of dogs to cats is $\dfrac{15}{5}$. (The ratio of cats to dogs is $\dfrac{5}{15}$.) Like any other fraction, this ratio can be simplified: $\dfrac{15}{5}$ can be simplified to $\dfrac{3}{1}$. In other words, for every 3 dogs, there is 1 cat.

The second form is *a:b.*

The ratio of dogs to cats is 15:5 or 3:1. The ratio of cats to dogs is 5:15 or 1:3.

Pay attention to what ratio is specified in the problem. Remember that the ratio of dogs to cats is different from the ratio of cats to dogs.

A **proportion** is a statement that two ratios are equal. To solve a proportion, cross multiply and solve for the variable.

$$\frac{x}{6} \diagdown \frac{2}{3}$$

$$3x = 12$$

$$x = 4$$

A **rate** is a ratio that compares quantities measured in different units. The most common example is **miles per hour**. Use the following formula for such problems:

$$\textbf{Distance = Rate} \times \textbf{Time}$$

Remember that although not all rates are speeds, this formula can be adapted to any rate.

# PROBABILITY

An **event** is a collection or set of possible outcomes. Suppose that a die with faces numbered 1, 2, 3, 4, 5, and 6 is rolled. All the possible outcomes are 1, 2, 3, 4, 5, and 6. Let $A$ be the event that a 1, 3, or 5 is rolled. The event $A$ is made up of the outcomes 1, 3, and 5. Thus, $A$ can also be described by saying that the number rolled is odd. A **possible outcome** is the elementary building block from which events are made up.

Of course, it is possible for an event to consist of a single possible outcome. For example, suppose that $B = \{4\}$; that is, the event $B$ is the result that a 4 is rolled. An event consisting of a single possible outcome is called an elementary event. Thus, $B$, which is $\{4\}$, is an elementary event.

To find the **probability** that an event will occur, use this formula:

$$\text{Probability} = \frac{\text{Number of desirable outcomes}}{\text{Number of possible outcomes}}$$

**KAPLAN
EXCLUSIVE TIPS**

" Probability is a part-to-whole ratio and can therefore never be greater than 1. "

**EXAMPLES**

If 12 books are on a shelf and 9 of them are mysteries, what is the probability of picking a mystery? $\frac{9}{12} = \frac{3}{4}$. This probability can also be expressed as 0.75 or 75%.

To find the probability that two **events** will occur, find the probability that the first event occurs and multiply this by the probability that the second event occurs—given that the first event occurs.

**EXAMPLES**

If there are 12 books on a shelf and 9 of them are mysteries, what is the probability of picking a mystery first and a non-mystery second if exactly two books are selected and none are replaced?

Probability of picking a mystery: $\frac{9}{12} = \frac{3}{4}$

Probability of picking a non-mystery: $\frac{3}{11}$

(Originally, there were 9 mysteries and 3 non-mysteries. After the mystery is selected, there are 8 mysteries and 3 non-mysteries; i.e., 11 books remaining.)

Probability of picking both books: $\frac{3}{4} \times \frac{3}{11} = \frac{9}{44}$

## STRANGE SYMBOLISM AND TERMINOLOGY

Some questions will be confusing because you're unfamiliar with the math concept being tested. Others will seem confusing because the math has literally been made up just for the purposes of the test. The test makers make up math symbols and terminology to test your ability to deal with unfamiliar concepts.

These problems aren't as hard as they seem. When you see a strange symbol, the question stem will *always* indicate what the symbol means. And if you see strange terminology, it will *always* be defined. The problems are essentially about following directions, so don't panic when you see them. All you have to do is slow down, read the problem, and follow the directions.

**EXAMPLE**

If $x<<>>y = \sqrt{x + y}$, what is $9<<>>16$?

All you have to do here is to substitute 9 and 16 into the defining equation:

$$\sqrt{9 + 16} = \sqrt{25} = 5$$

To "chomp" a number, take the sum of the digits of that number and divide this value by the number of digits.

What value do you get when you "chomp" 43,805?

$$4 + 3 + 8 + 0 + 5 = 20$$

$$20 \div 5 = 4$$

# PRACTICE QUESTIONS

1. Which of the following is not even?

   (A) 330
   (B) 436
   (C) 752
   (D) 861
   (E) 974

2. What is the least prime number greater than 50?

   (A) 51
   (B) 53
   (C) 55
   (D) 57
   (E) 59

3. Which of the following is a multiple of 2?

   (A) 271
   (B) 357
   (C) 463
   (D) 599
   (E) 756

4. $\dfrac{15 \times 7 \times 3}{9 \times 5 \times 2} =$

   (A) $\dfrac{2}{7}$

   (B) $\dfrac{3}{5}$

   (C) $3\dfrac{1}{2}$

   (D) 7

   (E) $7\dfrac{1}{2}$

5. What is the least common multiple of 18 and 24?

   (A) 6
   (B) 54
   (C) 72
   (D) 96
   (E) 432

6. Which of the following is a multiple of 3?

   (A) 115
   (B) 370
   (C) 465
   (D) 589
   (E) 890

7. $-6(3 - 4 \times 3) =$

   (A) −66
   (B) −54
   (C) −12
   (D) 18
   (E) 54

8. Which of the following is a multiple of 10?

   (A) 10,005
   (B) 10,030
   (C) 10,101
   (D) 100,005
   (E) 101,101

9. Which of the following is a multiple of both 5 and 2?

   (A) 2,203
   (B) 2,342
   (C) 1,005
   (D) 7,790
   (E) 9,821

10. Which of the following is a multiple of both 3 and 10?

    (A) 103
    (B) 130
    (C) 210
    (D) 310
    (E) 460

11. Which of the following is a multiple of 2, 3, and 5?

    (A) 165
    (B) 235
    (C) 350
    (D) 420
    (E) 532

12. Which of the following is an even multiple of both 3 and 5?

    (A) 135
    (B) 155
    (C) 250
    (D) 350
    (E) 390

13. Professor Jones bought a large carton of books. She gave 3 books to each student in her class, and there were no books left over. Which of the following could be the number of books she distributed?

    (A) 133
    (B) 143
    (C) 252
    (D) 271
    (E) 332

14. Two teams are having a contest. The prize is a box of candy that the members of the winning team will divide evenly. If team A wins, each player will get exactly 3 pieces of candy, and if team B wins, each player will get exactly 5 pieces. Which of the following could be the number of pieces of candy in the box?

    (A) 153
    (B) 325
    (C) 333
    (D) 425
    (E) 555

15. Three consecutive multiples of 4 have a sum of 60. What is the greatest of these numbers?

    (A) 8
    (B) 12
    (C) 16
    (D) 20
    (E) 24

16. Sheila cuts a 60-foot wire cable into equal strips of $\frac{4}{5}$ of a foot each. How many strips does she make?

    (A) 48
    (B) 51
    (C) 60
    (D) 70
    (E) 75

17. Which of the following is NOT odd?

    (A) 349
    (B) 537
    (C) 735
    (D) 841
    (E) 918

18. Which of the following can be the sum of two negative numbers?

    (A)  4
    (B)  2
    (C)  1
    (D)  0
    (E)  −1

19. Which of the following is NOT a prime number?

    (A)  2
    (B)  7
    (C)  17
    (D)  87
    (E)  101

20. All of the following can be the product of a negative integer and positive integer EXCEPT

    (A)  1
    (B)  −1
    (C)  −2
    (D)  −4
    (E)  −6

21. Susie and Dennis are training for a marathon. On Monday, they both run 3.2 miles. On Tuesday, Susie runs $5\frac{1}{5}$ miles and Dennis runs 3.6 miles. On Wednesday, Susie runs 4.8 miles and Dennis runs $2\frac{2}{5}$ miles. During those 3 days, how many more miles does Susie run than Dennis?

    (A)  4.8
    (B)  4
    (C)  3.2
    (D)  3
    (E)  2.4

22. Which number is a multiple of 60?

    (A)  213
    (B)  350
    (C)  540
    (D)  666
    (E)  1,060

23. Two odd integers and one even integer are multiplied together. Which of the following could be their product?

    (A)  1.5
    (B)  3
    (C)  6
    (D)  7.2
    (E)  15

24. If the number 9,899,399 is increased by 2,082, the result will be

    (A)  9,902,481
    (B)  9,901,481
    (C)  9,901,471
    (D)  9,891,481
    (E)  901,481

25. What is the sum of five consecutive integers if the middle one is 13?

    (A)  55
    (B)  60
    (C)  65
    (D)  70
    (E)  75

26. $\dfrac{4x^5}{2x^2} =$

(A) $2x^2$

(B) $2x^3$

(C) $2x^4$

(D) $4x^2$

(E) $4x^3$

27. $-2^3(1-2)^3 + (-2)^3 =$

(A) $-12$

(B) $-4$

(C) $0$

(D) $4$

(E) $12$

28. $n$ is an odd integer and $10 < n < 19$. What is the mean of all possible values of $n$?

(A) $13$

(B) $13.5$

(C) $14$

(D) $14.5$

(E) $15.5$

29. $a\Delta b = \dfrac{3a}{b}$. What is $\dfrac{14}{32}\Delta 1\dfrac{3}{4}$?

(A) $\dfrac{1}{4}$

(B) $\dfrac{1}{3}$

(C) $\dfrac{1}{2}$

(D) $\dfrac{3}{4}$

(E) $\dfrac{49}{64}$

30. Jon works 4.5 hours a day, 3 days each week after school. He is paid $7.25 per hour. How much is his weekly pay (rounded to the next highest cent)?

(A) $13.50

(B) $21.75

(C) $32.63

(D) $54

(E) $97.88

31. Zim buys a calculator that is marked 30% off. If he pays $35, what was the original price?

(A) $24.50

(B) $45.50

(C) $47

(D) $50

(E) $62.50

32. A museum records 16 visitors to an exhibit on Monday, 21 on Tuesday, 20 on Wednesday, 17 on Thursday, 19 on Friday, 21 on Saturday, and 17 on Sunday, what is the median number of visitors for the week?

(A) $18.5$

(B) $18.75$

(C) $19$

(D) $19.5$

(E) $19.75$

33. A bag contains 8 white, 4 red, 7 green, and 5 blue marbles. Eight marbles are withdrawn randomly. How many of the withdrawn marbles were white if the chance of drawing a white marble is now $\frac{1}{4}$?

    (A) 0

    (B) 3

    (C) 4

    (D) 5

    (E) 6

34. $\sqrt{1,500} =$

    (A) $10 + \sqrt{15}$

    (B) $10\sqrt{15}$

    (C) 25

    (D) $100 + \sqrt{15}$

    (E) $10\sqrt{150}$

35. $2(3 \times 2)^2 - 27(6 \div 2) + 3^2 =$

    (A) 72

    (B) 9

    (C) 3

    (D) 0

    (E) −24

36. Which of the following numbers is closest to the product of $48.9 \times 21.2$?

    (A) 10,000

    (B) 8,000

    (C) 1,000

    (D) 100

    (E) 70

37. $|16 - 25| + \sqrt{25 - 16} =$

    (A) −12

    (B) −6

    (C) 0

    (D) 6

    (E) 12

38. Which of the following is 81,455 rounded to the nearest 100?

    (A) 81,000

    (B) 81,400

    (C) 81,500

    (D) 82,000

    (E) 90,000

39. If 35% of $x$ is 7, what is $x$% of 35?

    (A) 7

    (B) 20

    (C) 28

    (D) 35

    (E) 42

40. A number is considered "blue" if the sum of its digits is equal to the product of its digits. Which of the following numbers is "blue"?

   (A) 111
   (B) 220
   (C) 321
   (D) 422
   (E) 521

41. To "fix" a number, you must perform the following four steps:

   Step 1: Raise the number to the third power.

   Step 2: Divide the result by 2.

   Step 3: Take the absolute value of the result of Step 2.

   Step 4: Round off this result to the nearest whole number.

   When you "fix" −3, you get

   (A) −13
   (B)    4
   (C)    5
   (D)   13
   (E)   14

42. When D is divided by 15, the result is 6 with a remainder of 2. What is the remainder when D is divided by 6?

   (A) 0
   (B) 1
   (C) 2
   (D) 3
   (E) 4

43. For any two numbers $a$ and $b$, $a ? b = (a + b)(a − b)$. For example, $10 ? 5 = (10 + 5)(10 − 5) = (15)(5) = 75$. The value of $7 ? 5$ is

   (A)  2
   (B) 12
   (C) 24
   (D) 36
   (E) 48

44. What is the greatest integer less than $\dfrac{71}{6}$?

   (A)  9
   (B) 10
   (C) 11
   (D) 12
   (E) 13

45. Which of the following is NOT less than 0.25?

   (A) $\dfrac{2}{9}$

   (B) $\dfrac{3}{14}$

   (C) $\dfrac{16}{64}$

   (D) $\dfrac{19}{80}$

   (E) $\dfrac{4}{17}$

46. If the average of five consecutive odd numbers is 11, then the largest number is

   (A) 17
   (B) 15
   (C) 13
   (D) 11
   (E)  9

# PRACTICE QUESTION ANSWERS

## 1. D

The way to tell if an integer is even is to look at the last digit to the right—the ones digit. If that digit is divisible by 2, or is 0, the number is even. Looking at the choices, only (D) ends in a number that isn't divisible by 2, so it is not even.

## 2. B

A prime number is an integer greater than 1 that is divisible by only two different positive integers, itself and 1. Of the choices, only (B), 53, and (E), 59, are prime. You want the least prime number greater than 50, so (B) is correct. Using the divisibility rules would quickly show you that 51 and 57 are divisible by 3, while 55 is divisible by 5.

## 3. E

If the ones digit of a number is even (0, 2, 4, 6, or 8), the number is even. The only choice whose last digit is even is (E), 756.

## 4. C

Before you do the multiplication, see which common factors in the numerator and denominator can be canceled. Canceling a 3 from the 3 in the numerator and the 9 in the denominator leaves $\frac{15 \times 7 \times 1}{3 \times 5 \times 2}$. Canceling a 5 from the 15 in the numerator and the 5 in the denominator leaves $\frac{3 \times 7 \times 1}{3 \times 1 \times 2}$. Canceling the 3 in the numerator and the 3 in the denominator leaves $\frac{7 \times 1}{1 \times 2} = \frac{7}{2} = 3\frac{1}{2}$, (C).

## 5. C

The least common multiple (LCM) of two integers is the product of their prime factors, each raised to the highest power with which it appears. The prime factorization of 18 is $2 \times 3^2$ and that of 24 is $2^3 \times 3$. So their LCM is $2^3 \times 3^2 = 8 \times 9 = 72$. You could also find their LCM by checking out the multiples of the larger integer until you find the one that's also a multiple of the smaller. Check out the multiples of 24: 24? No. 48? No. 72? Yes, $72 = 4 \times 18$.

## 6. C

If a number is divisible by 3, the sum of its digits will be divisible by 3. Checking the answer choices, only (C), 465, works since $4 + 6 + 5 = 15$, which is divisible by 3.

## 7. E

According to PEMDAS, start in the parentheses. Perform multiplication before subtraction: $-6(3 - 12)$. After the subtraction: $-6(-9)$. Since a negative times a negative is a positive, the answer is 54, (E).

## 8. B

If a number is divisible by 10, its last digit will be a 0. Only (B) fits this criterion.

## 9. D

If a number is divisible by both 5 and 2, then it must also be divisible by $5 \times 2$ or 10. Since a number divisible by 10 must have a 0 as its last digit, (D) is correct.

## 10. C

For a number to be divisible by 3 and 10, it must satisfy the divisibility rules of both: Its last digit must be 0, which automatically eliminates (A), and the sum of its digits must be divisible by 3. Checking the rest of the answer choices, only (C) is also divisible by 3, since $2 + 1 + 0 = 3$.

**11. D**

For a number to be a multiple of both 2 and 5, it must also be a multiple of 2 × 5 = 10. This means it must have a 0 as its last digit, which eliminates all but (C) and (D). To be a multiple of 3, the number's digits must sum to a multiple of 3. (D) is the only remaining choice that fits this requirement, since 4 + 2 + 0 = 6.

**12. E**

Since an even number is divisible by 2, the question is asking for a number that is divisible by 2, 3, and 5. If the number is divisible by 2 and 5, it must also be divisible by 10, so its last digit must be 0. To be a multiple of 3, its digits must sum to a multiple of 3. Eliminate (A) and (B) since they don't end in 0. Of the remaining choices, only (E) is a multiple of 3, since 3 + 9 + 0 = 12.

**13. C**

If Professor Jones was able to distribute all the books in groups of 3 without any left over, the number of books she started with was divisible by 3. Whichever choice is divisible by 3 must therefore be correct. For a number to be divisible by 3, the sum of its digits must also be divisible by 3. Only (C) fits this requirement: 2 + 5 + 2 = 9.

**14. E**

The problem tells you that the number of pieces of candy in the box can be evenly divided by 3 and 5. So the correct answer has a 0 or 5 as its last digit, and the sum of its digits is divisible by 3. Eliminate (A) and (C) since they don't end in either 0 or 5. Of the remaining choices, only (E) is also divisible by 3, since 5 + 5 + 5 = 15.

**15. E**

Use the answer choices to help find the solution. When backsolving, start with the middle choice, since it will help you determine if the correct answer needs to be greater or less than it. In this case, the middle choice is 16. The sum of 16 and 2 numbers that are each smaller than 16 has to be less than 3 × 16 or 48, so it is obviously too small. Therefore, (A) and (B) must also be too small, and you can eliminate all three. Try (D), 20. Again, 20 plus two numbers smaller than 20 will be less than 3 × 20 or 60, so it's not correct. The only choice remaining is (E), 24, so it must be correct. To prove it, 24 plus the two preceding consecutive multiples of 4, which are 16 and 20, do indeed sum to 60: 16 + 20 + 24 = 60.

**16. E**

When you're asked how many strips $\frac{4}{5}$ of a foot long can be cut from a 60-foot piece of wire, you're being asked how many times $\frac{4}{5}$ goes into 60, or what is $60 \div \frac{4}{5}$. Before you do the division, you can eliminate some unreasonable answer choices. Since $\frac{4}{5}$ is less than 1, $\frac{4}{5}$ must go into 60 more than 60 times. Eliminate (A), (B), and (C) because they're all less than or equal to 60. Dividing by a fraction is the same as multiplying by its reciprocal, so $60 \div \frac{4}{5} = 60 \times \frac{5}{4} = 75$.

**17. E**

If a number is odd, its last digit must be odd. (E) ends in an even digit, so it is not odd.

**18. E**

The sum of two negative numbers is always negative. (E) is the only negative choice, so it must be correct. If you're wondering how two negative numbers can add up to –1, remember that "number" doesn't necessarily mean "integer." It can also mean "fraction." For example, $\left(-\dfrac{1}{4}\right) + \left(-\dfrac{3}{4}\right) = -1$. Always read the questions carefully to see what types of numbers are involved.

### 19. D

A prime number has only two different positive factors, 1 and itself. The numbers 2, 7, and 17 are obviously prime, so eliminate them. Use the divisibility rules to check out the two remaining choices. Both end in an odd number, so neither is divisible by 2. But the digits of 87 sum to 15, which is a multiple of 3, so 87 is divisible by 3 and is therefore not prime.

### 20. A

The product of a positive integer and a negative integer is always negative. (A) is positive, so it couldn't be the product of a negative and a positive.

### 21. B

The simplest way to solve this problem is to convert the numbers so that they're all decimals or all fractions: $5\dfrac{1}{5} = 5\dfrac{2}{10} = 5.2$; $2\dfrac{2}{5} = 2\dfrac{4}{10} = 2.4$. Now you can more easily compare the distances. On Monday, they ran the same number of miles. On Tuesday, Susie ran 5.2 miles and Dennis ran 3.6 miles. The difference between the two amounts is 5.2 – 3.6, or 1.6, so on Tuesday Susie ran 1.6 more miles than Dennis did. On Wednesday, Susie ran 4.8 miles and Dennis ran 2.4. Then 4.8 – 2.4 = 2.4, so on Wednesday Susie ran 2.4 miles more than Dennis. The total difference for the three days is 1.6 + 2.4 = 4.0 more miles.

### 22. C

A number that is a multiple of 60 must be a multiple of every factor of 60. The factors of 60 are 1, 2, 3, 4, 5, 6, 10, 12, 15, 20, 30, and 60. (A) and (D) are not multiples of 10. (B) and (E) are not multiples of 3. The answer is 540, (C).

### 23. C

The product of three integers must be an integer, so eliminate (A) and (D). A product of integers that has at least one even factor is even, so the product of two odd integers and one even integer must be even. The only even choice is 6, (C).

### 24. B

This question is simply asking for the sum of 9,899,399 and 2,082, which is 9,901,481, (B).

### 25. C

If the middle of five consecutive integers is 13, the first two are 11 and 12 and the last two are 14 and 15. So the sum is 11 + 12 + 13 + 14 + 15 = 65. You could get to this answer more quickly if you knew that the middle term in a group of consecutive numbers is equal to the average of the group of numbers. In other words, the average of these five integers is 13, so their sum would be 13 × 5 = 65.

### 26. B

Simplify the expression by first simplifying the fraction $\dfrac{4}{2}$, which equals 2. Then, to divide the exponential expressions with the same base, subtract the exponents:

$$\frac{x^5}{x^2} = x^{5-2}$$

$$= x^3$$

So $\dfrac{4x^5}{2x^2} = 2x^3$

**27. C**

A negative number raised to an odd power is negative. Using PEMDAS,

$$-2^3(1-2)^3 + (-2)^3$$
$$= -2^3(-1)^3 + (-2)^3$$
$$= -8(-1) + (-8)$$
$$= 8 + (-8)$$
$$= 8 - 8$$
$$= 0$$

**28. C**

The mean (or average) is the sum of the terms divided by the number of terms. The numbers included are 11, 13, 15, and 17. Note that 19 is not in the set, since $n$ is less than 19. The average is $\frac{11 + 13 + 15 + 17}{4} = \frac{56}{4} = 14$. The average is an even number although the numbers in the set are all odd.

**29. D**

Substitute the number on the left for $a$ and the number on the right for $b$ in the formula given for the strange symbol. First, convert $b$ to an improper fraction: $\frac{7}{4}$. So the numerator is 3 times $\frac{14}{32}$, or (simplifying the fraction) 3 times $\frac{7}{16}$, or $\frac{21}{16}$. Dividing by $\frac{7}{4}$ is the same as multiplying by $\frac{4}{7}$. So we have $\frac{21}{16} \times \frac{4}{7}$ or $\frac{3}{4} \times \frac{1}{1} = \frac{3}{4}$.

**30. E**

Multiply the number of hours per day times the number of days times the rate per hour. $4.5 \times 3 \times 7.25 = 97.875$, which rounds to $97.88.

**31. D**

Let's say the original price is $x$ dollars. The price paid is 70 percent of the original price (100% minus 30%). So, $0.7x = 35$; $70x = 3,500$; $x = 50$.

**32. C**

The numbers for the week are 16, 21, 20, 17, 19, 21, 17. Listing them in ascending order, we have 16, 17, 17, 19, 20, 21, 21. There are an odd number of numbers, so the median is the number in the middle of the set: 19.

**33. C**

By adding the 8 white, 4 red, 7 green, and 5 blue marbles, we have a total of 24 marbles. If 8 are withdrawn, 16 remain in the bag. If the chance of drawing a white marble is now one-fourth, 4 white marbles remain in the bag, so 8 – 4, or 4 must have been drawn out.

**34. B**

To simplify the square root of a large number, break the number down into two or more factors and write the number as the product of the square roots of those factors. This is especially useful when one of the factors is a perfect square. In this case, break 1,500 down into two factors. $1,500 = 15 \times 100$, and 100 is a perfect square. So $1,500 = \sqrt{100 \times 15} = \sqrt{100} \times \sqrt{15} = 10\sqrt{15}$.

**35. D**

This is a basic arithmetic problem, and if you remember PEMDAS, it will be a breeze. PEMDAS tells you the order in which you need to do the different calculations: parentheses, exponents, multiplication and division, addition and subtraction. Take the expression and solve the parts in that order:

$$2(3 \times 2)^2 - 27(6 \div 2) + 3^2$$
$$= 2(6)^2 - 27(3) + 3^2$$
$$= 2(36) - 27(3) + 9$$
$$= 72 - 81 + 9$$
$$= -9 + 9$$
$$= 0$$

### 36. C

One way to solve this one would be to do the calculation. But this is really a test to see if you understand how to approximate a calculation by rounding off numbers. You could round off both numbers to the nearest whole number, but that wouldn't make the calculation much easier. And besides, the answer choices you're choosing between are pretty far apart, so you can probably round both numbers to the nearest ten. Then 48.9 is close to 50, so round it up to 50. And 21.2 is close to 20, so round it down to 20. Now the multiplication is $50 \times 20$ or 1,000, choice (C).

### 37. E

In terms of order of operations, treat absolute value bars and roots just like parentheses: Simplify them first. In this case, first find the value of $16 - 25$: $16 - 25 = -9$. The absolute value of a number is its distance from zero on the number line. Now $-9$ is 9 units from zero, so

$$|16 - 25| = |-9|$$
$$= 9$$

Now, simplify $\sqrt{25 - 16}$. $25 - 16 = 9$, so $\sqrt{25 - 16} = \sqrt{9}$. Because the radical sign is being used, simplify $\sqrt{9}$ by finding only the positive square root of 9, which is 3. The problem becomes $9 + 3$, which is 12, (E).

### 38. C

You're being asked whether 81,455 is closer to 81,400 or 81,500. Logically, because 81,455 is greater than 81,450 (the halfway point between 81,400 and 81,500), it is closer to 81,500. Formally, to round a number to the nearest hundred, consider the tens digit. If the tens digit is 5 or greater, round the hundreds digit up 1. If the tens digit is 4 or smaller, keep the same hundreds digit. Here the tens digit is 5, so round the hundreds digit up 1 from 4 to 5. To the nearest 100, 81,455 is 81,500, (C).

### 39. A

This problem is a snap if you remember that $a$% of $b = b$% of $a$. In this case, 35% of $x = x$% of 35, so $x$% of 35 is 7.

If you didn't remember that $a$% of $b = b$% of $a$, you could also have solved the statement that 35% of $x$ is 7 for $x$ and then found $x$% of 35. Percent × Whole = Part, so

$$\frac{35}{100}x = 7$$
$$35x = 700$$
$$x = 20$$

So $x$% of 35 is 20% of 35, which is 7, (A).

### 40. C

In this type of problem, you're given a rule or definition you've never heard before and then asked a question involving that new rule. In this example, you're given a definition of the term "blue": a number is "blue" if the sum of its digits is equal to the product of its digits. To solve, simply try each answer until you find the one that fits the definition of "blue." Only (C) is blue, because $3 + 2 + 1 = 3 \times 2 \times 1 = 6$.

### 41. E

This is another invented rule question. This time all you have to do is follow directions. To "fix" –3, you first raise it to the third power: $(-3)^3 = -27$. Then divide this result by 2: $-27 \div 2 = -13.5$. Next, take the absolute value of –13.5, which is just 13.5. Finally, round off this result to the nearest integer: 13.5 rounds up to 14, (E).

### 42. C

One way to do this problem is to realize that the remainder would have to be the same whether $D$ were divided by 15 or 6, since $D = 15 \times 6 + 2$. In other words, $D$ is 2 more than a multiple of both 15 and 6. Hence, the remainder is 2 regardless of whether $D$ is divided by 15 or 6.

Otherwise, find the actual value of $D$ by calculating:

$$D = 15 \times 6 + 2$$
$$= 90 + 2$$
$$= 92$$

Now divide $D$ by 6 to find the remainder: $92 \div 6 = 15$, with a remainder of 2. (C) is correct.

### 43. C

This is another follow-the-instructions problem. Just replace $a$ with 7 and $b$ with 5. So $7 \mathbin{?} 5 = (7 + 5)$ $(7 - 5) = (12)(2) = 24$, (C).

### 44. C

$\dfrac{71}{6} = 11\dfrac{5}{6}$, so the greatest integer less than $\dfrac{71}{6}$ is 11.

### 45. C

$0.25 = \dfrac{1}{4}$, so just find which choice is NOT less than $\dfrac{1}{4}$. (C), $\dfrac{16}{64}$, reduces to $\dfrac{1}{4}$ so it is equal to, not less than, 0.25.

### 46. B

The average of an odd number of consecutive numbers is equal to the middle term. Since 11 is the average of these five consecutive odd numbers, 11 is the third and middle term. So the five numbers are 7, 9, 11, 13, and 15. The largest number is 15.

# CHAPTER 12: ALGEBRA

Algebra problems will appear in two forms on the SSAT or ISEE: As regular math problems and as word problems. Word problems will be dealt with in another chapter. This chapter will give you a chance to review the basic algebra concepts that you'll see on the test. Chapter 14: Word Problems will build on these concepts and introduce word problem–specific skills.

## ALGEBRA CONCEPTS

### VOCABULARY

Algebra consists of the same basic operations as arithmetic, so in a sense, it can best be defined as abstract arithmetic. The difference is that letters, called *variables,* are often substituted for numbers. Before we discuss algebraic topics, let's review some important definitions.

A **variable** is a letter (usually lowercase) used to represent a numerical value that is unknown. The value of the variable may differ in any particular problem.

A **constant** is a value that does not change its value regardless of the problem. Constants are typically numbers.

A **term** is a variable, a constant, or the product of a constant and one or more variables. The variables may be raised to exponents. A term containing only a number is called a *constant term* because it contains no variable factors.

The **coefficient** of a term is understood to be the numerical factor of that term. If no numerical factor is present, the coefficient is understood to be 1 (or –1).

**EXAMPLES**

| Term | Variable | Coefficient | Constant |
|------|----------|-------------|----------|
| $5x$ | $x$ | 5 | 5 |
| $-3yz$ | $y, z$ | $-3$ | $-3$ |
| 12 | | | 12 |

**Like terms** are terms that contain exactly the same variables raised to exactly the same exponents. Like terms can be added and subtracted by combining the numerical coefficients and keeping the variable portion of the terms.

| Examples: | Can be simplified to: |
|-----------|----------------------|
| $7x + 5x$ | $12x$ |
| $3xy - 2 - xy$ | $2xy - 2$ |
| $8a^2b + 5ab^2 - 4a^2b$ | $4a^2b + 5ab^2$ (This expression cannot be simplified further because the exponents on the variables $a$ and $b$ are not the same.) |

In algebra, you work with expressions and equations. An algebraic **expression** contains one or more terms separated by addition and subtraction signs.

**EXAMPLES**

$$4x^3 + 12x^2 + 7x + 8$$
$$18a^3b^4 + 14a^2b^5 + 12a + 56$$

An algebraic **equation** is a statement that two expressions are equal. An equal sign, =, is used to indicate that the two expressions are equal.

**EXAMPLES**

$$5x + 10 = 4x + 26$$
$$x^2 + 5x + 12 = 3y + 4$$

A **polynomial** is an algebraic expression that is the sum of two or more terms. If a polynomial has two terms, it is called a **binomial**. If it has three terms, it is called a **trinomial**. If an expression only has one term, it is called a **monomial**.

**EXAMPLES**

| | |
|---|---|
| $16x^3 - 10x^2$ | binomial, polynomial |
| $-3a^3b^4 + 4a + 6$ | trinomial, polynomial |
| $13p^6k^9$ | monomial |

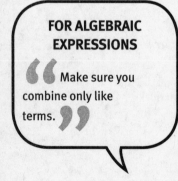

**FOR ALGEBRAIC EXPRESSIONS**

Make sure you combine only like terms.

## SUBSTITUTION

If a problem gives you the value for a variable, just substitute the value into the expression and solve. Make sure that you follow the correct order of operations and are careful with your calculations.

### EXAMPLE

If $x = 15$ and $y = 10$, what is the value of $4x(x - y)$?
Substitute 15 for $x$ and 10 for $y$.

$$4(15)(15 - 10) =$$

Then evaluate.

$$(60)(5) = 300$$

## SIMPLIFYING POLYNOMIAL EXPRESSIONS

To simplify a polynomial expression, remove all grouping symbols (parentheses) using distribution, simplify each term so that each variable appears no more than once in any one term, then combine like terms.

### EXAMPLES

$$6(3b - 4) = 18b - 24$$

$$-3(4x + 1) + 2 = -12x - 3 + 2$$
$$= -12x - 1$$

$$(2b)^3 - 5b^2(3b) = 8b^3 - 15b^3$$
$$= -7b^3$$

$$3a + 2b - 8a = 3a - 8a + 2b$$
$$= -5a + 2b \text{ or } 2b - 5a$$

$$(4w + 9h) - (3w - 4h) = 4w + 9h - 3w + 4h$$
$$= 4w - 3w + 9h + 4h$$
$$= w + 13h$$

## FACTORING POLYNOMIAL EXPRESSIONS

The main factoring method you need to master for the test is factoring using the **greatest common factor (GCF)** of an algebraic expression. The GCF of an expression consists of the largest numerical factor and the largest number of variable factors that can be factored out of all terms in the expression.

To find the GCF of an expression, first make sure that the expression is simplified. Second, find the largest factor common to all coefficients in the expression (it is possible to have a numerical GCF of 1). Finally, identify the variable factors common to all terms in the expression. The GCF will contain these factors raised to the lowest exponent given on the variable in any one term.

To write an expression in factored form, use the distributive property to write the GCF followed by the polynomial factor in parentheses.

**EXAMPLES**

$7y^3 + 14y^2 - 21y = 7y(y^2 + 2y - 3)$

$12ab^3 - 15a^2b^2 = 3ab^2(4b - 5a)$

In the first example, $7y$ is the GCF of the expression. In the second example, $3ab^2$ is the GCF of the expression.

## MULTIPLYING AND DIVIDING MONOMIALS AND BINOMIALS

To **add** or **subtract** terms consisting of a coefficient (the number in front of the variable) multiplied by a power (a power is a base raised to an exponent), both the base and the exponent *must* be the same. As long as the bases and the exponents are the same, you can add the coefficients.

$x^2 + x^2 = 2x^2$

$3x^4 - 2x^4 = x^4$

$x^2 + x^3$ cannot be combined.

$x^2 + y^2$ cannot be combined.

To **multiply** terms consisting of coefficients multiplied by powers having the same base, multiply the coefficients and add the exponents.

$2x^5 \times 8x^7 = (2 \times 8)(x^{5 + 7}) = 16x^{12}$

To **divide** terms consisting of coefficients multiplied by powers having the same base, divide the coefficients and subtract the exponents.

$6x^7 \div 2x^5 = (6 \div 2)(x^{7 - 5}) = 3x^2$

To **raise a power to an exponent,** multiply the exponents.

$(x^2)^4 = x^{2 \times 4} = x^8$

When you multiply monomials, multiply the coefficients of each term. (In other words, multiply the numbers that come before the variables.) Then, multiply the variables. Exponents of like variables should be added.

$$(6a)(4b) = (6 \times 4)(a \times b) = 24ab$$

$$(6a)(4ab) = (6 \times 4)(a \times a \times b) =$$

$$= (6 \times 4)(a^{1 + 1} \times b)$$

$$= 24a^2 b$$

When you divide monomials, divide the coefficient of the numerator by the coefficient of the denominator. When the same variable appears in both the numerator and the denominator, subtract the exponent of that variable in the denominator from the exponent of that variable in the numerator.

$$24a \div 3b = \frac{24a}{3b} = \frac{8a}{b}$$

$$40x^2 y^5 \div 5xy^2 z^4 = \frac{40x^2 y^5}{5xy^2 z^4} = \frac{8x^{2-1} y^{5-2}}{z^4} = \frac{8x^1 y^3}{z^4} = \frac{8xy^3}{z^4}$$

Remember that $x^1 = x$.

Use the FOIL method to **multiply binomials.** FOIL stands for **F**irst + **O**uter + **I**nner + **L**ast. Add these terms together for the most reduced equation, a *trinomial*.

$$(y + 1)(y + 2) = (y \times y) + (y \times 2) + (1 \times y) + (1 \times 2)$$

$$= y^2 + 2y + y + 2$$

$$= y^2 + 3y + 2$$

# WORKING WITH EQUATIONS

The key to **solving equations** is to do the same thing to both sides of the equation until you have your variable isolated on one side of the equation and all of the numbers on the other side.

$$12a + 8 = 23 - 3a$$

First, subtract 8 from each side so that the left side of the equation has only a variable term.

$$12a + 8 - 8 = 23 - 3a - 8$$

$$12a = 15 - 3a$$

Then, add $3a$ to each side so that the right side of the equation has only numbers.

$$12a + 3a = 15 - 3a + 3a$$

$$15a = 15$$

Finally, divide both sides by 15 to isolate the variable.

$$\frac{15a}{15} = \frac{15}{15}$$
$$a = 1$$

Sometimes you're given an equation with two variables and asked to **solve for one variable in terms of the other**. This means that you must isolate the variable for which you are solving on one side of the equation and put everything else on the other side. In other words, when you're done, you'll have $x$ (or whatever the variable is) on one side of the equation and an expression on the other side.

Solve $7x + 2y = 3x + 10y - 16$ for $x$ in terms of $y$.

Since you want to isolate $x$ on one side of the equation, begin by subtracting $2y$ from both sides.

$$7x + 2y - 2y = 3x + 10y - 16 - 2y$$
$$7x = 3x + 8y - 16$$

Then, subtract $3x$ from both sides to get all the $x$'s on one side of the equation.

$$7x - 3x = 3x + 8y - 16 - 3x$$
$$4x = 8y - 16$$

Finally, divide both sides by 4 to isolate $x$.

$$\frac{4x}{4} = \frac{8y - 16}{4}$$
$$x = 2y - 4$$

## PICKING NUMBERS

Picking Numbers is a useful strategy for avoiding tedious calculations. Instead of solving the equation and figuring out which answer choice matches your answer, you plug choices back into the equation until one fits.

Some typical questions that can be solved by Picking Numbers involve the following:

- Age stated in terms of variables
- Remainder
- Percentages or fractions of variables
- Even/odd variables
- Algebraic expressions in the answers

# WORKING WITH INEQUALITIES

Solving inequalities is very similar to solving equations—with two important differences:

1. When **multiplying or dividing both sides of an inequality by a negative number, the direction of the inequality must change.**

2. The **solution of an inequality** will be a **range of values for the variable,** rather than just one value.

When solving the inequality $-5a < 10$, for instance, it is correct to divide both sides of the inequality by $-5$. Because $-5$ is a negative number, the solution, after simplifying, would be $a > -2$, not $a < -2$.

If this is confusing, consider the rules for multiplying signed numbers. If $-5$ multiplied by some value must be less than 10, any positive number will do. That's because $-5$ multiplied by a positive number yields a negative number, and ALL negative numbers are less than 10. In addition, some negative numbers like $-1$ and $-\frac{1}{2}$ will also work; though when multiplied by $-5$, they yield positive results, and the positive product is less than 10. If $-5$ is multiplied by $-2$ or smaller numbers, however, the product becomes too large.

## EXAMPLES

$$4a + 6 > 2a + 10$$
$$4a - 2a > 10 - 6$$
$$2a > 4$$
$$a > 2$$

$$5(g - 6) \leq 6g + 18$$
$$5g - 30 \leq 6g + 18$$
$$5g - 6g \leq 18 + 30$$
$$-g \leq 48$$
$$g \geq -48$$

# PRACTICE QUESTIONS

1.  What is the value of $a(b-1) + \dfrac{bc}{2}$ if $a = 3$, $b = 6$, and $c = 5$?

    (A) 0
    (B) 15
    (C) 30
    (D) 45
    (E) 60

2.  If $\dfrac{c}{d} = 3$ and $d = 1$, then $3c + d =$

    (A) 3
    (B) 4
    (C) 6
    (D) 7
    (E) 10

3.  What is the value of $x$ in the equation $5x - 7 = y$, if $y = 8$?

    (A) −1
    (B) 1
    (C) 2
    (D) 3
    (E) 70

4.  What is the value of $x(y-2) + xz$, if $x = 2$, $y = 5$, and $z = 7$?

    (A) 12
    (B) 20
    (C) 22
    (D) 28
    (E) 32

5.  If $x = \sqrt{3}$, $y = 2$, and $z = \dfrac{1}{2}$, then $x^2 - 5yz + y^2 =$

    (A) 1
    (B) 2
    (C) 4
    (D) 7
    (E) 8

6.  If $x + y = 7$, what is the value of $2x + 2y - 2$?

    (A) 5
    (B) 9
    (C) 12
    (D) 14
    (E) 16

7.  What is the value of $a$ in the equation $3a - 6 = b$, if $b = 18$?

    (A) 4
    (B) 6
    (C) 8
    (D) 10
    (E) 18

8.  If $\dfrac{x}{y} = \dfrac{2}{5}$ and $x = 10$, $y =$

    (A) 4
    (B) 10
    (C) 15
    (D) 20
    (E) 25

9.  $-5n(3m - 2) =$

    (A) $-15mn + 10n$
    (B) $15mn - 10n$
    (C) $-8mn + 7n$
    (D) $8mn + 7n$
    (E) $-2mn - 7n$

10. What is the value of $(a + b)^2$, when $a = -1$ and $b = 3$?

    (A) 2
    (B) 4
    (C) 8
    (D) 10
    (E) 16

11. If $s - t = 5$, what is the value of $3s - 3t + 3$?

    (A) 2
    (B) 8
    (C) 11
    (D) 12
    (E) 18

12. $(3d - 7) - (5 - 2d) =$

    (A) $d - 12$
    (B) $5d - 2$
    (C) $5d + 12$
    (D) $5d - 12$
    (E) $8d + 5$

13. What is the value of $xyz + y(z - x) + 2x$ if $x = -2$, $y = 3$, and $z = 1$?

    (A) $-13$
    (B) $-7$
    (C) $-1$
    (D) 7
    (E) 19

14. If $3x + 7 = 14$, then $x =$

    (A) $-14$
    (B) 0
    (C) $\dfrac{7}{3}$
    (D) 3
    (E) 7

15. If $x$ is an integer, which of the following expressions is always even?

    (A) $2x + 1$
    (B) $3x + 2$
    (C) $4x + 3$
    (D) $5x + 4$
    (E) $6x + 2$

16. If $4z - 3 = -19$, then $z =$

    (A) $-16$
    (B) $-5\dfrac{1}{2}$
    (C) $-4$
    (D) 0
    (E) 4

17. If $3ab = 6$, what is the value of $a$ in terms of $b$?

    (A) 2
    (B) $\dfrac{2}{b}$
    (C) $\dfrac{2}{b^2}$
    (D) $2b$
    (E) $2b^2$

18. If $x$ and $y$ are integers, in which equation must $x$ be negative?

    (A) $xy = -1$
    (B) $xy^2 = -1$
    (C) $x^2y = -1$
    (D) $x^2y^2 = 1$
    (E) $xy^2 = 1$

19. If $n$ is an odd number, which of the following expressions is always odd?

    (A) $2n + 4$
    (B) $3n + 2$
    (C) $3n + 5$
    (D) $5n + 5$
    (E) $5n + 7$

20. If $5p + 12 = 17 - 4\left(\dfrac{p}{2} + 1\right)$, what is the value of $p$?

    (A) $\dfrac{1}{7}$

    (B) $\dfrac{1}{3}$

    (C) $\dfrac{6}{7}$

    (D) $1\dfrac{2}{7}$

    (E) $2$

21. If $\dfrac{2x}{5y} = 6$, what is the value of $y$, in terms of $x$?

    (A) $\dfrac{x}{15}$

    (B) $\dfrac{x}{2}$

    (C) $\dfrac{8}{2}$

    (D) $15x$

    (E) $\dfrac{30}{x}$

22. If $x$ is an odd integer and $y$ is an even integer, which of the following expressions MUST be odd?

    (A) $2x + y$

    (B) $2(x + y)$

    (C) $x^2 + y^2$

    (D) $xy + y$

    (E) $2x + y^2$

23. If $100 \div x = 10n$, then which of the following is equal to $nx$?

    (A) $10$

    (B) $10x$

    (C) $100$

    (D) $10xn$

    (E) $1,000$

24. For what value of $y$ is $4(y - 1) = 2(y + 2)$?

    (A) $0$

    (B) $2$

    (C) $4$

    (D) $6$

    (E) $8$

25. $$\dfrac{3}{4} + x = 8.3$$

    What is the value of $x$ in the equation above?

    (A) $4.9$

    (B) $6.75$

    (C) $7.55$

    (D) $8$

    (E) $9.05$

26. If $2(a + m) = 5m - 3 + a$, what is the value of $a$, in terms of $m$?

    (A) $\dfrac{3m}{2}$

    (B) $3$

    (C) $5m$

    (D) $4m + 33$

    (E) $3m - 3$

# PRACTICE QUESTION ANSWERS

## 1. C

Substitute $a = 3$, $b = 6$, and $c = 5$.

$$3(6 - 1) + \frac{6 \times 5}{2} = 3(5) + \frac{30}{2}$$
$$= 15 + 15$$
$$= 30$$

## 2. E

Since we're told the value of $d$, we can substitute it into the equation $\frac{c}{d} = 3$ to find the value of $c$. We are told that $d = 1$, so $\frac{c}{d} = 3$ can be rewritten as $\frac{c}{1} = 3$. Since $\frac{c}{1}$ is the same as $c$, we can rewrite the equation again as $c = 3$. Now we can substitute the values of $c$ and $d$ into the expression $3c + d$ to get $3(3) + 1 = 10$.

## 3. D

We are told that $y = 8$, so first we'll substitute 8 for $y$, and then we can solve for $x$.

$$5x - 7 = y$$
$$5x - 7 = 8$$

Now we can add 7 to both sides:

$$5x - 7 + 7 = 8 + 7$$
$$5x = 15$$

Next we divide both sides by 5:

$$\frac{5x}{5} = \frac{15}{5}$$
$$x = 3$$

## 4. B

Here we have three values to substitute. Remember, $xz$ means $x$ times $z$. After we substitute the values of $x$, $y$, and $z$, we will do the operations in PEMDAS order—parentheses, exponents, multiplication and division, addition and subtraction.

$$x(y - 2) + xz = 2(5 - 2) + 2 \times 7$$
$$= 2(3) + 2 \times 7$$
$$= 6 + 14$$
$$= 20$$

## 5. B

This is another "plug-in" question. Remember, $5yz$ means $5 \times y \times z$. First, we will replace $x$, $y$, and $z$ with the values given. Then we will carry out the indicated operations using PEMDAS.

$$x^2 - 5yz + y^2 = (\sqrt{3})^2 - 5 \times 2 \times \frac{1}{2} + 2^2$$
$$= 3 - 5 \times 2 \times \frac{1}{2} + 4$$
$$= 3 - 5 + 4$$
$$= -2 + 4$$
$$= 2$$

## 6. C

If you look carefully at the expression $2x + 2y - 2$, you should see some similarity to $x + y = 7$. If we ignore the $-2$ for a moment, $2x + 2y$ is really just twice $x + y$. If it helps to make it clearer, we can factor out the 2, making $2x + 2y$ into $2(x + y)$. Since $x + y = 7$, $2(x + y)$ must equal $2(7)$, or 14. If we replace $2x + 2y$ with 14, the expression $2x + 2y - 2$ becomes $14 - 2$, which equals 12, (C).

## 7. C

This question is solved the same way as question 3.

Plug in 18 for $b$ in the equation:

$$3a - 6 = 18$$

Isolate $a$ on one side of the equation:

$$3a = 18 + 6$$

$$3a = 24$$

Divide both sides by 3 to find the value of $a$: $a = 8$.

**8. E**

Substitute 10 for $x$ in the equation:

$$\frac{10}{y} = \frac{2}{5}$$

Cross multiply:

$$(10)(5) = (2)(y)$$
$$50 = 2y$$

Divide both sides by 2 to find the value of $y$:

$$\frac{50}{2} = \frac{2y}{2}$$
$$25 = y$$

**9. A**

Distribute $-5n$ to each term within the parentheses:

$$-5n(3m - 2) = (-5n)(3m) + (-5n)(-2)$$

Multiply:

$$= -15mn + 10n$$

Note that $(-5n)(-2) = +10n$, because a negative times a negative yields a positive.

**10. B**

Plug $a = -1$ and $b = 3$ into the expression:

$$(-1 + 3)^2 = (2)^2 = 4$$

**11. E**

The expression can be rewritten as $3(s - t) + 3$.

Plug in 5 for $s - t$:

$$3(5) + 3 = 15 + 3$$
$$= 18$$

**12. D**

Distribute the minus sign over the terms in parentheses: $3d - 7 - 5 - (-2d)$. Combine like terms:

$$3d - (-2d) - 7 - 5$$
$$5d - 12$$

$3d$ minus $-2d$ equals $+5d$, because subtraction is equivalent to "addition of the opposite." So $3d - (-2d)$ becomes $3d + (+2d)$, which is equal to $5d$.

**13. C**

Plug in $x = -2$, $y = 3$, and $z = 1$:

$$(-2)(3)(1) + 3[(1 - (-2)] + 2(-2)$$
$$= -6 + 3(3) - 4$$
$$= -6 + 9 - 4$$
$$= 3 - 4$$
$$= -1$$

**14. C**

We have to rearrange the equation until the $x$ is alone on one side of the equal sign. You must do the same thing to both sides of the equation. First, we will take away the 7:

$$3x + 7 = 14$$
$$3x + 7 - 7 = 14 - 7$$
$$3x = 7$$
$$\frac{3x}{3} = \frac{7}{3}$$
$$x = \frac{7}{3}$$

**15. E**

Notice that the question asks which expression is always even. (E), $6x + 2$, is correct because, first, the product of an even number and any integer is even, so $6x$ is even because 6 is even. Then, when two even numbers are added, their sum is also even, so $6x + 2$ is even. (A) and (C) are always odd regardless of what integer is substituted for x. (B) and (D) are even only when $x$ is even.

**16. C**

We must rearrange the equation until the $z$ is alone on one side of the equal sign. Anything we do to one side of the equation we must also do to the other side. First, we'll add 3 to both sides:

$$4z - 3 = -19$$
$$4z - 3 + 3 = -19 + 3$$
$$4z = -16$$

Next, we'll divide both sides by 4:

$$\frac{4z}{4} = -\frac{16}{4}$$
$$z = -4$$

## 17. B

Rearrange the equation until the variable $a$ is alone on one side of the equal sign.

$$3ab = 6$$
$$\frac{3ab}{3} = \frac{6}{3}$$
$$ab = 2$$
$$\frac{ab}{b} = \frac{2}{b}$$
$$a = \frac{2}{b}$$

## 18. B

Try each answer choice until you find the correct one.

(A) xy = –1. If the product of two integers is negative, then one of the two integers must be negative. In this case, x could be negative, but it's possible that y is negative and x is positive. We're looking for an equation where x will always have to be negative.

(B) $xy^2$ = –1. The exponent here applies only to the y, not to the x. The square of any non-zero number is positive, so whatever y is, $y^2$ must be positive. (We know that y isn't zero; if it were, then the product $xy^2$ would also be zero.) Since $y^2$ is positive and the product of $y^2$ and x is negative, x must be negative. (B) is the answer.

## 19. B

We're told that $n$ is odd, so we don't have to check to see what happens if $n$ is even. We do have to try each answer to see which one represents an odd number. Let's say $n = 3$ and replace all the $n$s with 3s.

(A) 2n + 4. 2(3) + 4 = 6 + 4 = 10. 10 is even.

(B) 3n + 2. 3(3) + 2 = 9 + 2 = 11. 11 is odd, so (B) is the answer.

## 20. A

This equation takes a few more steps to solve than the previous ones, but it follows the same rules.

First, we multiply using the distributive law:

$$5p + 12 = 17 - 4\left(\frac{p}{2} + 1\right)$$
$$5p + 12 = 17 + (-4)\left(\frac{p}{2}\right) + (-4)(1)$$
$$5p + 12 = 17 + \left(-\frac{4p}{2}\right) + (-4)$$

$\left(-\frac{4p}{2}\right)$ is equal to $-2p$, so $5p + 12 = 17 - 2p - 4$

Combine the integers on the right side:

$$5p + 12 = 13 - 2p$$

We can add $2p$ to each side to get all the $p$s on one side:

$$5p + 2p + 12 = 13 - 2p + 2p$$
$$7p + 12 = 13$$

Now we will subtract 12 from both sides:

$$7p + 12 - 12 = 13 - 12$$
$$7p = 1$$

And lastly, we divide both sides by 7:

$$\frac{7p}{7} = \frac{1}{7}$$
$$p = \frac{1}{7}$$

### 21. A

We want to rearrange the equation until $y$ is alone on one side of the equal sign. There's more than one way to do this, but here's one way:

$$\frac{2x}{5y} = 6$$

$$(5y)\frac{2x}{5y} = 6(5y)$$

$$2x = 30y$$

$$\frac{2x}{30} = y$$

$$\frac{x}{15} = y$$

### 22. C

This is another "try each answer" problem. We know that $x$ is odd and $y$ is even. Let's say that $x = 3$ and $y = 4$.

(A) $2x + y$. $2(3) + 4 = 6 + 4 = 10$. 10 is even, so this isn't correct.

(B) $2(x + y)$. $2(3 + 4) = 2(3 + 4) = 2(7) = 14$. 14 is even.

(C) $x^2 + y^2$. $3^2 + 4^2 = 9 + 16 = 25$. 25 is odd, so (C) is correct.

### 23. A

This problem looks harder than it really is. If

$$100 \div x = 10n, \text{ then}$$

$$(10n)(x) = 100 \text{ or}$$

$$10nx = 100$$

$$nx = 10, \text{ (A)}$$

### 24. C

Multiply through and solve for $y$ by isolating it on one side of the equation:

$$4(y - 1) = 2(y + 2)$$

$$4y - 4 = 2y + 4$$

$$2y - 4 = 4$$

$$2y = 8$$

$$\frac{2y}{2} = \frac{8}{2}$$

$$y = 4$$

### 25. C

Isolate $x$ on one side of the equation:

$$\frac{3}{4} + x = 8.3$$

$$\frac{3}{4} + x - \frac{3}{4} = 8.3 - \frac{3}{4}$$

$$x = 8.3 - \frac{3}{4}$$

Then $\frac{3}{4}$ can be rewritten as 0.75, and subtracting 0.75 from 8.3 gives you 7.55.

### 26. E

Multiply through and find $a$ in terms of $m$ by isolating $a$ on one side of the equation:

$$2(a + m) = 5m - 3 + a$$

$$2a + 2m = 5m - 3 + a$$

$$2a = 3m - 3 + a$$

$$a = 3m - 3$$

# CHAPTER 13: GEOMETRY

Like the rest of the math you'll see on your private school admissions test, the geometry will range from straightforward to difficult. You can count on seeing questions that test your knowledge of lines and angles, triangles, circles, and other assorted geometric figures. You will also see a little coordinate geometry. And finally, diagramless geometry can also show up in the form of word problems.

The most helpful thing you can do is review geometry content and practice a whole lot. If you're concerned about your math readiness, spend more time with the subjects that are less familiar to you. Make certain that you do all of the problems in the practice set even if you feel comfortable with the example questions presented.

It's important to know that unless otherwise indicated, *figures are drawn to scale*. That means you can usually eyeball the measurements of a figure.

## LINES AND ANGLES

### LINE SEGMENTS

Some of the most basic geometry problems deal with line segments. A **line segment** is a piece of a line, and it has an exact measurable length. A question might give you a segment divided into several pieces, provide the measurements of some of these pieces, and ask you for the measurement of a remaining piece.

If $PR = 12$ and $QR = 4$, $PQ =$

$PQ = PR - QR$

$PQ = 12 - 4$

$PQ = 8$

The point exactly in the middle of a line segment, halfway between the endpoints, is called the **midpoint** of the line segment. To **bisect** means to cut in half, so the midpoint of a line segment bisects that line segment.

$M$ is the midpoint of $AB$, so $AM = MB$.

## ANGLES

A **right angle** measures 90 degrees and is usually indicated in a diagram by a little box. The figure above is a right angle. Lines that intersect to form right angles are said to be **perpendicular**.

Angles that form **a straight line add up to 180 degrees**. In the figure above, $a + b = 180$.

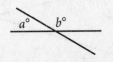

When two lines intersect, **adjacent angles are supplementary**, meaning they add up to 180 degrees. In the previous figure, $a + b = 180$.

**Angles around a point add up to 360 degrees.** In the figure above, $a + b + c + d + e = 360$.

When lines intersect, angles across the vertex from each other are called **vertical angles** and **are equal to each other**. Above, $a = c$ and $b = d$.

### PARALLEL LINES

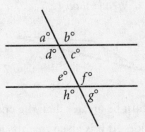

When parallel lines are crossed by a transversal:

- Corresponding angles are equal (for example, $a = e$).
- Alternate interior angles are equal ($d = f$).
- Same-side interior angles are supplementary ($c + f = 180$).
- All four acute angles are equal, as are all four obtuse angles.

## TRIANGLES

There are a few basic rules that apply to triangles in general.

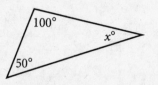

The three interior angles of any triangle add up to 180°. In the previous figure, $x + 50 + 100 = 180$, so $x = 30$.

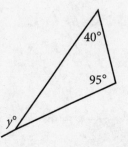

An exterior angle equals the sum of the remote interior angles. In the figure above, the exterior angle labeled $y°$ equals the sum of the remote interior angles: $y = 40 + 95 = 135$.

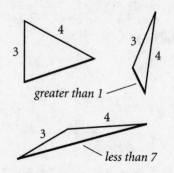

The length of one side of a triangle must be greater than the positive difference and less than the sum of the lengths of the other two sides. If it is given that the length of one side is 3 and the length of another side is 4, then the length of the third side must be greater than $4 - 3 = 1$ and less than $4 + 3 = 7$.

## TRIANGLES—PERIMETER AND AREA

The **perimeter** of a triangle is the sum of the lengths of its sides.

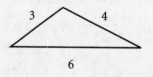

The perimeter of the triangle in the figure above is $3 + 4 + 6 = 13$.

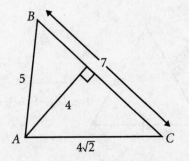

The **area** of a triangle is one-half base times height. The height is the perpendicular distance between the side that's chosen as the base and the opposite vertex. In this triangle, 4 is the height when the 7 is chosen as the base.

$$\text{Area} = \frac{1}{2}\,bh = \frac{1}{2}(7)(4) = 14$$

Be careful! Many students assume that the height and base are 5 and $4\sqrt{2}$. However, notice that there is no symbol indicating that those two sides are perpendicular. Look for the 90° sign in a figure to isolate the base and height.

## SIMILAR TRIANGLES

Similar triangles have the same shape: **Corresponding angles are equal, and corresponding sides are proportional.**

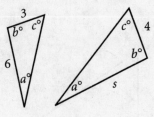

These triangles are similar because they have the same angles. The 3 corresponds to the 4, and the 6 corresponds to the *s*.

$$\frac{3}{4} = \frac{6}{s}$$
$$3s = 24$$
$$s = 8$$

## SPECIAL TRIANGLES

Special triangles are the isosceles, equilateral, and right triangles.

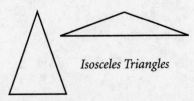

*Isosceles Triangles*

An **isosceles triangle** is a triangle that has two equal sides. Not only are two sides equal, but the angles opposite the equal sides, called base angles, are also equal.

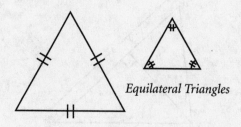

*Equilateral Triangles*

**Equilateral triangles** are triangles in which all three sides are equal. Since all the sides are equal, all the angles are also equal. All three angles in an equilateral triangle measure 60 degrees, regardless of the lengths of the sides.

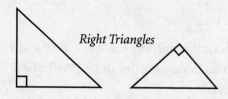

*Right Triangles*

A **right triangle** is a triangle with a right angle. Every right triangle has exactly two acute angles. The sides opposite the acute angles are called the **legs**. The side opposite the right angle is called the **hypotenuse**. Since it's opposite the largest angle, the hypotenuse is the longest side of a right triangle.

## RIGHT TRIANGLES

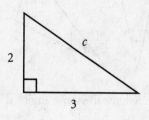

### PYTHAGOREAN THEOREM

The Pythagorean theorem is as follows:

$$(\text{leg}_1)^2 + (\text{leg}_2)^2 = (\text{hypotenuse})^2 \text{ or } a^2 + b^2 = c^2$$

If one leg is 2 and the other leg is 3, then

$$2^2 + 3^2 = c^2$$
$$c^2 = 4 + 9$$
$$c = \sqrt{13}$$

### PYTHAGOREAN "TRIPLETS"

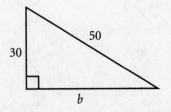

If a right triangle's leg-to-leg ratio is 3:4, or if the leg-to-hypotenuse ratio is 3:5 or 4:5, it's a 3-4-5 triangle and you don't need to use the Pythagorean theorem to find the third side. Just figure out what multiple of 3-4-5 it is. In this right triangle, one leg is 30 and the hypotenuse is 50. This is 10 times 3-4-5. The other leg, $b$, is 40.

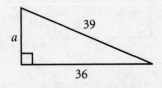

If a right triangle's leg-to-leg ratio is 5:12, or if the leg-to-hypotenuse ratio is 5:13 or 12:13, then it's a **5-12-13 triangle** and you don't need to use the Pythagorean theorem to find the third side. Just figure out what multiple of 5-12-13 it is. Here one leg is 36 and the hypotenuse is 39. This is 3 times 5-12-13. The other leg, $a$, is 15.

## SIDE-ANGLE RATIOS

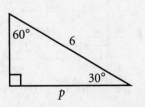

The sides of a 30-60-90 triangle are in a ratio of $x : x\sqrt{3} : 2x$. You don't need to use the Pythagorean theorem. If the hypotenuse is 6, then the shorter leg is half that, or 3; and then the longer leg, $p$, is equal to the short leg times $\sqrt{3}$, or $3\sqrt{3}$.

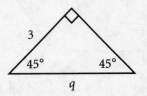

The sides of a 45-45-90 triangle are in a ratio of $x : x : x\sqrt{2}$. If one leg is 3, then the other leg is also 3, and the hypotenuse, $q$, is equal to a leg multiplied by $\sqrt{2}$, or $3\sqrt{2}$.

# QUADRILATERALS

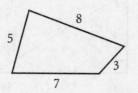

The **perimeter** of a polygon is the sum of the lengths of its sides. The perimeter of the quadrilateral in the figure above is $5 + 8 + 3 + 7 = 23$.

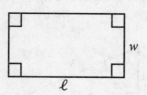

A **rectangle** is a parallelogram containing four right angles. Opposite sides are equal. The formula for the area of a rectangle is

**Area = (length)(width)**

In the figure above, $\ell$ = length and $w$ = width, so area = $\ell w$. Perimeter = $2(\ell + w)$.

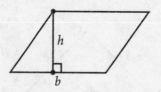

A **square** is a rectangle with four equal sides. The formula for the area of a square is

**Area = (side)$^2$**

In the figure above, $s$ = the length of a side, so area = $s^2$. Perimeter = $4s$.

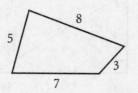

A **parallelogram** is a quadrilateral with two sets of parallel sides. Opposite sides are equal, as are opposite angles. The formula for the area of a parallelogram is

**Area = (base)(height)**

In the previous diagram, $h$ = height and $b$ = base, so area = $bh$.

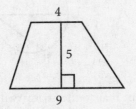

A **trapezoid** is a quadrilateral with one pair of parallel sides. The formula for the area of a trapezoid is

**Area = $\frac{1}{2}$ (sum of the lengths of the parallel sides)(height)**

In the figure above, the area of the trapezoid is $\frac{1}{2}(4 + 9)(5) = 32.5$

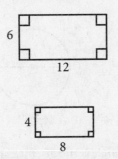

If two polygons are similar, then corresponding angles are equal and corresponding sides are in proportion.

The two rectangles above are similar because all the angles are right angles and each side of the larger rectangle is $1\frac{1}{2}$ times the corresponding side of the smaller.

# CIRCLES

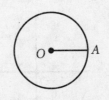

A **circle** is a figure each point of which is an equal distance from its center. In the diagram, $O$ is the center of the circle.

The **radius** of a circle is the straight-line distance from its center to any point on the circle. All radii of one circle have equal lengths. In the previous figure, $OA$ is a radius of circle $O$.

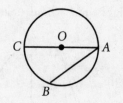

A **chord** is a line segment that connects any two points on a circle. Segments *AB* and *AC* are both chords. The largest chord that may be drawn in a circle will be a diameter of that circle.

A **diameter** of a circle is a chord that passes through the circle's center. All diameters are the same length and are equal to twice the radius. In the figure above, *AC* is a diameter of circle *O*.

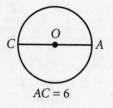

$AC = 6$

The **circumference** of a circle is the distance around it. It is equal to $\pi d$, or $2\pi r$. In this example, circumference = $\pi d = 6\pi$.

The **area** of a circle equals $\pi$ times the square of the radius, or $\pi r^2$. In this example, since *AC* is the diameter, $r = \dfrac{6}{2} = 3$, and area = $\pi r^2 = \pi(3^2) = 9\pi$.

## COORDINATE GEOMETRY

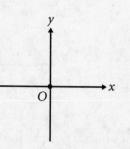

The previous diagram represents the **coordinate axes**—the perpendicular "number lines" in the coordinate plane. The horizontal line is called the **x-axis.** The vertical

> ### WHAT'S $\pi$?
>
> " $\pi$ is an infinite and nonrepeating decimal, but all you need to remember is that it's approximately 3.14. "

line is called the **y-axis**. In a coordinate plane, the point *O* at which the two axes intersect is called the **origin**.

The pair of numbers, written inside parentheses, that specify the location of a point in the coordinate plane are called **coordinates**. The first number is the **x-coordinate**, and the second number is the **y-coordinate**. The **origin** is the zero point on both axes, with coordinates (0, 0).

Starting at the origin:

| to the right: | *x* is positive. |
| to the left: | *x* is negative. |
| up: | *y* is positive. |
| down: | *y* is negative. |

The two axes divide the coordinate plane into four quadrants. When you know what quadrant a point lies in, you know the signs of its coordinates. A point in the upper left quadrant, for example, has a negative *x*-coordinate and a positive *y*-coordinate.

$$
\begin{array}{c|c}
\text{II} & \text{I} \\
(-,+) & (+,+) \\
\hline
(-,-) & (+,-) \\
\text{III} & \text{IV}
\end{array}
$$

## PLOTTING POINTS

If you were asked to graph the point (2, –3) you would start at the origin and count 2 units to the right and 3 down. To graph (–4, 5) you would start at the origin and go 4 units to the left and 5 units up.

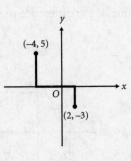

## SLOPE OF A LINE

To use two points to find the **slope of a line**, use the following formula:

$$\text{Slope} = \frac{\text{change in } y}{\text{change in } x} \text{ or slope} = \frac{y}{x} \text{ or } \frac{y_2 - y_1}{x_2 - x_1}.$$

### EXAMPLE

Calculate the slope of a line that contains the points $A(4, 6)$ and $B(0, -3)$.

$$\frac{y_2 - y_1}{x_2 - x_1} = \frac{-3 - 6}{0 - 4} = \frac{-9}{-4} = \frac{9}{4}$$

To use an equation of a line to find the slope, put the equation into the **slope-intercept form**:

$y = mx + b$, where the slope is $m$

### EXAMPLE

To find the slope of the equation $5x + 3y = 6$, rearrange it:

$5x + 3y = 6$

$3y = -5x + 6$      Subtract $5x$ from both sides of the equation.

$y = -\frac{5}{3}x + 2$      Isolate $y$ by dividing by 3.

The slope is $-\frac{5}{3}$.

## FIGURING LENGTHS

To find the length of a line segment **parallel to the *x*-axis** in the coordinate plane, calculate the absolute value of the difference of its $x$-coordinates.

To find the length of a line segment **parallel to the *y*-axis** in the coordinate plane, calculate the absolute value of the difference of its $y$-coordinates.

### EXAMPLE

**KAPLAN
EXCLUSIVE TIPS**

Length is always positive.

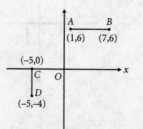

In the figure above, the length of $AB$ is $|7 - 1| = 6$. The length of $CD$ is $|0 - (-4)| = 4$.

## RETRACING A GEOMETRIC FIGURE

Some geometry questions ask you to determine whether a figure can be drawn without lifting the pencil. There's a simple rule for determining this: In any given figure, if exactly zero or two points have an odd number of intersecting line segments and/or curves, it can be drawn without lifting the pencil or retracing.

**EXAMPLE**

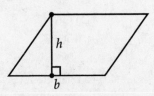

The figure above has two points that have three intersecting lines (an odd number), so it can be drawn without lifting your pencil.

# PRACTICE QUESTIONS

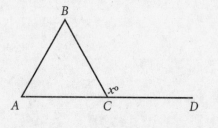

1. In the figure above, segments AB, BC, CD, and AC are all equal. What is the value of x?

   (A) 30
   (B) 45
   (C) 60
   (D) 90
   (E) 120

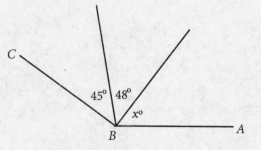

2. If the measure of angle ABC is 145°, what is the value of x?

   (A) 39
   (B) 45
   (C) 52
   (D) 55
   (E) 62

3. If the perimeter of a square is 32 meters, what is the area of the square, in square meters?

   (A) 16
   (B) 32
   (C) 48
   (D) 56
   (E) 64

4. In triangle XYZ the measure of angle Y is twice the measure of angle X, and the measure of Z is three times the measure of angle X. What is the degree measure of angle Y?

   (A) 15
   (B) 30
   (C) 45
   (D) 60
   (E) 90

5. The perimeter of triangle ABC is 24. If AB = 9 and BC = 7, then AC =

   (A) 6
   (B) 8
   (C) 10
   (D) 15
   (E) 17

6.  If the perimeter of an equilateral triangle is 150, what is the length of one of its sides?

    (A)  35

    (B)  40

    (C)  50

    (D)  75

    (E)  100

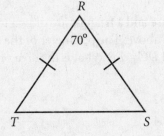

7.  In triangle *RST*, if *RS* = *RT*, what is the degree measure of angle *S*?

    (A)  40

    (B)  55

    (C)  70

    (D)  110

    (E)  It cannot be determined from the information given.

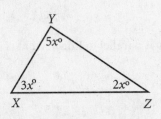

8.  In triangle *XYZ*, what is the degree measure of angle *YXZ*?

    (A)  18

    (B)  36

    (C)  54

    (D)  72

    (E)  90

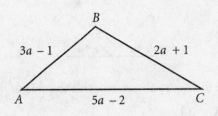

9.  If the perimeter of triangle *ABC* is 18, what is the length of *AC*?

    (A)  2

    (B)  4

    (C)  5

    (D)  6

    (E)  8

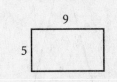

10. What is the area, in square units, of a square that has the same perimeter as the rectangle above?

    (A)  25

    (B)  36

    (C)  49

    (D)  64

    (E)  81

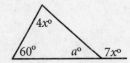

11. What is the value of *a* in the figure above?

    (A)  20

    (B)  40

    (C)  60

    (D)  80

    (E)  140

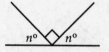

12. In the figure above, what is the value of *n*?

   (A)   30
   (B)   60
   (C)   45
   (D)   90
   (E)   135

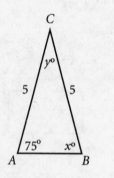

13. In the figure above, what is the value of $x - y$?

   (A)   30
   (B)   45
   (C)   75
   (D)   105
   (E)   150

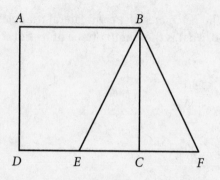

14. A square and a triangle are drawn together as shown above. The perimeter of the square is 64 and $DC = EF$. What is the area of triangle *BEF*?

   (A)   32
   (B)   64
   (C)   128
   (D)   256
   (E)   It cannot be determined from the information given.

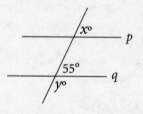

15. If line *p* is parallel to line *q*, what is the value of $x + y$?

   (A)   90
   (B)   110
   (C)   125
   (D)   180
   (E)   250

$2\sqrt{2}$

16. What is the area of the square above?

(A)  4

(B)  $4\sqrt{2}$

(C)  8

(D)  16

(E)  24

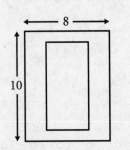

17. What is the area of the frame in the figure above if the inside picture has a length of 8 and a width of 4?

(A)  4

(B)  8

(C)  16

(D)  24

(E)  48

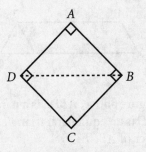

18. In the figure above, *ABCD* is a square, and the area of triangle *ABD* is 8. What is the area of square *ABCD*?

(A)  2

(B)  4

(C)  8

(D)  16

(E)  64

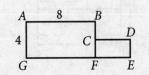

Note: Figure not drawn to scale.

19. In the figure above, *ABFG* and *CDEF* are rectangles, *CD* bisects *BF*, and *EF* has a length of 2. What is the area of the entire figure?

(A)  4

(B)  16

(C)  32

(D)  36

(E)  72

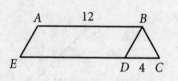

20. In the figure above, *ABDE* is a parallelogram, and *BCD* is an equilateral triangle. What is the perimeter of *ABCE*?

(A) 12

(B) 16

(C) 24

(D) 32

(E) 36

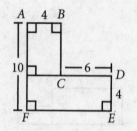

21. In the figure above, what is the perimeter of *ABCDEF*?

(A) 14

(B) 24

(C) 28

(D) 38

(E) 40

22. If the shaded regions are 4 rectangles, what is the area of the unshaded region?

(A)  9

(B)  12

(C)  16

(D)  19

(E)  20

```
A    B    C    D    E
•────•────•────•────•
```

Note: Figure not drawn to scale.

23. In the figure above, *AB* is twice the length of *BC*, *BC* = *CD*, and *DE* is triple the length of *CD*. If *AE* = 49, what is the length of *BD*?

(A) 14

(B) 21

(C) 28

(D) 30

(E) 35

8 inches

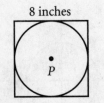

24. In the figure above, circle *P* is inscribed in a square with sides of 8 inches. What is the area of the circle?

(A) 4π square inches

(B) 16 square inches

(C) 8π square inches

(D) 16π square inches

(E) 32π square inches

25. What is the radius of a circle whose circumference is 36π?

(A) 3

(B) 6

(C) 8

(D) 18

(E) 36

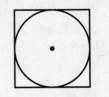

26. If the perimeter of the square is 36, what is the circumference of the circle?

(A) 6π

(B) 9π

(C) 12π

(D) 15π

(E) 18π

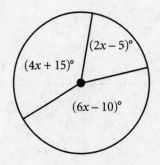

27. In the figure above, what is the value of *x*?

(A) 15

(B) 30

(C) 55

(D) 70

(E) 135

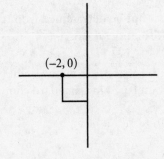

(−2, 0)

28. In the figure above, a square is graphed on the coordinate plane. If the coordinates of one corner are (−2, 0), what is the area of the square?

(A) $\frac{1}{4}$

(B) 1

(C) 2

(D) 4

(E) 16

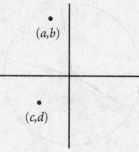

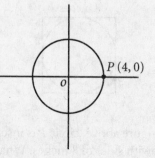

29. Points $(a, b)$ and $(c, d)$ are graphed in the coordinate plane as shown above. Which of the following statements MUST be true?

(A) $bd > ac$

(B) $c > ad$

(C) $b > acd$

(D) $bc > ad$

(E) It cannot be determined from the information given.

30. What is the distance from the point $(0, 6)$ to the point $(0, 8)$ in a standard coordinate plane?

(A) 2

(B) 7

(C) 10

(D) 12

(E) 14

31. Circle $O$ above has its center at the origin. If point $P$ lies on circle $O$, what is the area of circle $O$?

(A) $4\pi$

(B) $8\pi$

(C) $10\pi$

(D) $12\pi$

(E) $16\pi$

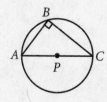

32. In the figure above, right triangle $ABC$ is inscribed in circle $P$, with $AC$ passing through center $P$. If $AB = 6$, and $BC = 8$, what is the area of the circle?

(A) $10\pi$

(B) $14\pi$

(C) $25\pi$

(D) $49\pi$

(E) $100\pi$

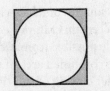

33. In the figure above, a circle is inscribed within a square. If the area of the circle is 25π, what is the perimeter of the shaded region?

   (A)   40 + 5π
   (B)   40 + 10π
   (C)  100 + 10π
   (D)  100 + 25π
   (E)   40 + 50π

34. What is the slope of the line that contains points (3, −5) and (−1, 7)?

   (A)  −3
   (B)  $-\dfrac{1}{3}$
   (C)  $-\dfrac{1}{4}$
   (D)  $\dfrac{1}{3}$
   (E)   3

35. If the circumference of a circle is 16π, what is its area?

   (A)    8π
   (B)   16π
   (C)   32π
   (D)   64π
   (E)  256π

36. What is the area of the square above with diagonals of length 6?

   (A)   9
   (B)  12
   (C)  $9\sqrt{2}$
   (D)  15
   (E)  18

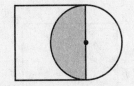

37. A square and a circle are drawn as shown above. The area of the square is 64. What is the area of the shaded region?

   (A)   4π
   (B)   8π
   (C)  16π
   (D)  32π
   (E)  It cannot be determined from the information given.

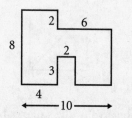

**38.** What is the area of the polygon above if each corner of the polygon is a right angle?

(A) 40

(B) 62

(C) 68

(D) 74

(E) 80

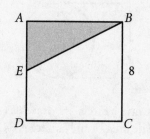

**39.** *ABCD* is a square. If *E* is the midpoint of *AD*, what is the area of the shaded region?

(A) 8

(B) 12

(C) 16

(D) 24

(E) 32

**40.** Circle *A* has radius *r* + 1. Circle *B* has radius *r* + 2. What is the positive difference between the circumference of circle *B* and the circumference of circle *A*?

(A) 1

(B) 2π

(C) 2π + 3

(D) 2π*r* + 3

(E) 2π(2*r* + 3)

**41.** Erica has 8 squares of felt, each with an area of 16. For a certain craft project, she cuts the largest circle possible from each square of felt. What is the combined area of the excess felt left over after cutting out all the circles?

(A) 4(4 − π)

(B) 8(4 − π)

(C) 8(π − 2)

(D) 32(4 − π)

(E) 8(16 − π)

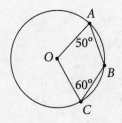

**42.** In the figure above, points *A*, *B*, and *C* lie on the circumference of the circle centered at *O*. If ∠*OAB* measures 50° and ∠*BCO* measures 60°, what is the degree measure of ∠*AOC*?

(A) 110

(B) 125

(C) 140

(D) 250

(E) It cannot be determined from the information given.

# PRACTICE QUESTION ANSWERS

**1. E**

Since $AB = BC = AC$, triangle $ABC$ is equilateral. Therefore, all of its angles are 60°. Since angle $BCD$ or $x$ is supplementary to angle $BCA$, a 60° angle, the value of $x$ is $180 - 60$ or 120.

**2. C**

Since the degree measure of angle $ABC$ is 145, $45 + 48 + x = 145$, $93 + x = 145$, and $x = 52$.

**3. E**

A square has four equal sides, so its perimeter is equal to $4s$, where $s$ is the length of a side of the square. Its perimeter is 32, so its side length is $32 \div 4 = 8$. The area of a square is equal to $s^2$, so the area of the square is $8^2$ or 64.

**4. D**

In any triangle, the measures of the three interior angles sum to 180°, so $X + Y + Z = 180$. Since the measure of angle $Y$ is twice the measure of angle $X$, $Y = 2X$. Similarly, $Z = 3X$. So $X + 2X + 3X = 180$, $6X = 180$ and $X = 30$. Since $Y = 2X$, the degree measure of angle $Y$ is $2 \times 30 = 60$.

**5. B**

The perimeter of a triangle is the sum of the lengths of its sides, in this case, $AB + BC + AC$. The perimeter of triangle $ABC$ is 24, so plugging in the given values, $9 + 7 + AC = 24$, $16 + AC = 24$, and $AC = 8$.

**6. C**

In an equilateral triangle, all three sides have equal length. The perimeter of a triangle is equal to the sum of the lengths of its three sides. Since all three sides are equal, each side must be $\frac{1}{3}$ of 150, or 50.

**7. B**

Since $RS$ and $RT$ are equal, the angles opposite them must be equal. Therefore, angle $T$ = angle $S$. Since the three angles of a triangle sum to 180, $70 + $ angle $S + $ angle $T = 180$ and angle $S + $ angle $T = 110$. Since the two angles, $S$ and $T$, are equal, each must be half of 110, or 55.

**8. C**

The three interior angles of a triangle add up to 180 degrees, so $2x + 3x + 5x = 180$, $10x = 180$ degrees and $x = 18$. So angle $YXZ$ has a degree measure of $3x = 3(18) = 54$.

**9. E**

The perimeter of triangle $ABC$ is 18, so $AB + BC + AC = 18$. Plugging in the algebraic expressions given for the length of each side, you get:

$$(3a - 1) + (2a + 1) + (5a - 2) = 18$$
$$10a - 2 = 18$$
$$10a = 20$$
$$a = 2$$

The length of $AC$ is given as $5a - 2$, so $AC = 5(2) - 2 = 8$.

**10. C**

The perimeter of a rectangle is $2(\ell + w)$, where $\ell$ represents its length and $w$ its width. The perimeter of this rectangle is $2(9 + 5) = 28$. A square has four equal sides, so a square with a perimeter of 28 has sides of length 7. The area of a square is equal to the length of a side squared, so the area of a square with a perimeter of 28 is $7^2$ or 49.

**11. B**

An exterior angle of a triangle equals the sum of the two remote interior angles. So $7x = 4x + 60$, $3x = 60$, and $x = 20$. So the angle marked $7x°$ has a degree measure of $7(20) = 140$. The angle marked $a°$ is supplementary to this angle, so its measure is $180 - 140 = 40$.

## 12. C

We are given a right angle, so that is $90°$. A straight angle contains $180°$, so $2n + 90 = 180$, $2n = 90$, and $n = 45$.

## 13. B

Since $AC = CB$, the angles opposite these sides are equal as well. So angle $CAB$ = angle $CBA$, and $x = 75$. The three interior angles of a triangle sum to 180 degrees, so $2(75) + y = 180$ and $y = 30$. The question asks for the value of $x - y$, or $75 - 30 = 45$.

## 14. C

The area of a triangle is equal to $\frac{1}{2}bh$. In triangle $BEF$, the height is $BC$ and the base is $EF$. The square's perimeter is 64, so each of its sides is a fourth of 64, or 16. Therefore, $BC = 16$. The question also states that $DC = EF$, so $EF = 16$ as well. Plugging into the formula, the area of triangle $BEF$ is $\frac{1}{2}(16 \times 16) = 128$.

## 15. D

When parallel lines are crossed by a transversal, all acute angles formed are equal, and all acute angles are supplementary to all obtuse angles. So in this diagram, the obtuse angle measuring $y°$ is supplementary to the acute angle measuring $x°$, so $x + y = 180$.

## 16. C

The area of a square is equal to the square of one of its sides. In this case, the square has a side length of $2\sqrt{2}$, so its area is $(2\sqrt{2})^2$ or $2 \times 2 \times \sqrt{2} \times \sqrt{2}$ or $4 \times 2 = 8$.

## 17. E

To find the area of the frame, find the area of the frame and picture combined (the outer rectangle) and subtract from it the area of the picture (the inner rectangle). The outer rectangle has area $10 \times 8 = 80$, the inner rectangle has area $8 \times 4 = 32$, so the area of the frame is $80 - 32 = 48$.

## 18. D

Diagonal $BD$ divides square $ABCD$ into two identical triangles. If the area of triangle $ABD$ is 8, the area of the square must be twice this, or 16.

## 19. D

The area of the entire figure is equal to the area of rectangle $ABFG$ plus the area of rectangle $CDEF$. The area of $ABFG$ is $8 \times 4 = 32$. So the area of the entire figure must be greater than 32, and at this point you can eliminate (A), (B), and (C). Since $BF$ has length 4, and $C$ bisects $BF$, $CF$ has length 2. The question states that $EF$ has length 2, so $CDEF$ is actually a square, and its area is $2^2$ or 4. So the area of the entire figure is $32 + 4 = 36$, choice (D).

## 20. E

The perimeter of $ABCE$ is equal to $AB + BC + CD + DE + EA$. Since triangle $BCD$ is equilateral, $BC = CD = BD = 4$. Because $ABDE$ is a parallelogram, $AB = DE = 12$ and $BD = EA = 4$. Therefore, the perimeter of $ABCE$ is $12 + 4 + 4 + 12 + 4 = 36$, choice (E).

## 21. E

Simply add the six sides of the L-shaped figure. Four of them are labeled, and you can use these to figure out the remaining two. The length of side *EF* must be equivalent to the sum of sides *AB* and *CD*, so 4 + 6 = 10 and *EF* = 10. The length of side *BC* is equivalent to the difference between sides *AF* and *DE*, so 10 − 4 = 6 and *BC* = 6. Therefore, the perimeter is 10 + 10 + 4 + 6 + 6 + 4 = 40.

## 22. A

Each of the shaded rectangles has a side of length 3 opposite the side contributing to the interior unshaded region. So the interior region, a square, has an area of $3^2$, or 9.

## 23. A

Let *BC* = *x*. *AB* has twice the length of *BC*, so it is 2*x*. *BC* = *CD*, so *CD* = *x*. *DE* is three times the length of *CD*, or 3*x*. Since *AE* = 49, 2*x* + *x* + *x* + 3*x* = 49, 7*x* = 49, and *x* = 7. *BD* is composed of segments *BC* and *CD*, so its length is 7 + 7 = 14.

## 24. D

Since circle *P* is inscribed within the square, its diameter is equal in length to a side of the square. Since the circle's diameter is 8, its radius is half this, or 4. Area of a circle = $\pi r^2$, where *r* is the radius, so the area of circle *P* is $\pi(4)^2 = 16\pi$ square inches.

## 25. D

Circumference of a circle = $2\pi r$, where *r* is the radius of the circle. So a circle with a circumference of 36π has a radius of $\frac{36\cancel{\pi}}{2\cancel{\pi}} = 18$.

## 26. B

The perimeter of the square is 36, and since all four sides are equal, one side has length 9. Since the circle is inscribed in the square, its diameter is equal in length to a side of the square, or 9. Circumference is π*d*, where *d* represents the diameter, so the circumference of the circle is 9π.

## 27. B

A circle contains 360°, so:

$$(4x + 15) + (2x - 5) + (6x - 10) = 360$$
$$4x + 2x + 6x + 15 - 5 - 10 = 360$$
$$12x = 360$$
$$x = 30$$

## 28. D

The area of a square is equal to the square of the length of one of its sides. Since one vertex (corner) of the square lies on the origin at (0, 0) and another vertex lies on the point (−2, 0), the length of a side of the square is the distance from the origin to the point (−2, 0). This can be found by calculating the absolute value of the difference between the *x*-coordinates of the points, namely |−2 − 0| = |−2| = 2. Therefore, the area of the square is $2^2 = 4$.

## 29. C

While there's no way to determine the numerical values of *a*, *b*, *c*, or *d*, from their positions on the coordinate plane, you do know that *a* is negative, *b* is positive, *c* is negative, and *d* is negative. Bearing in mind that a negative times a negative is a positive, consider each answer choice. (C) is indeed true: *b*, which is positive, is greater than the product *acd*, which is negative.

### 30. A

The points (0, 6) and (0, 8) have the same x-coordinate. That means that the segment that connects them is parallel to the y-axis. Therefore, all you have to do to figure out the distance is subtract the y-coordinate and find the absolute value of the difference. $|8 - 6| = 2$, so the distance between the points is 2.

### 31. E

$OP$ is the radius of the circle. Since $O$ has coordinates (0, 0), the length of $OP$ is $|4 - 0| = |4| = 4$. The area of a circle is $\pi r^2$ where $r$ is the radius, so the area of circle $O$ is $\pi(4)^2 = 16\pi$.

### 32. C

Right triangle $ABC$ has legs of 6 and 8, so the legs are in a ratio of 3:4 and the triangle is a multiple of the 3-4-5 right triangle. Since the $3 \times 2 = 6$ and $4 \times 2 = 8$, double the hypotenuse length of 5, and the hypotenuse of triangle $ABC$ equals 10. Notice that the hypotenuse is also the diameter of the circle. To find the area of the circle, we need its radius. Radius is half the diameter, so the radius of circle $P$ is 5. The area of a circle is $\pi r^2$ where $r$ is the radius, so the area of circle $P$ is $\pi(5)^2 = 25\pi$.

### 33. B

The area of a circle is $\pi r^2$ where $r$ is the radius, and since the area of the circle is $25\pi$, its radius is 5. Circumference is equal to $2\pi r$, or $2\pi(5) = 10\pi$. Only (B) and (C) contain $10\pi$, so you can eliminate (A), (D), and (E). Since the circle is inscribed within the square, its diameter is equal to a side of the square. The diameter of the circle is $2r$ or 10, so a side of the square is 10 and its perimeter is $4(10) = 40$. Therefore, the perimeter of the shaded region is $40 + 10\pi$, choice (B).

### 34. A

Slope of a line is defined by the formula $\dfrac{y_2 - y_1}{x_2 - x_1}$, where $(x_1, y_1)$ and $(x_2, y_2)$ represent two points on the line. Substitute the given coordinates into the formula (it doesn't matter which you designate as point 1 or point 2; just be consistent):

$$\text{slope} = \frac{y_2 - y_1}{x_2 - x_1} = \frac{7 - (-5)}{-1 - 3}$$

$$= \frac{12}{-4}$$

$$= -3$$

### 35. D

The circumference of a circle is $2\pi r$, where $r$ is the radius, so a circle whose circumference is $16\pi$ has a radius of $\dfrac{16\pi}{2\pi} = 8$. The area of a circle is $\pi r^2$, so in this case the area is $\pi(8)^2 = 64\pi$, (D).

### 36. E

Since all sides of a square are equal, notice that the diagonal of the square is also the hypotenuse of an isosceles right triangle. Use this information to determine the length of a side of the square, marked $s$ in the figure. The ratio of the sides in such a triangle is $x : x : x\sqrt{2}$. Since $x\sqrt{2}$ represents the hypotenuse, which is equal to 6, solve the equation $x\sqrt{2} = 6$. Divide by $\sqrt{2}$ to get $x = \dfrac{6}{\sqrt{2}}$. So the length of a side of the square is $\dfrac{6}{\sqrt{2}}$. The area of a square is therefore $\left(\dfrac{6}{\sqrt{2}}\right)^2 = \dfrac{36}{2} = 18$.

**37. B**

The shaded region represents one-half the area of the circle. Find the length of the radius to determine this area. Notice that the diameter of the circle is equal to a side of the square. Since the area of the square is 64, it has a side length of 8 (because $8^2 = 64$). So the diameter of the circle is 8, and its radius is 4. The area of the circle is $\pi r^2$, or $\pi(4)^2 = 16\pi$. This isn't the answer though; the shaded region is only half the circle, so its area is $8\pi$.

**38. B**

Think of the figure as a rectangle with two rectangular bites taken out of it. Sketch in lines to make one large rectangle (see diagram below):

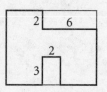

Now find the area of the large rectangle, and subtract the areas of the two rectangular pieces that weren't in the original figure. The area of a rectangle is length times width. Since the length of the large rectangle is 10, and its width is 8, its area is $10 \times 8 = 80$. The rectangular bite taken out of the top right corner has dimensions 6 and 2, so its area is $6 \times 2$ or 12. The bite taken out of the bottom has dimensions 2 and 3, so its area is $2 \times 3 = 6$. To find the area of the polygon, subtract the areas of the two bites from the area of the large rectangle: $80 - (12 + 6) = 80 - 18 = 62$, (B).

**39. C**

Since *ABCD* is a square, all four sides have the same length, and the corners meet at right angles. The area you're looking for is that of a triangle, and since all corners of the square are right angles, angle *EAB* is a right angle, which makes triangle *EAB* a right triangle. The area of a right triangle is $\frac{1}{2}(\text{leg}_1)(\text{leg}_2)$. The diagram shows that *BC* has length 8, so *AB* = *AD* = 8. Point *E* is the midpoint of *AD*, so *AE* is 4. Now that you have the lengths of both legs, you can substitute into the formula: $\frac{1}{2}(AB)(AE) = \frac{1}{2}(8)(4) = 16$, (C).

**40. B**

The circumference of a circle is equal to $2\pi r$, where *r* is the radius. The circumference of circle *A* is $2\pi(r + 1) = 2\pi r + 2\pi$. The circumference of circle *B* is $2\pi(r + 2) = 2\pi r + 4\pi$. So the positive difference between the two circumferences is simply $2\pi$.

**41. D**

A square with area 16 has sides of length 4. Therefore, the largest circle that could possibly be cut from such a square would have a diameter of 4.

Such a circle would have a radius of 2, making its area $\pi(2)^2 = 4\pi$. So the amount of felt left after cutting such a circle from one of the squares of felt would be $16 - 4\pi$, or $4(4 - \pi)$. There are 8 such squares, so the total area of the leftover felt is $8 \times 4(4 - \pi) = 32(4 - \pi)$, (D).

**42. C**

The key to solving this problem is to draw in *OB*:

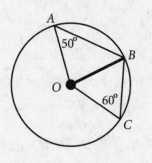

Because *OA*, *OB*, and *OC* are all radii of the same circle, triangle *AOB* and triangle *BOC* are both isosceles triangles, each therefore having equal base angles:

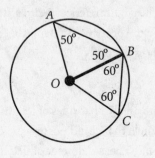

Using the fact that the three interior angles of a triangle add up to 180°, you can figure out that the vertex angles measure 80° and 60° as shown:

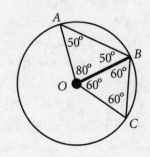

Angle *AOC* measures 80 + 60 = 140, (C).

# CHAPTER 14: WORD PROBLEMS

Word Problems. Two simple words that evoke more fear and loathing than most other math concepts and question types combined.

When the subject of word problems arises, you might envision the following nightmare:

> Two trains are loaded with equal amounts of rock salt and ball bearings. Train A leaves Frogboro at 10:00 A.M. carrying 62 passengers. Train B leaves Toadville at 11:30 A.M. carrying 104 passengers. If Train A is traveling at a speed of 85 mph and makes four stops, and Train B is traveling at an average speed of 86 mph and makes three stops, and the trains both arrive at Lizard Hollow at 4:30 P.M., what is the average weight of the passengers on Train B?

The good news is that you won't see anything this ugly. SSAT and ISEE word problems are pretty straightforward. Generally, all you have to do is translate the prose to math and solve.

The bad news is that you can expect to see a lot of word problems on your test. Keep in mind that, while word problems are generally algebra problems, they can contain other math concepts.

## TRANSLATION

Many word problems seem tricky because it's hard to figure out what they're asking. It can be difficult to translate English into math. The following table lists some common words and phrases that turn up in word problems, along with their mathematical translations.

| When you see: | Think: |
|---|---|
| sum, plus, more than, added to, combined total | + |
| minus, less than, difference between, decreased by | − |
| is, was, equals, is equivalent to, is the same as, adds up to | = |
| times, product, multiplied by, of, twice, double, triple | × |
| divided by, over, quotient, per, out of, into | ÷ |
| what, how much, how many, a number | $x$, $n$, etc. |

Now, try translating the following phrases from English to math.

**English**                                                  **Math**

1. $y$ is 5 more than $x$.                                   _____

2. $r$ equals half of $s$.                                   _____

3. $x$ is twice as great as $y$.                             _____

4. 2 less than $m$ is equal to $n$.                          _____

5. The product of $a$ and $b$ is 3 more than their sum.      _____

Now let's look at how you did:

1. $y = x + 5$

2. $r = \dfrac{1}{2}s$ or $2r = s$

3. $x = 2y$

4. $n = m - 2$

5. $ab = (a + b) + 3$

**TRANSLATE THE STORY**

" In some questions, the translation will be embedded within a "story." Don't be put off by the details of the scenario—it's the numbers that matter. Focus on the math and translate. "

# SYMBOLISM WORD PROBLEMS

Word problems, by definition, require you to translate English to math. But some word problems contain an extra level of translation. *Symbolism* word problems are like any other word problem; just translate the English and the symbols into math and then solve.

**EXAMPLE**

Assume that the notation □ ($w$, $x$, $y$, $z$) means "Divide the sum of $w$ and $x$ by $y$ and multiply the result by $z$." What is the value of

□ (10, 4, 7, 8) + □ (2, 6, 4, 5)?

**KAPLAN EXCLUSIVE TIPS**

" If you see a symbol you've never seen before, it's usually a safe bet that the test maker just made it up! "

First, translate the English/symbols into math.

$$\square \, (w, x, y, z) \text{ means } \frac{w + x}{y} \times z$$

Next, substitute the given values into the expression.

$$\square \, (10, 4, 7, 8) + \square \, (2, 6, 4, 5) = \frac{10 + 4}{7} \times 8 \; + \; \frac{2 + 6}{4} \times 5$$

$$= 16 + 10$$

$$= 26$$

# WORD PROBLEMS WITH FORMULAS

Some of the more difficult word problems may involve translations into mathematical formulas. For example, you might see questions dealing with averages, rates, or areas of geometric figures. Since the SSAT and ISEE does *not* provide formulas for you, you'll have to know these going in.

### EXAMPLE

If a truck travels at 50 miles per hour for $6\frac{1}{2}$ hours, how far will the truck travel?

(A)  600 miles

(B)  425 miles

(C)  325 miles

(D)  300 miles

(E)  500 miles

To answer this question, you need to remember that Distance = Rate × Time. Once you note the formula, you can just plug in the numbers.

$$D = 50 \times 6.5$$
$$D = 325 \text{ miles, (C)}.$$

# BACKDOOR STRATEGIES

Word problems are extraordinarily susceptible to backdoor strategies. Here's a quick recap of Kaplan's **Picking Numbers** and **Backsolving** Strategies.

### PICKING NUMBERS

**Step 1.**  Pick simple, easy-to-use numbers for each variable.

**Step 2.**  Solve the problem using the numbers you pick.

**Step 3.**  Substitute your numbers into each answer choice. The choice that gives you the same numerical solution you arrived at in step 2 is correct.

Here are a few things to remember:

- You can Pick Numbers when the answer choices contain variables.

- Pick easy numbers rather than realistic ones. Keep the numbers small and manageable.

- You have to try all the answer choices. If more than one works, pick another set of numbers.

- Don't pick the same number for more than one variable.

- When picking a number for a remainder problem, add the remainder to the number you're dividing by.

- Always pick 100 for percent questions.

## EXAMPLE

The average of four numbers is $n$. If three of the numbers are $n + 3$, $n + 5$, and $n - 2$, what is the value of the fourth number?

(A) $n - 6$

(B) $n - 4$

(C) $n$

(D) $n + 2$

(E) $n + 4$

Pick an easy number for $n$, such as 10. If the average of four numbers is 10, the sum of the four numbers is 40 ($4 \times 10 = 40$). If three of the numbers are $n + 3$, $n + 5$, and $n - 2$, then those three numbers are $10 + 3$, $10 + 5$, and $10 - 2$—13, 15, and 8. Then $13 + 15 + 8 = 36$. The sum of the four numbers must equal 40, so the remaining number is 4. If you plug 10 in for $n$ in each of the answer choices, only (A) gives you 4.

## BACKSOLVING

- You can Backsolve when the answer choices are only numbers.

- Always start with the middle answer choice, (C).

- If the middle answer choice is not correct, you can usually eliminate two more choices simply by determining whether the value you're looking for must be higher or lower.

**EXAMPLE**

Mike has *n* Hawaiian shirts, and Adam has 3 times as many Hawaiian shirts. If Adam gives Mike six Hawaiian shirts, both boys would have an equal number of Hawaiian shirts. How many Hawaiian shirts does Mike have?

(A)  3

(B)  6

(C)  9

(D)  15

(E)  18

Start with the middle answer choice, 9. If Mike has 9 shirts, then Adam has three times as many, or 27. If Adam gives Mike 6 shirts, Adam now has 21 and Mike has 15. This is not equal, so (C) is not correct. Since Adam was left with too many shirts when Mike had 9, Mike must have fewer than 9. Try (B). If Mike has 6 shirts, then Adam has 18. If Adam gives Mike 6, then they both have 12 shirts. Bingo, (B) is correct.

# ROMAN NUMERAL WORD PROBLEMS

You might see a Roman numeral problem on your test. If you do, keep a few things in mind. In keeping with the problem style, let's lay them out in Roman numerals . . .

  I.  You don't have to work with the statements in the order they are given. Deal with them in whatever order is easiest for you.

 II.  If you find a statement that is true, eliminate all of the choices that *don't* include it.

III.  If you find a statement that is false, eliminate all of the choices that *do* include it.

**EXAMPLE**

If the product of the positive numbers *x* and *y* is 20 and *x* is less than 4, which of the following must be true?

  I.  *y* is greater than 5.
 II.  The sum of *x* and *y* is greater than 10.
III.  Twice the product of *x* and *y* is equal to 40.

(A)  I only

(B)  II only

(C)  I and III only

(D)  II and III only

(E)  I, II, and III

We're told that $xy = 20$ and $x < 4$. Now let's look at the statements. Statement I says that $y > 5$. Since $xy = 20$, $y = \dfrac{20}{x}$. When $x = 4$, $y = 5$. If we replace $x$ with a smaller number than 4 in $\dfrac{20}{x}$, then $\dfrac{20}{x}$, which is $y$, will be greater than 5. Statement I must be true. Statement I must be part of the correct answer. Eliminate choices (B) and (D). Statement II says that $x + y > 10$. Try picking some values such that $xy = 20$ and $x < 4$. If $x = 3$, then $y = \dfrac{20}{x} = \dfrac{20}{3} = 6\dfrac{2}{3}$. The sum of $x$ and $y$ is not greater than 10. Statement II does not have to be true. It will not be part of the correct answer. Eliminate (E). Statement III says that $2(xy) = 40$, or $2xy = 40$. The question stem says that $xy = 20$. Multiplying both sides of the equation $xy = 20$ by 2, we have that $2(xy) = 2(20)$, or $2xy = 40$. Statement III must be true. (C) is correct.

Now it's time to put all of your skills into play with some practice questions. Remember to translate the English to math, don't get intimidated, and keep your cool. Good luck!

# PRACTICE QUESTIONS

1. During a sale, a bookstore sold $\frac{1}{2}$ of all its books in stock. On the following day, the bookstore sold 4,000 more books. Now, only $\frac{1}{10}$ of the books in stock before the sale are remaining in the store. How many books were in stock before the sale?

   (A)  8,000
   (B)  10,000
   (C)  12,000
   (D)  15,000
   (E)  20,000

2. Brad bought an MP3 player on sale at a 20% discount from its regular price of $118. If there is an 8% sales tax that is calculated on the sale price, how much did Brad pay?

   (A)  $23.60
   (B)  $86.85
   (C)  $94.40
   (D)  $101.95
   (E)  $127.44

3. Sheila charges $5 per haircut during the week. On Saturday, she charges $7.50. If Sheila has six customers each day of the week except Sunday, how much money does she earn in five weekdays and Saturday?

   (A)  $150
   (B)  $175
   (C)  $180
   (D)  $195
   (E)  $210

4. The original price of a television decreases by 20 percent. By what percent must the discounted price increase to reach its original value?

   (A)  15%
   (B)  20%
   (C)  25%
   (D)  30%
   (E)  40%

5. Ed has 100 dollars more than Robert. After Ed spends 20 dollars on groceries, Ed has five times as much money as Robert. How much money does Robert have?

   (A)  $20
   (B)  $30
   (C)  $40
   (D)  $50
   (E)  $120

6. A worker earns $15 an hour for the first 40 hours he works each week and one and a half times this much for every hour over 40 hours. If he earned $667.50 for one week's work, how many hours did he work?

   (A)  40
   (B)  41
   (C)  42
   (D)  43
   (E)  44

7. Liza has 40 less than three times the number of books that Janice has. If $B$ is equal to the number of books that Janice has, which of the following expressions shows the total number of books that Liza and Janice have together?

   (A) $3B - 40$

   (B) $3B + 40$

   (C) $4B - 40$

   (D) $4B$

   (E) $4B + 40$

8. If $a @ b = \dfrac{ab}{a-b}$, which of the following does $3 @ 2$ equal?

   (A) $2 @ 3$

   (B) $6 @ 1$

   (C) $6 @ 2$

   (D) $6 @ 3$

   (E) $8 @ 4$

9. If William divides the amount of money he has by 5, and he adds $8, the result will be $20. If $X$ is equal to the number of dollars that William has, which of the following equations shows this relationship?

   (A) $(X \div 8) + 5 = 20$

   (B) $(X \div 5) + 8 = 20$

   (C) $(X + 8) \div 5 = 20$

   (D) $(X + 5) \div 8 = 20$

   (E) $8(X + 5) = 20$

10. If a six-sided pencil with a trademark on one of its sides is rolled on a table, what is the probability that the side with the trademark is not touching the surface of the table when the pencil stops?

    (A) $\dfrac{1}{6}$

    (B) $\dfrac{1}{3}$

    (C) $\dfrac{1}{2}$

    (D) $\dfrac{2}{3}$

    (E) $\dfrac{5}{6}$

11. Yesterday, a store sold 8 times as many hats as it sold coats. It also sold 3 times as many sweaters as it sold coats. What could be the total number of hats, sweaters, and coats that were sold?

    (A) 16

    (B) 21

    (C) 25

    (D) 36

    (E) 54

12. Five hundred eighty-seven people are travelling by bus for a field trip. If each bus seats 48 people and all the buses are filled to capacity except one, how many people sit in the unfilled bus?

    (A) 37

    (B) 36

    (C) 12

    (D) 11

    (E) 7

13. Rose has finished $\frac{5}{6}$ of her novel after one week of reading. If she reads an additional tenth of the novel during the next two days, what part of the novel will she have read?

(A) $\frac{1}{10}$

(B) $\frac{7}{15}$

(C) $\frac{4}{5}$

(D) $\frac{14}{15}$

(E) $\frac{29}{30}$

14. A farmer has $4\frac{2}{3}$ acres of land for growing corn and $2\frac{1}{2}$ times as many acres for growing wheat. How many acres does she have for wheat?

(A) $2\frac{2}{3}$

(B) $4\frac{1}{2}$

(C) $8\frac{1}{6}$

(D) $10\frac{1}{2}$

(E) $11\frac{2}{3}$

15. Joyce baked 42 biscuits for her 12 guests. If 6 biscuits remain uneaten, what is the average number of biscuits that the guests ate?

(A) 2

(B) 3

(C) 4

(D) 6

(E) 12

16. The average weight of Jake, Ken, and Larry is 60 kilograms. If Jake and Ken both weigh 50 kilograms, how much, in kilograms, does Larry weigh?

(A) 40

(B) 50

(C) 60

(D) 70

(E) 80

17. If 3 added to 4 times a number is 11, the number must be

(A) 1

(B) 2

(C) 3

(D) 4

(E) 5

18. The sum of 8 and a certain number is equal to 20 minus the same number. What is the number?

(A) 2

(B) 4

(C) 6

(D) 10

(E) 14

19. Liz worked 3 hours less than twice as many hours as Rachel did. If $W$ is the number of hours Rachel worked, which of the following expressions shows the total number of hours worked by Liz and Rachel together?

(A) $2W - 3$

(B) $2W + 3$

(C) $3W - 3$

(D) $3W + 3$

(E) $4W - 2$

20. The area of a circle is $\pi r^2$, where $r$ is the radius. If the circumference of a circle is $h\pi$, what is the area of the circle, in terms of $h$?

   (A) $h^2 r^2$

   (B) $\dfrac{\pi h^2}{4}$

   (C) $\dfrac{\pi h^2}{2}$

   (D) $\pi h^2$

   (E) $4\pi h^2$

21. If $m \neq 0$, $m \neq 1$, and $m \ddagger = \dfrac{m}{m^2 - m}$, what is the value of $(6\ddagger) - (-5\ddagger)$?

   (A) $\dfrac{1}{30}$

   (B) $\dfrac{1}{20}$

   (C) $\dfrac{1}{4}$

   (D) $\dfrac{11}{30}$

   (E) $\dfrac{9}{20}$

22. Five less than 3 times a certain number is equal to twice the original number plus 7. What is the original number?

   (A) 2

   (B) $2\dfrac{2}{5}$

   (C) 6

   (D) 11

   (E) 12

23. The volume of a sphere is $\dfrac{4}{3}\pi r^3$, where $r$ is the radius. What is the volume of a sphere with a radius of 3, in terms of $\pi$?

   (A) $4\pi$

   (B) $8\pi$

   (C) $16\pi$

   (D) $36\pi$

   (E) $72\pi$

# PRACTICE QUESTION ANSWERS

## 1. B

Call the original number of books in stock $N$. On the first day of the sale, $\frac{1}{2}$ of all the books in stock were sold. So on the first day of the sale, $\frac{1}{2}N$ books were sold. After the first day of the sale, $N - \frac{1}{2}N$ books remained. On the next day, 4,000 more books were sold. So after two days of the sale, $N - \frac{1}{2}N - 4{,}000$ books remained. We are told that after two days of the sale, $\frac{1}{10}$ of the books in stock before the sale remained in the store. So the number of books that remained in the store after two days of the sale was $\frac{1}{10}N$. Thus, $N - \frac{1}{2}N - 4{,}000 = \frac{1}{10}N$. Solve for $N$.

$$N - \frac{1}{2}N - 4{,}000 = \frac{1}{10}N$$

$$\frac{1}{2}N - 4{,}000 = \frac{1}{10}N$$

$$\frac{1}{2}N - \frac{1}{10}N = 4{,}000$$

$$\frac{5}{10}N - \frac{1}{10}N = 4{,}000$$

$$\frac{4}{10}N = 4{,}000$$

$$\frac{2}{5}N = 4{,}000$$

$$N = 4{,}000\left(\frac{5}{2}\right)$$

$$= 2{,}000\,(5)$$

$$= 10{,}000$$

## 2. D

This problem needs to be done in several steps. First, find out the sale price of the MP3 player. The discount was 20%, so the sale price was 80% of the original price.

$$\text{Percent} \times \text{Whole} = \text{Part}$$

$$80\% \times \$118 = \text{Sale Price}$$

$$0.80 \times \$118 = \text{Sale Price}$$

$$\$94.40 = \text{Sale Price}$$

Now figure out how much tax Brad paid. The tax was 8% of the sale price.

$$\text{Percent} \times \text{Whole} = \text{Part}$$

$$8\% \times \$94.40 = \text{Tax}$$

$$0.08 \times \$94.40 = \text{Tax}$$

$$\$7.5520 = \text{Tax}$$

$$\$7.55 = \text{Tax}$$

Now just add the tax to the sale price.

$$\$94.40 + 7.55 = \$101.95$$

## 3. D

Each weekday, Sheila earns $\$5 \times 6$ haircuts = \$30. Each Saturday, Sheila earns $\$7.50 \times 6$ haircuts = \$45. In five weekdays, she earns $5 \times \$30 = \$150$. In one Saturday, she earns \$45. So in five weekdays plus one Saturday, she earns $\$150 + \$45$, or \$195.

## 4. C

It is important to note that while the value of the television decreases and increases by the same dollar amount, it doesn't increase and decrease by the same percent. Let's pick \$100 for the price of the television. If the price decreases by 20%, and since 20% of \$100 is \$20, the price decreases by \$20. The new price is $\$100 - \$20$, or \$80. For the new price to reach the original price ($100), it must be increased by $20. Twenty dollars is $\frac{1}{4}$ of 80, or 25% of $80. The new price must be increased by 25%, choice (C).

**5.  A**

Translate to get two equations. Let $E$ be the amount Ed has and $R$ be the amount Robert has. "Ed has $100 more than Robert" becomes $E = R + 100$. "Ed spends $20" means he'll have $20 less, or $E - 20$. "Five times as much as Robert" becomes $5R$. Therefore, $E - 20 = 5R$. Substitute $R + 100$ for $E$ in the second equation and solve for $R$:

$$(R + 100) - 20 = 5R$$
$$R + 80 = 5R$$
$$80 = 4R$$
$$20 = R, \text{ so Robert has } \$20$$

**6.  D**

Run the answer choices through the information in the stem to see which one gives a total of $667.50. Since the answer choices are in numerical order, start with the middle choice, (C). If he works for 42 hours, he earns $15 per hour for the first 40 hours, or $600, and he earns $1\frac{1}{2}$ times his normal rate for the two extra hours. So $\frac{3}{2}$ times $15 is $22.50 per hour, and since he worked 2 hours at that rate, he made an additional $45. The total is $645, which isn't enough. So (C) is too small, as are (A) and (B). Now try (D). He still earns $600 for the first 40 hours, but now you have to multiply the overtime rate, $22.50, by 3, which gives you $67.50. The total is $667.50, which means that (D) is correct.

Another way to approach the question is to see that for the first 40 hours, the worker earns $15 an hour:

40 hours × $15 an hour = $600. For any additional hours, he earns one and a half times $15. So 1.5 × $15 = $22.50 per hour. If he earned $667.50 in one week, $600 was earned in the first 40 hours and the remaining $67.50 was earned working additional hours. To find out how many additional hours the worker worked, divide the amount earned ($67.50) by the amount earned per hour ($22.50). And $67.50 ÷ $22.50 = 3. So 40 hours + 3 additional hours equals 43 hours.

**7.  C**

This is a straightforward translation problem. You're told that Janice has $B$ books. Liza has 40 less than three times the number of books Janice has, which you can translate as $L = 3B - 40$. The total number they have together equals $B + (3B - 40)$, or $4B - 40$.

**8.  D**

Substitute the given values. Then try the values in each answer choice until you find the one that produces the same result. Substituting 3 and 2 yields $\frac{(3)(2)}{3 - 2} = \frac{6}{1} = 6$. So you're looking for the answer choice that produces a result of 6. Only (D) does: $\frac{(6)(3)}{6 - 3} = \frac{18}{3} = 6$.

**9.  B**

This problem asks you to translate English sentences into math.

The amount of money William has is $X$.
This amount divided by 5: $(X \div 5)$.
Add 8 dollars: $(X \div 5) + 8$.
The result is 20 dollars: $(X \div 5) + 8 = 20$, choice (B). Since division comes before addition in the order of operations, the parentheses aren't really necessary.

## 10. E

The probability of an event happening is the ratio of the number of desired outcomes to the number of possible outcomes, or

$$\text{Probability} = \frac{\text{Number of desired outcomes}}{\text{Number of possible outcomes}}$$

One side of the pencil has the trademark on it, and the other five sides are blank. When any one of the five blank sides is touching the surface of the table, the marked side cannot be touching the table. So there are five different ways for the pencil to lie on the table without the marked side touching the surface. The total number of possible sides for the pencil to lie on is six. The probability that the trademark will not be touching the surface of the table when the pencil stops rolling is $\frac{5}{6}$, choice (E).

## 11. D

Let $x$ be the number of coats that the store sold yesterday. Keep in mind that $x$ must be an integer. The store sold 8 times the number of hats as coats yesterday. So the store sold $8x$ hats. The store sold 3 times the number of sweaters as coats yesterday. So the store sold $3x$ sweaters. The total number of hats, sweaters, and coats that the store sold was $8x + 3x + x = 12x$. Since $x$ is an integer, $12x$ must be a multiple of 12. Only (D), 36, is a multiple of 12 ($36 = 3 \times 12$).

## 12. D

There are 587 people traveling, and each bus holds 48 people. Therefore, $587 \div 48 = 12$ with a remainder of 11. So 12 buses are full, and 11 people remain to ride in the unfilled bus.

## 13. D

Rose read $\frac{5}{6}$ of the novel and plans to read another $\frac{1}{10}$, which will result in her having read $\frac{5}{6} + \frac{1}{10}$ of the novel. Add these two fractions, using 30 as the common denominator: $\frac{5}{6} + \frac{1}{10} = \frac{25}{30} + \frac{3}{30} = \frac{28}{30} = \frac{14}{15}$.

## 14. E

The farmer has $4\frac{2}{3} \times 2\frac{1}{2}$ acres for growing wheat. Change these mixed numbers to fractions in order to multiply: $\frac{\overset{7}{\cancel{14}}}{3} \times \frac{5}{\underset{1}{\cancel{2}}} = \frac{35}{3} = 11\frac{2}{3}$ acres.

## 15. B

If 6 biscuits remain, $42 - 6 = 36$ were eaten by the 12 guests.

$\text{Average} = \dfrac{\text{Sum of the terms}}{\text{Number of the terms}}$, so the average number of biscuits eaten by the guests is $\frac{36}{12} = 3$.

## 16. E

$$\text{Average} = \frac{\text{Sum of the terms}}{\text{Number of the terms}}$$
$$60 = \frac{\text{Total weight}}{3}$$
$$60 \times 3 = \text{Total weight}$$
$$180 = \text{Total weight}$$

Jake and Ken each weigh 50 kilograms, so $50 + 50 +$ Larry's weight $= 180$ kilograms. Doing the math, Larry must weigh 80 kilograms.

## 17. B

Let the number be $x$. Translating gives you $3 + 4x = 11$. Therefore, $4x = 8$ and $x = 2$.

## 18. C

Translate from English to math. The sum of 8 and $b$ is $8 + b$. The question states that this is equal to 20 minus the same number, or $20 - b$. So your equation is $8 + b = 20 - b$, and you can solve for $b$:

$$8 + b = 20 - b$$
$$8 + 2b = 20$$
$$2b = 12$$
$$b = 6$$

**19. C**

Rachel worked $W$ hours, and Liz worked 3 hours less than twice as many hours as Rachel, or $2W - 3$. Add these expressions to find the total number of hours worked by Liz and Rachel together:

$$W + 2W - 3 = 3W - 3$$

**20. B**

Circumference of a circle is $\pi$ times diameter, so a circumference of $h\pi$ means a diameter of $h$. The radius is half the diameter, or $\dfrac{h}{2}$. Substitute $\dfrac{h}{2}$ into the area formula:

$$\pi \left(\frac{h}{2}\right)^2 = \pi \left(\frac{h^2}{4}\right) = \frac{h^2\pi}{4}$$

**21. D**

Substitute into the expression that defines the symbol ‡:

$$(6\ddagger) - (-5)\ddagger = \frac{6}{6^2 - 6} - \frac{-5}{(-5)^2 - (-5)}$$
$$= \frac{6}{36 - 6} - \frac{-5}{25 + 5}$$
$$= \frac{6}{30} - \frac{-5}{30}$$
$$= \frac{6}{30} + \frac{5}{30}$$
$$= \frac{11}{30}$$

At two points in your calculation, it is crucial to remember that subtracting a negative is the same as adding a positive.

**22. E**

Call the unknown number $x$. Five less than 3 times the number, or $3x - 5$, equals twice the original number plus 7, or $2x + 7$. So $3x - 5 = 2x + 7$. Solve for $x$:

$$3x - 5 = 2x + 7$$
$$x - 5 = 7$$
$$x = 12$$

**23. D**

Substitute the value of $r = 3$ into the formula and simplify:

$$\text{volume} = \frac{4}{3}\pi(3)^3$$
$$= \frac{4}{3}\pi(27)$$
$$= 36\pi$$

# CHAPTER 15: MANAGING YOUR STRESS

Is it starting to feel like as though your whole life is a buildup to the SSAT or ISEE? You really want to go to a certain school, and you know your parents want you to as well. You have worried about the test for months and spent at least a few hours in solid preparation for it. As the test gets closer, you may find your anxiety is on the rise. Don't worry. After the preparation you've received from this book, you're in good shape for the test.

To calm any pretest jitters you may have, this chapter leads you through a sane itinerary for the last week.

## THE WEEK BEFORE THE TEST

- Focus on strategy and backup plans.

- Practice strategies you had the best success rate with.

- Decide and know **exactly** how you're going to approach each section and question type.

- Sit down and do practice problems or complete extra drills you might have skipped the first time through.

- Practice waking up early and eating breakfast so that you'll be alert in the morning on Test Day.

## THE DAYS JUST BEFORE THE TEST

- The best test takers do less and less as the test approaches. Taper off your study schedule and take it easy. Give yourself time off, especially the evening before the exam. By that time, if you've studied well, everything you need to know is firmly stored in your memory bank.

- Positive self-talk can be extremely liberating and invigorating, especially as the test looms closer. Tell yourself things such as "I will do well," rather than "I hope things go well";

"I can" rather than "I cannot." Replace any negative thoughts with affirming statements that boost your self-esteem.

- Get your act together sooner rather than later. Have everything (including choice of clothing) laid out in advance. Most importantly, make sure you know where the test will be held and the easiest, quickest way to get there. You'll have great peace of mind by knowing that all the little details—gas in the car, directions, etc.—are set before the day of the test.

- Go to the test site a few days in advance, particularly if you are especially anxious. If at all possible, find out what room your part of the alphabet is assigned to and try to sit there (by yourself) for a while. Better yet, bring some practice material and do a section or two.

- Forgo any practice on the day before the test. It's in your best interest to marshal your physical and psychological resources for 24 hours or so. Even race horses are kept in the paddock and treated like royalty the day before a race. Keep the upcoming test out of your consciousness; go to a movie, take a pleasant hike, or just relax. Don't eat junk food or tons of sugar. And, of course, get plenty of rest the night before—just don't go to bed too early. It's hard to fall asleep earlier than you're used to, and you don't want to lie there worrying about the test.

## THE NIGHT BEFORE THE TEST

Don't study. Get together the following items:

- Your admission/registration ticket
- Photo ID
- A watch (choose one that is easy to read)
- Slightly dull No. 2 pencils (so they fill in the ovals faster)
- Pencil sharpener
- Erasers
- Clothes you'll wear (Dress in layers! The climate at the test location may vary, as may your body temperature. Make sure you can warm up or cool down easily.)
- Snacks (easy to open or partially unwrapped)
- Money
- Packet of tissues

Relax the night before the test. Read a good book, take a bubble bath, watch TV. Get a good night's sleep. Go to bed at a reasonable hour and leave yourself extra time in the morning.

# THE MORNING OF THE TEST

Eat breakfast. Make it something substantial and nutritious, but don't deviate too much from your everyday pattern.

Dress in layers so that you can adjust to the temperature of the test room.

Read something to warm up your brain before the test starts.

Be sure to get there early. Leave enough time to allow for traffic, mass transit delays, your dad getting lost en route, and any other snag that could slow you down.

# DURING THE TEST

Don't be shaken. If you find your confidence slipping, remind yourself how well you've prepared. You know the structure of the test; you know the instructions; you've studied for every question type.

The biggest stress monster will be the test itself. Fear not; there are methods of quelling your stress during the test.

- Keep moving forward instead of getting bogged down in a difficult question. You don't have to get everything right to achieve a fine score. So don't linger out of desperation on a question that is going nowhere even after you've spent considerable time on it. The best test takers skip difficult material temporarily in search of the easier stuff. They mark the ones that require extra time and thought.

- Don't be thrown if other test takers seem to be working more busily and furiously than you are. Don't mistake other people's sheer activity as a sign of progress and higher scores.

- *Keep breathing!* Weak test takers tend to share one major trait: They don't breathe properly as the test proceeds. They might hold their breath without realizing it, or breathe erratically or arrhythmically. Improper breathing hurts confidence and accuracy. Just as importantly, it interferes with clear thinking.

Some quick isometrics during the test—especially if concentration is wandering or energy is waning—can help. Try this:

- Put your palms together and press intensely for a few seconds. Concentrate on the tension you feel through your palms, wrists, forearms, and up into your biceps and shoulders. Then, quickly release the pressure. Feel the difference as you let go. Focus on the warm relaxation that floods through the muscles.

**THE NIGHT BEFORE THE TEST, DO NOT**

- try to copy the dictionary onto your fingernails

- stay up all night watching all the *Friday the 13th* movies

- eat a large double anchovy and pepper pizza with a case of chocolate soda

- send away for brochures for clown school

- start making flashcards

- tattoo yourself

**WHAT ARE "SIGNS OF A WINNER," ALEX?**

Here's some advice from a Kaplan instructor who won big on Jeopardy!™ In the green room before the show, he noticed that the contestants who were quiet and "within themselves" were the ones who did great on the show. The contestants who didn't perform as well were those who were cramming facts and talking a lot before the show. Lesson: Spend the final hours before the test getting sleep, meditating, and generally relaxing.

Here's another isometric that will relieve tension in both your neck and eye muscles.

- Slowly rotate your head from side to side, turning your head and eyes to look as far back over each shoulder as you can. Feel the muscles stretch on one side of your neck as they contract on the other. Repeat five times in each direction.

Now you're ready to return to the task.

With what you've just learned here, you're armed and ready to do battle with the test. This book and your studies will give you the information you'll need to answer the questions. It's all firmly planted in your mind. You also know how to deal with any excess tension that might come along, both when you're studying for and taking the exam. You've experienced everything you need to tame your test anxiety and stress. You're going to get a great score.

Even if something goes really wrong, don't panic. If the test booklet is defective—two pages are stuck together or the ink has run—try to stay calm. Raise your hand and tell the proctor you need a new book. If you accidentally misgrid your answer page or put the answers in the wrong section, again don't panic. The proctor might be able to arrange for you to regrid your test after it's over, when it won't cost you any time.

## AFTER THE TEST

Once the test is over, put it out of your mind. Start thinking about more interesting things. You might walk out of the test thinking that you blew it. You probably didn't. You tend to remember the questions that stumped you, not the many that you knew.

# Part Four

# SSAT PRACTICE TESTS AND EXPLANATIONS

# SSAT TEST OVERVIEW

## TOTAL TIME

Approximately two and a half hours, plus two brief breaks.

## QUESTIONS

Aside from the essay, all questions are multiple-choice in format, with all answer choices labeled (A)–(E).

## CONTENT

The SSAT tests Math, Reading, Writing, and Verbal skills. There are two Math sections, one Verbal section, one Reading section, and one unscored Essay.

## PACING

You are not expected to complete all items on the SSAT. This is particularly true if you are at the low end of the age range of test takers for your level. The best approach to pacing is to work as quickly as you can without losing accuracy. Further, if a question is giving you difficulty, circle it and move on. You can always come back to it later, but you shouldn't waste time on a question that is stumping you when you could be gaining valuable points elsewhere.

## GUESSING

You receive 1 point for each question answered correctly. For those questions you answer incorrectly, you lose $\frac{1}{4}$ point. As a result, guess *only* when you can do so intelligently. In other words, don't guess wildly, but *do* guess if you can eliminate at least one answer choice as clearly wrong.

# CHAPTER 16: SSAT PRACTICE TEST 1: UPPER-LEVEL

## HOW TO TAKE THIS PRACTICE TEST

Before taking this practice test, find a quiet room where you can work uninterrupted for two and a half hours. Make sure you have a comfortable desk and several No. 2 pencils.

Use the answer sheet provided to record your answers. (You can cut it out or photocopy it.)

Once you start this practice test, don't stop until you've finished. Remember—you can review any questions within a section, but you may not go backward or forward a section.

You'll find answer explanations following the test. Scoring information is in chapter 19.

Good luck.

# SSAT Practice Test 1: Upper-Level Answer Sheet

**Remove (or photocopy) the answer sheet and use it to complete the practice test.**

Start with number 1 for each section. If a section has fewer questions than answer spaces, leave the extra spaces blank.

## SECTION 2

| | | | | |
|---|---|---|---|---|
| 1 Ⓐ Ⓑ Ⓒ Ⓓ Ⓔ | 6 Ⓐ Ⓑ Ⓒ Ⓓ Ⓔ | 11 Ⓐ Ⓑ Ⓒ Ⓓ Ⓔ | 16 Ⓐ Ⓑ Ⓒ Ⓓ Ⓔ | 21 Ⓐ Ⓑ Ⓒ Ⓓ Ⓔ |
| 2 Ⓐ Ⓑ Ⓒ Ⓓ Ⓔ | 7 Ⓐ Ⓑ Ⓒ Ⓓ Ⓔ | 12 Ⓐ Ⓑ Ⓒ Ⓓ Ⓔ | 17 Ⓐ Ⓑ Ⓒ Ⓓ Ⓔ | 22 Ⓐ Ⓑ Ⓒ Ⓓ Ⓔ |
| 3 Ⓐ Ⓑ Ⓒ Ⓓ Ⓔ | 8 Ⓐ Ⓑ Ⓒ Ⓓ Ⓔ | 13 Ⓐ Ⓑ Ⓒ Ⓓ Ⓔ | 18 Ⓐ Ⓑ Ⓒ Ⓓ Ⓔ | 23 Ⓐ Ⓑ Ⓒ Ⓓ Ⓔ |
| 4 Ⓐ Ⓑ Ⓒ Ⓓ Ⓔ | 9 Ⓐ Ⓑ Ⓒ Ⓓ Ⓔ | 14 Ⓐ Ⓑ Ⓒ Ⓓ Ⓔ | 19 Ⓐ Ⓑ Ⓒ Ⓓ Ⓔ | 24 Ⓐ Ⓑ Ⓒ Ⓓ Ⓔ |
| 5 Ⓐ Ⓑ Ⓒ Ⓓ Ⓔ | 10 Ⓐ Ⓑ Ⓒ Ⓓ Ⓔ | 15 Ⓐ Ⓑ Ⓒ Ⓓ Ⓔ | 20 Ⓐ Ⓑ Ⓒ Ⓓ Ⓔ | 25 Ⓐ Ⓑ Ⓒ Ⓓ Ⓔ |

# right in section 2

# wrong in section 2

## SECTION 3

| | | | | |
|---|---|---|---|---|
| 1 Ⓐ Ⓑ Ⓒ Ⓓ Ⓔ | 9 Ⓐ Ⓑ Ⓒ Ⓓ Ⓔ | 17 Ⓐ Ⓑ Ⓒ Ⓓ Ⓔ | 25 Ⓐ Ⓑ Ⓒ Ⓓ Ⓔ | 33 Ⓐ Ⓑ Ⓒ Ⓓ Ⓔ |
| 2 Ⓐ Ⓑ Ⓒ Ⓓ Ⓔ | 10 Ⓐ Ⓑ Ⓒ Ⓓ Ⓔ | 18 Ⓐ Ⓑ Ⓒ Ⓓ Ⓔ | 26 Ⓐ Ⓑ Ⓒ Ⓓ Ⓔ | 34 Ⓐ Ⓑ Ⓒ Ⓓ Ⓔ |
| 3 Ⓐ Ⓑ Ⓒ Ⓓ Ⓔ | 11 Ⓐ Ⓑ Ⓒ Ⓓ Ⓔ | 19 Ⓐ Ⓑ Ⓒ Ⓓ Ⓔ | 27 Ⓐ Ⓑ Ⓒ Ⓓ Ⓔ | 35 Ⓐ Ⓑ Ⓒ Ⓓ Ⓔ |
| 4 Ⓐ Ⓑ Ⓒ Ⓓ Ⓔ | 12 Ⓐ Ⓑ Ⓒ Ⓓ Ⓔ | 20 Ⓐ Ⓑ Ⓒ Ⓓ Ⓔ | 28 Ⓐ Ⓑ Ⓒ Ⓓ Ⓔ | 36 Ⓐ Ⓑ Ⓒ Ⓓ Ⓔ |
| 5 Ⓐ Ⓑ Ⓒ Ⓓ Ⓔ | 13 Ⓐ Ⓑ Ⓒ Ⓓ Ⓔ | 21 Ⓐ Ⓑ Ⓒ Ⓓ Ⓔ | 29 Ⓐ Ⓑ Ⓒ Ⓓ Ⓔ | 37 Ⓐ Ⓑ Ⓒ Ⓓ Ⓔ |
| 6 Ⓐ Ⓑ Ⓒ Ⓓ Ⓔ | 14 Ⓐ Ⓑ Ⓒ Ⓓ Ⓔ | 22 Ⓐ Ⓑ Ⓒ Ⓓ Ⓔ | 30 Ⓐ Ⓑ Ⓒ Ⓓ Ⓔ | 38 Ⓐ Ⓑ Ⓒ Ⓓ Ⓔ |
| 7 Ⓐ Ⓑ Ⓒ Ⓓ Ⓔ | 15 Ⓐ Ⓑ Ⓒ Ⓓ Ⓔ | 23 Ⓐ Ⓑ Ⓒ Ⓓ Ⓔ | 31 Ⓐ Ⓑ Ⓒ Ⓓ Ⓔ | 39 Ⓐ Ⓑ Ⓒ Ⓓ Ⓔ |
| 8 Ⓐ Ⓑ Ⓒ Ⓓ Ⓔ | 16 Ⓐ Ⓑ Ⓒ Ⓓ Ⓔ | 24 Ⓐ Ⓑ Ⓒ Ⓓ Ⓔ | 32 Ⓐ Ⓑ Ⓒ Ⓓ Ⓔ | 40 Ⓐ Ⓑ Ⓒ Ⓓ Ⓔ |

# right in section 3

# wrong in section 3

## SECTION 4

| | | | | |
|---|---|---|---|---|
| 1 Ⓐ Ⓑ Ⓒ Ⓓ Ⓔ | 13 Ⓐ Ⓑ Ⓒ Ⓓ Ⓔ | 25 Ⓐ Ⓑ Ⓒ Ⓓ Ⓔ | 37 Ⓐ Ⓑ Ⓒ Ⓓ Ⓔ | 49 Ⓐ Ⓑ Ⓒ Ⓓ Ⓔ |
| 2 Ⓐ Ⓑ Ⓒ Ⓓ Ⓔ | 14 Ⓐ Ⓑ Ⓒ Ⓓ Ⓔ | 26 Ⓐ Ⓑ Ⓒ Ⓓ Ⓔ | 38 Ⓐ Ⓑ Ⓒ Ⓓ Ⓔ | 50 Ⓐ Ⓑ Ⓒ Ⓓ Ⓔ |
| 3 Ⓐ Ⓑ Ⓒ Ⓓ Ⓔ | 15 Ⓐ Ⓑ Ⓒ Ⓓ Ⓔ | 27 Ⓐ Ⓑ Ⓒ Ⓓ Ⓔ | 39 Ⓐ Ⓑ Ⓒ Ⓓ Ⓔ | 51 Ⓐ Ⓑ Ⓒ Ⓓ Ⓔ |
| 4 Ⓐ Ⓑ Ⓒ Ⓓ Ⓔ | 16 Ⓐ Ⓑ Ⓒ Ⓓ Ⓔ | 28 Ⓐ Ⓑ Ⓒ Ⓓ Ⓔ | 40 Ⓐ Ⓑ Ⓒ Ⓓ Ⓔ | 52 Ⓐ Ⓑ Ⓒ Ⓓ Ⓔ |
| 5 Ⓐ Ⓑ Ⓒ Ⓓ Ⓔ | 17 Ⓐ Ⓑ Ⓒ Ⓓ Ⓔ | 29 Ⓐ Ⓑ Ⓒ Ⓓ Ⓔ | 41 Ⓐ Ⓑ Ⓒ Ⓓ Ⓔ | 53 Ⓐ Ⓑ Ⓒ Ⓓ Ⓔ |
| 6 Ⓐ Ⓑ Ⓒ Ⓓ Ⓔ | 18 Ⓐ Ⓑ Ⓒ Ⓓ Ⓔ | 30 Ⓐ Ⓑ Ⓒ Ⓓ Ⓔ | 42 Ⓐ Ⓑ Ⓒ Ⓓ Ⓔ | 54 Ⓐ Ⓑ Ⓒ Ⓓ Ⓔ |
| 7 Ⓐ Ⓑ Ⓒ Ⓓ Ⓔ | 19 Ⓐ Ⓑ Ⓒ Ⓓ Ⓔ | 31 Ⓐ Ⓑ Ⓒ Ⓓ Ⓔ | 43 Ⓐ Ⓑ Ⓒ Ⓓ Ⓔ | 55 Ⓐ Ⓑ Ⓒ Ⓓ Ⓔ |
| 8 Ⓐ Ⓑ Ⓒ Ⓓ Ⓔ | 20 Ⓐ Ⓑ Ⓒ Ⓓ Ⓔ | 32 Ⓐ Ⓑ Ⓒ Ⓓ Ⓔ | 44 Ⓐ Ⓑ Ⓒ Ⓓ Ⓔ | 56 Ⓐ Ⓑ Ⓒ Ⓓ Ⓔ |
| 9 Ⓐ Ⓑ Ⓒ Ⓓ Ⓔ | 21 Ⓐ Ⓑ Ⓒ Ⓓ Ⓔ | 33 Ⓐ Ⓑ Ⓒ Ⓓ Ⓔ | 45 Ⓐ Ⓑ Ⓒ Ⓓ Ⓔ | 57 Ⓐ Ⓑ Ⓒ Ⓓ Ⓔ |
| 10 Ⓐ Ⓑ Ⓒ Ⓓ Ⓔ | 22 Ⓐ Ⓑ Ⓒ Ⓓ Ⓔ | 34 Ⓐ Ⓑ Ⓒ Ⓓ Ⓔ | 46 Ⓐ Ⓑ Ⓒ Ⓓ Ⓔ | 58 Ⓐ Ⓑ Ⓒ Ⓓ Ⓔ |
| 11 Ⓐ Ⓑ Ⓒ Ⓓ Ⓔ | 23 Ⓐ Ⓑ Ⓒ Ⓓ Ⓔ | 35 Ⓐ Ⓑ Ⓒ Ⓓ Ⓔ | 47 Ⓐ Ⓑ Ⓒ Ⓓ Ⓔ | 59 Ⓐ Ⓑ Ⓒ Ⓓ Ⓔ |
| 12 Ⓐ Ⓑ Ⓒ Ⓓ Ⓔ | 24 Ⓐ Ⓑ Ⓒ Ⓓ Ⓔ | 36 Ⓐ Ⓑ Ⓒ Ⓓ Ⓔ | 48 Ⓐ Ⓑ Ⓒ Ⓓ Ⓔ | 60 Ⓐ Ⓑ Ⓒ Ⓓ Ⓔ |

# right in section 4

# wrong in section 4

## SECTION 5

| | | | | |
|---|---|---|---|---|
| 1 Ⓐ Ⓑ Ⓒ Ⓓ Ⓔ | 6 Ⓐ Ⓑ Ⓒ Ⓓ Ⓔ | 11 Ⓐ Ⓑ Ⓒ Ⓓ Ⓔ | 16 Ⓐ Ⓑ Ⓒ Ⓓ Ⓔ | 21 Ⓐ Ⓑ Ⓒ Ⓓ Ⓔ |
| 2 Ⓐ Ⓑ Ⓒ Ⓓ Ⓔ | 7 Ⓐ Ⓑ Ⓒ Ⓓ Ⓔ | 12 Ⓐ Ⓑ Ⓒ Ⓓ Ⓔ | 17 Ⓐ Ⓑ Ⓒ Ⓓ Ⓔ | 22 Ⓐ Ⓑ Ⓒ Ⓓ Ⓔ |
| 3 Ⓐ Ⓑ Ⓒ Ⓓ Ⓔ | 8 Ⓐ Ⓑ Ⓒ Ⓓ Ⓔ | 13 Ⓐ Ⓑ Ⓒ Ⓓ Ⓔ | 18 Ⓐ Ⓑ Ⓒ Ⓓ Ⓔ | 23 Ⓐ Ⓑ Ⓒ Ⓓ Ⓔ |
| 4 Ⓐ Ⓑ Ⓒ Ⓓ Ⓔ | 9 Ⓐ Ⓑ Ⓒ Ⓓ Ⓔ | 14 Ⓐ Ⓑ Ⓒ Ⓓ Ⓔ | 19 Ⓐ Ⓑ Ⓒ Ⓓ Ⓔ | 24 Ⓐ Ⓑ Ⓒ Ⓓ Ⓔ |
| 5 Ⓐ Ⓑ Ⓒ Ⓓ Ⓔ | 10 Ⓐ Ⓑ Ⓒ Ⓓ Ⓔ | 15 Ⓐ Ⓑ Ⓒ Ⓓ Ⓔ | 20 Ⓐ Ⓑ Ⓒ Ⓓ Ⓔ | 25 Ⓐ Ⓑ Ⓒ Ⓓ Ⓔ |

# right in section 5

# wrong in section 5

# SECTION 1
Time—25 Minutes

**Directions:** Read the following topics carefully. Take a few minutes to select the topic you find more interesting. Think about the selected topic and organize your thoughts on scrap paper before you begin writing.

**Topic A:** I opened the window and immediately saw…

**Topic B:** Where is your favorite place to read and why?

Circle your selection: Topic A or Topic B. Write your essay for the selected topic on the paper provided. Your essay should NOT exceed two pages and must be written in pencil. Be sure that your handwriting is legible and that you stay within the lines and margins.

GO ON TO THE NEXT PAGE

_____

_____

_____

_____

_____

_____

_____

_____

_____

_____

_____

_____

_____

_____

_____

_____

_____

_____

_____

_____

_____

_____

_____

IF YOU FINISH BEFORE TIME IS CALLED, YOU MAY CHECK YOUR WORK ON
THIS SECTION ONLY. DO NOT TURN TO ANY OTHER SECTION IN THE TEST.

**STOP**

# SECTION 2

Time—30 Minutes
25 Questions

In this section, there are five possible answers after each problem. Choose which one is best. You may use the blank space at the right for scratch work.

Note: Figures provided with the problems are drawn with the greatest possible accuracy, UNLESS stated "Not Drawn to Scale."

USE THIS SPACE FOR FIGURING.

1. Each member of a club sold the same number of raffle tickets. If the club sold a total of 120 tickets, which of the following CANNOT be the number of tickets sold by each member?

   (A)  2
   (B)  8
   (C)  10
   (D)  12
   (E)  16

2. According to the graph in Figure 1, about how many students are art majors?

   (A)  200
   (B)  225
   (C)  280
   (D)  300
   (E)  360

MAJORS OF 900 STUDENTS

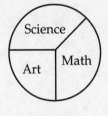

Figure 1

3. Sean arrives home 14 minutes before midnight, and his sister gets home 25 minutes later. When does Sean's sister arrive home?

   (A)  11 minutes before midnight
   (B)  11 minutes after midnight
   (C)  14 minutes after midnight
   (D)  25 minutes after midnight
   (E)  39 minutes after midnight

GO ON TO THE NEXT PAGE

4. Which of the following is closest to $0.52 \times 78$?

(A) $\frac{1}{5}$ of 70

(B) $\frac{1}{5}$ of 80

(C) $\frac{2}{5}$ of 70

(D) $\frac{1}{2}$ of 70

(E) $\frac{1}{2}$ of 80

USE THIS SPACE FOR FIGURING.

**Questions 5–6 refer to the graph in Figure 2.**

5. Brian's summer savings are greater than James's summer savings by how many dollars?

(A)   3
(B)   4
(C)   100
(D)   150
(E)   200

SUMMER SAVINGS

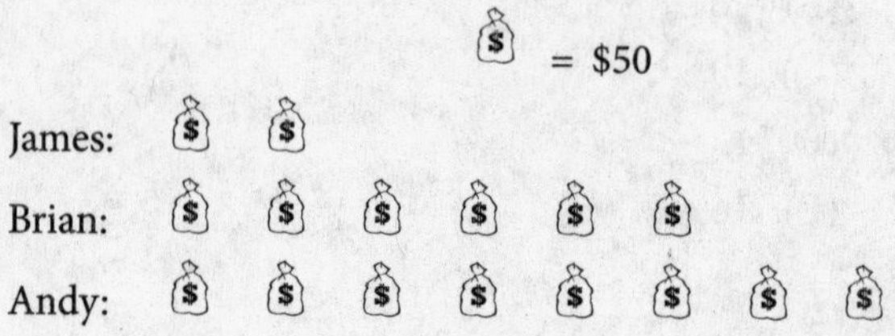

Figure 2

6. The amount of money saved by Andy is how many times the amount of money saved by James?

(A)   3
(B)   4
(C)   6
(D   300
(E)  400

GO ON TO THE NEXT PAGE

7. How many students are in a class if 30 percent of the class is equal to 30 students?

(A) 10

(B) 90

(C) 100

(D) 900

(E) It cannot be determined from the information given.

8. Each of the following is less than 2 EXCEPT

(A) $\dfrac{15}{8}$

(B) $\dfrac{45}{22}$

(C) $\dfrac{99}{50}$

(D) $\dfrac{180}{100}$

(E) $\dfrac{701}{400}$

9. The sides and angles of triangles $ABC$, $BDE$, $BCE$, and $CEF$ in Figure 3 are all equal. Which of the following is the longest path from $A$ to $F$?

(A) $A - C - B - D - F$

(B) $A - B - E - C - F$

(C) $A - B - C - E - F$

(D) $A - C - E - F$

(E) $A - B - D - F$

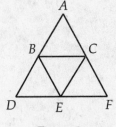

Figure 3

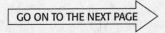

10. Which of the following is closest to 80.08?

  (A)    80
  (B)  80.01
  (C)  80.1
  (D)    81
  (E)    90

11. If $\frac{1}{3}$ of a number is less than 12, then the number is always

  (A)  less than 36
  (B)  equal to 4
  (C)  greater than 4
  (D)  equal to 36
  (E)  greater than 36

12. In a basketball game, Team A scored 39 points, and Team B scored more points than Team A. If Team B has 5 players, the average score of the players on Team B must have been at least how many points?

  (A)   1
  (B)   5
  (C)   6
  (D)   8
  (E)  12

13. In the triangle shown in Figure 4, what is the value of $a$ ?

  (A)  4
  (B)  6
  (C)  8
  (D)  9
  (E)  It cannot be determined from the information given.

USE THIS SPACE FOR FIGURING.

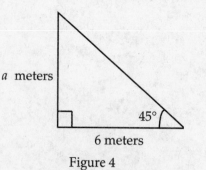

Figure 4

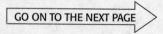
GO ON TO THE NEXT PAGE

14. A man bought a piece of land for 40 thousand dollars. Then he spent 2 million dollars to build a house on it. The cost of the house is how many times the cost of the land?

(A)   5
(B)   20
(C)   50
(D)  200
(E)  500

USE THIS SPACE FOR FIGURING.

15. If $(x - y) + 2 = 6$ and $y$ is less than 3, which of the following CANNOT be the value of $x$ ?

(A)  −3
(B)   0
(C)  $1\frac{1}{2}$
(D)   4
(E)   8

16. In Figure 5, the distance from $A$ to $D$ is 55, and the distance from $A$ to $B$ is equal to the distance from $C$ to $D$. If the distance from $A$ to $B$ is twice the distance from $B$ to $C$, how far apart are $B$ and $D$ ?

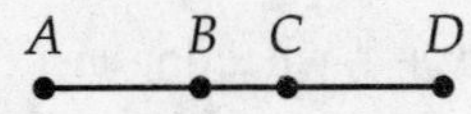

(A)  11
(B)  30
(C)  33
(D)  44
(E)  45

Figure 5

GO ON TO THE NEXT PAGE

17. A book is placed on a flat table surface, as shown in Figure 6. Which of the following best shows all of the points where the book touches the table?

(A)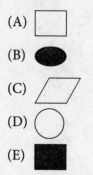

(B)

(C)

(D)

(E)

USE THIS SPACE FOR FIGURING.

Figure 6

18. Which of the following can be expressed as $(J + 2) \times 3$, where $J$ is a whole number?

(A) 40

(B) 52

(C) 65

(D) 74

(E) 81

19. If $a - 7 = 3b + 4$, what does $a + 5$ equal?

(A) $b - 1$

(B) $4b - 1$

(C) $3b + 9$

(D) $3b + 16$

(E) It cannot be determined from the information given.

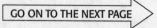
GO ON TO THE NEXT PAGE

20. According to a census report for Country A, 21.5 out of every 100 families live in rural areas. Based on this report, how many of the 2 million families in Country A live in rural areas?

    (A) 430,000
    (B) 215,000
    (C) 43,000
    (D) 4,300
    (E) 430

USE THIS SPACE FOR FIGURING.

21. Bob is $x$ years old, and Jerry is 7 years older. In terms of $x$, what was the sum of their ages, in years, 5 years ago?

    (A) $2x + 3$
    (B) $2x + 2$
    (C) $2x - 3$
    (D) $x - 3$
    (E) $x - 10$

22. A game show contestant answered exactly 20 percent of the questions correctly. Of the first 15 questions, he answered 4 correctly. If he answered only one of the remaining questions correctly, which of the following must be true?

    I. There were a total of 20 questions.

    II. He answered 10 percent of the remaining questions correctly.

    III. He didn't answer 9 of the remaining questions correctly.

    (A) I only
    (B) II only
    (C) I and II only
    (D) II and III only
    (E) I, II, and III

GO ON TO THE NEXT PAGE

23. If $C$ is the product of consecutive integers $A$ and $B$, then $C$ must be

(A) greater than $A + B$

(B) a negative integer

(C) a positive integer

(D) an even integer

(E) an odd integer

24. A 20 percent discount is offered on all sweaters at Store S. If a cotton sweater is on sale for $48.00 and a wool sweater is on sale for $64.00, what was the difference in price of the sweaters before the discount?

(A) $16.00

(B) $19.20

(C) $20.00

(D) $24.00

(E) $32.00

25. The maximum load that a railway car can carry is $17\frac{1}{3}$ tons of freight. If a train has 36 railway cars, and each of these carries $\frac{5}{9}$ of a ton less than its maximum load, how many tons of freight is the train carrying?

(A) 604

(B) $612\frac{7}{9}$

(C) $640\frac{5}{9}$

(D) 648

(E) 660

USE THIS SPACE FOR FIGURING.

IF YOU FINISH BEFORE TIME IS CALLED, YOU MAY CHECK YOUR WORK ON THIS SECTION ONLY. DO NOT TURN TO ANY OTHER SECTION IN THE TEST.

STOP

# SECTION 3

Time—40 Minutes
40 Questions

**Read each passage carefully and then answer the questions about it. For each question, decide on the basis of the passage which one of the choices best answers the question.**

Typical lemurs are primates with bodies similar to those of monkeys but with pointed muzzles and large eyes; most have long, bushy
*Line* tails. Their fur is woolly and may be colored red,
(5) gray, brown, or black. The name of the lemur stems from the Latin *lemures,* the Roman name for vampire-like ghosts of the dead, which these large-eyed creatures were thought to resemble. Found only off the east coast of Africa on the island of
(10) Madagascar and neighboring islands, lemurs spend some time on the ground but most often are in the trees, building nests high in the branches. Besides leaves, lemurs eat eggs, fruit, insects, and small animals. They are active throughout the day and
(15) night and are reputed to be gentle, friendly creatures. Besides typical lemurs, the lemur family includes avahi, aye-aye, loris, and galogo. However, contrary to popular belief, the so-called flying lemur is not even a primate, much less a
(20) true lemur; it is, in fact, a member of an altogether different order of mammals known as *Dermoptera.*

1.  The style of the passage is most like that found in a

    (A)  biology textbook
    (B)  novel about Madagascar
    (C)  zoologist's diary
    (D)  tourist's guidebook
    (E)  personal letter

2.  Which of the following would be the best title for this passage?

    (A)  The Lemur: Friend or Foe?
    (B)  Madagascar's Loneliest Hunters
    (C)  Facts About Lemurs
    (D)  African Vampires
    (E)  The Diet of the Lemur

3.  According to the passage, all of the following are true about lemurs EXCEPT

    (A)  they spend much of their time in trees
    (B)  most have long, bushy tails
    (C)  the flying lemur is not a true lemur
    (D)  they eat only fruits and leaves
    (E)  the body of the lemur resembles the body of the monkey

4.  The passage suggests that

    (A)  the typical lemur is a member of an order of mammals known as *Dermoptera*
    (B)  flying lemurs are only active during the night
    (C)  the lemur is not an aggressive animal
    (D)  lemurs spend most of their time on the ground
    (E)  flying lemurs can only be found on Madagascar and neighboring islands

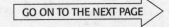
GO ON TO THE NEXT PAGE

5.  According to the passage, it is reasonable to assume that

    (A)  flying lemurs resemble typical lemurs

    (B)  typical lemurs are herbivores

    (C)  their large eyes mean that lemurs come out only at night

    (D)  aye-ayes are primates

    (E)  lemurs' pointed muzzles give them an excellent sense of smell

     Before a joint session of Congress in January 1918, President Woodrow Wilson outlined his plan for a post–World War I peace settlement. Known as
Line the Fourteen Points, Wilson's plan is best
(5) remembered for its first point, which declared that international diplomacy should be conducted in the open and that quiet, unpublicized diplomacy should be made illegal. Wilson believed that public diplomacy would end the threat of war by
(10) preventing immoral national leaders from secretly plotting aggressive actions against others.
     Although Wilson was a highly intelligent and well-meaning man, he lacked insight into the complexities of international politics. Contrary to
(15) Wilson's belief, war rarely results from the behind-the-scenes plotting of unscrupulous national leaders. Rather, war usually stems from unresolved disagreements among nations— disagreements over territory, access to resources,
(20) and so forth. Even if quiet diplomacy could be eliminated, these disagreements would still remain, as would the threat of war.

6.  The second paragraph of this passage is primarily about

    (A)  a post–World War I peace settlement

    (B)  diplomacy's role in international politics

    (C)  disagreements among nations

    (D)  the actual causes of war

    (E)  the first point in Wilson's Fourteen Points

7.  The attitude of the writer toward the subject is

    (A)  calculating

    (B)  suspicious

    (C)  opinionated

    (D)  cheerful

    (E)  apologetic

8.  The author would most likely agree that war between country A and country B would result from which of the following situations?

    (A)  A dispute over ownership of a piece of land bordering both countries

    (B)  An agreement by a leader in country A to tax imports from a third country

    (C)  The capture of a spy from country A in country B

    (D)  An unpublicized agreement by country A to sell weapons to country B

    (E)  A secret alliance made between country A and another country

9.  Why does the author say that open diplomacy would not prevent war?

    (A)  Quiet diplomacy will always be a part of international relations.

    (B)  War breaks out because immoral rulers make decisions in secret.

    (C)  Open diplomacy is not a solution to the problems which lead to war.

    (D)  Disagreements over territory and resources rarely lead to conflict.

    (E)  International relations are too complex to be conducted in the public eye.

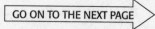

GO ON TO THE NEXT PAGE

10. All of the following questions can be answered by the passage EXCEPT:

    (A) Does the author think the Fourteen Points was a good plan?

    (B) According to the author, why does war usually start?

    (C) Did Wilson support public diplomacy or concealed diplomacy?

    (D) Does the author feel he or she understands international politics better than Wilson did?

    (E) How does the author think the threat of war could be eliminated for good?

11. Which of the following is the author most likely to discuss next?

    (A) Wilson's domestic policies in the post–World War I period

    (B) The impact of import taxes on foreign trade relations

    (C) An example of a war that resulted from a territorial or resource dispute

    (D) The events leading up to World War I

    (E) Other examples of Wilson's intelligence

Live thy Life,
    Young and old,
Like yon oak,
*Line*    Bright in spring,
(5)  Living gold;

Summer-rich
    Then: and then
Autumn-changed,
Soberer-hued
(10)    Gold again.

All his leaves
    Fall'n at length,
Look, he stands,
Trunk and bough,
(15)    Naked strength.

"The Oak," by Lord Alfred Tennyson

12. In this poem, the seasons represent different

    (A) kinds of trees

    (B) times of day

    (C) stages of life

    (D) styles of dress

    (E) periods of history

13. The "he" mentioned in line 13 refers to

    (A) the poet

    (B) life

    (C) the oak

    (D) autumn

    (E) the reader

GO ON TO THE NEXT PAGE

14. What does "Gold again" in line 10 signify?

(A) The arrival of autumn

(B) The richness of summer

(C) The increased wealth of the narrator

(D) The color of oak trees

(E) The revival of the past

15. During which season is the oak referred to as "Living gold"?

(A) Spring

(B) Summer

(C) Autumn

(D) Winter

(E) This description does not refer to a season.

16. With which of the following statements about life would the speaker be most likely to agree?

(A) People should live every period of their lives to the fullest.

(B) It is important to try to accomplish something during one's lifetime.

(C) Life is too short to spend time doing unpleasant things.

(D) The seasons are unpredictable.

(E) Trees are an integral part of the enjoyment of life.

17. All of the following can describe the tone of the poem EXCEPT

(A) optimistic

(B) passionate

(C) pompous

(D) hopeful

(E) thoughtful

       Tea is consumed by more people and in greater amounts than any other beverage in the world, with the exception of water. The tea plant, from whose
*Line* leaves tea is made, is native to India, China,
(5) and Japan and was first cultivated for use by the Chinese in prehistoric times. The plant, which is characterized as an evergreen, can reach a height of about thirty feet but is usually pruned down to three or four feet for cultivation. It has dark green
(10) leaves and cream-colored, fragrant blossoms.

       Cultivation of the tea plant requires a great deal of effort. The plant must grow in a warm, wet climate in a carefully protected, well-drained area. Its leaves must be picked by hand. (Cultivation in
(15) North America has been attempted, but was found to be impractical because of a shortage of cheap labor.) Today, the plant is cultivated in the lands to which it is native, as well as in Sri Lanka, Indonesia, Taiwan, and South America.
(20)      Tea was probably first used as a vegetable relish and for medicinal purposes. In the 1400s Chinese and Japanese Buddhists developed a semireligious ceremony surrounding tea drinking. It was not until after 1700, however, that tea was first imported
(25) into Europe. Today, the United Kingdom imports more tea than does any other nation— almost one-third of the world's production. The United States is also a large importer, but Americans have seemed to prefer coffee ever since
(30) the famous Boston Tea Party in 1773.

18. This passage is mainly about

(A) the tea plant

(B) the uses of the tea plant

(C) tea drinking throughout history

(D) the tea trade

(E) the cultivation of the tea plant

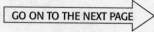 GO ON TO THE NEXT PAGE

19. According to the passage, the tea plant

    (A) was first cultivated in Japan in prehistoric times

    (B) requires well-drained soil to grow properly

    (C) is the largest import of the United Kingdom

    (D) has odorless flowers

    (E) is native to South America

20. Why is a large supply of cheap labor important for the cultivation of tea?

    (A) Since the tea plant can reach a height of thirty feet, several workers are required to harvest each plant.

    (B) Since tea is exported all over the world, a lot of people are needed to handle the trade complications that arise.

    (C) Since tea has been around since prehistoric times, many workers are employed to protect it and ensure that it doesn't die out.

    (D) Since England and China are far away from each other, many workers are required to coordinate tea shipments and deliveries.

    (E) Since the tea plant is handpicked, many laborers are needed at harvest time.

21. The style in the passage is most like that found in a

    (A) newspaper article

    (B) passage in an encyclopedia

    (C) cookbook

    (D) journal entry

    (E) history textbook

22. Which of the following is the author most likely to discuss next?

    (A) The details and aftermath of the Boston Tea Party

    (B) Other major imports of the United Kingdom and United States

    (C) Current trends in tea consumption

    (D) Other examples of plants that have a medicinal value

    (E) A description of what China was like in prehistoric times

23. The purpose of the second paragraph is to

    (A) describe the role of tea in religious ceremonies

    (B) explain why Americans prefer coffee

    (C) discuss historical uses of tea

    (D) describe the cultivation of tea

    (E) question the importance of tea

GO ON TO THE NEXT PAGE

There were moments of waiting. The youth
thought of the village street at home before the
arrival of the circus parade on a day in the spring.
*Line* He remembered how he had stood, a small thrillful
(5) boy, prepared to follow the band in its faded
chariot. He saw the yellow road, the lines of
expectant people, and the sober houses. He
particularly remembered an old fellow who used to
sit upon a cracker box in front of the store and
(10) pretend to despise such exhibitions. A thousand
details of color and form surged in his mind.

Someone cried, "Here they come!" There was
rustling and muttering among the men.

They displayed a feverish desire to have every
(15) possible cartridge ready to their hands. The boxes
were pulled around into various positions and
adjusted with great care.

The tall soldier, having prepared his rifle,
produced a red handkerchief of some kind. He was
(20) engaged in knitting it about his throat with
exquisite attention to its position, when the cry
was repeated up and down the line in a muffled
roar of sound.

"Here they come! Here they come!" Gun locks
(25) clicked.

Across the smoke-infested fields came a brown
swarm of running men who were giving shrill
yells. They came on, stooping and swinging their
rifles at all angles. A flag, tilted forward, sped near
(30) the front.

24. In the first paragraph, the youth is primarily
concerned with

(A) reliving a fond childhood memory
(B) describing a turning point in his life
(C) preparing for the upcoming battle
(D) planning his day at the circus
(E) watching a soldier tie a handkerchief

25. What is meant by the exclamation "Here they
come!" in line 12?

(A) A band in a chariot is approaching.
(B) The circus is coming to town.
(C) The enemy soldiers are advancing.
(D) A group of men selling handkerchiefs is
on its way.
(E) The youth's family is arriving to save him.

26. The tone of the passage undergoes a change
from the first to the second paragraph that can
best be described as a movement from

(A) anger to amusement
(B) reminiscence to anticipation
(C) informality to formality
(D) reluctance to fear
(E) respect to indifference

27. According to the passage, all of the following
are ways the soldiers prepare for battle EXCEPT

(A) gathering cartridges
(B) positioning ammunition
(C) priming their guns
(D) tying handkerchiefs
(E) saddling horses

28. Why are the men in the last paragraph
carrying a flag?

(A) It is going to be raised in the youth's
village.
(B) It needs to be protected from gunfire.
(C) It is going to be burned in a public
demonstration.
(D) It represents the side they are fighting for.
(E) It has been damaged and needs to be
mended.

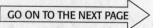
GO ON TO THE NEXT PAGE

Acupuncture is a type of medical therapy that has been part of Chinese medicine since ancient times. It involves the insertion of thin,
*Line* solid needles into specific sites on the body's
(5) surface. The belief is that the application of a needle at one particular point produces a specific response at a second point. It is based on the ancient Chinese philosophy that human beings are miniature versions of the universe and that the
(10) forces that control nature also control health. These forces are divided between two main principles called the yin and the yang, which have an opposite but complementary effect on each other. For example, one force keeps the body's
(15) temperature from rising too high, and the other keeps it from dropping too low. When they are in balance, the body maintains a constant, normal state. Disease occurs when these forces get out of balance.
(20) Although acupuncture had been used in Western countries during many periods, it was not until the 1970s that it gained widespread interest, when it was determined that it could be used to control pain during surgery. The mechanism for its
(25) effectiveness is still a mystery, but it has become a very popular technique in many countries for the treatment of various diseases and medical problems.

29. Which of the following is true about acupuncture?

  I. Although originally only a part of Chinese medicine, it is now practiced in many Western countries.

  II. It has been used to control pain during surgery since ancient times.

  III. The mechanism for its effectiveness was discovered during the 1970s.

  (A) I only
  (B) I and II only
  (C) I and III only
  (D) II and III only
  (E) I, II, and III

30. This passage is primarily about

  (A) various diseases that are particularly common among the Chinese
  (B) the meaning and use of the yin and the yang
  (C) different types of medical therapies and their relative effectiveness
  (D) the historical and philosophical background of acupuncture
  (E) modern uses of acupuncture both in China and in Western countries

31. According to the passage, acupuncture is based on

  (A) the idea that the human body is a model of the universe and is therefore controlled by the forces of nature
  (B) a firm belief in the Chinese gods known as the yin and the yang
  (C) an ancient Chinese religious ceremony that involves the insertion of needles into the body
  (D) a philosophy of health and disease that originated in China but has been totally changed by Western countries
  (E) the ideas of an astronomer who was attempting to study the universe in ancient times

32. According to the passage, the yin and the yang are principles that represent

  (A) high and low extremes of temperature
  (B) states of health and disease
  (C) similar treatments for different diseases
  (D) competing, balancing forces within the body
  (E) the ideas of comfort and pain

GO ON TO THE NEXT PAGE

33. The author includes the example of the yin and the yang controlling the extremes of body temperature in order to

   (A) back up her claim that the forces within the body mirror the forces of the universe

   (B) clarify how these forces have a complementary effect on each other

   (C) provide proof that acupuncture is an effective medical therapy

   (D) suggest a possible explanation for why people sometimes run high fevers

   (E) highlight a feature of the body that acupuncture has not yet been shown to influence

34. The author's tone in this passage could best be described as

   (A) critical

   (B) admiring

   (C) bitter

   (D) serene

   (E) neutral

   The painter Georgia O'Keeffe was born in Wisconsin in 1887, and grew up on her family's farm. At seventeen she left for Chicago and New
Line York, but she never lost her bond with the land.
(5) Like most painters, O'Keeffe painted the things that were most important to her, and she became famous for her simplified paintings of nature. During a visit to New Mexico in 1929, O'Keeffe was moved by the desert's stark beauty, and she
(10) began to paint many of its images. From about 1930 until her death in 1986, her true home was in the western desert, and bleached bones, barren hills, and colorful flowers were her characteristic subjects.

(15)   O'Keeffe is widely considered to have been a pioneering American modernist painter. While most early modern American artists were strongly influenced by European art, O'Keeffe's position was more independent.
(20)   Almost from the beginning, her work was more identifiably American—in its simplified and idealized treatment of color, light, space, and natural forms. Her paintings are generally considered "semiabstract," because, while they
(25) often depict recognizable images and objects, they don't present those images in a very detailed or realistic way. Rather, the colors and shapes in her paintings are often so reduced and simplified that they begin to take on a life of their own,
(30) independent from the real-life objects they are taken from.

35. According to the passage, all of the following strongly influenced O'Keeffe's paintings EXCEPT

   (A) her rural upbringing

   (B) her life in the West

   (C) the work of artists in other countries

   (D) the appearance of the natural landscape

   (E) animal and plant forms

GO ON TO THE NEXT PAGE ▷

36. O'Keeffe's relationship to nature is most similar to

(A) a photographer's relationship to a model

(B) a writer's relationship to a publisher

(C) a student's relationship to a part-time job

(D) a sculptor's relationship to an art dealer

(E) a carpenter's relationship to a hammer

37. O'Keeffe's paintings have been called "semiabstract" because they

(A) involve a carefully realistic use of color and light

(B) depict common, everyday things

(C) show recognizable scenes from nature

(D) depict familiar things in an unrealistic way

(E) refer directly to real-life activities

38. According to the passage, O'Keeffe is considered an artistic pioneer because

(A) her work became influential in Europe

(B) she painted the American Southwest

(C) her paintings had a definite American style

(D) she painted things that were familiar to her

(E) her work was very abstract

39. The passage's main point about O'Keeffe is that she

(A) was the best painter of her generation

(B) was a distinctive modern American painter

(C) liked to paint only what was familiar to her

(D) never developed fully enough as an abstract artist

(E) used colors and shapes that are too reduced and simple

40. It can be inferred from the passage that modern European art of the time

(A) did not depict images of the desert

(B) was extremely abstract

(C) did not portray natural shapes in a simple, idealistic manner

(D) was not influenced by rural landscapes

(E) approached colors in a semiabstract manner

IF YOU FINISH BEFORE TIME IS CALLED, YOU MAY CHECK YOUR WORK ON THIS SECTION ONLY. DO NOT TURN TO ANY OTHER SECTION IN THE TEST.    STOP

# SECTION 4

Time—30 Minutes
60 Questions

This section consists of two different types of questions. There are directions for each type.

Each of the following questions consists of one word followed by five words or phrases. You are to select the one word or phrase whose meaning is closest to the word in capital letters.

1. PLEAD:

   (A) strike
   (B) cry
   (C) tease
   (D) beg
   (E) try

2. PROWL:

   (A) growl
   (B) sneak
   (C) scrub
   (D) leave
   (E) fight

3. VESSEL:

   (A) blood
   (B) decoration
   (C) car
   (D) account
   (E) container

4. APPROVE:

   (A) withhold information
   (B) regard innocently
   (C) watch attentively
   (D) judge favorably
   (E) consider carefully

5. SEEP:

   (A) ooze
   (B) gurgle
   (C) liquefy
   (D) stick
   (E) fall

6. VEX:

   (A) scribble
   (B) locate
   (C) scream
   (D) play
   (E) irritate

7. DOZE:

   (A) graze
   (B) sleep
   (C) refresh
   (D) bore
   (E) ignore

8. BOUNTY:

   (A) outside border
   (B) new harvest
   (C) woven basket
   (D) upper limit
   (E) generous gift

GO ON TO THE NEXT PAGE

9. COARSE:

   (A) sifted
   (B) sticky
   (C) unpopular
   (D) difficult
   (E) rough

10. MEEK:

   (A) submissive
   (B) old
   (C) tiny
   (D) worried
   (E) quick

11. SATURATE:

   (A) anger
   (B) measure
   (C) soak
   (D) boil
   (E) pour

12. GENTEEL:

   (A) timid
   (B) loud
   (C) stupid
   (D) harmless
   (E) refined

13. WINSOME:

   (A) athletic
   (B) charming
   (C) critical
   (D) small
   (E) shy

14. REPROACH:

   (A) retreat
   (B) blame
   (C) insist
   (D) complain
   (E) whine

15. DEMONSTRATE:

   (A) object
   (B) show
   (C) require
   (D) renew
   (E) imply

16. CAMOUFLAGE:

   (A) jewelry
   (B) outfit
   (C) disguise
   (D) outlook
   (E) helmet

17. AGHAST:

   (A) shocked
   (B) swollen
   (C) irritated
   (D) nasty
   (E) rude

18. RECOLLECT:

   (A) invent
   (B) remove
   (C) discover
   (D) reject
   (E) remember

 GO ON TO THE NEXT PAGE

19. INITIATE:

    (A) gather
    (B) try
    (C) start
    (D) command
    (E) celebrate

20. SUFFOCATE:

    (A) give instruction
    (B) pull out
    (C) make willing
    (D) surround completely
    (E) deprive of air

21. PREVAIL:

    (A) triumph
    (B) predict
    (C) entrust
    (D) cover
    (E) enlighten

22. PRANCE:

    (A) boast
    (B) lead
    (C) strut
    (D) pry
    (E) sing

23. PROFOUND:

    (A) stubborn
    (B) unfounded
    (C) perplexing
    (D) absurd
    (E) deep

24. LIMBER:

    (A) supple
    (B) wooden
    (C) skinny
    (D) sober
    (E) sociable

25. TERMINATE:

    (A) extend
    (B) renew
    (C) finalize
    (D) sell
    (E) end

26. CONTEMPLATE:

    (A) ponder
    (B) reject
    (C) founder
    (D) dominate
    (E) deserve

27. CAPRICE:

    (A) idea
    (B) mistake
    (C) whim
    (D) decision
    (E) guess

28. ADAGE:

    (A) permission
    (B) disdain
    (C) humor
    (D) prevention
    (E) proverb

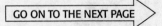
GO ON TO THE NEXT PAGE

29. DIN:

   (A) outline
   (B) clamor
   (C) improvement
   (D) demonstration
   (E) pressure

30. EXPUNGE:

   (A) erase
   (B) handle
   (C) label
   (D) assault
   (E) keep

**The following questions ask you to find relationships between words. For each question, select the choice that best completes the meaning of the sentence.**

31. Pilot is to airplane as

   (A) team is to players
   (B) horse is to cart
   (C) captain is to ship
   (D) passenger is to train
   (E) army is to country

32. Snake is to python as dog is to

   (A) terrier
   (B) canine
   (C) pet
   (D) mammal
   (E) quadruped

33. Mayor is to city as

   (A) governor is to state
   (B) member is to union
   (C) board is to district
   (D) secretary is to committee
   (E) citizen is to legislature

34. Paper is to novel as

   (A) person is to poll
   (B) paint is to brush
   (C) canvas is to portrait
   (D) back is to chair
   (E) color is to palette

35. Refined is to vulgar as

   (A) calm is to placid
   (B) submissive is to recalcitrant
   (C) happy is to ecstatic
   (D) helpful is to victorious
   (E) tranquil is to forgivable

36. Whip is to lash as

   (A) stick is to throw
   (B) shoe is to walk
   (C) saddle is to sit
   (D) food is to eat
   (E) club is to beat

37. Migrate is to swan as

   (A) hibernate is to groundhog
   (B) pet is to dog
   (C) reproduce is to fish
   (D) sting is to bee
   (E) pounce is to cat

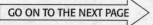 GO ON TO THE NEXT PAGE

38. Weather is to meteorologist as vegetation is to

(A) driver

(B) artist

(C) oceanographer

(D) hunter

(E) botanist

39. Track is to horse racing as

(A) circus is to elephant

(B) court is to tennis

(C) net is to basketball

(D) goal is to football

(E) air is to bird

40. Director is to actor as coach is to

(A) executive

(B) player

(C) chorus

(D) airplane

(E) officer

41. Dessert is to meal as

(A) finale is to performance

(B) lunch is to breakfast

(C) fork is to spoon

(D) plate is to table

(E) ocean is to river

42. Confirm is to deny as

(A) accept is to reject

(B) assert is to proclaim

(C) contend is to imply

(D) pull is to tug

(E) simplify is to organize

43. Tower is to airport as lighthouse is to

(A) museum

(B) jet

(C) park

(D) farm

(E) shoreline

44. Fidelity is to unfaithfulness as

(A) loyalty is to honor

(B) friendship is to gossip

(C) honesty is to deceit

(D) laziness is to slothfulness

(E) intelligence is to unconcern

45. Widespread is to limited as

(A) encompassed is to surrounded

(B) enlarged is to big

(C) broad is to narrow

(D) unusual is to strange

(E) provincial is to international

46. Saw is to carpenter as plow is to

(A) banker

(B) surveyor

(C) farmer

(D) physician

(E) steelworker

47. Sword is to fence as glove is to

(A) box

(B) soccer

(C) hockey

(D) baseball

(E) golf

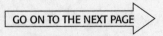GO ON TO THE NEXT PAGE

48. Encourage is to demand as

    (A) insinuate is to hint
    (B) fire is to dismiss
    (C) suggest is to order
    (D) motivate is to undermine
    (E) condemn is to reprimand

49. Grin is to delight as

    (A) anxiety is to confusion
    (B) frown is to dismay
    (C) perspiration is to exhaustion
    (D) laugh is to happiness
    (E) resignation is to uncertainty

50. Mysterious is to understandable as

    (A) unknown is to indefinable
    (B) doubtful is to incredulous
    (C) skillful is to swift
    (D) clouded is to warm
    (E) obscure is to clear

51. Injury is to heal as malfunction is to

    (A) repair
    (B) bandage
    (C) misinterpret
    (D) throw
    (E) disassemble

52. Jog is to sprint as trot is to

    (A) ramble
    (B) gallop
    (C) roam
    (D) saunter
    (E) soar

53. Bone is to body as

    (A) floor is to house
    (B) motor is to boat
    (C) driver is to car
    (D) knob is to door
    (E) beam is to building

54. Amorphous is to shape as odorless is to

    (A) appearance
    (B) weight
    (C) worth
    (D) scent
    (E) anger

55. Vain is to humble as

    (A) anxious is to boisterous
    (B) cantankerous is to thoughtless
    (C) judicious is to lenient
    (D) authoritative is to discursive
    (E) extroverted is to shy

56. Test is to study as

    (A) job is to apply
    (B) train is to practice
    (C) play is to rehearse
    (D) office is to employ
    (E) income is to work

57. Smile is to frown as cheer is to

    (A) jeer
    (B) wince
    (C) laugh
    (D) extricate
    (E) leap

GO ON TO THE NEXT PAGE

58. Banana is to peel as

    (A) egg is to crack

    (B) carrot is to uproot

    (C) apple is to core

    (D) bread is to slice

    (E) corn is to husk

59. Touch is to tactile as

    (A) sound is to noise

    (B) smell is to olfactory

    (C) mouth is to oral

    (D) eye is to visual

    (E) taste is to sense

60. Articulateness is to speech as

    (A) etiquette is to society

    (B) music is to note

    (C) ballet is to form

    (D) legibility is to handwriting

    (E) painting is to palette

IF YOU FINISH BEFORE TIME IS CALLED, YOU MAY CHECK YOUR WORK ON THIS SECTION ONLY. DO NOT TURN TO ANY OTHER SECTION IN THE TEST.

# SECTION 5

Time—30 Minutes
25 Questions

In this section, there are five possible answers after each problem. Choose which one is best. You may use the blank space at the right of the page for scratch work.

Note: Figures provided with the problems are drawn with the greatest possible accuracy, UNLESS stated "Not Drawn to Scale."

1. The crown in Figure 1 is made up of toothpicks that each have the same length. If each toothpick is 2 meters long and each side is equal to one toothpick, what is the perimeter of the crown in meters?

    (A)  5
    (B)  7
    (C)  10
    (D)  12
    (E)  14

USE THIS SPACE FOR FIGURING.

Figure 1

2. $D$ is an odd number between 4 and 11. If $D$ is also between 7 and 18, what is the value of $D$?

    (A)  5
    (B)  7
    (C)  8
    (D)  9
    (E)  11

3. Gary has a collection of 16 different operas, and his roommate Paul has a collection of 18 different operas. If Paul and Gary have 4 operas common to both record collections, how many different operas do they have between them?

    (A)  18
    (B)  30
    (C)  34
    (D)  36
    (E)  38

4.  If $\frac{1}{9}G = 18$, then $\frac{1}{3}G =$

(A)   6

(B)   9

(C)  36

(D)  54

(E)  63

**USE THIS SPACE FOR FIGURING.**

5.  A model sailboat floating on the water is attached to a string 1 meter long, as shown in Figure 2. If the string is tied to a post on the edge of the dock, which of the following best shows the area of water on which the sailboat can float?

Figure 2

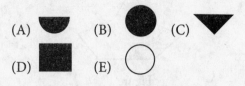

6.  At a party, there are exactly 4 times as many adults as children. Which of the following could be the total number of people at this party?

(A) 14

(B) 16

(C) 21

(D) 25

(E) 29

7.  Using a pair of scissors, which of the following can be made from a 20 cm by 28 cm rectangular sheet of paper by one straight cut?

   I. Triangle

  II. Square

 III. Rectangle

(A) I only

(B) II only

(C) III only

(D) I and II only

(E) I, II, and III

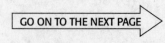
GO ON TO THE NEXT PAGE

8.  According to the graph in Figure 3, the average number of students taking the swimming class during the four months of March through June was

   (A) 50
   (B) 55
   (C) 60
   (D) 65
   (E) 70

**Questions 9–10 refer to the following definition.**

For all real numbers $n$ and $r$, $n \clubsuit r = (n - 1) - \dfrac{n}{r}$.

EXAMPLE: $5 \clubsuit 3 = (5 - 1) - \dfrac{5}{3} = 4 - \dfrac{5}{3} = 2\dfrac{1}{3}$.

9.  What is the value of $4 \clubsuit 2$?

   (A)  1
   (B)  2
   (C)  6
   (D)  8
   (E) 16

10. If $Q \clubsuit 2 = 4$, then $Q =$

   (A) 10
   (B)  8
   (C)  6
   (D)  4
   (E)  2

USE THIS SPACE FOR FIGURING.

NUMBER OF STUDENTS TAKING
SWIMMING CLASS

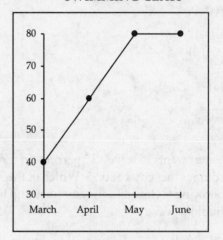

Figure 3

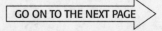

11. If Henry traveled at a rate of 45 miles per hour, how many hours did it take him to drive 225 miles?

(A) 3

(B) 4

(C) $4\frac{1}{2}$

(D) 5

(E) $5\frac{1}{2}$

USE THIS SPACE FOR FIGURING.

12. Robert wants to leave a 15 percent tip for a dinner that costs $20.95. Which of the following is closest to the amount of tip he should leave?

(A) $2.70

(B) $3.00

(C) $3.15

(D) $3.50

(E) $3.75

13. Juan studied from 4:00 P.M. to 6:00 P.M. and finished one-third of his assignments. He is taking a break and wants to finish his homework by 10:30 P.M. If he plans to continue working at the same rate, what is the latest that he can return to his studies?

(A) 6:30 P.M.

(B) 7:00 P.M.

(C) 7:30 P.M.

(D) 8:00 P.M.

(E) 8:30 P.M.

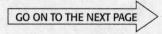
GO ON TO THE NEXT PAGE

14. Mrs. Brown and her *z* children each ate 2 peaches. What's the total number of peaches they ate?

   (A)  $z + 1$
   (B)  $z + 2$
   (C)   $2z$
   (D)  $2z + 1$
   (E)  $2z + 2$

USE THIS SPACE FOR FIGURING.

15. Which figure can be drawn WITHOUT lifting the pencil or retracing?

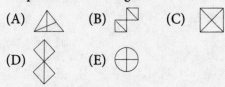

16. If 0.59 is about $\dfrac{N}{5}$, then *N* is closest to which of the following?

   (A)  0.3
   (B)   1
   (C)   2
   (D)   3
   (E)  30

17. If the largest of 7 consecutive integers is 25, what is the average of the 7 integers?

   (A)  24
   (B)  22
   (C)  21
   (D)  20
   (E)  16

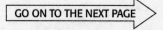 GO ON TO THE NEXT PAGE

18. The price of a box of raisins increased from $0.93 to $1.08. The increase in price is closest to what percent?

(A) 1%

(B) 14%

(C) 15%

(D) 16%

(E) 20%

$$21\overline{)Q}^{15}$$

$$15\overline{)S}^{21} \text{ remainder } 8$$

19. In the division problems shown above, $S - Q =$

(A) 6

(B) 8

(C) 15

(D) 18

(E) 21

20. What is the least number of square tiles with side 6 cm needed to cover a rectangular floor 72 cm long and 48 cm wide?

(A) 14

(B) 72

(C) 96

(D) 144

(E) 192

USE THIS SPACE FOR FIGURING.

GO ON TO THE NEXT PAGE

21. It takes Craig 5 minutes to type *n* pages. At this rate, how many minutes will it take him to type 20 pages?

(A)  $\dfrac{n}{100}$

(B)  $\dfrac{4}{n}$

(C)  $\dfrac{100}{n}$

(D)  $4n$

(E)  $100n$

USE THIS SPACE FOR FIGURING.

22. The width of a rectangular swimming pool is one-quarter of its length. If the length is 60 meters, what is the perimeter of the pool?

(A)  60 m
(B)  120 m
(C)  150 m
(D)  180 m
(E)  240 m

23. The price of a dress at a department store decreases by 20 percent every month it is not sold. After 3 months, the current price of the unsold dress is approximately what percent of the original price?

(A)  40%
(B)  50%
(C)  60%
(D)  70%
(E)  80%

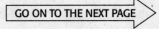
GO ON TO THE NEXT PAGE

24. If $p$ is a positive integer and $n$ is a negative integer, which of the following is greatest?

   (A) $\dfrac{p}{n}$

   (B) $\dfrac{n}{p}$

   (C) $\dfrac{1}{p-n}$

   (D) $\dfrac{1}{n-p}$

   (E) It cannot be determined from the information given.

25. At a party, 2/3 of the guests drank only soda and 1/4 of the guests drank only juice. If the remaining 5 guests had nothing to drink, then how many guests were at the party.

   (A) 60
   (B) 50
   (C) 45
   (D) 30
   (E) 25

USE THIS SPACE FOR FIGURING.

IF YOU FINISH BEFORE TIME IS CALLED, YOU MAY CHECK YOUR WORK ON THIS SECTION ONLY. DO NOT TURN TO ANY OTHER SECTION IN THE TEST.

# ANSWER KEY

**Section 2**

| | | | | |
|---|---|---|---|---|
| 1. E | 5. D | 36. A | 26. A | 57. A |
| 2. B | 6. D | 37. D | 27. C | 58. E |
| 3. B | 7. C | 38. C | 28. E | 59. B |
| 4. E | 8. A | 39. B | 29. B | 60. D |
| 5. E | 9. C | 40. C | 30. A | **Section 5** |
| 6. B | 10. E | **Section 4** | 31. C | 1. E |
| 7. C | 11. C | 1. D | 32. A | 2. D |
| 8. B | 12. C | 2. B | 33. A | 3. B |
| 9. A | 13. C | 3. E | 34. C | 4. D |
| 10. C | 14. A | 4. D | 35. B | 5. A |
| 11. A | 15. A | 5. A | 36. E | 6. D |
| 12. D | 16. A | 6. E | 37. A | 7. E |
| 13. B | 17. C | 7. B | 38. E | 8. D |
| 14. C | 18. A | 8. E | 39. B | 9. A |
| 15. E | 19. B | 9. E | 40. B | 10. A |
| 16. C | 20. E | 10. A | 41. A | 11. D |
| 17. E | 21. B | 11. C | 42. A | 12. C |
| 18. E | 22. C | 12. E | 43. E | 13. A |
| 19. D | 23. D | 13. B | 44. C | 14. E |
| 20. A | 24. A | 14. B | 45. C | 15. D |
| 21. C | 25. C | 15. B | 46. C | 16. D |
| 22. D | 26. B | 16. C | 47. A | 17. B |
| 23. D | 27. E | 17. A | 48. C | 18. D |
| 24. C | 28. D | 18. E | 49. B | 19. B |
| 25. A | 29. A | 19. C | 50. E | 20. C |
| **Section 3** | 30. D | 20. E | 51. A | 21. C |
| 1. A | 31. A | 21. A | 52. B | 22. C |
| 2. C | 32. D | 22. C | 53. E | 23. B |
| 3. D | 33. B | 23. E | 54. D | 24. C |
| 4. C | 34. B | 24. A | 55. E | 25. A |
| | 35. C | 25. E | 56. C | |

# SSAT PRACTICE TEST 1: UPPER-LEVEL: ASSESS YOUR STRENGTHS

Use the following tables to determine which topics and chapters you need to review most. If you need help with your essay, be sure to review Chapter 9: The Essay and Chapter 26: Writing Skills.

| Topic | Question |
|---|---|
| Math I | Section 2, questions 1–25 |
| Reading Comprehension | Section 3, questions 1–40 |
| Verbal: Synonyms | Section 4, questions 1–30 |
| Verbal: Analogies | Section 4, questions 31–60 |
| Math II | Section 5, questions 1–25 |

| Topic | Number of Questions on Test | Number Correct | If you struggled with these questions, study… |
|---|---|---|---|
| Math I | 25 | | Chapters 10–14 and Chapter 25 |
| Reading Comprehension | 40 | | Chapter 8 |
| Verbal: Synonyms | 30 | | Chapters 7 and 24 |
| Verbal: Analogies | 30 | | Chapters 2 and 24 |
| Math II | 25 | | Chapters 10–14 and Chapter 25 |

# ANSWERS AND EXPLANATIONS

## SECTION 2: MATH

**1. E**

We need an answer here that is not a factor of 120. In other words, a number which will not evenly divide into 120. Only (E), 16, is not a factor of 120.

**2. B**

Recall that all figures on the SSAT are always drawn to scale unless stated otherwise. Extending the vertical line segment boundary of the art slice upward and extending the horizontal line segment boundary of the art slice to the right shows that the art slice is about 25% of the pie. Twenty-five percent or $\frac{1}{4}$ of 900 (the total number of students) is 225 art students.

**3. B**

Sean's sister must arrive $(25 - 14)$ or 11 minutes after midnight because it takes 14 minutes to reach midnight and 11 more minutes to add up to 25 minutes.

**4. E**

The key here is to make what you are given look like the answer choices. No calculation is needed. Round off 0.52 to 0.5 or $\frac{1}{2}$ and round 78 to 80.

**5. E**

Careful! The question asks for dollars. Each sack of money = $50 as is noted in the table. Brian has 4 more sacks than James, so the amount more than James that Brian saved is 4 times $50 which equals $200.

**6. B**

We must determine how much was saved by Andy and how much was saved by James and compare the two. Andy saved 8 sacks, which is 8 times $50 or $400, and James saved 2 sacks, which is 2 times $50 or $100. Thus, Andy's $400 is 4 times James's $100.

**7. C**

Using the formula Part = Percent × Whole, 30 = 30% × $N$ (total number of students). We need to isolate the total number of students ($N$). Thirty percent = $\frac{30}{100}$, so the equation can be written as $30 = \frac{30}{100} \times N$. Now multiply both sides of this equation by $\frac{100}{30}$; the $N$ is now by itself once $\frac{30}{100}$ and $\frac{100}{30}$ cancel out to 1. Multiplying $30 \times \frac{100}{30}$ gives a value of 100 for $N$.

**8. B**

Because of the word *except,* we need to determine which fraction is *not* less than 2. So we are looking for a fraction that is greater than or equal to 2. In order to determine this, make all of the fractions improper: With (A), $\frac{15}{8} = 1\frac{7}{8}$. The only fraction where the denominator can be divided into the numerator with a result of at least 2 is (B): $\frac{45}{22} = 2\frac{1}{22}$.

**9. A**

We are told all the sides are equal. Thus, set each segment = 1 and add. With (A), $A - C - B - D - F = 1$ ($A$ to $C$) + 1 ($C$ to $B$) + 1 ($B$ to $D$) + 2 ($D$ to $E$ and then $E$ to $F$) = 5. (B) counts to 4; hence, cross it out. (C) counts to 4 also, so cross it out. (D) counts to 3, and (E) counts to 4. The longest path is 5, so (A) is correct.

## 10. C

Scan the answer choices. (A), 80, is 80.08 − 80 = 0.08 away from 80.08. (B), 80.01, is 80.08 − 80.01 = 0.07 away from 80.08. (C), 80.1, is 80.1 − 80.08 = 0.02 away from 80.08. (D), 81, is 0.92 away from 80.08; and (E), 90, is more than 9 away from 80.08. The question asks for the choice closest to 80.08, and thus (C), 80.1, is correct.

## 11. A

Call the number $N$. Write an inequality using the information given. Remember, *of* means multiply, $\frac{1}{3} \times N < 12$. We need to isolate $N$, our unknown value. Multiplying both sides by the reciprocal of $\frac{1}{3}$, which is 3, produces a result of $N < 12 \times 3$, and thus $N < 36$. (A) is correct.

## 12. D

The minimum number of points Team B could have scored is 1 more than Team A, or 40. Using the average formula, Average = $\frac{\text{Sum of the terms}}{\text{Number of terms}}$, we can plug in our given information: Average = $\frac{40 \text{ points}}{5 \text{ players}}$. Thus the average score of the players on Team B must have been at least 8 points per player.

## 13. B

The sum of the 3 interior angles of any triangle is 180 degrees. Figure 4 indicates that two of the angles have degree measures of 90 and 45. So the degree measure of the third angle is 180 − 90 − 45 = 45. So this is a 45–45–90 triangle. In any triangle, the sides opposite two equal angles must be equal. Hence, $a = 6$.

## 14. C

Here, we need to divide 40,000 into 2,000,000: $\frac{2,000,000}{40,000}$. Simply cancel out 4 zeros from the bottom and 4 zeros from the top. We now have $\frac{200}{4}$, which equals 50.

## 15. E

The question states that $y$ is less than 3, and we want the value that $x$ cannot equal, so let's solve the equation for $x$ in terms of $y$ and see if we can conclude something about $x$. The equation is $x - y + 2 = 6$. First subtract 2 from both sides. Then $x - y = 6 - 2$, or $x - y = 4$. Adding $y$ to both sides, we have that $x = y + 4$. Since $y$ is less than 3, $y + 4$ must be less than 7. Now $x = y + 4$, so $x$ must be less than 7. Look for a choice that is not less than 7. Only (E), 8, is not less than 7. So $x$ cannot be 8, and (E) is correct.

## 16. C

Segment $AD = 55$. Because the length of $AB$ is 2 times the length of $BC$, let $BC = x$ and let $AB = 2x$. Since $AB = CD$, let $CD = 2x$ also. The total length of $AD = AB + BC + CD = 2x + x + 2x = 5x = 55$. Hence, $x = 11$ and $BD = BC + CD = x + 2x = 3x = 3 \times 11 = 33$.

## 17. E

The question asks for all the points. (A) is incorrect because it only includes the rectangular boundary of the set of all the points that touch the table; it does not include the points inside this rectangle that also touch the surface of the table. (E) indicates all the points and is correct.

## 18. E

The question is not asking for a value of $J$. Indeed, $J$ could be any whole number. The question is asking for the answer choice that can be written in the form $(J + 2) \times 3$, where $J$ is a whole number. Since 3 is a factor of $(J + 2) \times 3$, the choice we're looking for must be a multiple of 3. A whole number is a multiple of 3 if and only if the sum of its digits is a multiple of 3. Looking at the answer choices, only the sum of the digits of (E), 81, is a multiple of 3. That is, the sum of the digits of 81 is $8 + 1 = 9$, which is a multiple of 3. So (E) is correct.

### 19. D

Using the information given, isolate $a$: $a = 3b + 4 + 7 = 3b + 11$. Thus, $a = 3b + 11$. Next add 5 to both sides of this equation: $a + 5 = 3b + 11 + 5 = 3b + 16$.

### 20. A

They give us 21.5 out of 100, which is easily translated into 21.5%. Hence, 21.5% of (multiplication) 2,000,000 is $\frac{21.5}{100} \times 2,000,000$. Cancel out two zeros from the 100 in the denominator and from the 2,000,000 in the numerator to get $21.5 \times 20,000 = 430,000$.

### 21. C

Translate from English into math. Let Bob's current age = $x$, and let Jerry's current age = $x + 7$. To find their ages 5 years ago, subtract 5 years from each current age: 5 years ago Bob was $x - 5$, and Jerry was $x + 7 - 5 = x + 2$. The sum of Bob and Jerry's ages 5 years ago was $x - 5 + x + 2 = 2x - 3$.

### 22. D

The contestant answered a total of 5 questions correctly. Using our percent formula, Percent $\times$ Whole = Part, 20% $\times$ total number of questions = 5. Multiply both sides of the equation by $\frac{100}{20}$ (the reciprocal of 20%), and the total number of questions = 25. Thus, statement I is incorrect so eliminate (A), (C), and (E). For statement II, there were 25 − 15 =

10 questions remaining, and 1 of these 10 questions was answered correctly. So he answered $\frac{1}{10}$, or 10% of the remaining questions correctly, so statement II is true. (Also, both remaining answer choices, (B) and (D), contain this Roman numeral.) Finally, statement III is true because 1 of the remaining 10 questions was answered correctly so 9 of these 10 were not answered correctly. Eliminate choice (B). (D) remains and is correct.

### 23. D

This problem is perfect for our Picking Numbers strategy. $C = A \times B$. Pick two consecutive numbers for $A$ and $B$ such as 2 and 3. Their product is 6 and positive. However, if we selected 1 and 0, the product would be 0, which is neither positive nor negative. Because the integers are consecutive, one of the integers must be even, or a multiple of 2, and hence the product of any two consecutive integers must be even. (D) is correct.

### 24. C

Be careful here. The question asks for the difference before the discount. The sweaters were sold for 100% − 20% of their old price. Using our percent formula, Part = Percent $\times$ Whole, we have that 48 = 80% $\times$ old price. Convert 80% to $\frac{80}{100}$ and multiply both sides by $\frac{100}{80}$. We now have $\frac{100}{80} \times 48$ = old price. Canceling yields $60. Use the percent formula for the wool sweater, and you have the equation $64 = 80% $\times$ old price. You'll find that its original price was $80. The difference is $80 − $60 = $20.

## 25. A

The maximum load that a car can carry is $17\frac{1}{3}$ tons. If each car carries the maximum load minus $\frac{5}{9}$ of a ton, then each car carries $17\frac{1}{3} - \frac{5}{9} = \frac{52}{3} - \frac{5}{9} = \frac{52}{3} \times \frac{3}{3} - \frac{5}{9} = \frac{156-5}{9} = \frac{151}{9}$ tons. Next, multiply this amount carried in each car by 36 cars and get $\frac{151}{9} \times 36$ tons. Cancel the 9 into the 36 and get $151 \times 4 = 604$.

# SECTION 3: READING COMPREHENSION

## LEMURS PASSAGE

This fact-based passage introduces us to the lemur, a monkey-like animal that lives chiefly in Madagascar. We're given various information about lemurs: their physical characteristics, the origin of their name, where they're found, and so on.

### 1. A

The author's style is straightforward and informative, like the style of a biology textbook. A zoologist's diary would more likely be in the first-person ("June 20: Saw two lemurs in a jungle in southern Madagascar."), and a tourist's guidebook would go into less scientific detail and would place lemurs in a specific location. ("Be sure to check out the lemurs in Avahi National Park.")

### 2. C

Summarize the passage in your own mind. You might have come up with something like "Things to Know about Lemurs." (C) restates this idea. The passage doesn't mention whether lemurs hunt alone or in groups, so (B) is incorrect, and the rest of the answer choices focus on details.

### 3. D

You're looking for the detail that's false. The author states that lemurs eat "leaves . . . eggs, fruit, insects, and small animals," so (D) must be incorrect.

### 4. C

In the second half of the paragraph, the author states that lemurs "are reputed to be gentle, friendly creatures." If they're "gentle" and "friendly," you can infer that they're not very aggressive. (A) is contradicted in the final sentence of the passage. (B) and (D) are refuted when the author says that lemurs "are active throughout the day and night" and "most often are in the trees." We don't know enough about the flying lemur to infer that it can only be found in and around Madagascar, so (E) is incorrect.

### 5. D

(A) and (E) cannot be verified using the passage. (B) is incorrect because the passage states that "lemurs eat eggs ... insects, and small animals" (lines 13–14). (C) is incorrect because the passage says that lemurs "are active throughout the day" (line 14). (D) is correct because aye-ayes are in the lemur family and lemurs are primates.

## WOODROW WILSON PASSAGE

This historical passage focuses on President Woodrow Wilson and his post-World War I peace settlement—specifically, on the Fourteen-Point Plan, which called for the abolition of secret diplomacy. Wilson considered open negotiations vital for peace, but in paragraph 2 the author disagrees, arguing that Wilson's view was too simplistic.

### 6. D

The first and second sentences of each paragraph usually reveal the paragraph's topic. In this case, it's the second sentence: Wilson was wrong—war stems not from secret deals by national leaders but from "unresolved disagreements among nations." (A) and (E) summarize the topic of paragraph 1, not paragraph 2. (B) is too general; the paragraph mainly discusses why one form of diplomacy usually fails to avert wars. Not all disagreements among nations lead to war, so (C) is also too broad.

**7. C**

We're told that Wilson called for an end to secret negotiations as a way to end war and then that Wilson was wrong—that "he lacked insight into the complexities of international politics." Clearly, the author disagrees with Wilson. (A) is tempting, given the author's "realpolitik" attitude, but she isn't being Machiavellian; she's simply stating why Wilson's idea was wrong. (B) and (D) are too emotional, and (E) is incorrect because the author doesn't apologize for criticizing Wilson.

**8. A**

The scenario in (A) is the closest parallel to the author's thinking. As the next-to-last sentence of the passage puts it, "war usually stems from unresolved disagreements among nations . . . over territory . . . ." (B)'s scenario is an economic trade agreement involving a third country—not very likely to lead to war. The other answer choices involve secret deals or covert activity of the kind that Wilson—not the author—thought would lead to war.

**9. C**

Look at the last two sentences of the text. According to the author, open diplomacy can't solve the kinds of problems that lead to war. (A)'s assertion that quiet diplomacy will always be with us doesn't explain why open diplomacy won't prevent war.

**10. E**

To find the correct answer, try to answer each of the questions in the choices. (A) is answered in lines 14–15; the author says Wilson's first point on diplomacy was wrong. (B) is answered in lines 17–19; wars usually result from disagreements among nations. (C) is answered in line 7; Wilson supported open (public) diplomacy. (D) is answered in the second paragraph; the author says Wilson "lacked insight into the complexities of international politics" (lines 13–14), and then the author proceeds to present his or her knowledge or international politics. (E) is the answer because the passage does not tackle ways to eliminate the threat of war.

**11. C**

To imagine where the author might go next, retrace the steps of the argument: 1) Wilson offered a peace proposal that argued for open diplomacy, which he thought would end wars; 2) Wilson failed to grasp that secret diplomacy is not the cause of most wars, which occur because of unresolved disputes among nations over such things as territory and resources. Having disagreed with Wilson, it's most likely that the author will try to illustrate this last point by giving an example of a war that occurred because of a territorial or resource dispute. (A), (D), and (E) suggest that the author will return to the subjects of President Wilson or World War I, but the text moves beyond Wilson to discuss the cause of war.

## POETRY PASSAGE

You are likely to see one poem on the SSAT. When you do, be alert for tone and the use of metaphor. Here, an oak tree is used as a metaphor—for living our lives as an oak tree does, in accordance with nature and the change of seasons. The first three lines of the poem generate its central metaphor: "Live thy life, Young and old, Like yon oak…" ("Yon" is short for "yonder," meaning "that oak over there.") In other words, "Live your life, at all ages, like that oak tree does."

### 12. C

You're asked to infer the poem's central metaphor. What do the seasons represent? The successive stages of life, (C): Spring is youth, summer is maturity, autumn is middle age, and winter is old age.

### 13. C

Who is the "he" of line 13? The entire stanza provides clues: "he" has lost his leaves, "he" stands, "trunk and bough, naked strength." "He," then, is the oak tree.

### 14. A

The second stanza shows the oak tree in summer and in autumn; "gold again" refers to the seasonally changed color of the oak tree's leaves, so (A) is best here. (B), (C), and (E) are pretty easily eliminated, and (D) isn't right because the arrival of autumn signals a change in foliage—and the quoted phrase refers to the latter, not the former.

### 15. A

This is a Detail question. The oak is referred to as "Living gold" in line 5 of the poem; the previous line says, "Bright in spring."

### 16. A

This question basically asks for the statement that mirrors the poem's Big Idea, which is that we should be like the oak tree, living each season of our lives as well as we can. (A) restates this best. (B) is

wrong because "something" can apparently be accomplished at any point in one's life; what about the other "seasons"? (C) makes little sense, and (D) contradicts the poem. (E) dispenses with the poem's central metaphor altogether: It's not that a good life includes the enjoyment of trees; it's that a good life is lived as a tree lives its life.

### 17. C

Think about how the poem would sound if you read it aloud. It would sound as if the poet were giving you advice on living life to the fullest. That rules out (A), (D), and (E). The poem is optimistic (seeking the best possible outcome), hopeful, and helpful; that leaves passionate (expressing intense feeling) and pompous (arrogant). The poem does sound intense, so the answer is (C).

## TEA PASSAGE

This passage is about tea—the plant, and the history of its cultivation and uses. Paragraph 1 describes its universal appeal, its origin, and its description and look. Paragraph 2 describes the difficulties of cultivating tea and where the plant is currently grown. The final paragraph summarizes tea's history, from ancient times to today.

### 18. A

The choice that best sums up the passage is (A). The other answer choices each touch on only one aspect of the text.

### 19. B

(A) is wrong because tea was first cultivated in China. (C) distorts lines 25–27: The author states that the United Kingdom is the world's largest importer of tea, not that tea is the United Kingdom's largest import.

**20. E**

The phrase "cheap labor" in the question stem is also found in paragraph 2, which states that, since tea leaves "must be picked by hand," cultivation in North America "was found to be impractical because of a shortage of cheap labor." In other words, tea cultivation requires a supply of cheap labor because the leaves must be handpicked. (A) contradicts paragraph 1, which says that tea plants are "usually pruned down to three or four feet for cultivation." (B) and (C) are never mentioned, and (D) incorrectly reduces the world's cultivation and consumption of tea to two countries, England and China.

**21. B**

The author's style is informative, offering an encyclopedic summary of the cultivation and uses of tea.

**22. C**

Since paragraph 3 summarizes the historic uses of tea, beginning with ancient times and ending with consumption today, it's likely that the author will continue to discuss current consumption trends. (A) temptingly mentions the last detail in the passage, but the Boston Tea Party is only an aside, a lighthearted explanation of why consumption of tea in the United States today lags behind that of coffee.

**23. D**

Paragraph 2 describes the difficulties of cultivating tea and where it is currently cultivated.

## FICTION PASSAGE

This passage reflects the thoughts going through a soldier's mind in the final moments before battle. Notice how the two lines of dialogue toward the end of the passage increase the tension of the imminent attack. Be alert for shifts of tone and perspective and the use of metaphor.

**24. A**

After the teaser in the opening sentence (moments of waiting for what?), the first paragraph details the youth's childhood memory of the circus in town, (A). The circus's arrival couldn't be called a turning point in his life—it was simply a fond memory—so (B) is incorrect. (D) is incorrect because he wasn't planning his day at the circus; he was simply enjoying the day as a spectator. Neither (C) nor (E) are discussed in the first paragraph, so they are incorrect as well.

**25. C**

The text jumps from one "scene" to another. That is, the quoted exclamation breaks us away from the youth's daydream of the circus and into the reality of his current situation. A fellow soldier has shouted that the enemy is approaching, (C), and we are jolted into the reality of the situation. (A) and (B) wrongly assume that the exclamation is part of the youth's memory, and (D) and (E) are completely unwarranted inferences.

**26. B**

As we have just seen in the previous question, the youth reminisces in paragraph 1. As we jump to the next paragraph and to the reality of the battle, the men prepare with anticipation. No other answer choice fits.

## 27. E

Horses are never mentioned here; all the soldiers are on foot.

## 28. D

Why do soldiers carry a flag? In the same way flags are raised on ships in the ocean, raising a flag on land is meant to represent one's side or country. (A) is tempting, but true only if the enemy wins. (B) makes no sense, since the flag is carried at the front of a charging line of soldiers.

## ACUPUNCTURE PASSAGE

This modified science passage discusses acupuncture, an ancient Chinese form of medical therapy. There's very little science in the passage. Instead, the author describes the thinking behind acupuncture and gives a brief history of its use in Western countries.

## 29. A

A Roman Numeral question. The only true statement, according to the passage, is statement I: Acupuncture was first practiced in China, but it is now practiced in many Western countries as well. Statement II is false: According to the first sentence of paragraph 2, acupuncture was not used to control pain during surgery until the 1970s. And the final sentence of the passage disputes statement III: The mechanism for its effectiveness "is still a mystery."

## 30. D

The author tells us what acupuncture involves, the ancient Chinese philosophy on which it's based, and how it recently spread to the West. The passage is primarily about the historical and philosophical background of acupuncture, (D). (A) is not mentioned, and (B) focuses too narrowly on the first paragraph. (C) is too general.

## 31. A

Paragraph 1 states that acupuncture is based on the ancient Chinese belief that "human beings are miniature versions of the universe" and that the same forces control nature and health. Yin and yang are not Chinese gods, (B); they're principles. And contrary to (D), Western countries have not "totally changed" the Chinese philosophy of health and disease. They may have ignored it or failed to understand it, but they did not change it.

## 32. D

Yin and yang have "an opposite but complementary effect on each other. . . . When they are in balance, the body maintains a constant, normal [i.e., healthy] state." (A) names an example of how the two principles operate, not what they represent. (B) wrongly states that one principle is healthy and the other unhealthy, but it's a balance of both that maintains health and an imbalance that results in sickness.

## 33. B

When yin and yang are in balance, the body is healthy, but when they're out of balance, disease occurs. These two forces work together, or complement, each other. The claim in (A) was made by ancient Chinese philosophy, and there is no actual proof in the passage for (C). The author does not mention any part of the body that isn't influenced by acupuncture, so (E) is incorrect.

## 34. B

Are the author's points positive, negative, or neutral? The author sticks to pointing out what acupuncture is and how it has become a popular form of treatment. The author doesn't talk about the negative aspects, so the tone is positive. That rules out (A), (C), and (E), leaving "admiring" and "serene." Next, think about how the passage would sound if you read it aloud. Does it sound as if the author holds acupuncture with high regard and respect (admiring), or does it sound calm and peaceful (serene)? Clearly, the author is excited about acupuncture and admires its effectiveness. (B) is the answer.

## O'KEEFFE PASSAGE

The final passage is about the American painter Georgia O'Keeffe—her life, her fame, and the subjects of her paintings. The opening sentence of paragraph 2 sums up the main point: O'Keeffe is "widely considered to have been a pioneering American modernist painter."

### 35. C

(C) is contradicted by paragraph 2, which states that O'Keeffe was "more independent" than most other early modern American artists, who were "strongly influenced by European art." The other choices can be found in the passage as influences on O'Keeffe.

### 36. A

O'Keeffe was the artist, and nature was her favorite subject. Do this one as you would an Analogy. The relationship of artist to subject is repeated in (A): The model *is* the photographer's subject. Similarly, nature is O'Keeffe's subject.

### 37. D

Why are the paintings "semiabstract" (line 24)? (B) and (C) are only half the answer: It was her treatment of these objects and scenes—the way she painted them—that made them "semiabstract."

### 38. C

According to paragraph 2, O'Keeffe was unlike her contemporary American painters—"independent," not influenced by European art. Her work was "identifiably American," which makes (C) correct. (B) and (D) are factually true, but they're not the reason why she's considered a pioneer. And (E) is incorrect since O'Keeffe's work was considered "semiabstract," not very abstract.

### 39. B

The main point is summed up in the opening sentence of paragraph 2. The author never claims that O'Keeffe was the best painter of her generation, (A), or that she didn't develop a fully abstract style, (D), or even that her colors and shapes were too simple, (E). (C) is plausible (though we never learn that O'Keeffe painted only familiar subjects), but it's not the main point.

### 40. C

We're told that European art strongly influenced most American artists of O'Keeffe's time. Unlike European art, however, O'Keeffe's paintings offered a "simplified and idealized treatment of color, light, space, and natural forms." Since European art was different from O'Keeffe's art, we can infer that it did not portray natural shapes in a simple, idealistic way, making (C) correct. No other answer choice can be inferred.

## SECTION 4: VERBAL

### SYNONYMS

### 1. D

To plead is to appeal earnestly or desperately—to beg.

**2.  B**

To prowl is to move around secretly, stealthily—in other words, to sneak.

**3.  E**

A vessel, such as a bowl or glass, is a container for holding something.

**4.  D**

To approve means to judge favorably.

**5.  A**

To seep means to flow through little cracks, or to ooze.

**6.  E**

To vex means to anger, or irritate.

**7.  B**

To doze is to sleep lightly. You might doze because someone bores you, but the two words are not synonymous.

**8.  E**

A bounty is a reward or gift.

**9.  E**

Something coarse is harsh or rough.

**10.  A**

Meek means mild mannered or submissive.

**11.  C**

To saturate is to wet something thoroughly or soak it. You saturate a sponge in water, for example.

**12.  E**

Genteel describes something elegant, aristocratic, or refined.

**13.  B**

Winsome means pleasing or charming, such as a winsome smile.

**14.  B**

To reproach means to express disapproval or disappointment in someone. (D) is tempting, but you can complain without blaming anything specific.

**15.  B**

To demonstrate means to explain clearly or show.

**16.  C**

A camouflage is a disguise or a concealment. An outfit, (B), may or may not be a camouflage.

**17.  A**

Aghast is an adjective that means to be struck with amazement or horror—in other words, to be shocked.

**18.  E**

To recollect means to remember.

**19.  C**

To initiate means to begin or start.

**20.  E**

To suffocate is to choke or deprive of air.

**21.  A**

To prevail means to win, overcome, or triumph.

**22.  C**

To prance is to walk in a cocky way or to strut. The closest wrong answer choice, in attitude at least, is (A), but boasting is not a way of walking.

**23. E**

Profound means deep-seated or intense. A parent has a profound love for his or her child.

**24. A**

Limber means flexible, lithe, nimble, or supple. (B), wooden, is a good antonym for limber.

**25. E**

To terminate means to finish or bring to an end.

**26. A**

To contemplate means to think about or ponder.

**27. C**

A caprice is a sudden fancy or whim. (A) is tempting, but not all ideas are whims or caprices.

**28. E**

An adage is a common saying or proverb.

**29. B**

A din is a loud, confused mixture of noises—in other words, a clamor.

**30. A**

To expunge is to get rid of, obliterate, erase.

## ANALOGIES

**31. C**

A pilot directs a plane as a captain directs a ship.

**32. A**

One breed of snake is a python. One breed of dog is a terrier. The relationships in the other answer choices are in the wrong order as compared to the stem words. In other words, a python is a subset of the snake family, and that same relationship is not reflected in (B)–(E). Quadruped, by the way, means four-legged.

**33. A**

A mayor is the highest official in a city. A governor is the highest official in a state. The suggested bridge easily eliminates (B), (C), and (E). With (D), a secretary is not usually the highest official on a committee—the chairperson is.

**34. C**

Paper is the material upon which a novel is written. Similarly, canvas is the material upon which a portrait is painted.

**35. B**

Refined is the opposite of vulgar. In (B), submissive is the opposite of recalcitrant, which means stubbornly defiant. (A) contains synonyms, not opposites. In (C), ecstatic is an extreme state of happiness. And the word pairs in (D) and (E) have no obvious relationship to each other.

**36. E**

You use a whip to lash something. You use a club to beat something. As for (A), you may throw a stick at someone, but that's not the relationship needed here.

**37. A**

To migrate is to travel seasonally. In the winter, swans migrate. In the winter, groundhogs hibernate (hide and sleep). Petting is something a person does to a dog, so (B) is incorrect, and (C), (D), and (E) are not specifically done in the winter—even though they all are things these animals do.

## 38. E

Flip the words: A meteorologist studies weather. Similarly, a botanist studies plants or vegetation.

## 39. B

Again, flip the pairs: Horse racing is done, or played, on a track. Tennis is played on a court.

## 40. B

A director tells an actor what to do, the way a coach tells a player what to do.

## 41. A

The relationship here is one of order or sequence. A dessert is eaten at the end of a meal. A finale is played at the end of a performance. Lunch is eaten after breakfast, but it's a different meal, not part of the same one, so the bridge doesn't fit.

## 42. A

The words in the stem are opposites. The only pair of opposites among the choices is in (A): Accept is the opposite of reject, as confirm is the opposite of deny.

## 43. E

A tower is the tall structure that enables planes to navigate safely at an airport. A lighthouse is the tall structure that enables ships to navigate safely near the shoreline.

## 44. C

Fidelity is the opposite or absence of unfaithfulness. Honesty is the opposite or absence of deceit. The words in (A) and (D) are synonyms, and there's no clear relationship between the words in (B) and (E).

## 45. C

If something is widespread, it's not limited. If something is broad, it's not narrow. The words in (A) are synonyms, as are the words in (B) and (D). (E) is a little tough: International seems to suggest sophisticated, which is the opposite of provincial, but the words are in the opposite order as those presented in the stem.

## 46. C

A saw is a tool used by a carpenter. A plow is a tool used by a farmer. No other occupation listed here requires the use of a plow.

## 47. A

A sword is used against an opponent in fencing just as a glove is used in boxing.

## 48. C

Here the relationship is one of degree, with the second word being much stronger than the first. You can encourage or suggest that someone do something, and they may or may not do it. But if you demand or order them to do it, then they must. The words in (A) and (B) are synonyms, and the words in (D) are opposites. Condemn in (E) is stronger than reprimand, not the other way around, so the order is wrong.

## 49. B

A grin is a facial expression showing delight. A frown is a facial expression showing dismay (dismay is a mixture of fear and discouragement). A laugh in (D) expresses happiness, but it isn't precisely a facial expression.

## 50. E

Something mysterious is not understandable. Something obscure is not clear.

### 51. A

When an injury heals, it disappears. When a malfunction is repaired, it disappears. In both cases, the thing that heals or is repaired gets better, which is why (E) is not quite right.

### 52. B

A jog is a slow run; a sprint is a fast run. A trot is a slow run for a horse, while a gallop is a fast run. (C) means to wander about—not at a great speed, while (D) means to stroll. (E) means flying, not running.

### 53. E

A bone is one part of the structural system of the body—the system that holds it up. Similarly, a beam—a long piece of timber or steel—is one part of the structural system that holds up a building. (A) may be tempting, but floors don't generally connect to other floors the way beams and bones do.

### 54. D

Amorphous means "without shape." So amorphous is to shape as odorless is to odor, or scent.

### 55. E

Another relationship of opposites. A vain person is, by definition, not humble. Similarly, an extroverted or outgoing person is, by definition, not shy. (A) may be tempting since boisterous means noisy and exuberant. But anxious people aren't by definition quiet; one may be anxious and act boisterously—by talking too much out of nervousness, for example. Cantankerous in (B) means bad tempered and quarrelsome, and discursive in (D) means to talk in a rambling way.

### 56. C

You study for a test the way you rehearse for a play. One is preparation for the other. (A) seems close, but apply is not quite "preparation" for a job.

### 57. A

You smile when you're happy and frown when you're sad or angry. You cheer to signal your approval and jeer your disapproval of a sports team, for example. Wince, in (B), means to express pain.

### 58. E

To peel a banana is to pull off its outer covering. To husk an ear of corn is to pull off its outer covering (also called a husk).

### 59. B

Tactile refers to anything perceptible through the sense of touch, just as olfactory refers to anything perceptible through the sense of smell. If they had been correct, (D) would have read, "sight is to visual," and (C), "taste is to oral."

### 60. D

Articulateness is the quality of speaking or writing in a clear manner. Similarly, legibility refers to clear, understandable handwriting.

## SECTION 5: MATH

### 1. E

The perimeter of a polygon is the sum of the lengths of its sides. Label each of the sides with a value of 2 and add.

### 2. D

(C) can be immediately eliminated because it is an even integer and we are looking for an odd. Since $D$ is an odd integer between 4 and 11, $D$ must be one of the integers 5, 7, or 9. Since $D$ is also between 7 and 18, $D$ must be one of the integers 9, 11, 13, 15, or 17. The only choice that meets both requirements is (D), 9. Notice that (E), 11, is not between 4 and 11.

**3.  B**

Gary and Paul have a total of 16 + 18 = 34 operas put together. This number is equal to the number of operas that only Gary has plus the number of operas that only Paul has plus twice the number of operas that they both have in common. The number that they have in common was counted twice: once in the number of operas that Gary has and once in the number of operas that Paul has. Since the number of operas that they have in common should only be counted once, subtract the 4 they have in common from 34, and the result is 30 different operas.

**4.  D**

Solve for $G$ by multiplying both sides by the reciprocal of $\frac{1}{9}$: $G = 18 \times \frac{9}{1} = 162$. Substitute 162 for $G$ into the expression $\frac{1}{3} G$, and you will get $\frac{1}{3} G = \frac{1}{3} \times 162 = 54$.

**5.  A**

The boat can swing out and around as far as the line extends or the wind can push it anywhere within this semicircle. If you chose (B), you assumed the boat could float onto the dock. You want the choice indicating all the points of the semicircle shaded, which is (A).

**6.  D**

Let $x$ = the number of children. Hence, $4x$ = the number of adults. The total number of people is then $x + 4x = 5x$. The key to solving this is to keep in mind that $x$ must be an integer. It is because of this that $5x$ must be a multiple of 5. Therefore the answer must be a multiple of 5. (D), 25, is correct.

**7.  E**

Draw a figure! With a diagonal cut, triangles can be created. By cutting to decrease the length 28 of the rectangle by 8 with a cut parallel to the sides of length 20, a square can be created. Cutting anywhere parallel to any side of the original rectangle, a rectangle with new dimensions can be created.

**8.  D**

We must note how many students were in the class each month. March = 40, April = 60, May = 80, and June = 80. Use the formula

$$\text{Average} = \frac{\text{Sum of the terms}}{\text{Number of terms}}.$$ Here, the average is

$$\frac{40 + 60 + 80 + 80}{4} = \frac{260}{4} = 65.$$

**9.  A**

The value of $n$ is 4, and the value of $r$ is 2. Simply substitute these values into the equation that defines the symbol: $4 \clubsuit 2 = (4 - 1) - \frac{4}{2} = 3 - \frac{4}{2} = 3 - 2 = 1$, (A).

**10. A**

Here, you are given $n = Q$ and $r = 2$. Use the equation given in the definition to set $Q \clubsuit 2$ equal to 4 and solve for $Q$: $(Q - 1) - \frac{Q}{2} = 4$. First, eliminate the denominator by multiplying both sides by 2: $2(Q - 1) - Q = 8$. Then, distribute the 2 through the parentheses: $2Q - 2 - Q = 8$. Third, isolate the $Q$: $Q = 10$, (A).

**11. D**

You might find the formula Rate × Time = Distance easier to use than a proportion. Either will work, so use the one with which you're more comfortable.

$$\frac{45 \text{ miles}}{1 \text{ hour}} = \frac{225 \text{ miles}}{t \text{ hours}}$$
$$45t = 225$$
$$t = 5$$

or

$$45 \text{ miles per hour} \times t \text{ hours} = 225 \text{ miles}$$
$$45t = 225$$
$$t = 5$$

### 12. C

Use the percent formula, Part = Percent × Whole. Here, tip = 15% of \$20.95 = 15% × \$20.95. Round the \$20.95 to \$21.00 and evaluate: $\frac{15}{100} \times 21 = \frac{3}{20} \times 21 = \frac{63}{20} = 3\frac{3}{20} = \$3.15$.

### 13. A

Break down the problem into steps. Juan finishes one-third of his homework in 2 hours. Thus, he has two-thirds still left to do. If it takes 2 hours to do one-third, it must take 4 hours to do two-thirds (twice as much). Finally, subtract 4 hours from 10:30 P.M, and we are left with 6:30 P.M.

### 14. E

Mrs. Brown ate 2 peaches, plus each child ate 2 peaches. She has $z$ children, so 2 for each of $z$ children and 2 for Mrs. Brown = $2z + 2$.

### 15. D

You'll recall the rule for geometry questions that ask about drawing figures in one fluid motion without lifting the pencil. In any given figure, if exactly zero or two points have an odd number of intersecting line segments and/or curves, it can be drawn without lifting the pencil or retracing. (A), (B), (C), and (E) are incorrect because they all have four points at which three line segments intersect. Four points is too many. (D) is the answer because it has two points that have three (an odd number) intersecting lines.

### 16. D

Round 0.59 to 0.6. Now, $0.6 = \frac{N}{5}$. Isolate the $N$ by multiplying both sides by 5. Then $N = 3$. (Be careful placing the decimal point.)

### 17. B

The consecutive integers must be 19, 20, 21, 22, 23, 24, and 25. The average of an odd number of equally spaced numbers is always the middle one. Consecutive integers are an instance of equally spaced numbers. The answer is 22.

### 18. D

The percent increase can be found using this formula: $\frac{\text{New price} - \text{Old price}}{\text{Old price}} \times 100\%$. Here, the percent increase is $\frac{1.08 - 0.93}{0.93} \times 100\% = \frac{0.15}{0.93} \times 100\% = \frac{15}{93} \times 100\% = \frac{5}{31} \times 100\% \approx 16\%$.

### 19. B

To find $Q$, use the first division problem. $Q = 15 \times 21 = 315$. To find $S$, use the second division problem. Then $S = 21 \times 15 + 8$. We already know that $15 \times 21 = 315$, so add 8 to the value 315 of $Q$ to get 323. Finally, $S - Q = 323 - 315 = 8$. Notice that this is also the remainder of the second division problem.

### 20. C

The area of the floor is found by multiplying $72 \times 48$. Dividing this result by the area of a single tile, which is $6 \times 6$, gives us the number of tiles needed. In the fraction $\frac{72 \times 48}{6 \times 6}$, cancel the 6s, leaving $12 \times 8 = 96$.

### 21. C

Set up a ratio here. $n$ pages is to 5 minutes as 20 pages is to how many minutes? Let's call $x$ the number of minutes it will take to type 20 pages. Therefore $\frac{n}{5} = \frac{20}{x}$. Cross-multiplying, we get $xn = 100$. Finally, isolate the $x$ by dividing each side by $n$: $x = \frac{100}{n}$, choice (C).

## 22. C

Draw a figure. The length is 60, and the width is $\frac{1}{4}$ of 60 or $\frac{1}{4} \times 60 = 15$. The perimeter is simply the sum of the lengths of all the sides: $60 + 60 + 15 + 15 = 150$ meters.

## 23. B

Pick 100 when dealing with percent problems. If the dress was $100 the first month, the second month it costs 80% of 100 or $80, and the third month it costs 80% of 80, which is $64. After 3 months it costs 80% of $64, which is about $51. So, after 3 months, the cost is about 50% of the original price.

## 24. C

Picking Numbers is your best option here. If $p = 4$ and $n = -2$, then the results are: (A), $-2$; (B), $-\frac{1}{2}$; (C), $\frac{1}{6}$; (D), $-\frac{1}{6}$. The greatest value is thus $\frac{1}{6}$, making (C) the correct choice. This question can also be solved by realizing that for any positive integer $p$ and any negative integer $n$, (A), (B), and (D) will be negative, while (C) will be positive.

## 25. A

Backsolving is a great way to get around setting up a complicated Algebra equation. Call the total number of guests $G$.

$\frac{2}{3} G$ had only soda, $\frac{1}{4} G$ had only juice, and the remaining 5 had nothing at all. That's enough information to find $G$.

$$\frac{2}{3} G + \frac{1}{4} G + 5 = G$$

$$\frac{8}{12} G + \frac{3}{12} G + 5 = G$$

$$\frac{11}{12} G + 5 = G$$

$$5 = G - \frac{11}{12} G$$

$$5 = \frac{1}{12} G$$

$$5(12) = G$$

$$60 = G$$

To Backsolve, start in the middle:

(C) $\frac{2}{3} (45) + \frac{1}{4} (45) + 5 = 30 + 11\frac{1}{4} + 5 = 46\frac{1}{4}$.

A fractional number of people can't attend a party, and this doesn't add up to the original number, so it doesn't work. Try a larger number and eliminate (D) and (E).

(B) $\frac{2}{3} (50) + \frac{1}{4} (50) + 5 = 33\frac{1}{3} + 12\frac{1}{2} + 5 = 50\frac{5}{6}$.

Again, you need a larger number.

(A) $\frac{2}{3} (60) + \frac{1}{4} (60) + 5 = 40 + 15 + 5 = 60$.

That works perfectly.

# CHAPTER 17: SSAT PRACTICE TEST 2: MIDDLE-LEVEL

## HOW TO TAKE THIS PRACTICE TEST

Before taking this practice test, find a quiet room where you can work uninterrupted for two and a half hours. Make sure you have a comfortable desk and several No. 2 pencils.

Use the answer sheet provided to record your answers. (You can cut it out or photocopy it.)

Once you start this practice test, don't stop until you've finished. Remember—you can review any questions within a section, but you may not go backward or forward a section.

You'll find answer explanations following the test. Scoring information can be found in chapter 19.

Good luck.

# SSAT Practice Test 2: Middle-Level Answer Sheet

**Remove (or photocopy) this answer sheet and use it to complete the practice test.**

Start with number 1 for each section. If a section has fewer questions than answer spaces, leave the extra spaces blank.

**SECTION 2**

1 Ⓐ Ⓑ Ⓒ Ⓓ Ⓔ   6 Ⓐ Ⓑ Ⓒ Ⓓ Ⓔ   11 Ⓐ Ⓑ Ⓒ Ⓓ Ⓔ   16 Ⓐ Ⓑ Ⓒ Ⓓ Ⓔ   21 Ⓐ Ⓑ Ⓒ Ⓓ Ⓔ
2 Ⓐ Ⓑ Ⓒ Ⓓ Ⓔ   7 Ⓐ Ⓑ Ⓒ Ⓓ Ⓔ   12 Ⓐ Ⓑ Ⓒ Ⓓ Ⓔ   17 Ⓐ Ⓑ Ⓒ Ⓓ Ⓔ   22 Ⓐ Ⓑ Ⓒ Ⓓ Ⓔ
3 Ⓐ Ⓑ Ⓒ Ⓓ Ⓔ   8 Ⓐ Ⓑ Ⓒ Ⓓ Ⓔ   13 Ⓐ Ⓑ Ⓒ Ⓓ Ⓔ   18 Ⓐ Ⓑ Ⓒ Ⓓ Ⓔ   23 Ⓐ Ⓑ Ⓒ Ⓓ Ⓔ
4 Ⓐ Ⓑ Ⓒ Ⓓ Ⓔ   9 Ⓐ Ⓑ Ⓒ Ⓓ Ⓔ   14 Ⓐ Ⓑ Ⓒ Ⓓ Ⓔ   19 Ⓐ Ⓑ Ⓒ Ⓓ Ⓔ   24 Ⓐ Ⓑ Ⓒ Ⓓ Ⓔ
5 Ⓐ Ⓑ Ⓒ Ⓓ Ⓔ   10 Ⓐ Ⓑ Ⓒ Ⓓ Ⓔ   15 Ⓐ Ⓑ Ⓒ Ⓓ Ⓔ   20 Ⓐ Ⓑ Ⓒ Ⓓ Ⓔ   25 Ⓐ Ⓑ Ⓒ Ⓓ Ⓔ

# right in section 2

# wrong in section 2

**SECTION 3**

1 Ⓐ Ⓑ Ⓒ Ⓓ Ⓔ   9 Ⓐ Ⓑ Ⓒ Ⓓ Ⓔ   17 Ⓐ Ⓑ Ⓒ Ⓓ Ⓔ   25 Ⓐ Ⓑ Ⓒ Ⓓ Ⓔ   33 Ⓐ Ⓑ Ⓒ Ⓓ Ⓔ
2 Ⓐ Ⓑ Ⓒ Ⓓ Ⓔ   10 Ⓐ Ⓑ Ⓒ Ⓓ Ⓔ   18 Ⓐ Ⓑ Ⓒ Ⓓ Ⓔ   26 Ⓐ Ⓑ Ⓒ Ⓓ Ⓔ   34 Ⓐ Ⓑ Ⓒ Ⓓ Ⓔ
3 Ⓐ Ⓑ Ⓒ Ⓓ Ⓔ   11 Ⓐ Ⓑ Ⓒ Ⓓ Ⓔ   19 Ⓐ Ⓑ Ⓒ Ⓓ Ⓔ   27 Ⓐ Ⓑ Ⓒ Ⓓ Ⓔ   35 Ⓐ Ⓑ Ⓒ Ⓓ Ⓔ
4 Ⓐ Ⓑ Ⓒ Ⓓ Ⓔ   12 Ⓐ Ⓑ Ⓒ Ⓓ Ⓔ   20 Ⓐ Ⓑ Ⓒ Ⓓ Ⓔ   28 Ⓐ Ⓑ Ⓒ Ⓓ Ⓔ   36 Ⓐ Ⓑ Ⓒ Ⓓ Ⓔ
5 Ⓐ Ⓑ Ⓒ Ⓓ Ⓔ   13 Ⓐ Ⓑ Ⓒ Ⓓ Ⓔ   21 Ⓐ Ⓑ Ⓒ Ⓓ Ⓔ   29 Ⓐ Ⓑ Ⓒ Ⓓ Ⓔ   37 Ⓐ Ⓑ Ⓒ Ⓓ Ⓔ
6 Ⓐ Ⓑ Ⓒ Ⓓ Ⓔ   14 Ⓐ Ⓑ Ⓒ Ⓓ Ⓔ   22 Ⓐ Ⓑ Ⓒ Ⓓ Ⓔ   30 Ⓐ Ⓑ Ⓒ Ⓓ Ⓔ   38 Ⓐ Ⓑ Ⓒ Ⓓ Ⓔ
7 Ⓐ Ⓑ Ⓒ Ⓓ Ⓔ   15 Ⓐ Ⓑ Ⓒ Ⓓ Ⓔ   23 Ⓐ Ⓑ Ⓒ Ⓓ Ⓔ   31 Ⓐ Ⓑ Ⓒ Ⓓ Ⓔ   39 Ⓐ Ⓑ Ⓒ Ⓓ Ⓔ
8 Ⓐ Ⓑ Ⓒ Ⓓ Ⓔ   16 Ⓐ Ⓑ Ⓒ Ⓓ Ⓔ   24 Ⓐ Ⓑ Ⓒ Ⓓ Ⓔ   32 Ⓐ Ⓑ Ⓒ Ⓓ Ⓔ   40 Ⓐ Ⓑ Ⓒ Ⓓ Ⓔ

# right in section 3

# wrong in section 3

**SECTION 4**

1 Ⓐ Ⓑ Ⓒ Ⓓ Ⓔ    13 Ⓐ Ⓑ Ⓒ Ⓓ Ⓔ   25 Ⓐ Ⓑ Ⓒ Ⓓ Ⓔ   37 Ⓐ Ⓑ Ⓒ Ⓓ Ⓔ   49 Ⓐ Ⓑ Ⓒ Ⓓ Ⓔ
2 Ⓐ Ⓑ Ⓒ Ⓓ Ⓔ    14 Ⓐ Ⓑ Ⓒ Ⓓ Ⓔ   26 Ⓐ Ⓑ Ⓒ Ⓓ Ⓔ   38 Ⓐ Ⓑ Ⓒ Ⓓ Ⓔ   50 Ⓐ Ⓑ Ⓒ Ⓓ Ⓔ
3 Ⓐ Ⓑ Ⓒ Ⓓ Ⓔ    15 Ⓐ Ⓑ Ⓒ Ⓓ Ⓔ   27 Ⓐ Ⓑ Ⓒ Ⓓ Ⓔ   39 Ⓐ Ⓑ Ⓒ Ⓓ Ⓔ   51 Ⓐ Ⓑ Ⓒ Ⓓ Ⓔ
4 Ⓐ Ⓑ Ⓒ Ⓓ Ⓔ    16 Ⓐ Ⓑ Ⓒ Ⓓ Ⓔ   28 Ⓐ Ⓑ Ⓒ Ⓓ Ⓔ   40 Ⓐ Ⓑ Ⓒ Ⓓ Ⓔ   52 Ⓐ Ⓑ Ⓒ Ⓓ Ⓔ
5 Ⓐ Ⓑ Ⓒ Ⓓ Ⓔ    17 Ⓐ Ⓑ Ⓒ Ⓓ Ⓔ   29 Ⓐ Ⓑ Ⓒ Ⓓ Ⓔ   41 Ⓐ Ⓑ Ⓒ Ⓓ Ⓔ   53 Ⓐ Ⓑ Ⓒ Ⓓ Ⓔ
6 Ⓐ Ⓑ Ⓒ Ⓓ Ⓔ    18 Ⓐ Ⓑ Ⓒ Ⓓ Ⓔ   30 Ⓐ Ⓑ Ⓒ Ⓓ Ⓔ   42 Ⓐ Ⓑ Ⓒ Ⓓ Ⓔ   54 Ⓐ Ⓑ Ⓒ Ⓓ Ⓔ
7 Ⓐ Ⓑ Ⓒ Ⓓ Ⓔ    19 Ⓐ Ⓑ Ⓒ Ⓓ Ⓔ   31 Ⓐ Ⓑ Ⓒ Ⓓ Ⓔ   43 Ⓐ Ⓑ Ⓒ Ⓓ Ⓔ   55 Ⓐ Ⓑ Ⓒ Ⓓ Ⓔ
8 Ⓐ Ⓑ Ⓒ Ⓓ Ⓔ    20 Ⓐ Ⓑ Ⓒ Ⓓ Ⓔ   32 Ⓐ Ⓑ Ⓒ Ⓓ Ⓔ   44 Ⓐ Ⓑ Ⓒ Ⓓ Ⓔ   56 Ⓐ Ⓑ Ⓒ Ⓓ Ⓔ
9 Ⓐ Ⓑ Ⓒ Ⓓ Ⓔ    21 Ⓐ Ⓑ Ⓒ Ⓓ Ⓔ   33 Ⓐ Ⓑ Ⓒ Ⓓ Ⓔ   45 Ⓐ Ⓑ Ⓒ Ⓓ Ⓔ   57 Ⓐ Ⓑ Ⓒ Ⓓ Ⓔ
10 Ⓐ Ⓑ Ⓒ Ⓓ Ⓔ   22 Ⓐ Ⓑ Ⓒ Ⓓ Ⓔ   34 Ⓐ Ⓑ Ⓒ Ⓓ Ⓔ   46 Ⓐ Ⓑ Ⓒ Ⓓ Ⓔ   58 Ⓐ Ⓑ Ⓒ Ⓓ Ⓔ
11 Ⓐ Ⓑ Ⓒ Ⓓ Ⓔ   23 Ⓐ Ⓑ Ⓒ Ⓓ Ⓔ   35 Ⓐ Ⓑ Ⓒ Ⓓ Ⓔ   47 Ⓐ Ⓑ Ⓒ Ⓓ Ⓔ   59 Ⓐ Ⓑ Ⓒ Ⓓ Ⓔ
12 Ⓐ Ⓑ Ⓒ Ⓓ Ⓔ   24 Ⓐ Ⓑ Ⓒ Ⓓ Ⓔ   36 Ⓐ Ⓑ Ⓒ Ⓓ Ⓔ   48 Ⓐ Ⓑ Ⓒ Ⓓ Ⓔ   60 Ⓐ Ⓑ Ⓒ Ⓓ Ⓔ

# right in section 4

# wrong in section 4

**SECTION 5**

1 Ⓐ Ⓑ Ⓒ Ⓓ Ⓔ   6 Ⓐ Ⓑ Ⓒ Ⓓ Ⓔ   11 Ⓐ Ⓑ Ⓒ Ⓓ Ⓔ   16 Ⓐ Ⓑ Ⓒ Ⓓ Ⓔ   21 Ⓐ Ⓑ Ⓒ Ⓓ Ⓔ
2 Ⓐ Ⓑ Ⓒ Ⓓ Ⓔ   7 Ⓐ Ⓑ Ⓒ Ⓓ Ⓔ   12 Ⓐ Ⓑ Ⓒ Ⓓ Ⓔ   17 Ⓐ Ⓑ Ⓒ Ⓓ Ⓔ   22 Ⓐ Ⓑ Ⓒ Ⓓ Ⓔ
3 Ⓐ Ⓑ Ⓒ Ⓓ Ⓔ   8 Ⓐ Ⓑ Ⓒ Ⓓ Ⓔ   13 Ⓐ Ⓑ Ⓒ Ⓓ Ⓔ   18 Ⓐ Ⓑ Ⓒ Ⓓ Ⓔ   23 Ⓐ Ⓑ Ⓒ Ⓓ Ⓔ
4 Ⓐ Ⓑ Ⓒ Ⓓ Ⓔ   9 Ⓐ Ⓑ Ⓒ Ⓓ Ⓔ   14 Ⓐ Ⓑ Ⓒ Ⓓ Ⓔ   19 Ⓐ Ⓑ Ⓒ Ⓓ Ⓔ   24 Ⓐ Ⓑ Ⓒ Ⓓ Ⓔ
5 Ⓐ Ⓑ Ⓒ Ⓓ Ⓔ   10 Ⓐ Ⓑ Ⓒ Ⓓ Ⓔ   15 Ⓐ Ⓑ Ⓒ Ⓓ Ⓔ   20 Ⓐ Ⓑ Ⓒ Ⓓ Ⓔ   25 Ⓐ Ⓑ Ⓒ Ⓓ Ⓔ

# right in section 5

# wrong in section 5

# SECTION 1

Time—25 Minutes

**Directions:** Read the following topics carefully. Take a few minutes to select the topic you find more interesting. Think about the selected topic and organize your thoughts on scrap paper before you begin writing.

**Topic A:** I had thirty minutes to complete the mission.

**Topic B:** I opened the door and suddenly …

Circle your selection: Topic A or Topic B. Write your essay for the selected topic on the paper provided. Your essay should NOT exceed two pages and must be written in pencil. Be sure that your handwriting is legible and that you stay within the lines and margins.

_____

_____

_____

_____

_____

_____

_____

_____

_____

_____

_____

_____

_____

_____

_____

GO ON TO THE NEXT PAGE ⟶

_____

_____

_____

_____

_____

_____

_____

_____

_____

_____

_____

_____

_____

_____

_____

_____

_____

_____

_____

_____

IF YOU FINISH BEFORE TIME IS CALLED, YOU MAY CHECK YOUR WORK ON
THIS SECTION ONLY. DO NOT TURN TO ANY OTHER SECTION IN THE TEST.

STOP

# SECTION 2

Time—30 Minutes
25 Questions

In this section, there are five possible answers after each problem. Choose which one is best. You may use the blank space at the right of the page for scratch work.

Note: Figures provided with the problems are drawn with the greatest possible accuracy, UNLESS stated "Not Drawn to Scale."

USE THIS SPACE FOR FIGURING.

1. The polygon in Figure 1 has a perimeter of 30. If each side of the polygon has the same length, what is the length of one side?

(A) 3
(B) 4
(C) 5
(D) 6
(E) 7

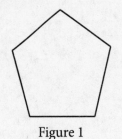

Figure 1

2. Mr. Stuart sold peppermint candy to 25 customers and caramel candy to 17 customers. If 4 of these customers bought both types of candy, how many bought only caramel candy?

(A) 29
(B) 25
(C) 21
(D) 17
(E) 13

3. In a bag of 24 balloons, there is an equal number of balloons of each color. Which of the following CANNOT be the number of different colors in the bag?

(A) 2
(B) 3
(C) 4
(D) 5
(E) 6

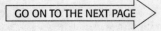

GO ON TO THE NEXT PAGE

4. Which of the following is a whole number that is both less than 13 and between 11 and 18?

(A)  11
(B)  12
(C) 12.5
(D)  13
(E)  14

USE THIS SPACE FOR FIGURING.

5. According to the graph in Figure 2, Susan spent about how many hours watching movies?

(A) 2
(B) 3
(C) 4
(D) 6
(E) 9

HOW SUSAN SPENT 12 HOURS
WATCHING TV

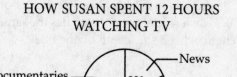
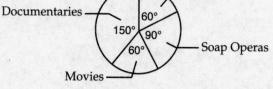

Figure 2

6. If $\frac{1}{2}R = 16$, then $\frac{3}{4}R =$

(A) 24
(B) 20
(C) 16
(D) 12
(E)  8

7. Which of the following is closest to $\frac{1}{4}$ of 59?

(A) $0.26 \times 50$
(B) $0.41 \times 50$
(C) $0.26 \times 60$
(D) $0.41 \times 60$
(E) $41 \times 60$

GO ON TO THE NEXT PAGE

8.  According to the graph in Figure 3, the average sales of Company M from 1993 to 1997 was

    (A)  $250,000
    (B)  $260,000
    (C)  $265,000
    (D)  $270,000
    (E)  $275,000

**Questions 9–10 refer to the following definition.**

For all real numbers $u$ and $v$, $u \, ø \, v = u - \left(1-\dfrac{1}{v}\right)$.

(Example: $3 \, ø \, 2 = 3 - \left(1-\dfrac{1}{2}\right) = 3 - \dfrac{1}{2} = 2\dfrac{1}{2}$)

9.  Which of the following is equal to $5 \, ø \, 5$?

    (A)  0
    (B)  1
    (C)  $4\dfrac{1}{5}$
    (D)  $4\dfrac{4}{5}$
    (E)  25

10. If $a \, ø \, 3 = 4\dfrac{1}{3}$, then $a =$

    (A)  $\dfrac{2}{3}$
    (B)  3
    (C)  4
    (D)  $4\dfrac{2}{3}$
    (E)  5

USE THIS SPACE FOR FIGURING.

SALES OF COMPANY M: 1993–1997

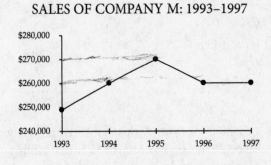

Figure 3

GO ON TO THE NEXT PAGE

11. Twenty percent of 64 is equal to 5 percent of what number?

   (A)  16
   (B)  20
   (C)  64
   (D) 128
   (E) 256

USE THIS SPACE FOR FIGURING.

12. During the 4 fishing trips that Rich and Andy made, Rich caught a total of 35 fish. If Andy caught more fish than Rich, Andy must have caught an average of a least how many fish per trip?

   (A)  $8\frac{3}{4}$
   (B)    9
   (C)   36
   (D)  140
   (E)  144

13. Jeff, Todd, and Lee were hired by their father to work on the yard, and each was paid at the same hourly rate. Jeff worked 4 hours, Todd worked 6 hours, and Lee worked 8 hours. If the 3 boys together earned $27, how much did Lee earn?

   (A)  $8
   (B)  $12
   (C)  $15
   (D)  $16
   (E)  $27

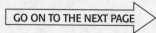
GO ON TO THE NEXT PAGE

14. Johnny picked apples from 9:00 A.M. to 11:30 A.M. and gathered 200 apples. He wants to pick a total of at least 600 apples before 7:15 P.M. If he plans to pick apples at the same rate, what is the latest time that he can start picking apples again?

(A) 1:15 P.M.

(B) 1:45 P.M.

(C) 2:15 P.M.

(D) 2:45 P.M.

(E) 3:15 P.M.

15. If 0.88 equals $8W$, what is the value of $W$?

(A) 0.11

(B) 0.9

(C) 1.1

(D) 9

(E) 11

16. In the triangle shown in Figure 4, what is the value of $r$?

(A) 50

(B) 60

(C) 70

(D) 80

(E) It cannot be determined from the information given.

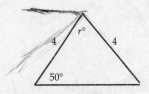

Figure 4

17. A company's income increased from 9 thousand dollars in 1958 to 4.5 million dollars in 1988. Its income in 1988 was how many times its income in 1958?

(A)    200

(B)    500

(C)    2,000

(D)    5,000

(E)  20,000

USE THIS SPACE FOR FIGURING.

GO ON TO THE NEXT PAGE

18. Which of the following can be expressed as $(5 \times R) + 2$, where $R$ is a whole number?

(A) 25

(B) 33

(C) 47

(D) 56

(E) 68

USE THIS SPACE FOR FIGURING.

19. Which of the following can be drawn without lifting the pencil or retracing?

(A)

(B)

(C)

(D) 

(E) 

20. If the population of Country X increased by 10 percent each year over a 2-year period, what was the total percent increase in the population over the entire period?

(A)   2%

(B)  10%

(C)  11%

(D)  20%

(E)  21%

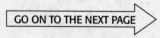 GO ON TO THE NEXT PAGE

21. If $z = y + 2$, what does $2z + 1$ equal?

    (A)  $y + 3$
    (B)  $2y + 3$
    (C)  $2y + 5$
    (D)  $2y + 6$
    (E)  It cannot be determined from the information given.

USE THIS SPACE FOR FIGURING.

22. If $x$ is greater than 0 but less than 1, and $y$ is greater than $x$, which of the following is the LEAST?

    (A)  $\dfrac{y}{x}$

    (B)  $\dfrac{x}{y}$

    (C)  $xy$

    (D)  $\dfrac{1}{x-y}$

    (E)  It cannot be determined from the information given.

23. In a restaurant, there are $x$ tables that can each seat 6 people, and there are $y$ tables that can each seat 5 people. What is the maximum number of people that may be seated?

    (A)  $5x + 6y$
    (B)  $6x + 5y$
    (C)  $11x + 11y$
    (D)  $11xy$
    (E)  $30xy$

GO ON TO THE NEXT PAGE

24. Mrs. Smith bought 3 square pieces of fabric. A side of the largest piece is 3 times as long as a side of the middle one, and a side of the middle one is 3 times as long as a side of the smallest one. The area of the largest piece is how many times the area of the smallest piece?

(A) 112
(B) 81
(C) 27
(D) 9
(E) 3

USE THIS SPACE FOR FIGURING.

25. Mr. Dali's car uses $\frac{3}{4}$ gallons of gas each time he drives to work. If his gas tank holds exactly 9 gallons of gas, how many tanks of gas does he need to make 18 trips to work?

(A) $1\frac{1}{2}$
(B) $2\frac{1}{2}$
(C) 4
(D) 6
(E) 9

IF YOU FINISH BEFORE TIME IS CALLED, YOU MAY CHECK YOUR WORK ON THIS SECTION ONLY. DO NOT TURN TO ANY OTHER SECTION IN THE TEST.  STOP

# SECTION 3

Time—40 Minutes
40 Questions

**Read each passage carefully and then answer the questions about it. For each question, decide on the basis of the passage which one of the choices best answers the question.**

Scott Joplin composed approximately 60 works during his lifetime, including 41 piano pieces called "rags," many songs and marches, and an
*Line* opera entitled *Treemonisha*. His most significant
(5) creative contribution was to the development of ragtime, a type of instrumental music marked by its distinctive, choppy rhythm. Joplin's rhythmic diversity was very important to the development of ragtime as a genre, a unique musical form. In
(10) 1899, his "Maple Leaf Rag" became the most popular piano rag of the time and he was dubbed the "King of Ragtime." Despite all of those accomplishments, he was not considered a serious composer during his lifetime. It was not until 59
(15) years after his death that he was properly recognized: In 1976, he was awarded the Pulitzer Prize for music, at last receiving the praise he deserved.

1. The term "rag," as it is used in the passage, refers to

    (A) a specific piece of operatic music

    (B) a genre of dance music

    (C) a piece of piano music known for its unique rhythm

    (D) a kind of instrumental music played by marching bands

    (E) a style of songs invented by Joplin

2. This passage deals primarily with

    (A) the fact that Joplin was not taken seriously during his lifetime

    (B) the history and development of ragtime music

    (C) the diversity of styles in which Joplin composed

    (D) how Joplin came to win the Pulitzer Prize

    (E) Joplin's contributions to and accomplishments in the world of music

3. According to the passage, Joplin died in

    (A) 1899

    (B) 1917

    (C) 1941

    (D) 1959

    (E) 1976

4. When discussing Scott Joplin, the author's tone in this passage could best be described as

    (A) indifferent

    (B) amused

    (C) envious

    (D) resentful

    (E) appreciative

GO ON TO THE NEXT PAGE

5. It can be inferred from the passage that a genre is

(A) a particular type of ragtime music

(B) a distinct category or style

(C) a term that Joplin coined when he created ragtime

(D) a rhythmic style characteristic of Joplin's period

(E) an early form of "rag"

6. From this passage, it can be inferred that

(A) although people liked Joplin's work, they did not appreciate its value while he was alive

(B) Joplin died a destitute musician

(C) ragtime wouldn't have existed had Joplin not written "Maple Leaf Rag"

(D) all of Joplin's piano pieces were rags

(E) Joplin played a lot of venues to popularize ragtime

Thousands of species of birds exist today, and nearly every species has its own special courtship procedures and "identification checks."
*Line* Identification checks are important, because if
(5) birds of different species mate, any offspring will usually be sterile or badly adapted to their surroundings.

Plumage often plays a key role in both identification and courtship. In breeding season,
(10) male birds often acquire distinctive plumage which they use to attract females who will, in turn, only respond to males with the correct markings. In some species, the females are more brightly colored, and the courtship roles are

(15) reversed. Distinctive behavioral changes can also be important aspects of courtship and breeding activity. Aggressiveness between males, and sometimes between females, is quite common. Some birds, like whooping cranes and trumpeter
(20) swans, perform wonderfully elaborate courtship dances in which both sexes are enthusiastic participants.

Bird sounds are often a very central part of identification and courtship behavior between
(25) individuals in a given species. When a female migrates in the spring to her breeding region, she often encounters numerous birds of different species. By its singing, the male of a species both identifies itself and communicates to females of
(30) that species that it is in breeding condition. This information allows a female to predict a male's response to her approach. Later, after mating has taken place, the note patterns of a particular male's song enable a nesting female to continue to
(35) identify her own partner.

7. The author implies that a bird engages in identification and courtship procedures mainly in order to

(A) find a better nesting spot

(B) find the most colorful partner it can

(C) attract a mate of its own species

(D) increase its control over its nesting partner

(E) try to dominate the bird population of a given area

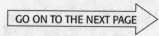
GO ON TO THE NEXT PAGE

8. According to the passage, a feature of the male songbird is its ability to

   I. attract a female of its own species

   II. intimidate rival males

   III. communicate its identity to its mate

   (A) I only

   (B) III only

   (C) I and II only

   (D) I and III only

   (E) I, II, and III

9. The author uses the whooping crane as an example of a bird that

   (A) seldom participates in courtship procedures

   (B) acquires a distinctive breeding plumage

   (C) behaves in an unusual and noteworthy way during courtship

   (D) reverses the normal male and female courtship roles

   (E) displays unusual aggressiveness while courting

10. According to the passage, matings between birds of different species

   (A) are quite common

   (B) produce more sturdy offspring

   (C) may help to establish a permanent new species

   (D) do not usually result in healthy offspring

   (E) have never happened

11. The passage is primarily about

   (A) causes of aggression between male birds

   (B) several courtship and identification methods used by birds

   (C) the breeding season of birds

   (D) the role of bird sounds in courtship identification

   (E) why birds migrate to particular breeding regions

12. This passage most likely comes from

   (A) a website on identifying birds

   (B) a book on birds and mating

   (C) a personal letter from a bird-watcher

   (D) a novel about breeding birds

   (E) a news article on endangered birds

   More than 1,500 Native American languages have thus far been discovered by linguists. Edward Sapir, a pioneer in the field of Native American
Line linguistics, grouped these languages into six
(5) "families" more than three-quarters of a century ago.
   Ever since that time, the classification of Native American languages has been a source of controversy. A small group of linguists has recently
(10) argued that all Native American languages fit into three linguistic families. These scholars believe that similarities and differences among words and sounds leave no doubt about the validity of their classification scheme. The vast majority of
(15) linguists, however, reject both the methods and conclusions of these scholars, arguing that linguistic science has not yet advanced far enough to be able to group Native American languages into a few families. According to these scholars,
(20) Native American languages have diverged to such an extent over the centuries that it may never be possible to group them in distinct language families.

GO ON TO THE NEXT PAGE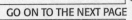

13. This passage is primarily about

   (A) the classification of Native American languages

   (B) the six families of Native American languages

   (C) scholars' views about language

   (D) the similarities and differences between words of Native American languages

   (E) linguistic debates about how to group languages

14. The scholars who believe that Native American languages can be classified into three families apparently believe that

   (A) these languages have diverged significantly over the last 75 years

   (B) languages can be classified according to the degree of similarities and differences between words

   (C) linguistic science has not advanced far enough to safely classify languages so narrowly

   (D) languages are all related by their common origins

   (E) distinct language families have their own peculiar grammatical rules

15. The style of the passage is most like that found in a

   (A) personal letter written by a linguistics student

   (B) textbook about linguistics

   (C) novel about Native American tribes

   (D) diary of a linguist

   (E) biography of Edward Sapir

16. It can be inferred that the classification of Native American languages has been a source of controversy because

   (A) scholars do not agree on the method for classifying languages

   (B) languages have split in several directions

   (C) linguistics is a very new field

   (D) there is not enough known about Native American vocabulary

   (E) Native Americans dislike such classifications

17. Which of the following questions is answered by the passage?

   (A) Did Edward Sapir study languages other than Native American languages?

   (B) How many languages are in a typical linguistic family?

   (C) How many Native American languages are yet to discovered?

   (D) In what ways have Native American languages changed over time?

   (E) Into how many families did Edward Sapir classify Native American languages?

18. As used in the passage, "extent" (line 21) most nearly means

   (A) limit

   (B) language

   (C) range

   (D) time

   (E) duration

GO ON TO THE NEXT PAGE

Hope is the thing with feathers
That perches in the soul,
And sings the tune without the words
And never stops at all,
Line
(5) And sweetest in the gale is heard;
And sore must be the storm
That could abash[1] the little bird
That kept so many warm.

(10) I've heard it in the chillest land,
And on the strangest sea;
Yet, never, in extremity,
It asked a crumb of me.

[1]discourage
"Hope," by Emily Dickinson

19. In this poem, hope is compared to

(A) a gale
(B) a sea
(C) a storm
(D) a bird
(E) a song

20. What is the poet saying in the last stanza of the poem?

(A) It is terrible to imagine a world without hope, and we must therefore do everything possible to preserve our hopes.

(B) The bird continues to sing through all conditions.

(C) Hope can be found anywhere and never asks anything in return for its loyalty.

(D) The bird is very hungry because it is constantly singing and never takes any time to eat.

(E) The potential for hope is always present, but it takes a great effort to make it a reality.

21. The lines "the little bird/That kept so many warm" in the second stanza refer to the fact that

(A) the feathers of birds have traditionally provided protection against the cold

(B) hope has comforted a great many people over the years

(C) the bird provided protection before it was destroyed in a storm

(D) hope has often proven useless in the face of real problems

(E) hope is a good last resort when faced with a difficult situation

22. The attitude of the speaker in this poem can best be described as

(A) angry
(B) unconcerned
(C) respectful
(D) nervous
(E) grateful

23. The term "sore" (line 6) most nearly means

(A) hurt
(B) angry
(C) severe
(D) kind
(E) wet

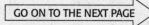GO ON TO THE NEXT PAGE

Although recycling has taken place in various forms for some time, today we are being asked to regard recycling as not only an important, but even *Line* a necessary measure.
(5)  Recycling, in its broadest sense, refers to the remaking of waste products and other used materials for practical purposes. For example, an old soda bottle can be returned, washed, and used as a bottle again, or it can be ground down and its
(10) glass can be employed for another useful purpose. Since fixing up old things is often cheaper than making brand new ones, this saves money. More importantly, it saves resources and reduces the amount of waste produced.
(15)  Businesses have been performing large-scale recycling for some time, based primarily on the goal of saving money. However, the amount of residential waste, that is, the waste produced at home, has been steadily increasing, and the role of the individual in
(20) the recycling campaign has been seriously underemphasized. Although it is true that we, as individuals, cannot reduce the overall amount of waste significantly or save large amounts of money and resources on our own, taken collectively, we can
(25) have an important impact. Our increased efforts toward recycling can have a dramatic effect on the future availability of resources and the condition of the environment. It is our duty to ourselves and to our fellow human beings to pitch in and help protect
(30) what remains of it.

24. According to the passage, which of the following is true?

I.  Recycling increases the amount of waste produced

II.  Reusing waste products can be very economical

III.  The amount of waste produced in the home has been continuously growing

(A) II only

(B) I and II only

(C) I and III only

(D) II and III only

(E) I, II, and III

25. The author would most likely agree that

(A) recycling is a good idea for big businesses but, on an individual level, it makes very little difference

(B) although businesses recycle to save money, individuals are motivated to recycle by a desire to serve the general good of society

(C) recycling is extremely important and everyone has a responsibility to contribute to the overall effort to preserve our environment

(D) although our natural resources are limited, we only live once and we shouldn't concentrate on conservation to such a degree that it interferes with our enjoyment of life

(E) recycling is a very expensive process and should be left to the owners of big businesses

26. All of the following are examples of recycling EXCEPT

(A) turning old newspapers into cardboard

(B) melting down scraps of metal and recasting them

(C) washing out empty soda bottles and using them as vases

(D) selling a piece of jewelry and using the money to buy a car

(E) crushing old cans and reusing the aluminum to make new ones

27. The tone of this passage is

(A) insistent

(B) relaxed

(C) formal

(D) amused

(E) disinterested

GO ON TO THE NEXT PAGE

28. Which of the following is the author most likely to discuss next?

    (A) The current problem of toxic waste disposal

    (B) The negative aspects of recycling and the many problems that can develop when it is done too much

    (C) Different ways that an old bottle can be either reused or remade into an entirely different object

    (D) Other important differences between the way businesses and residences are run

    (E) Examples of ways in which people can recycle their own waste and help out on an individual basis

29. What can be said about the author based on lines 15–17?

    (A) She is only interested in the economic aspects of recycling.

    (B) She believes that businesses are motivated to recycle primarily for monetary gain.

    (C) She knows little about the possible financial savings of recycling.

    (D) She is more concerned with the environmental benefits of recycling than the economic rewards.

    (E) She values recycling even though it results in the production of greater amounts of waste.

    Most of us who live in relatively mild climates rarely view bad weather as more than an inconvenience, but in certain, less fortunate parts
*Line* of the world, a change in weather can have
*(5)* disastrous consequences for an entire society. Weather fluctuations along the northwest coast of South America, for instance, can periodically have a dramatic effect on the area's fishing villages.

    Under normal circumstances, the cold, steadily
*(10)* flowing waters of the Humboldt Current bring nutrients up from the sea floor along the coast, providing a dependable food supply for fish and squid. For centuries, the fishing villages have depended on this rich ocean harvest for food and
*(15)* trade. Occasionally, however, global weather patterns cause the current to fail, setting off a deadly chain reaction. Without nutrients, the fish and squid die, depriving the villagers of their livelihood. This destructive weather phenomenon,
*(20)* called "El Niño" (The Boy Child) because it occurs at Christmastime, has sometimes forced entire villages to disband and move elsewhere to avoid starvation.

30. According to the passage, the Humboldt Current flows

    (A) only at Christmastime

    (B) without fail

    (C) east to west

    (D) along the northwest coast of South America

    (E) through warm water

31. This passage is mainly about

    (A) how the economy of South American villages depends exclusively on fishing

    (B) the importance of fish and squid in the food chain

    (C) the advantages of living in a mild climate

    (D) the undependable nature of the Humboldt Current

    (E) how changes in weather patterns can have a dramatic effect on the way people live

GO ON TO THE NEXT PAGE

32. According to the passage, all of the following are true EXCEPT

    (A) the actions of the Humboldt Current help provide nutrients for fish and squid

    (B) the Humboldt Current affects the survival of fishing on the northwest coast of South America

    (C) the warm waters of the Humboldt Current affect the climate of nearby land masses

    (D) the failure of the Humboldt Current can set off a deadly chain reaction

    (E) the Humboldt Current sometimes fails as a result of global weather patterns

33. Which of the following would be the best title for this passage?

    (A) An Example of Weather's Social Impact

    (B) Fishing Villages of South America

    (C) El Niño: A Christmas Occurrence

    (D) Fish and Squid: A Rich Ocean Harvest

    (E) The Impact of Fishing on Coastal Villages

34. The author's attitude toward the villagers along the northwest coast of South America can best be described as

    (A) sympathetic

    (B) unconcerned

    (C) condescending

    (D) angry

    (E) emotional

35. Which of the following is an example of a chain reaction?

    (A) Forest fires kill off thousands of acres of land, destroying valuable resources.

    (B) When temperatures start to fall, many birds fly south to spend winter in warm climates.

    (C) Earthquakes cause extensive damage to property and often result in the loss of human life.

    (D) Global warming causes glaciers to melt, resulting in rising water levels, which reduce the amount of habitable land.

    (E) The moon revolves around the earth, and the earth revolves around the sun.

World War II left much of Western Europe deeply scarred in many ways. Economically, it was devastated. In early 1948, as the Cold War
*Line* developed between the United States and the
(5) Soviet Union and political tensions rose, U.S. policymakers decided that substantial financial assistance would be required to maintain a state of political stability. This conclusion led Secretary of State George C. Marshall to
(10) announce a proposal: European countries were advised to draw up a unified plan for reconstruction, to be funded by the United States.

This European Recovery Program, also known as the Marshall Plan, provided economic and
(15) technical assistance to 16 countries. Between 1948 and 1952, participating countries received a combined total of 12 billion dollars in U.S. aid. In the end, the program was seen as a great success; it revived the economies of Western Europe and
(20) set them on a course for future growth.

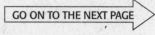
GO ON TO THE NEXT PAGE

36. Which of the following would be the best title for this passage?

    (A) The Aftermath of World War II
    (B) The Marshall Plan: A Program for European Reconstruction
    (C) The Economic Destruction of Europe
    (D) George C. Marshall: The Man behind the Plan
    (E) Western European Recovery

37. The tone of the author toward the Marshall Plan is

    (A) objective
    (B) excited
    (C) insistent
    (D) anxious
    (E) unfavorable

38. All of the following are true about the Marshall Plan EXCEPT

    (A) it provided economic assistance to 16 countries
    (B) it went into action in 1948
    (C) it supplied economic aid for a period spanning four years
    (D) it gave each of the participating countries 12 billion dollars
    (E) it was considered a great long-term success

39. The passage suggests that the driving force behind the Marshall Plan was

    (A) a formal request for aid by European leaders
    (B) fear of economic repercussions for the U.S. economy
    (C) George C. Marshall's desire to improve his political career and public image
    (D) a joint U.S.-Soviet agreement to assist the countries of Western Europe
    (E) the increase in tension between the United States and the Soviet Union

40. Which of the following would the author be most likely to discuss next?

    (A) Developments in the Cold War during and after the years of the Marshall Plan
    (B) The events leading up to Western Europe's economic collapse
    (C) The detailed effects of the Marshall Plan on specific countries
    (D) Other successful economic recovery programs employed throughout history
    (E) How George C. Marshall became the U.S. Secretary of State

IF YOU FINISH BEFORE TIME IS CALLED, YOU MAY CHECK YOUR WORK ON THIS SECTION ONLY. DO NOT TURN TO ANY OTHER SECTION IN THE TEST.

STOP

# SECTION 4

Time—30 Minutes
60 Questions

This section consists of two different types of questions. There are directions for each type.

Each of the following questions consists of one word followed by five words or phrases. You are to select the one word or phrase whose meaning is closest to the word in capital letters.

1. HARSH:

   (A) cold
   (B) angry
   (C) poor
   (D) useless
   (E) severe

2. INDICATE:

   (A) meet with
   (B) look at
   (C) help with
   (D) point out
   (E) search for

3. BLEAK:

   (A) unknown
   (B) quiet
   (C) cheerless
   (D) trembling
   (E) timid

4. SECURE:

   (A) unseen
   (B) aware
   (C) secret
   (D) safe
   (E) knotty

5. ALIEN:

   (A) strange
   (B) futile
   (C) valuable
   (D) brutal
   (E) unclear

6. CHRONIC:

   (A) persistent
   (B) difficult
   (C) doubtful
   (D) legal
   (E) elaborate

7. QUENCH:

   (A) complete
   (B) compare
   (C) demean
   (D) satisfy
   (E) withdraw

8. SEVERE:

   (A) frozen
   (B) extreme
   (C) long
   (D) limited
   (E) essential

GO ON TO THE NEXT PAGE

9. RANSACK:

   (A) search thoroughly
   (B) act quickly
   (C) cover completely
   (D) make secure
   (E) denounce publicly

10. SUMMIT:

   (A) plateau
   (B) landscape
   (C) slope
   (D) island
   (E) peak

11. TUMULT:

   (A) annoyance
   (B) commotion
   (C) insignificance
   (D) disagreement
   (E) blockage

12. RETARD:

   (A) turn around
   (B) push apart
   (C) slow down
   (D) change position
   (E) see through

13. ANTIDOTE:

   (A) fantasy
   (B) remedy
   (C) substitute
   (D) award
   (E) decoration

14. SOLITARY:

   (A) mindful
   (B) careless
   (C) friendly
   (D) alone
   (E) troubled

15. CAMOUFLAGE:

   (A) obstacle
   (B) range
   (C) emergency
   (D) disguise
   (E) amount

16. EXPEL:

   (A) finish off
   (B) teach
   (C) question
   (D) scold
   (E) cast out

17. LUNGE:

   (A) pursue
   (B) turn
   (C) thrust
   (D) restore
   (E) startle

18. BREVITY:

   (A) ambition
   (B) consistency
   (C) conflict
   (D) imagination
   (E) shortness

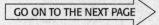
GO ON TO THE NEXT PAGE

19. MARVEL:

(A) discard
(B) usurp
(C) confuse
(D) point
(E) wonder

20. CANDOR:

(A) majesty
(B) daring
(C) honesty
(D) perception
(E) fatigue

21. CONVENE:

(A) clarify
(B) serve
(C) assemble
(D) elect
(E) dignify

22. CATASTROPHE:

(A) illusion
(B) disaster
(C) indication
(D) warning
(E) estimate

23. GREGARIOUS:

(A) sloppy
(B) sociable
(C) happy
(D) intelligent
(E) talented

24. DEXTERITY:

(A) secrecy
(B) equality
(C) reserve
(D) nimbleness
(E) determination

25. IMMINENT:

(A) intense
(B) impressive
(C) proper
(D) observable
(E) forthcoming

26. ANIMOSITY:

(A) doubt
(B) hatred
(C) sadness
(D) illness
(E) guilt

27. AMEND:

(A) create
(B) address
(C) observe
(D) exclude
(E) improve

28. DESPONDENT:

(A) depressed
(B) unintended
(C) artificial
(D) literary
(E) unconcerned

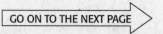

29. UNFLINCHING:

(A) uncommitted

(B) distinct

(C) uncompromising

(D) transitory

(E) invalid

30. REPUDIATE:

(A) renounce

(B) impede

(C) provoke

(D) divert

(E) submit

**The following questions ask you to find relationships between words. For each question, select the choice that best completes the meaning of the sentence.**

31. Sun is to solar as

(A) earth is to terrestrial

(B) pond is to marine

(C) ground is to subterranean

(D) tower is to architectural

(E) planet is to lunar

32. Botany is to plants as meteorology is to

(A) weather

(B) flora

(C) health

(D) language

(E) style

33. Hammer is to nail as

(A) axe is to wood

(B) lathe is to molding

(C) chisel is to marble

(D) nut is to bolt

(E) screwdriver is to screw

34. Bone is to mammal as girder is to

(A) skyscraper

(B) steel

(C) rivet

(D) crane

(E) concrete

35. Human is to primate as

(A) kangaroo is to vegetarian

(B) snake is to reptile

(C) disease is to bacterium

(D) bird is to amphibian

(E) dog is to pet

36. Tremor is to earthquake as

(A) eye is to hurricane

(B) desert is to sandstorm

(C) faucet is to deluge

(D) wind is to tornado

(E) flood is to river

GO ON TO THE NEXT PAGE

37. Amusing is to uproarious as

   (A) silly is to serious
   (B) dead is to immortal
   (C) interesting is to mesmerizing
   (D) humorous is to dull
   (E) worthless is to valuable

38. Fickle is to steadfast as tempestuous is to

   (A) worth
   (B) open
   (C) inspiration
   (D) peace
   (E) ire

39. School is to fish as

   (A) fin is to shark
   (B) library is to student
   (C) flock is to bird
   (D) leg is to frog
   (E) college is to mascot

40. Cartographer is to map as chef is to

   (A) flower
   (B) silverware
   (C) table
   (D) meal
   (E) ingredient

41. Throne is to monarch as

   (A) miter is to pope
   (B) bench is to judge
   (C) lobby is to doorman
   (D) armchair is to general
   (E) ship is to captain

42. Canal is to river as

   (A) boat is to driftwood
   (B) puddle is to lake
   (C) hammer is to mallet
   (D) mine is to cavern
   (E) telephone is to computer

43. Milk is to sour as bread is to

   (A) bent
   (B) stale
   (C) folded
   (D) baked
   (E) hot

44. Ore is to mine as

   (A) apple is to peel
   (B) water is to purify
   (C) batter is to stir
   (D) grain is to plow
   (E) oil is to drill

45. Weight is to scale as

   (A) distance is to speedometer
   (B) number is to slide rule
   (C) length is to thermometer
   (D) reading is to gauge
   (E) altitude is to altimeter

46. Porcupine is to quill as

   (A) bat is to wing
   (B) horse is to tail
   (C) skunk is to odor
   (D) oyster is to pearl
   (E) tiger is to stripe

GO ON TO THE NEXT PAGE

47. Jar is to contain as pillar is to

(A) stand
(B) ascend
(C) prepare
(D) support
(E) swing

48. Irrigate is to dry as

(A) soften is to uneven
(B) smooth is to coarse
(C) purify is to distasteful
(D) depend is to supportive
(E) ferment is to salty

49. Electricity is to wire as

(A) sound is to radio
(B) water is to aqueduct
(C) music is to instrument
(D) light is to bulb
(E) river is to bank

50. Contempt is to sneer as

(A) shame is to shrug
(B) anger is to laugh
(C) enjoyment is to groan
(D) agreement is to grimace
(E) displeasure is to frown

51. Building is to foundation as plant is to

(A) pane
(B) grotto
(C) primer
(D) floor
(E) root

52. Nose is to olfactory as ear is to

(A) beautiful
(B) edible
(C) auditory
(D) raspy
(E) allergic

53. Irk is to soothing as support is to

(A) conciliating
(B) elevating
(C) undermining
(D) irritating
(E) vilifying

54. Illegible is to read as

(A) invisible is to see
(B) illegal is to act
(C) broken is to fix
(D) irreparable is to break
(E) intense is to strain

55. Tact is to diplomat as

(A) parsimony is to philanthropist
(B) agility is to gymnast
(C) vulnerability is to victim
(D) training is to physician
(E) bias is to judge

GO ON TO THE NEXT PAGE

56. Ravenous is to hunger as

    (A) pliable is to obstinacy

    (B) agitated is to placidity

    (C) concerned is to apathy

    (D) smart is to tenacity

    (E) furious is to indignation

57. Amplify is to sound as bolster is to

    (A) smell

    (B) courage

    (C) insomnia

    (D) light

    (E) silence

58. Auditorium is to lecture as

    (A) theater is to concert

    (B) attic is to storage

    (C) temple is to religion

    (D) cafeteria is to food

    (E) target is to arrow

59. Philanthropic is to benevolence as

    (A) smooth is to surface

    (B) ostentatious is to reserve

    (C) miserly is to stinginess

    (D) devout is to malice

    (E) realistic is to plan

60. Spurious is to authenticity as

    (A) lavish is to expense

    (B) abject is to subjectivity

    (C) affluent is to character

    (D) laughable is to seriousness

    (E) totalitarian is to completeness

# SECTION 5

Time—30 Minutes
25 Questions

---

In this section, there are five possible answers after each question. Choose which one is best. You may use the blank space at the right of the page for scratch work.

Note: Figures are drawn with the greatest possible accuracy, UNLESS stated "Not Drawn to Scale."

---

1. Justine bought a comic book at $5 above the cover price. A year later she sold the book for $9 less than she paid. At what price did Justine sell the book?

   (A)  $14 below the cover price
   (B)  $4 below the cover price
   (C)  The cover price
   (D)  $4 above the cover price
   (E)  $14 above the cover price

USE THIS SPACE FOR FIGURING.

**Questions 2–3 refer to the graph in Figure 1.**

2. How many fewer boxes of cereal were sold in February than in March?

   (A)  2
   (B)  3
   (C)  20
   (D)  40
   (E)  60

3. The number of boxes sold in January was how many times the number of boxes sold in February?

   (A)  2
   (B)  $2\frac{1}{2}$
   (C)  3
   (D)  40
   (E)  60

CEREAL SALES AT STORE X

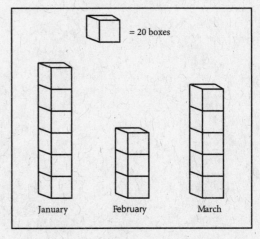

Figure 1

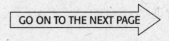

4.  Team A has 4 times as many losses as it had ties in a season. If Team A won none of its games, which could be the total number of games it played that season?

    (A)  12
    (B)  15
    (C)  18
    (D)  21
    (E)  26

5.  Figure 2 contains rectangles and a triangle. How many different rectangles are there in Figure 2?

    (A)   5
    (B)   7
    (C)   9
    (D)  10
    (E)  12

6.  Which of the following is NOT less than $\frac{1}{4}$?

    (A)  $\frac{2}{9}$

    (B)  $\frac{3}{14}$

    (C)  $\frac{14}{64}$

    (D)  $\frac{19}{70}$

    (E)  $\frac{27}{125}$

USE THIS SPACE FOR FIGURING.

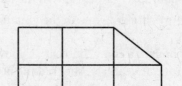

Figure 2

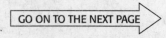

7. In Figure 3, the sides of triangles *ABC* and *FGH*, and of squares *BCFE* and *CDGF*, are all equal in length. Which of the following is the longest path from *A* to *H* ?

   (A)  *A – B – C – F – H*

   (B)  *A – B – E – F – H*

   (C)  *A – C – D – G – H*

   (D)  *A – B – E – G – H*

   (E)  *A – C – F – G – H*

8. If $5\frac{1}{3} \times (14 - x) = 0$, then what does $x$ equal?

   (A)  0

   (B)  1

   (C)  $5\frac{1}{3}$

   (D)  14

   (E)  It cannot be determined from the information given.

9. Which of the following is closest to 1.18?

   (A)  12

   (B)  2.2

   (C)  1.9

   (D)  1.1

   (E)  1

10. If $X$ is greater than 15, then $\frac{1}{3}$ of $X$ must always be

   (A)  less than 5

   (B)  equal to 5

   (C)  greater than 5

   (D)  equal to 45

   (E)  less than 45

USE THIS SPACE FOR FIGURING.

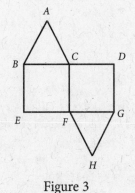

Figure 3

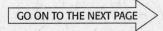
GO ON TO THE NEXT PAGE

11. Of the following, 35 percent of $26.95 is closest to

(A)  $7.00

(B)  $9.45

(C)  $10.50

(D)  $11.15

(E)  $12.25

12. If a factory can make 600 nails every 3 minutes, how long would it take to make 27,000 nails?

(A)  45 minutes

(B)  1 hour

(C)  1 hour 45 minutes

(D)  2 hours 15 minutes

(E)  3 hours 15 minutes

13. Sally has $x$ dollars and receives $100 for her birthday. She then buys a bicycle that costs $125. How many dollars does Sally have remaining?

(A)  $x + 125$

(B)  $x + 100$

(C)  $x + 25$

(D)  $x - 25$

(E)  $x - 100$

14. If $\dfrac{A+B}{3} = 4$ and $A$ is greater than 1, which of the following could NOT be the value of $B$ ?

(A)  −3

(B)  0

(C)  1

(D)  2

(E)  12

USE THIS SPACE FOR FIGURING.

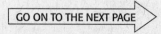
GO ON TO THE NEXT PAGE

15. The average of five numbers is 10. If two of the five numbers are removed, the average of the remaining three numbers is 9. What is the sum of the two numbers that were removed?

    (A) 17
    (B) 18
    (C) 21
    (D) 22
    (E) 23

USE THIS SPACE FOR FIGURING.

16. The bottom of the shopping bag shown in Figure 4 is placed flat on a table. Except for the handles, this shopping bag is constructed with rectangular pieces of paper. Which of the following diagrams best represents all the points where the shopping bag touches the table?

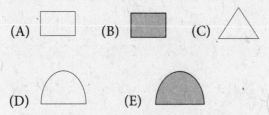

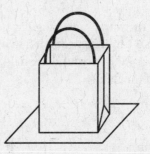

Figure 4

17. The number of students in a certain school is expected to increase from 1,086 students in 2010 to 1,448 students in 2011. What is the expected increase to the nearest percent?

    (A) 20%
    (B) 33%
    (C) 37%
    (D) 40%
    (E) 45%

GO ON TO THE NEXT PAGE

18. In Figure 5, the distance between *W* and *Y* is three times the distance between *W* and *X*, and the distance between *X* and *Z* is twice the distance between *X* and *Y*. If the distance from *W* to *X* is 2, how far apart are *W* and *Z*?

   (A) 10
   (B) 12
   (C) 14
   (D) 16
   (E) 18

USE THIS SPACE FOR FIGURING.

$$W \quad X \quad\quad Y \quad\quad Z$$

Figure 5

19. A fence surrounds a rectangular field whose length is 3 times its width. If 240 meters of the fence is used to surround the field, what is the width of the field?

   (A) 30 m
   (B) 40 m
   (C) 60 m
   (D) 80 m
   (E) 90 m

20. Ms. Kirschner receives $50 for every $900 she collects from stock sales. How much does she receive if she collects $18,000 from stock sales?

   (A)   $100
   (B)   $180
   (C) $1,000
   (D) $1,200
   (E) $1,800

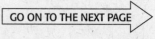
GO ON TO THE NEXT PAGE

21. What is the greatest number of rectangles 4 centimeters wide and 6 centimeters long that can be cut from a square piece of paper with a side of 24 centimeters?

(A)  2
(B)  10
(C)  24
(D  36
(E)  48

USE THIS SPACE FOR FIGURING.

22. $R$ is the sum of consecutive integers $S$ and $T$. If $S$ and $T$ are negative, which of the following is ALWAYS true?

(A)  $R = -4$
(B)  $R = -1$
(C)  $R$ is less than either $S$ or $T$.
(D)  $R$ is greater than either $S$ or $T$.
(E)  $R + S + T$ is positive.

23. Initially, Greg had a total of 60 DVDs and CDs in his collection. He then sold $\frac{1}{8}$ of his CDs and $\frac{1}{2}$ of his DVDs. If the number of DVDs he sold is twice the number of CDs he sold, how many DVDs did he sell?

(A)  4
(B)  5
(C)  8
(D)  10
(E)  20

GO ON TO THE NEXT PAGE

24. Mary saved exactly 60 percent of the total allowance she received in the last two weeks, and she spent the rest. If she received $20 for allowance each week and spent $12 of her first week's allowance, which of the following MUST be true?

I. She saved a total of $24.

II. She spent $6 of her second week's allowance.

III. She saved 80 percent of her second week's allowance.

(A) None
(B) I only
(C) II only
(D) I and III only
(E) I, II, and III

25. Paul and Bill each received a raise of 20 percent. If Paul now earns $4.50 per hour while Bill earns $5.40 per hour, Bill earned how much more per hour than Paul before their raises?

(A) $0.70
(B) $0.73
(C) $0.75
(D) $0.80
(E) $0.90

USE THIS SPACE FOR FIGURING.

IF YOU FINISH BEFORE TIME IS CALLED, YOU MAY CHECK YOUR WORK ON THIS SECTION ONLY. DO NOT TURN TO ANY OTHER SECTION IN THE TEST.

STOP

# ANSWER KEY

**Section 2**

1. D
2. E
3. D
4. B
5. A
6. A
7. C
8. B
9. C
10. E
11. E
12. B
13. B
14. C
15. A
16. D
17. B
18. C
19. C
20. E
21. C
22. D
23. B
24. B
25. A

**Section 3**

1. C
2. E
3. B
4. E

5. B
6. A
7. C
8. D
9. C
10. D
11. B
12. B
13. A
14. B
15. B
16. A
17. E
18. C
19. D
20. C
21. B
22. E
23. C
24. D
25. C
26. D
27. A
28. E
29. B
30. D
31. E
32. C
33. A
34. A
35. D

36. B
37. A
38. D
39. E
40. C

**Section 4**

1. E
2. D
3. C
4. D
5. A
6. A
7. D
8. B
9. A
10. E
11. B
12. C
13. B
14. D
15. D
16. E
17. C
18. E
19. E
20. C
21. C
22. B
23. B
24. D
25. E

26. B
27. E
28. A
29. C
30. A
31. A
32. A
33. E
34. A
35. B
36. D
37. C
38. D
39. C
40. D
41. B
42. D
43. B
44. E
45. E
46. C
47. D
48. B
49. B
50. E
51. E
52. C
53. C
54. A
55. B
56. E

57. B
58. A
59. C
60. D

**Section 5**

1. B
2. D
3. A
4. B
5. E
6. D
7. D
8. D
9. D
10. C
11. B
12. D
13. D
14. E
15. E
16. B
17. B
18. A
19. A
20. C
21. C
22. C
23. D
24. D
25. C

# SSAT PRACTICE TEST 2: MIDDLE-LEVEL: ASSESS YOUR STRENGTHS

Use the following tables to determine which topics and chapters you need to review most. If you need help with your essay, be sure to review Chapter 9: The Essay and Chapter 26: Writing Skills.

| Topic | Question |
| --- | --- |
| Math I | Section 2, questions 1–25 |
| Reading Comprehension | Section 3, questions 1–40 |
| Verbal: Synonyms | Section 4, questions 1–30 |
| Verbal: Analogies | Section 4, questions 31–60 |
| Math II | Section 5, questions 1–25 |

| Topic | Number of Questions on Test | Number Correct | If you struggled with these questions, study… |
| --- | --- | --- | --- |
| Math I | 25 | | Chapters 10–14 and Chapter 25 |
| Reading Comprehension | 40 | | Chapter 8 |
| Verbal: Synonyms | 30 | | Chapters 7 and 24 |
| Verbal: Analogies | 30 | | Chapters 2 and 24 |
| Math II | 25 | | Chapters 10–14 and Chapter 25 |

# ANSWERS AND EXPLANATIONS

## SECTION 2: MATH

**1. D**

With a perimeter of 30 and 5 sides of equal length, the length of one side is $\frac{30}{5}$, or 6.

**2. E**

There were a total of 17 customers who bought caramel candy. Subtract from these the 4 who bought both, and you are left with the 13 who bought only caramel.

**3. D**

Only factors of 24 (numbers that can be divided evenly into 24) can be the number of different colors in the bag. Since 5 is not a factor of 24, (D), 5, is the correct choice.

**4. B**

Since the whole number is less than 13 and also between 11 and 18, it must be between 11 and 13. We can immediately eliminate (C) because we need a whole number. (D) and (E) are out, too, because 13 and 14 are not "less than 13." And (A) is incorrect because 11 is not "between 11 and 18." Therefore, the number must be 12, choice (B).

**5. A**

Movies take up 60 degrees of 360 degrees, one-sixth of the pie chart. So Susan spent about one-sixth of 12 hours, or 2 hours, watching movies.

**6. A**

To solve for $R$, multiply both sides of the equation by 2; hence, $R = 32$. Plug 32 for $R$ into the expression $\frac{3}{4}R$, and you find that $\frac{3}{4}R = \frac{3}{4} \times 32 = 24$.

**7. C**

The fraction $\frac{1}{4}$ has a decimal value of 0.25; thus (B), (D), and (E) can be eliminated. Fifty-nine rounded to the nearest ten is 60; indeed, 59 is much closer to 60 than to 50, so (C) is correct.

**8. B**

There is no calculation necessary on this problem. Three of the five points lie on the horizontal $260,000 line, and the only other two points are the identical distance above and below the line. Thus, $260,000 is the correct answer.

**9. C**

This problem calls for substitution. $u = 5$ and $v = 5$. Plugging these values in yields $5 \emptyset 5 = 5 - (1 - \frac{1}{5}) = 5 - \frac{4}{5} = 4\frac{1}{5}$; (C) is correct.

**10. E**

This problem calls for substitution. $u = a$, $v = 3$, and $a \emptyset 3 = 4\frac{1}{3}$. Using the definition for the left side of this equation, which is $a \emptyset 3$, we have $a - (1 - \frac{1}{3}) = 4\frac{1}{3}$; then $a - \frac{2}{3} = 4\frac{1}{3}$ and $a = 5$.

**11. E**

Call the unknown number $x$ and translate the information in the question into math. Remember that *of* means "times." Twenty percent of 64 means $\frac{20}{100}(64)$, and 5% of $x$ means $\frac{5}{100}x$. Then 20% of 64 is equal to 5% of $x$ means that $\frac{20}{100}(64) = \frac{5}{100}x$. Reducing $\frac{20}{100}$ and $\frac{5}{100}$ yields $\frac{1}{5}(64) = \frac{1}{20}x$. Isolate the $x$ by multiplying both sides by 20. Then $x = \frac{1}{5}(64) \times 20 = \frac{64 \times 20}{5} = 64 \times 4 = 256$.

## 12. B

The minimum number of fish Andy could have caught was 36, or 1 more than Rich caught. Use the average formula, Average = $\dfrac{\text{Sum of the terms}}{\text{Number of terms}}$. Sum of the terms = 36, and number of terms (or number of fishing trips) = 4. Hence, Andy must have caught an average of at least $\dfrac{36}{4} = 9$ fish per trip.

## 13. B

We need to set up an equation here. We know all the boys earned the same amount per hour, so 4 × Rate + 6 × Rate + 8 × Rate = 27. Thus, 18 × Rate = 27 and the Rate = $\dfrac{27}{18}$ = $1.50 per hour. Lee worked 8 hours, so Lee earned 8 × $1.50 = $12.

## 14. C

Johnny has already picked 200 apples in 2.5 hours. He must pick an additional 600 − 200 = 400 apples. Call the number of additional hours that Johnny must spend picking apples $x$. To find $x$, set up a ratio and solve for $x$ : $\dfrac{200 \text{ apples}}{2.5 \text{ hours}} = \dfrac{400 \text{ apples}}{x \text{ hours}}$. Since the numerator of the fraction on the right is equal to twice the numerator of the fraction on the left, the denominator of the fraction on the right must also be equal to twice the denominator of the fraction on the left. So $x = 2 \times 2.5 = 5$. Since Johnny must work an additional 5 hours, the latest time that he can begin picking apples again is 5 hours earlier than 7:15 P.M. So 2:15 P.M. is the latest that Johnny can start picking apples again.

## 15. A

Set up an equation: $8W = 0.88$. Isolate the $W$ by dividing each side by 8. $W = \dfrac{0.88}{8} = 0.11$.

## 16. D

Figure 4 indicates that the legs of two sides of the triangle are equal and thus the triangle is isosceles. Angles that are opposite equal sides must be equal. Thus, each of the two base angles is 50 degrees, and we know that the sum of the three interior angles of any triangle is 180 degrees, so $r = 180 - 50 - 50 = 80$ .

## 17. B

To determine how many times the income of 1988 was of the income of 1958, divide the 1988 income by the 1958 income. Then the number we are seeking is $\dfrac{4,500,000}{9,000}$. Dividing the numerator and the denominator by 1,000, we have $\dfrac{4,500}{9} = 500$.

## 18. C

The correct answer choice, when 2 is subtracted from it, must be a multiple of 5. A number is a multiple of 5 only if its ones digit is a 5 or a 0. Looking at the choices, 25 − 2 = 23 is not a multiple of 5, so eliminate choice (A). 33 − 2 = 31 is not a multiple of 5, so eliminate (B). 47 − 2 = 45, which is a multiple of 5. So (C) is correct.

## 19. C

Recall Kaplan's strategy: A figure can be drawn without lifting the pencil or retracing if there are exactly 0 or 2 points where an odd number of lines intersect. (C) has no points where an odd number of lines intersect. Hence, this is the correct answer.

## 20. E

Pick 100 as the initial population of Country X. The increase for the first year was $\dfrac{10}{100}$ of 100 = 10, and the total at the end of the first year was 100 + 10 or 110 people. The increase for the second year was $\dfrac{10}{100}$ of 110 = 11, and the total at the end of the second year was 110 + 11 or 121 people. The population increased from 100 to 121 over the two-year period. The increase in the population was 121 − 100 = 21. Hence, the percent increase in the population over the entire two-year period was $\frac{21}{100}$ or 21%.

**21. C**

The value of $z$ is given to us in terms of $y$; we need to multiply this value by 2 and add 1. Hence, 2$z$ + 1 = 2($y$ + 2) + 1 = 2$y$ + 4 + 1 = 2$y$ + 5, (C).

**22. D**

Picking numbers for $x$ and $y$ is a foolproof method for solving this problem. Pick a positive fraction for $x$ that is less than 1, such as $\frac{1}{2}$. Then pick a positive value for $y$ that is greater than $x$, which in this case means that the $y$ that we pick must also be greater than $\frac{1}{2}$. Remember, the question says that $y$ is greater than $x$ and the numbers you pick must always be consistent with the question stem. So let's pick 1 for $y$. So we're letting $x$ be $\frac{1}{2}$ and $y$ be 1. With these values, (A) is 2, (B) and (C) are both $\frac{1}{2}$, and (D) is −2. Further examining (D), we see that the denominator, $x − y$, has a larger positive number $y$ subtracted from a smaller positive number $x$. So $x − y$ will always be negative. Therefore $\frac{1}{x − y}$ will also always be negative.

**23. B**

If 6 people can sit at each of $x$ tables and 5 people can sit at each of $y$ tables, then the maximum number of people that may be seated is 6$x$ + 5$y$.

**24. B**

Draw 3 squares: big, bigger, and biggest. Let the side of the middle fabric piece be 9. The side of the largest fabric piece must be three times this, or 27. Likewise, the side of the smallest square piece must be 3. The area of the largest piece is 27 × 27 = 729, and the area of the smallest piece is 9. Now determine the number of times that 9 goes into 729: $\frac{729}{9} = 81$.

**25. A**

Begin by determining how many gallons of gas it takes to make the 18 trips: $\frac{3}{4} \times 18 = \frac{27}{2} = 13.5$ gallons. If there are 9 gallons in a tank, Mr. Dali will need $\frac{13.5}{9} = 1.5$ tanks of gas.

## SECTION 3: READING COMPREHENSION

### SCOTT JOPLIN PASSAGE

First up is a brief history passage about Scott Joplin, a composer best known for his ragtime music. Don't try to absorb all the details, even in a brief passage like this. Just get a feel for the Big Idea, which is that Joplin was instrumental in developing the ragtime genre but wasn't recognized as a serious composer until almost 60 years after his death.

**1. C**

Lines 2–3 note that Joplin composed 41 piano pieces known as "rags," the only time the word is used in the passage. (C), then, must be correct. (E) is tempting, but the genre or style of songs Joplin invented is described as "ragtime," not "rag." (A)'s "operatic" is incorrect; Joplin's *Treemonisha* was his only opera. (B) and (D) are incorrect because ragtime is never described as "dance" music or as being played by marching bands.

## 2.   E

Only (E) has the proper scope here. (A) and
(B) focus too narrowly on details. It was Joplin's
"rhythmic diversity," not his stylistic diversity, (C),
that distinguished his composing. The passage
doesn't say how Joplin finally won the Pulitzer, (D).

## 3.   B

The passage states that Joplin received the Pulitzer in
1976, "59 years after his death." Subtract 59 from 76
and you get 17, so Joplin died in 1917, choice (B).

## 4.   E

The author discusses Joplin's "significant creative
contribution" to music, his great popularity, and
how he "at last" received "the praise he deserved."
Thus, (E)'s "appreciative" best sums up the author's
tone toward Joplin.

## 5.   B

The passage states that Joplin was instrumental in
developing ragtime "as a genre, a unique musical
form." Therefore, (B) is the correct inference: A
genre is a distinct category or style. While ragtime
is an example of a musical genre, a genre is not an
example of a particular type of ragtime, (A). There's
no evidence that Joplin coined the term *genre,* (C).

## 6.   A

Lines 13–14 say "he was not considered a serious
composer during his lifetime," even though his
"Maple Leaf Rag" was "the most popular piano
rag of the time" (lines 10–11). That says his work
was liked but people didn't appreciate it as serious
music. The last sentence says he wasn't celebrated
until 59 years after he died, making (A) correct.

(C) is incorrect because line 5 says he made a
"contribution" to ragtime; he didn't invent it.

## BIRD COURTSHIP PASSAGE

Next up is a science passage about the courtship
procedures and "identification checks" used by
birds during courtship and mating. Paragraph 1
introduces the topic, paragraph 2 details the roles of
plumage and aggressive behavior, and paragraph 3
discusses the role of sounds in the birds' courting and
mating rituals.

## 7.   C

This Inference question is answered in the
opening paragraph. The author states that the
bird's identification and courtship procedures are
important "because if birds of different species mate,
any offspring" will be sterile and have a low chance
for survival. Thus, the procedures are important
because they help a bird find a mate of its own
species. (B) focuses too narrowly on a detail from
paragraph 2.

## 8.   D

The answer lies in paragraph 3, which states that a
male's singing tells females of its species that "it is
in breeding condition," I. After mating, the singing
enables the nesting female "to continue to identify"
her partner, III. The passage does not mention that
male birds use sound to intimidate male rivals, II, so
I and III only are correct.

## 9.   C

This Detail question focuses on the last sentence of
paragraph 2. There we learn that whooping cranes
"perform wonderfully elaborate courtship dances."

So the whooping crane is an example of a bird that behaves in an unusual, noteworthy way during courtship, and (C) is correct. (B), (D), and (E) incorrectly mention other details from paragraph 2—plumage, reversed roles, and aggressiveness.

## 10. D

The answer here is taken from the same sentence—the last of paragraph 1—that answered question 7. If birds of different species mate, "any offspring will usually be sterile or badly adapted to their surroundings." This point is restated in (D). (B) is the opposite of the correct choice. The frequency of interspecies mating, (A), is not mentioned in the passage, but it must happen occasionally, contrary to (E), or the author wouldn't warn against its dangers. The idea of a new species evolving, (C), is not discussed.

## 11. B

This time the Big Idea question comes near the end of the set. The passage is about the various courtship behaviors and "identification checks" used by birds, which makes (B) correct. (A) and (E) raise issues not debated in the passage. (C) and (D) focus too narrowly on details.

## 12. B

Think about where you would most likely find this passage. (C) and (D) are incorrect because the passage contains nothing personal or fictional, just facts. (E) is incorrect because the passage does not talk about endangered birds. (A) is incorrect. The passage discusses how birds of the same species identify one another in order to mate, not how you would identify birds, so (B) is correct.

## NATIVE AMERICAN PASSAGE

Next up is a brief passage about the 1,500 Native American languages that have been discovered by linguists. The Big Idea here is simple: A pioneering linguist originally divided these 1,500 languages into six main groups; a recent group of scholars thinks they can all be divided into three broader groups, but other scholars disagree with this new theory.

## 13. A

(A) is the most specific and accurate, and it's correct here. (B) leaves out the recent debate over the revised classification of Native American languages into three groups. (C) and (E) are too broad; they could be talking about any group of languages, not just Native American languages. And (D) focuses too narrowly on a detail from paragraph 2.

## 14. B

According to paragraph 2, scholars believe Native American languages can be classified into only three families because of "similarities and differences among words and sounds." (B) can be inferred from this statement. (A) distorts a detail from paragraph 1. (C) is the argument of those who think Native American languages can't be classified into three families. (D) is too broad, and (E) is beyond the scope of the passage.

## 15. B

Where would you be likely to come upon this passage? In a discussion of Native American languages or a linguistics textbook (B). (A), (C), and (D) are incorrect because there's nothing either personal or fictional in the text; it's just a series of factual statements. And while Sapir pioneered the field of Native American linguistics, the passage doesn't contain any significant biographical information about his life, (E).

## 16. A

Why is classifying Native American languages controversial? Those who group them into three families have "no doubt about the validity" of their theory. But "the vast majority of linguists" argue that "linguistic science has not yet advanced far enough" to group 1,500 languages into only three families. So the controversy exists because scholars do not yet agree on how to classify languages, and (A) is correct. (B) is a point argued by linguists who think Native American languages might never be properly grouped into families, but it's not the source of the controversy. We don't know when the field of linguistics was founded, but even though it hasn't "advanced far enough," it is not a "very new" field, as (C) suggests. There's no evidence for (D) or (E).

## 17. E

Paragraph 1 states that Sapir classified Native American languages into six families. None of the other questions is answered in the passage.

## 18. C

Look at the sentence "extent" appears in. The author says the languages have "diverged" so much that it would be impossible to classify them into three linguistic families. Therefore, the answer needs to mean something close to "wide". (C) is the answer.

## POETRY PASSAGE

Next up is a famous poem by Emily Dickinson. The first stanza creates a metaphor of hope as a bird that lives inside us and never stops singing. The second stanza says that the bird of hope sings even in bad weather (i.e., bad times). And in the final stanza, the poet claims that, while she has heard the bird of hope singing in distant places, "It never asked a crumb of me."

## 19. D

Hope is "the thing with feathers" in stanza 1 and "the little bird" in stanza 2, so (D) is correct. (A), (B), and (C) are trials and dangers that the bird/hope faces; (E) is what the bird sings.

## 20. C

Paraphrase the final stanza: "I've heard the bird of hope in far-off places, and it never asked me for anything." This points to (C) as correct. (A) is incorrect because the poem says nothing about a world without hope or about preserving hope at all costs. (B) summarizes the second stanza, not the third. (D) takes the poem literally to the point of absurdity; the "crumb" line doesn't mean that the bird is always hungry, but rather that it gives its song of hope freely. And (E) is incorrect because, according to the poet, hope is always present; no great effort is required to make it so.

## 21. B

Remember you're dealing with metaphor. This poem isn't about a bird; it's comparing hope to a bird that never stops singing. The statement that it "kept so many warm" means that hope has given comfort to a lot of people; therefore, (B) is correct. (A) and (C) take the poem literally. (D) is pessimistic where the poet is optimistic about hope, and (E) implies that hope *only* works in the worst of situations. But the poet is saying that hope is helpful *even* in the worst of situations.

## 22. E

The poet likens hope to a bird that, thankfully, is always there to help people, never asking anything in return. Her tone is one of gratitude, making choice (E) correct. (C) is the closest character, but "respectful" is too formal, too distancing. Hope in this poem isn't a great person or awesome display of nature; it's a little bird "that perches in the soul."

### 23. C

Figure out what the poet is saying in the lines "sore" appears in. The poet is saying only the worst of storms could discourage the bird. The only choice that comes close to meaning "worst" is "severe," (C).

## RECYCLING PASSAGE

The next passage is about recycling, the remaking of waste products and materials for practical purposes. In paragraph 1, we learn that recycling is now considered a necessity, that it saves money and resources and reduces waste. In paragraph 2, the author focuses on residential recycling—what we as private citizens can do to reduce waste.

### 24. D

Statement I is false: Recycling "reduces the amount of waste produced" (lines 13–14). This eliminates (B), (C), and (E). Since statement II is included in both of the remaining answer choices, it must be true, and it is: We're told twice that recycling can save money. Statement III, then, is the crucial one. And it's true: Lines 17–19 state that "the amount of...waste produced at home has been steadily increasing." So only Statements II and III are true, and choice (D) is correct.

### 25. C

(A) is easily eliminated: The author thinks the individual's role in recycling "has been seriously underemphasized." The first half of (B) is correct: Businesses do recycle to save money. But the

second half is incorrect: The author doesn't think individuals are motivated to recycle by a sense of the greater good—but the author does think that we should be so motivated. This point is restated in correct choice (C). (D) says we shouldn't recycle, which the author would certainly disagree with, and (E) claims that recycling is only the responsibility of businesses, which goes against the thrust of paragraph 2.

### 26. D

You're looking for the choice that is not an example of recycling, which the author defines in lines 5–7 as "the remaking of waste products and other used materials for practical purposes." Using this definition, (A), (B), and (E) are easily checked off as examples of recycling. (C) involves a second use for empty soda bottles, as does the author's example in lines 8–10. This leaves (D): Selling jewelry to buy a car is not recycling, because the jewelry is not a waste product that's being remade.

### 27. A

The author argues that recycling is "important... even...necessary," that "it is our duty to ourselves and to our fellow human beings." These and similar signals throughout the passage reveal the author's tone as insistent, (A). By the same token, (B), (D), and (E) are easy to eliminate. (C) may be tempting since the author tells us that the future of humanity is at stake, but (A) remains the best choice, because more than being formal, the author is trying to motivate us to do something (recycle).

### 28. E

Paragraph 3 argues that individuals can and must learn to recycle their waste products. You can predict, then, that the author will go on to suggest one or more ways in which individuals can pitch in to help the recycling effort, a point restated in (E). There's no evidence to suggest (A) or (B). (C) wrongly suggests the author will return to a detail from the previous paragraph. And (D) doesn't even mention recycling.

### 29. B

In lines 15–17, the author states that businesses recycle "based primarily on the goal of saving money." So you can infer that the author believes that businesses recycle primarily for financial gain, (B). (A) is incorrect because the economics of recycling are of greatest interest to businesses, not to the author. Nor can it be inferred from the passage that the author's knowledge of the financial aspects of recycling, (C), is limited. And while (D) is probably true, it can't be inferred from lines 15–17.

## El Niño Passage

The passage begins with a statement that, although bad weather is usually only an "inconvenience" for us, it can have "disastrous consequences" for communities in other parts of the world. The remainder of the passage describes an example of this disastrous bad weather: El Niño, a change in the Humboldt Current (an ocean current) that disrupts marine life and can thereby threaten villagers on the northwest coast of South America with starvation.

### 30. D

The Humboldt Current flows off the northwest coast of South America, making (D) correct. Each of the other choices contradicts the passage. El Niño occurs only at Christmastime (A), but the Humboldt Current flows all year long. The Humboldt Current does fail when El Niño occurs (B). The passage does not state the directional flow of the Humboldt Current, (C),

but does state that it is a cold-water current, not a hot-water current, (E).

### 31. E

The bulk of the passage concerns what happens when the Humboldt Current fails, which makes (D) very tempting, but the Big Idea of the passage is really stated in the first sentence: Changes in weather patterns can dramatically affect the way people live, making (E) correct here. Remember, the Humboldt Current and El Niño information is there only to back up this claim by the author. (A), (B), and (C) focus on details and should have been easier to eliminate.

### 32. C

Here you're looking for the one choice that isn't true. Only (C) is not confirmed in the passage. As we noted in question 30, the Humboldt Current carries cold water, not warm; the passage also never states that the current affects "the climate of nearby land masses."

### 33. A

If you answered question 31 correctly, you probably answered this one correctly too. This passage is not about El Niño; El Niño is discussed in order to prove the author's larger point: that bad weather can harm communities. This means that (A), not (C), is the correct answer.

### 34. A

We're told that bad weather can have a "dramatic effect" on these villages, "depriving" them "of their livelihood." The author's attitude toward the villagers, then, is—what? Not condescending, (C), angry, (D), or emotional, (E). And though the author doesn't express undue alarm, you wouldn't say she was simply unconcerned about the villagers, as (B) puts it. No, the author's attitude is best described as sympathetic, (A). The villagers occasionally have this awful problem, and the author expresses concern about it.

### 35. D

The "chain reaction" described in the passage is as follows: the current fails, stopping the flow of nutrients to the fish and squid, which die, thereby harming the villagers. A chain reaction then, is not a pair but a series of causally linked occurrences. (A), (B), and (C), concern only a pair—not a chain—of occurrences. The best example of a chain reaction in the choices is therefore (D), where global warming leads to melted glaciers, which lead to higher water levels and then less available land for people. (E) gives two phenomena that occur at the same time.

## MARSHALL PLAN PASSAGE

The final passage is a history passage about the Marshall Plan, an American scheme to help rebuild Europe after World War II. Paragraph 1 sets the scene, explaining that the United States believed that Europe's economic devastation needed to be cured in order to keep it from falling under the domination of the Soviet Union. Paragraph 2 explains that in 1948, U.S. Secretary of State George Marshall instituted the Marshall Plan, which distributed 12 billion dollars among 16 different European countries over the next four years.

### 36. B

The answer will probably mention the Marshall Plan and how it helped Europe; (B) fits this bill nicely. (A) and (E) are way too broad. (C) describes what happened during World War II that made the Marshall Plan so necessary but says nothing about the Plan itself. (D) suggests that the passage is about Marshall himself, when the author actually tells

you nothing more than Marshall's name and job—Secretary of State.

### 37. A

The author's tone is not noticeably positive (B) or negative (E). It betrays no personal feelings such as insistence, (C), or anxiety, (D). Instead, it's objective.

### 38. D

This is a Detail question that careful readers will get. Paragraph 2 states that the Marshall Plan doled out "a combined total of $12 billion" to the 16 "participating countries." So each country did not get $12 billion. All of the other statements are substantiated in the passage.

### 39. E

What was the driving force behind the Marshall Plan? Early in paragraph 1, we learn that post-World War II Western Europe was economically devastated and that when tensions between the United States and the Soviet Union escalated, U.S. policymakers felt "substantial financial assistance" was needed in Western Europe "to maintain a state of political stability." This points to (E). None of the other choices draws a correct inference from the passage.

### 40. C

The first paragraph describes the postwar economic and political problems that the Marshall Plan was intended to solve, and paragraph 2 describes, in general terms, how much money was distributed and how well the plan worked. You can infer, then, that the author will go on to talk about specifics—how the Plan's money was put to work in some or all of the 16 participating countries. (A) wrongly sees the Cold War, not the Marshall Plan, as the focus of the passage. (B) goes back in time, to events before the

Marshall Plan was ever dreamed up. Other economic recovery plans are never mentioned, and (E) is also unwarranted.

## SECTION 4: VERBAL

### SYNONYMS

**1. E**

Harsh means rough or overly demanding—in other words, severe, (E). A crime might be punished by a harsh penalty, for example. One can be angry, (B), without being harsh; these words are not synonyms.

**2. D**

Indicate means to show, state, or point out.

**3. C**

Bleak means desolate and barren, or cheerless, (C). "We camped out in a bleak wilderness."

**4. D**

Secure means free from danger or safe.

**5. A**

Alien means foreign or strange.

**6. A**

Chronic means frequently occurring, habitual, or persistent, (A), as in a "chronic cough."

**7. D**

To quench a thirst means to slake or satisfy it, (D).

**8. B**

Severe, as we saw in question 1, means harsh, overly demanding, or extreme, (B). Severe cold leaves you frozen, (A), but severe and frozen are not synonyms. Don't just think associatively; look for the word that's closest in meaning to the stem word.

**9. A**

When thieves ransack an apartment, they turn it upside down looking for things to steal. In other words, to ransack is to search thoroughly, (A).

**10. E**

The summit is the top of something, as in the summit of a mountain peak, which makes (E) correct.

**11. B**

A tumult is a loud noise, an uproar, or commotion, (B).

**12. C**

To retard means to delay the progress of, hold back, or slow down, (C).

**13. B**

An antidote is a cure or remedy, (B), such as an antidote for poison.

**14. D**

Solitary is the state of being secluded or alone, (D).

**15. D**

To camouflage means to hide or disguise, (D).

**16. E**

To expel means to drive out, to reject, or to cast out, (E).

**17. C**

To lunge is to make a sudden forward stride or leap. A lunge—especially with a weapon—is also called a thrust, (C). To pursue, (A), means to chase, that is, to follow with the intent of overtaking. Pursuit may begin with a lunge, but the two verbs are not synonyms. In similar fashion, a lunge may involve a turn, (B), or startle someone, (E), but these words are not synonyms of lunge, either.

**18. E**

Brevity is the quality of being brief, which means of short duration—so shortness, (E), is correct.

**19. E**

To marvel is to feel surprise, amazed curiosity, or wonder, (E).

**20. C**

Candor is truthfulness, or honesty, (C). To be daring, (B), is to be bold but not necessarily honest.

**21. C**

To convene is to meet or to assemble, (C). The closest distracters, (B) and (D), are actions associated with meetings that are convened, but they're not synonyms.

**22. B**

A catastrophe is a great misfortune, a terrible occurrence, or a disaster, (B).

**23. B**

Gregarious means talkative, outgoing, or sociable, (B).

**24. D**

Dexterity is mental or physical skill and quickness. The best synonym here is nimbleness, (D).

**25. E**

To say that something is imminent means that it's about to happen, that it is forthcoming, (E).

**26. B**

Animosity is hostility, ill will, or resentment. The best synonym here is hatred, (B).

**27. E**

To amend means to change, alter, or improve, (E).

**28. A**

Someone who feels despondent is very sad or depressed, (A).

**29. C**

Unflinching means not flinching or shrinking from; it's the quality of being steadfast. The best synonym here is uncompromising, (C). (A) and (D) are near-antonyms for unflinching.

**30. A**

To repudiate means to cast off, disown, or refuse to have anything to do with. The choice with the closest meaning to repudiate is renounce, (A). To impede, (B), is to slow or interfere with someone's progress.

## ANALOGIES

**31. A**

Anything having to do with the sun is solar. In the same way, anything having to do with the earth is terrestrial, (A). Marine refers to a sea or ocean, not to a pond. Subterranean refers to what is below the ground, not to the ground itself. You might suspect (E), but lunar refers to anything having to do with the moon, not planets.

**32. A**

Botany is the study of plants. Similarly, meteorology is the study of weather, (A). Flora is the generic word for plant life or vegetation.

**33. E**

You use a hammer to *put in* a nail. In the same way, you use a screwdriver to *put in* a screw, (E). You use an axe to chop wood, a lathe to smooth or shape molding, a chisel to chip marble, and a nut to secure a bolt.

**34. A**

A bone is part of the structural system that supports a mammal. A girder is part of the structural system that supports a skyscraper, (A). The other choices are also part of the structural system that supports a skyscraper, not the skyscraper itself.

**35. B**

A primate is an order of mammals that includes monkeys, apes, and humans. So a human is one species of the primate order, just as a snake is one species of the order of reptiles. Vegetarians are not an order in the same way as primates and reptiles. A disease is not necessarily bacterial in nature. Birds are mammals, not amphibians; amphibians are a class in the animal kingdom that includes frogs and toads.

**36. D**

A tremor is a quivering motion of the earth. A powerful tremor may be an earthquake. In the same way, wind is a motion of the air, and a powerful wind may be a tornado, (D). The analogy isn't exact here, but it's better than the other choices. An eye is the calm center of a hurricane, (A); a powerful desert is not a sandstorm, (B). A faucet is a man-made object through which water flows; a deluge, (C), is a great flood. And a powerful flood, (E), is not a river.

**37. C**

Something tremendously amusing is uproarious; similarly, something tremendously interesting is hypnotic, fascinating, or mesmerizing, (C).

**38. D**

Being fickle, or inconstant, is the opposite of steadfastness. In the same way, being tempestuous, or stormy, is the opposite of peacefulness, (D). Ire, (E), means anger.

**39. C**

A group of fish is called a school, just as a group of birds is called a flock.

**40. D**

A cartographer is a designer of maps, just as a chef is a designer of meals.

**41. B**

A throne is the official chair for a monarch, just as a bench is the official chair for a judge, (B). A miter, (A), is the headdress worn by bishops.

**42. D**

A canal is a man-made river, just as a mine is a man-made cavern, (D). It's stretching things to call a boat a man-made piece of driftwood, (A), even though both float.

**43. B**

When milk goes bad it gets sour; when bread goes bad it gets stale, (B).

**44. E**

Ore is mined to bring it up out of the earth, just as oil is drilled to bring it up out of the earth, (E). Grain is plowed, (D), but it's not found buried in the earth.

**45. E**

Weight is measured on a scale, just as altitude is measured on an altimeter. Speed, not distance, is measured on a speedometer (A). (B) is a little tricky: Numbers are measured on a slide rule, but only special kinds of numbers called logarithms.

**46. C**

A porcupine protects itself with quills. In a similar fashion, a skunk protects itself with odor.

## 47. D

The purpose of a jar is to contain, just as the purpose of a pillar is to support, (D).

## 48. B

Irrigate means to flush with liquid. So you irrigate something that is dry, just as you smooth something that's coarse, (B). (A) and (C) are tempting but not as good. You soften something that's hard, not uneven. And you purify something that's impure, or tainted. To ferment something is to induce a chemical process that makes alcohol; this has nothing to do with saltiness.

## 49. B

Electricity flows through a wire, just as water flows through an aqueduct. Sound is broadcast from a radio, choice (A), which is not the same thing. (C) and (D) have similar problems; in each case the music or light is emitted from the object, it doesn't flow through it. And in (E), a river is contained by its bank.

## 50. E

You can express contempt with a sneer. In the same way, you express displeasure with a frown, (E). Each of the other actions is inappropriately matched to its emotion.

## 51. E

The base of a building is its foundation. The base of a plant is its root, (E). If you chose (A), (C), or (D), you were probably confusing the vegetative meaning of "plant" with, say, a manufacturing plant. A grotto is a cave.

## 52. C

Olfactory refers to anything having to do with the sense of smell. So our bridge could be, *The nose is the organ of the olfactory sense*. Similarly, the ear is the organ of the sense of hearing or auditory sense, (C).

## 53. C

Irk means to annoy, disgust, or irritate. So the relationship here is of opposites: Something that irks is not soothing. In the same way, something that supports is not weakening or undermining, (C). Irritating, (D), is second-best here; it would go better with soothing than with support.

## 54. A

Something illegible is impossible to read, just as something invisible is impossible to see, (A). Something broken is not by definition impossible to fix.

## 55. B

Tact is sensitivity, or the ability to do or say the right thing with people. So tact is a necessary quality for a diplomat. In the same way, agility is a necessary quality for a gymnast, which makes (B) correct. Parsimony, (A), or stinginess, is a quality a philanthropist will not have, since a philanthropist is someone who gives generous amounts of money to charity. Similarly, a judge, (E), should be unbiased, not biased, which means having a declared preference for one side or the other. Victims may be vulnerable, (C), but you wouldn't ordinarily say that vulnerability is a necessary quality for being a victim. And training in (D) is too vague; it's not a quality specific to the practice of medicine.

## 56. E

Ravenous means extremely hungry. So to be ravenous is to be in an extreme state of hunger. In the same way, to be furious is to be in an extreme state of indignation, (E). None of the other choices has a first word that's an extreme version of the second word. Pliable, (A), means flexible, while obstinacy is stubbornness, so these words are opposites. The same is true for (B) and (C). Tenacity, (D), is stubborn persistence; being smart is not being in an extreme state of tenacity.

### 57. B

To amplify sound is to make it stronger or louder. To bolster something means to strengthen it. In the same way, then, to bolster courage is to make it stronger. Getting the right answer here depends a little on knowing common usage. You can't bolster a smell, (A), insomnia or sleeplessness, (C), or light, (D), or silence, (E).

### 58. A

Reverse the order of the stem pair: You attend a lecture in an auditorium. In the same way, you attend a concert in a theater, (A). This bridge clearly doesn't work on (B), (D), or (E). One attends religious services, not religion itself, in a temple, (C).

### 59. C

Philanthropic means generous, giving; benevolence is the quality of generosity. So our bridge might be, *A philanthropic act is evidence of benevolence.* In the same way, a miserly act is evidence of stinginess, (C). Ostentatious, (B), means showy or extravagant.

### 60. D

Spurious is simply a fancy word meaning fake. So we've got a relationship of opposites here: Something spurious has no authenticity. Similarly, something laughable has no seriousness, (D). Lavish, (A), means extravagantly expensive. Abject means miserable; subjectivity may or may not be miserable, (B). There's no obvious bridge between the words in (C), and in (E), totalitarian refers to an imposing system of government, so it is not the opposite of completeness.

## SECTION 5: MATH

### 1. B

Begin with $5 + cover price – $9 and simplify it: cover price – $4, which means $4 below the cover price. (B) is correct.

### 2. D

Note here that each cube = 20 boxes. February has two cubes less than March, hence $2(20) = 40$ boxes less.

### 3. A

In January, 6 cubes were sold, and in February, 3 cubes were sold. Thus, in January, the number of boxes sold was $\frac{6}{3} = 2$ times the number of boxes sold in February. It is not necessary to perform the calculation using the fact that 20 boxes are represented by each cube.

### 4. B

Let $x$ = the number of ties for Team A; keep in mind that $x$ is an integer here. Thus, Team A had $4x$ losses. Adding the losses and ties (there were no wins), the number of games the team played was $x + 4x = 5x$. Thus, the correct answer choice must be a multiple of 5 (because $x$ is an integer). Only (B), 15, is a multiple of 5.

### 5. E

In order to make the discussion simpler, the five rectangles that are in the figure to begin with have been labeled.

Systematically count the different rectangles in the figure. There are 5 rectangles in the figure to begin with, which we will call basic rectangles. Next, let's count the number of rectangles that are made up of 2 basic rectangles. Rectangles made up of 2 basic rectangles can be formed from basic rectangles A and B, C and D, D and E, A and C, and B and D. There are 5 rectangles made up of 2 basic rectangles. Next, let's count the number of rectangles that can be made up of 3 basic rectangles. There is just one such rectangle. This is the rectangle that is made up of the 3 basic rectangles at the bottom, rectangles C, D, and E. Next, let's count the number of rectangles that can be made up of 4 basic rectangles. There is just one such rectangle, the rectangle that is made up of basic rectangles A, B, C, and D. There are no other rectangles that can be made up of basic rectangles. There is a total of 5 + 5 + 1 + 1 = 12 different rectangles in the figure.

## 6.  D

We are looking for the fraction that is NOT less than $\frac{1}{4}$, that is, a fraction that is greater than or equal to $\frac{1}{4}$. (D) is correct because $\frac{1}{4} = \frac{19}{19 \times 4} = \frac{19}{76}$ is less than $\frac{19}{70}$ because $\frac{19}{70}$ has a smaller denominator. Looking at the other choices, since $\frac{2}{8} = \frac{1}{4}$, $\frac{2}{9}$ must be less than $\frac{1}{4}$ (since 9 is a greater denominator).

Since $\frac{3}{12} = \frac{1}{4}$, $\frac{3}{14}$ must be less than $\frac{1}{4}$ (due to the greater denominator, 14). Reducing $\frac{14}{64}$, we get $\frac{7}{32}$ and since $\frac{8}{32} = \frac{1}{4}$, $\frac{14}{64} = \frac{7}{32}$ is less than $\frac{1}{4}$. Since $\frac{1}{4} = \frac{27}{27 \times 4} = \frac{27}{108}$, then $\frac{27}{125}$ is less than $\frac{27}{108} = \frac{1}{4}$.

## 7.  D

Begin by labeling each side 1. Using the answer choices, count the lengths of 1 in the path: (A) = 4, (B) = 4, (C) = 4, (D) = 5, and (E) = 4. (D) is the longest path.

## 8.  D

No lengthy calculation is needed here. In order for a product of numbers to equal 0, at least one of the numbers must equal zero. Since $5\frac{1}{3}$ is not 0, the other factor, $14 - x$, must equal 0. So $14 - x = 0$, and $x = 14$.

## 9.  D

Since 1.18 has 2 places after the decimal point, write each answer choice with 2 places after the decimal point. (A) and (B) are more than 1.00 away from 1.18. (C), 1.90, is more than 0.70 away from 1.18, (D), 1.10, is 0.08 away from 1.18, and (E), 1.00, is 0.18 away from 1.18.

## 10.  C

Write out the given inequality: $X > 15$. Next multiply both sides by $\frac{1}{3}$ (or divide both sides by 3). We now have $\frac{1}{3}X > \frac{15}{3}$ and $\frac{1}{3}X > 5$, (C).

## 11.  B

Round $26.95 to 27.00. Then we have $\frac{35}{100} \times 27 = ?$ Canceling yields $\frac{7}{20} \times 27 = \frac{189}{20} = 9.45$.

### 12. D

Let $T$ be the number of minutes. Set up a ratio:

$\frac{600}{3} = \frac{27,000}{T}$. Reduce $\frac{600}{3}$ to $\frac{200}{1}$. Then $\frac{200}{1} = $

$\frac{27,000}{T}$. Next cross-multiply: $200T = 27,000$.

Divide both sides by 100: $2T = 270$, and thus
$T = 135$. Put this into the time format of hours and
minutes by dividing 135 minutes by 60 minutes per
hour and we have $2\frac{1}{4}$ hours, which is 2 hours and
15 minutes.

### 13. D

Translate what is stated in the question step-by-step.
To begin with, Sally has $x$ dollars. After she receives
100 dollars, she has $x + 100$ dollars. She spends
125 dollars, so she has $(x + 100) - 125$ dollars left.
Now simplify $(x + 100) - 125$: $(x + 100) - 125 = x +$
$100 - 125 = x - 25$. Sally has $x - 25$ dollars left, so
(D) is correct.

### 14. E

Begin by multiplying both sides by 3 to eliminate
the denominator. Then $A + B = 12$. If $A$ is greater
than 1, then $B$ must be less than 11. Thus (E), 12,
could not be the value of $B$.

### 15. E

Use the average formula, which is Average =
$\frac{\text{Sum of the terms}}{\text{Number of terms}}$. Call $X$ the sum of all 5 numbers.
Then $\frac{X}{5} = 10$, so $X = 50$. Call $Y$ the sum of the
3 remaining numbers. Then $\frac{Y}{3} = 9$, so $Y = 27$.

Subtracting from the sum of all 5 numbers the sum of
the 3 numbers that remain leaves the sum of the
2 numbers that were removed. So the sum of the
2 numbers that were removed is $X - Y = 50 - 27 = 23$.

### 16. B

The bottom surface of the bag is a rectangle and all
points are inside the rectangle, so choice (A) can be
eliminated. (B) is correct.

### 17. B

The formula for percent increase is Percent

increase = $\frac{\text{New value} - \text{Old value}}{\text{Old value}} \times 100\%$. Here,

$\frac{1,448 - 1,086}{1,086} \times 100\% = \frac{362}{1,086} \times 100\% = \frac{1}{3} \times 100\%$

$= 33\frac{1}{3}\%$, so (B) is the best choice.

### 18. A

Let the length of $WX$ be represented by $a$. Then
the length of $WY$ is $3a$. The length of $XY$ must be
$3a - a = 2a$. Then, the length of $XZ$ must be $2 \times 2a =$
$4a$. So $WZ = WX + XZ = a + 4a = 5a = 5(2) = 10$.

### 19. A

Draw a rectangle. Label its width $w$ and its length
$3w$. The perimeter is 240, thus $3w + w + 3w + w =$
$240$, so $8w = 240$ and $w = 30$.

### 20. C

The phrase "for every" indicates a ratio is needed.
Call the amount she receives from the $18,000
collection $x$. Here set up $\frac{50}{900} = \frac{x}{18,000}$. After

cancellation on the left we have $\frac{1}{18} = \frac{x}{18,000}$.

Cross-multiply and get $18x = 18,000$. Solve for $x$ by
dividing each side by 18, and $x = 1,000$.

### 21. C

We need to find out how many $4 \times 6$ rectangles fit
into a square with a side of 24. Use our area formula
$A = L \times W$: $\frac{24 \times 24}{4 \times 6} = 24$.

## 22. C

Pick Numbers. Let $S = -2$ and $T = -3$. Thus, we have $R = -5$. Taking this value for $R$ through our choices, only (C) fits.

## 23. D

Call the number of DVDs Greg has $d$ and the number of CDs he has $c$. Our first equation is $d + c = 60$. The second equation is $\frac{1}{2}r = 2(\frac{1}{8}c)$. So $\frac{1}{2}r = \frac{1}{4}c$ and $c = 4 \times \frac{1}{2}r = 2d$. Now, substitute $2d$ for $c$ in the first equation, $d + c = 60$. Then $d + 2d = 60$, $3d = 60$, and $d = \frac{60}{3} = 20$. The problem asks how many DVDs he sold, which is $\frac{1}{2}(20) = 10$.

## 24. D

Mary received $20 each week for 2 weeks and saved 60% of this or $\frac{60}{100}(\$40) = \$24$. Since she saved only $8 the first week, she must have saved $16 the second week. Looking at the Roman numeral statements, I is true so eliminate (A) and (C). Looking at statement II, $20 - $16 = $4 was spent during the second week, not $6, so it is not true. Eliminate (E). Finally in III, the percent of the second week's allowance that she saved was $\frac{16}{20} \times 100\% = \frac{4}{5} \times 100\% = 80\%$, so statement III is true. (D) is correct.

## 25. C

First work with Paul: Original wage + 20% of his original wage = $4.50. Convert this into the equation: $x + 0.20x = 4.50$, $1.2x = 4.50$, and $x = \$3.75$. Set up a similar equation for Bill: $y + 0.20y = 5.40$ and $1.2y = 5.40$, so $y = \$4.50$. Hence, $4.50 - $3.75 = $0.75.

# CHAPTER 18: SSAT PRACTICE TEST 3: ELEMENTARY-LEVEL

## HOW TO TAKE THIS PRACTICE TEST

Before taking this practice test, find a quiet room where you can work uninterrupted for two and a half hours. Make sure you have a comfortable desk and several No. 2 pencils.

Use the answer sheet provided to record your answers. (You can cut it out or photocopy it.)

Once you start this practice test, don't stop until you've finished. Remember—you can review any questions within a section, but you may not go backward or forward a section.

You'll find answer explanations following the test. Scoring information can be found in chapter 19.

Good luck.

# SSAT Practice Test 3: Elementary-Level Answer Sheet

**Remove (or photocopy) the answer sheet and use it to complete the practice test.**

Start with number 1 for each section. If a section has fewer questions than answer spaces, leave the extra spaces blank.

---

**SECTION 1**

| 1 Ⓐ Ⓑ Ⓒ Ⓓ Ⓔ | 7 Ⓐ Ⓑ Ⓒ Ⓓ Ⓔ | 13 Ⓐ Ⓑ Ⓒ Ⓓ Ⓔ | 19 Ⓐ Ⓑ Ⓒ Ⓓ Ⓔ | 25 Ⓐ Ⓑ Ⓒ Ⓓ Ⓔ |
| 2 Ⓐ Ⓑ Ⓒ Ⓓ Ⓔ | 8 Ⓐ Ⓑ Ⓒ Ⓓ Ⓔ | 14 Ⓐ Ⓑ Ⓒ Ⓓ Ⓔ | 20 Ⓐ Ⓑ Ⓒ Ⓓ Ⓔ | 26 Ⓐ Ⓑ Ⓒ Ⓓ Ⓔ |
| 3 Ⓐ Ⓑ Ⓒ Ⓓ Ⓔ | 9 Ⓐ Ⓑ Ⓒ Ⓓ Ⓔ | 15 Ⓐ Ⓑ Ⓒ Ⓓ Ⓔ | 21 Ⓐ Ⓑ Ⓒ Ⓓ Ⓔ | 27 Ⓐ Ⓑ Ⓒ Ⓓ Ⓔ |
| 4 Ⓐ Ⓑ Ⓒ Ⓓ Ⓔ | 10 Ⓐ Ⓑ Ⓒ Ⓓ Ⓔ | 16 Ⓐ Ⓑ Ⓒ Ⓓ Ⓔ | 22 Ⓐ Ⓑ Ⓒ Ⓓ Ⓔ | 28 Ⓐ Ⓑ Ⓒ Ⓓ Ⓔ |
| 5 Ⓐ Ⓑ Ⓒ Ⓓ Ⓔ | 11 Ⓐ Ⓑ Ⓒ Ⓓ Ⓔ | 17 Ⓐ Ⓑ Ⓒ Ⓓ Ⓔ | 23 Ⓐ Ⓑ Ⓒ Ⓓ Ⓔ | 29 Ⓐ Ⓑ Ⓒ Ⓓ Ⓔ |
| 6 Ⓐ Ⓑ Ⓒ Ⓓ Ⓔ | 12 Ⓐ Ⓑ Ⓒ Ⓓ Ⓔ | 18 Ⓐ Ⓑ Ⓒ Ⓓ Ⓔ | 24 Ⓐ Ⓑ Ⓒ Ⓓ Ⓔ | 30 Ⓐ Ⓑ Ⓒ Ⓓ Ⓔ |

# right in section 1

# wrong in section 1

---

**SECTION 2**

| 1 Ⓐ Ⓑ Ⓒ Ⓓ Ⓔ | 7 Ⓐ Ⓑ Ⓒ Ⓓ Ⓔ | 13 Ⓐ Ⓑ Ⓒ Ⓓ Ⓔ | 19 Ⓐ Ⓑ Ⓒ Ⓓ Ⓔ | 25 Ⓐ Ⓑ Ⓒ Ⓓ Ⓔ |
| 2 Ⓐ Ⓑ Ⓒ Ⓓ Ⓔ | 8 Ⓐ Ⓑ Ⓒ Ⓓ Ⓔ | 14 Ⓐ Ⓑ Ⓒ Ⓓ Ⓔ | 20 Ⓐ Ⓑ Ⓒ Ⓓ Ⓔ | 26 Ⓐ Ⓑ Ⓒ Ⓓ Ⓔ |
| 3 Ⓐ Ⓑ Ⓒ Ⓓ Ⓔ | 9 Ⓐ Ⓑ Ⓒ Ⓓ Ⓔ | 15 Ⓐ Ⓑ Ⓒ Ⓓ Ⓔ | 21 Ⓐ Ⓑ Ⓒ Ⓓ Ⓔ | 27 Ⓐ Ⓑ Ⓒ Ⓓ Ⓔ |
| 4 Ⓐ Ⓑ Ⓒ Ⓓ Ⓔ | 10 Ⓐ Ⓑ Ⓒ Ⓓ Ⓔ | 16 Ⓐ Ⓑ Ⓒ Ⓓ Ⓔ | 22 Ⓐ Ⓑ Ⓒ Ⓓ Ⓔ | 28 Ⓐ Ⓑ Ⓒ Ⓓ Ⓔ |
| 5 Ⓐ Ⓑ Ⓒ Ⓓ Ⓔ | 11 Ⓐ Ⓑ Ⓒ Ⓓ Ⓔ | 17 Ⓐ Ⓑ Ⓒ Ⓓ Ⓔ | 23 Ⓐ Ⓑ Ⓒ Ⓓ Ⓔ | 29 Ⓐ Ⓑ Ⓒ Ⓓ Ⓔ |
| 6 Ⓐ Ⓑ Ⓒ Ⓓ Ⓔ | 12 Ⓐ Ⓑ Ⓒ Ⓓ Ⓔ | 18 Ⓐ Ⓑ Ⓒ Ⓓ Ⓔ | 24 Ⓐ Ⓑ Ⓒ Ⓓ Ⓔ | 30 Ⓐ Ⓑ Ⓒ Ⓓ Ⓔ |

# right in section 2

# wrong in section 2

---

**SECTION 3**

| 1 Ⓐ Ⓑ Ⓒ Ⓓ Ⓔ | 7 Ⓐ Ⓑ Ⓒ Ⓓ Ⓔ | 13 Ⓐ Ⓑ Ⓒ Ⓓ Ⓔ | 19 Ⓐ Ⓑ Ⓒ Ⓓ Ⓔ | 25 Ⓐ Ⓑ Ⓒ Ⓓ Ⓔ |
| 2 Ⓐ Ⓑ Ⓒ Ⓓ Ⓔ | 8 Ⓐ Ⓑ Ⓒ Ⓓ Ⓔ | 14 Ⓐ Ⓑ Ⓒ Ⓓ Ⓔ | 20 Ⓐ Ⓑ Ⓒ Ⓓ Ⓔ | 26 Ⓐ Ⓑ Ⓒ Ⓓ Ⓔ |
| 3 Ⓐ Ⓑ Ⓒ Ⓓ Ⓔ | 9 Ⓐ Ⓑ Ⓒ Ⓓ Ⓔ | 15 Ⓐ Ⓑ Ⓒ Ⓓ Ⓔ | 21 Ⓐ Ⓑ Ⓒ Ⓓ Ⓔ | 27 Ⓐ Ⓑ Ⓒ Ⓓ Ⓔ |
| 4 Ⓐ Ⓑ Ⓒ Ⓓ Ⓔ | 10 Ⓐ Ⓑ Ⓒ Ⓓ Ⓔ | 16 Ⓐ Ⓑ Ⓒ Ⓓ Ⓔ | 22 Ⓐ Ⓑ Ⓒ Ⓓ Ⓔ | 28 Ⓐ Ⓑ Ⓒ Ⓓ Ⓔ |
| 5 Ⓐ Ⓑ Ⓒ Ⓓ Ⓔ | 11 Ⓐ Ⓑ Ⓒ Ⓓ Ⓔ | 17 Ⓐ Ⓑ Ⓒ Ⓓ Ⓔ | 23 Ⓐ Ⓑ Ⓒ Ⓓ Ⓔ | 29 Ⓐ Ⓑ Ⓒ Ⓓ Ⓔ |
| 6 Ⓐ Ⓑ Ⓒ Ⓓ Ⓔ | 12 Ⓐ Ⓑ Ⓒ Ⓓ Ⓔ | 18 Ⓐ Ⓑ Ⓒ Ⓓ Ⓔ | 24 Ⓐ Ⓑ Ⓒ Ⓓ Ⓔ | 30 Ⓐ Ⓑ Ⓒ Ⓓ Ⓔ |

# right in section 3

# wrong in section 3

# SECTION 1

Time—30 Minutes

30 Questions

In this section, there are five possible answers after each question. Choose which one is best. You may use the blank space at the right of the page for scratch work.

Note: Figures are drawn with the greatest possible accuracy, UNLESS stated "Not Drawn to Scale."

1. Which of the following shapes can be folded to create a cube with no overlapping flaps?

USE THIS SPACE FOR FIGURING.

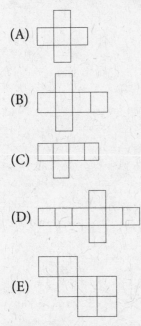

(A)

(B)

(C)

(D)

(E)

2. Of the following, 20 percent of $19.95 is closest to

(A)   $1.95
(B)   $2
(C)   $4
(D)   $5
(E)   $20

GO ON TO THE NEXT PAGE

3. Dividing 93 by 5 leaves a remainder of

(A) 18

(B) 5

(C) 4

(D) 3

(E) 2

4. If $7,000 + \square - 500 = 9,500$, then $\square =$

(A) 200

(B) 300

(C) 2,000

(D) 2,500

(E) 3,000

5. The width of a rectangle is one-third of its length. If the length is 12, what is its perimeter?

(A) 3

(B) 4

(C) 16

(D) 24

(E) 32

6. What is the value of $a$ in Figure 1?

(A) 30

(B) 60

(C) 90

(D) 120

(E) It cannot be determined from the information given.

7. Of the following, which number is the greatest?

(A) 0.08

(B) 0.7899

(C) 0.7923

(D) 0.792

(E) 0.79

USE THIS SPACE FOR FIGURING.

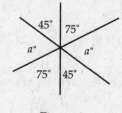

Figure 1

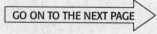

8. "When 4 is added to three times a number $N$, the result is 36." Which of the following equations represents this statement?

   (A) $4N + 3 = 36$

   (B) $36 + 4N = 3$

   (C) $36N + 3 = 4$

   (D) $3N + 4 = 36$

   (E) $36 - 4N = 3$

9. If $N + 5$ is an odd, whole number, then $N$ could be which of the following?

   (A) 5

   (B) 3

   (C) $\dfrac{1}{2}$

   (D) 0

   (E) $-7$

USE THIS SPACE FOR FIGURING.

10. A bull is tied to a seven-foot leash in the center of a square pen, as shown in Figure 2. If a side of the pen is 14 feet in length, which figure best shows the shape and size of the area in which the bull can move?

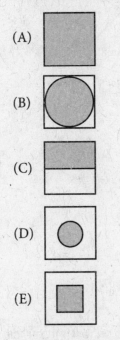

(A)

(B)

(C)

(D)

(E)

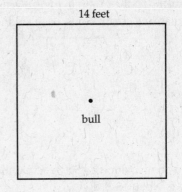

Figure 2

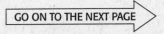
GO ON TO THE NEXT PAGE

11. $\dfrac{7}{8} - \dfrac{5}{8} =$

(A)  0.58

(B)  0.5

(C)  0.375

(D)  0.25

(E)  0.125

USE THIS SPACE FOR FIGURING.

12. At sunset the temperature was 20 degrees. By midnight, it had dropped another 32 degrees. What was the temperature at midnight?

(A) 12 degrees below zero

(B) 6 degrees below zero

(C) 0 degrees

(D) 12 degrees above zero

(E) 20 degrees above zero

13. According to the graph in Figure 3, how many chocolate ice cream cones were sold?

(A)  25

(B)  30

(C)  50

(D)  75

(E)  100

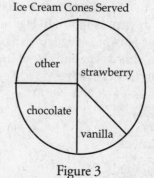

Flavors of 300
Ice Cream Cones Served

Figure 3

14. When 36 is divided by 5, the remainder is the same as when 65 is divided by

(A)  10

(B)  9

(C)  8

(D)  7

(E)  6

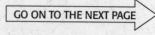
GO ON TO THE NEXT PAGE

15. According to the graph in Figure 4, what is the average number of emergency calls made from Monday through Thursday?

(A)   500

(B)   750

(C)   875

(D)  1,000

(E)  1,125

USE THIS SPACE FOR FIGURING.

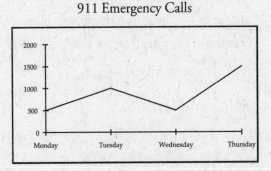

911 Emergency Calls

Figure 4

**Questions 16–18 refer to the following definition.**

For all real numbers $y$ and $z$, let $y @ z = y \times z - 2$.

16. $3 @ 7 =$

(A) 15

(B) 19

(C) 21

(D) 25

(E) 27

17. If $y @ 4 = 6$, then $y$ must equal

(A)   1

(B)   2

(C)   4

(D)   6

(E)  12

18. If $y = \dfrac{1}{4}$, for what value of $z$ will $y @ z$ equal 0 ?

(A)  −4

(B)   4

(C)   6

(D)   8

(E)  10

GO ON TO THE NEXT PAGE

19. A class of 25 girls and 15 boys built a haunted house for the Halloween carnival. If $\frac{1}{5}$ of the girls and $\frac{2}{3}$ of the boys participated, what fraction of the total class participated?

(A) $\frac{1}{5}$

(B) $\frac{3}{8}$

(C) $\frac{3}{7}$

(D) $\frac{3}{5}$

(E) $\frac{13}{15}$

20. The ratio of 7 to 4 is equal to the ratio of 28 to what number?

(A) 7

(B) 8

(C) 12

(D) 14

(E) 16

21. Which figure CANNOT be drawn without lifting the pencil or retracing?

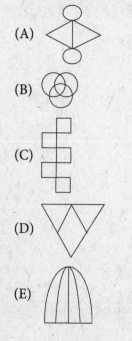

(A)

(B)

(C)

(D)

(E)

USE THIS SPACE FOR FIGURING.

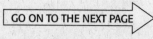

22. Sparkly stickers are $0.50 and smelly stickers are $0.60. If Jill buys 5 sparkly stickers and 8 smelly stickers, what is her change from $10? (Stickers are not taxable.)

    (A) $1.20
    (B) $2
    (C) $2.70
    (D) $3
    (E) $7.30

23. Greg read from 5:00 P.M. to 5:45 P.M. and finished one-third of his book. He wants to finish reading his book by 11:00 P.M. If he plans to read at the same rate, what is the latest time he can start reading again?

    (A) 7:15 P.M.
    (B) 8:00 P.M.
    (C) 8:45 P.M.
    (D) 9:30 P.M.
    (E) 10:15 P.M.

24. The map in Figure 5 shows all the paths that connect $X$ and $Y$, and all distances are expressed in miles. How many paths are there from $X$ to $Y$ measuring exactly seven miles?

    (A) 2
    (B) 3
    (C) 4
    (D) 5
    (E) 6

25. A palindrome is a number that is unchanged when the order of its digits is reversed. For example, 232 is a palindrome. Which of the following is one more than a palindrome?

    (A) 7,336
    (B) 373
    (C) 8,337
    (D) 7,338
    (E) 8,338

USE THIS SPACE FOR FIGURING.

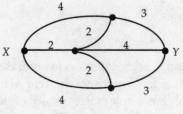

Figure 5

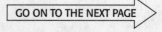 GO ON TO THE NEXT PAGE

26. $2,600 - 402 =$

(A) 2,208

(B) 2,202

(C) 2,198

(D) 2,192

(E) 2,098

USE THIS SPACE FOR FIGURING.

27. Sari has a strip of ribbon $2\frac{2}{5}$ inches long that
she wants to cut into 6 equal-length pieces.
How long will each piece be in inches?

(A) 0.20 inches

(B) 0.25 inches

(C) 0.30 inches

(D) 0.40 inches

(E) 0.50 inches

28. $7.7 - 4.07$ is closest to which of the following?

(A) 30

(B) 4

(C) 3.7

(D) 3.6

(E) 3

29. Alan has three times as many erasers as Roy.
Lance has 2 more erasers than Alan. If Roy
only has whole erasers, which of the following
could be the number of erasers that Lance has?

(A) 12

(B) 16

(C) 19

(D) 20

(E) 22

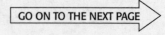
GO ON TO THE NEXT PAGE

1, 2 3 4 . 4 3 2

     ↑        ↑

     X       Y

**USE THIS SPACE FOR FIGURING.**

30. How many times larger is the value of 3 in the X place of the numeral above than the 3 in the Y place?

(A)     1
(B)    10
(C)   100
(D)  1,000
(E)  10,000

# SECTION 2

Time—20 Minutes
30 Questions

This section consists of two different types of questions. There are directions for each type.

Each of the following questions consists of one word followed by five words or phrases. You are to select the one word or phrase whose meaning is closest to the word in capital letters.

1. PHOBIA:

(A) illumination
(B) retraction
(C) anxiety
(D) height
(E) dismissal

2. PROPEL:

(A) intend
(B) belie
(C) fly
(D) project
(E) repel

3. CODDLE:

(A) baby
(B) waddle
(C) carry
(D) riddle
(E) assume

4. KEEN:

(A) sharp
(B) nice
(C) forgiving
(D) dense
(E) rotund

5. MURKY:

(A) religious
(B) musty
(C) sentimental
(D) gloomy
(E) forgetful

6. ADHERE:

(A) connect
(B) alter
(C) stick
(D) listen
(E) complete

7. POMPOUS:

(A) flat
(B) concerned
(C) arranged
(D) colorful
(E) pretentious

8. FATAL:

(A) childish
(B) painful
(C) accidental
(D) social
(E) lethal

GO ON TO THE NEXT PAGE

9. FREQUENT:

   (A) general
   (B) frail
   (C) locomotive
   (D) various
   (E) habitual

10. INDUSTRY:

   (A) element
   (B) accusation
   (C) diligence
   (D) phobia
   (E) warehouse

11. CONDONE:

   (A) respect
   (B) approve
   (C) give
   (D) stifle
   (E) elevate

12. SENTRY:

   (A) watch
   (B) beginning
   (C) row
   (D) revolutionary
   (E) companion

13. ORBIT:

   (A) program
   (B) inertia
   (C) revolution
   (D) galaxy
   (E) project

14. IMMINENT:

   (A) impenetrable
   (B) impossible
   (C) immature
   (D) implicated
   (E) impending

15. SPURN:

   (A) unearth
   (B) incinerate
   (C) twirl
   (D) reject
   (E) clash

**The following questions ask you to find relationships between words. For each question, select the choice that best completes the meaning of the sentence.**

16. Scissors is to cut as pencil is to

   (A) snip
   (B) write
   (C) raze
   (D) turn
   (E) read

17. Bread is to crust as orange is to

   (A) butter
   (B) pudding
   (C) rind
   (D) tree
   (E) lemon

GO ON TO THE NEXT PAGE

18. Team is to captain as

   (A) sport is to player

   (B) paper is to reporter

   (C) republic is to president

   (D) game to opponent

   (E) navy is to ensign

19. Ruler is to measure as camera is to

   (A) piano

   (B) lung

   (C) soul

   (D) limb

   (E) photograph

20. Tiptoe is to walk as

   (A) whisper is to speech

   (B) dance is to rhythm

   (C) tumble is to tree

   (D) rasp is to throat

   (E) press is to wrinkle

21. Nap is to sleep as snack is to

   (A) rest

   (B) meal

   (C) biscuit

   (D) part

   (E) age

22. Fossil is to petrified as

   (A) solution is to dissolved

   (B) wood is to hard

   (C) snowflake is wet

   (D) fog is to dense

   (E) gully is to craggy

23. Careful is to picky as

   (A) tired is to exhausted

   (B) alert is to asleep

   (C) concerned is to grateful

   (D) forgiving is to peaceful

   (E) fancy is to short

24. Frog is to amphibian as whale is to

   (A) mammal

   (B) toad

   (C) sea

   (D) branch

   (E) fur

25. Dentist is to drill as

   (A) surgeon is to scalpel

   (B) doctor is to stretcher

   (C) farmer is to grain

   (D) manager is to computer

   (E) pilot is to wing

26. Pebble is to rock as drop is to

   (A) boulder

   (B) fountain

   (C) sand

   (D) liquid

   (E) grain

27. Levee is to river as

   (A) sail is to boat

   (B) bridge is to truck

   (C) train is to track

   (D) path is to forest

   (E) shoulder is to road

GO ON TO THE NEXT PAGE

28. Fan is to air as heart is to

    (A) power
    (B) heat
    (C) lung
    (D) wind
    (E) blood

29. Quill is to porcupine as

    (A) needle is to thread
    (B) wing is to duck
    (C) pouch is to kangaroo
    (D) tail is to pig
    (E) scent is to skunk

30. Caterpillar is to butterfly as

    (A) salmon is to fish
    (B) egg is to dinosaur
    (C) tadpole is to frog
    (D) nest is to chick
    (E) worm is to bait

IF YOU FINISH BEFORE TIME IS CALLED, YOU MAY CHECK YOUR WORK ON
THIS SECTION ONLY. DO NOT TURN TO ANY OTHER SECTION IN THE TEST.

STOP

# SECTION 3

Time—30 Minutes
28 Questions

Read each passage carefully and then answer the questions about it. For each question, decide on the basis of the passage which one of the choices best answers the question.

When I was a boy, there was but one permanent ambition among my comrades in our village on the west bank of the Mississippi River. That was, to be
Line a steamboat-man. We had transient ambitions of
(5) other sorts, but they were only transient. When a circus came and went, it left us all burning to become clowns; the first minstrel show that came to our section left us all suffering to try that kind of life; now and then we had a hope that if we loved
(10) and were good, God would permit us to be pirates. These ambitions faded out, each in its turn; but the ambition to be a steamboat-man always remained.

*From* Life on the Mississippi *by Mark Twain*

1. The author's intent in this passage is to

   (A) explain how he chose his adult profession

   (B) describe the life of a steamboat-man

   (C) convey some of his childhood aspirations

   (D) compare the merits of several different occupations

   (E) present a social history of the Mississippi

2. According to the passage, the author considered all of the following as possible careers EXCEPT

   (A) steamboat-man

   (B) clown

   (C) minstrel

   (D) writer

   (E) pirate

3. As it is used in line 5, the word "transient" means

   (A) appealing

   (B) relative

   (C) short-lived

   (D) disastrous

   (E) equal

4. The author most likely uses the phrase "all burning to become clowns" in order to

   (A) provide an example of the boys' fleeting ambitions

   (B) illustrate the lack of cultural life in Mississippi

   (C) encourage his readers to follow similar career paths

   (D) clarify why the boys all wanted to be steamboat-men

   (E) show the kind of people that traveled on steamboats

5. Which of the following best describes the effect of the phrase "if we loved and were good, God would permit us to be pirates"?

   (A) Pathos

   (B) Humor

   (C) Exaggeration

   (D) Mockery

   (E) Rhyme

GO ON TO THE NEXT PAGE

6.  The attitude of the author toward the subject is

    (A) nostalgic
    (B) regretful
    (C) optimistic
    (D) cynical
    (E) somber

7.  The reader can infer from the passage that

    (A) the author and his friends looked forward to leaving the village
    (B) no girls hoped to navigate the river by steamboat
    (C) the author became a steamboat-man
    (D) the author regrets not becoming a pirate
    (E) the author disliked growing up on the Mississippi River

    Alchemy is the name given to the attempt
    to change lead, copper, and other metals into
    silver or gold. Today, alchemy is regarded as a
*Line* pseudoscience. Its associations with astrology and
  (5) the occult suggest primitive superstition to the
    modern mind, and the alchemist is generally
    portrayed by historians as a charlatan obsessed
    with dreams of impossible wealth. For many
    centuries, however, alchemy was a highly
(10) respected art. In the search for the elusive secret to
    making gold, alchemists helped develop many of
    the apparatuses and procedures that are used in
    laboratories today. Moreover, the results of their
    experiments laid the basic conceptual framework
(15) of the modern science of chemistry.

8.  The passage is mainly about the

    (A) early history of a scientific field
    (B) manufacture of gold from other metals
    (C) mystery surrounding the origins of chemistry
    (D) links among chemistry, astrology, and sociology
    (E) specific results of alchemists' experiments

9.  According to the passage, alchemists are generally portrayed in history books as

    (A) wealthy businessmen
    (B) rogues motivated by greed
    (C) talented but misunderstood individuals
    (D) the ancestors of today's chemists
    (E) brilliant scientists

10. It can be inferred from the passage that a "charlatan" (line 7)

    (A) existed only in the Middle Ages
    (B) is not respected by historians
    (C) practiced an early form of chemistry
    (D) uses his research for criminal purposes
    (E) understood the secret to making gold

11. The style of the passage is most like that found in a

    (A) scientist's diary
    (B) novel about alchemists
    (C) history textbook
    (D) newspaper article
    (E) personal letter

12. With which of the following statements would the author most likely agree?

    (A) Few alchemists ever became wealthy from their work.
    (B) Alchemy was a primitive, superstitious field of science.
    (C) Alchemy is becoming increasingly respectable among today's chemists.
    (D) Astrology and the occult also deserve consideration as legitimate sciences.
    (E) Alchemists helped pave the way for scientists today.

GO ON TO THE NEXT PAGE

13. The following questions are all answered by the passage EXCEPT:

(A) What did alchemists hope to achieve?

(B) What have alchemists contributed to science?

(C) How do historians view alchemy?

(D) How did alchemists turn metals into gold?

(E) Has the general consensus always been that alchemists were charlatans?

14. Which of these titles is the most appropriate for the passage?

(A) Alchemy as Art

(B) Turning Copper to Gold

(C) In Pursuit of Wealth

(D) Alchemists: Charlatans or Scientists?

(E) Alchemy's Contributions to Science

On May 18, 1980, in Washington State, the
volcano Mount Saint Helens erupted, sending a
cloud of dust 15 miles into the air. The explosion
Line was not unexpected; the earth's crust had shaken
(5) for weeks beforehand, providing people in the
surrounding area with plenty of advance warning.
In spite of these danger signals, no one was
prepared for the extent of the blast; over the course
of several weeks, the volcano's eruption ripped the
(10) top 1,300 feet off the mountain, resulting in a
landslide that was the largest in recorded history.
540 million tons of ash from the volcano were
spread over three states, altering the earth's
weather patterns for several years afterward. One
(15) thing missing from the initial eruption was fluid
lava usually identified with volcanic activity. Later
eruptions emitted a thick and oozing lava. Thick
lava is easily outrun because it moves extremely
slowly.  In addition, thick lava creates taller
(20) volcanoes because it often cools and hardens
instead of flowing down the volcano's sides.

15. This passage is primarily about

(A) the geological history of Washington State

(B) the difficulty of predicting volcanic activity

(C) a contrast between different forms of lava

(D) a story of an unusual geological event

(E) the factors that cause landslides

16. As used in line 6, the word "advance" means

(A) ahead of time

(B) moving forward

(C) in the past

(D) undetected

(E) extremely urgent

17. According to the passage, all of the following were caused by the Mount Saint Helens eruption EXCEPT

(A) tidal waves

(B) streams of lava

(C) a massive landslide

(D) changes in the earth's climate

(E) the emission of clouds of ash

18. It can be inferred from the passage that fluid lava (lines 15 and 16)

(A) is very thick

(B) creates tall volcanoes

(C) is only found in the United States

(D) is not easily outrun

(E) destroyed many forests in Washington

GO ON TO THE NEXT PAGE

19. The author's style is best described as

    (A) surprised

    (B) dramatic

    (C) skeptical

    (D) informative

    (E) mysterious

20. The author most likely mentions "providing people in the surrounding area with plenty of advance warning" in order to

    (A) show that experts thought they knew what was coming

    (B) indicate that no one was hurt in the blast

    (C) criticize people who did not evacuate on time

    (D) describe how experts were not seeing fluid lava

    (E) convey the importance of volcano warning systems

The cowboy of the American West is an enduring icon in popular culture, but Hawaiian cowboys predated their American counterparts by
*Line* several decades. In 1792, King Kamehameha the
(5) Great of Hawaii received gifts of beef cattle, goats, sheep, and horses from Captain George Vancouver. The introduction of these unfamiliar animals caused unrest among the native islanders, because the unruly animals often trampled the crops in
(10) their fields. Initially, the king protected his imports from wrathful Hawaiians under kapu laws. But in 1830, Kamehameha III decided to hire a few Spanish vaqueros from California to keep the animals under control. Soon the Hawaiians were
(15) riding, roping, and lassoing alongside the Spanish cowboys.

21. It can be inferred from the passage that the American cowboy

    (A) taught the Hawaiians how to ride and lasso

    (B) accompanied the shipment of horses and cattle to Hawaii

    (C) did not understand the Hawaiians' opposition to horses

    (D) emerged in the West later than his counterpart in Hawaii

    (E) was not able to lasso as well as the Hawaiian cowboy

22. According to the passage, all of the following are true about horses and cattle EXCEPT

    (A) they were unfamiliar to Hawaiians before 1792

    (B) they were introduced to Hawaii in the 18th century

    (C) they were protected by Hawaiian law

    (D) they were found to be too expensive to import

    (E) they were destructive to Hawaiian property

23. According to the passage, the Hawaiian cowboys

    I. were taught to ride by the Spanish vaqueros

    II. existed earlier than the American cowboys

    III. proved better at roping and lassoing than their American counterparts

    (A) I only

    (B) II only

    (C) I and II only

    (D) II and III only

    (E) I, II, and III

GO ON TO THE NEXT PAGE

24. This passage is primarily about

   (A) the roping of cattle

   (B) the history of King Kamehameha

   (C) the Spanish relationship with Hawaii

   (D) the history of horses in Hawaii

   (E) the introduction of cowboys to Hawaii

25. The attitude of the writer toward the subject is

   (A) biased

   (B) condescending

   (C) neutral

   (D) elated

   (E) confused

26. As it is used in line 11, "wrathful" most nearly means

   (A) tolerant

   (B) enraged

   (C) accommodating

   (D) confused

   (E) vengeful

27. Which of the following questions is NOT answered by the passage?

   (A) How did Hawaiians view Capt. George Vancouver's gifts?

   (B) What effect did the vaqueros have on the animals?

   (C) What can be implied about the author's attitude toward the cowboys?

   (D) For how many years did the animals cause unrest in Hawaii?

   (E) How did the king use kapu laws in Hawaii to protect animals?

28. This passage was likely taken from

   (A) a historical journal

   (B) a cowboy movie script

   (C) a political novel

   (D) an epic poem

   (E) a travel advertisement

IF YOU FINISH BEFORE TIME IS CALLED, YOU MAY CHECK YOUR WORK ON THIS SECTION ONLY. DO NOT TURN TO ANY OTHER SECTION IN THE TEST.

STOP

# SECTION 4

Time—15 Minutes

**Directions:** Write an essay on the following prompt on the paper provided. Your essay should not exceed two pages and must be written in ink. Erasing is not allowed.

Look at the picture and write a story about what has happened. Be sure that your story includes a beginning, middle, and conclusion.

_____

_____

_____

_____

_____

_____

GO ON TO THE NEXT PAGE ▷

_____
_____
_____
_____
_____
_____
_____
_____
_____
_____
_____
_____
_____
_____
_____
_____
_____
_____
_____
_____
_____
_____

IF YOU FINISH BEFORE TIME IS CALLED, YOU MAY CHECK YOUR WORK ON THIS SECTION ONLY. DO NOT TURN TO ANY OTHER SECTION IN THE TEST.

STOP

# ANSWER KEY

| **Section 1** | 19. B | 7. E | 26. D | 14. E |
|---|---|---|---|---|
| 1. B | 20. E | 8. E | 27. E | 15. D |
| 2. C | 21. E | 9. E | 28. E | 16. A |
| 3. D | 22. C | 10. C | 29. E | 17. A |
| 4. E | 23. D | 11. B | 30. C | 18. D |
| 5. E | 24. C | 12. A | **Section 3** | 19. D |
| 6. B | 25. D | 13. C | 1. C | 20. A |
| 7. C | 26. C | 14. E | 2. D | 21. D |
| 8. D | 27. D | 15. D | 3. C | 22. D |
| 9. D | 28. D | 16. B | 4. A | 23. C |
| 10. B | 29. D | 17. C | 5. B | 24. E |
| 11. D | 30. D | 18. C | 6. A | 25. C |
| 12. A | **Section 2** | 19. E | 7. A | 26. E |
| 13. D | 1. C | 20. A | 8. A | 27. E |
| 14. C | 2. D | 21. B | 9. B | 28. A |
| 15. C | 3. A | 22. A | 10. B | |
| 16. B | 4. A | 23. A | 11. C | |
| 17. B | 5. D | 24. A | 12. E | |
| 18. D | 6. C | 25. A | 13. D | |

# SSAT PRACTICE TEST 3: ELEMENTARY-LEVEL: ASSESS YOUR STRENGTHS

Use the following tables to determine which topics and chapters you need to review most. If you need help with your essay, be sure to review Chapter 9: The Essay and Chapter 26: Writing Skills.

| Topic | Question |
|---|---|
| Math I | Section 1, questions 1–30 |
| Verbal: Synonyms | Section 2, questions 1–15 |
| Verbal: Analogies | Section 2, questions 16–30 |
| Reading Comprehension | Section 3, questions 1–28 |

| Topic | Number of Questions | Number Correct | If you struggled with these questions, study… |
|---|---|---|---|
| Math I | 30 | | Chapters 10–14 and Chapter 25 |
| Verbal: Synonyms | 15 | | Chapters 7 and 24 |
| Verbal: Analogies | 15 | | Chapters 2 and 24 |
| Reading Comprehension | 28 | | Chapter 8 |

# ANSWERS AND EXPLANATIONS

## SECTION 1: MATH

### 1.  B

Remember, a cube has six faces. Since you're asked which shape can be folded into a cube with no overlapping flaps, the answer must contain exactly six faces. The only choice that does so is (B).

### 2.  C

You know $19.95 is close to $20. Twenty percent of $20 is $4, (C).

### 3.  D

Five will divide evenly into numbers that end in 5 or 0. You are asked to divide 93 by 5. The largest number less than 93 that 5 divides into evenly is 90. This means that 5 will divide into 93 with a remainder of 3.

### 4.  E

This question is essentially an algebra question. Just isolate the $\square$ and solve.

$$7{,}000 + \square - 500 = 9{,}500$$
$$7{,}000 + \square = 10{,}000$$
$$\square = 3{,}000$$

### 5.  E

The perimeter of a rectangle is equal to $2(l + w)$, where $l$ and $w$ represent the length and width, respectively. The length of the rectangle is 12, so you need to find its width in order to solve. You're also told that the width of the rectangle is one-third of its length, so $\dfrac{12}{3}$, or 4, is its width. Plugging in the

formula, the perimeter is equal to $2(12 + 4) = 2(16) = 32$, choice (E).

### 6.  B

Angles around a point add up to 360°, so you can write the following equation to solve for $a$:

$$45 + 75 + a + 45 + 75 + a = 360$$
$$2a + 240 = 360$$
$$2a = 120$$
$$a = 60$$

### 7.  C

The easiest way to solve is to compare each answer choice, looking for the largest digit in each place holder. The largest tenths digit, for example, is 7. Eliminate (A) since its tenths digit is 0. In the hundredths place the largest digit is 9. (B) is out, too, since its hundredths digit is 8. (E) doesn't have a thousandths, so it is understood to be 0, which is less than the 2 that appears in the thousandths places in (C) and (D). (D) doesn't have a digit in the ten-thousandths place, so it is understood to be 0. It can be eliminated since it is less than the 3 in the ten-thousandths place in (C). (C) is the largest.

### 8.  D

Break this question down into parts, translating as you go. You're told that 4 added to 3 times a number $N$ results in 36. Three times $N$ can be represented algebraically as $3N$, and adding 4 to that can be written as $3N + 4$. The result is 36, so $3N + 4 = 36$, (D).

### 9.  D

You are looking for the choice that, when added to 5, will result in an odd, whole number. Try each answer choice to see which does:

(A) $5 + 5 = 10$; not odd

(B) $3 + 5 = 8$; not odd

(C) $\frac{1}{2} + 5 = 5\frac{1}{2}$; not a whole number

(D) $0 + 5 = 5$; an odd, whole number!

(E) $-7 + 5 = -2$; not odd

## 10. B

Try drawing in the bull's leash to get a sense of how far it can graze. Since the length of the fence is 14 feet, and the length of the rope is 7 feet, the bull will just be able to reach the center of each side but not the corners. In other words, the bull will be able to graze in a circle with radius 7, as shown in (B). Though (D) also represents the region as a circle, it is too small.

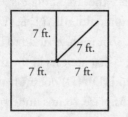

## 11. D

A quick look at the answer choices tells you that your answer needs to be in decimal form. So, first convert to decimal form, then subtract: $0.875 - 0.625 = 0.25$. Another approach is to subract the fractions to get $\frac{7}{8} - \frac{5}{8} = \frac{2}{8}$. Since $\frac{2}{8} = \frac{1}{4}$, convert $\frac{1}{4}$ to 0.25.

## 12. A

The temperature was originally 20 degrees. It then dropped 32 degrees, so you need to subtract 32 from 20: $20 - 32 = -12$. So the temperature at midnight was $-12$, or 12 degrees below zero, (A).

## 13. D

According to the graph, the slice labeled   represents $\frac{1}{4}$ of the entire pie. Since a total of 300 cones were sold, $\frac{1}{4} \times 300 = 75$ chocolate cones were sold.

## 14. C

First determine what the remainder is when 36 is divided by 5. Five goes into 36 seven times with a remainder of 1. So you need to find which choice will divide into 65 and leave a remainder of 1. Since $8 \times 8 = 64$, 65 will leave a remainder of 1 when divided by 8. The answer is (C).

## 15. C

The average formula is Average $= \dfrac{\text{Sum of the terms}}{\text{Number of terms}}$. Look at the graph to find the number of 911 calls made for each of the four days and plug them into the formula:

$$\frac{500 + 1{,}000 + 500 + 1{,}500}{4} = \frac{3{,}500}{4} = 875$$

## 16. B

This is a straightforward symbolism problem. Plug in the values for $y$ and $z$ and solve.

$$y @ z = y \times z - 2$$
$$3 @ 7 = 3 \times 7 - 2$$
$$= 21 - 2$$
$$= 19$$

## 17. B

Plug the given information into the equation and solve for $y$.

$$y @ z = y \times z - 2$$
$$y @ 4 = 6$$
$$4y - 2 = 6$$
$$4y = 8$$
$$y = 2$$

**18. D**

Plug the given information into the equation and solve for $z$.

$$y @ z = y \times z - 2$$
$$\frac{1}{4} @ z = 0$$
$$\frac{1}{4} \times z - 2 = 0$$
$$\frac{1}{4}z = 2$$
$$z = 8$$

**19. B**

There are 25 girls and 15 boys in the class, a total of 40 students. One-fifth of the girls, or $\frac{25}{5} = 5$, and two-thirds of the boys, or $\frac{2}{3} \times 15 = 10$, ran the haunted house. So a total of $5 + 10 = 15$ students participated. Since the class has 40 students in all, $\frac{15}{40} = \frac{3}{8}$ of all the students participated.

**20. E**

Set up a proportion, letting $N$ equal the number you are looking for:

$$\frac{7}{4} = \frac{28}{N}$$
$$4 \times 28 = 7N$$
$$112 = 7N$$
$$16 = N$$

**21. E**

Here is the rule for whether you can retrace a figure without having to lift your pencil: If exactly zero or two points have an odd number of intersecting line segments and/or curves, the figure can be drawn without lifting. So, for example, if a figure has three places where an odd number of line segments

intersect, you would have to lift your pencil to retrace it. Also, the number of points a figure has with an even number of intersecting line segments is irrelevant.

Count the number of line segments that meet at each point of intersection. Find all the points that bring together an odd number of line segments. If you find zero or two points that meet this condition, the diagram can be drawn without lifting your pencil.

So, in this question, the only figure that doesn't fit this criteria is (E). There are six points of intersection, four of which have an odd number of intersecting segments.

**22. C**

To find Jill's change, you need to know how much money she spent. Then subtract that amount from $10. Jill bought five sparkly stickers at $0.50 each and eight smelly stickers at $0.60 each:

$$(5)(0.50) + (8)(0.60) = \$7.30$$
$$\$10 - \$7.30 = \$2.70$$

**23. D**

Greg spent 45 minutes to finish one-third of the book. He still has two-thirds left to read, twice as much as he has already read. So he'll need to spend twice the time he already spent—an hour and a half. To finish by 11 P.M., he needs to start an hour and a half before 11 P.M., or at 9:30 P.M.

## 24. C

Work systematically, checking one route at a time and keeping careful track of each path. There is a total of 4 paths from $X$ to $Y$ with a total length 7, as shown in the figures below:

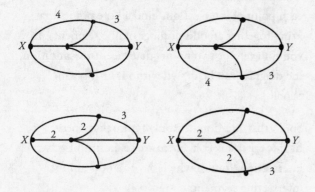

## 25. D

You need the answer choice that is 1 more than a palindrome, so you should be able to subtract 1 from the correct answer choice and end up with a palindrome. (A) gives you the number 7,336. One less than 7,336 is 7,335, which is not a palindrome. Same thing for (B), (C), and (E). In (D), 1 less than the answer choice is 7,337, which is a palindrome.

## 26. C

Don't try to save time by doing Arithmetic problems in your head. You'll avoid mistakes by taking the extra time to work them out on paper:
2,600 − 402 = 2,198

## 27. D

Some questions require you to convert between fractions and decimals to select the correct answer. First, convert the mixed fraction into an improper fraction:

$2\frac{2}{5}$ inches $= \frac{(2 \times 5) + 2}{5} = \frac{12}{5}$ inches

Now, divide the fraction by 6:

$\dfrac{\frac{12}{5} \text{ inches}}{6} = \frac{12}{30} = \frac{2}{5}$ inches

$\frac{2}{5} = \frac{4}{10} = 0.4$ inches

## 28. D

When a problem has more than one step, take it one step at a time. Rewrite 7.7 as 7.70 and begin by doing the subtraction. 7.70 − 4.07 = 3.63. Of the choices, 3.63 is closest to (D).

## 29. D

Whenever a problem looks vague, Pick Numbers. If Roy has 1 eraser, Alan has 3 × 1 = 3, and Lance has 3 + 2 = 5. If Roy has 2 erasers, Alan has 3 × 2 = 6, and Lance has 6 + 2 = 8.

In fact, Lance's number is always 2 more than a multiple of 3. The only choice that consistently works is (D).

## 30. D

To find a ratio between values, divide one number by the other. Divide the $X$ value by the $Y$ value to determine how many times larger $X$ is than $Y$.

$\dfrac{30}{0.03} \times \dfrac{100}{100} = \dfrac{3,000}{3} = 1,000$ times larger.

# SECTION 2: VERBAL

## SYNONYMS

### 1. C

To have a phobia is to have great fear or anxiety about something. To have a phobia of snakes is to have a fear of snakes.

### 2. D

To propel something is to thrust it forward or to project it. A strong wind can propel a ship through the water. Note that "project" is used as a verb here, not as a noun. Your answer must always be the same word form as that of the stem word.

**3. A**

To coddle something is to treat it gently or to baby it. Too much coddling of a child, for example, may cause him to be insufficiently prepared to face the harsh realities of life.

**4. A**

To be keen is to be very smart or sharp. A keen mind is good at solving problems.

**5. D**

If something is murky, it is dark and mysterious, or gloomy. Murky water is hard to see through.

**6. C**

If you adhere to a decision, you stay with it or stick to it. Adhesive tape is sticky tape—it adheres.

**7. E**

To be pompous is to be stuck up or pretentious. A pompous person feels and acts as though he is more important than he is.

**8. E**

Something that is fatal will kill you; it is lethal. A fatal blow is a blow that kills a person.

**9. E**

Something frequent happens regularly; it is habitual. A frequent flyer is a person who flies all the time.

**10. C**

Industry is commonly thought of as manufacturing, but it also means hard work, or diligence. A person who possesses great industry is a person who is very diligent.

**11. B**

To condone something is to approve of something or to support it. If one condones a certain type of behavior, then one approves of it.

**12. A**

A sentry is a group of people who look out for certain things—a watch. During war, the sentry looks out for the enemy.

**13. C**

An orbit occurs when one object circles around another object; it is a revolution. When the moon orbits the earth, it makes a revolution. Don't be misled by the fact that revolution also means a war, as in the American Revolution. If a word has more than one meaning, make sure you consider them all before deciding that an answer choice is incorrect.

**14. E**

An imminent event is just about to happen—it is impending. For centuries, people have believed that the end of the world is imminent.

**15. D**

To spurn someone is to scorn or reject someone. A spurned friend is a rejected friend.

## ANALOGIES

**16. B**

Scissors are specifically used to cut, just as a pencil is specifically used to write.

**17. C**

The outer shell of bread is the crust. The outer shell of an orange is the rind.

**18. C**

A captain is the leader of a team, just as a president is the leader of a republic. Watch out for (A)—it mentions the word "sports," which fits the subject matter of the stem pair but does not match the bridge.

**19. E**

A ruler is a tool used to measure something, just as a camera is a tool used to photograph something.

**20. A**

Tiptoe is a quiet kind of walk, as whisper is a quiet kind of speech. A rasp (D) is a harsh sound in one's throat.

**21. B**

A nap is a short sleep just as a snack is a short meal. A biscuit can be a type of snack, but we are looking for a word that fits the bridge "is a short."

**22. A**

A fossil is a substance that is petrified. A solution is a substance that is dissolved. Wood (B) is not necessarily hard, nor are snowflakes (C) necessarily wet.

**23. A**

To be picky is to be extremely careful. Similarly, to be exhausted is to be extremely tired. To be alert (B) is to be awake.

**24. A**

A frog is a type of amphibian, as a whale is a type of mammal.

**25. A**

A dentist uses a drill in the way that a surgeon uses a scalpel. A doctor doesn't use a stretcher—his patients do. And though a farmer may harvest grain, he does not by definition use it.

**26. D**

A pebble is a tiny bit of rock, just as a drop is a tiny bit of liquid.

**27. E**

A levee is the border of a river, just as a shoulder is the border of a road. A path may or may not go through a forest.

**28. E**

A fan by definition circulates air, and a heart circulates blood.

**29. E**

A quill is a porcupine's means of defense just as a scent is a skunk's means of defense. Wings (B) are a duck's means of flight.

**30. C**

A caterpillar is an animal that turns into a butterfly. A tadpole is an animal that turns into a frog.

## SECTION 3: READING COMPREHENSION

### FICTION PASSAGE

First up is a narrative passage. The author is reminiscing about his childhood and some of the fantasies that he and his peers had about their future professions. As with all fiction passages, pay close attention to shifts in tone and uses of simile, metaphor, and irony as you read.

**1. C**

This is a Main Idea question. You first need to summarize what the passage is about. The first two sentences contain the author's main idea: He and his peers wanted nothing more than to be steamboatmen. This is essentially what (C) states.

(A) is tricky; it mentions a profession, but we were never told that the author chose to be a steamboatman in adulthood.

## 2. D

We are asked to determine which profession the author did not consider. The easiest way to do this is to eliminate all choices that he did consider. By just looking back at the text, we can identify all choices except (D). Being a writer is never mentioned.

## 3. C

After the author uses the word "transient," he explains that while he and his friends had other professional aspirations, those desires went away. Only the desire to be a steamboat-man remained. In other words, the other desires were "short-lived" as in (C).

## 4. A

Immediately before line 6, we are told that the author and his friends had "transient ambitions." In other words, they had ambitions that disappeared very quickly. The phrase "all burning to become clowns" is an example of such a fleeting ambition.

## 5. B

This question is a little tricky. After the friends considered being clowns and minstrels, they dreamt of becoming pirates. The fact that the boys wanted to become pirates is in itself comical, but with the added reference about God permitting that if they were good, the lightheartedness and humor become evident. If you weren't sure about the answer, try the other choices. It couldn't be (E), because there is no rhyme here, and it couldn't be (D), because Twain isn't making fun of anyone. Pathos means sympathy, sorrow, so (A) is definitely out, too. (C) is wrong since nothing is being exaggerated.

## 6. A

The author is fondly looking back on his childhood days. Somber, cynical, and regretful are too negative; the author is not saying anything negative. Neither is he hopeful about the future or optimistic. So the only answer choice that makes sense is (A), nostalgic. Nostalgic means reminiscing about the old days.

## 7. A

The author and his friends dreamed about piloting steamboats. Their "transient ambitions"—clowns with the circus, traveling minstrels, pirates—were all jobs that would have required them to travel away from the village, so (A) is the answer. (B) is incorrect because girls are not mentioned in the passage. (C) and (E) might be true, but they can't be proved with this passage. (D) is incorrect because if the author regrets not becoming something, it's most likely a steamboat-man.

## ALCHEMY PASSAGE

Next up we have a science passage about alchemy. The first half describes alchemy and the unfavorable way in which it has been viewed by history. The second half of the passage explains the positive aspects of alchemy and how it paved the way for modern science.

## 8. A

Remember to summarize the main point to yourself before going to the questions. Here, the passage provides a brief history of alchemy. (A) best restates this idea. (B) is incorrect because gold was never actually manufactured.

## 9. B

Lines 6–8 state that "the alchemist is generally portrayed by historians as a charlatan obsessed with dreams of impossible wealth." In other words, historians feel that the alchemists were greedy. (B) restates this idea. Be careful of (D): It contains information stated in the passage, but this isn't the view of historians, which is what the question asks for.

## 10. B

Infer means to draw a conclusion. Read the surrounding lines: They tell you that a "charlatan" was portrayed as obsessively greedy by historians—so you can infer that historians did not respect "charlatans"—(B).

## 11. C

To determine where this passage most likely came from, you need to consider the author's tone and purpose. Does the passage sound positive, negative, or neutral? Does the author seem to be trying to convince us of something? In fact, the author's tone sounds very detached—as you do when you are explaining something. So a history book is the logical place to find this type of passage. The text doesn't sound like news, so (D) is out.

## 12. E

To answer this question you need to understand the author's point of view. The author makes it clear that while alchemy was viewed with disdain by historians, it did make a positive contribution to the sciences. (E) reflects this attitude. Watch out for choices that contain information not expressly stated in the passage—(A), (C), and (D). (B) is tricky: Even though the text says that historians felt alchemy was primitive and superstitious, we don't know if the author thinks this is the case.

## 13. D

To find the answer, try to use the passage to answer each question. (D) cannot be answered using the passage, which says only that alchemists attempted to change metals into gold and makes no mention of successful attempts. It does not say how alchemists make gold. The other choices can be answered by

the passage. (A) is answered in lines 2–3: "change lead, copper, and other metals into silver or gold." (B) is answered in lines 11–13: "alchemists helped develop many of the apparatuses and procedures that are used in laboratories today." (C) is answered in lines 6–8: "the alchemist is generally portrayed by historians as a charlatan obsessed with dreams of impossible wealth." (E) is answered in lines 8–10: "For many centuries ... alchemy was a highly respected art."

## 14. E

This is a Main Idea question. Although the passage talks about what alchemy is and how alchemists were viewed, those were not the goals of the author, so (A), (B), (C), and (D) are not correct. The author spends lines 10–15 supporting alchemy's influences on modern science, making (E) the answer.

## MOUNT SAINT HELENS PASSAGE

This is a science passage describing the eruption of the volcano Mount Saint Helens and its effects. The first part of the passage focuses on the physical results of the eruption, while the last part describes the kind of lava emitted.

## 15. D

As you were reading the passage, you should have tried to summarize the point. The text describes Mount Saint Helens, its eruption, and what the eruption produced. (A) is far too broad, and (C) and (E) are too narrow and detailed. The information in (B) is not discussed.

## 16. A

Lines 3–6 state, "The explosion was not unexpected; the earth's crust had shaken for weeks beforehand, providing people in the surrounding area with plenty of advance warning." In other words, the shaking of the crust warned people of the impending volcano; "advance," therefore, means ahead of time. While "moving forward" (B) is one definition for advance, it is not the meaning that works in this context.

## 17. A

You need to identify the answer choice that contains information not mentioned in the passage. If something leaps out at you immediately, there's a good chance that it's the answer. If not, eliminate all answer choices that are mentioned in the passage until one remains. Only tidal waves aren't mentioned.

## 18. D

Fluid lava, in the question stem, is thin, flowing lava. The text states, "Thick lava is easily outrun because it moves extremely slowly." Since thin and thick lava would naturally have opposite characteristics, we can assume that thin lava is not easily outrun—(D).

## 19. D

The author isn't speaking in praise of something, nor is he trying to persuade his readers of a certain point of view. His tone is informative and balanced. (D) is the best choice.

## 20. A

The author offers that phrase as a contrast to the next sentence: "In spite of these danger signals, no one was prepared for the extent of the blast." (A) is correct because these lines, to paraphrase, are saying that people were prepared and knew about the blast, but no one expected such a major explosion, which the author goes on to discuss. (D) might be true, that experts were not seeing fluid lava in the blast, but it does not have to do with the phrase in question.

## HAWAIIAN COWBOY PASSAGE

This humanities passage discusses how the cowboy came to Hawaii. The author explains that while the word *cowboy* conjures up an image of the American West, the Hawaiian cowboy actually emerged earlier than his Western counterpart.

## 21. D

The first sentence of the text tells us that American cowboys emerged later than Hawaiian ones. This is what (D) states. (A) contradicts the text, and (B), (C), and (E) present details not discussed in the text.

## 22. D

Here you have to research which answer choice was not mentioned in the passage. If something leaps out at you immediately, there's a good chance that that is the answer. If not, use process of elimination by looking back at the text. The only answer choice not mentioned is (D).

## 23. C

Evaluate each Roman numeral one at a time, eliminating answer choices as you go. I is supported directly by lines in the text, so it is correct. We can now eliminate (B) and (D) because they do not contain I. II is also supported in the text, so it, too, is true. That means (A) can be eliminated. Finally, III is not supported by the passage, so it is not true. The answer must therefore be (C).

## 24. E

The passage discusses how the cowboy came to Hawaii, which is what (E) states. (A), (B), and (C) don't get the focus of the passage right, while (D) focuses too much on one detail. Even though the introduction of horses is mentioned in the text, it isn't the point of the entire passage.

## 25. C

The author isn't excited or confused, so (D) and (E) are out right away. Biased means prejudiced toward a point of view, and condescending means negative, and the tone was neither one of these things, so (A) and (B) are incorrect, too. His tone is informative and balanced, so (C) is the answer.

## 26. E

(A) and (C) are almost antonyms of "wrathful." (D) doesn't make sense in context. (B) is close, but (E) is more accurate. Lines 10–12 say the king felt the need to protect the troublemaking animals from the people. He wouldn't need to protect the animals if the people were merely enraged, or angry.

## 27. E

Find the right answer by using the passage to answer the questions asked in the choices. (A) is answered in line 9: The Hawaiians found the animals unruly for ruining their crops. (B) is answered in lines 14–16: With the help of the vaqueros, the animals were able to become cowboys and control the animals. (C) is answered in the first lines: The author calls Western cowboys icons but wants to clarify that by the time the West's cowboys entered pop culture, the Hawaiians had already had cowboys for decades. (D) is answered by subtracting line 4's year—1792—from line 12's year—1830. (E) cannot be answered using the passage. Kapu laws are mentioned in lines 12–13, but the passage doesn't say what they were or how they were used.

## 28. A

This passage focuses on the emergency of how the cowboy culture emerged in Hawaii. This account could be an excerpt from a peer-reviewed journal, perhaps focusing upon Hawaiian history. (A) best fits this description. Strategic elimination can also be used to arrive at the correct answer. (B) seems illogical, because the script of a movie would include directions or dialogue between characters. A movie, just like a novel like choice (C), also implies that the context could be fictional. Both choices can be eliminated. An epic poem is more narrative, and would indicate more information about the heroic deeds of cowboys, for example. (E) is tempting, perhaps, because Hawaii is a popular travel destination, but the context of this passage is too historical to be part of a marketing advertisement.

# CHAPTER 19: SCORING YOUR SSAT PRACTICE TEST

Your SSAT score is calculated by using a formula that cannot be directly applied to your practice tests. Therefore, it is impossible to provide a completely accurate score for your practice tests. Nevertheless, you'll understandably want to get an idea of how well you have performed.

Follow the steps described below to obtain a rough approximation of what your score on the actual SSAT might be. First, add up the number of questions you got right and the number of questions you got wrong. Questions left blank are worth zero points. Then, do the math, based on the following:

|  | Verbal (60 questions total) | (Quantitative) Math (50 questions total) | Reading Comprehension (40 questions total) |
|---|---|---|---|
| + 1 point for each right answer | _____ | _____ | _____ |
| $-\frac{1}{4}$ point for each wrong answer | _____ | _____ | _____ |
| TOTAL: | _____ | _____ | _____ |

This is called your **raw score.** Next, take your raw score and look at the following chart, which *approximates* a conversion to a **scaled score.** A scaled score takes into account the range in difficulty level of the various editions of the test.

Again, while the following scores and percentiles are close approximations, they do not reflect the official scores and percentiles used on the SSAT. Among other contributing factors, your actual test score will take into account the group of students to whom you will be compared to on your test administration.

## UPPER- AND MIDDLE-LEVEL SCORES

Upper-level scores are based on a scale of 500–800. Middle-level scores are based on a scale of 440–710. Once you have looked up your scaled score, refer to the 50th Percentile score chart below: This will tell you the score at which equal numbers of students scored above and below you. With this information, you will be able to gauge how well you have done with respect to other students.

### SCALED SCORES

| Raw Score | Upper Level | | | Middle Level | | |
|---|---|---|---|---|---|---|
| | Reading | Verbal | Math* | Reading | Verbal | Math* |
| 60 | | 800 | | | 710 | |
| 55 | | 800 | | | 710 | |
| 50 | | 779 | 800 | | 700 | 710 |
| 45 | | 752 | 782 | | 681 | 698 |
| 40 | 800 | 725 | 755 | 710 | 652 | 672 |
| 35 | 722 | 698 | 725 | 669 | 623 | 654 |
| 30 | 692 | 671 | 698 | 639 | 592 | 622 |
| 25 | 662 | 644 | 668 | 609 | 565 | 590 |
| 20 | 632 | 617 | 641 | 589 | 551 | 579 |
| 15 | 602 | 590 | 614 | 559 | 533 | 554 |
| 10 | 572 | 563 | 584 | 529 | 502 | 524 |
| 5 | 542 | 533 | 557 | 499 | 472 | 497 |
| 0 | 512 | 506 | 530 | 469 | 449 | 470 |
| –5 or lower | 500 | 500 | 500 | 440 | 440 | 440 |

*Both math sections have been combined. Add together both of your scores for those sections.

### MEDIAN SCORE: 50TH PERCENTILE

| Grade | Reading | Verbal | Math |
|---|---|---|---|
| 5 | 592 | 590 | 589 |
| 6 | 594 | 613 | 597 |
| 7 | 610 | 639 | 614 |
| 8 | 629 | 662 | 647 |
| 9 | 644 | 683 | 668 |
| 10 | 647 | 671 | 692 |
| 11 | 626 | 653 | 689 |

## ELEMENTARY-LEVEL SCORES

Elementary-level test scores are based on a scale of 300–600. Once you have looked up your scaled score, refer to the 50th Percentile score chart below: That chart will tell you the score at which equal numbers of students scored above and below you. This way, you will be able to gauge how well you have done with respect to other students.

### SCALED SCORES

| Raw Score | Reading | Verbal | Math |
|---|---|---|---|
| 30 | | 600 | 600 |
| 28 | 600 | 560 | 555 |
| 25 | 550 | 520 | 520 |
| 20 | 500 | 480 | 490 |
| 15 | 450 | 440 | 450 |
| 10 | 400 | 390 | 400 |
| 5 | 350 | 340 | 350 |
| 0 | 310 | 310 | 310 |
| −5 or lower | 300 | 300 | 300 |

### MEDIAN SCORE: 50TH PERCENTILE

| Grade | Reading | Verbal | Math |
|---|---|---|---|
| 3 | 450 | 450 | 450 |
| 4 | 450 | 450 | 450 |

| Part Five |

# ISEE PRACTICE TESTS AND EXPLANATIONS

# ISEE TEST OVERVIEW

## TOTAL TIME

Approximately 3 hours.

## QUESTIONS

Aside from the essay, all questions are multiple-choice format, with all answer choices labeled (A)–(D).

## CONTENT

The ISEE tests Math, Reading Comprehension, and Verbal skills. There are two scored Math sections, one scored Reading Comprehension section, one scored Verbal section, and one unscored Essay.

## PACING

You are not expected to complete all items on the ISEE. This is particularly true if you are at the low end of the age range of test takers for your level. The best approach to pacing is to work as quickly as you can without losing accuracy. Further, if a question is giving you difficulty, circle it and move on. You can always come back to it later, but you shouldn't waste time on a question that is stumping you when you could be gaining valuable points elsewhere.

## GUESSING

There is no guessing penalty on the ISEE. You receive 1 point for each question that you answer correctly. You don't lose any points for questions left blank or for questions answered incorrectly. As a result, it's always to your advantage to guess on questions you don't know. However, it's better to answer questions correctly, so only guess if you try to answer the question and can't figure it out, or if you are running out of time.

# CHAPTER 20: ISEE PRACTICE TEST 1: UPPER- AND MIDDLE-LEVEL

## HOW TO TAKE THIS PRACTICE TEST

Before taking this practice test, find a quiet room where you can work uninterrupted for three hours. Make sure you have a comfortable desk and several No. 2 pencils.

Use the answer sheet provided to record your answers. (You can cut it out or photocopy it.)

Once you start this practice test, don't stop until you have finished. Remember—you can review any questions within a section, but you may not go backward or forward a section.

You'll find answer explanations following the test.

Note: There are no major differences between the Middle- and Upper-level ISEE tests, and most of the questions on both tests are appropriate to either the Middle or Upper levels.

The practice test here covers both levels. If you are taking this as a Middle-level test, you may find a few of the questions to be too difficult. Don't worry—just do the best you can, and know that on Test Day, you will see only those questions that are appropriate to your level. Remember, too, that your scores will be based on how you compare to others taking the Middle-level test.

Good luck.

# ISEE Practice Test 1: Upper- and Middle-Level Answer Sheet

**Remove (or photocopy) the answer sheet and use it to complete the practice test.**

Start with number 1 for each section. If a section has fewer questions than answer spaces, leave the extra spaces blank.

## SECTION 1

| 1 A B C D | 9 A B C D | 17 A B C D | 25 A B C D | 33 A B C D |
| 2 A B C D | 10 A B C D | 18 A B C D | 26 A B C D | 34 A B C D |
| 3 A B C D | 11 A B C D | 19 A B C D | 27 A B C D | 35 A B C D |
| 4 A B C D | 12 A B C D | 20 A B C D | 28 A B C D | 36 A B C D |
| 5 A B C D | 13 A B C D | 21 A B C D | 29 A B C D | 37 A B C D |
| 6 A B C D | 14 A B C D | 22 A B C D | 30 A B C D | 38 A B C D |
| 7 A B C D | 15 A B C D | 23 A B C D | 31 A B C D | 39 A B C D |
| 8 A B C D | 16 A B C D | 24 A B C D | 32 A B C D | 40 A B C D |

# right in section 1

# wrong in section 1

## SECTION 2

| 1 A B C D | 9 A B C D | 17 A B C D | 25 A B C D | 33 A B C D |
| 2 A B C D | 10 A B C D | 18 A B C D | 26 A B C D | 34 A B C D |
| 3 A B C D | 11 A B C D | 19 A B C D | 27 A B C D | 35 A B C D |
| 4 A B C D | 12 A B C D | 20 A B C D | 28 A B C D | 36 A B C D |
| 5 A B C D | 13 A B C D | 21 A B C D | 29 A B C D | 37 A B C D |
| 6 A B C D | 14 A B C D | 22 A B C D | 30 A B C D | 38 A B C D |
| 7 A B C D | 15 A B C D | 23 A B C D | 31 A B C D | 39 A B C D |
| 8 A B C D | 16 A B C D | 24 A B C D | 32 A B C D | 40 A B C D |

# right in section 2

# wrong in section 2

## SECTION 3

| 1 A B C D | 9 A B C D | 17 A B C D | 25 A B C D | 33 A B C D |
| 2 A B C D | 10 A B C D | 18 A B C D | 26 A B C D | 34 A B C D |
| 3 A B C D | 11 A B C D | 19 A B C D | 27 A B C D | 35 A B C D |
| 4 A B C D | 12 A B C D | 20 A B C D | 28 A B C D | 36 A B C D |
| 5 A B C D | 13 A B C D | 21 A B C D | 29 A B C D | 37 A B C D |
| 6 A B C D | 14 A B C D | 22 A B C D | 30 A B C D | 38 A B C D |
| 7 A B C D | 15 A B C D | 23 A B C D | 31 A B C D | 39 A B C D |
| 8 A B C D | 16 A B C D | 24 A B C D | 32 A B C D | 40 A B C D |

# right in section 3

# wrong in section 3

## SECTION 4

| 1 A B C D | 11 A B C D | 21 A B C D | 31 A B C D | 41 A B C D |
| 2 A B C D | 12 A B C D | 22 A B C D | 32 A B C D | 42 A B C D |
| 3 A B C D | 13 A B C D | 23 A B C D | 33 A B C D | 43 A B C D |
| 4 A B C D | 14 A B C D | 24 A B C D | 34 A B C D | 44 A B C D |
| 5 A B C D | 15 A B C D | 25 A B C D | 35 A B C D | 45 A B C D |
| 6 A B C D | 16 A B C D | 26 A B C D | 36 A B C D | 46 A B C D |
| 7 A B C D | 17 A B C D | 27 A B C D | 37 A B C D | 47 A B C D |
| 8 A B C D | 18 A B C D | 28 A B C D | 38 A B C D | 48 A B C D |
| 9 A B C D | 19 A B C D | 29 A B C D | 39 A B C D | 49 A B C D |
| 10 A B C D | 20 A B C D | 30 A B C D | 40 A B C D | 50 A B C D |

# right in section 4

# wrong in section 4

*→ positive or negative? (prefixes)*

*→ root word*

*→ related word*

*→ where have you heard the word before*

# SECTION 1

Time—20 Minutes
40 Questions

This section consists of two different types of questions. There are directions for each type.

Each of the following questions consists of one word followed by five words or phrases. Select the one word or phrase whose meaning is closest to the word in capital letters.

1. EXCESS:

   (A) exit
   (B) surplus
   (C) disorder
   (D) end

2. REIMBURSE:

   (A) punish
   (B) divert
   (C) compensate
   (D) recollect

3. ASTOUND:

   (A) stun
   (B) laugh
   (C) suspend
   (D) scold

4. MASSIVE:

   (A) high
   (B) inferior
   (C) huge
   (D) ancient

5. DIN:

   (A) departure
   (B) clamor
   (C) code
   (D) supper

6. SCARCE:

   (A) delicious
   (B) afraid
   (C) thin
   (D) rare

7. DECEIT:

   (A) civility
   (B) trickery
   (C) rudeness
   (D) despair

8. HALLOWED:

   (A) carved
   (B) distinguished
   (C) empty
   (D) sacred

*→ if 2 answer choices mean the same thing, eliminate them!*

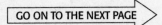
GO ON TO THE NEXT PAGE

9. APPREHENSION:

(A) appreciation

(B) worry

(C) aggravation

(D) elevation

10. BLEAK:

(A) charming

(B) warm

(C) drowsy

(D) dreary

11. OFFEND:

(A) divulge

(B) betray

(C) soothe

(D) insult

12. VIGOROUS:

(A) robust

(B) hungry

(C) destructive

(D) lovely

13. DESPONDENT:

(A) heightened

(B) annoyed

(C) relaxed

(D) depressed

14. SATIATE:

(A) prolong

(B) elongate

(C) seal

(D) satisfy

15. SPONTANEOUS:

(A) impulsive

(B) excitable

(C) ingenious

(D) dazzling

16. WAN:

(A) short

(B) pale

(C) foreign

(D) insincere

17. ABHOR:

(A) despise

(B) horrify

(C) avoid

(D) deny

18. APPARITION:

(A) clothing

(B) ghost

(C) guard

(D) wall

19. BENEVOLENT:

(A) disobedient

(B) charitable

(C) sensitive

(D) widespread

20. TOLERANT:

(A) open-minded

(B) friendly

(C) grave

(D) ambitious

GO ON TO THE NEXT PAGE

**Directions:** Select the word(s) that best fit the meaning of each sentence.

21. The ____ writer was on her 12th novel.

    (A) myopic
    (B) prolific
    (C) nefarious
    (D) elusive

22. Though underfunded, the school made the best of its ____ resources.

    (A) meager
    (B) emphatic
    (C) acrid
    (D) belittled

23. The advent of the computer chip made Frank's job _____.

    (A) exuberant
    (B) eminent
    (C) belligerent
    (D) obsolete

24. All efforts to save the nature preserve proved _____.

    (A) inextricable
    (B) insular
    (C) glib
    (D) futile

25. Except for periods where they function as "loners," wolves are generally ____ animals, living in packs.

    (A) carnivorous
    (B) fearsome
    (C) social
    (D) wild

26. The company employed many unproductive employees who had a(n) ____ approach to their work.

    (A) creative
    (B) discontented
    (C) independent
    (D) lackadaisical

27. The recent forest fire, which ____ the mountains of Indonesia, was the most severe ____ disaster the region has ever experienced.

    (A) destroyed .. inflammable
    (B) devastated .. environmental
    (C) singed .. intangible
    (D) burned .. scientific

28. Despite his ____ beginnings as the son of a minor tribal chieftain, the warrior became one of the greatest ____ in Asia.

    (A) humble .. rulers
    (B) luxurious .. leaders
    (C) innocent .. monarchs
    (D) regal .. kings

29. Although Angela was an interior decorator, her home was ____ decorated.

    (A) sufficiently
    (B) impressively
    (C) modestly
    (D) amply

30. Beneath the calm surface of the lake, marine creatures ____ continually for food.

    (A) qualified
    (B) survived
    (C) contested
    (D) gathered

GO ON TO THE NEXT PAGE

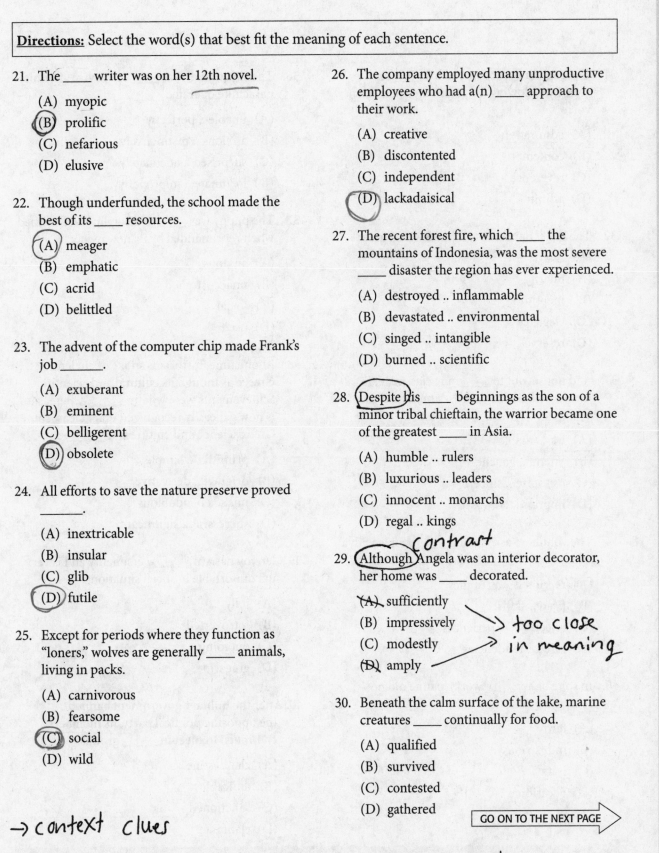

31. The captain demonstrated his _____ for the crew by bellowing his commands in a harsh voice.

   (A) admiration
   (B) contempt
   (C) reverence
   (D) affinity

32. The ballet dancers performed with a grace and _____ that left the audience breathless.

   (A) hilarity
   (B) ineptitude
   (C) elegance
   (D) reserve

33. I did not set out to _____ my classmate; I meant well, but my words came across as _____.

   (A) irk .. affable
   (B) offend .. gauche
   (C) ostracize .. sincere
   (D) impress .. confused

34. The volunteer association _____ people with a wide range of _____ to staff their offices.

   (A) recruited .. attributes
   (B) fired .. skills
   (C) rejected .. experiences
   (D) hired .. tendencies

35. In spite of her _____ work, Joanne did not receive a promotion.

   (A) tardy
   (B) industrious
   (C) irate
   (D) occasional

36. The sky jumper was _____ to survive after his parachute operated _____ .

   (A) unable .. perfectly
   (B) anxious .. instinctively
   (C) surprised .. adequately
   (D) fortunate .. improperly

37. The puppy was _____ to discipline and whined when reprimanded by its new owner.

   (A) anxious
   (B) unaccustomed
   (C) jovial
   (D) used

38. At one time, historians spoke of ancient Greece as though its cultural and scientific achievements were wholly _____, whereas it is now generally recognized that at least some Greek science and culture was _____.

   (A) primitive .. simple
   (B) original .. derivative
   (C) mistaken .. dubious
   (D) successful .. significant

*Contrast*

39. Jeremy has a(n) _____ personality and is very uncomfortable in social situations.

   (A) jolly
   (B) introverted
   (C) outgoing
   (D) gregarious

40. After the military government banned the opposing political party, its members continued to meet in _____ groups.

   (A) clandestine
   (B) amicable
   (C) sanctioned
   (D) elaborate

IF YOU FINISH BEFORE TIME IS CALLED, YOU MAY CHECK YOUR WORK ON THIS SECTION ONLY. DO NOT TURN TO ANY OTHER SECTION IN THE TEST.    STOP

# SECTION 2

Time—35 Minutes

37 Questions

---

In this section there are four possible answers after each question. Choose which one is best. You may use the blank space at the right of the page for scratch work.

Note: Figures are drawn with the greatest possible accuracy, UNLESS stated "Not Drawn to Scale."

---

1. Two radii of a circle combine to form a diameter if they meet at an angle whose measure in degrees is

    (A)  90 degrees

    (B) 120 degrees

    (C) 180 degrees

    (D) 240 degrees

USE THIS SPACE FOR FIGURING.

2. The price of a stock doubled from Monday to Tuesday. What is the percent increase in the price of the stock from Monday to Tuesday?

    (A)  50%

    (B) 100%

    (C) 150%

    (D) 200%

3. Which of the following is true?

    (A) $0.2 \times 0.2 = 0.4$

    (B) $0.2 \times 2 = 0.04$

    (C) $\dfrac{0.2}{2} = 0.1$

    (D) $\dfrac{0.2}{0.1} = 0.01$

4. A square has a perimeter of 8. What is the length of one of its sides?

    (A)  2

    (B)  4

    (C)  8

    (D) 16

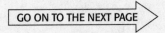
GO ON TO THE NEXT PAGE

**USE THIS SPACE FOR FIGURING.**

5. All of the following are equal to $\frac{1}{3}$ EXCEPT

   (A) $\frac{6}{18}$

   (B) $\frac{10}{30}$

   (C) $\frac{11}{33}$

   (D) $\frac{7}{24}$

6. If $N$ is an integer, which of the following MUST be odd?

   (A) $2N$

   (B) $N + 1$

   (C) $2N + 1$

   (D) $3N + 1$

7. If $\frac{700}{x} = 35$, then $x =$

   (A) 2

   (B) 5

   (C) 20

   (D) 200

8. Which of the following is closest to 15%?

   (A) $\frac{1}{7}$

   (B) $\frac{1}{5}$

   (C) $\frac{1}{4}$

   (D) $\frac{1}{3}$

9. When $A$ is divided by 5 it leaves a remainder of 3. What is the remainder when $A + 2$ is divided by 5?

   (A) 0

   (B) 1

   (C) 2

   (D) 3

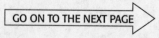

10. The difference between 30% of 400 and 15% of 400 is

(A) 200

(B) 150

(C) 60

(D) 30

USE THIS SPACE FOR FIGURING.

11. If $\dfrac{x}{3} = \dfrac{y}{6} = 3$, what is the value of $x + y$?

(A) 27

(B) 21

(C) 18

(D) 9

12. In the triangle in Figure 1, $x =$

(A) 50

(B) 60

(C) 80

(D) 100

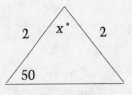

Figure 1

13. In Figure 2, if triangle $ABC$ and triangle $CED$ are equilateral, then the measure in degrees of angle $BCE$ is

(A) 60

(B) 90

(C) 120

(D) 180

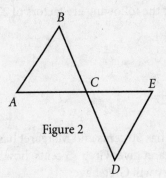

Figure 2

14. If 9 is added to the product of 12 and 4, the result is

(A) 17

(B) 25

(C) 57

(D) 84

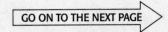

GO ON TO THE NEXT PAGE

15. If 45 is divided by the product of 3 and 5, the result is

    (A)  3
    (B)  5
    (C)  9
    (D) 15

16. Joe shoveled snow for $2\frac{1}{3}$ hours in the morning and then for another $1\frac{3}{4}$ hours in the afternoon. How many hours did he shovel in total?

    (A)  $3\frac{1}{6}$

    (B)  $3\frac{5}{6}$

    (C)  $4\frac{1}{12}$

    (D)  7

17. All of the following are factors of 27 EXCEPT

    (A)  1
    (B)  3
    (C)  7
    (D) 27

18. Greg has 50 cents and Margaret has $5. If Margaret gives Greg 75 cents, how much money will Greg have?

    (A)   $1
    (B)  $1.25
    (C)  $1.50
    (D)  $5.50

USE THIS SPACE FOR FIGURING.

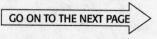

GO ON TO THE NEXT PAGE

19. $\frac{1}{2} + \frac{1}{6} =$

USE THIS SPACE FOR FIGURING.

    (A)   $\frac{1}{3}$

    (B)   $\frac{2}{3}$

    (C)   $\frac{5}{6}$

    (D)   $\frac{1}{12}$

20. How many integers are there from 1,960 to 1,980, inclusive?

    (A)   10

    (B)   20

    (C)   21

    (D)   30

21. If $n^* = 2n + 4$, what is the value of $10^*$?

    (A)   14

    (B)   24

    (C)   40

    (D)   44

22. If $a + b = 6$, then which expression is equal to $b$?

    (A)   $b = a - 6$

    (B)   $b = 6 - a$

    (C)   $b = 6a$

    (D)   $b = \frac{6}{a}$

GO ON TO THE NEXT PAGE

**Directions: In questions 23–37, note the given information, if any, and then compare the quantity in Column A to the quantity in Column B. Choose on you answer sheet grid**

**A**  if the quantity in Column A is greater

**B**  if the quantity in Column B is greater

**C**  if the two quantities are equal

**D**  if the relationship cannot be determined from the information given

|  Column A | Column B |
| --- | --- |

USE THIS SPACE FOR FIGURING.

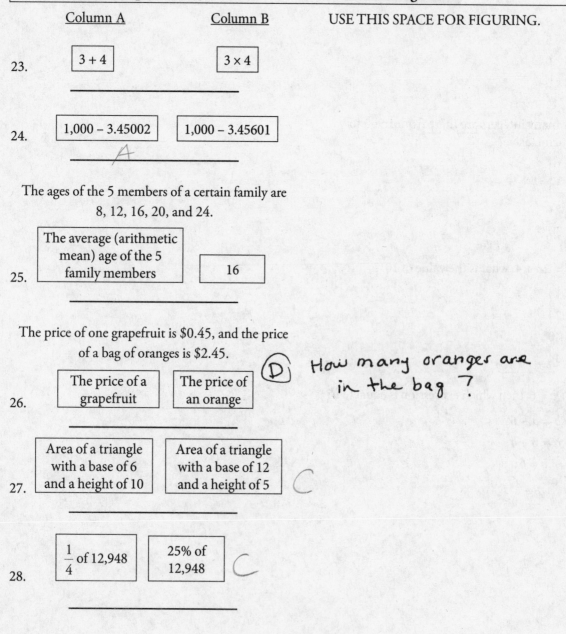

23.  $3 + 4$     $3 \times 4$

24.  $1{,}000 - 3.45002$     $1{,}000 - 3.45601$

*A*

The ages of the 5 members of a certain family are
8, 12, 16, 20, and 24.

25.  The average (arithmetic mean) age of the 5 family members     16

The price of one grapefruit is $0.45, and the price of a bag of oranges is $2.45.

26.  The price of a grapefruit     The price of an orange

Ⓓ How many oranges are in the bag?

27.  Area of a triangle with a base of 6 and a height of 10     Area of a triangle with a base of 12 and a height of 5

*C*

28.  $\frac{1}{4}$ of 12,948     25% of 12,948

*C*

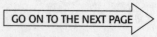
GO ON TO THE NEXT PAGE

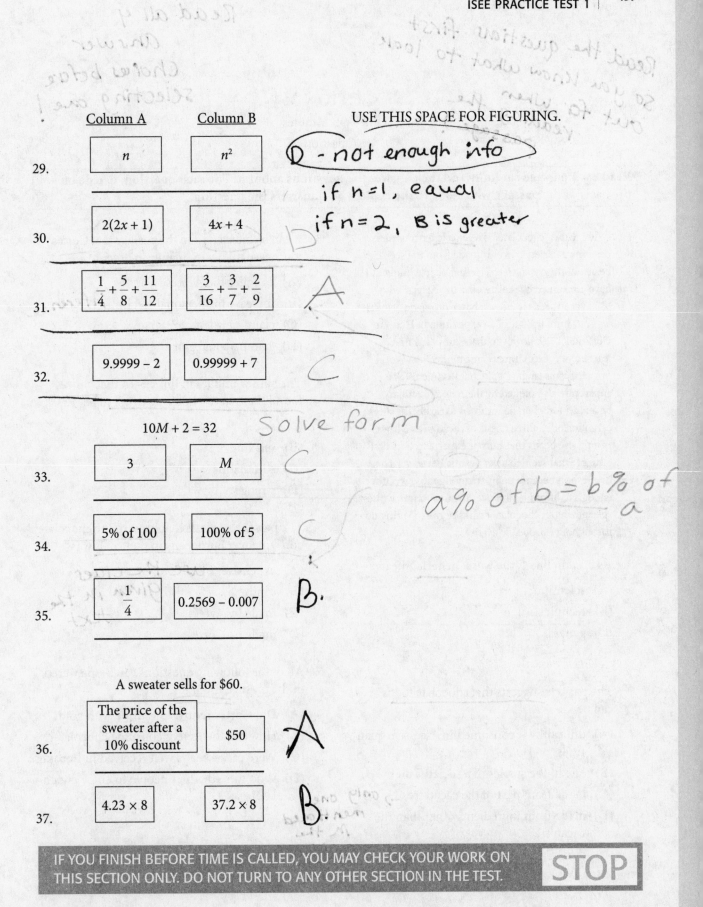

USE THIS SPACE FOR FIGURING.

| | Column A | Column B |
|---|---|---|
| 29. | $n$ | $n^2$ |
| 30. | $2(2x + 1)$ | $4x + 4$ |
| 31. | $\dfrac{1}{4} + \dfrac{5}{8} + \dfrac{11}{12}$ | $\dfrac{3}{16} + \dfrac{3}{7} + \dfrac{2}{9}$ |
| 32. | $9.9999 - 2$ | $0.99999 + 7$ |

$$10M + 2 = 32$$

| | Column A | Column B |
|---|---|---|
| 33. | 3 | $M$ |
| 34. | 5% of 100 | 100% of 5 |
| 35. | $\dfrac{1}{4}$ | $0.2569 - 0.007$ |

A sweater sells for $60.

| | Column A | Column B |
|---|---|---|
| 36. | The price of the sweater after a 10% discount | $50 |
| 37. | $4.23 \times 8$ | $37.2 \times 8$ |

Handwritten notes:

D - not enough info
if n=1, equal
if n=2, B is greater

Solve form

a% of b = b% of a

IF YOU FINISH BEFORE TIME IS CALLED, YOU MAY CHECK YOUR WORK ON THIS SECTION ONLY. DO NOT TURN TO ANY OTHER SECTION IN THE TEST.   **STOP**

*[Handwritten annotations: "Read the questions first so you know what to look out for when reading the passage!" and "Read all 4 answer choices before selecting one!"]*

# SECTION 3

Time—35 Minutes

36 Questions

Read each passage carefully and then answer the questions about it. For each question, decide on the basis of the passage which one of the choices best answers the question.

The word "chocolate" is a generic term used to describe a variety of foods made from the seeds, or beans, of the cacao tree. The first people known to
Line have consumed chocolate were the Aztecs, who
(5) used cacao seeds to brew a bitter, aromatic drink. It was not until the Mexican expedition of Hernan Cortes in 1519, however, that Europeans first learned of cacao. Cortes came to the New World primarily in search of gold, but his interest was
(10) apparently also piqued by the Aztecs' peculiar beverage, for when he returned to Spain, his ship's cargo included three chests of cacao beans. It was from these beans that Europe experienced its first taste of what seemed a very exotic beverage. The
(15) drink soon became popular among those wealthy enough to afford it, and over the next century cafes specializing in chocolate drinks began to spring up throughout Europe.

1. As used in line 1, the word "generic" means

    (A) scientific
    (B) technical
    (C) general
    (D) obscure

2. The passage suggests that chocolate foods can be

    (A) unhealthy if consumed in excessive quantities
    (B) one of the staples of a society's diet
    (C) made from part of the cacao tree *[handwritten: → only one mentioned in the passage]*
    (D) made from ingredients other than the cacao tree

3. It can be inferred from the passage that Cortes journeyed to Mexico mainly in order to

    (A) conquer the Aztecs
    (B) increase his personal wealth *[handwritten: inference]*
    (C) claim new land for Spain
    (D) gain personal glory

4. The author implies in lines 9–14 that Cortes found the Aztecs' chocolate drink to be

    (A) sweet
    (B) relaxing
    (C) stimulating
    (D) strange

5. The passage suggests that most of the chocolate consumed by Europeans in the 1500s was

    (A) expensive *[handwritten: use the clues given in the text]*
    (B) candy
    (C) made by Aztecs
    (D) made by Cortes

6. All of the following questions can be answered in the passage EXCEPT:

    (A) Did Cortes return to Europe with gold?
    (B) How did the Aztecs consume chocolate?
    (C) Were cacao beans well received in Europe?
    (D) Who were the first people to enjoy chocolate?

GO ON TO THE NEXT PAGE

It has been known for some time that wolves
live and hunt in hierarchically structured packs,
organized in a kind of "pecking order" similar to
*Line* that found in flocks of birds. At the top of the
(5) hierarchy in any wolf pack are the senior males,
dominating the others in all matters of privilege
and leadership. As many as three other distinct
subgroups may exist within a pack: mature wolves
with subordinate status in the hierarchy;
(10) immature wolves (who will not be treated as adults
until their second year); and outcast wolves
rejected by the rest of the pack. Each individual
wolf, moreover, occupies a specific position within
these subgroups, taking precedence over wolves of
(15) lower rank in the selection of food, mates, and
resting places and holding a greater share of the
responsibility for protecting the pack from strange
wolves and other dangers.

7. According to the passage, wolves and birds are
similar in that they both

   (A) mate for life
   (B) become adults at two years of age
   (C) defer to senior females
   (D) live in structured groups

8. The passage suggests that our knowledge of the
social hierarchies of wolves is

   (A) mostly theoretical
   (B) not a recent discovery
   (C) based on observations of individual
   wolves
   (D) in need of long-range studies

9. What is implied in the passage about outcast
wolves?

   (A) They never share the pack's food.
   (B) They sometimes kill the pack's young.
   (C) Their status is lower than that of imma-
   ture wolves.
   (D) They are incapable of protecting the pack
   from strange wolves.

10. According to the passage, the structure of a wolf
pack is determined by each wolf's share of all of
the following EXCEPT

   (A) food
   (B) water
   (C) resting place
   (D) mate

11. The author's attitude toward the subject may
best be described as

   (A) admiring
   (B) critical
   (C) informative
   (D) indifferent

12. As used in line 9, the word "subordinate" most
nearly means

   (A) top
   (B) inferior
   (C) short
   (D) immature

GO ON TO THE NEXT PAGE ⟩

The Romantic poets in nineteenth-century Britain prided themselves on their rejection of many of the traditional practices of English poetry.
*Line* William Wordsworth, one of the leaders of the
(5) Romantic movement, wished to avoid what he considered the emotional insincerity and affectation characteristic of much earlier poetry; instead he attempted to achieve spontaneity and naturalness of expression in his verse. According
(10) to Wordsworth, a poet should be "a man speaking to men" rather than a detached observer delivering pronouncements from an ivory tower. John Keats, Wordsworth's younger contemporary, brought a similar attitude to his poetry. Keats tried to make
(15) even the structure of his sentences seem unpremeditated. "If poetry," he claimed, "comes not as naturally as the leaves to a tree, it had better not come at all."

13. The passage is primarily concerned with

   (A) describing an artistic movement
   (B) detailing the achievements of William Wordsworth
   (C) criticizing traditional English poetry
   (D) providing information about John Keats

14. As used in line 3, the word "traditional" means

   (A) conservative
   (B) formal
   (C) boring
   (D) standard

15. It is implied by the passage that

   (A) the Romantic poets wrote better poetry than their predecessors did
   (B) Keats imitated Wordsworth's poetry
   (C) Keats is considered a Romantic poet
   (D) Keats only wrote poetry about nature

16. By the statement that a poet should be "a man speaking to men," Wordsworth probably meant that poetry should

   (A) be written in the form of a dialogue
   (B) always be read aloud to an audience
   (C) not be written by women
   (D) have the directness and spontaneity of real speech

17. All of the following are true about Wordsworth and Keats EXCEPT

   (A) both were Romantic poets
   (B) both wrote with a naturalness of expression
   (C) both liked poetry that was told from an angle of a detached observer
   (D) both wanted to stray from traditional English poetry

18. Where would this passage most likely be found?

   (A) A review of a book on Romantic poets
   (B) A biography of Wordsworth
   (C) A research paper on Romantic poets
   (D) A love letter from Wordsworth

GO ON TO THE NEXT PAGE

Edward Stratmeyer, the creator of the Hardy
Boys, Nancy Drew, and the Bobbsey Twins, did not
gain enormous commercial success through luck
Line  alone. His books, in which young amateur
(5)   detectives had fantastic adventures and always
saved the day, had a particular appeal in the time
they were written. When Stratmeyer himself was a
boy, the harsh economics of an industrializing
America quickly forced children to become adults.
(10)  By 1900, however, prosperity began to prolong
childhood, creating a new stage of life—
adolescence. From 1900 to 1930, the heyday of
Stratmeyer's career, adolescence came of age. Child
labor laws made schooling compulsory until
(15)  the age of sixteen. Young Americans, with more
free time than the working youth of the previous
century, looked to fiction and fantasy for
adventure. Stratmeyer, writing under a variety of
pseudonyms, responded to the needs of his readers
(20)  with a slew of heroic super-teens.

19. The passage primarily serves to explain

(A) the universal appeal of Stratmeyer's
characters

(B) the benefits of mandatory schooling for
teenagers

(C) the underlying reason for a writer's
popularity

(D) the economic boom created by child
labor laws

20. The passage suggests that the appeal of
Stratmeyer's fictional heroes lay partly in the
fact that

(A) they worked long hours in industrial jobs

(B) their activities were not restricted by
fictional parents

(C) they were the same age as his readers

(D) they were based on young people
Stratmeyer actually knew

21. According to the passage, children under
sixteen during the 1930s

(A) led lives of fun and adventure

(B) were better off financially than ever before

(C) began to lose interest in Stratmeyer's
books

(D) were legally required to attend school

22. According to the passage, Stratmeyer wrote his
books

(A) in a single thirty-year span

(B) using a series of pseudonyms

(C) to pay off family debts

(D) without ever gaining commercial success

23. As used in line 10, "prosperity" most closely
means

(A) success

(B) failure

(C) medicine

(D) life

24. The author's attitude toward Stratmeyer can
best be described as

(A) surprised

(B) tired

(C) admiring

(D) scornful

GO ON TO THE NEXT PAGE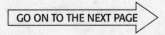

The ventriloquist's "dummy," the wooden
figure that a ventriloquist uses to create the
illusion of "throwing" his or her voice, was first
*Line* developed in the 1880s. On the outside, the first
(5) dummies looked very much like those used
today—with much the same exaggerated mouth
and range of movement. On the inside, however,
the best of these wooden figures were a curious
fusion of engineering feats and sculpture.
(10) Underneath the wig, the back of the dummy's head
opened up, revealing tangled innards of metal and
wire, screws, and levers. Arguably the most
mechanically complex figures were made by
the McElroy brothers, who together created one
(15) hundred figures in the ten years prior to the Second
World War. The mechanical brain of the McElroy
dummy was assembled from some 300 different
springs, pieces of metal, typewriter keys, and
bicycle spokes—a synergistic effort comparable to
(20) the work of the Wright Brothers.

25. The primary purpose of the passage is to

(A) compare the achievements of two different
families of inventors

(B) relate the history of the ventriloquist's art

(C) compare the ventriloquists' dummies of
the 19th century with those produced
today

(D) describe the complex craftsmanship
behind early ventriloquists' dummies

26. It can be inferred from the passage that the
outward appearance of ventriloquists' dummies

(A) is meant to seem as lifelike as possible

(B) has not changed much since they were
invented

(C) depends on what mechanical devices are
inside them

(D) changed after the work of the McElroy
brothers

27. The passage suggests that the most complex
dummies are

(A) created using scientific and artistic craftsmanship

(B) able to fool the most discerning observer

(C) those with the widest range of movement

(D) those made since the end of the Second
World War

28. The author probably argues that the McElroy
brothers' dummies were "a synergistic effort"
(line 19) because

(A) the McElroys were related to the Wright
Brothers

(B) the McElroys borrowed design concepts
from other inventors

(C) the McElroys worked together on the
design

(D) their dummies required so much energy
to operate

29. The author's attitude toward the McElroy
brothers can best be described as

(A) skeptical

(B) puzzled

(C) elated

(D) appreciative

30. All the following questions can be answered by
the passage EXCEPT:

(A) How does a ventriloquist throw his or her
voice?

(B) What is a dummy?

(C) How did the McElroy brothers' dummies
differ from others?

(D) Did the McElroy brothers start making
dummies before or after the war?

GO ON TO THE NEXT PAGE ▷

In 1916, James VanDerZee opened a photography studio in New York City's Harlem. It was the eve of the Harlem Renaissance—the
Line decade-long flowering of art and culture that
(5) established Harlem as the most artistically vigorous African-American community in the nation. For some 40 years, VanDerZee captured the life and spirit of that burgeoning community, producing thousands of portraits, not only of
(10) notables but of ordinary citizens—parents and children, brides and grooms, church groups, and women's clubs. Critics consider these images important today not only for their record of Harlem life, but for their reflection of their
(15) subjects' keen sense of the importance of their culture. VanDerZee's carefully staged photographs spotlighted his subjects' pride and self-assurance. His unique vision recorded a time, place, and culture that might otherwise have slipped away.

31. This passage focuses primarily on

   (A) the cultural achievements of the Harlem Renaissance

   (B) the history of African-American photography

   (C) the creative influences that shaped one photographer's career

   (D) the cultural record left by a Harlem photographer

32. It can be inferred from the passage that VanDerZee opened his studio

   (A) just before the Harlem Renaissance began

   (B) in order to photograph African-American celebrities

   (C) without having previous photographic experience

   (D) with financial support from his community

33. The passage most likely describes the subjects of VanDerZee's photographs (lines 7–12) in order to

   (A) demonstrate the artist's flair for composition

   (B) show that his work represented the whole community

   (C) highlight the self-assurance of Harlem residents

   (D) reflect upon the nature of photography

34. The author's attitude toward VanDerZee can best be described as

   (A) neutral

   (B) condescending

   (C) admiring

   (D) generous

35. Which of the following statements is NOT true?

   (A) VanDerZee helped trigger the Harlem Renaissance

   (B) If it weren't for VanDerZee, a part of Harlem life would have been forgotten

   (C) The Harlem Renaissance helped establish the neighborhood as an artistic community

   (D) VanDerZee captured the lives of a variety of people in Harlem

36. As used in line 8, "burgeoning" means

   (A) beautiful

   (B) barren

   (C) quiet

   (D) thriving

IF YOU FINISH BEFORE TIME IS CALLED, YOU MAY CHECK YOUR WORK ON THIS SECTION ONLY. DO NOT TURN TO ANY OTHER SECTION IN THE TEST.

STOP

# SECTION 4

Time—40 Minutes

47 Questions

In this section there are four possible answers after each question. Choose which one is best. You may use the blank space at the right of the page for scratch work.

Note: Figures are drawn with the greatest possible accuracy, UNLESS stated "Not Drawn to Scale."

1. Ralph is twice as old as Howie. If Ralph is $x$ years old, how many years old is Howie, in terms of $x$?

   (A) $0.5x$

   (B) $2x$

   (C) $x + 2$

   (D) $x - 2$

USE THIS SPACE FOR FIGURING.

2. A bag contains only blue and red marbles. If there are three blue marbles for every red marble, what fraction of all the marbles is red?

   (A) $\dfrac{1}{4}$

   (B) $\dfrac{1}{3}$

   (C) $\dfrac{1}{2}$

   (D) $\dfrac{3}{4}$

3. On Monday the temperatures of four different cities were $55°$, $-18°$, $25°$, and $-15°$. What was the average (arithmetic mean) temperature on Monday for these four cities?

   (A) $103°$

   (B) $20°$

   (C) $12°$

   (D) $11.75°$

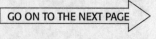

Questions 4–5 refer to the graph in Figure 1.

USE THIS SPACE FOR FIGURING.

4. Approximately how many medium-sized shirts were sold?

   (A) 300
   (B) 400
   (C) 500
   (D) 600

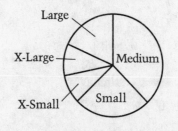

September Sales
for Ace T-Shirt Co.

Total Sales: 1,200 shirts

Figure 1

5. If each shirt sells for $5.95, approximately how much was spent on small-sized shirts?

   (A)  $300
   (B)  $900
   (C) $1,800
   (D) $3,600

6. How many seconds are there in $\frac{1}{20}$ of a minute?

   (A)  2
   (B)  3
   (C) 20
   (D) 30

7. What is the greatest number of squares, each measuring 2 centimeters by 2 centimeters, that can be cut from a rectangle with a length of 8 centimeters and a width of 6 centimeters?

   (A) 48
   (B) 12
   (C)  8
   (D)  6

8. Five percent of the guests at a Halloween party were dressed as witches. If there were 8 witches at the party, how many guests were at the party?

   (A)  40
   (B)  80
   (C) 160
   (D) 200

GO ON TO THE NEXT PAGE ⟩

Questions 9–10 refer to the following definition.

For all real numbers $a$ and $b$, $a@b = (a \times b) - (a + b)$.

Example: $6 @ 5 = (6 \times 5) - (6 + 5) = 30 - 11 = 19$.

USE THIS SPACE FOR FIGURING.

9.  $9@8 =$

(A) 73

(B) 72

(C) 71

(D) 55

10. If $10@N = -1$, then $N =$

(A)  0

(B)  1

(C)  9

(D) 11

11. A CD collection was divided among six people so that each received the same number of CDs. Which of the following could be the number of CDs in the collection?

(A) 10

(B) 15

(C) 21

(D) 24

12. At which of the following times is the smaller angle formed by the minute hand and the hour hand of a clock less than 90 degrees?

(A) 1:30

(B) 3:00

(C) 4:30

(D) 6:00

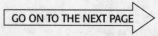

GO ON TO THE NEXT PAGE

13. Carol spent $\frac{1}{2}$ of her day at work, and $\frac{2}{3}$ of her time at work in meetings. What fraction of her entire day did Carol spend in meetings?

(A) $\frac{1}{2}$

(B) $\frac{1}{3}$

(C) $\frac{1}{5}$

(D) $\frac{1}{6}$

14. If $\frac{1}{2} \times S = 0.2$, then $S =$

(A) $\frac{2}{5}$

(B) $\frac{1}{4}$

(C) $\frac{1}{5}$

(D) $\frac{1}{10}$

15. If 50% of a number equals 75, then 10% of the number equals

(A)  15

(B)  30

(C)  60

(D) 150

16. If $\frac{1}{2} + \frac{1}{3} = \frac{M}{12}$, then $M =$

(A)  8

(B)  9

(C) 10

(D) 11

USE THIS SPACE FOR FIGURING.

GO ON TO THE NEXT PAGE

17. The perimeter of a rectangle is 32. If its length is three times as long as its width, what is its width?

(A) 12
(B) 8
(C) 6
(D) 4

USE THIS SPACE FOR FIGURING.

$$2,955 \times A = 35,460$$
$$11,820 \times B = 35,460$$
$$3,940 \times C = 35,460$$
$$7,092 \times D = 35,460$$

18. If each of the above equations is correctly solved, which of the following has the greatest value?

(A) $A$
(B) $B$
(C) $C$
(D) $D$

19. In a certain garage, 3 out of every 10 cars are foreign. If there are 180 cars at the garage, how many of them are foreign?

(A) 27
(B) 45
(C) 54
(D) 60

20. If $N_{\dot{c}} = N \times 10$, then $30_{\dot{c}} + 2_{\dot{c}} =$

(A) 32
(B) 302
(C) 320
(D) 3,200

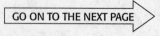
GO ON TO THE NEXT PAGE

21. Patricia began reading from the beginning of page 42 of a book and stopped at the end of page 83. How many pages did she read?

    (A)  40
    (B)  41
    (C)  42
    (D)  43

USE THIS SPACE FOR FIGURING.

22. In Figure 2, if $AB = 8$ and $AC = 14$, how far is the midpoint of $AB$ from the midpoint of $BC$?

    (A)  3
    (B)  4
    (C)  7
    (D)  8

```
|————————————|————————|
A            B        C
```
Figure 2

23. Judy has six more baseball cards than her brother. How many would she have to give him so that they would have an equal number of cards?

    (A)  6
    (B)  4
    (C)  3
    (D)  2

24. Fred averaged 168 on the first three games he bowled. What must he score on his fourth game in order to raise his average 5 points?

    (A)  158
    (B)  163
    (C)  178
    (D)  188

25. Which of the following equations could NEVER be true?

    (A)  $N \times 0 = N$
    (B)  $1 \times N = N$
    (C)  $N \times N = N$
    (D)  $N - 1 = N$

GO ON TO THE NEXT PAGE

26. If $X$ is the set of numbers greater than 6 and $Y$ is the set of numbers less than 11, how many whole numbers exist that are in both sets?

    (A) 4

    (B) 5

    (C) 6

    (D) Infinitely many

USE THIS SPACE FOR FIGURING.

27. Mary has 30% more money than June has. If June has $65, how much money does Mary have?

    (A) $84.50

    (B)    $80

    (C)    $50

    (D) $45.50

28. If 9 is $x$ percent of 90, what is 50 percent of $x$?

    (A)   5

    (B)  10

    (C)  15

    (D)  18

29. A certain machine caps 5 bottles every 2 seconds. At this rate, how many bottles will be capped in 1 minute?

    (A)   75

    (B)  150

    (C)  225

    (D)  300

30. What is 5 percent of 20 percent of 100?

    (A)   1

    (B)   5

    (C)  20

    (D)  25

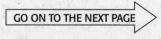
GO ON TO THE NEXT PAGE

31. If an exam had 10 questions and Keith answered 2 questions incorrectly, what percent of the questions did he answer incorrectly?

    (A)  2%
    (B) 10%
    (C) 12%
    (D) 20%

32. The difference between 6,985 and 3,001 is approximately

    (A) 3,000
    (B) 3,500
    (C) 4,000
    (D) 4,500

33. One and one-third minus five-sixths equals

    (A) $\dfrac{1}{4}$

    (B) $\dfrac{1}{3}$

    (C) $\dfrac{1}{2}$

    (D) $\dfrac{3}{4}$

34. Patty and Liza went out for lunch. Patty paid $3.30 for a drink and two hot dogs. Liza paid $2.15 for a drink and one hot dog. How much did a hot dog cost?

    (A) $0.90
    (B) $1.15
    (C) $1.30
    (D) $1.65

USE THIS SPACE FOR FIGURING.

GO ON TO THE NEXT PAGE

35. If one-fourth of a number is 3, what is one-third of the same number?

(A) 1

(B) 2

(C) 3

(D) 4

36. $2 \times 4 \times 7 \times 9$ is equal to the product of 18 and

(A) 8

(B) 14

(C) 28

(D) 36

37. If $12 + P = 20 - 2 \times 3$, then $P =$

(A) 2

(B) 14

(C) 36

(D) 42

38. One-tenth of 99 is

(A) 0.99

(B) 9.9

(C) 99

(D) 99.9

39. Twenty percent of 30 is

(A) 6

(B) 8

(C) 10

(D) 12.5

40. $\dfrac{64}{2 \times 4} =$

(A) 8

(B) 24

(C) 42

(D) 128

USE THIS SPACE FOR FIGURING.

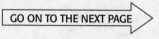

**USE THIS SPACE FOR FIGURING.**

41. $\dfrac{81}{9} + 2 =$

(A)  3

(B)  6

(C)  8

(D)  11

42. In a certain class, there are 6 girls for every 2 boys. What is the ratio of the number of girls to the entire class?

(A)  12:1

(B)  8:6

(C)  6:2

(D)  3:4

43. If $\dfrac{28}{a} = \dfrac{48}{12}$, then $a =$

(A)  7

(B)  8

(C)  9

(D)  10

44. If Set $A$ contains all integers greater than 8, and Set $B$ contains all integers less than 30, which of the following numbers could be in both sets?

(A)  0

(B)  2

(C)  4

(D)  9

45. $\dfrac{18 + 16}{4}$ equals

(A)  8

(B)  8.5

(C)  9

(D)  22

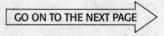

GO ON TO THE NEXT PAGE

46. When an integer is multiplied by itself, it can end in all of the following EXCEPT

   (A)  1
   (B)  3
   (C)  5
   (D)  6

47. If 20 percent of $J$ is 1,500, what is 15 percent of $J$?

   (A)  1,125
   (B)  3,000
   (C)  5,125
   (D)  6,000

USE THIS SPACE FOR FIGURING.

# SECTION 5

Time—30 Minutes

**Directions:** Write an essay on the following prompt on the paper provided. Your essay should NOT exceed two pages and must be written in blue or black ink. Erasing is not allowed.

**Prompt:** What is your favorite academic subject? Explain why you feel this way.

Do you agree or disagree with this statement? Use examples from history, literature, or your own personal experience to support your point of view.

_[handwritten margin note: might give a quote or saying going 2 reasons]_

_____

_____

_____

_____

_____

_____

_____

_____

_____

_____

_____

_____

_____

_____

_____

_____

_____

_____

GO ON TO THE NEXT PAGE →

# ANSWER KEY

| **Section 1** | 33. B | 25. C | 20. C | 16. C |
|---|---|---|---|---|
| 1. B | 34. A | 26. D | 21. D | 17. D |
| 2. C | 35. B | 27. C | 22. B | 18. A |
| 3. A | 36. D | 28. C | 23. A | 19. C |
| 4. C | 37. B | 29. D | 24. C | 20. C |
| 5. B | 38. B | 30. B | 25. D | 21. C |
| 6. D | 39. B | 31. A | 26. B | 22. C |
| 7. B | 40. A | 32. B | 27. A | 23. C |
| 8. D | **Section 2** | 33. C | 28. C | 24. D |
| 9. B | 1. C | 34. C | 29. D | 25. D |
| 10. D | 2. B | 35. A | 30. A | 26. A |
| 11. D | 3. C | 36. A | 31. D | 27. A |
| 12. A | 4. A | 37. B | 32. A | 28. A |
| 13. D | 5. D | **Section 3** | 33. B | 29. B |
| 14. D | 6. C | 1. C | 34. C | 30. A |
| 15. A | 7. C | 2. C | 35. A | 31. D |
| 16. B | 8. A | 3. B | 36. D | 32. C |
| 17. A | 9. A | 4. D | **Section 4** | 33. C |
| 18. B | 10. C | 5. A | 1. A | 34. B |
| 19. B | 11. A | 6. A | 2. A | 35. D |
| 20. A | 12. C | 7. D | 3. D | 36. C |
| 21. B | 13. C | 8. B | 4. B | 37. A |
| 22. A | 14. C | 9. C | 5. C | 38. B |
| 23. D | 15. A | 10. B | 6. B | 39. A |
| 24. D | 16. C | 11. D | 7. B | 40. A |
| 25. C | 17. C | 12. B | 8. C | 41. D |
| 26. D | 18. B | 13. A | 9. D | 42. D |
| 27. B | 19. B | 14. D | 10. B | 43. A |
| 28. A | 20. C | 15. C | 11. D | 44. D |
| 29. C | 21. B | 16. D | 12. C | 45. B |
| 30. C | 22. B | 17. C | 13. B | 46. B |
| 31. B | 23. B | 18. C | 14. A | 47. A |
| 32. C | 24. A | 19. C | 15. A | |

# ISEE PRACTICE TEST 1: UPPER- AND MIDDLE-LEVEL: ASSESS YOUR STRENGTHS

Use the following tables to determine which topics and chapters you need to review most. If you need help with your essay, be sure to review Chapter 9: The Essay and Chapter 26: Writing Skills.

| Topic | Question |
|---|---|
| Verbal: Synonyms | Section 1, questions 1–20 |
| Verbal: Sentence Completions | Section 1, questions 21–40 |
| Quantitative Reasoning: Word Problems | Section 2, questions 1–22 |
| Quantitative Reasoning: Quantitative Comparison | Section 2, questions 23–37 |
| Reading Comprehension | Section 3, questions 1–36 |
| Mathematics Achievement | Section 4, questions 1–47 |

| Topic | Number of Questions on Test | Number Correct | If you struggled with these questions, study… |
|---|---|---|---|
| Verbal: Synonyms | 20 | | Chapters 7 and 24 |
| Verbal: Sentence Completions | 20 | | Chapter 4 |
| Quantitative Reasoning: Word Problems | 22 | | Chapters 10–14 and Chapter 25 |
| Quantitative Reasoning: Quantitative Comparison | 15 | | Chapter 5 |
| Reading Comprehension | 36 | | Chapter 8 |
| Mathematics Achievement | 47 | | Chapters 10–14 and Chapter 25 |

# ANSWERS AND EXPLANATIONS

## SECTION 1: VERBAL REASONING

### SYNONYMS

**1.  B**

An excess is an extra amount of something—a surplus.

**2.  C**

To reimburse someone is to pay him back or to compensate him.

**3.  A**

When you astound someone, you greatly surprise or stun her.

**4.  C**

Something that is massive is extremely large or huge.

**5.  B**

Din refers to a large and distracting sound or a clamor.

**6.  D**

When something is scarce there is not a lot of it; it is very rare.

**7.  B**

If you accuse someone of deceit, you are accusing him of being untruthful or of trickery.

**8.  D**

You often hear the expression "hallowed ground," which means sacred ground.

**9.  B**

If you have apprehension about something, you have an acute concern or worry about it.

**10.  D**

When something is bleak, like the weather, it is very harsh or dreary.

**11.  D**

To offend someone is to be extremely rude to her or to insult her.

**12.  A**

Someone who is vigorous is very lively and healthy—robust.

**13.  D**

A despondent person feels hopeless and depressed.

**14.  D**

If you are very hungry and then eat a large meal, you can say that your appetite has been satiated or satisfied.

**15.  A**

Spontaneous actions or behavior occur with no apparent reason or cause—they are impulsive.

**16.  B**

Someone whose face is wan is sickly and pale.

**17.  A**

If you abhor liver or brussel sprouts, you dislike them immensely—you despise them.

**18.  B**

If you see an apparition on Halloween, you are seeing something resembling a ghost.

**19.  B**

A person who is benevolent is kind and giving—charitable.

**20.  A**

A tolerant person does not become angry or intimidated by new and strange ideas because she is open-minded.

## SENTENCE COMPLETIONS

### 21. B

This author has written a lot of novels, so we need a word that describes an author who writes a great deal. Prolific means producing abundant works.

### 22. A

The school has managed in this situation in spite of a lack of funds. Meager means deficient in quantity or scant. Don't be misled by (D), belittled. True, it has to do with little, but in an emotional sense. One feels belittled by public criticism.

### 23. D

With the advent, or arrival, of the computer chip, Frank's job became "something." Common sense tells us that his job became outdated or extinct. Obsolete means just that: no longer useful.

### 24. D

There were efforts to do something to the nature preserve. Whatever those efforts were, we can infer from the word "proved" that they were unsuccessful. Inextricable, (A), looks tempting, as it means incapable of being disentangled (think of extricating yourself from something), but it doesn't make sense here. Futile, (D), means having no useful result or ineffective.

### 25. C

The clue "except for" indicates that you're looking for the opposite of "loners"—social, (C).

### 26. D

"Unproductive" is the clue here—it suggests that the company employs people who don't work hard. In other words, they have a lackadaisical approach to their work.

### 27. B

Environmental, (B), is the only word that fits the second blank—a forest fire "devastated the region" fits the first blank.

### 28. A

"Despite" is a clue that indicates contrast—in spite of his humble beginnings, the chieftain became one of the greatest rulers.

### 29. C

Another contrast question—in spite of Angela's job as an interior decorator, her home might be modestly decorated.

### 30. C

Contested is the only word that fits the context here—you can't gather, qualify, or survive for food if you're a marine creature.

### 31. B

You're looking for a negative word here—contempt, (B), fits the captain's attitude best.

### 32. C

Which word goes best with grace? Grace and (C), elegance, are the two words that best describe a ballet dancer.

### 33. B

You're looking for negative words here for both blanks, so you can eliminate choices (A), (C), and (D).

### 34. A

The word "staff" indicates that the volunteer association is either (A), recruiting, or (D), hiring. "Attributes" is the word that best fits the idea of job qualifications.

**35. B**

The phrase "in spite of" indicates a contrast or paradox—you can tell that Joanne didn't get the promotion even though she worked hard. (B), industrious, is the only word that works.

**36. D**

The sky diver's reaction has to be consistent with his parachute—if it opened improperly, then he would be fortunate to survive.

**37. B**

The logic of the sentence suggests that the puppy would only whine if unaccustomed, or unused to, discipline.

**38. B**

The clue word "whereas" tells you this is a contrast question, so you need a choice with contrasting words. Only choice (B) provides the needed contrast.

**39. B**

Another word for "uncomfortable in social situations" is (B), introverted.

**40. A**

You're looking for a word that means secret. You may have heard the word "clandestine" on the news or in spy movies. It means secret, or undercover.

## SECTION 2: QUANTITATIVE REASONING

### WORD PROBLEMS

**1. C**

A diameter is a chord that runs straight through the center of a circle. Two radii will form a diameter if they form a straight line, as shown in the figure below. A straight angle has 180°, so (C) is correct.

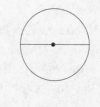

**2. B**

If the price of the stock doubled, it increased by its full price, or 100%, (B). If this isn't clear, pick a number for the original price of the stock, say $100. On Tuesday it would be twice this, or $200. So the increase is $200 − $100 = $100; $100 is 100% of $100, so again (B) is correct.

**3. C**

Evaluate each choice to see which is true:

(A) $0.2 \times 0.2 = 0.04$, not 0.4, so (A) is false.

(B) $0.2 \times 2 = 0.4$, not 0.04, so (B) is false.

(C) $0.2 \div 2 = 0.1$, so (C) is true.

(D) $0.2 \div 0.1 = 2$, not 0.01, so (D) is false.

**4. A**

A square has 4 equal sides, so its perimeter is equal to $4s$, where $s$ represents the length of one of its sides. So $4s = 8$, and a side of the square has length 2.

**5. D**

Evaluate each choice to see which is not equal to $\frac{1}{3}$:

(A) $\frac{6}{18} = \frac{1}{3}$ (when you factor out a 6)

(B) $\frac{10}{30} = \frac{1}{3}$ (when you factor out a 10)

(C) $\frac{11}{33} = \frac{1}{3}$ (when you factor out an 11)

(D) $\frac{7}{24} \neq \frac{1}{3}$

**6. C**

Pick numbers for $N$ and see which of the choices must be odd. The question says must, not can, so the correct choice will be the one that is odd no matter what number you pick. Start with $N = 1$:

(A) $2N = 2$; even so eliminate (A). Any integer multiplied by 2 will be even.

(B) $N + 1 = 2$; even, so eliminate (B).

(C) $2N + 1 = 3$; odd. To see if this is always the case, try $N = 2$: $2N + 1 = 5$; odd, so (C) is correct. Since any integer multiplied by 2 will be even, $2N + 1$ will always be odd.

(D) If $N = 1$, $3N + 1 = 4$; even, so eliminate (D).

**7. C**

You know $\dfrac{700}{x} = 35$, so $35x = 700$ and $700 \div 35 = 20$. Thus, $x = 20$.

**8. A**

Fifteen percent $= \dfrac{15}{100} = 0.15$. Convert each choice to a decimal to see which comes closest to 0.15.

(A) $\dfrac{1}{7} = 0.142...$

(B) $\dfrac{1}{5} = 0.2$

(C) $\dfrac{1}{4} = 0.25$

(D) $\dfrac{1}{3} = 0.0\overline{33}$

Of the choices, 0.142 is closest to 0.15, so (A) is correct.

**9. A**

Pick a number for $A$. Since $A$ leaves a remainder of 3 when divided by 5, let $A = 5 + 3 = 8$. You're asked for the remainder when $A + 2$, or 10, is divided by 5. Because 10 is divisible by 5, it leaves a remainder of 0.

**10. C**

You could figure out 30% of 400, then figure out 15% of 400, and then find their difference, but it's not necessary. The difference between 30% of a number and 15% of that same number is 30% − 15% = 15% of that number. Then 15% of 400 is 60, so (C) is correct.

**11. A**

Since $\dfrac{x}{3}$ and $\dfrac{y}{6}$ both equal 3, $\dfrac{x}{3} = 3$, and $x = 3 \times 3 = 9$ and $\dfrac{y}{6} = 3$, so $y = 3 \times 6 = 18$. So $x + y = 9 + 18 = 27$.

**12. C**

The triangle in Figure 1 is isosceles, since it has two sides of length 2. Therefore, the angles opposite these sides are also equal, and the unidentified base angle must equal 50°. The interior angles of a triangle sum to 180°, so $50 + 50 + x = 180$, $100 + x = 180$, and $x = 80$.

**13. C**

Since triangle $ABC$ is equilateral, it has three 60° angles. Therefore, $\angle BCA$ is 60°. $\angle BCE$ is supplementary to $\angle BCA$, so $60 + \angle BCE = 180$ and $\angle BCE = 120$.

**14. C**

The product of two numbers is the result of multiplying them together, so the product of 12 and 4 is $12 \times 4 = 48$. Adding 9 to 48 gives you 57, (C).

**15. A**

The product of 3 and 5 is equal to $3 \times 5 = 15$. $45 \div 15 = 3$, (A).

**16. C**

Joe shoveled for a total of $2\dfrac{1}{3} + 1\dfrac{3}{4}$ hours. To add, first convert to improper fractions: $\dfrac{7}{3} + \dfrac{7}{4}$. Then find a common denominator: $\dfrac{28}{12} + \dfrac{21}{12} = \dfrac{49}{12}$. Lastly, convert to a mixed number: $= 4\dfrac{1}{12}$.

**17. C**

Evaluate each choice to see whether it is a factor of 27:

(A) $1 \times 27 = 27$, so 1 is a factor.

(B) $3 \times 9 = 27$, so 3 is a factor.

(C) 7 is *not* a factor of 27.

(D) $27 \times 1 = 27$, so 27 is a factor.

**18. B**

Greg has $0.50 and is given $0.75, for a total of $1.25, (B).

**19. B**

$\frac{1}{2} + \frac{1}{6} = \frac{3}{6} + \frac{1}{6} = \frac{4}{6} = \frac{2}{3}$, (B)

**20. C**

To find the number of integers in an inclusive range, subtract the first integer from the last integer, and then add 1: $1,980 - 1,960 = 20$; $20 + 1 = 21$, choice (C).

**21. B**

Plug in 10 for $n$ in the equation. So, $10* = 2(10) + 4 = 20 + 4 = 24$.

**22. B**

If $a + b = 6$, in order to solve for $b$, you need to move $a$ to the right side of the equation by subtracting it from 6. So, $b = 6 - a$.

## QUANTITATIVE COMPARISON

**23. B**

In Column A, $3 + 4 = 7$. In Column B, $3 \times 4 = 12$. Since Column B is greater, (B) is correct.

**24. A**

You don't need to figure out the differences to answer this QC. In both cases you're subtracting some number from 1,000. Since you're subtracting more

from 1,000 in Column B, the difference in Column B is smaller than the difference in Column A.

**25. C**

$$\text{Average} = \frac{\text{Sum of terms}}{\text{Number of terms}}, \text{ so here:}$$

$$\text{Average age} = \frac{8 + 12 + 16 + 20 + 24}{5}$$

$$= \frac{80}{5}$$

$$= 16$$

You could have saved time if you remembered that the average of a group of consecutive integers is equal to the middle value. The ages of the family happen to be consecutive multiples of 4, so their average is the middle value, or 16.

**26. D**

You're told that a grapefruit costs $0.45, so that's the value in Column A. You're told that a bag of oranges costs $2.45, but you're given no information about the number of oranges in the bag. If there were 2 oranges in the bag, each would cost about $1.25, and Column B would be greater. But if there were 10 oranges in the bag, each would cost about $0.25, and Column A would be greater. As it stands, you are not given enough information to determine which column is larger, so (D) is correct.

**27. C**

Area of a triangle is equal to $\frac{1}{2}$(base)(height). In Column A you have $\frac{1}{2}(6)(10) = 30$. In Column B you have $\frac{1}{2}(12)(5) = 30$. The columns are equal, so (C) is correct.

**28. C**

In Column A you have $\frac{1}{4}$ of 12,948, and in Column B you have 25% of 12,948. Since $\frac{1}{4} = 25\%$, the columns will be equal. Notice that you didn't need to do any calculation to solve this problem—in fact, calculating would waste time you could use to answer other questions.

**29. D**

Pick Numbers for $n$. If $n = 1$, Column A is 1 and Column B is $1^2 = 1$, and the columns are equal. But if $n = 2$, Column A is 2, and Column B is $2^2 = 4$, and Column B is greater. Since there is more than one possible relationship between the columns, (D) is correct.

**30. B**

Multiplying through Column A gives you $4x + 2$. Compare piece by piece: While you may not know the value of $4x$, it will be the same in both columns. Looking at the second piece in each column, 4 is greater than 2, so Column B is greater.

**31. A**

It's not necessary—and is actually a waste of time—to find common denominators and calculate the sum in each column. Compare piece by piece. The first piece in Column A is $\frac{1}{4}$, and the first piece in Column B is $\frac{3}{16}$; $\frac{1}{4} = \frac{4}{16}$, so the first piece in A is bigger. The second piece in A is $\frac{5}{8}$, which is a little more than $\frac{1}{2}$, and the second piece in B is $\frac{3}{7}$, which is a little less than $\frac{1}{2}$. Therefore the second piece in A is greater. The third piece in A is $\frac{11}{12}$, which is greater than $\frac{1}{2}$, and the third piece in B is $\frac{2}{9}$, which is less than $\frac{1}{2}$. So the third piece in A is also greater, and Column A is greater.

**32. B**

The value in Column A is 7.9999, and the value in Column B is 7.99999. Column A only shows four places to the right of the decimal place, so any other places are understood to be zeros. Therefore Column A is actually 7.99990. So Column B is 0.00009 greater than Column A.

**33. C**

$10M + 2 = 32$, so $10M = 30$ and $M = 3$. Therefore the columns are equal.

**34. C**

This question is a breeze if you remember that $a$% of $b = b$% of $a$. If not, work it out. In Column A, 5% of 100 is 5. In Column B, 100% of 5 is 5. The columns are equal, so (C) is correct.

**35. A**

Put the columns in the same form so that they're easier to compare. In Column A, $\frac{1}{4} = 0.25$. In Column B, $0.2569 - 0.007 = 0.2499$, just less than 0.25 in Column A.

**36. A**

A 10 percent discount on a price of $60 is $6, so the sale price is $60 − $6 = $54. This is greater than $50 in Column B.

**37. B**

Comparing piece by piece, you see that the second pieces in both columns, namely 8, are equal. Since $4.23 < 37.2$, the first piece in B, 37.2, is greater, so Column B is greater.

## SECTION 3: READING COMPREHENSION

### CHOCOLATE PASSAGE

The first passage is about chocolate, which comes from the seeds, or beans, of the cacao tree. You're told that chocolate was first known to have been consumed (in drink form) by the Aztec people of Mexico, that the Spanish explorer Cortes learned of chocolate in 1519 on his expedition among the Aztecs, and that he brought three chests of cacao beans back to Spain. Over the next century, the passage concludes, the chocolate drink became popular with the wealthy throughout Europe.

**1. C**

Chocolate, we learn, is a "generic" term that describes "a variety of foods." Generic means general or relating to a whole group.

**2. C**

The passage's first sentence says that chocolate can be "made from the seeds, or beans, of the cacao tree." Since seeds are a part of the tree, (C) is correct. The healthiness of chocolate, (A), is not mentioned; we don't know whether it's a main food or staple of any society, (B); and we don't know what other ingredients, if any, go into making chocolate, (D).

**3. B**

Stick to what the passage actually says. "Cortes came to the New World primarily in search of gold... ." Therefore, (B) is correct: He came to amass wealth—i.e., to get rich.

**4. D**

We learn that Cortes's "interest was... piqued by the Aztec's peculiar beverage." The word "peculiar" suggests that Cortes found the Aztecs' chocolate

drinks strange, (D). Several lines earlier, we learn that the drink was bitter, so (A) is incorrect. And the passage doesn't say whether the drink was relaxing, (B), or stimulating, (C).

**5. A**

This question points you to the passage's final sentence. It says there that, in the century after its introduction to Europe, the chocolate drink "became popular among those wealthy enough to afford it," which implies that chocolate was very expensive in Europe at that time, (A). This early European chocolate was a drink, not a candy, (B). As far as we know, Aztecs were not imported to make the drink, (C), only the cacao beans were. And the passage never suggests that Cortes himself made most of the chocolate consumed in Europe during the entire 16th century, (D).

**6. A**

Find the right answer by using the passage to answer the questions asked in the choices. (B) is answered in line 5; they "used cacao seeds to brew a bitter, aromatic drink." Line 15 says drinks made from cacao beans "became popular" in Europe, so (C) is incorrect. (D) is answered in lines 3–4; the passage says that "the first people known to have consumed chocolate were the Aztecs." (A) is the answer because the passage does not say whether Cortes returned with gold in his cargo, only that he returned with "chests of cacao beans."

### WOLVES PASSAGE

The next passage is about the structured packs that wolves live in. These packs are described as hierarchies similar to the "pecking order" of birds. Senior male wolves are at the top of the hierarchy, followed by mature wolves, young or immature wolves, and outcast wolves. We learn that a wolf's place in the hierarchy determines its selection of "food, mates, and resting places" and how much responsibility each wolf is given in terms of protecting the pack from danger.

### 7. D

Wolves are compared with birds only in the first sentence, where the wolf pack structure is compared to the pecking order of a bird flock. So both species live in structured groups, and (D) is correct. We don't learn whether birds or wolves mate for life, (A), when birds become "adults," (B), or whether either species defers to senior females, (C).

### 8. B

The passage's opening sentence notes that "it has been known for some time" that wolves live in structured packs; therefore, our knowledge of such packs is not a recent discovery, (B). (A) is incorrect because the information given is not theoretical. (C) is presumably incorrect because information about wolf packs must come from observations of the packs themselves, not individual wolves. And (D) is never suggested.

### 9. C

Outcast wolves are only mentioned in the third sentence, where we learn that they are fourth in order of importance, behind senior males, mature wolves, and immature wolves. So (C) is correct: The status of outcast wolves is lower than that of immature wolves. (A), (B), and (D) are all plausible statements, but none of them is implied in the passage.

### 10. B

The passage's final sentence says that the order of the pack determines the selection of "food, mates, and resting places," which eliminates choices (A), (C), and (D). It's plausible that a wolf's share of water,

(B), would also be determined by the pack structure, but this is never mentioned, so (B) is correct.

### 11. D

The author's attitude toward wolf packs may best be described as indifferent because no opinion is expressed, (D).

### 12. B

Look at the sentence "subordinate" appears in. It talks about hierarchy, and the word modifies "status," so you know that the answer will have something to do with where the mature wolves fall in the hierarchy. That rules out (C) and (D). The sentence also calls the mature wolves a subgroup, putting them below senior males. That means their status is inferior to that of the senior males (B).

## ROMANTICS PASSAGE

The third passage is about the Romantic poets, a group of writers in 19th-century England who "prided themselves on their rejection of" earlier English poetry. In other words, the Romantic poets tried to write differently than their predecessors. In support of this thesis, you're told about how two major Romantic poets, Wordsworth and Keats, rejected pre-Romantic poems as insincere and affected and tried to write more spontaneous-seeming poems.

### 13. A

The best choice is (A): The passage describes an artistic movement, the Romantic movement in British poetry. (B) and (D) are equally incorrect, as each focuses on only one Romantic poet. And while (C) describes how the Romantics felt about earlier English poetry—they were critical of it—it doesn't sum up the passage, which also describes the kind of poetry the Romantics themselves tried to write.

### 14. D

The word "traditional" is used here to describe earlier British poetry. The Romantics rebelled against what they saw as the usual or standard practices of earlier poets, so (D) is correct. (A), (B), and (C) are all fairly plausible in context, but they don't have the equivalent meaning of "traditional."

### 15. C

Which of these statements is implied in the passage? (C): Since Keats was Wordsworth's contemporary, and brought a similar attitude to his poetry as this leader of the Romantic movement did, Keats must also be a Romantic poet. (A) isn't implied; all we know about Romantic poetry is that it was different from earlier poetry, not that it was better (even if the Romantics themselves thought it was). Similarly, (B) is incorrect because we only know that Keats brought an attitude to his writing that was similar to Wordsworth's—we don't know if the younger man actually imitated his older contemporary or not. And while Keats said that poetry should be written "as naturally as the leaves to a tree," this is a comment about spontaneity—it doesn't imply that Keats's poems are actually about nature (D).

### 16. D

In the sentence just before the quoted one, we learn that Wordsworth "attempted to achieve spontaneity and naturalness of expression" in his poems. Therefore, (D) is correct. (A), (B), and (C) all interpret Wordsworth's statement too literally. Wordsworth meant that poetry should *seem* like spontaneous speech, not that it should actually be written in dialogue form, or always read aloud, or only be written by men.

### 17. C

Try to find facts in the passage to back up each statement. (A) is in lines 4–5 and 12–13. (B) is in line 9. (D) is in lines 2–3. (C) is contradicted in lines 10–11.

### 18. C

Think about where you would most likely find this passage. (A) is incorrect because a review would most likely include opinions, which are not offered in the passage. (B) is incorrect because the focus of the passage is on Romantic poets in general, not just Wordsworth. (D) is incorrect because the passage has no passion and doesn't take the tone of a love letter. (C) is the most likely answer because the passage offers facts on Romantic poets.

## STRATMEYER PASSAGE

The fourth passage is about Edward Stratmeyer, a writer who created those fictional teen heroes and heroines the Hardy Boys, Nancy Drew, and the Bobbsey Twins. The author gives some biographical information about Stratmeyer, but the passage's main thrust is that he was so successful because his career coincided with the growth of a new population segment—adolescents. Labor laws passed early in the 20th century required children to stay in school until the age of 16, which gave them more free time than they'd ever had before. Wanting adventure, they read Stratmeyer's books.

### 19. C

As noted above, the main thrust of the passage is not the universal appeal of Stratmeyer's characters, (A); how mandatory schooling benefited teenagers, (B); or the boom created by labor laws, (D). Instead, the author is interested in telling us why Stratmeyer was so popular.

## 20. C

The second sentence describes the adventurous young heroes of Stratmeyer's books as having particular appeal; the final sentence notes that Stratmeyer satisfied his readers' needs with a "slew of heroic super-teens." Since Stratmeyer's readers were mostly teenagers, you can infer that his fictional heroes appealed to them at least partly because readers and heroes were the same age, (C). (A), (B), and (D) are not mentioned in the passage.

## 21. D

The passage states that, by 1930, adolescence had come of age, because labor laws required children to be in school until the age of sixteen, which makes (D) correct. (A) distorts the passage: By 1930, adolescents had more free time, but it was Stratmeyer's heroes who led lives of fun and adventure. (B) distorts the fourth sentence, which notes that, by 1900, the nation was more prosperous—not that teens themselves were. (C) is tricky. 1930 is described as the end of the heyday of Stratmeyer's career, but that doesn't necessarily mean his reading audience started to drop. It may just as well mean he stopped writing so many books.

## 22. B

(A) is incorrect because the 30-year span was the heyday, or best part, of Stratmeyer's career. This doesn't mean he wrote all his books within that span. The passage doesn't mention that his family was in debt, (C), and we know from the first sentence that, contrary to (D), he enjoyed enormous commercial success. This leaves correct choice (B): As the final sentence describes in passing, Stratmeyer wrote his books "under a variety of pseudonyms," or false names.

## 23. A

Look at the sentence "prosperity" appears in. The author says that "prosperity began to prolong childhood." That sounds as if "prosperity" is something positive, meaning (B) is incorrect. (D) doesn't make sense, so it's incorrect. That leaves success and medicine. Medicine is not mentioned in the passage, so the answer is (A).

## 24. C

Questions about the author's attitude are generally asking about the tone of the passage. Are the author's points positive, negative, or neutral? The author uses phrases such as "did not gain enormous commercial success through luck alone" and "responded to the needs of his readers with a slew of heroic super-teens." Those show that the author had a positive attitude, and that rules out (B) and (D). Next, think about how the passage would sound if you read it aloud. Does it sound as if the author didn't think Stratmeyer would be successful, or does it sound as if the author respected Stratmeyer's work? (C) is correct.

## DUMMIES PASSAGE

The fifth passage is about ventriloquists' dummies. The author tells you when dummies were first developed and that early dummies looked much like those of today on the outside but, on the inside, were a complicated mixture of "engineering feats and sculpture." The passage goes on to describe the inside of early dummy heads, especially the dummies made by the McElroy brothers, whose creations are said to have rivaled those of the Wright Brothers—inventors of the airplane—in complexity.

## 25. D

The author's primary purpose here is to describe early ventriloquists' dummies—the care and craft that went into making them. This point is restated in correct choice (D). The two inventing families mentioned in (A)—the McElroy and Wright Brothers—are only compared briefly in the passage's last sentence, making this a poor choice for a primary purpose question. (B) is too general, and as for (C), the passage compares early dummies with today's dummies only to tell us that both had similar exteriors. But the bulk of the passage is about the interiors of early dummies, and we learn nothing about the insides of today's dummies, so (D) remains best.

## 26. B

As described in the last question, the outsides of dummies are only mentioned in sentence 2: The outsides of early ones "looked very much like those used today." So you can infer (B), that outwardly, dummies haven't changed much since they were invented. (A) is not indicated, since at least one feature, the mouth, has always been "exaggerated." (C) is wrong because the outward appearance has remained the same even though the insides have changed over the years.

## 27. A

Correct choice (A) restates sentence 3: The interiors of the best dummies "were a curious fusion of engineering feats and sculpture"—that is, a mix of science and art. With their exaggerated features, even the best-made dummies aren't meant to fool the observer, (B); it's the "throwing" of the ventriloquist's voice that does the fooling. (C) distorts the point, in sentence 2, that dummies from all eras have similar range of movement. And the McElroy brothers' dummies, arguably the best ever made, were constructed before World War II, not after (D).

## 28. C

A "synergistic effort" describes two things working together so that the effect of the whole is more than the effect of the parts working separately. We know that the McElroy brothers worked together on their puppets, making (C) the correct answer. There's no evidence for (A). (B) and (D) are never mentioned.

## 29. D

The author clearly admires the work of the McElroy brothers, so (A) and (B) are easily eliminated. Elated, (C), means extremely happy, which doesn't seem fitting in the context of what is essentially a dry, expository passage.

## 30. A

Find the right answer by using the passage to answer the questions asked in the choices. (B) is answered in lines 1–3. (C) is in lines 12–13. (D) is answered in lines 14–16. (A) is not addressed in the passage.

## PHOTOGRAPHY PASSAGE

The sixth and last passage on this test is about James VanDerZee, a photographer who worked in Harlem. We learn that VanDerZee's career started in 1916, just before an African-American cultural boom known as the Harlem Renaissance, and that, in a career spanning 40 years, he took thousands of photographs of Harlem residents. The passage states that these photographs—of celebrities and unknown citizens alike—are now considered an important cultural record of a proud community.

## 31. D

The main focus of this passage is clearly on the work of VanDerZee, how he created an important cultural record. (D), which restates this idea, is thus the correct answer. (A) is too broad in scope and too narrow in time frame: VanDerZee was just one artist among many who made up the Harlem Renaissance, and that "decade-long flowering" spanned only one-fourth of his productive career. (B) is similarly too broad, since VanDerZee is the only African-American photographer mentioned in the passage. And (C) is incorrect because we're never told what creative influences shaped VanDerZee's career.

## 32. A

The passage states that VanDerZee opened his studio in 1916, on "the eve of the Harlem Renaissance." As it does in "Christmas Eve," the word "eve" means, literally or figuratively, the night before. So we can infer that 1916 was just before the beginning of the Harlem Renaissance, and (A) is correct. (B) is unlikely, since the passage states that VanDerZee photographed thousands of noncelebrities. In fact, we really know nothing (and so can infer nothing) of his original intentions, of his experience prior to opening the studio, (C), or of who bankrolled his studio, (D).

## 33. B

Sentence 3 describes VanDerZee's Harlem subjects as representing "the life and spirit of that burgeoning community." It also notes that they were not only "notables," or celebrities, but also "ordinary citizens." In other words, VanDerZee's subjects represented the entire Harlem community, and (B) is correct. The artist's flair for photographic composition, (A), and the self-assurance of his subjects, (C), are described further down in the passage, not in the lines in question. And (D) is too abstract and theoretical; the author wants to tell you whose pictures VanDerZee took, not to expound on the nature of photography in general.

## 34. C

The author describes VanDerZee as capturing the life of a community, as an artist respected by critics who had a "unique vision." In other words, the author admires VanDerZee, and (C) is correct. Neutral, (A), implies that the author doesn't feel one way or the other about VanDerZee, which clearly isn't the case. Condescending, (B), is a negative word that means "looking down on," and it's also inappropriate. Generous, (D), seems to imply that the author is somehow giving VanDerZee the benefit of the doubt, looking kindly on a career that really wasn't as great as the author says it was. No such attitude is hinted at in the passage, so (C) is best.

## 35. A

Try to find facts in the passage to back up each statement. (B) is supported by lines 18–19; the author says that he "recorded a time, place and culture that might otherwise have slipped away." (C) is found in lines 5–7; the author says the Harlem Renaissance "established Harlem as the most artistically vigorous African-American community in the nation." (D) is described in lines 10–12; he produced portraits of "parents and children, brides and grooms, church groups, and women's clubs." (A) is not true because the passage says the photographer opened his studio on "the eve of the Harlem Renaissance," meaning it was on the verge of occurring when he arrived in Harlem.

## 36. D

Look at the sentence "burgeoning" appears in. "VanDerZee captured the life and spirit of that burgeoning community." That shows that the answer has something to do with something lively, ruling out (B) and (C). That leaves "beautiful" and "thriving." (D) is the answer.

## SECTION 4: MATHEMATICS ACHIEVEMENT

**1. A**

Ralph's age is represented by $x$. Since Ralph is twice as old as Howie, Howie is half as old as Ralph, or $0.5x$.

**2. A**

If there are 3 blue marbles for every red marble, 1 out of every 4 marbles is red. Therefore, red marbles represent $\frac{1}{4}$ of all the marbles.

**3. D**

Average = $\frac{\text{Sum of terms}}{\text{Number of terms}}$, so the average temperature on Monday was

$$\text{Average} = \frac{55° + (-18°) + 25° + (-15°)}{4}$$

$$= \frac{80° + (-33°)}{4}$$

$$= 11\frac{3}{4}° = 11.75°$$

**4. B**

Looking at the pie chart, you can see that the slice that represents medium shirts represents about $\frac{1}{3}$ of the pie. The entire pie represents 1,200 shirts, so $\frac{1}{3}$ represents 400 shirts, (B).

**5. C**

The slice that represents small shirts represents about $\frac{1}{4}$ of the pie. Since the whole pie is 1,200 shirts, there were 300 small shirts sold. Each shirt sold for $5.95. The question asks approximately how much was spent on the small shirts, so estimate the price of a shirt to be $6 to make the calculation easier. The choices are pretty far apart, so it's okay to do this. $300 \times \$6 = \$1,800$, so (C) is correct.

**6. B**

There are 60 seconds in a minute, so in $\frac{1}{20}$ of a minute there are $60 \times \frac{1}{20} = \frac{60}{20} = 3$ seconds.

**7. B**

Sketch yourself a diagram:

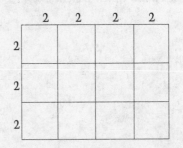

The 8-inch length can be divided into four 2-inch segments, and the 6-inch width can be divided into three 2-inch segments, which gives you a total of $4 \times 3 = 12$ squares.

**8. C**

Five percent of the guests at the party were witches. There were 8 witches, so 8 represents 5 percent = $\frac{5}{100} = \frac{1}{20}$ of the guests. The total number of guests is $20 \times 8 = 160$.

**9. D**

Just plug into the formula: $9@8 = (9 \times 8) - (9 + 8) = 72 - 17 = 55$.

**10. B**

Plug into the formula and solve for $N$:

$$10@N = -1$$
$$(10 \times N) - (10 + N) = -1$$
$$10N - 10 - N = -1$$
$$9N - 10 = -1$$
$$9N = 9$$
$$N = 1$$

**11. D**

If a CD collection can be evenly divided among 6 people, the number of CDs must be a multiple of 6. Only (D), 24, is a multiple of 6, since $6 \times 4 = 24$.

**12. C**

Make yourself a few quick sketches:

1:30          3:00

4:30          6:00

Only at 4:30 is the smaller angle less than 90°, so (C) is correct.

**13. B**

Carol spent $\frac{1}{2}$ of her day at work and $\frac{2}{3}$ of that time in meetings. So the amount of time she spent in meetings was $\frac{1}{2} \times \frac{2}{3} = \frac{2}{6} = \frac{1}{3}$ of her day.

**14. A**

If $\frac{1}{2} S = 0.2$, $S$ is twice that, or $2 \times 0.2 = 0.4$. The answer choices are all given as fractions, so convert 0.4 to a fraction: 0.4 is four-tenths, or $\frac{4}{10}$, which reduces to $\frac{2}{5}$, (A).

**15. A**

Ten percent is one-fifth of 50%, so if 50% of a number is 75, 10% of that same number is $\frac{1}{5} \times 75 = 15$.

**16. C**

$$\frac{1}{2} + \frac{1}{3} = \frac{M}{12}$$
$$\frac{6}{12} + \frac{4}{12} = \frac{10}{12}$$

So $M = 10$.

**17. D**

Let $w$ = the width of the rectangle. Its length is three times its width, or $3w$. Perimeter is equal to $2(l + w)$, where $l$ and $w$ represent length and width respectively. The perimeter is 32, so $2(l + w) = 32$. Plug in $3w$ for $l$: $2(3w + w) = 32$; $8w = 32$; $w = 4$.

**18. A**

It is possible to solve for each of the four variables, but it is really a waste of time. Note that each of the equations is equal to 35,460. Therefore, the largest variable will be the one with the smallest coefficient, because it takes fewer of a larger number to come up with the same product. Looking at the equations, you see that since 2,955 is the smallest coefficient, $A$ must have the greatest value.

**19. C**

Let $x$ = the number of foreign cars and set up a proportion.

$$\frac{3}{10} = \frac{x}{180}$$
$$(3)(180) = 10x$$
$$540 = 10x$$
$$54 = x$$

**20. C**

Plug in and solve.

If $N_\xi = N \times 10$, $30_\xi + 2_\xi = 30 \times 10 + 2 \times 10$
$$= 300 + 20$$
$$= 320$$

**21. C**

To find the number of integers in an inclusive range, subtract the smaller integer from the larger and then add 1: $83 - 42 = 41 + 1 = 42$, (C).

**22. C**

Looking at the figure, you can see that $AB + BC = AC$. Therefore, $8 + BC = 14$, and $BC = 6$. The midpoint of $AB$ divides it into two segments of length 4, and the midpoint of $BC$ divides it into two segments of length 3. Therefore the distance between their midpoints is $4 + 3 = 7$.

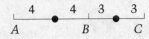

**23. C**

Judy has 6 cards more than her brother. For each to have an equal number, she would have to split her 6 extra cards between them, that is, give him 3, while keeping 3 for herself. If this isn't clear, Pick Numbers. Say Judy's brother had 4 cards. That would mean Judy had $4 + 6 = 10$ cards. If she gave him 3, she'd have $10 - 3 = 7$, and he would have $4 + 3 = 7$.

**24. D**

Since Average $= \dfrac{\text{Sum of terms}}{\text{Number of terms}}$, Average $\times$ Number of terms = Sum of terms. If Fred averaged 168 for his first three games, that means he scored a total of $3 \times 168 = 504$ points. With his last game Fred wants to score enough to raise his average by 5 points, bringing it up to $168 + 5 = 173$. That means he needs to score a total of $173 \times 4 = 692$ for all four games. Since he scored 504 in the first three games, he'd need to score $692 - 504 = 188$ in his last game.

**25. D**

Evaluate each statement. If you can come up with even one value for $N$ that makes the statement true, eliminate it.

A: If $N = 0$, $0 \times 0 = 0$, and the statement is true—eliminate.

B: If $N = 1$, $1 \times 1 = 1$, and the statement is true—eliminate.

C: If $N = 1$, $1 \times 1 = 1$, and the statement is true—eliminate.

D: $N - 1 = N$, so $N = N + 1$. There is no value of $N$ for which adding 1 to it will result in a sum of $N$, so this statement can never be true.

**26. A**

To find the numbers that are in both sets, start listing the integers greater than 6, but stop before you hit 11: 7, 8, 9, 10. There are 4, so (A) is correct.

**27. A**

If June has $65, Mary has $65 + 30\%(\$65) = \$65 + \$19.50 = \$84.50$.

**28. A**

Nine is $\dfrac{1}{10}$, or 10%, of 90, so $x = 10$. Then 50%, or $\dfrac{1}{2}$, of $10 = 5$.

**29. B**

Let $x$ = the number of bottles capped in 1 minute and set up a proportion. Be sure to convert 1 minute into 60 seconds.

$$\frac{5}{2} = \frac{x}{60}$$
$$(5)(60) = 2x$$
$$300 = 2x$$
$$150 = x$$

**30. A**

Take this problem in steps: 20% of 100 is 20; 5% of 20 is $(0.05)(20) = 1$.

**31. D**

Keith answered 2 out of 10 questions, or $\frac{2}{10}$, incorrectly. Then $\frac{2}{10} = \frac{1}{5}$, or 20%, choice (D).

**32. C**

You know 6,985 is approximately 7,000 and 3,001 is approximately 3,000. Therefore the difference between 6,985 and 3,001 is approximately 7,000 − 3,000 = 4,000, (C).

**33. C**

Convert to improper fractions: $1\frac{1}{3} - \frac{5}{6} = \frac{4}{3} - \frac{5}{6}$.

Find a common denominator: $\frac{16}{12} - \frac{10}{12} = \frac{6}{12} = \frac{1}{2}$.

**34. B**

Patty bought 2 hot dogs and a soda, and Liza bought 1 hot dog and a soda. Therefore the difference in what they paid, or $3.30 − $2.15 = $1.15, is the price of 1 hot dog.

**35. D**

If one-fourth of a number is 3, the number is $4 \times 3 = 12$. One-third of 12 is 4, (D).

**36. C**

Rewrite $2 \times 4 \times 7 \times 9$ as $(2 \times 9)(4 \times 7)$ or $18 \times 28$. (C) is correct.

**37. A**

$12 + P = 20 - 2 \times 3$

$12 + P = 20 - 6$

$12 + P = 14$

$\quad\quad P = 2$

**38. B**

One-tenth or 0.1 of 99 is 9.9, (B).

**39. A**

Twenty percent or $\frac{1}{5}$ of 30 is 6, (A).

**40. A**

$\frac{64}{2 \times 4} = \frac{64}{8} = 8$, (A).

**41. D**

$\frac{81}{9} + 2 = 9 + 2 = 11$, (D).

**42. D**

If there are 6 girls for every 2 boys, the ratio of girls to the entire class is 6:(6 + 2) or 6:8, which reduces to 3:4, (D).

**43. A**

So $\frac{48}{12} = \frac{4}{1}$, so $\frac{28}{a} = \frac{4}{1}$. Cross-multiply to get $28 = 4a$, and $a = 7$, (A).

**44. D**

For a number to be in both sets, it must be greater than 8 and less than 30. The only choice that falls in this range is 9, (D).

**45. B**

You can determine $\frac{18+16}{4} = \frac{34}{4} = 8\frac{1}{2} = 8.5$, (B).

**46. B**

Pick Numbers. All of the choices, except (B), can be ruled out by squaring the first few integers. $1^2 = 1$; $5^2 = 25$; $6^2 = 36$. Nothing squared ends in 3.

**47. A**

If $0.2J = 1,500$, then $J = 0.1,500 = 7,500$. So $0.15J = 0.15(7,500) = 1,125$.

# CHAPTER 21: ISEE PRACTICE TEST 2: UPPER- AND MIDDLE-LEVEL

## HOW TO TAKE THIS PRACTICE TEST

Before taking this practice test, find a quiet room where you can work uninterrupted for three hours. Make sure you have a comfortable desk and several No. 2 pencils.

Use the answer sheet provided to record your answers. (You can cut it out or photocopy it.)

Once you start this practice test, don't stop until you have finished. Remember—you can review any questions within a section, but you may not go backward or forward a section.

You'll find answer explanations following the test.

Note: There are no major differences between the Middle- and Upper-level ISEE tests, and most of the questions on both tests are appropriate to either the Middle or Upper levels.

The practice test here covers both levels. If you are taking this as a Middle-level test, you may find a few of the questions to be too difficult. Don't worry—just do the best you can, and know that on Test Day, you will see only those questions that are appropriate to your level. Remember, too, that your scores will be based on how you compare to others taking the Middle-level test.

Good luck.

# ISEE Practice Test 2: Upper- and Middle-Level Answer Sheet

**Remove (or photocopy) the answer sheet and use it to complete the practice test.**
Start with number 1 for each section. If a section has fewer questions than answer spaces, leave the extra spaces blank.

## SECTION 1

| 1 Ⓐ Ⓑ Ⓒ Ⓓ | 9 Ⓐ Ⓑ Ⓒ Ⓓ | 17 Ⓐ Ⓑ Ⓒ Ⓓ | 25 Ⓐ Ⓑ Ⓒ Ⓓ | 33 Ⓐ Ⓑ Ⓒ Ⓓ |
| 2 Ⓐ Ⓑ Ⓒ Ⓓ | 10 Ⓐ Ⓑ Ⓒ Ⓓ | 18 Ⓐ Ⓑ Ⓒ Ⓓ | 26 Ⓐ Ⓑ Ⓒ Ⓓ | 34 Ⓐ Ⓑ Ⓒ Ⓓ |
| 3 Ⓐ Ⓑ Ⓒ Ⓓ | 11 Ⓐ Ⓑ Ⓒ Ⓓ | 19 Ⓐ Ⓑ Ⓒ Ⓓ | 27 Ⓐ Ⓑ Ⓒ Ⓓ | 35 Ⓐ Ⓑ Ⓒ Ⓓ |
| 4 Ⓐ Ⓑ Ⓒ Ⓓ | 12 Ⓐ Ⓑ Ⓒ Ⓓ | 20 Ⓐ Ⓑ Ⓒ Ⓓ | 28 Ⓐ Ⓑ Ⓒ Ⓓ | 36 Ⓐ Ⓑ Ⓒ Ⓓ |
| 5 Ⓐ Ⓑ Ⓒ Ⓓ | 13 Ⓐ Ⓑ Ⓒ Ⓓ | 21 Ⓐ Ⓑ Ⓒ Ⓓ | 29 Ⓐ Ⓑ Ⓒ Ⓓ | 37 Ⓐ Ⓑ Ⓒ Ⓓ |
| 6 Ⓐ Ⓑ Ⓒ Ⓓ | 14 Ⓐ Ⓑ Ⓒ Ⓓ | 22 Ⓐ Ⓑ Ⓒ Ⓓ | 30 Ⓐ Ⓑ Ⓒ Ⓓ | 38 Ⓐ Ⓑ Ⓒ Ⓓ |
| 7 Ⓐ Ⓑ Ⓒ Ⓓ | 15 Ⓐ Ⓑ Ⓒ Ⓓ | 23 Ⓐ Ⓑ Ⓒ Ⓓ | 31 Ⓐ Ⓑ Ⓒ Ⓓ | 39 Ⓐ Ⓑ Ⓒ Ⓓ |
| 8 Ⓐ Ⓑ Ⓒ Ⓓ | 16 Ⓐ Ⓑ Ⓒ Ⓓ | 24 Ⓐ Ⓑ Ⓒ Ⓓ | 32 Ⓐ Ⓑ Ⓒ Ⓓ | 40 Ⓐ Ⓑ Ⓒ Ⓓ |

# right in section 1

# wrong in section 1

## SECTION 2

| 1 Ⓐ Ⓑ Ⓒ Ⓓ | 9 Ⓐ Ⓑ Ⓒ Ⓓ | 17 Ⓐ Ⓑ Ⓒ Ⓓ | 25 Ⓐ Ⓑ Ⓒ Ⓓ | 33 Ⓐ Ⓑ Ⓒ Ⓓ |
| 2 Ⓐ Ⓑ Ⓒ Ⓓ | 10 Ⓐ Ⓑ Ⓒ Ⓓ | 18 Ⓐ Ⓑ Ⓒ Ⓓ | 26 Ⓐ Ⓑ Ⓒ Ⓓ | 34 Ⓐ Ⓑ Ⓒ Ⓓ |
| 3 Ⓐ Ⓑ Ⓒ Ⓓ | 11 Ⓐ Ⓑ Ⓒ Ⓓ | 19 Ⓐ Ⓑ Ⓒ Ⓓ | 27 Ⓐ Ⓑ Ⓒ Ⓓ | 35 Ⓐ Ⓑ Ⓒ Ⓓ |
| 4 Ⓐ Ⓑ Ⓒ Ⓓ | 12 Ⓐ Ⓑ Ⓒ Ⓓ | 20 Ⓐ Ⓑ Ⓒ Ⓓ | 28 Ⓐ Ⓑ Ⓒ Ⓓ | 36 Ⓐ Ⓑ Ⓒ Ⓓ |
| 5 Ⓐ Ⓑ Ⓒ Ⓓ | 13 Ⓐ Ⓑ Ⓒ Ⓓ | 21 Ⓐ Ⓑ Ⓒ Ⓓ | 29 Ⓐ Ⓑ Ⓒ Ⓓ | 37 Ⓐ Ⓑ Ⓒ Ⓓ |
| 6 Ⓐ Ⓑ Ⓒ Ⓓ | 14 Ⓐ Ⓑ Ⓒ Ⓓ | 22 Ⓐ Ⓑ Ⓒ Ⓓ | 30 Ⓐ Ⓑ Ⓒ Ⓓ | 38 Ⓐ Ⓑ Ⓒ Ⓓ |
| 7 Ⓐ Ⓑ Ⓒ Ⓓ | 15 Ⓐ Ⓑ Ⓒ Ⓓ | 23 Ⓐ Ⓑ Ⓒ Ⓓ | 31 Ⓐ Ⓑ Ⓒ Ⓓ | 39 Ⓐ Ⓑ Ⓒ Ⓓ |
| 8 Ⓐ Ⓑ Ⓒ Ⓓ | 16 Ⓐ Ⓑ Ⓒ Ⓓ | 24 Ⓐ Ⓑ Ⓒ Ⓓ | 32 Ⓐ Ⓑ Ⓒ Ⓓ | 40 Ⓐ Ⓑ Ⓒ Ⓓ |

# right in section 2

# wrong in section 2

## SECTION 3

| 1 Ⓐ Ⓑ Ⓒ Ⓓ | 9 Ⓐ Ⓑ Ⓒ Ⓓ | 17 Ⓐ Ⓑ Ⓒ Ⓓ | 25 Ⓐ Ⓑ Ⓒ Ⓓ | 33 Ⓐ Ⓑ Ⓒ Ⓓ |
| 2 Ⓐ Ⓑ Ⓒ Ⓓ | 10 Ⓐ Ⓑ Ⓒ Ⓓ | 18 Ⓐ Ⓑ Ⓒ Ⓓ | 26 Ⓐ Ⓑ Ⓒ Ⓓ | 34 Ⓐ Ⓑ Ⓒ Ⓓ |
| 3 Ⓐ Ⓑ Ⓒ Ⓓ | 11 Ⓐ Ⓑ Ⓒ Ⓓ | 19 Ⓐ Ⓑ Ⓒ Ⓓ | 27 Ⓐ Ⓑ Ⓒ Ⓓ | 35 Ⓐ Ⓑ Ⓒ Ⓓ |
| 4 Ⓐ Ⓑ Ⓒ Ⓓ | 12 Ⓐ Ⓑ Ⓒ Ⓓ | 20 Ⓐ Ⓑ Ⓒ Ⓓ | 28 Ⓐ Ⓑ Ⓒ Ⓓ | 36 Ⓐ Ⓑ Ⓒ Ⓓ |
| 5 Ⓐ Ⓑ Ⓒ Ⓓ | 13 Ⓐ Ⓑ Ⓒ Ⓓ | 21 Ⓐ Ⓑ Ⓒ Ⓓ | 29 Ⓐ Ⓑ Ⓒ Ⓓ | 37 Ⓐ Ⓑ Ⓒ Ⓓ |
| 6 Ⓐ Ⓑ Ⓒ Ⓓ | 14 Ⓐ Ⓑ Ⓒ Ⓓ | 22 Ⓐ Ⓑ Ⓒ Ⓓ | 30 Ⓐ Ⓑ Ⓒ Ⓓ | 38 Ⓐ Ⓑ Ⓒ Ⓓ |
| 7 Ⓐ Ⓑ Ⓒ Ⓓ | 15 Ⓐ Ⓑ Ⓒ Ⓓ | 23 Ⓐ Ⓑ Ⓒ Ⓓ | 31 Ⓐ Ⓑ Ⓒ Ⓓ | 39 Ⓐ Ⓑ Ⓒ Ⓓ |
| 8 Ⓐ Ⓑ Ⓒ Ⓓ | 16 Ⓐ Ⓑ Ⓒ Ⓓ | 24 Ⓐ Ⓑ Ⓒ Ⓓ | 32 Ⓐ Ⓑ Ⓒ Ⓓ | 40 Ⓐ Ⓑ Ⓒ Ⓓ |

# right in section 3

# wrong in section 3

## SECTION 4

| 1 Ⓐ Ⓑ Ⓒ Ⓓ | 11 Ⓐ Ⓑ Ⓒ Ⓓ | 21 Ⓐ Ⓑ Ⓒ Ⓓ | 31 Ⓐ Ⓑ Ⓒ Ⓓ | 41 Ⓐ Ⓑ Ⓒ Ⓓ |
| 2 Ⓐ Ⓑ Ⓒ Ⓓ | 12 Ⓐ Ⓑ Ⓒ Ⓓ | 22 Ⓐ Ⓑ Ⓒ Ⓓ | 32 Ⓐ Ⓑ Ⓒ Ⓓ | 42 Ⓐ Ⓑ Ⓒ Ⓓ |
| 3 Ⓐ Ⓑ Ⓒ Ⓓ | 13 Ⓐ Ⓑ Ⓒ Ⓓ | 23 Ⓐ Ⓑ Ⓒ Ⓓ | 33 Ⓐ Ⓑ Ⓒ Ⓓ | 43 Ⓐ Ⓑ Ⓒ Ⓓ |
| 4 Ⓐ Ⓑ Ⓒ Ⓓ | 14 Ⓐ Ⓑ Ⓒ Ⓓ | 24 Ⓐ Ⓑ Ⓒ Ⓓ | 34 Ⓐ Ⓑ Ⓒ Ⓓ | 44 Ⓐ Ⓑ Ⓒ Ⓓ |
| 5 Ⓐ Ⓑ Ⓒ Ⓓ | 15 Ⓐ Ⓑ Ⓒ Ⓓ | 25 Ⓐ Ⓑ Ⓒ Ⓓ | 35 Ⓐ Ⓑ Ⓒ Ⓓ | 45 Ⓐ Ⓑ Ⓒ Ⓓ |
| 6 Ⓐ Ⓑ Ⓒ Ⓓ | 16 Ⓐ Ⓑ Ⓒ Ⓓ | 26 Ⓐ Ⓑ Ⓒ Ⓓ | 36 Ⓐ Ⓑ Ⓒ Ⓓ | 46 Ⓐ Ⓑ Ⓒ Ⓓ |
| 7 Ⓐ Ⓑ Ⓒ Ⓓ | 17 Ⓐ Ⓑ Ⓒ Ⓓ | 27 Ⓐ Ⓑ Ⓒ Ⓓ | 37 Ⓐ Ⓑ Ⓒ Ⓓ | 47 Ⓐ Ⓑ Ⓒ Ⓓ |
| 8 Ⓐ Ⓑ Ⓒ Ⓓ | 18 Ⓐ Ⓑ Ⓒ Ⓓ | 28 Ⓐ Ⓑ Ⓒ Ⓓ | 38 Ⓐ Ⓑ Ⓒ Ⓓ | 48 Ⓐ Ⓑ Ⓒ Ⓓ |
| 9 Ⓐ Ⓑ Ⓒ Ⓓ | 19 Ⓐ Ⓑ Ⓒ Ⓓ | 29 Ⓐ Ⓑ Ⓒ Ⓓ | 39 Ⓐ Ⓑ Ⓒ Ⓓ | 49 Ⓐ Ⓑ Ⓒ Ⓓ |
| 10 Ⓐ Ⓑ Ⓒ Ⓓ | 20 Ⓐ Ⓑ Ⓒ Ⓓ | 30 Ⓐ Ⓑ Ⓒ Ⓓ | 40 Ⓐ Ⓑ Ⓒ Ⓓ | 50 Ⓐ Ⓑ Ⓒ Ⓓ |

# right in section 4

# wrong in section 4

# SECTION 1

Time—20 Minutes
40 Questions

This section consists of two different types of questions. There are directions for each type.

Each of the following questions consists of one word followed by four words or phrases. Select the one word or phrase whose meaning is closest to the word in capital letters.

1. DESECRATE:

   (A) defend
   (B) deny
   (C) describe
   (D) defile

2. LAUD:

   (A) touch
   (B) praise
   (C) insult
   (D) hear

3. AVERT:

   (A) vindicate
   (B) prevent
   (C) explain
   (D) dislike

4. PIETY:

   (A) rarity
   (B) smell
   (C) faith
   (D) meal

5. AMORAL:

   (A) unethical
   (B) lovable
   (C) transparent
   (D) imaginary

6. CANDOR:

   (A) odor
   (B) honesty
   (C) ability
   (D) wealth

7. HAUGHTINESS:

   (A) heat
   (B) height
   (C) rudeness
   (D) arrogance

8. VERIFY:

   (A) complete
   (B) prove
   (C) violate
   (D) consume

9. DECEIVE:

   (A) trick
   (B) empty
   (C) dye
   (D) view

10. FICTION:

    (A) presumption
    (B) growth
    (C) falsehood
    (D) wound

GO ON TO THE NEXT PAGE

11. HARDY:

    (A) healthy
    (B) mysterious
    (C) firm
    (D) obese

12. LYRICAL:

    (A) mythical
    (B) bright
    (C) musical
    (D) wet

13. METAMORPHOSIS:

    (A) change
    (B) compliment
    (C) rejection
    (D) meeting

14. LAMENT:

    (A) support
    (B) decline
    (C) solidify
    (D) grieve

15. ARID:

    (A) light
    (B) clean
    (C) worried
    (D) dry

16. PERCEPTIVE:

    (A) confused
    (B) round
    (C) observant
    (D) imbued

17. ADAMANT:

    (A) thin
    (B) enlarged
    (C) admiring
    (D) stubborn

18. NEUTRAL:

    (A) inventive
    (B) foreign
    (C) unbiased
    (D) detailed

19. DOCILE:

    (A) old
    (B) tame
    (C) active
    (D) rare

20. WARINESS:

    (A) extremity
    (B) caution
    (C) superiority
    (D) mobility

**Directions:** Select the word(s) that best fits the meaning of each sentence.

21. Raccoons are _____ : they come out at night to look for food and sleep during the day.

    (A) nocturnal
    (B) friendly
    (C) precocious
    (D) monolithic

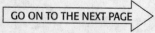
GO ON TO THE NEXT PAGE

22. Normally _____ , Jenny lacked her usual _____ when I called her and invited her to a movie.

    (A) absurd .. severity
    (B) scornful .. predilection
    (C) amiable .. enthusiasm
    (D) distraught .. cheeriness

23. The soap opera regularly dwells on the _____ aspects of life; just last week two characters died.

    (A) morbid
    (B) presumptuous
    (C) exciting
    (D) expensive

24. Once a(n) _____ gathering, the Greek festival has, in recent times, become highly _____ .

    (A) urban .. contemporary
    (B) religious .. commercialized
    (C) mournful .. gloomy
    (D) parallel .. transformed

25. The candidate changed his positions on so many issues that people began to think he was _____.

    (A) reliable
    (B) dependent
    (C) aloof
    (D) flighty

26. Melanie danced with such _____, that no one could _____ her talent any longer.

    (A) speed.. ascertain
    (B) grace .. affirm
    (C) agility .. question
    (D) melancholy .. deny

27. Sandy showed genuine _____ when she was caught: she cried and promised never to hurt anyone again.

    (A) remorse
    (B) melodrama
    (C) wit
    (D) enthusiasm

28. The _____ journey _____ us all; even my dog sat down to take a rest.

    (A) panoramic .. exhausted
    (B) tortuous .. invigorated
    (C) strenuous .. fatigued
    (D) arduous .. rejuvenated

29. Relying on every conceivable gimmick and stereotype, the latest Hollywood movie is not only _____ but _____ .

    (A) dull .. ambivalent
    (B) predictable .. absurd
    (C) complete .. erudite
    (D) boring .. enlightening

30. Lara not only respected her grandfather, she _____ him.

    (A) feared
    (B) retired
    (C) resembled
    (D) revered

31. That Chinese pieces of silk dating over 1,500 years old have been found in Egypt is _____ since the landscape between these two countries includes arid deserts and several _____ mountain ranges.

    (A) known .. required
    (B) impressive .. reduced
    (C) predictable .. steep
    (D) incredible .. massive

32. At first the empty house seemed frightening with all its cobwebs and creaking shutters, but we soon realized that it was quite _____ .

    (A) benign
    (B) deceptive
    (C) affluent
    (D) obliterated

33. Once a _____ propagated only by science fiction movies, the possibility of life on Mars has recently become more _____ .

    (A) wish .. doubtful
    (B) myth .. plausible
    (C) story .. impossible
    (D) hypothesis .. empty

34. Many writers of the 20th century were influenced by Hemingway's _____ writing style and consequently discontinued the _____ language characteristic of the 19th century novel.

    (A) sparse .. verbose
    (B) dull .. insipid
    (C) peaceful .. descriptive
    (D) complete .. florid

35. Dave never failed to charm listeners with his _____ stories.

    (A) lethargic
    (B) wan
    (C) insufferable
    (D) engaging

36. Screaming and laughing, the students were _____ by their _____ experience on the white-water raft.

    (A) amused .. tepid
    (B) irritated .. continued
    (C) exhilarated .. first
    (D) frightened .. secure

37. Highly influenced by Frank Lloyd Wright's principles of design, the architect E. Fay Jones has built homes reputed to equal—and even _____ —Wright's successes at building in harmony with natural surroundings.

    (A) echo
    (B) question
    (C) reconstruct
    (D) surpass

38. Weighing more than 70 tons, brachiosaurus was a(n) _____ creature, yet its brain was quite _____ .

    (A) intelligent .. enormous
    (B) gargantuan .. small
    (C) minute .. tiny
    (D) prodigious .. extant

39. Trumpets, including Pacific conch-shell trumpets, African ivory trumpets, orchestral valve trumpets, and tubas, comprise one of the most _____ categories of wind instruments.

    (A) excessive
    (B) discordant
    (C) coherent
    (D) diverse

40. The _____ nature of the platypus makes it difficult to spot, even in the _____ space of a zoological exhibit.

    (A) elusive .. confined
    (B) crafty .. massive
    (C) playful .. structured
    (D) slothful .. open

IF YOU FINISH BEFORE TIME IS CALLED, YOU MAY CHECK YOUR WORK ON THIS SECTION ONLY. DO NOT TURN TO ANY OTHER SECTION IN THE TEST.

STOP

# SECTION 2
Time—35 Minutes
37 Questions

In this section there are four possible answers after each question. Choose which one is best. You may use the blank space at the right of the page for scratch work.

Note: Figures are drawn with the greatest possible accuracy, UNLESS stated "Not Drawn to Scale."

1. If $Q + 7 - 8 + 3 = 23$, what is the value of $Q$?

   (A) 19
   (B) 20
   (C) 21
   (D) 22

   USE THIS SPACE FOR FIGURING.

2. A kilogram is equal to how many grams?

   (A) −1,000
   (B) −100
   (C) 100
   (D) 1,000

3. What is the value of $\frac{1}{9} + \frac{7}{12} + \frac{5}{6}$ ?

   (A) $\frac{9}{13}$
   (B) $1\frac{19}{36}$
   (C) $1\frac{2}{3}$
   (D) 2

4. What is 15% of 60?

   (A) 6
   (B) 9
   (C) 12
   (D) 15

5. If $a + 2 > 5$ and $a - 4 < 1$, which of the following is a possible value for $a$?

   (A) 2
   (B) 3
   (C) 4
   (D) 5

USE THIS SPACE FOR FIGURING.

6. If $2x + 4 = 26$, then $x + 4 =$

   (A)  9
   (B)  11
   (C)  13
   (D)  15

7. If the perimeter of an equilateral hexagon is 42, what is the sum of the lengths of 2 sides?

   (A)  6
   (B)  7
   (C)  12
   (D)  14

8. If Angelo earns $2,000 per month and spends 30% of his monthly earnings on rent, how much does he pay for rent each month?

   (A) $510
   (B) $600
   (C) $610
   (D) $680

9. A farmer pays $58 for 6 new chickens. How many eggs must the farmer sell at 16 cents apiece in order to pay for the chickens?

   (A) 360
   (B) 361
   (C) 362
   (D) 363

GO ON TO THE NEXT PAGE

10. A certain moped needs 12 gallons of fuel to go 48 miles. At this rate, how many gallons of fuel are needed to go 60 miles?

(A) 4

(B) 5

(C) 15

(D) 24

USE THIS SPACE FOR FIGURING.

11. $1\frac{6}{11} + 1\frac{7}{22} =$

(A) $2\frac{13}{33}$

(B) $2\frac{19}{22}$

(C) $2\frac{10}{11}$

(D) $2\frac{21}{22}$

12. If the average of 6 numbers is 9, what is the sum of those numbers?

(A) 15

(B) 30

(C) 54

(D) 96

13. If $\frac{1}{2} > x > 0$ and $\frac{1}{3} > x > \frac{1}{10}$, which of the following is a possible value for $x$?

(A) $\frac{2}{3}$

(B) 0.47

(C) $\frac{1}{5}$

(D) $\frac{1}{20}$

14. If $3a + 6a = 36$, what is the value of $a$?

   (A) 1

   (B) 2

   (C) 3

   (D) 4

15. What is $\dfrac{1}{4}$ of 0.72?

   (A) 0.018

   (B) 0.18

   (C) 1.8

   (D) 18

16. In Figure 1, what is the total area?

   (A) 10

   (B) 24

   (C) 28

   (D) 45

17. How many different prime factors are there of 48?

   (A) 1

   (B) 2

   (C) 3

   (D) 4

18. Which of the following is a factor of 36 but not of 48?

   (A) 3

   (B) 6

   (C) 12

   (D) 18

19. If Figure 2 is a cube, what is its volume?

   (A) 125

   (B) 100

   (C) 50

   (D) 25

USE THIS SPACE FOR FIGURING.

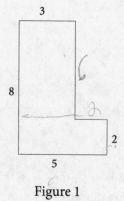

Figure 1

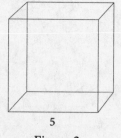

Figure 2

GO ON TO THE NEXT PAGE

20. While studying for a history test, it took Jake 1 hour 15 minutes to review the first 30 pages. If he continues to study at the same pace, how long will it take him to review the remaining 70 pages?

   (A) 2 hours 30 minutes

   (B) 2 hours 37 minutes

   (C) 2 hours 45 minutes

   (D) 2 hours 55 minutes

21. Mary types 12 words every 20 seconds. At this rate, how many words does she type every 2 minutes?

   (A) 18

   (B) 36

   (C) 42

   (D) 72

22. If $r = 8$, then $(r + 4)^2 =$

   (A)  24

   (B)  64

   (C)  80

   (D)  144

USE THIS SPACE FOR FIGURING.

**Directions:** In questions 23–35, note the given information, if any, and then compare the quantity in Column A to the quantity in Column B. Next to the number of each question write

**A** if the quantity in Column A is greater

**B** if the quantity in Column B is greater

**C** if the two quantities are equal

**D** if the relationship cannot be determined from the information given

Column A          Column B

USE THIS SPACE FOR FIGURING.

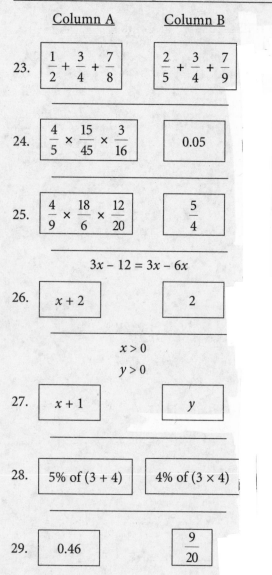

23. $\dfrac{1}{2} + \dfrac{3}{4} + \dfrac{7}{8}$    $\dfrac{2}{5} + \dfrac{3}{4} + \dfrac{7}{9}$

24. $\dfrac{4}{5} \times \dfrac{15}{45} \times \dfrac{3}{16}$    $0.05$

25. $\dfrac{4}{9} \times \dfrac{18}{6} \times \dfrac{12}{20}$    $\dfrac{5}{4}$

$3x - 12 = 3x - 6x$

26. $x + 2$    $2$

$x > 0$

$y > 0$

27. $x + 1$    $y$

28. $5\%$ of $(3 + 4)$    $4\%$ of $(3 \times 4)$

29. $0.46$    $\dfrac{9}{20}$

GO ON TO THE NEXT PAGE

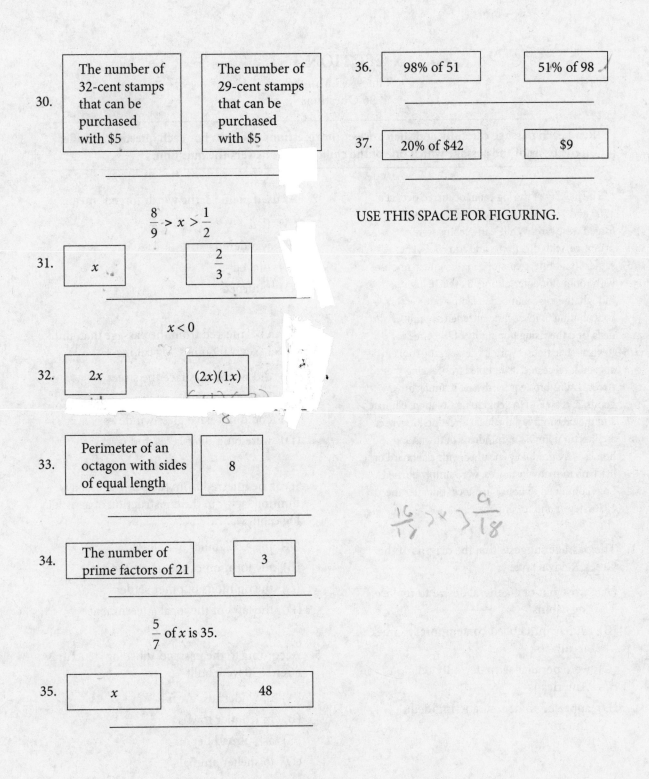

30.

| The number of 32-cent stamps that can be purchased with $5 | The number of 29-cent stamps that can be purchased with $5 |

31.

$$\frac{8}{9} > x > \frac{1}{2}$$

| $x$ | $\frac{2}{3}$ |

32.

$$x < 0$$

| $2x$ | $(2x)(1x)$ |

33.

| Perimeter of an octagon with sides of equal length | 8 |

34.

| The number of prime factors of 21 | 3 |

35.

$$\frac{5}{7} \text{ of } x \text{ is } 35.$$

| $x$ | 48 |

36.

| 98% of 51 | 51% of 98 |

37.

| 20% of $42 | $9 |

USE THIS SPACE FOR FIGURING.

$$\frac{16}{18} > x > \frac{9}{18}$$

IF YOU FINISH BEFORE TIME IS CALLED, YOU MAY CHECK YOUR WORK ON THIS SECTION ONLY. DO NOT TURN TO ANY OTHER SECTION IN THE TEST.

# SECTION 3

Time—35 Minutes
36 Questions

---

**Read each passage carefully and then answer the questions about it. For each question, decide on the basis of the passage which one of the choices best answers the question.**

---

The heyday of the log cabin occurred between 1780 and 1850, when a great number of settlers forged westward. While early cabins were
*Line* primitive, with dirt floors and sod roofs, later
(5) settlers built fine, two-story, log-hewn farmhouses with rooms for entertaining. By the 1840s, though, the log cabin began fading out. Factors contributing to its decline included sawmills, nails, and the rising popularity of the Greek
(10) Revival-style house, with its democratic roots in ancient Greece and its templed front facing the street. Trains brought hardware, manufactured goods, and an end to geographic isolation. Climate and the proximity of the local forest no longer set
(15) architectural limits. In hundreds of towns, log homes were gradually sheathed with clapboard or brick or, in many instances, were simply burned. Logs continued to house livestock, but after the 1850s, fewer and fewer people.

1. The passage suggests that the origins of the Greek Revival style

   (A) arose out of a general desire to replace log cabins

   (B) widely influenced contemporary Greek architects

   (C) were popular with devoutly religious Americans

   (D) appealed to democratic-minded Americans

2. As used in line 3, the word "forged" means

   (A) fled

   (B) wandered

   (C) moved

   (D) returned

3. It can be inferred from the passage that, unlike Greek Revival homes, log cabins

   (A) did not always face the street

   (B) lacked indoor plumbing

   (C) could not have glass windows

   (D) were built near lakes and rivers

4. It can be inferred from the passage that a limiting factor in the construction of a settler's log cabin was often

   (A) the availability of nails

   (B) the location of the nearest forest

   (C) the opinions of other settlers

   (D) the laws of the local government

5. According to the passage, most log structures after 1850 were built

   (A) in wilderness areas

   (B) in frontier towns

   (C) as railroad depots

   (D) to shelter animals

GO ON TO THE NEXT PAGE ⟹

6. Which of the following questions is NOT answered in the passage?

   (A) In their heyday, were log cabins common in the West?

   (B) When did log cabins finally disappear?

   (C) Why was the Greek Revival–style house popular?

   (D) How did log cabins in the 1780s differ from log cabins in the 1840s?

   The plague, or Black Death, struck Europe in a series of outbreaks in the 13th and 14th centuries, killing an estimated one-third of the continent's population. The epidemic wrought enormous
*Line*
(5) changes in European society, some of which, ironically, were beneficial. Reform in the medical profession, which had mostly failed to relieve the suffering, was one of the most immediate benefits. A great many doctors died or simply ran away
(10) during the plague. By the 1300s, many universities were lacking professors of medicine and surgery. Into this void rushed people with new ideas. In addition, ordinary people began acquiring medical guides and taking command of their own health.
(15) Gradually, more medical texts began to appear in everyday languages rather than in Latin, making medical knowledge more accessible.

7. The passage focuses primarily on

   (A) the enormous loss of life caused by the plague

   (B) the lack of qualified doctors during the plague

   (C) one positive result of a catastrophic event

   (D) the translation of medical texts into everyday language

8. As used in line 4, the word "wrought" means

   (A) caused

   (B) needed

   (C) accelerated

   (D) offered

9. The passage suggests that, prior to the plague outbreaks, European medicine was

   (A) hampered by a shortage of doctors

   (B) available only to university students

   (C) in need of sweeping changes

   (D) practiced mainly in Latin-speaking countries

10. It can be inferred from the passage that after the 1300s, medical texts

   (A) included information on how to cure the plague

   (B) were more easily available to the general population

   (C) were no longer written in Latin

   (D) were not written by university professors

11. Which of the following best describes the tone of the article?

   (A) Mournful

   (B) Sarcastic

   (C) Favorable

   (D) Sensible

12. All of the following are outcomes of the plague EXCEPT

   (A) medical information was made more accessible to people

   (B) people started learning Latin to understand the medical texts

   (C) people with new ideas on medicine started teaching medicine and surgery

   (D) a lot of people died from the plague

In the sport of orienteering, competitors use a map and compass to navigate their way cross-country along an unfamiliar course. The novice

*Line* quickly finds, however, that the most important
(5) question in orienteering is not compass bearing but choice of route. There are almost always several different ways to get from one point to another, and the beeline on a direct compass bearing over a mountain is seldom the best.
(10) Indeed, orienteers tend to disdain beelining over obstacles as a crude approach; they aspire to intellectual finesse. If climbing 20 feet in elevation requires the time and energy it would take to travel 250 feet on level ground—the sort of quick
(15) calculation orienteers are always making—then it may be better to follow a prominent contour along one flank of the mountain or even to stick to the safety of a trail looping around the base.

13. The passage suggests that a hiker with a map and compass is NOT orienteering if she

   (A) climbs more than one mountain per route

   (B) travels over a known, familiar route

   (C) takes more than one route per day

   (D) follows a direct path over an obstacle

14. According to the passage, an orienteer places greatest importance on

   (A) maintaining a single compass bearing

   (B) avoiding hazardous terrain

   (C) overcoming obstacles as fast as possible

   (D) choosing the best route available

15. It can be inferred from the passage that most orienteers would consider a competitor who climbs a mountain in order to take the most direct route to be

   (A) gaining a major advantage

   (B) lacking sophistication

   (C) breaking the rules

   (D) endangering other competitors

16. The passage suggests that one skill orienteers require is the ability to

   (A) run while carrying a backpack

   (B) swim long distances

   (C) set up a campsite

   (D) make rapid calculations

17. As used in line 12, "finesse" means

   (A) skill

   (B) movement

   (C) inefficiency

   (D) devotion

18. Which of the following best describes the author's attitude toward the subject?

   (A) Respect

   (B) Disdain

   (C) Indifference

   (D) Appreciation

Researchers have identified two phenomena that in previous literature were confounded under the category of nightmares. On the one hand,

*Line* there is the true nightmare, which is an actual,
(5) detailed dream. On the other there is the "night terror," from which the sleeper, often a child, suddenly awakes in great fright with no memory of a dream, often screaming and sometimes going off in a sleepwalking trance. Night terrors are seldom
(10) of serious consequence, no matter how horrifying they may appear to anxious parents. Outside of taking commonsense precautions—such as making sure a sleepwalker does not go to bed near an open window or on a balcony—there is nothing
(15) much to do about them. A child's night terrors can be reduced somewhat with a consistent sleep schedule and by avoiding excessive fatigue. Excessive concern or medication should usually be avoided.

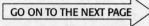 GO ON TO THE NEXT PAGE

19. As used in line 2, the word "confounded" means

   (A) entitled
   (B) confused
   (C) written
   (D) underappreciated

20. The passage suggests that, until recently, sleep researchers

   (A) knew very little about the nature of dreams
   (B) studied only adult sleeping habits, not those of children
   (C) did not differentiate between nightmares and night terrors
   (D) prescribed medication for children suffering from night terrors

21. According to the passage, a nightmare is a

   (A) full-fledged dream
   (B) dream fragment
   (C) hallucination
   (D) trancelike state

22. The passage implies that parents of children who experience night terrors

   (A) tend to dismiss them as inconsequential
   (B) also suffered night terrors when they were children
   (C) find their occurrence nearly as frightening as the children themselves do
   (D) should consult a doctor as soon as possible

23. Which of the following questions is NOT answered in the passage?

   (A) What is the difference between nightmares and night terrors?
   (B) What are some precautions parents can take to ensure the safety of children who experience night terrors?
   (C) Does a child who is frightened upon waking from a night terror remember dreaming?
   (D) Why does a consistent sleep schedule reduce the incidence of night terrors?

24. According to the passage, how are night terrors different from nightmares?

   (A) One is remembered by the sleeper, and the other is not.
   (B) One happens when the person is asleep, and the other does not.
   (C) One will bring harm to the sleeper, and the other will not.
   (D) One requires hospitalization, while the other does not.

The Neanderthal was an early human that flourished throughout Europe and western Asia between 35,000 and 85,000 years ago. Physically,
Line Neanderthals differed from modern humans in
(5) many important ways. They had massive limb bones, a barrel chest, thick brow ridges, a receding forehead, and a bunlike bulge on the back of the skull. Yet despite Neanderthals' reputation for low intelligence, there is nothing that clearly
(10) distinguishes a Neanderthal's brain from that of modern humans—except for the fact that, on average, Neanderthal versions were slightly larger. Combining enormous physical strength with manifest intelligence, Neanderthals appeared to
(15) be supremely well adapted. Nevertheless, around 35,000 years ago, they vanished from the face of the earth. The question of what became of the Neanderthals still baffles paleontologists and is perhaps the most talked-about issue in human
(20) origins research today.

25. It can be inferred from the passage that most Neanderthals probably had

(A) big arms
(B) wide-set eyes
(C) bowed legs
(D) narrow feet

26. According to the passage, Neanderthals lived

(A) in caves and mud dwellings
(B) by hunting in packs
(C) in Europe and Asia
(D) on all the continents

27. Based on information in the passage, modern humans, when compared with Neanderthals, probably have

(A) superior eyesight
(B) a better sense of smell
(C) less physical strength
(D) more body hair

28. The passage suggests that modern humans tend to think of Neanderthals as

(A) peaceful
(B) skilled artists
(C) farmers
(D) unintelligent

29. According to the passage, one question paleontologists are still trying to solve is

(A) what constituted the basic Neanderthal diet
(B) what were the Neanderthals' migratory patterns
(C) why the Neanderthal species became extinct
(D) where the Neanderthals originally came from

30. Where would this passage most likely be found?

(A) A short story about cavemen
(B) A research paper on early humans
(C) A letter from an explorer's encounter with a Neanderthal
(D) A textbook in health class

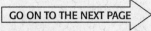
GO ON TO THE NEXT PAGE

Coyotes are one of the most primitive of living dogs. According to the fossil record, a close relative of the contemporary coyote existed here two to
Line three million years ago. It in turn seems to have
(5) descended from a group of small canids that was widely dispersed throughout the world and that also gave rise to the jackals of Eurasia and Africa. One to two million years ago, a division occurred in North America between the coyote and the
(10) wolf. Time passed, and glaciers advanced and receded. Mammoths, saber-toothed tigers, and dire wolves (canids with enormous heads) came and went. Native horses left the continent over land bridges, and others returned on galleons. Through
(15) it all, coyotes remained basically the same—primitive in evolutionary terms but marvelously flexible, always progressive and innovative—riding out, adjusting to and exploiting the changes.

31. The primary focus of the passage is on

   (A) the ability of the coyote species to survive unchanged

   (B) the unfortunate extinction of many prehistoric life forms

   (C) the changing nature of animal life in prehistoric times

   (D) the evolutionary division between coyotes and wolves

32. The passage suggests that modern dogs are

   (A) direct descendants of dire wolves

   (B) native to North America but not to Eurasia

   (C) genetically related to coyotes

   (D) lacking in evolutionary flexibility

33. According to the passage, a close relative of the coyote existed in North America

   (A) ten million years ago

   (B) seven million years ago

   (C) five million years ago

   (D) two million years ago

34. The author probably mentions mammoths and saber-toothed tigers in order to give examples of

   (A) the coyote's more distant relatives

   (B) animals that did not leave North America by land bridge

   (C) species that the jackal hunted into extinction

   (D) species that failed to adapt as the coyote did

35. When the passage states that "others returned on galleons" (line 14), it most probably means that

   (A) some species of horse became extinct, then others appeared

   (B) horses were reintroduced to North America when Europeans brought them by ship

   (C) some coyotes were introduced into Africa and Eurasia

   (D) prehistoric horses and dire wolves became extinct at roughly the same time

36. All the following are true EXCEPT

   (A) mammoths and dire wolves no longer exist

   (B) horses were in North America before the Europeans brought them here

   (C) coyotes are related to wolves

   (D) coyotes are not good at adapting to change

IF YOU FINISH BEFORE TIME IS CALLED, YOU MAY CHECK YOUR WORK ON THIS SECTION ONLY. DO NOT TURN TO ANY OTHER SECTION IN THE TEST.

STOP

# SECTION 4

Time—40 Minutes
47 Questions

In this section there are four possible answers after each question. Choose which one is best. You may use the blank space at the right of the page for scratch work.

Note: Figures are drawn with the greatest possible accuracy, UNLESS stated "Not Drawn to Scale."

1. What are all the values of $x$ for which $(x - 2)(x + 5) = 0$?

    (A) $-5$

    (B) $-2$

    (C) 2 and $-5$

    (D) $-2$ and $-5$

2. Patty uses 2 gallons of paint to cover 875 square feet of surface. At this rate, how many gallons will she need to cover 4,375 square feet of surface?

    (A) 4

    (B) 5

    (C) 8

    (D) 10

3. What is the area of a triangle with a base of 4 inches and a height of 6 inches?

    (A) 10

    (B) 12

    (C) 20

    (D) 24

4. An equilateral triangle has sides of lengths $3x + 1$ and $x + 7$. What is the length of one side?

    (A) 3

    (B) 5

    (C) 8

    (D) 10

USE THIS SPACE FOR FIGURING.

GO ON TO THE NEXT PAGE

5. $(65 \times 10^2) + (31 \times 10^3) + 12 =$

(A) 375,120

(B) 37,512

(C) 3,751.20

(D) 375.12

USE THIS SPACE FOR FIGURING.

6. Mr. Richman purchased a boat for $120,000. If the boat loses 20% of its value when placed in the water, how much did Mr. Richman lose in the value of his boat on its first use?

(A) $2,400

(B) $9,600

(C) $24,000

(D) $96,000

7. A dog is chained by a flexible leash to a stake in the ground in the center of his yard. If the leash is 8 meters long, what is the area in square meters in which he is able to run?

(A) 8

(B) 16

(C) $8\pi$

(D) $64\pi$

8. If Megan needs to drive 328 miles in 4 hours, at what rate of speed must she drive?

(A) 92 miles per hour

(B) 82 miles per hour

(C) 72 miles per hour

(D) 67 miles per hour

9. If a jet travels at a constant rate of 270 miles per hour, approximately how many hours will it take to reach its destination 3,300 miles away?

   (A) 23.68
   (B) 18.91
   (C) 15.38
   (D) 12.22

10. If $a = 3$ and $b = 4$, what is the value of $a^2 + 2ab + b^2$?

    (A) 14
    (B) 24
    (C) 49
    (D) 144

11. If $x - y = 5$ and $4x + 6y = 20$, then $x + y =$

    (A) 3
    (B) 4
    (C) 5
    (D) 6

12. How many distinct prime factors are there of 726?

    (A) 2
    (B) 3
    (C) 4
    (D) 5

13. If $n$ is an odd number, which of the following MUST be even?

    (A) $-2n - 1$
    (B) $2n + 1$
    (C) $2n - 1$
    (D) $4n$

USE THIS SPACE FOR FIGURING.

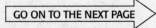

14. If Jamie is in school for 6 hours per day, 5 days per week, how many seconds does Jamie spend in school in one week?

   (A)  1,108,000
   (B)    180,000
   (C)    108,000
   (D)     18,000

USE THIS SPACE FOR FIGURING.

15. If it is snowing at a rate of 3.5 inches per hour and the storm is expected to continue at the same rate for the next 4 days, how many inches of snow accumulation can be expected?

   (A)  84
   (B)  168
   (C)  226
   (D)  336

16. Nicholas is $x$ years old, and Billy is three times as old as Nicholas. What was the sum of their ages, in years, 5 years ago?

   (A)  $x - 5$
   (B)  $2x + 2$
   (C)  $3x - 10$
   (D)  $4x - 10$

17. In a certain class, there are twice as many boys as girls. If the total number of students in the class is 36, how many boys are there?

   (A)  24
   (B)  18
   (C)  12
   (D)  9

18. At a party, $\frac{1}{3}$ of the guests drank only soda, and $\frac{2}{5}$ of the guests drank only juice. If the remaining 16 guests had nothing to drink, then how many guests were at the party?

    (A) 60
    (B) 50
    (C) 45
    (D) 30

19. If $x$ and $y$ are consecutive integers such that $xy = 6$ and $y$ is greater than $x$, which of the following statements MUST be true?

    I. $x + y = 5$
    II. $x$ is less than 6
    III. $\frac{x}{y} = \frac{2}{3}$

    (A) I only
    (B) II only
    (C) I and II only
    (D) I and III only

20. Jenny has $y$ baseball cards. She gives 5 cards to each of three different friends and in return receives 2 cards from each friend. How many cards does Jenny have after the exchange?

    (A) $y - 9$
    (B) $y - 5$
    (C) $y + 3$
    (D) $y + 5$

USE THIS SPACE FOR FIGURING.

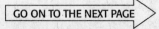

GO ON TO THE NEXT PAGE

21. If two fair coins are tossed simultaneously, what is the probability that two tails are thrown?

    (A) 1

    (B) $\dfrac{1}{2}$

    (C) $\dfrac{1}{4}$

    (D) $\dfrac{1}{8}$

22. A photocopier makes copies at a constant rate of 15 copies per minute. A certain copy job requires 600 copies. What fraction of the job will the machine finish in 5 minutes?

    (A) $\dfrac{1}{200}$

    (B) $\dfrac{1}{40}$

    (C) $\dfrac{1}{8}$

    (D) $\dfrac{1}{5}$

23. Which of the following is a possible value of $z$ if $2(z-3) > 6$ and $z + 4 < 15$ ?

    (A) 3

    (B) 6

    (C) 7

    (D) 11

24. In a certain library there are 3 fiction books for every 8 nonfiction books. If the library has 600 nonfiction books, how many books does it have?

    (A) 2,200

    (B) 1,400

    (C) 825

    (D) 800

USE THIS SPACE FOR FIGURING.

25. If $x + y$ equals an odd number and $x + z$ equals an even number, each of the following could be true EXCEPT

(A)  $x$ is even and $y$ is odd

(B)  $y$ is even and $z$ is odd

(C)  $x$ and $z$ are even and $y$ is odd

(D)  $x$ and $y$ are even and $z$ is odd

26. On the first test, Ted scored 7 percentage points above the passing grade. On the second test he scored 12 percentage points lower than he did on his first test. His score on the second test was

(A)  19 percentage points below the passing grade

(B)  12 percentage points below the passing grade

(C)  5 percentage points below the passing grade

(D)  2 percentage points above the passing grade

27. In a class, 70 percent of the students are right-handed, and the rest are left-handed. If 70 percent of the left-handed students have brown eyes, then left-handed students with brown eyes make up what percent of the entire class?

(A)  14%

(B)  21%

(C)  30%

(D)  49%

Questions 28 and 29 refer to the following definition:
For all real numbers $q$ and $r$, let $q//r = (qr) - (q - r)$.

28.  $8//2 =$

(A)  6

(B)  8

(C)  10

(D)  16

USE THIS SPACE FOR FIGURING.

29. If $P//3 = 11$, then $P =$

    (A) 3
    (B) 4
    (C) 6
    (D) 7

30. If the product of integers $a$ and $b$ is 16 and $a$ is greater than 4, then which of the following MUST be true?

    I. $b = 2$
    II. The sum of $a$ and $b$ is greater than zero
    III. $a$ is greater than $b$

    (A) II only
    (B) III only
    (C) I and II only
    (D) II and III only

31. In Figure 1, what is the value of $x$ ?

    (A) 20
    (B) 30
    (C) 45
    (D) 90

32. In Figure 2, the distance from $B$ to $C$ is twice the distance from $A$ to $B$, and the distance from $C$ to $D$ is equal to half the distance from $A$ to $C$. If the distance from $B$ to $C$ is 12, what is the distance from $A$ to $D$ ?

    (A) 18
    (B) 24
    (C) 27
    (D) 32

USE THIS SPACE FOR FIGURING.

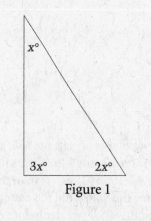
Figure 1

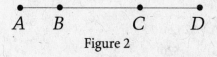
Figure 2

GO ON TO THE NEXT PAGE

33. What is the greatest number of squares with sides of 2 centimeters that can be cut from a square with an area of 36 square centimeters?

(A)  4

(B)  9

(C) 18

(D) 36

34. If $x = 4y + 3$, then what does $x - 5$ equal?

(A) $4y - 8$

(B) $4y - 2$

(C) $4y + 5$

(D) $5y - 8$

35. A grocer buys oranges at a price of 4 for $1 and then sells them in his store for 40 cents each. How many oranges must he sell to earn a profit of $3?

(A)  2

(B) 10

(C) 15

(D) 20

36. A wool sweater is on sale for $63, and a cotton sweater is on sale for $45. If the sale price for each sweater is 10% less than the original price, how much less did the cotton sweater cost than the wool sweater before either went on sale?

(A) $23.50

(B)  $20

(C) $19.80

(D)  $18

USE THIS SPACE FOR FIGURING.

GO ON TO THE NEXT PAGE

USE THIS SPACE FOR FIGURING.

37. John finished $\frac{1}{3}$ of his homework assignment between 6:00 P.M. and 7:30 P.M. He needs to finish the assignment by 11:00 P.M. If he works at the same rate, what is the latest time that he can return to his homework?

(A) 7:45 P.M.

(B) 8:00 P.M.

(C) 8:30 P.M.

(D) 9:30 P.M.

38. There are twice as many men as women on a track team. Medals were given to $\frac{1}{3}$ of the women. If there are 45 men and women on the team, how many women received medals?

(A) 5

(B) 6

(C) 10

(D) 11

39. If $m$ is greater than $n$, and $n$ is greater than 4, which of the following is LEAST?

(A) $\dfrac{1}{4m}$

(B) $\dfrac{1}{4n}$

(C) $\dfrac{1}{4 + m}$

(D) $\dfrac{1}{4 + n}$

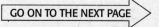
GO ON TO THE NEXT PAGE

40. If $\frac{1}{5}$ of a number is less than 20, the number must be

    (A) less than 4
    (B) equal to 4
    (C) greater than 4
    (D) less than 100

41. A six-story apartment building has $x$ apartments on each of its lower 3 floors and $y$ apartments on each of its upper 3 floors. If 3 people live in each apartment, how many people live in the building?

    (A) $3x + 3y$
    (B) $3x + 3y + 3$
    (C) $9x + 9y$
    (D) $3x + 3y + 18$

42. Joe spent 20% of his allowance on CDs. Then he spent 10% of what was left on a movie. After the movie, he was left with what percent of his original allowance?

    (A) 65%
    (B) 70%
    (C) 72%
    (D) 75%

43. Each of the $n$ members in an organization may invite up to 3 guests to a conference. What is the maximum number of members and guests who might attend the conference?

    (A) $n + 3$
    (B) $3n$
    (C) $3n + 4$
    (D) $4n$

USE THIS SPACE FOR FIGURING.

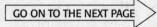
GO ON TO THE NEXT PAGE

44. A square rug with each side 4 meters long is placed on a square floor. If each side of the rug is one-third the length of one side of the floor, what is the area, in square meters, of the floor?

    (A) 144
    (B)  96
    (C)  64
    (D)  16

USE THIS SPACE FOR FIGURING.

45. Figure 3 is composed of six squares. How many rectangles are there in the figure?

    (A) 20
    (B) 18
    (C) 15
    (D) 12

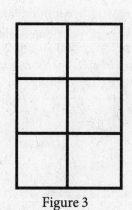

Figure 3

46. When Mr. Jones arrived at the grocery store, there were 8 cases of soda on the shelf. One case contained 11 cans of soda, and each of the others contained 6. If Mr. Jones bought all 8 cases, how many cans of soda did he purchase at this store?

    (A) 53
    (B) 54
    (C) 57
    (D) 59

47. When the sum of a set of numbers is divided by the average (arithmetic mean) of these numbers, the result is *j*. What does *j* represent?

    (A) Half of the sum of the numbers in the set
    (B) The average of the numbers in the set
    (C) Half of the average of the numbers in the set
    (D) The quantity of numbers in the set

IF YOU FINISH BEFORE TIME IS CALLED, YOU MAY CHECK YOUR WORK ON THIS SECTION ONLY. DO NOT TURN TO ANY OTHER SECTION IN THE TEST.    STOP

# SECTION 5
Time—30 Minutes

**Directions:** Write an essay on the following prompt on the paper provided. Your essay should NOT exceed two pages and must be written in ink. Erasing is not allowed.

**Prompt:** Technology makes the world smaller every day.

Do you agree or disagree with this statement? Use examples from history, literature, or your own personal experience to support your point of view.

_____

_____

_____

_____

_____

_____

_____

_____

_____

_____

_____

_____

_____

_____

_____

_____

_____

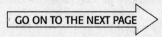

# ANSWER KEY

| **Section 1** | 33. B | 25. B | 20. C | 16. D |
|---|---|---|---|---|
| 1. D | 34. A | 26. A | 21. A | 17. A |
| 2. B | 35. D | 27. D | 22. C | 18. A |
| 3. B | 36. C | 28. B | 23. D | 19. B |
| 4. C | 37. D | 29. A | 24. A | 20. A |
| 5. A | 38. B | 30. B | 25. A | 21. C |
| 6. B | 39. D | 31. D | 26. C | 22. C |
| 7. D | 40. A | 32. B | 27. C | 23. C |
| 8. B | **Section 2** | 33. D | 28. D | 24. C |
| 9. A | 1. C | 34. B | 29. C | 25. D |
| 10. C | 2. D | 35. A | 30. B | 26. C |
| 11. A | 3. B | 36. C | 31. A | 27. B |
| 12. C | 4. B | 37. B | 32. C | 28. C |
| 13. A | 5. C | **Section 3** | 33. D | 29. B |
| 14. D | 6. D | 1. D | 34. D | 30. D |
| 15. D | 7. D | 2. C | 35. B | 31. B |
| 16. C | 8. B | 3. A | 36. D | 32. C |
| 17. D | 9. D | 4. B | **Section 4** | 33. B |
| 18. C | 10. C | 5. D | 1. C | 34. B |
| 19. B | 11. B | 6. B | 2. D | 35. D |
| 20. B | 12. C | 7. C | 3. B | 36. B |
| 21. A | 13. C | 8. A | 4. D | 37. B |
| 22. C | 14. D | 9. C | 5. B | 38. A |
| 23. A | 15. B | 10. B | 6. C | 39. A |
| 24. B | 16. C | 11. D | 7. D | 40. D |
| 25. D | 17. B | 12. B | 8. B | 41. C |
| 26. C | 18. D | 13. B | 9. D | 42. C |
| 27. A | 19. A | 14. D | 10. C | 43. D |
| 28. C | 20. D | 15. B | 11. C | 44. A |
| 29. B | 21. D | 16. D | 12. B | 45. B |
| 30. D | 22. D | 17. A | 13. D | 46. A |
| 31. D | 23. A | 18. A | 14. C | 47. D |
| 32. A | 24. C | 19. B | 15. D | |

# ISEE PRACTICE TEST 2: UPPER- AND MIDDLE-LEVEL: ASSESS YOUR STRENGTHS

Use the following tables to determine which topics and chapters you need to review most. If you need help with your essay, be sure to review Chapter 9: The Essay and Chapter 26: Writing Skills.

| Topic | Question |
|---|---|
| Verbal: Synonyms | Section 1, questions 1–20 |
| Verbal: Sentence Completions | Section 1, questions 21–40 |
| Quantitative Reasoning: Word Problems | Section 2, questions 1–22 |
| Quantitative Reasoning: Quantitative Comparison | Section 2, questions 23–37 |
| Reading Comprehension | Section 3, questions 1–36 |
| Mathematics Achievement | Section 4, questions 1–47 |

| Topic | Number of Questions on Test | Number Correct | If you struggled with these questions, study… |
|---|---|---|---|
| Verbal: Synonyms | 20 | | Chapters 7 and 24 |
| Verbal: Sentence Completions | 20 | | Chapter 4 |
| Quantitative Reasoning: Word Problems | 22 | | Chapters 10–14 and Chapter 25 |
| Quantitative Reasoning: Quantitative Comparison | 15 | | Chapter 5 |
| Reading Comprehension | 36 | | Chapter 8 |
| Mathematics Achievement | 47 | | Chapters 10–14 and Chapter 25 |

# ANSWERS AND EXPLANATIONS

## SECTION 1: VERBAL REASONING

### SYNONYMS

**1. D**

To desecrate is to commit a sacrilegious act—to defile.

**2. B**

To laud is to praise in a lavish manner (e.g. "The spectators lauded the efforts of the competing athletes.").

**3. B**

To avert is to prevent something from occurring (e.g, "The disaster was averted by the air-traffic controller.").

**4. C**

Piety is another word for religious faith.

**5. A**

Amoral means without "without moral code." Ethics are a kind of moral code, so unethical is the best choice here.

**6. B**

Candor means honesty—a "candid camera," for example, is one that shows real-life events.

**7. D**

Haughtiness means excessive pride—arrogance. (C), rudeness, might have been a tempting distractor, but rude people aren't necessarily haughty.

**8. B**

To verify means to prove something (e.g., "The existence of UFOs has never been verified.").

**9. A**

To deceive means to trick.

**10. C**

Look for secondary definitions—a fiction is a story that is untrue, so one possible meaning for fiction is falsehood (e.g., "His reputation was largely based on the fiction that he had fought in World War II.").

**11. A**

Something that's hardy is healthy (e.g., "a hardy troop of soldiers").

**12. C**

Something that's lyrical is like a singing voice—it's musical.

**13. A**

Use roots here—*meta* means change, and *morph* means shape. So the closest synonym is change.

**14. D**

To lament for someone or something is to grieve.

**15. D**

Something that's arid is dry (e.g., an arid desert). Word association could have worked here if you thought of *Arrid* the deodorant.

**16. C**

A perceptive person is observant—he or she is able to perceive things quickly and understand them.

**17. D**

An adamant person is convinced, resolute—stubborn (e.g., "Dave was adamant about his decision to buy a Range Rover™.").

**18. C**

Neutral people or parties are impartial. They don't take sides—they're unbiased.

**19. B**

Docile means tame (e.g., "The aggressive dog became docile in later life.").

**20. B**

Wariness means caution—if you're wary, you're apprehensive about a situation.

## SENTENCE COMPLETIONS

**21. A**

The clue words "come out at night" indicate that raccoons are nocturnal.

**22. C**

The two clue words "normally" and "usual" suggest that both blanks mean more or less the same—(C), amiable .. enthusiasm, works best here.

**23. A**

Death is a morbid subject, making (A) the best choice here.

**24. B**

You're looking for a contrast here; once a religious festival (B), the event is now commercialized.

**25. D**

A person who is constantly changing his views is described as flighty.

**26. C**

You're looking for a positive word for the first blank and a word meaning "deny" or "criticize" for

the second blank. (C), agility .. question, fits this description.

**27. A**

Predict a synonym for "guilt" here—(A), remorse, is the correct answer.

**28. C**

The first blank should mean "tiring," so rule out (A). The only choice that means "tired" for the second blank is (C), fatigued. So strenuous .. fatigued is the correct answer.

**29. B**

The phrase "not only . . . but . . ." indicates that the second word is slightly more extreme than the first. Since you're looking for negative-sounding words, (B), predictable .. absurd, fits best.

**30. D**

Predict a more extreme version of "respect" for the blank here; revered works best in this context.

**31. D**

The first blank here should express the writer's incredulity—after all, it's pretty amazing that Chinese silk showed up in Egypt. (D), incredible .. massive, best explains why this fact is so amazing.

**32. A**

"At first" should have clued you into the contrast here—the house seemed frightening, but later proved benign, or friendly.

**33. B**

You're looking for a contrast—once just a myth, UFO stories are now thought plausible or believable.

### 34. A

Again, there should be a contrast here—(A), sparse, means terse, brief, minimal, and verbose means excessively wordy.

### 35. D

The clue "charm his listeners" suggests a positive word here, such as (D), engaging.

### 36. C

Exhilarated best captures the mixture of fear and enjoyment suggested by the sentence—consistent with a first trip on a raft.

### 37. D

The key phrase here is "to equal and even—Wright's successes." So we're looking for a word meaning more than equal. Choice (D), surpass, works nicely.

### 38. B

"Weighing more than seventy tons" leads us to predict a word like large or gigantic for the first blank. The word "yet" sets up a contrast for the second blank. We want a word like small for the second blank. Only (B), gargantuan, and (D), prodigious, work for the first blank. Of these two options, only choice (B), small, works for the second blank. So (B) is correct.

### 39. D

We are looking for a word that covers the wide variety of trumpets described in this sentence. Look for a word that means "varied" among the answer choices. Choice (D), diverse, works best.

### 40. A

Take this two-blank sentence one word at a time. For the first blank, we're looking for a word that works

with "difficult to spot." Elusive, (A), and crafty, (B), are the only choices that work. For the second blank, we're looking for a word that sets up a contrast with "difficult to spot." Choice (A), confined, works here.

## SECTION 2: QUANTITATIVE REASONING

### WORD PROBLEMS

**1. C**

$$Q + 7 - 8 + 3 = 23$$
$$Q + 2 = 23$$
$$Q = 21$$

**2. D**

A kilogram is equal to 1,000 grams. Remember, *kilo* means 1,000. A kilometer, for example, equals 1,000 meters.

**3. B**

To solve this problem, you need to find a common denominator. In this case, the lowest common denominator is 36.

$$\frac{1}{9} + \frac{7}{12} + \frac{5}{6} = \frac{4}{36} + \frac{21}{36} + \frac{30}{36}$$
$$= \frac{55}{36}$$
$$= 1\frac{19}{36}$$

**4. B**

$$15\% \text{ of } 60 = (15\%)(60)$$
$$= (0.15)(60)$$
$$= 9$$

## 5.  C

To solve this problem, you first need to determine the limits of possible values for *a*:

$$a + 2 > 5$$
$$a > 3$$
$$a - 4 < 1$$
$$a < 5$$

So *a* is between 3 and 5. The only value from the answer choices that fits in the limits is (C), 4.

## 6.  D

To solve this equation, we first need to find the value of *x*.

$$2x + 4 = 26$$
$$2x = 22, \text{ so } x = 11.$$

Therefore, 11 + 4 = 15.

## 7.  D

The key to solving this problem is to take in the information one piece at a time. We're told that we have an equilateral hexagon. *Equilateral* means that all sides are equal. A hexagon has 6 sides. If we divide 6 into 42, we have the measure of one side: 7. So two sides would total 14.

## 8.  B

Angelo earns $2,000. Of this money, he spends 30% on rent. We can easily turn this information into an equation.

$$\text{Rent} = 30\% \text{ of } \$2,000$$
$$= (0.30)(\$2,000)$$
$$= \$600$$

## 9.  D

The eggs cost 16 cents apiece. We need to figure out how many eggs can make up for the cost of 6 new chickens or 58 dollars. In other words, how many times does 16 cents divide into 58 dollars. Set this problem up as you would any division problem, paying attention to decimal places.

$$0.16\overline{)58.00}$$

$$16\overline{)5800.0}^{362.5}$$

Since the famer cannot sell half of an egg, he must sell 363 eggs.

## 10. C

Notice the use of the word "rate" in this problem. Don't be fooled by the terms "fuel" and "miles"—this is a straightforward rate problem, and you want to set it up as such. Twelve gallons of fuel for 48 miles is the same as how many gallons for 60 miles?

$$\frac{12}{48} = \frac{x}{60}$$
$$48x = 12 \times 60$$
$$x = \frac{720}{48} = 15$$

## 11. B

To add mixed numbers, add the whole number parts and add the fraction parts. (Sometimes the sum of the fraction parts will be greater than 1, in which case you would need to make some adjustments.) To add the fraction parts, find a common denominator.

$$1\frac{6}{11} + 1\frac{7}{22} = 2 + \frac{6}{11} + \frac{7}{22}$$
$$= 2 + \frac{12}{22} + \frac{7}{22}$$
$$= 2\frac{19}{22}$$

**12. C**

Use the average formula:

$$\text{Average} = \frac{\text{Sum of the items}}{\text{Number of items}}$$

$$9 = \frac{\text{Sum}}{6}$$

$$\text{Sum} = 9 \times 6 = 54$$

**13. C**

Let's consider each answer choice. (A) gives us the value $\frac{2}{3}$. But we know that $x$ must be smaller than $\frac{1}{2}$, and since $\frac{2}{3}$ is not, we can eliminate it. (B) proposes 0.47, but $x$ must be smaller than $\frac{1}{3}$, and 0.47 is not. (C) gives us $\frac{1}{5}$, which is smaller than $\frac{1}{3}$ but larger than $\frac{1}{10}$—it fits the given criteria. Since there can only be one correct answer, there is no reason to check the last answer choice. Choice (D) is incorrect because $\frac{1}{20}$ is less than $\frac{1}{10}$ and $x$ can not be less than $\frac{1}{10}$.

**14. D**

The best way to solve this problem is to solve for $a$.

$$3a + 6a = 36$$

$$9a = 36$$

$$a = 4$$

**15. B**

The easiest way to solve this problem is to convert $\frac{1}{4}$ to a decimal, 0.25, and then multiply. Again, make sure that you remember to count your decimal places.

$$(0.72) \times (0.25) = 0.18$$

**16. C**

The easiest way to solve this problem is to break the diagram on the right into two rectangles. Then solve for each area and add them together.

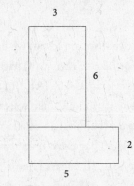

The area of the rectangle on top is $3 \times 6 = 18$. The area of the rectangle on bottom is $5 \times 2 = 10$. The total area is $18 + 10 = 28$.

**17. B**

First you need to break down 48 into its prime factors, and then you can determine how may *different* ones there are.

$$48 = 2 \times 24$$
$$= 2 \times 2 \times 12$$
$$= 2 \times 2 \times 2 \times 6$$
$$= 2 \times 2 \times 2 \times 2 \times 3$$

There are only two different prime factors for 48: 2 and 3.

**18. D**

Remember as you do this problem that a factor is a number that divides evenly into another number. Again, the easiest way to solve this problem is to consider each factor individually. (A) cannot be the answer because 3 is a factor of 36 and also 48. Ditto for (B), 6, and (C), 12. The answer must be (D), 18.

## 19. A

The formula for the volume of a cube is the length of a side cubed. We are told that the length of one side is 5. Five cubed equals 125, (A).

## 20. D

Doubling the rate that we are given, we have 2 hours and 30 minutes for Jake to review 60 pages. We know that the answer cannot be (A). But we need to figure out how long it will take Jake to review those final 10 pages. To do that, we can divide the rate it takes Jake to review 30 pages by 3; that will give us the rate it takes to read 10 pages. Then 1 hour and 15 minutes is the same as 75 minutes. A third of 75 is 25—we know it will take Jake 25 minutes to read 10 pages. Put it all together: 2 hours and 30 minutes plus 25 minutes gives us 2 hours and 55 minutes for Jake to read his history book.

## 21. D

If Mary types 12 words in 20 seconds, then she types 36 words in 60 seconds, or 1 minute. Thus, she types twice that, or 72 words, in 2 minutes.

## 22. D

Just substitute 8 for $r$ in the equation: $(8 + 4)^2 =$ $(12)^2 = 12 \times 12 = 144$.

## QUANTITATIVE COMPARISONS

## 23. A

Remember to compare, not calculate: There is no reason to look for common denominators and solve here. The $\frac{1}{2}$ in Column A is just slightly larger than the $\frac{2}{5}$ in Column B. Both columns contain $\frac{3}{4}$. The $\frac{7}{8}$ in Column A is also larger than the $\frac{7}{9}$ in Column

B, so overall, whatever the total value, Column A is larger than Column B.

## 24. C

Put the expressions in Column A and Column B in the same form so they are easy to compare. First, simplify the value under Column A. It's easy to multiply these fractions together because they cancel easily, giving us a final value of $\frac{1}{20}$, which in decimal form is 0.05. The columns are equal.

## 25. B

This problem is similar to the one above. First simplify the value under Column A, making sure that you cancel whenever possible. Under Column A we end up with the value $\frac{4}{5}$, which is less than 1. The value under Column B is $\frac{5}{4}$, which is greater than 1. So, the answer is (B).

## 26. A

The fastest way to solve this problem is to determine the value of $x$.

$$3x - 12 = 3x - 6x$$
$$-12 = -6x$$
$$2 = x$$

So $x$ equals 2. If you add 2 to $x$, you get 4, a value larger than the 2 in Column B. So Column A is larger.

## 27. D

The answer to this problem is (D). All we know about $x$ and $y$ is that both are positive. We don't know their relative values: We don't know if $x$ is greater than $y$ or vise versa. Consequently, we can't determine if adding the number 1 to the value of $x$ would make Column A greater, less than, or equal to the value under Column B. The answer here must therefore be (D).

**28. B**

Find the value of each column:

$$5\% \text{ of } (3 + 4) = 5\% \text{ of } 7$$
$$= (0.05)(7)$$
$$= 0.35$$
$$4\% \text{ of } (3 \times 4) = 4\% \text{ of } 12$$
$$= (0.04)(12)$$
$$= 0.48$$

**29. A**

The easiest way to solve this problem is to change the value under Column B, a fraction, into a decimal. Thus, $\frac{9}{20}$ is the same as $\frac{45}{100}$ or 0.45. Column A, with a value of 0.46, is larger than Column B.

**30. B**

This problem requires no math at all. You are given a certain amount of money—5 dollars. Can you buy more expensive items (32-cent stamps) or more cheap items (29-cent stamps) with this money? You can buy more of the cheaper items, so the answer must be Column B.

**31. D**

You're given that $x$ is between $\frac{8}{9}$ and $\frac{1}{2}$, and you're asked to compare $x$ to $\frac{2}{3}$. The fraction $\frac{2}{3}$ is between $\frac{8}{9}$ and $\frac{1}{2}$, but so are lots of other fractions, some less than $\frac{2}{3}$ and others greater than $\frac{2}{3}$. Column A could be greater than, equal to, or less than Column B, so the answer is (D).

**32. B**

This is another problem that takes no math at all. We are told that $x$ is negative. Before you start plugging in values for $x$, you should take a look at the expression under Column B: $(2x)(1x)$. If you multiplied these $x$'s together, whatever the value, the result would be positive. The value under Column A, however, would remain negative. Since a positive is always greater than a negative, the answer has to be (B).

**33. D**

Don't be fooled by the number 8 under Column B. Column A asks you to find the perimeter of an octagon with sides of equal length. The problem is, we don't know what those lengths are. One side could equal 1, in which case the answer would be (C). One side could be 2, in which case the answer would be (A). We already have two possibilities, which tells us that the correct answer must be (D).

**34. B**

The factors of 21 are 1, 3, 7, and 21. Of these only two are prime. Compare that to the value under Column B, 3, and the answer is (B).

**35. A**

Translate the expression into an equation: $\frac{5}{7}$ of $x$ is 35.

$$\frac{5}{7}x = 35$$
$$x = 35 \times \frac{7}{5}$$
$$x = 49$$

**36. C**

Remember the saying "A percent of B is equal to B percent of A"? If you do, then this question is a breeze. If not, you want to commit that rule to memory. In this case, 98% of 51 is $0.98 \times 51 = 49.98$, and 51% of 98 is 0.51 × 98 = 49.98. The columns are equal.

### 37. B

There are a few ways to solve this problem. The first is to actually calculate the math. Twenty percent of 42 is the same as (0.20)(42) or 8.4. The other way to do this problem is to realize that 20% of 42 is the same as taking $\frac{1}{5}$ of 42. We know that $\frac{1}{5}$ of 45 is 9, the value under Column B. But we want $\frac{1}{5}$ of 42, which will be less than 9. In either case, the answer must be (B).

## SECTION 3: READING COMPREHENSION

### LOG CABINS PASSAGE

The first passage is about log cabins and the era of their greatest popularity—a period from 1780 to 1850. The author describes early simple cabins and grand later ones and then discusses the factors that led to a decline in the log cabin's popularity, factors like the greater availability of hardware and building materials, the rising popularity of the Greek Revival style of house, and the spread of the railroads. The passage ends with a brief description of what happened to most log cabins as their heyday ended.

### 1. D

The Greek Revival style is described as becoming increasingly popular, "with [i.e., because of] its democratic roots in ancient Greece...." So the origins of the new style lay in the ancient democracy of Greece —a fact that might well have appealed to the citizens of a young democratic nation like the United States—and (D) is the best answer. The passage never suggests that there had been a general desire to replace log cabins, (A), and never mentions contemporary Greek architects, (B), or devoutly religious Americans, (C).

### 2. C

The first sentence says that "a great number of settlers forged westward." What word plugs in best for "forged"? (C)'s moved. Fled, (A), incorrectly implies that the settlers were running away from something; wandered, (B), implies that their movements were aimless, without purpose. Returned, (D), suggests that the settlers had already been out west, which makes little sense in context.

### 3. A

The author indicates that Greek Revival houses became more popular than log cabins for two reasons: the democratic roots of the Greek Revival style and the templed fronts of these houses, which faced the street. This last feature—that the fronts of Greek Revival houses faced the street—suggests that log cabins became less popular because they didn't always face the street, which makes (A) correct. The passage doesn't suggest that either style of house had indoor plumbing, (B), or that log cabins could not have glass windows, (C). And while log cabins may well have been built near lakes and rivers, (D), there's no suggestion that Greek Revival homes were not. So (A) is the correct answer.

### 4. B

The question stem's reference to limiting factors in the architecture of log cabins recalls sentence 6: "Climate and the proximity of the local forest no longer set architectural limits." What does this mean? It means that, with the new railroads bringing lumber and hardware to formerly isolated regions, a settler's choice of which house to build was no longer dictated by local weather and the distance to the nearest forest. (B) restates this latter point, and it's correct. (A) is incorrect because, unlike logs from the local forest, nails were not widely available. (C) and (D) bring up issues that aren't mentioned at all in the passage and so cannot be inferred.

**5. D**

The passage's final sentence notes that, after the 1850s, log structures housed livestock but "fewer and fewer people." So most log structures built after 1850 housed animals, (D).

**6. B**

Find the right answer by using the passage to answer the questions asked in the choices. (A) can be answered in lines 1–3; log cabins actually grew in popularity because settlers were moving west. (C) is answered in lines 10–12; the style's "democratic roots in ancient Greece and its templed front facing the street" were desirable. (D) can be answered in lines 3–6; log cabins grew from being primitive to being sophisticated, two-story houses. (B) is the answer because the author does not say log cabins have disappeared.

## PLAGUE PASSAGE

Next up is a passage about the plague, an epidemic that killed one-third of the people in Europe in the 13th and 14th centuries. The author says that, ironically, the plague brought about some beneficial changes in European society. One of these changes—the focal point of the passage—was in the medical profession. The plague created a shortage of doctors, allowing people with new ideas to enter the profession. In addition, having been failed by the old doctors with their Latin medical texts, ordinary people began clamoring for medical texts printed in everyday languages. These were eventually published, making medical knowledge more accessible to everyone.

**7. C**

As noted above, the primary focus of the passage is how at least one good thing came out of the terrible tragedy of the plague. (C) correctly restates this idea. (A) and (B) focus too narrowly on details mentioned in sentences 1 and 4. (D) is closer to the mark, but it too is a detail, not the larger focus of the passage.

**8. A**

Plug the choices into the sentence in question, and (A) is correct: The epidemic caused enormous changes in European society. The changes were needed, (B), but needed by the society, not by the plague itself. Accelerated, (C), means moved faster, which implies that the changes were already occurring before the plague. But the passage never suggests that this was so. Offered, (D), doesn't work at all.

**9. C**

Sentence 6 says that, when the plague created a shortage of doctors, "people with new ideas" rushed in to fill the void, bringing needed reform (sentence 3) to the medical profession. This suggests that, prior to the plague, the medical profession was in need of new ideas—sweeping changes—which makes (C) correct. The shortage of doctors, (A), occurred during and after the plague, not before it. As for (B), while sentence 5 says that universities were short on medical professors, there's no evidence that medical care was available only to students in the pre-plague years. And (D) distorts the final sentence, which says that people demanded medical texts printed in their own languages, not the language of Latin. This doesn't mean that, before the plague, medicine was only practiced in Latin-speaking countries. (Latin is, in fact, and was even then, a "dead" language, the language of the long-vanquished Roman Empire.)

**10. B**

Take another look at the last sentence of the passage. It says that medical texts gradually began to be published in everyday languages instead of in Latin, "making medical knowledge more accessible." You can infer from this that, after the 1300s, easy-to-read medical texts were probably more available to the general public, an idea restated in choice (B). The passage never indicates that a cure for the plague, (A), would soon be found (in fact, it would not be found for several centuries). As for (C), just because more medical texts were published in everyday languages after the plague doesn't mean that, a hundred years later, none were written in Latin. Finally, (D) is completely unsupported by the passage.

## 11. D

Are the author's points positive, negative, or neutral? The author talks about the negative effects of the plague, but he or she focuses more on the positive effects. The author says that medical knowledge became more accessible to people and that it led to medical reform. That rules out (A) and (B), leaving favorable and sensible. Next, think about how the passage would sound if you read it aloud. Does it sound as if the author expresses approval about the outcome of the plague (favorable), or does it sound as if he or she has based his argument on sound reasoning (sensible)? Although, the author recognizes that the plague had positive effects, he or she also points out the negative—one-third of the European population died. (D) is the better answer.

## 12. B

Try to find each of the choices in the passage. (A) is in lines 15–17; the author says new medical texts in everyday languages made "medical knowledge more accessible." (C) is in lines 10–12; people with new ideas took the place of doctors who died or fled during the plague. (D) is in lines 3–4. (B) is

the answer because it is not fully addressed in the passage. The author says in lines 15–17 that medical texts began appearing in languages other than Latin, but that doesn't mean more people did not learn Latin.

## ORIENTEERING PASSAGE

The fourth passage is about the sport of orienteering, in which competitors make their way across unfamiliar terrain using only a map and a compass. The author focuses on the notion that the most important element of orienteering is choosing a good route. Why? Because the shortest route from point A to point B is rarely the fastest or easiest way.

## 13. B

What defines orienteering, if not having a compass and a map? Orienteers have to "navigate their way cross-country along an unfamiliar course." Therefore, a hiker with a map and compass is NOT orienteering if she travels over a known, familiar route, and (B) is correct. (A) and (C) propose rules that are never mentioned in the passage. (D) describes an orienteer who takes the "crude" approach.

## 14. D

As sentence 2 puts it, "the most important question in orienteering is not compass bearing but choice of route," which eliminates (A) and makes (D) correct. While it is no doubt important to avoid hazardous terrain, (B), and to overcome obstacles quickly, (C), the passage places the highest priority on the choice of route.

## 15. B

The competitor in question climbs a mountain to take the most direct route, but sentences 3 and 4 say that this is "seldom the best" and that orienteers "tend to disdain" competitors who do so as crude and lacking intellectual finesse, or sophistication, (B). (A) is incorrect because the competitor's beeline approach will probably put him at a disadvantage in terms of both time and energy. The beeline approach may be stupid, but the author never says it's against the rules, (C), or that it can endanger other competitors, (D). So (B) is correct.

### 16. D

The passage never mentions running or backpacks, (A), swimming, (B), or setting up campsites, (C). So (D) must be correct. In fact, the final sentence of the passage notes that orienteers "are always making" quick calculations of the times and distances involved in various possible routes.

### 17. A

Look at the sentence "finesse" appears in. The author contrasts "intellectual finesse" with "beelining over obstacles," which means orienteers would rather use their minds before acting, so you know the answer's not (B). (C) is wrong, too, because "intellectual inefficiency" doesn't make sense. That leaves "skill" (ability) and "devotion" (dedication). (A) is the answer.

### 18. A

Questions about the author's attitude are generally asking about the tone of the passage. Are the author's points positive, negative, or neutral? The passage doesn't discuss downfalls or troubles orienteers might have, but it does talk about their "intellectual finesse" and the "quick calculation orienteers are always making." That rules out (B) and (C), leaving "respect" and "appreciative." Next, think about how the passage would sound if you read it aloud. Does

it sound as if the author is holding orienteers in high regard, or does it sound as if the author is showing gratitude to orienteers? (A) is the answer.

## NIGHT TERRORS PASSAGE

Next up is a passage about two psychological phenomena: first, nightmares, and second, something called night terrors. In the latter the sleeper, usually a child, wakes up in great fright with no memory of having dreamed. The passage begins with the statement that, while nightmares and night terrors used to be confused with each other, researchers now know they are two different phenomena. The rest of the passage focuses on night terrors, noting that they're not really dangerous and that parents should use common sense, taking precautions and not worrying unduly.

### 19. B

Two phenomena, long "confounded" under one heading, are now known to be separate things. The word in question, then, should mean confused, or mixed up, (B). None of the other words means anything remotely similar to "confounded."

### 20. C

The correct answer, (C), restates the first sentence of the passage. None of the other choices are suggested, not even (D), which is a distorted echo of the passage's final sentence. The author says that children suffering from night terrors should usually not be medicated. This is a far cry from saying that sleep researchers used to prescribe medication for such children but have recently stopped.

### 21. A

Sentence 2 says that a nightmare "is an actual, detailed dream." (A) correctly restates this fact.

No mention is made of dream fragments, (B), hallucinations, (C), or trances, (D).

## 22. C

What do we know about the parents of children who suffer from night terrors? That these parents themselves sometimes find their child's experience "horrifying" and that a child suffering from night terrors can make a parent "anxious." We can infer, then, that the parents find night terrors nearly as frightening as the children do, and (C) is correct. (A) is the opposite of what the author says. (B) makes an unwarranted leap; the passage never suggests that these parents also suffered night terrors when they were children. And the last sentence of the passage implies, if anything, that a doctor usually should not be consulted at all, rather than as soon as possible, (D).

## 23. D

The difference between nightmares and night terrors, (A), is defined in sentences 2 and 3. The question in (B) is answered in the second-to-last sentence of the passage. Sentence 3 notes that the child waking from a night terror does not remember dreaming, (C). This leaves (D) as correct, and indeed, the author merely advises a sleep schedule, never explaining why a sleep schedule helps reduce night terrors.

## 24. A

How would you answer this question in your own words? Lines 3 and 5 use contrast phrases: "On the one hand" and "On the other." Those are hints to where to find the difference between nightmares and night terrors. (B) is incorrect, and (C) and (D) are not addressed in the passage.

## NEANDERTHALS PASSAGE

This passage is about the Neanderthal, an early human that lived in Europe and Asia until about 35,000 years ago. The passage puts forth two ideas: first, that Neanderthals were physically very different from modern humans and second, that despite their reputation to the contrary, Neanderthals were probably quite intelligent. The passage concludes with a teaser: The disappearance of this capable creature mystifies and fascinates scientists and is "perhaps the most talked-about issue in human origins research today."

## 25. A

All four choices are physical attributes of the Neanderthal. In the author's description of Neanderthals, found in sentence 3, "massive limb bones" are the first item on the list. A "limb" is an arm or a leg, so you can infer from this that most Neanderthals had big arms, (A). You can't infer, however, that their legs were bowed, (C), because "bowed" implies shape, not size. The set of Neanderthal eyes, (A), and the breadth of their feet, (D), are never mentioned.

## 26. C

The opening sentence says that Neanderthals lived "throughout Europe and western Asia," which makes (C) correct. The passage never says what kind of dwellings they lived in, (A), how they hunted, (B), or whether they lived on all the continents, (D).

## 27. C

The author says that Neanderthals, unlike modern humans, had "massive limb bones," and "enormous physical strength." Modern humans, then probably have less physical strength than their Neanderthal cousins, and (C) is correct. No information is given on either species' eyesight, (A), sense of smell, (B), or amount of body hair, (D).

## 28. D

The only reference to what modern humans think of Neanderthals comes at the beginning of sentence 4: "yet despite the Neanderthals' reputation for low intelligence...." (D) is thus the correct inference.

## 29. C

The word "question" appears only once in the passage, in the final sentence. We know from the previous sentence that Neanderthals vanished or died out around 35,000 years ago. "The question of what became of the Neanderthals...." Therefore, (C) is correct. The questions of the Neanderthals' diet, (A), migratory patterns, (B), and origins, (D), are never raised in the passage.

## 30. B

Think about where you would most likely find this passage. (A) is incorrect because the passage contains nothing fictional. (C) is incorrect because it is unlikely an explorer would encounter Neanderthals, who lived at least 35,000 years ago. (D) is incorrect because the passage doesn't discuss nutrition, exercise, or any other health topic. (B) is the answer because the passage sticks to facts about Neanderthals.

## COYOTES PASSAGE

The final passage is about coyotes. The author's main focus is not on the behavioral habits of living coyotes, but rather on the evolution of the coyote as found in the fossil record. Both the coyote and the wolf, we learn, had a common ancestor living in North America as long as three million years ago.

One or two million years ago, the coyote and the wolf became separate species. As time passed, other species such as the mammoth and the saber-toothed tiger lived and became extinct, but the coyote endured—basically the same primitive animal, but still marvelously adaptable to its environment.

## 31. A

In most passages, the main idea is stated in the first or second sentence. Here the main idea becomes clear only at the end: that the coyote has endured for millions of years without evolving into a more advanced species. This point is restated in correct choice (A). (B) focuses on a detail, how other species came and went. But these species are described in order to provide a contrast with the coyote, which not only avoided extinction but did so without evolving. (C) has the same problem: The author's point is that, unlike other animals, the coyote did not change—it survived by staying the same. And (D) is a passing detail found in sentence 4—not significant enough to be the primary focus of the passage.

## 32. C

"Modern" dogs are mentioned only in the first sentence, which says that coyotes are "one of the most primitive of living dogs." This suggests that modern dogs are relatives of coyotes, as stated in (C). Dire wolves are extinct "canids"; we don't know from the passage whether they're related to modern dogs or not, but it's a pretty safe bet that modern dogs are not "direct descendants of dire wolves," as (A) suggests. Where modern dogs live, (B), is not mentioned, but again, common sense suggests they're found everywhere, not just in North America. The evolutionary flexibility of modern dogs (D) is not discussed in the passage.

**33. D**

Sentence 2 says that "a close relative of the contemporary coyote existed here two to three million years ago." The choice closest to this estimate is (D), and it's correct.

**34. D**

Why does the author mention mammoths and saber-tooth tigers? Because they lived and became extinct, while the ever-adaptable coyote endured. In other words, these species died out because they failed to adapt as the coyote did, and (D) is correct. Neither animal in question is described as a relative of the coyote, (A). Unlike wild horses, mammoths and tigers are not described as having left North America by land bridge, (C), but that's beside the point. These species died out because they couldn't adapt—as the coyote did. And the author never says that jackals hunted any species into extinction, (D).

**35. B**

Here's a word-in-context question that really requires you to know the meaning of the word—the word, in this case, being "galleon." Maybe you've come across it in pirate stories; a galleon is a kind of ship. So the idea that other horses "returned on galleons" means that horses, who had left North America by land bridge, returned to the continent when brought by ship, making (B) correct. None of the other choices picks up on the proper meaning of "galleon."

**36. D**

Try to find evidence in the passage supporting each of the choices. (A) is found in lines 11–13: "Mammoths ... and dire wolves ... came and went." (B) is in lines 13–14: "Native horses left the continent ... and others returned in galleons." (C) is in lines 8–10: "a division occurred in North America between the coyote and the wolf." (D) is the answer because it is incorrect. The passage says they have existed a long time, living even as "time passed, and glaciers advanced and receded" (lines 10–11) and that they have always adjusted to the changes (lines 17–18).

## SECTION 4: MATHEMATICS ACHIEVEMENT

**1. C**

$(x - 2)(x + 5)$ will equal 0 when either factor $(x - 2)$ or $(x + 5)$ is 0. That's when $x$ is 2 or –5.

**2. D**

Set up a proportion. Here 2 gallons for 875 square feet is the same as $x$ gallons for 4,375 square feet:

$$\frac{2}{875} = \frac{x}{4,375}$$
$$875x = 2 \times 4,375$$
$$875x = 8,750$$
$$x = \frac{8,750}{875} = 10$$

**3. B**

Use the formula for the area of a triangle:

$$\text{Area} = \frac{1}{2} \, (\text{base})(\text{height})$$
$$= \frac{1}{2} \, (4 \text{ in.})(6 \text{ in.}) = 12 \text{ sq. in.}$$

**4. D**

The sides of an equilateral triangle are equal in length, so $3x + 1$ and $x + 7$ are equal:

$$3x + 1 = x + 7$$
$$3x - x = 7 - 1$$
$$2x = 6$$
$$x = 3$$

Plug $x = 3$ back into either of the expressions, and you'll find that the length of each side is 10.

**5.  B**

Sixty-five times $10^2$ means 65 times 100, or 6,500. Thirty-one times $10^3$ means 31 times 1,000, or 31,000. Add 6,500 and 31,000 and 12 and you get 37,512.

**6.  C**

He lost 20% of $120,000, which is 0.20 times $120,000, or $24,000.

**7.  D**

The dog can run in a circular area with radius of 8 meters. Use the formula for the area of a circle:

$$\text{Area} = \pi(\text{radius})^2$$
$$= \pi(8 \text{ meters})^2$$
$$= 64\pi \text{ square meters}$$

**8.  B**

Rate is distance divided by time. So 328 miles divided by 4 hours is $\frac{328}{4} = 82$ miles per hour.

**9.  D**

If distance equals rate times time, then time equals distance divided by rate. Here the distance is 3,300 miles and the rate is 270 miles per hour. And 3,300 miles divided by 270 miles per hour is $\frac{3.300}{270} \oplus 12.22$ hours.

**10.  C**

Plug $a = 3$ and $b = 4$ into the expression:

$$a^2 + 2ab + b^2 = 3^2 + 2(3)(4) + 4^2$$
$$= 9 + 24 + 16$$
$$= 49$$

**11.  C**

Look what happens when you just add the equations as presented:

$$x - y = 5$$
$$\underline{4x + 6y = 20}$$
$$5x + 5y = 25$$

Now just divide both sides by 5, and you get $x + y = 5$.

**12.  B**

Break 726 down to its prime factorization by factoring out any prime factor you see one at a time:

$$726 = 2 \times 363$$
$$= 2 \times 3 \times 121$$
$$= 2 \times 3 \times 11 \times 11$$

The distinct prime factors are 2, 3, and 11. That's 3 distinct prime factors.

**13.  D**

Plug any odd number in for $n$ and evaluate the answer choices. If you take $n = 3$, you'll find that (A) is $-2(3) - 1 = -7$; (B) is $2(3) + 1 = 7$; (C) is $2(3) - 1 = 5$; and (D) is $4(3) = 12$. Only (D) is even.

**14.  C**

Six hours a day for 5 days is 30 hours; 30 hours is $30 \times 60 = 1,800$ minutes; and 1,800 minutes is $1,800 \times 60 = 108,000$ seconds.

**15.  D**

There are $4 \times 24 = 96$ hours in 4 days. Then 96 hours of snow at 3.5 inches per hour is $96 \times 3.5 = 336$ inches.

**16.  D**

Today Nicholas is $x$ years old and Billy is $3x$ years old. Five years ago Nicholas was $x - 5$ years old and Nicholas was $3x - 5$, so the sum of their ages was $(x - 5) + (3x - 5) = 4x - 10$.

### 17. A

If there are twice as many boys as girls, then $\frac{2}{5}$ of the students are boys and $\frac{1}{3}$ are girls. Two-thirds of 36 is 24.

### 18. A

The $\frac{1}{3}$ who drank soda only and the $\frac{2}{5}$ who drank juice only account for $\frac{1}{3} + \frac{2}{5} = \frac{5}{15} + \frac{6}{15} = \frac{11}{15}$ of the guests. The 16 who drank nothing therefore account for the other $\frac{4}{15}$. So you want to find out what number multiplied by $\frac{4}{15}$ will give you 16: $\frac{4}{15}x = 16$; $x = 16 \times \frac{15}{4} = 4 \times 15 = 60$.

### 19. B

You might think that $x$ has to be 2 and $y$ has to be 3, but in fact there's another pair of consecutive integers that have a product of 6: –3 and –2. So what you know is that either $x = 2$ and $y = 3$, or $x = -3$ and $y = -2$. All three statements are true in the first case (when $x$ and $y$ are positive), but only statement II is true in the second case (when $x$ and $y$ are negative).

### 20. A

She starts with $y$ cards. Giving away 5 to each of 3 friends means giving away $3 \times 5 = 15$, leaving her with $y - 15$. Receiving 2 from each of 3 friends means receiving $3 \times 2 = 6$, leaving her with $y - 15 + 6 = y - 9$.

### 21. C

For each coin the probability of tails is $\frac{1}{2}$. The combined probability is the product of the separate probabilities: $\frac{1}{2} \times \frac{1}{2} = \frac{1}{4}$.

### 22. C

Five minutes at 15 copies per minute is $5 \times 15 = 75$ copies. Then 75 out of 600 is $\frac{75}{600} = \frac{1}{8}$.

### 23. C

Simplify each inequality:

$$2(z - 3) > 6$$
$$2z - 6 > 6$$
$$2z > 6 + 6$$
$$2z > 12$$
$$z > 6$$
$$z + 4 < 15$$
$$z < 15 - 4$$
$$z < 11$$

So $z$ is between 6 and 11. The only answer choice that qualifies is (C), 7.

### 24. C

Three fiction books for every 8 nonfiction books means that 8 out of $3 + 8$, or $\frac{8}{11}$, of all the books are nonfiction. The 600 nonfiction books are $\frac{8}{11}$ of the number you're looking for, so:

$$\frac{8}{11}x = 600$$
$$x = 600 \times \frac{11}{8} = \frac{6,600}{8} = 825$$

### 25. D

(D) is impossible because if $x$ and $y$ were even and $z$ were odd, then $x + y$ would be even and $x + z$ would be odd.

### 26. C

If you call the passing grade $x$, then his second score was $x + 7$, and his third score was $x + 7 - 12 = x - 5$, which is 5 less than $x$.

## 27. B

If 70 percent are right-handed and the rest are left-handed, then $100 - 70 = 30$ percent are left-handed. Of that 30 percent, 70 percent have brown eyes. Seventy percent of 30 percent is $(0.70)(0.30) = 0.21$, or 21 percent.

## 28. C

Plug $q = 8$ and $r = 2$ into the definition:

$$q//r = (qr) - (q - r)$$
$$8//2 = (8 \times 2) - (8 - 2)$$
$$= 16 - 6 = 10$$

## 29. B

Plug $q = P$ and $r = 3$ into the definition:

$$q//r = (qr) - (q - r)$$
$$P//3 = (P \times 3) - (P - 3)$$
$$= 3P - P + 3$$
$$= 2P + 3$$

Set that equal to 11 and solve for $P$:

$$2P + 3 = 11$$
$$2P = 11 - 3$$
$$2P = 8$$
$$P = 4$$

## 30. D

Since $a$ is anything greater than 4, $a$ can be 8 or 16, so $b$ doesn't have to be 2—which eliminates statement I. But you do know that $b$ has to be positive, because $a$ is positive (it's greater than 4) and the product of $a$ and $b$ is positive (it's 16). Therefore the sum of $a$ and $b$ is positive, and statement II is true. And lastly, when $a = 8$, $b = 2$; and when $a = 16$, $b = 1$. Thus, $a$ is greater than $b$, and statement III is true.

## 31. B

The three angles have to add up to 180°, so:

$$x + 2x + 3x = 180$$
$$6x = 180$$
$$x = 30$$

## 32. C

$AB$ is half of $BC$, which is given as 12, so $AB = 6$, and $AC = 6 + 12 = 18$. $CD$ is half of $AC$, so $CD = 9$, and thus $AD = AB + BC + CD = 6 + 12 + 9 = 27$.

## 33. B

A square with an area of 36 square centimeters has sides of length 6 centimeters. Thus each side of the large square gets cut into thirds, and the whole large square gets divided into $3 \times 3 = 9$ smaller squares:

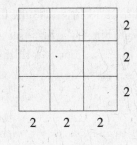

## 34. B

Just subtract 5 from both sides of the given equation:

$$x = 4y + 3$$
$$x - 5 = 4y + 3 - 5$$
$$= 4y - 2$$

## 35. D

Four for a dollar means 25 cents each. Selling them for 40 cents each means a profit of 15 cents on every orange sold. To get a total profit of $3.00, he must sell $\dfrac{\$3.00}{\$0.15} = \dfrac{300}{15} = 20$ oranges.

## 36. B

Each sale price is 90% of the original price. Sixty-three dollars is 90% of what?

$$0.90x = \$63$$

$$x = \$\frac{63}{0.90} = \$70$$

The original price of the wool sweater was $70. And $45 is 90% of what?

$$0.90y = \$45$$

$$y = \$\frac{45}{0.90} = \$50$$

The original price of the cotton sweater was $50. The difference was $20.

## 37. B

It took him a hour and a half to do the first one-third, so it will take him twice that long—or 3 hours—to do the remaining two-thirds. To finish by 11:00 P.M., he must resume by 8:00 P.M.

## 38. A

If there are twice as many men as women on the team, then two-thirds of the team members are men and one-third are women. One-third of 45 is 15, so there are 15 women. One-third of those 15 women received medals, so that's 5 women medal winners.

## 39. A

The four fractions you're comparing all have the same numerator (1) and they all have positive denominators, so the fraction with the least value must be the one with the greatest denominator. $m$ is greater than $n$, so $4m$ is greater than $4n$, and $4 + m$ is greater than $4 + n$. That eliminates (B) and (D). And since $m$ is greater than 4, $4m$ is greater than $4 + m$. Thus, (A) has the greatest denominator and therefore the least value.

## 40. D

Translate into algebra. If one-fifth of a number is less than 20, then:

$$\frac{1}{5}x < 20$$

$$x < 20 \times \frac{5}{1}$$

$$x < 100$$

## 41. C

The lower three floors have a total of $3x$ apartments. The upper three floors have a total of $3y$ apartments. That's a total of $3x + 3y$ apartments in the building. If there are 3 people in each apartment, then the total number of people is 3 times $(3x + 3y)$, or $9x + 9y$.

## 42. C

After spending 20% on CDs, Joe had 80% left. He then spent 10% of that, or 8% of the original amount, leaving
$100\% - (20\% + 8\%) = 72\%$.

## 43. D

If every one of the $n$ members invited 3 guests, that would be a total of $3n$ guests. $n$ members plus $3n$ guests adds up to $n + 3n = 4n$ attendees.

## 44. A

If each side of the 4-by-4 rug is one-third of the sides of the floor, then it's a 12-by-12 floor, which would have an area of 144 square meters.

### 45. B

Each of the six squares is a rectangle.

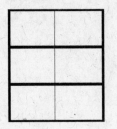

Plus there are these two rectangles:

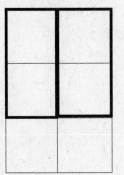

And these two:

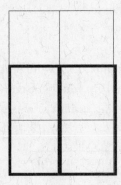

And these two:

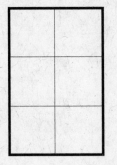

Plus this one:

And this one:

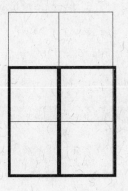

And lastly this one:

That's a total of 6 + 3 + 2 + 2 + 2 + 1 + 1 + 1 = 18.

## 46. A

Mr. Jones bought 1 case with 11 cans and 7 cases
with 6 cans each, so he bought $1(11) + 7(6)$ or $11 +$
$42 = 53$ cans of soda.

## 47. D

Translating complicated word problems into written
equations can help you figure out where to get
started. Solve for $j$ using the average formula:

$$\text{Average} = \frac{\text{Sum of terms}}{\text{Number of terms}}$$

Now, express this as $\dfrac{\text{Sum of terms}}{\text{Average of terms}} = \text{Number} = j.$

# CHAPTER 22: ISEE PRACTICE TEST 3: LOWER-LEVEL

## HOW TO TAKE THIS PRACTICE TEST

Before taking this practice test, find a quiet room where you can work uninterrupted for three hours. Make sure you have a comfortable desk and several No. 2 pencils.

Use the answer sheet provided to record your answers. (You can cut it out or photocopy it.)

Once you start this practice test, don't stop until you've finished. Remember—you can review any questions within a section, but you may not go backward or forward a section.

You'll find answer explanations following the test.

Good luck.

# ISEE Practice Test 3: Lower-Level Answer Sheet

**Remove (or photocopy) the answer sheet and use it to complete the practice test.**

Start with number 1 for each section. If a section has fewer questions than answer spaces, leave the extra spaces blank.

## SECTION 1

1 Ⓐ Ⓑ Ⓒ Ⓓ  9 Ⓐ Ⓑ Ⓒ Ⓓ  17 Ⓐ Ⓑ Ⓒ Ⓓ  25 Ⓐ Ⓑ Ⓒ Ⓓ  33 Ⓐ Ⓑ Ⓒ Ⓓ
2 Ⓐ Ⓑ Ⓒ Ⓓ  10 Ⓐ Ⓑ Ⓒ Ⓓ  18 Ⓐ Ⓑ Ⓒ Ⓓ  26 Ⓐ Ⓑ Ⓒ Ⓓ  34 Ⓐ Ⓑ Ⓒ Ⓓ
3 Ⓐ Ⓑ Ⓒ Ⓓ  11 Ⓐ Ⓑ Ⓒ Ⓓ  19 Ⓐ Ⓑ Ⓒ Ⓓ  27 Ⓐ Ⓑ Ⓒ Ⓓ  35 Ⓐ Ⓑ Ⓒ Ⓓ
4 Ⓐ Ⓑ Ⓒ Ⓓ  12 Ⓐ Ⓑ Ⓒ Ⓓ  20 Ⓐ Ⓑ Ⓒ Ⓓ  28 Ⓐ Ⓑ Ⓒ Ⓓ  36 Ⓐ Ⓑ Ⓒ Ⓓ
5 Ⓐ Ⓑ Ⓒ Ⓓ  13 Ⓐ Ⓑ Ⓒ Ⓓ  21 Ⓐ Ⓑ Ⓒ Ⓓ  29 Ⓐ Ⓑ Ⓒ Ⓓ  37 Ⓐ Ⓑ Ⓒ Ⓓ
6 Ⓐ Ⓑ Ⓒ Ⓓ  14 Ⓐ Ⓑ Ⓒ Ⓓ  22 Ⓐ Ⓑ Ⓒ Ⓓ  30 Ⓐ Ⓑ Ⓒ Ⓓ  38 Ⓐ Ⓑ Ⓒ Ⓓ
7 Ⓐ Ⓑ Ⓒ Ⓓ  15 Ⓐ Ⓑ Ⓒ Ⓓ  23 Ⓐ Ⓑ Ⓒ Ⓓ  31 Ⓐ Ⓑ Ⓒ Ⓓ  39 Ⓐ Ⓑ Ⓒ Ⓓ
8 Ⓐ Ⓑ Ⓒ Ⓓ  16 Ⓐ Ⓑ Ⓒ Ⓓ  24 Ⓐ Ⓑ Ⓒ Ⓓ  32 Ⓐ Ⓑ Ⓒ Ⓓ  40 Ⓐ Ⓑ Ⓒ Ⓓ

# right in section 1

# wrong in section 1

## SECTION 2

1 Ⓐ Ⓑ Ⓒ Ⓓ  9 Ⓐ Ⓑ Ⓒ Ⓓ  17 Ⓐ Ⓑ Ⓒ Ⓓ  25 Ⓐ Ⓑ Ⓒ Ⓓ  33 Ⓐ Ⓑ Ⓒ Ⓓ
2 Ⓐ Ⓑ Ⓒ Ⓓ  10 Ⓐ Ⓑ Ⓒ Ⓓ  18 Ⓐ Ⓑ Ⓒ Ⓓ  26 Ⓐ Ⓑ Ⓒ Ⓓ  34 Ⓐ Ⓑ Ⓒ Ⓓ
3 Ⓐ Ⓑ Ⓒ Ⓓ  11 Ⓐ Ⓑ Ⓒ Ⓓ  19 Ⓐ Ⓑ Ⓒ Ⓓ  27 Ⓐ Ⓑ Ⓒ Ⓓ  35 Ⓐ Ⓑ Ⓒ Ⓓ
4 Ⓐ Ⓑ Ⓒ Ⓓ  12 Ⓐ Ⓑ Ⓒ Ⓓ  20 Ⓐ Ⓑ Ⓒ Ⓓ  28 Ⓐ Ⓑ Ⓒ Ⓓ  36 Ⓐ Ⓑ Ⓒ Ⓓ
5 Ⓐ Ⓑ Ⓒ Ⓓ  13 Ⓐ Ⓑ Ⓒ Ⓓ  21 Ⓐ Ⓑ Ⓒ Ⓓ  29 Ⓐ Ⓑ Ⓒ Ⓓ  37 Ⓐ Ⓑ Ⓒ Ⓓ
6 Ⓐ Ⓑ Ⓒ Ⓓ  14 Ⓐ Ⓑ Ⓒ Ⓓ  22 Ⓐ Ⓑ Ⓒ Ⓓ  30 Ⓐ Ⓑ Ⓒ Ⓓ  38 Ⓐ Ⓑ Ⓒ Ⓓ
7 Ⓐ Ⓑ Ⓒ Ⓓ  15 Ⓐ Ⓑ Ⓒ Ⓓ  23 Ⓐ Ⓑ Ⓒ Ⓓ  31 Ⓐ Ⓑ Ⓒ Ⓓ  39 Ⓐ Ⓑ Ⓒ Ⓓ
8 Ⓐ Ⓑ Ⓒ Ⓓ  16 Ⓐ Ⓑ Ⓒ Ⓓ  24 Ⓐ Ⓑ Ⓒ Ⓓ  32 Ⓐ Ⓑ Ⓒ Ⓓ  40 Ⓐ Ⓑ Ⓒ Ⓓ

# right in section 2

# wrong in section 2

## SECTION 3

1 Ⓐ Ⓑ Ⓒ Ⓓ  9 Ⓐ Ⓑ Ⓒ Ⓓ  17 Ⓐ Ⓑ Ⓒ Ⓓ  25 Ⓐ Ⓑ Ⓒ Ⓓ  33 Ⓐ Ⓑ Ⓒ Ⓓ
2 Ⓐ Ⓑ Ⓒ Ⓓ  10 Ⓐ Ⓑ Ⓒ Ⓓ  18 Ⓐ Ⓑ Ⓒ Ⓓ  26 Ⓐ Ⓑ Ⓒ Ⓓ  34 Ⓐ Ⓑ Ⓒ Ⓓ
3 Ⓐ Ⓑ Ⓒ Ⓓ  11 Ⓐ Ⓑ Ⓒ Ⓓ  19 Ⓐ Ⓑ Ⓒ Ⓓ  27 Ⓐ Ⓑ Ⓒ Ⓓ  35 Ⓐ Ⓑ Ⓒ Ⓓ
4 Ⓐ Ⓑ Ⓒ Ⓓ  12 Ⓐ Ⓑ Ⓒ Ⓓ  20 Ⓐ Ⓑ Ⓒ Ⓓ  28 Ⓐ Ⓑ Ⓒ Ⓓ  36 Ⓐ Ⓑ Ⓒ Ⓓ
5 Ⓐ Ⓑ Ⓒ Ⓓ  13 Ⓐ Ⓑ Ⓒ Ⓓ  21 Ⓐ Ⓑ Ⓒ Ⓓ  29 Ⓐ Ⓑ Ⓒ Ⓓ  37 Ⓐ Ⓑ Ⓒ Ⓓ
6 Ⓐ Ⓑ Ⓒ Ⓓ  14 Ⓐ Ⓑ Ⓒ Ⓓ  22 Ⓐ Ⓑ Ⓒ Ⓓ  30 Ⓐ Ⓑ Ⓒ Ⓓ  38 Ⓐ Ⓑ Ⓒ Ⓓ
7 Ⓐ Ⓑ Ⓒ Ⓓ  15 Ⓐ Ⓑ Ⓒ Ⓓ  23 Ⓐ Ⓑ Ⓒ Ⓓ  31 Ⓐ Ⓑ Ⓒ Ⓓ  39 Ⓐ Ⓑ Ⓒ Ⓓ
8 Ⓐ Ⓑ Ⓒ Ⓓ  16 Ⓐ Ⓑ Ⓒ Ⓓ  24 Ⓐ Ⓑ Ⓒ Ⓓ  32 Ⓐ Ⓑ Ⓒ Ⓓ  40 Ⓐ Ⓑ Ⓒ Ⓓ

# right in section 3

# wrong in section 3

## SECTION 4

1 Ⓐ Ⓑ Ⓒ Ⓓ  9 Ⓐ Ⓑ Ⓒ Ⓓ  17 Ⓐ Ⓑ Ⓒ Ⓓ  25 Ⓐ Ⓑ Ⓒ Ⓓ  33 Ⓐ Ⓑ Ⓒ Ⓓ
2 Ⓐ Ⓑ Ⓒ Ⓓ  10 Ⓐ Ⓑ Ⓒ Ⓓ  18 Ⓐ Ⓑ Ⓒ Ⓓ  26 Ⓐ Ⓑ Ⓒ Ⓓ  34 Ⓐ Ⓑ Ⓒ Ⓓ
3 Ⓐ Ⓑ Ⓒ Ⓓ  11 Ⓐ Ⓑ Ⓒ Ⓓ  19 Ⓐ Ⓑ Ⓒ Ⓓ  27 Ⓐ Ⓑ Ⓒ Ⓓ  35 Ⓐ Ⓑ Ⓒ Ⓓ
4 Ⓐ Ⓑ Ⓒ Ⓓ  12 Ⓐ Ⓑ Ⓒ Ⓓ  20 Ⓐ Ⓑ Ⓒ Ⓓ  28 Ⓐ Ⓑ Ⓒ Ⓓ  36 Ⓐ Ⓑ Ⓒ Ⓓ
5 Ⓐ Ⓑ Ⓒ Ⓓ  13 Ⓐ Ⓑ Ⓒ Ⓓ  21 Ⓐ Ⓑ Ⓒ Ⓓ  29 Ⓐ Ⓑ Ⓒ Ⓓ  37 Ⓐ Ⓑ Ⓒ Ⓓ
6 Ⓐ Ⓑ Ⓒ Ⓓ  14 Ⓐ Ⓑ Ⓒ Ⓓ  22 Ⓐ Ⓑ Ⓒ Ⓓ  30 Ⓐ Ⓑ Ⓒ Ⓓ  38 Ⓐ Ⓑ Ⓒ Ⓓ
7 Ⓐ Ⓑ Ⓒ Ⓓ  15 Ⓐ Ⓑ Ⓒ Ⓓ  23 Ⓐ Ⓑ Ⓒ Ⓓ  31 Ⓐ Ⓑ Ⓒ Ⓓ  39 Ⓐ Ⓑ Ⓒ Ⓓ
8 Ⓐ Ⓑ Ⓒ Ⓓ  16 Ⓐ Ⓑ Ⓒ Ⓓ  24 Ⓐ Ⓑ Ⓒ Ⓓ  32 Ⓐ Ⓑ Ⓒ Ⓓ  40 Ⓐ Ⓑ Ⓒ Ⓓ

# right in section 4

# wrong in section 4

# SECTION 1

Time—20 Minutes

34 Questions

This section consists of two different types of questions. There are directions for each type.

Each of the following questions consists of one word followed by four words or phrases. Select the one word or phrase whose meaning is closest to the word in capital letters.

1. DECLINE:

(A) decrease

(B) promote

(C) delete

(D) agree

2. DELICATE:

(A) strong

(B) fragile

(C) low

(D) delicious

3. JUBILEE:

(A) confidence

(B) chaos

(C) design

(D) festival

4. LIBERATE:

(A) release

(B) work

(C) chase

(D) hope

5. TRANSFORM:

(A) open

(B) submit

(C) change

(D) keep

6. COLLIDE:

(A) forget

(B) crash

(C) amplify

(D) plan

7. PROCLAIM:

(A) behave

(B) preclude

(C) submit

(D) announce

8. SYMPATHY:

(A) understanding

(B) harmony

(C) affection

(D) responsibility

9. INVENTION:

(A) interpretation

(B) party

(C) delegation

(D) creation

10. AUTHORITY:

(A) expert

(B) respect

(C) bravery

(D) rivalry

GO ON TO THE NEXT PAGE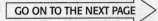

11. ILLUSTRATE:

    (A) cover
    (B) draw
    (C) simulate
    (D) waste

12. COMMOTION:

    (A) happiness
    (B) trick
    (C) uproar
    (D) collaboration

13. EXHAUSTED:

    (A) clumsy
    (B) tired
    (C) accountable
    (D) excited

14. TREAD:

    (A) scatter
    (B) help
    (C) alarm
    (D) walk

15. MENTOR:

    (A) symbol
    (B) artist
    (C) collector
    (D) counselor

16. REACTION:

    (A) selection
    (B) response
    (C) care
    (D) achievement

17. DWINDLE:

    (A) ridicule
    (B) thwart
    (C) shrink
    (D) tarnish

**Directions:** Select the word(s) that best fit the meaning of each sentence.

18. Although Mrs. Brown had taught long division to her students numerous times, she decided to take the time to _____ it once more.

    (A) admonish
    (B) request
    (C) explain
    (D) employ

19. Keesha's _____ nature would not allow her to ignore others who were feeling sad or lonely.

    (A) terse
    (B) intellectual
    (C) secure
    (D) compassionate

20. The toddler was so _____ that he often hid behind his mother's legs when introduced to strangers.

    (A) hyper
    (B) timid
    (C) young
    (D) disobedient

21. Alex often felt _____ after earning a high score on a test.

    (A) distressed
    (B) proud
    (C) helpless
    (D) intimidated

GO ON TO THE NEXT PAGE

22. The low, gray clouds made the sky look _____.

    (A) trite
    (B) ominous
    (C) intentional
    (D) luminous

23. Judy noticed that the native vegetation created a _____ over the swamp.

    (A) canopy
    (B) hazard
    (C) reef
    (D) lagoon

24. Ling needed to win one more match in order to be the _____ of the tournament.

    (A) creator
    (B) center
    (C) choice
    (D) champion

25. Phoebe was _____ after she finished running the Boston Marathon.

    (A) conservative
    (B) fortunate
    (C) jubilant
    (D) confused

26. Jeff spilled grape juice on his essay, but it wasn't a big deal since he could just print out a _____ copy.

    (A) duplicate
    (B) creative
    (C) symbolic
    (D) previous

27. A _____ summer day for the young mother and her son included a two-mile walk around the neighborhood.

    (A) naïve
    (B) typical
    (C) confidential
    (D) dire

28. Even though Mischa was guilty, she tried to _____ it.

    (A) tell
    (B) shout
    (C) propose
    (D) deny

29. Highway traffic was _____ due to the accident up ahead.

    (A) tight
    (B) stalled
    (C) reinforced
    (D) fatigued

30. The police officer told Clay he needed to _____ his speed on the road.

    (A) simplify
    (B) join
    (C) reduce
    (D) practice

31. In order to do well in school, the football player had to _____ his time between his practice and his studies.

    (A) balance
    (B) entertain
    (C) connect
    (D) perform

GO ON TO THE NEXT PAGE

32. Allison left a note on the counter to _____ her father to buy more milk.

    (A) confront
    (B) urge
    (C) taunt
    (D) remind

33. The puppy looked _____ when he realized he was going to be left behind.

    (A) relieved
    (B) dejected
    (C) hungry
    (D) excited

34. The _____ solution to a problem takes both sides into account.

    (A) incredible
    (B) malicious
    (C) ideal
    (D) unexpected

# SECTION 2

Time—35 Minutes
38 Questions

---

In this section there are four possible answers after each question. Choose which one is best. You may use the blank space at the right of the page for scratch work.

Note: Figures are drawn with the greatest possible accuracy, UNLESS stated "Not Drawn to Scale."

---

1. If $8 - x = 4$, and $10 + y = 12$, then $x - y =$

   (A) 2

   (B) 3

   (C) 4

   (D) 5

USE THIS SPACE FOR FIGURING.

2. Twenty students brought animals to school for pet day. Eight students brought dogs, four students brought birds, two brought cats, and the rest brought other animals. What fraction of the students brought other animals?

   (A) $\dfrac{3}{10}$

   (B) $\dfrac{6}{14}$

   (C) $\dfrac{10}{12}$

   (D) $\dfrac{3}{20}$

3. $8 \times 2 \times 6 \times 2$ is equal to the product of 16 and

   (A) 4

   (B) 8

   (C) 12

   (D) 16

4. Jennifer and José each swam five laps in 15 minutes. At the same rate of speed, how long would they need in order to swim 35 laps?

   (A) 35 minutes

   (B) 75 minutes

   (C) 105 minutes

   (D) 175 minutes

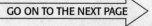
GO ON TO THE NEXT PAGE

5. A square has a perimeter of 16. What is the length of one side?

   (A) 2

   (B) 4

   (C) 6

   (D) 8

6. Which of the following is the smallest?

   (A) 0.0005

   (B)  0.005

   (C)   0.05

   (D)    0.5

7. Which of the following is equal to two-thirds?

   (A) $\dfrac{4}{12}$

   (B) $\dfrac{6}{12}$

   (C) $\dfrac{10}{15}$

   (D) $\dfrac{12}{15}$

8. Which fruit is included in the shaded section of Figure 1?

   (A) Apples

   (B) Peaches

   (C) Grapes

   (D) Bananas

9. Which of the following numbers is NOT a prime factor of 90?

   (A) 2

   (B) 3

   (C) 5

   (D) 9

USE THIS SPACE FOR FIGURING.

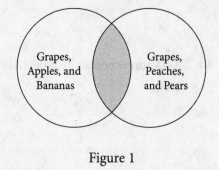

Figure 1

10. In a semester of 40 school days, Mrs. Alvarez was out sick twice. What percent of the time was she out sick?

    (A)   3 percent
    (B)   4 percent
    (C)   5 percent
    (D)  10 percent

11. To which number is the arrow pointing in Figure 2?

    (A)  $\dfrac{3}{8}$

    (B)  $3\dfrac{3}{8}$

    (C)  $3\dfrac{2}{4}$

    (D)  $3\dfrac{5}{8}$

12. In the Venn diagram in Figure 3, the shaded region shows people who drive

    (A)  cars and trucks
    (B)  trucks and motorcycles
    (C)  cars and motorcycles
    (D)  cars, trucks, and motorcycles

13. The record for the 100-yard dash was 13.71 seconds. Andrew beat the record by a tenth of a second. What was Andrew's time?

    (A)  13.61 seconds
    (B)  13.72 seconds
    (C)  13.82 seconds
    (D)  14.71 seconds

USE THIS SPACE FOR FIGURING

Figure 2

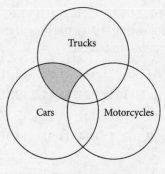

Figure 3

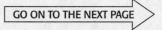

GO ON TO THE NEXT PAGE

14. During a 24-hour day, Shannon's cat sleeps $\frac{5}{6}$ of the time. How many hours does the cat sleep?

(A) 16 hours

(B) 18 hours

(C) 20 hours

(D) 22 hours

15. Kurt has four boxes. He wants to use the box with the smallest volume. Which box should Kurt use?

(A) 2" high × 3" wide × 4" long

(B) 2" high × 4" wide × 5" long

(C) 3" high × 4" wide × 5" long

(D) 4" high × 5" wide × 6" long

16. The populations of four small towns are 11,361, 11,924, 12,102, and 11,642. Which of the following shows the populations in order of smallest to largest?

(A) 11,361, 11,642, 11,924, 12,102

(B) 11,361, 11,924, 11,642, 12,102

(C) 11,642, 11,924, 11,361, 12,102

(D) 12,102, 11,624, 11,924, 11,361

17. Which of these numbers is equal to $\frac{65}{100}$?

(A) 0.065

(B) 0.65

(C) 6.5

(D) 65

18. Look at this series: 1, 3, 7, 15, 31, 63, …. What number comes next?

(A) 64

(B) 126

(C) 127

(D) 133

USE THIS SPACE FOR FIGURING.

19. Christopher is nine times the age of his 4-year-old son. How old is Christopher?

    (A) 30 years old
    (B) 32 years old
    (C) 34 years old
    (D) 36 years old

20. Darby was making a fruit smoothie. The ingredients included 15 percent yogurt, 40 percent ice, and 10 percent bananas. The only other thing she put in was frozen strawberries. What fractional part of the smoothie was made up of strawberries?

    (A) $\dfrac{7}{20}$

    (B) $\dfrac{55}{100}$

    (C) $\dfrac{13}{20}$

    (D) $\dfrac{65}{100}$

21. What place does the 5 take in 23.654?

    (A) Tenths
    (B) Hundredths
    (C) Thousandths
    (D) Ten-thousandths

22. Ms. Campton's classroom is 15 feet long and 22 feet wide. What is the area of her classroom?

    (A)  37 square feet
    (B)  74 square feet
    (C) 300 square feet
    (D) 330 square feet

USE THIS SPACE FOR FIGURING.

GO ON TO THE NEXT PAGE

23. The O'Malleys have a rectangular pool that is 16' long and 8' wide. Their next-door neighbors want to build a congruent pool. What measurements will the neighbors' pool have?

    (A)  8' × 8'
    (B)  8' × 16'
    (C)  24' × 2'
    (D)  16' × 16'

24. Casey makes a 30 percent profit for every sale she makes selling cosmetics. If she sells $300 worth of cosmetics, how much money will she make?

    (A)  $30
    (B)  $90
    (C)  $100
    (D)  $200

25. Which of the following does NOT equal $\frac{1}{4}$?

    (A)  $\frac{2}{8}$
    (B)  $\frac{3}{12}$
    (C)  $\frac{4}{16}$
    (D)  $\frac{8}{20}$

26. Approximately how long is the drive from point A to point B in Figure 4?

    (A)  12 miles
    (B)  14 miles
    (C)  16 miles
    (D)  20 miles

USE THIS SPACE FOR FIGURING.

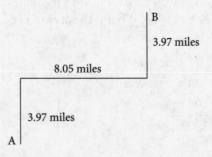

Figure 4

27. Cecile received $10 as an allowance. She spent $1.15 on ice cream and $3.49 on a magazine. How much does Cecile have left?

    (A) $4.64
    (B) $5.36
    (C) $6.51
    (D) $8.85

28. The school bus can hold 50 children. Which two classes can use the school bus for their field trip?

    (A) A class of 14 and a class of 32
    (B) A class of 15 and a class of 36
    (C) A class of 25 and a class of 26
    (D) A class of 30 and a class of 25

29. Rover's dog food costs $19.85 for a 20-pound bag. Trixie's cat food costs $9.24 for a 10-pound bag. Which of the following costs more?

    (A) One bag of dog food
    (B) Two bags of cat food
    (C) One bag of dog food and two bags of cat food cost the same.
    (D) The answer cannot be determined from the information given.

30. In a grocery cart, there is an equal number of vegetables, fruits, and breads. How many items could be in the cart?

    (A) 14
    (B) 38
    (C) 42
    (D) 56

31. Which transformation has been applied to the shape in Figure 5?

    (A) A reflection
    (B) A slide
    (C) A turn
    (D) A slide followed by a turn

USE THIS SPACE FOR FIGURING.

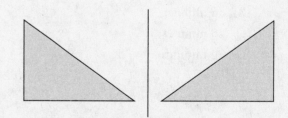

Figure 5

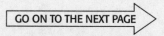

GO ON TO THE NEXT PAGE

32. Libby types 75 words per minute. How many words does she type per second?

   (A) 0.75
   (B) 1.25
   (C)  2
   (D) 7.5

33. In a geography class of 24 students, each student had to select a state on which to give a three-minute report. How long did the presentations last in total?

   (A) 1 hour 6 minutes
   (B) 1 hour 12 minutes
   (C) 1 hour 15 minutes
   (D) 1 hour 30 minutes

34. If the shaded section of the circle in Figure 6 signifies 850 types of flowers, how many flowers could the unshaded section represent?

   (A) 750
   (B) 800
   (C) 850
   (D) 900

35. Rebecca, Ian, and Clare were driving at the same speed. It took Rebecca 20 minutes to drive 15 miles. How long did it take Ian to drive 30 miles?

   (A) 40 minutes
   (B) 50 minutes
   (C) 60 minutes
   (D) 70 minutes

USE THIS SPACE FOR FIGURING.

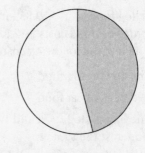

Figure 6

36. In a jar, there are equal numbers of red, green, and yellow marbles. Which of the following could be the number of marbles in the jar?

    (A) 35
    (B) 47
    (C) 58
    (D) 72

37. In a survey of 45 students, twice as many students preferred dogs to cats than preferred cats to dogs. If all students preferred either a dog or a cat, how many people preferred dogs?

    (A) 15
    (B) 20
    (C) 25
    (D) 30

38. Which of these is a whole number greater than 15?

    (A)   14
    (B) 15.5
    (C) $16\frac{1}{2}$
    (D)   18

USE THIS SPACE FOR FIGURING.

# SECTION 3

Time—25 Minutes
25 Questions

---

**Read each passage carefully and then answer the questions about it. For each question, decide on the basis of the passage which one of the choices best answers the question.**

---

Whale sharks (*Rhincodon typus*) are not whales and they are not mammals. They are the largest fish in the world. An average whale shark is around
Line 25 feet long, but they can reach up to 40 feet long.
(5) As with most sharks, the females are larger than the males.

You would think that with such a massive body this shark would be a fierce predator, but this mammoth fish is quite mild-mannered. It likes its
(10) solitude. Its mouth, which looks quite threatening, can open up to four feet wide and has about 310 rows of teeth, or about 3,000 teeth in all. The interesting thing is, this gentle giant doesn't even really use the teeth. Instead, it filters plankton and
(15) krill through its gills for nourishment by simply opening its enormous mouth to take in a large amount of water. The plankton stay in the mouth for nourishment while the water strains through gills in the side of the mouth. Even though a whale
(20) shark has a huge body, its gullet is relatively small. So while a whale shark could fit larger food into its mouth, it would not be able to swallow it.

Whale sharks are quite beautiful. Their back and
(25) sides are a reddish or greenish-brown. The top of the body has white or yellowish spots and stripes of varying sizes, and the underside is whitish or yellowish-white. A diver looking for such beauty has nothing to fear: Whale sharks are harmless to
(30) people, and if met by a diver, would probably ignore him completely. They live in the open seas all over the world, preferring to stay in areas close to the equator for the mild temperatures. They reach adulthood at 25 to 30 years of age, and they may
(35) live to be 100 years old.

1. The purpose of this passage is to
   (A) explain why whale sharks are harmless to people
   (B) explain why whale sharks are fish instead of mammals
   (C) describe whale sharks
   (D) explain how divers should deal with whale sharks

2. Most female sharks are
   (A) larger than the males
   (B) more beautiful than the males
   (C) more dangerous than the males
   (D) smaller than the males

3. What is a predator?
   (A) A fish
   (B) A hunter
   (C) A mammal
   (D) A gentle giant

4. Which of the following is NOT true about whale sharks?
   (A) They use all 3,000 teeth.
   (B) They have mouths that can open up to four feet wide.
   (C) They cannot swallow a large amount of food.
   (D) They eat mostly plankton and krill.

GO ON TO THE NEXT PAGE

5. If a scuba diver came across a whale shark, the whale shark would probably

   (A) swim away

   (B) open its enormous mouth

   (C) keep its eye on the diver

   (D) pay no attention to the diver

   There is nothing I like so well on a summer day as to hear the ding-ding song of the ice cream truck as it's coming around the corner. That tune of "Do
*Line* Your Ears Hang Low" makes my heart jump. I race
(5) out the door to catch the truck before I miss it, but not before grabbing some change from the kitchen counter that my parents have left. It's something to do—something to cool me off—and it's the highlight of a typical lazy day.
(10) Once I catch the truck, I've got all the time in the world to hem and haw about what to get. I like to read through the entire side-of-the-truck menu, chatting with the girl behind the counter. I usually like an orange push-up, though occasionally I'll get
(15) an ice cream sandwich. I have to eat it slowly enough to enjoy it, but fast enough so that it doesn't drip down my arm. Finding this balance is tricky, and sometimes depends on whether the sky is cloudy or clear.
(20) Lots of my neighbors race out of their houses the way I do, hoping to get there in time. I'm usually first since my house is the closest to the corner, and if I can catch the truck, then they are usually all safe. Often, though, if I miss it, they
(25) miss it too. If that's the case, imagine how disappointed I am. If there's no change to grab from the counter or if the truck is going too fast, I get outside just in time to see its taillights turn off my street. On those days, I'm not allowed to go
(30) that far to catch it. But when I do make it in time, that ice cream song stays with me for the rest of the day.

6. The purpose of the passage is to

   (A) challenge the reader to run to the ice cream truck

   (B) prove that ice cream is the best treat on a summer day

   (C) describe a summer treat

   (D) teach the reader a new song

7. What does it mean to "hem and haw"?

   (A) To take one's time in choosing

   (B) To buy more than one thing

   (C) To halt

   (D) To choose quickly

8. This passage is written in the

   (A) first person

   (B) second person

   (C) third person

   (D) fourth person

9. All of the following are true EXCEPT

   (A) the ice cream truck makes this person feel happy

   (B) this person is not allowed to leave the street where she lives

   (C) this person always gets an orange push-up

   (D) other people in the neighborhood enjoy the ice cream truck too

10. The main character is probably a

    (A) baby

    (B) toddler

    (C) parent

    (D) child

In May, Bailey moved into a new house. His large, fenced-in yard had potential, but the grass needed to be weeded and some flowers needed to be
*Line* planted. Bailey invited some friends to his house to
(5) help. He provided good music, plenty of snacks, and cold drinks. Everyone was amazed how much they were able to accomplish in that one day!

Bailey and Nolan started by weeding the front yard. Then they planted ferns and marigolds
(10) underneath the olive tree. They planted a bleeding heart vine and some red impatiens along the front of the fence. Bailey left plenty of room between the impatiens for the roses he would plant in the fall.

Janet focused on the side of the back porch. She
(15) filled some holes with dirt, and then she hoed the ground to make it level. She alternated planting gardenias and black-eyed Susans. She knew that gardenia blooms would smell lovely, and the bright yellow flowers would be pleasing to the eye.
(20) Together these plants made an attractive garden bed.

Meanwhile, Christina and Akiko worked along the back of the porch. They laid 10 large stepping stones in even spaces, and in between each stone, planted red, orange, yellow, and pink purslane
(25) ground cover. They knew that the plants would grow all around the stones to create a charming walkway.

Lilia and Nathan cleared weeds along the whole right-side fence. This was back-breaking
(30) work, but the weeds had to go! Then they planted red bougainvillea and blue plumbago bushes. There was still space to plant some smaller annuals, but Bailey would have to do that another day.
(35) After hours of work in the hot sun, the friends were exhausted. They spent the rest of the afternoon resting, talking, and laughing on the porch, surrounded by the results of their hard work. Thanks to the help of so many friends,
(40) Bailey's new house looks loved.

11. In paragraph 1, what does it mean that the yard had potential?

(A) There was the possibility that the yard would look good.

(B) The yard was full of weeds and needed work.

(C) The yard had no flowers.

(D) Someone had been taking care of the yard.

12. Bailey wants his yard to look

(A) unusual

(B) busy

(C) charming

(D) exhausting

13. Bailey and Nolan

(A) weeded the backyard

(B) planted an olive tree

(C) planted roses

(D) planted ferns and marigolds

14. What did Janet do first?

(A) She planted gardenias

(B) She planted black-eyed Susans

(C) She smoothed the ground

(D) She filled in some holes

15. Lilia and Nathan did all of the following EXCEPT

(A) plant some small annuals

(B) plant bougainvillea

(C) plant plumbago bushes

(D) pull out weeds

GO ON TO THE NEXT PAGE

"Come on, come on," you think. "I can see the top!" You're almost there. The top. The summit. Your goal. The sun is beating down on your back *Line* and you are there, in the moment, looking upward.
(5) Whatever you do, you cannot look down. Leg muscles shaking, fingertips clutching their hold, you think, "I can do this!"

This is rock climbing at its best. There's the challenge to face, the fear to overcome, the
(10) muscles to test, and finally, the exhilaration to feel. But would you rather ride horses? Hike? Do gymnastics? Do you stick your toe in the water first before jumping in? Or do you dive headfirst? Cautious, careful, or crazy, one week at an
(15) adventure camp could change your whole attitude about yourself and level of confidence.

Maybe you're thinking that "real kids" don't get to do these things. You're wrong. You don't even have to be an athlete. Today there are thousands of
(20) adventure camps across the country. So what are you waiting for? Sign up and go! What you do with your experience will be up to you.

16. What is the purpose of this passage?

(A) To teach you about backpacking

(B) To challenge you to change your lifestyle

(C) To excite you about going to adventure camp

(D) To encourage you have a better attitude

17. What is "exhilaration" (paragraph 2)?

(A) Fear

(B) Heat

(C) Understanding

(D) Excitement

18. Which of the following statements is NOT listed as a part of rock climbing?

(A) The challenge of reaching the summit

(B) Overcoming your fear

(C) Testing your muscles

(D) Spending time with friends

19. Why would someone choose to go to an adventure camp?

(A) To challenge himself

(B) To climb a mountain

(C) To do gymnastics

(D) To go hiking

20. What kind of person sticks her toe in the water before going in?

(A) A risk taker

(B) An adventurous person

(C) A cautious person

(D) A mountain climber

Here's what to do for the dogs while we're out of town:

Fido likes to go out first thing in the morning *Line* and then before bed. There's no need to go out with
(5) her, just open the door and she'll go right into the yard. If she needs to go in the middle of the day, she'll stare at you intently and grunt. Both dogs like a little walk in the morning and again at around 4:30. After the morning walk, you can give
(10) them some bread as a treat.

Samson has to take arthritis pills: Two in the morning and one in the evening. Use peanut butter or bread to hide the pills so that he'll eat them. Fido gets two vitamins in the morning, which she
(15) loves, so you don't have to camouflage her pills.

I'm leaving peanut butter treats, chew sticks, bacon, and sausages in the fridge. Use anything you want! If you need more food, that's in the garage. We leave the food bowl filled up all day so
(20) the dogs can eat whenever they are hungry. Please make sure they always have cold water in their bowls.

Thanks for all of your help! See you on Saturday!
(25) Oh, one last thing: If you decide to take the dogs to your house, don't forget to take the dog bed, along with a blanket, so you can cover up Samson if it starts to thunder.

21. What is the purpose of this passage?

    (A) To give directions for feeding two dogs

    (B) To give directions for taking care of two dogs

    (C) To give directions for walking two dogs

    (D) To give directions for giving medicine to two dogs

22. When do the dogs eat?

    (A) Whenever they are hungry

    (B) After their morning walk

    (C) In the afternoon

    (D) After their afternoon walk

23. Why do Samson's pills have to be hidden in peanut butter or bread?

    (A) He will spit them out otherwise.

    (B) He might otherwise try to eat Fido's vitamins.

    (C) He likes peanut butter or bread as a breakfast treat.

    (D) He is spoiled.

24. How does Fido let you know if she needs to go out?

    (A) She barks.

    (B) She only needs to go out during her regular walks.

    (C) She paces around the room.

    (D) She stares and grunts.

25. After their morning walk, the dogs get what treat?

    (A) Sausages

    (B) A piece of bread

    (C) Dog food

    (D) A peanut butter treat

IF YOU FINISH BEFORE TIME IS CALLED, YOU MAY CHECK YOUR WORK ON THIS SECTION ONLY. DO NOT TURN TO ANY OTHER SECTION IN THE TEST.    STOP

# SECTION 4

Time—30 Minutes
30 Questions

**In this section there are four possible answers after each question. Choose which one is best.**

**Note: Figures are drawn with the greatest possible accuracy, UNLESS stated "Not Drawn to Scale."**

1. Which is fifty-three thousand, nine hundred fourteen?

   (A)  53,914
   (B)  503,914
   (C)  530,914
   (D)  539,014

2. Which is the largest fraction?

   (A)  $\dfrac{6}{18}$
   (B)  $\dfrac{1}{2}$
   (C)  $\dfrac{5}{6}$
   (D)  $\dfrac{9}{10}$

3. $\dfrac{1}{5} + \dfrac{2}{3} =$

   (A)  $\dfrac{3}{15}$
   (B)  $\dfrac{2}{8}$
   (C)  $\dfrac{3}{8}$
   (D)  $\dfrac{13}{15}$

4. $400 + 950 =$

   (A)    990
   (B)  1,350
   (C)  4,950
   (D)  9,450

USE THIS SPACE FOR FIGURING.

GO ON TO THE NEXT PAGE

5. What is the product of 11 and 3?

   (A) 0.273

   (B) 3.66

   (C) 14

   (D) 33

6. What is 5,772 divided by 6?

   (A) 662

   (B) 912

   (C) 962

   (D) 1,012

7. ___ + 8 − 19 = 50

   (A) 11

   (B) 31

   (C) 39

   (D) 61

8. $15 \times 300 =$

   (A) 45

   (B) 450

   (C) 4,500

   (D) 45,000

9. $53.09 − 9.34 =$

   (A) 40.31

   (B) 42.25

   (C) 43.25

   (D) 43.75

10. $\dfrac{?}{15} = \dfrac{2}{3}$

   (A) 2

   (B) 4

   (C) 5

   (D) 10

USE THIS SPACE FOR FIGURING.

GO ON TO THE NEXT PAGE

11. Marla twirls her hair once every six seconds. How many times does she twirl her hair in a minute?

    (A)  6
    (B)  8
    (C) 10
    (D) 12

12. __ + 16 − 5 = 40

    What is the missing number?

    (A) 24
    (B) 29
    (C) 31
    (D) 33

13. A puppy weighed four pounds when he was six weeks old. Now that he is six months old, he has gained 80 percent more weight. How much does the puppy weigh now?

    (A)   7 pounds
    (B)  7.2 pounds
    (C) 12.8 pounds
    (D)  32 pounds

14. If $x = 5$, which of these statements is true?

    (A) $x + 8 = 11 + 3$
    (B) $x + 9 = 6 + 8$
    (C) $x + 10 = 15 − 5$
    (D) $x + 11 = 14 + 5$

15. What is the missing number in the pattern in Figure 1?

    (A) 16
    (B) 17
    (C) 18
    (D) 19

USE THIS SPACE FOR FIGURING.

| −3 | 9 |
|----|----|
| 0 | 12 |
| 3 | 15 |
| 6 | ? |

Figure 1

16. If $n = 9$, which of these number sentences is true?

   (A) $2n - 6 = 14$
   (B) $3(n - 3) = 18$
   (C) $4(n + 5) = 18$
   (D) $5n + 8 = 22$

17. What is the sum of 25 and 30?

   (A) 5
   (B) 55
   (C) 75
   (D) 750

18. Devon bought $8.96 worth of gas. He paid with a 20 dollar bill. How much change did he receive?

   (A) $11.04
   (B) $11.96
   (C) $12.14
   (D) $12.96

19. $500 - 409 = $ ___

   (A) 91
   (B) 109
   (C) 101
   (D) 191

20. What is the product of 5 and 20?

   (A) 4
   (B) 25
   (C) 75
   (D) 100

USE THIS SPACE FOR FIGURING.

GO ON TO THE NEXT PAGE

21. If $8 + a = 15$ and $6 + b = 14$, then what is $a + b$?

    (A) 12

    (B) 13

    (C) 14

    (D) 15

22. If $a = b$ and $b = c$, then

    (A) $a + b = c$

    (B) $a = c$

    (C) $bc = a$

    (D) $c + b = a$

23. The diameter of the circle in Figure 2 is 8 cm. What is the radius? NOTE: The radius is the length halfway across the circle.

    (A) 4 cm

    (B) 8 cm

    (C) 10 cm

    (D) 16 cm

24. What is the perimeter of the rectangle in Figure 3?

    (A) 18 in.

    (B) 30 in.

    (C) 36 in.

    (D) 72 in.

25. When folded on the lines, what will the shape in Figure 4 become?

    (A) Cylinder

    (B) Cube

    (C) Square pyramid

    (D) Sphere

USE THIS SPACE FOR FIGURING.

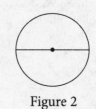

Figure 2

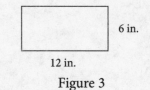

12 in.

6 in.

Figure 3

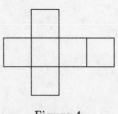

Figure 4

26. What is the volume of the box in Figure 5?

    (A) 12 cubic feet
    (B) 24 cubic feet
    (C) 48 cubic feet
    (D) 60 cubic feet

27. $5.123 + 2.627 =$

    (A) 7.65
    (B) 7.743
    (C) 7.749
    (D) 7.75

28. $10,000 - 45n =$

    (A)    $955n$
    (B)    $9,955n$
    (C)  $99,955n$
    (D) The answer cannot be determined from the information given.

29. Which of the following is closest to 100.11?

    (A) 99.11
    (B)   101
    (C) 100.1
    (D)   100

USE THIS SPACE FOR FIGURING.

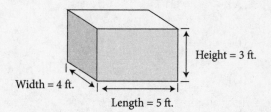

Figure 5

GO ON TO THE NEXT PAGE

USE THIS SPACE FOR FIGURING.

30. $\dfrac{1}{4} + \dfrac{5}{8} =$

(A) $\dfrac{1}{2}$

(B) $\dfrac{3}{4}$

(C) $\dfrac{5}{6}$

(D) $\dfrac{7}{8}$

# SECTION 5

Time—30 Minutes

Write an essay on the following prompt on the paper provided. Your essay should not exceed two pages and must be written in ink. You must use a black or blue pen. Erasing is not allowed.

**Prompt:** Write about a time when you made a mistake.

_____

_____

_____

_____

_____

_____

_____

_____

_____

_____

_____

_____

_____

_____

_____

_____

_____

_____

 GO ON TO THE NEXT PAGE

_____

_____

_____

_____

_____

_____

_____

_____

_____

_____

_____

_____

_____

_____

_____

_____

_____

_____

IF YOU FINISH BEFORE TIME IS CALLED, YOU MAY CHECK YOUR WORK ON
THIS SECTION ONLY. DO NOT TURN TO ANY OTHER SECTION IN THE TEST.

STOP

# ANSWER KEY

| **Section 1** | | 31. A | | 27. B | | 19. A | | 24. C |
|---|---|---|---|---|---|---|---|---|
| 1. A | | 32. D | | 28. A | | 20. C | | 25. B |
| 2. B | | 33. B | | 29. A | | 21. B | | 26. D |
| 3. D | | 34. C | | 30. C | | 22. A | | 27. D |
| 4. A | | **Section 2** | | 31. A | | 23. A | | 28. D |
| 5. C | | 1. A | | 32. B | | 24. D | | 29. C |
| 6. B | | 2. A | | 33. B | | 25. B | | 30. D |
| 7. D | | 3. C | | 34. D | | **Section 4** | | |
| 8. A | | 4. C | | 35. A | | 1. A | | |
| 9. D | | 5. B | | 36. D | | 2. D | | |
| 10. A | | 6. A | | 37. D | | 3. D | | |
| 11. B | | 7. C | | 38. D | | 4. B | | |
| 12. C | | 8. C | | **Section 3** | | 5. D | | |
| 13. B | | 9. D | | 1. C | | 6. C | | |
| 14. D | | 10. C | | 2. A | | 7. D | | |
| 15. D | | 11. B | | 3. B | | 8. C | | |
| 16. B | | 12. A | | 4. A | | 9. D | | |
| 17. C | | 13. A | | 5. D | | 10. D | | |
| 18. C | | 14. C | | 6. C | | 11. C | | |
| 19. D | | 15. A | | 7. A | | 12. B | | |
| 20. B | | 16. A | | 8. A | | 13. B | | |
| 21. B | | 17. B | | 9. C | | 14. B | | |
| 22. B | | 18. C | | 10. D | | 15. C | | |
| 23. A | | 19. D | | 11. A | | 16. B | | |
| 24. D | | 20. A | | 12. C | | 17. B | | |
| 25. C | | 21. B | | 13. D | | 18. A | | |
| 26. A | | 22. D | | 14. D | | 19. A | | |
| 27. B | | 23. B | | 15. A | | 20. D | | |
| 28. D | | 24. B | | 16. C | | 21. D | | |
| 29. B | | 25. D | | 17. D | | 22. B | | |
| 30. C | | 26. C | | 18. D | | 23. A | | |

# ISEE PRACTICE TEST 3: LOWER-LEVEL: ASSESS YOUR STRENGTHS

Use the following tables to determine which topics and chapters you need to review most. If you need help with your essay, be sure to review Chapter 9: The Essay and Chapter 26: Writing Skills.

| Topic | Question |
|---|---|
| Verbal: Synonyms | Section 1, questions 1–17 |
| Verbal: Sentence Completions | Section 1, questions 18–34 |
| Quantitative Reasoning | Section 2, questions 1–38 |
| Reading Comprehension | Section 3, questions 1–25 |
| Mathematics Achievement | Section 4, questions 1–30 |

| Topic | Number of Questions on Test | Number Correct | If you struggled with these questions, study… |
|---|---|---|---|
| Verbal: Synonyms | 17 | | Chapters 7 and 24 |
| Verbal: Sentence Completions | 17 | | Chapter 4 |
| Quantitative Reasoning | 38 | | Chapters 10–14 and Chapter 25 |
| Reading Comprehension | 25 | | Chapter 8 |
| Mathematics Achievement | 30 | | Chapters 10–14 and Chapter 25 |

# ANSWERS AND EXPLANATIONS

## SECTION 1: VERBAL REASONING

### SYNONYMS

**1. A**

To decline is to deteriorate or decrease.

**2. B**

Something delicate is also fragile, as in a delicate glass vase. Do not be misled by (D) just because its beginning letters are similar to that of the original word.

**3. D**

A jubilee is a celebration, such as an anniversary or festival.

**4. A**

To liberate is to set free or release from captivity.

**5. C**

When you transform your life, you change it.

**6. B**

When two items collide, they crash into each other.

**7. D**

To proclaim something means to announce it.

**8. A**

To show sympathy for another is to express sorrow and understanding of that person's feelings.

**9. D**

An invention is a new idea or creation.

**10. A**

An authority is an expert.

**11. B**

To illustrate is to draw.

**12. C**

To cause a commotion is to create a fuss or uproar. A collaboration is something that involves the participation of several people.

**13. B**

When you feel exhausted, you are extremely tired.

**14. D**

Tread is another word for walk.

**15. D**

A mentor is a tutor or coach. (D), counselor, is the closest in meaning.

**16. B**

A reaction is a response.

**17. C**

To dwindle means to shrink or become steadily less, such as a dwindling bank account.

### SENTENCE COMPLETIONS

**18. C**

The sentence implies that the students need long division to be explained again. "Although" is a key word here: It suggests that you will need to repeat an idea again in the second clause. The verb "had taught" is closely related to explain. Numerous means many, so she had taught them many times before. Admonish means to caution, which does not make sense. Request means to ask for, and employ means to use.

### 19. D

The blank requires you to fill in a word with the same meaning as *not ignoring others who are feeling sad or lonely*. A compassionate person is concerned for others. A terse person is dismissive or brief, an intellectual person thinks academically, and an insecure person lacks confidence; none of these have anything to do with being concerned for others.

### 20. B

Hiding behind your mother's legs would suggest you are timid or shy. A toddler would probably be young as well, but being young does not explain why he would hide when meeting strangers. He might also be disobedient, but that, too, does not explain why he would hide.

### 21. B

Earning a high score is something one would be proud of. Feeling distressed (upset) would be the opposite of how you would feel under these circumstances. Neither would you feel helpless (defenseless). Intimidated means nervous or anxious, so that answer choice is incorrect as well.

### 22. B

Low, gray clouds are a sign of something—probably something bad or negative. Ominous means threatening and is the correct answer. Trite means commonplace and unoriginal. Intentional means on purpose.

### 23. A

A canopy is a covering. From the other words in the sentence, we know we need something "created" by the vegetation. No other choice fits.

### 24. D

Ling is winning "in order to be" something. The only answer choice that makes sense is (D). A champion is a winner in a competition.

### 25. C

We know that Phoebe finished running the marathon, so she must be very happy. Jubilant means filled with joy, and it is the right answer. She might feel also fortunate (lucky), but between the two answer choices (B) and (C), jubilant is the better choice: We do not know for certain that she would feel lucky, but we can be fairly certain that she would feel happy.

### 26. A

Jeff needs to print out a new copy of his essay. (A), duplicate (double or identical) copy is what he would need to print. Don't be misled by (D), a previous copy: Previous means earlier or prior, and it is not right here. You wouldn't print out an earlier copy; you would print out an identical copy.

### 27. B

It seems as though a walk around the neighborhood is something the mother and son do on a daily basis—in other words, on a typical day or a regular day. Naïve means inexperienced or innocent, confidential means private, and dire means terrible.

**28. D**

"Even though" tells us there must be a contrast here. We are told that Mischa is guilty, so the contrast is probably something that has to do with denying the truth—declaring it untrue.

**29. B**

An accident on the highway would make traffic come to a standstill. That's another way of saying stalled traffic, (B). You might suspect (A) is correct, but it is not appropriate to say tight traffic. Fatigued means tired, and traffic cannot be tired.

**30. C**

A police officer would want Clay to lower, or reduce, his speed.

**31. A**

The football player would have to balance, or divide fairly, his time between practice and studying if he wants to do well in school. Entertain makes no sense here; nor does connect or perform.

**32. D**

The note is intended to remind her father. Don't be tricked by (B): It seems like it might be acceptable to say that she urged her father to get more milk, but then when you see (D) as an option, you see *remind* is the best possible answer choice.

**33. B**

Since the puppy was going to be left behind, we probably need a word that means unhappy. Dejected means unhappy. The puppy would not be relieved or excited if he were left behind, so (A) and (D) are incorrect.

**34. C**

The ideal solution would be the best solution. It means the perfect solution.

## SECTION 2: QUANTITATIVE REASONING

**1. A**

$8 - x = 4$, so $x = 4$. $10 + y = 12$, so $y = 2$. That means $x - y$ is the same as $4 - 2$.

**2. A**

First, figure out how many students brought other pets. Fourteen students brought dogs, birds, and cats, so that means six students brought other pets. The fraction is $\frac{6}{20}$, which reduces to $\frac{3}{10}$. You might have incorrectly chosen (B) since it has the number 6 in it.

**3. C**

You have $8 \times 2 = 16$ and $6 \times 2 = 12$. So $8 \times 2 \times 6 \times 2$ equals 16 times 12, (C).

**4. C**

Five laps in 15 minutes means 3 minutes per lap. If Jennifer and José want to swim 35 laps at 3 minutes each, that would take 105 minutes.

**5. B**

A square has 4 equal sides. Sixteen divided by 4 is 4. If you divided by 2, you might have gotten an incorrect answer of 8, (D).

**6. A**

The decimal 0.0005 is equivalent to $\frac{5}{10,000}$, which is the smallest number given. The farther away a digit is to the right of the decimal point, the smaller the place that digit is in.

**7. C**

Two-thirds is equal to $\frac{10}{15}$ because $2 \times 5 = 10$ and $3 \times 5 = 15$.

**8. C**

Grapes are the only fruit included in both circles.

**9. D**

A prime number is a number greater than 1 that can be divided evenly only by itself and by 1. Nine is not a prime number because it can be divided by 3. You might have suspected (D) was incorrect because 90 is divisible by 9, but 9 is not prime.

**10. C**

Divide 2 by 40 to get 0.05, which is the same as 5 percent. You might have guessed 4 percent since the original number was 40, but that would be incorrect.

**11. B**

The interval from 3 to 4 is divided into 8 equal segments, so each segment has a length of $\frac{1}{8}$. Since there are 3 segments to where the arrow is pointing, the arrow is pointing to $3\frac{3}{8}$.

**12. A**

The shaded region shows people who drive cars and trucks. You might have guessed (D), since cars, trucks, and motorcycles are all included in the diagram, but the question asks you to look at the shaded region.

**13. A**

Since this is a race time, for Andrew to beat the record means his time is 0.1 second less than the record. Line up the decimal points to solve:

$$\begin{array}{r} 13.71 \\ -\ 0.1 \\ \hline 13.61 \end{array}$$

**14. C**

$\frac{5}{6}$ of 24 is $\frac{5}{6} \times 24 = 20$ hours.

**15. A**

Volume is length × width × height. The box with the smallest volume is the one in (A), $2 \times 3 \times 4 = 24$ cubic inches.

**16. A**

(A) shows the numbers from smallest to largest.

**17. B**

The decimal $0.65 = \frac{65}{100}$ (sixty-five hundredths). (D), 65, is tempting, but you must remember to change your fraction to a decimal.

**18. C**

The pattern is that each number adds twice the difference between the previous two terms: +2, +4, +8, +16, +32, +64, and so on. $63 + 64 = 127$.

**19. D**

To find Christopher's age, multiply his son's age (4) by 9.

**20. A**

You have 15 + 40 + 10 = 65 percent. Subtract that number from 100 percent and you get 35 percent. Then $\frac{35}{100}$ reduces to $\frac{7}{20}$. If you forgot to subtract from 100, you might have gotten wrong answer (C).

**21. B**

The 5 is in the hundredths place. From the decimal, moving right, the places are as follows: tenths, hundredths, thousandths.

**22. D**

Area equals length × width. If you had added instead of multiplied, except for the unit square feet, you would have gotten an incorrect answer of (A).

**23. B**

Congruent pools have the same measurements. A congruent figure is the same shape and size as the original figure.

**24. B**

The decimal equivalent of 30% is 0.3. So 0.3 × 300 = $90.

**25. D**

The fraction $\frac{8}{20}$ reduces to $\frac{2}{5}$, not $\frac{1}{4}$. You can use the process of elimination to solve this question.

**26. C**

Let's approximate: 4 miles plus 4 miles plus 8 miles—the drive is about 16 miles.

**27. B**

Cecile spent a total of $1.15 + $3.49 = $4.64. From $10.00, that means $5.36 is left. Make sure to line up the decimal points when calculating.

**28. A**

The number of students cannot exceed 50. (A) is the only combination of classes that is less than or equal to 50.

**29. A**

One bag of dog food costs $19.85; 2 bags of cat food would cost $18.48.

**30. C**

The number of items in the cart must be a multiple of 3. Forty-two is divisible by 3 without a remainder, so 42 is a multiple of 3.

**31. A**

The shape has been reflected (flipped as if in a mirror).

**32. B**

Divide 75 by 60 to find the answer. (A) and (D) are tricky because you might think you should be dividing by 10 or 100, but they are incorrect.

**33. B**

Multiply 24 by 3 to get 72 minutes. Since there are 60 minutes in an hour, that's the same as 1 hour 12 minutes.

**34. D**

More of the circle is unshaded, so the number has to be higher than 850.

**35. A**

Fifteen miles divided by 20 minutes = 0.75 miles per minute. Thirty miles divided by 0.75 miles per minute = 40 minutes. You could also have realized that if Rebecca and Ian are driving at the same speed, it will take Ian twice as long to drive twice as far. 2 × 20 = 40 minutes. If you had added Rebecca's 20 minutes to her 30 miles, you would have gotten the number in incorrect answer (B).

### 36. D

The number must be divisible by 3 with no remainder.

### 37. D

Solve this problem by thinking of three groups: one group that likes cats and two groups that like dogs. Divide 45 by 3 to see that there are 15 students in each group. There are 2 dog groups, so multiply 15 × 2 to get 30.

### 38. D

A whole number has no fraction or decimal point. Also, the number has to be greater than 15, so (D) is the only possible answer.

## SECTION 3: READING COMPREHENSION

### WHALE SHARKS PASSAGE

### 1. C

This is a descriptive passage. The other three answer choices are details included in the passage, but none gives the purpose or main idea of the passage.

### 2. A

The passage states that most female sharks are larger than the males. As for (B), the passage does state that whale sharks are beautiful, though it doesn't say anything about the females being more beautiful than the males.

### 3. B

A predator is a hunter—one that preys or destroys. The meaning is implied by the text: "You would think that with such a massive body this shark would be a fierce predator, but this mammoth fish is quite docile. It likes its solitude." The other three answer choices are words used in the passage, but none of them mean the same thing as predator.

### 4. A

The whale shark's teeth are largely useless. Since you are asked which answer choice is NOT true, you can go back to the passage to find the three that are true. Then, use the process of elimination.

### 5. D

You can reread the last paragraph of the passage to find out that whale sharks will probably ignore divers, or pay no attention to them.

## ICE CREAM TRUCK PASSAGE

### 6. C

The function of the passage is to describe a summer treat. It does not challenge, prove, or teach anything.

### 7. A

To "hem and haw" means to take one's time in choosing. Read the context of the words surrounding this phrase, and you will see that it suggests taking one's time.

**8. A**

When a passage uses the author's own voice, and when it uses the pronouns *I* and *me*, it is written in first person. That means the story is told from the author's perspective.

**9. C**

You must find the answer choice that is NOT true here. (C) is not true: Though the author usually gets an orange push-up, that's not always the case. The other three answer choices are indeed stated in the passage.

**10. D**

Since the writer needs permission to grab change and run to catch the truck but is not allowed off of the street, she is probably a child. A baby or toddler would not be able to run out to the ice cream truck, and a parent would not need permission to go to the ice cream truck.

## YARD WORK PASSAGE

**11. A**

"The yard had potential" means the yard could look good if some work was done to it. You may have chosen (B) because the yard was indeed full of weeds and it did need work, but since that's not what the question asked, it is incorrect.

**12. C**

Bailey wanted the yard to look charming. He and his friends were busy all day, but that is not how the yard looked.

**13. D**

Bailey and Nolan planted ferns and marigolds under an olive tree that was already there. You might have chosen the incorrect answer of (A). Bailey and Nolan did some weeding, but they weeded in the front yard, not the back.

**14. D**

Janet had to fill in the holes before she could do the rest of her work.

**15. A**

Lilia and Nathan left room to plant annuals at a later time, but they did not actually do it that day.

## ADVENTURE CAMPS PASSAGE

**16. C**

The purpose of the passage is to excite you about going to adventure camp. It does not challenge you to change your life, only to try something new.

**17. D**

The meaning of exhilaration is implied in the sentence. It means excitement or stimulation.

**18. D**

Use the process of elimination to see that being with friends is not mentioned.

**19. A**

One might do yoga or climb a mountain or go backpacking while there, but no matter what activity one chose, adventure camp would challenge a kid.

## 20. C

A cautious person would test the water before jumping into it.

## DOG CARE PASSAGE

### 21. B

The passage is intended to give directions for taking care of Samson and Fido. Feeding, walking, and giving medicine are mentioned, but those answers are all details that are part of the overall care. The main idea of the passage is reflected in (B).

### 22. A

Since the dog food bowl is left full all day, the dogs can eat whenever they are hungry.

### 23. A

Since the pills have to be hidden in bread or peanut butter, Samson must not like the taste of them. He would probably spit them out if given them plain. Chances are, he likes the taste of peanut butter or bread. He may also be spoiled, but that doesn't explain why he needs his pills hidden in something sweet.

### 24. D

Fido stares and grunts when she needs to go out. The other three choices are not mentioned in the text.

### 25. B

The dogs get a piece of bread as a breakfast treat. Though the text does mention the other choices, you are asked to identify the treat the dogs get after their morning walk.

## SECTION 4: MATH ACHIEVEMENT

### 1. A

To solve, read each answer choice individually:

(A) Fifty-three thousand, nine hundred fourteen—YES

(B) Five hundred three thousand, nine hundred fourteen—NO

(C) Five hundred thirty thousand, nine hundred fourteen—NO

(D) Five hundred thirty-nine thousand, fourteen—NO

### 2. D

You know $\frac{6}{18}$ is less than $\frac{1}{2}$ because the numerator 6 of $\frac{6}{18}$ is less than half of the denominator 18. Also, $\frac{1}{2}$ is less than each of $\frac{5}{6}$ and $\frac{9}{10}$ because the numerator of each of those two fractions is greater than half of the denominator. So we must compare $\frac{5}{6}$ with $\frac{9}{10}$ to find the greatest fraction. The easiest way to compare these fractions is to convert them to decimals: $\frac{5}{6} = 0.8\overline{3}$ and $\frac{9}{10} = 0.9$. So $\frac{9}{10}$ is the largest fraction.

### 3. D

$\frac{1}{5} + \frac{2}{3} = \frac{3}{15} + \frac{10}{15} = \frac{13}{15}$. You might have chosen (C) if you had simply added the numerators and denominators together, but that is not the correct way to solve.

### 4. B

$400 + 950 = 1,350$

### 5. D

The product is the answer when you multiply: $11 \times 3 = 33$. If you didn't know that product means to multiply, you might have added and gotten (C), which is 14.

**6. C**

$5{,}772 \div 6 = 962$.

**7. D**

To solve, turn the question around: $50 + 19 - 8 = \underline{\hspace{1em}}$. If you forgot to change your signs, you would get 39, which is (C). You have to change + to − when you move the numbers across the equal sign. The answer is 61.

**8. C**

$15 \times 300 = 4{,}500$. A good rule of thumb is that there are the same number of zeros at the end of a number in the question as in the answer.

**9. D**

Line up the decimal points before you subtract. You have to borrow in order to find the answer.

$$
\begin{array}{r}
12 \\
4\,\cancel{2}. \\
\cancel{5}\,\cancel{3}.\cancel{0}\,9 \\
-\ 9.34 \\
\hline
43.75
\end{array}
$$

**10. D**

Convert $\dfrac{2}{3}$ to a fraction with a denominator of 15. Since $3 \times 5 = 15$, then $\dfrac{2}{3} = \dfrac{2 \times 5}{3 \times 15} = \dfrac{10}{15}$. So ? is 10.

**11. C**

There are 60 seconds in a minute. Sixty divided by $6 = 10$. She twirls her hair 10 times in a minute.

**12. B**

This question would be a good one to Backsolve. Plug in the answer choices and see which one works. You could also move the numbers across the equal

signs. You have to change + to − and you have to change − to + . So $\underline{\hspace{1em}} = 40 - 16 + 5$. The answer is 29.

**13. B**

Eighty percent is the same as 0.80. To find out how much weight the puppy has gained, multiply: $4 \times 0.80 = 3.2$. Add the original weight (4 pounds) to the gained weight (3.2). Then $4 + 3.2 = 7.2$.

**14. B**

Substitute in 5 for $x$ and see which answer choice results in a true statement. When you solve, choice (B) becomes $14 = 14$, which is the only true statement here.

**15. C**

The numbers on the right-hand column skip by threes: 9, 12, 15 (and are 12 more than the number in the left column). Fifteen plus 3 is 18 (and 6 plus 12 is 18), so that must be the missing number.

**16. B**

Plug 9 into each answer choice. For (B), after you have substituted, you must find the value of what is in parentheses first, then multiply by 3. If you tried to multiply before you subtracted, you would have gotten an incorrect value.

**17. B**

The sum is the result of addition. So $25 + 30 = 55$. If you multiplied the numbers, you would have gotten (D), which is incorrect.

**18. A**

You have $20 – $8.96 = $11.04. You must line up the decimal points and borrow.

**19. A**

You must borrow to solve this subtraction question.

$$
\begin{array}{r}
\overset{\overset{10}{\cancel{5}}}{5}\,\cancel{0}\,\cancel{0} \\
-\ 4\ 0\ 9 \\
\hline
9\ 1
\end{array}
$$

**20. D**

The product is the result of multiplication. Here, $5 \times 20 = 100$. If you added you might have come up with (B), which is incorrect.

**21. D**

If $8 + a = 15$, then $a = 15 - 8 = 7$. If $6 + b = 14$, then $b = 14 - 6 = 8$. $a = 7$ and $b = 8$, so $a + b$ is the same as $7 + 8$.

**22. B**

If $a = b$ and $b = c$ then it follows logically that $a = c$.

**23. A**

The diameter is the full length across the circle. The radius is the length halfway across. If we're given that the diameter is 8 cm, the radius is half of that: 4 cm. If you doubled the length of 8 cm, you would have gotten 16, which would have been incorrect.

**24. C**

To find the perimeter, add the lengths of all four sides: $12 + 6 + 12 + 6 = 36$ inches.

**25. B**

A cube is made up of six squares. The six squares in the figure can be folded into a cube.

**26. D**

Volume = Length × Width × Height. The volume in cubic feet is $5 \times 4 \times 3 = 60$.

**27. D**

Line up the decimal points to add.

$$
\begin{array}{r}
5.123 \\
2.627 \\
\hline
7.750
\end{array}
$$

**28. D**

Since $n$ is unknown, the answer cannot be determined.

**29. C**

There is only 0.01 difference between 100.11 and 100.1. If you weren't sure, you could subtract for each to solve.

**30. D**

Find a common denominator. The lowest common denominator is 8. Convert $\frac{1}{4}$ to $\frac{2}{8}$.

Then add: $\frac{2}{8} + \frac{5}{8} = \frac{7}{8}$.

# CHAPTER 23: SCORING YOUR ISEE PRACTICE TEST

The ISEE calculates scores by using a formula that compares each student's score against the scores of other students of the same grade level. The governing board of the ISEE does not release any information about how scores are actually calculated, so we are unable to provide you with a scaled score on your practice tests.

So, rather than worrying over what the numbers mean, just concentrate on improving your performance. Look over all the answers and explanations we have provided. Since you won't know how hard the actual test will be on test day, or how other students will do, simply focusing on performing your best in your practice will put you in the right frame of mind to do just that on test day.

| Part Six |

# LEARNING RESOURCES

# CHAPTER 24: VOCABULARY REFERENCE

## ROOT LIST

| ROOT | MEANING | EXAMPLES |
|---|---|---|
| A, AN | *not, without* | amoral, atrophy, asymmetrical, anarchy, anesthetic, anonymity, anomaly, annul |
| AB, A | *from, away, apart* | abnegate, abortive, abrogate, abscond, absolve, abstemious, abstruse, avert, aversion, abnormal, abdicate, aberration, abhor, abject, abjure, ablution |
| AC, ACR | *sharp, sour* | acid, acerbic, exacerbate, acute, acuity, acumen, acrid, acrimony |
| AD, A | *to, toward* | adhere, adjacent, adjunct, admonish, adroit, adumbrate, advent, abeyance, abet, accede, accretion, acquiesce, affluent, aggrandize, aggregate, alleviate, alliteration, allude, allure, ascribe, aspersion, aspire, assail, assonance, attest |
| ALI, ALTR | *another* | alias, alienate, inalienable, altruism |
| AM, AMI | *love* | amorous, amicable, amiable, amity |
| AMBI, AMPHI | *both* | ambiguous, ambivalent, ambidextrous, amphibious |
| AMBL, AMBUL | *walk* | amble, ambulatory, perambulator, somnambulist |
| ANIM | *mind, spirit, breath* | animal, animosity, unanimous, magnanimous |
| ANN, ENN | *year* | annual, annuity, superannuated, biennial, perennial |
| ANTE, ANT | *before* | antecedent, antediluvian, antebellum, antepenultimate, anterior, antiquity, antiquated, anticipate |
| ANTHROP | *human* | anthropology, anthropomorphic, misanthrope, philanthropy |

| ROOT | MEANING | EXAMPLES |
|---|---|---|
| ANTI, ANT | *against, opposite* | antidote, antipathy, antithesis, antacid, antagonist, antonym |
| AUD | *hear* | audio, audience, audition, auditory, audible |
| AUTO | *self* | autobiography, autocrat, autonomous |
| BELLI, BELL | *war* | belligerent, bellicose, antebellum, rebellion |
| BENE, BEN | *good* | benevolent, benefactor, beneficent, benign |
| BI | *two* | bicycle, bisect, bilateral, bilingual, biped |
| BIBLIO | *book* | Bible, bibliography, bibliophile |
| BIO | *life* | biography, biology, amphibious, symbiotic, macrobiotics |
| BURS | *money, purse* | reimburse, disburse, bursar |
| CAD, CAS, CID | *happen, fall* | accident, cadence, cascade, deciduous |
| CAP, CIP | *head* | captain, decapitate, capitulate, precipitous, precipitate, recapitulate |
| CAP, CAPT, CEPT, CIP | *take, hold, seize* | capable, capacious, captivate, deception, intercept, precept, inception, anticipate, emancipate, incipient, percipient |
| CARN | *flesh* | carnal, carnage, carnival, carnivorous, incarnate, incarnadine |
| CED, CESS | *yield, go* | cede, precede, accede, recede, antecedent, intercede, secede, cession, cease, cessation, incessant |
| CHROM | *color* | chrome, chromatic, monochrome |
| CHRON | *time* | chronology, chronic, anachronism |
| CIDE | *murder* | suicide, homicide, regicide, patricide |
| CIRCUM | *around* | circumference, circumlocution, circumnavigate, circumscribe, circumspect, circumvent |
| CLIN, CLIV | *slope* | incline, declivity, proclivity |
| CLUD, CLUS, CLAUS, CLOIS | *shut, close* | conclude, reclusive, claustrophobia, cloister, preclude, occlude |

| ROOT | MEANING | EXAMPLES |
|---|---|---|
| CO, COM, CON | *with, together* | coeducation, coagulate, coalesce, coerce, cogent, collateral, colloquial, colloquy, commensurate, commodious, compassion, compatriot, complacent, compliant, complicity, compunction, concerto, conciliatory, concord, concur, condone, conflagration, congeal, congenial, congenital, conglomerate, conjure, conjugal, conscientious, consecrate, consensus, consonant, constrained, contentious, contrite, contusion, convalescence, convene, convivial, convoke, convoluted, congress |
| COGN, GNO | *know* | recognize, cognition, cognizance, incognito, diagnosis, agnostic, prognosis, gnostic, ignorant |
| CONTRA | *against* | controversy, incontrovertible, contravene, contradict |
| CORP | *body* | corpse, corporeal, corpulence |
| COSMO, COSM | *world* | cosmopolitan, cosmos, microcosm, macrocosm |
| CRAC, CRAT | *rule, power* | democracy, bureaucracy, theocracy, autocrat, aristocrat, technocrat |
| CRED | *trust, believe* | incredible, credulous, credence |
| CRESC, CRET | *grow* | crescent, crescendo, accretion |
| CULP | *blame, fault* | culprit, culpable, inculpate, exculpate |
| CURR, CURS | *run* | current, concur, cursory, precursor, incursion |
| DE | *down, out, apart* | depart, debase, debilitate, declivity, decry, deface, defamatory, defunct, delegate, demarcation, demean, demur, deplete, deplore, depravity, deprecate, deride, derivative, desist, detest |
| DEC | *ten, tenth* | decade, decimal, decathlon, decimate |
| DEMO, DEM | *people* | democrat, demographics, demagogue, epidemic, pandemic, endemic |
| DI, DIURN | *day* | diary, diurnal, quotidian |
| DIA | *across* | diagonal, diatribe, diaphanous |
| DIC, DICT | *speak* | diction, interdict, predict, abdicate, indict, verdict, dictum |

| ROOT | MEANING | EXAMPLES |
|------|---------|----------|
| DIS, DIF, DI | *not, apart, away* | disaffected, disband, disbar, disburse, discern, discordant, discredit, discursive, disheveled, disparage, disparate, dispassionate, dispirit, dissemble, disseminate, dissension, dissipate, dissonant, dissuade, distend, differentiate, diffidence, diffuse, digress, divert |
| DOC, DOCT | *teach* | doctrine, docile, doctrinaire |
| DOL | *pain* | condolence, doleful, dolorous, indolent |
| DUC, DUCT | *lead* | seduce, induce, conduct, viaduct, induct |
| EGO | *self* | ego, egoist, egocentric |
| EN, EM | *in, into* | enter, entice, encumber, endemic, ensconce, enthrall, entreat, embellish, embezzle, embroil, empathy |
| ERR | *wander* | erratic, aberration, errant |
| EU | *well, good* | eulogy, euphemism, euphony, euphoria, eurythmics, euthanasia |
| EX, E | *out, out of* | exit, exacerbate, excerpt, excommunicate, exculpate, execrable, exhume, exonerate, exorbitant, exorcise, expatriate, expedient, expiate, expunge, expurgate, extenuate, extort, extremity, extricate, extrinsic, exult, evoke, evict, evince, elicit, egress, egregious |
| FAC, FIC, FECT, FY, FEA | *make, do* | factory, facility, benefactor, malefactor, fiction, fictive, beneficent, affect, confection, refectory, magnify, unify, rectify, vilify, feasible |
| FAL, FALS | *deceive* | false, infallible, fallacious |
| FERV | *boil* | fervent, fervid, effervescent |
| FID | *faith, trust* | confident, diffidence, perfidious, fidelity |
| FLU, FLUX | *flow* | fluent, flux, affluent, confluence, effluvia, superfluous |
| FORE | *before* | forecast, foreboding, forestall |
| FRAG, FRAC | *break* | fragment, fracture, diffract, fractious, refract |
| FUS | *pour* | profuse, infusion, effusive, diffuse |
| GEN | *birth, class, kin* | generation, congenital, homogeneous, heterogeneous, ingenious, engender, progenitor, progeny |

| ROOT | MEANING | EXAMPLES |
|---|---|---|
| GRAD, GRESS | *step* | graduate, gradual, retrograde, centigrade, degrade, gradation, gradient, progress, congress, digress, transgress, ingress, egress |
| GRAPH, GRAM | *writing* | biography, bibliography, epigraph, grammar, epigram |
| GRAT | *pleasing* | grateful, gratitude, gratis, ingrate, congratulate, gratuitous, gratuity |
| GRAV, GRIEV | *heavy* | grave, gravity, aggravate, grieve, aggrieve, grievous |
| GREG | *crowd, flock* | segregate, gregarious, egregious, congregate, aggregate |
| HABIT, HIBIT | *have, hold* | habit, inhibit, cohabit, habitat |
| HAP | *by chance* | happen, haphazard, hapless, mishap |
| HELIO, HELI | *sun* | heliocentric, helium, heliotrope, aphelion, perihelion |
| HETERO | *other* | heterosexual, heterogeneous, heterodox |
| HOL | *whole* | holocaust, catholic, holistic |
| HOMO | *same* | homosexual, homogenize, homogeneous, homonym |
| HOMO | *man* | *Homo sapiens*, homicide, bonhomie |
| HYDR | *water* | hydrant, hydrate, dehydration |
| HYPER | *too much, excess* | hyperactive, hyperbole, hyperventilate |
| HYPO | *too little, under* | hypodermic, hypothermia, hypochondria, hypothesis, hypothetical |
| IN, IG, IL, IM, IR | *not* | incorrigible, indefatigable, indelible, indubitable, inept, inert, inexorable, insatiable, insentient, insolvent, insomnia, interminable, intractable, incessant, inextricable, infallible, infamy, innumerable, inoperable, insipid, intemperate, intrepid, inviolable, ignorant, ignominious, ignoble, illicit, illimitable, immaculate, immutable, impasse, impeccable, impecunious, impertinent, implacable, impotent, impregnable, improvident, impassioned, impervious, irregular |
| IN, IL, IM, IR | *in, on, into* | invade, inaugurate, incandescent, incarcerate, incense, indenture, induct, ingratiate, introvert, incarnate, inception, incisive, infer, infusion, ingress, innate, inquest, inscribe, insinuate, inter, illustrate, imbue, immerse, implicate, irrigate, irritate |

| ROOT | MEANING | EXAMPLES |
|---|---|---|
| INTER | *between, among* | intercede, intercept, interdiction, interject, interlocutor, interloper, intermediary, intermittent, interpolate, interpose, interregnum, interrogate, intersect, intervene |
| INTRA, INTR | *within* | intrastate, intravenous, intramural, intrinsic |
| IT, ITER | *between, among* | transit, itinerant, reiterate, transitory |
| JECT, JET | *throw* | eject, interject, abject, trajectory, jettison |
| JOUR | *day* | journal, adjourn, sojourn |
| JUD | *judge* | judge, judicious, prejudice, adjudicate |
| JUNCT, JUG | *join* | junction, adjunct, injunction, conjugal, subjugate |
| JUR | *swear, law* | jury, abjure, adjure, conjure, perjure, jurisprudence |
| LAT | *side* | lateral, collateral, unilateral, bilateral, quadrilateral |
| LAV, LAU, LU | *wash* | lavatory, laundry, ablution, antediluvian |
| LEG, LEC, LEX | *read, speak* | legible, lecture, lexicon |
| LEV | *light* | elevate, levitate, levity, alleviate |
| LIBER | *free* | liberty, liberal, libertarian, libertine |
| LIG, LECT | *choose, gather* | eligible, elect, select |
| LIG, LI, LY | *bind* | ligament, oblige, religion, liable, liaison, lien, ally |
| LING, LANG | *tongue* | lingo, language, linguistics, bilingual |
| LITER | *letter* | literate, alliteration, literal |
| LITH | *stone* | monolith, lithograph, megalith |
| LOQU, LOC, LOG | *speech, thought* | eloquent, loquacious, colloquial, colloquy, soliloquy, circumlocution, interlocutor, monologue, dialogue, eulogy, philology, neologism |
| LUC, LUM | *light* | lucid, illuminate, elucidate, pellucid, translucent |
| LUD, LUS | *play* | ludicrous, allude, delusion, allusion, illusory |
| MACRO | *great* | macrocosm, macrobiotics |
| MAG, MAJ, MAS, MAX | *great* | magnify, magnanimous, magnate, magnitude majesty, master, maximum |
| MAL | *bad* | malady, maladroit, malevolent, malodorous |
| MAN | *hand* | manual, manuscript, emancipate, manifest |
| MAR | *sea* | submarine, marine, maritime |
| MATER, MATR | *mother* | maternal, matron, matrilineal |
| MEDI | *middle* | intermediary, medieval, mediate |
| MEGA | *great* | megaphone, megalomania, megaton, megalith |
| MEMOR, MEMEN | *remember* | memory, memento, memorabilia, memoir |

| ROOT | MEANING | EXAMPLES |
|---|---|---|
| METER, METR, MENS | *measure* | meter, thermometer, perimeter, metronome, commensurate |
| MICRO | *small* | microscope, microorganism, microcosm, microbe |
| MIS | *wrong, bad, hate* | misunderstand, misanthrope, misapprehension, misconstrue, misnomer, mishap |
| MIT, MISS | *send* | transmit, emit, missive |
| MOLL | *soft* | mollify, emollient, mollusk |
| MON, MONIT | *warn* | admonish, monitor, premonition |
| MONO | *one* | monologue, monotonous, monogamy, monolith, monochrome |
| MOR | *custom, manner* | moral, mores, morose |
| MOR, MORT | *dead* | morbid, moribund, mortal, amortize |
| MORPH | *shape* | amorphous, anthropomorphic, metamorphosis, morphology |
| MOV, MOT, MOB, MOM | *move* | remove, motion, mobile, momentum, momentous |
| MUT | *change* | mutate, mutability, immutable, commute |
| NAT, NASC | *born* | native, nativity, natal, neonate, innate, cognate, nascent, renascent, renaissance |
| NAU, NAV | *ship, sailor* | nautical, nauseous, navy, circumnavigate |
| NEG | *not, deny* | negative, abnegate, renege |
| NEO | *new* | neoclassical, neophyte, neologism, neonate |
| NIHIL | *none, nothing* | annihilation, nihilism |
| NOM, NYM | *name* | nominate, nomenclature, nominal, cognomen, misnomer, ignominious, antonym, homonym, pseudonym, synonym, anonymity |
| NOX, NIC, NEC, NOC | *harm* | obnoxious, noxious, pernicious, internecine, innocuous |
| NOV | *new* | novelty, innovation, novitiate |
| NUMER | *number* | numeral, numerous, innumerable, enumerate |
| OB | *against* | obstruct, obdurate, obfuscate, obnoxious, obsequious, obstinate, obstreperous, obtrusive |
| OMNI | *all* | omnipresent, omnipotent, omniscient, omnivorous |
| ONER | *burden* | onerous, onus, exonerate |
| OPER | *work* | operate, cooperate, inoperable |
| PAC | *peace* | pacify, pacifist, pacific |

| ROOT | MEANING | EXAMPLES |
|------|---------|----------|
| PALP | *feel* | palpable, palpitation |
| PAN | *all* | panorama, panacea, panegyric, pandemic, panoply |
| PATER, PATR | *father* | paternal, paternity, patriot, compatriot, expatriate, patrimony, patricide, patrician |
| PATH, PASS | *feel, suffer* | sympathy, antipathy, empathy, apathy, pathos, impassioned |
| PEC | *money* | pecuniary, impecunious, peculation |
| PED, POD | *foot* | pedestrian, pediment, expedient, biped, quadruped, tripod |
| PEL, PULS | *drive* | compel, compelling, expel, propel, compulsion |
| PEN | *almost* | peninsula, penultimate, penumbra |
| PEND, PENS | *hang* | pendant, pendulous, compendium, suspense, propensity |
| PER | *through, by, for, throughout* | perambulator, percipient, perfunctory, permeable, perspicacious, pertinacious, perturbation, perusal, perennial, peregrinate |
| PER | *against, destruction* | perfidious, pernicious, perjure |
| PERI | *around* | perimeter, periphery, perihelion, peripatetic |
| PET | *seek, go toward* | petition, impetus, impetuous, petulant, centripetal |
| PHIL | *love* | philosopher, philanderer, philanthropy, bibliophile, philology |
| PHOB | *fear* | phobia, claustrophobia, xenophobia |
| PHON | *sound* | phonograph, megaphone, euphony, phonetics, phonics |
| PLAC | *calm, please* | placate, implacable, placid, complacent |
| PON, POS | *put, place* | postpone, proponent, exponent, preposition, posit, interpose, juxtaposition, depose |
| PORT | *carry* | portable, deportment, rapport |
| POT | *drink* | potion, potable |
| POT | *power* | potential, potent, impotent, potentate, omnipotence |
| PRE | *before* | precede, precipitate, preclude, precocious, precursor, predilection, predisposition, preponderance, prepossessing, presage, prescient, prejudice, predict, premonition, preposition |
| PRIM, PRI | *first* | prime, primary, primal, primeval, primordial, pristine |

| ROOT | MEANING | EXAMPLES |
|------|---------|----------|
| PRO | *ahead, forth* | proceed, proclivity, procrastinator, profane, profuse, progenitor, progeny, prognosis, prologue, promontory, propel, proponent, propose, proscribe, protestation, provoke |
| PROTO | *first* | prototype, protagonist, protocol |
| PROX, PROP | *near* | approximate, proximity, propinquity |
| PSEUDO | *false* | pseudoscientific, pseudonym |
| PYR | *fire* | pyre, pyrotechnics, pyromania |
| QUAD, QUAR, QUAT | *four* | quadrilateral, quadrant, quadruped, quarter, quarantine, quaternary |
| QUES, QUER, QUIS, QUIR | *question* | quest, inquest, query, querulous, inquisitive, inquiry |
| QUIE | *quiet* | disquiet, acquiesce, quiescent, requiem |
| QUINT, QUIN | *five* | quintuplets, quintessence |
| RADI, RAMI | *branch* | radius, radiate, radiant, eradicate, ramification |
| RECT, REG | *straight, rule* | rectangle, rectitude, rectify, regular |
| REG | *king, rule* | regal, regent, interregnum |
| RETRO | *backward* | retrospective, retroactive, retrograde |
| RID, RIS | *laugh* | ridiculous, deride, derision |
| ROG | *ask* | interrogate, derogatory, abrogate, arrogate, arrogant |
| RUD | *rough, crude* | rude, rudimentary |
| RUPT | *break* | disrupt, interrupt, rupture, erupt |
| SACR, SANCT | *holy* | sacred, sacrilege, consecrate, sanctify, sanction, sacrosanct |
| SCRIB, SCRIPT, SCRIV | *write* | scribe, ascribe, circumscribe, inscribe, proscribe, script, manuscript, scrivener |
| SE | *apart, away* | separate, segregate, secede, sedition |
| SEC, SECT, SEG | *cut* | sector, dissect, bisect, intersect, segment, secant |
| SED, SID | *sit* | sedate, sedentary, supersede, reside, residence, assiduous, insidious |
| SEM | *seed, sow* | seminar, seminal, disseminate |
| SEN | *old* | senior, senile, senescent |
| SENT, SENS | *feel, think* | sentiment, sentient, nonsense, assent, consensus, sensual |
| SEQU, SECU | *follow* | sequence, sequel, subsequent, obsequious, obsequy, non sequitur, consecutive |
| SIM, SEM | *similar, same* | similar, verisimilitude, semblance, dissemble, |

| ROOT | MEANING | EXAMPLES |
|------|---------|----------|
| SIGN | *mark, sign* | signal, designation, assignation |
| SIN | *curve* | sine curve, sinuous, insinuate |
| SOL | *sun* | solar, parasol, solarium, solstice |
| SOL | *alone* | solo, solitude, soliloquy, solipsism |
| SOMN | *sleep* | insomnia, somnolent, somnambulist |
| SON | *sound* | sonic, consonance, dissonance, assonance, sonorous, resonate |
| SOPH | *wisdom* | philosopher, sophistry, sophisticated, sophomoric |
| SPEC, SPIC | *see, look* | spectator, circumspect, retrospective, perspective, perspicacious |
| SPER | *hope* | prosper, prosperous, despair, desperate |
| SPERS, SPAR | *scatter* | disperse, aspersion, sparse, disparate |
| SPIR | *breathe* | respire, inspire, spiritual, aspire, transpire |
| STRICT, STRING | *bind* | strict, stricture, constrict, stringent, astringent |
| STRUCT, STRU | *build* | structure, obstruct, construe |
| SUB | *under* | subconscious, subjugate, subliminal, subpoena, subsequent, subterranean, subvert |
| SUMM | *highest* | summit, summary, consummate |
| SUPER, SUR | *above* | supervise, supercilious, supersede, superannuated, superfluous, insurmountable, surfeit |
| SURGE, SURRECT | *rise* | surge, resurgent, insurgent, insurrection |
| SYN, SYM | *together* | synthesis, sympathy, synonym, syncopation, synopsis, symposium, symbiosis |
| TACIT, TIC | *silent* | tacit, taciturn, reticent |
| TACT, TAG, TANG | *touch* | tact, tactile, contagious, tangent, tangential, tangible |
| TEN, TIN, TAIN | *hold, twist* | detention, tenable, tenacious, pertinacious, retinue, retain |
| TEND, TENS, TENT | *stretch* | intend, distend, tension, tensile, ostensible, contentious |
| TERM | *end* | terminal, terminus, terminate, interminable |
| TERR | *earth, land* | terrain, terrestrial, extraterrestrial, subterranean |
| TEST | *witness* | testify, attest, testimonial, testament, detest, protestation |
| THE | *god* | atheist, theology, apotheosis, theocracy |
| THERM | *heat* | thermometer, thermal, thermonuclear, hypothermia |
| TIM | *fear, frightened* | timid, intimidate, timorous |

| ROOT | MEANING | EXAMPLES |
| --- | --- | --- |
| TOP | *place* | topic, topography, utopia |
| TORT | *twist* | distort, extort, tortuous |
| TORP | *stiff, numb* | torpedo, torpid, torpor |
| TOX | *poison* | toxic, toxin, intoxication |
| TRACT | *draw* | tractor, intractable, protract |
| TRANS | *across, over, through, beyond* | transport, transgress, transient, transitory, translucent, transmutation, transpire, intransigent |
| TREM, TREP | *shake* | tremble, tremor, tremulous, trepidation, intrepid |
| TURB | *shake* | disturb, turbulent, perturbation |
| UMBR | *shadow* | umbrella, umbrage, adumbrate, penumbra |
| UNI, UN | *one* | unify, unilateral, unanimous |
| URB | *city* | urban, suburban, urbane |
| VAC | *empty* | vacant, evacuate, vacuous |
| VAL, VAIL | *value, strength* | valid, valor, ambivalent, convalescence, avail, prevail, countervail |
| VEN, VENT | *come* | convene, contravene, intervene, venue, convention, circumvent, advent, adventitious |
| VER | *true* | verify, verity, verisimilitude, veracious, aver, verdict |
| VERB | *word* | verbal, verbose, verbiage, verbatim |
| VERT, VERS | *turn* | avert, convert, revert, incontrovertible, divert, subvert, versatile, aversion |
| VICT, VINC | *conquer* | victory, conviction, evict, evince, invincible |
| VID, VIS | *see* | evident, vision, visage, supervise |
| VIL | *base, mean* | vile, vilify, revile |
| VIV, VIT | *life* | vivid, convivial, vivacious, vital |
| VOC, VOK, VOW | *call, voice* | vocal, equivocate, vociferous, convoke, evoke, invoke, avow |
| VOL | *wish* | voluntary, malevolent, benevolent, volition |
| VOLV, VOLUT | *turn, roll* | revolve, evolve, convoluted |
| VOR | *eat* | devour, carnivorous, omnivorous, voracious |

## VOCABULARY LIST

| WORD | DEFINITION, CONTEXT, SYNONYMS |
|---|---|
| **ABDICATE** | to give up a position, right, or power<br>*With the angry mob clamoring outside the palace, the king* abdicated *his throne and fled with his queen.*<br>Synonyms: **quit, resign, renounce, step down** |
| **ABDUCT** | to carry, take, or lead away forcefully and wrongfully<br>*The kidnappers planned to* abduct *the child and hold her for ransom.*<br>Synonyms: **kidnap, carry off** |
| **ABHOR** | to hate, to view with repugnance, to detest<br>*After repeated failure to learn the Pythagorean theorem, Susan began to* abhor *geometry.*<br>Synonyms: **hate, loathe, abominate** |
| **ABSURD** | ridiculously unreasonable, lacking logic<br>*Ironing one's underwear is* absurd.<br>Synonyms: **ridiculous, ludicrous, preposterous, bizarre** |
| **ABYSS** | deep hole; deep immeasurable space, gulf, or cavity<br>*Looking down into the* abyss *was terrifying, for I could not see the bottom.*<br>Synonyms: **chasm, pit** |
| **ACCELERATE** | to increase in speed, cause to move faster<br>*The new disease has spread like wildfire, causing researchers to* accelerate *their search for a cure.*<br>Synonyms: **speed up, hasten, expedite** |
| **ACCLAIM** | (n) praise, enthusiastic approval<br>*The artist won international* acclaim; *critics and viewers all over the world were intrigued by the works.*<br>Synonyms: **praise, approval**<br>(v) to approve, to welcome with applause and praise<br>*The critic was eager to* acclaim *the actress for her performance.*<br>Synonyms: **cheer, applaud, praise, honor** |
| **ACUTE** | sharp in some way (as in an acute angle) or sharp in intellect; crucial<br>*There is an* acute *shortage of food will ultimately result in a famine if something is not done soon to increase the food supply.*<br>Synonyms: **perceptive, sharp, keen, shrewd, crucial** |
| **ADAGE** | old saying, proverb<br>*"A penny saved is a penny earned" is a popular* adage.<br>Synonyms: **proverb, maxim** |

| WORD | DEFINITION, CONTEXT, SYNONYMS |
|---|---|
| ADHERE | to stick fast; to hold to<br><br>*(1) After we put glue on his pants, John* adhered *to the chair.*<br><br>*(2) He was a strict Catholic who* adhered *to all the teachings of the Church.*<br><br>Synonyms: **stick to** (like glue or adhesive tape); **follow** |
| ADJOURN | to postpone; to suspend (a meeting) for a period of time<br><br>*Since it was late in the day, the prosecutor moved that the court* adjourn *for the day.*<br><br>Synonyms: **suspend, recess, postpone** |
| ADJUNCT | something or someone associated with another but in a defendant or secondary position<br><br>*An* adjunct *professor is one not given the same full-time status as other faculty members.*<br><br>Synonyms: **additional, supporting, assisting, accessory** |
| ADMONISH | to scold (sometimes in a good natured way); to urge to duty, remind; to advise against something<br><br>*My mother began to* admonish *me about my poor grades.*<br><br>Synonyms: **warn, caution, scold** |
| ADORN | to decorate or add beauty to, for instance with ornaments; to make pleasing, more attractive<br><br>*She* adorned *her hair with flowers.*<br><br>Synonyms: **decorate, ornament, embellish** |
| ADVERSARY | opponent or enemy<br><br>*Democrats and Republicans are usually* adversaries *in the political world.*<br><br>Synonyms: **enemy, foe, opponent** |
| AERONAUTIC | relating to aircraft<br><br>*The Air Force's Stealth plane is reported to be a masterpiece of* aeronautic *design.* |
| AFFABLE | pleasantly easy to get along with; friendly and warm<br><br>*He was an* affable *host and made us feel right at home.*<br><br>Synonyms: **agreeable, amiable** |
| AFFECTATION | attempt to appear to be what one is not for the purpose of impressing others (for instance, pretending to have a pretentiously cultured accent)<br><br>*Justin once spent three months in France and has now acquired the silly* affectation *of using French phrases in casual conversation.*<br><br>Synonyms: **pretension, unnaturalness, artificiality, mannerism, pretense, airs, sham, facade, pose, posture** |

| WORD | DEFINITION, CONTEXT, SYNONYMS |
|---|---|
| AGHAST | overcome by surprise, disgust, or amazement; seized with terror; shocked<br><br>*The investigator was* aghast *at the horrible conditions in the nursing home.*<br><br>Synonyms: **astounded, dismayed, appalled, astonished, shocked** |
| AGILITY | condition of being able to move quickly and easily or being mentally alert<br><br>*Strength and* agility *are important for an athlete.*<br><br>Synonyms: **skillfulness, dexterity, nimbleness** |
| AGITATE | to shake or grow excited; to move around a lot, to disturb or excite emotionally<br><br>*The bat's flight into the classroom managed to* agitate *the teacher so much that he went home early.*<br><br>Synonyms: **disturb, upset, stir up** (like a washing machine) |
| AIMLESS | lacking purpose or goals<br><br>*After its engine died, the boat drifted* aimlessly *for days.*<br><br>Synonyms: **purposeless, haphazard, accidental** |
| ALLEVIATE | to make easier to bear, lessen<br><br>*This medicine will help to* alleviate *the pain.*<br><br>Synonyms: **relieve, allay, assuage, ease, decrease, lessen, mitigate** |
| ALLURE | fascination, appeal<br><br>*Video games have an* allure *that some people find impossible to resist.*<br><br>Synonyms: **temptation, attraction, fascination** |
| ALOOF | distant in relations with other people<br><br>*The newcomer remained* aloof *from all our activities and therefore made no new friends.*<br><br>Synonyms: **detached, cool, blase, remote** |
| ALTRUISTIC | concerned for the welfare of others<br><br>*The* altruistic *woman gave out money to all who seemed needy.*<br><br>Synonyms: **benevolent, charitable, compassionate, humane** |
| AMATEUR | (n) someone not paid to engage in a hobby, sport, art, etc.<br><br>*Since professionals couldn't play, only* amateur *athletes were allowed to participate in the Olympics.*<br><br>Synonyms: **devotee, dabbler, enthusiast, buff, nonprofessional**<br><br>(adj) like an amateur<br><br>*The brilliant author James Joyce was an* amateur *singer.* |

| WORD | DEFINITION, CONTEXT, SYNONYMS |
|---|---|
| AMEND | to improve; to alter; to add to, or subtract from by formal procedure<br><br>*Congress will* amend *the bill so that the president will sign it.*<br><br>Synonyms: **alter, improve, repair, mend, make better, ameliorate** |
| AMOROUS | having to do with love<br><br>*The love-sick young poet wrote many* amorous *poems about his girlfriend.*<br><br>Synonyms: **romantic, erotic** |
| AMORPHOUS | lacking a specific shape<br><br>*In the movie* The Blob, *the creature was an* amorphous *one that was constantly changing shape.*<br><br>Synonyms: **shapeless, vague** |
| AMPHIBIAN | animal at home both on land and in the water<br><br>*A frog, which lives both on land and in the water, is an* amphibian. |
| ANGULAR | having clear angles or thin and bony facial features.<br><br>*The figures on the left side of the painting are very* angular, *whereas the figures on the right are rounded.*<br><br>Synonyms: **lanky, gaunt, bony** |
| ANIMOSITY | feeling of ill will, intense dislike for someone or something<br><br>*The deep-rooted* animosity *between them made it difficult for the brothers to work together.*<br><br>Synonyms: **ill will, ill feeling, bitterness, rancor, acrimony** |
| ANNIHILATE | to destroy completely<br><br>*The first troops to land on the beach during the invasion were* annihilated *by the powerful artillery of the enemy.*<br><br>Synonyms: **destroy, devastate, demolish** |
| ANTIDOTE | remedy to relieve the effects of poison<br><br>*The first aid kit included an* antidote *for snake bite.*<br><br>Synonyms: **remedy, counteragent, neutralizer** |
| APERTURE | opening<br><br>*The* aperture *of a camera lens is a circular opening of variable diameter that regulates the amount of light entering the lens.*<br><br>Synonyms: **hole, gap, space, opening, crack** |
| AQUEOUS | similar to, or composed of water<br><br>*The inside of an eyeball is filled with an* aqueous *substance.*<br><br>Synonyms: **watery, aquatic, hydrous, liquid** |

| WORD | DEFINITION, CONTEXT, SYNONYMS |
|---|---|
| ARDENT | characterized by passion or desire<br><br>*After a 25-game losing streak, even the Mets' most* ardent *fans realized the team wouldn't finish first.*<br><br>Synonyms: **passionate, enthusiastic, fervent** |
| ARID | very dry, lacking moisture; unproductive, unimaginative<br><br>*The* arid *farmland produced no crops.*<br><br>Synonyms: **dry, parched, barren, dull, uninteresting, insipid** |
| AROMA | pleasing fragrance; any odor or smell<br><br>*The* aroma *in the bakery made her mouth water.*<br><br>Synonyms: **smell, fragrance, odor** |
| ARTICULATE | (adj) well-spoken, lucidly presented<br><br>*Joe's* articulate *argument was so persuasive that we all agreed with him.*<br><br>Synonyms: **eloquent, glib**<br><br>(v) to pronounce clearly<br><br>*The great actor* articulated *every word so clearly it was easy to understand him.*<br><br>Synonyms: **enunciate** |
| ARTIFICE | (1) trickery, clever ruse<br><br>*Ralph's use of rubber masks proved to be a brilliant* artifice.<br><br>Synonyms: **stratagem, trick, ploy, deception, ruse, maneuver**<br><br>(2) ability to create or imagine<br><br>*Many question the meaningfulness of Jamie's science fiction novel, but its fantastic images and ingenious plot cannot fail to impress one with his sheer* artifice.<br><br>Synonyms: **creativity, inventiveness, innovation, resourcefulness, imagination, ingenuity** |
| ASCERTAIN | to find out or discover by examination<br><br>*Try though he did, the archaeologist couldn't* ascertain *the correct age of the Piltdown man's skeleton.*<br><br>Synonyms: **determine, discover, unearth, find out** |
| ASSAILABLE | able to be attacked or assaulted by blows or words<br><br>*Carcassonne was widely thought to be an* unassailable *fortress after it resisted a siege by Charlemagne.*<br><br>Synonyms: **vulnerable, exposed, unprotected** |

| WORD | DEFINITION, CONTEXT, SYNONYMS |
|---|---|
| ASTOUND | to overwhelm with amazement<br><br>*The extent of his great knowledge never ceases to* astound *me.*<br><br>Synonyms: **amaze, stupefy, stun** |
| ASTUTE | shrewd and perceptive; able to understand clearly and quickly<br><br>*The novelist Judy Blume is an* astute *judge of human character.*<br><br>Synonyms: **keen, discerning, penetrating, incisive, perceptive, crafty, foxy, wily, shrewd** |
| ATROCITY | horrible act<br><br>*During the Indian bid for freedom from British colonial rule, a British officer committed the* atrocity *of slaughtering a large congregation of peaceful Indian demonstrators.*<br><br>Synonyms: **horror, barbarity, outrage** |
| AUDACITY | boldness or daring, especially with disregard for personal safety<br><br>*He had the* audacity *to insult the president to his face.*<br><br>Synonyms: **boldness, daring, impudence** |
| AUTHORITATIVE | having great authority<br><br>*J. R. R. Tolkien, who had written many books about Old English poetry, was widely considered to be the most* authoritative *scholar in the field.*<br><br>Synonyms: **masterful** |
| BANAL | boringly predictable<br><br>*A boring conversation is likely to be full of* banal *statements like "Have a nice day."*<br><br>Synonyms: **boring, dull, bland, insipid** |
| BANISH | to send away, condemn to exile; drive or put away<br><br>*After the incident with the food fight, Arthur was* banished *from the lunchroom.*<br><br>Synonyms: **send away, get rid of, expel, exile, deport** |
| BARRIER | anything that makes progress harder or impossible; a limit or boundary<br><br>*(1) The Pythagorean theorem has been a* barrier *to Donald's complete understanding of geometry.*<br>*(2) To discourage visitors, Janet built a* barrier *in front of the entrance to her room.*<br><br>Synonyms: **obstacle** |
| BEGUILE | to delude, deceive by trickery<br><br>Beguiled *by the supernatural songs of the Sirens, Odysseus wanted to abandon all his men and forget his family.*<br><br>Synonyms: **charm, allure, bewitch, captivate** |

| WORD | DEFINITION, CONTEXT, SYNONYMS |
|---|---|
| BELLIGERENCE | aggressive hostility<br>*A soldier can be shocked by the* belligerence *of his enemy.*<br>Synonyms: **aggressiveness, combativeness** |
| BENEFACTOR | someone giving financial or general assistance<br>*A wealthy alumnus who gives $5 million to his old college would be considered a great* benefactor.<br>Synonyms: **patron, backer, donor** |
| BENEFICIAL | advantageous, helpful, conferring benefit<br>*Eating vegetables and getting 8 hours of sleep are* beneficial *to your health, but they sure aren't much fun.*<br>Synonyms: **advantageous, favorable** |
| BENEVOLENCE | inclination to do good deeds<br>*The* benevolence *of the generous donor was recognized by a plaque.*<br>Synonyms: **largess** |
| BEWILDERED | completely confused or puzzled, perplexed<br>*I was* bewildered *by the complex algebra problem.*<br>Synonyms: **confused, puzzled, perplexed** |
| BIAS | (n) prejudice, particular tendency<br>*Racial* bias *in employment is illegal in the United States.*<br>Synonyms: **partiality**<br>(v) to cause prejudice in (a person); to influence unfairly<br>*The article is not accurate and may* bias *some readers.* |
| BILE | ill temper, irritability<br>*Mr. Watkins is harsh when he grades essays; his comments reveal his* bile *and sharp tongue.*<br>Synonyms: **bitterness** |
| BLISS | supreme happiness, utter joy or contentment; heaven, paradise<br>*For lovers of ice cream, this new flavor is absolute* bliss.<br>Synonyms: **joy, delight, ecstasy** |
| BOISTEROUS | loud and unrestrained<br>*The* boisterous *party made so much noise last night that I got no sleep.*<br>Synonyms: **loud, noisy, raucous** |
| BOTANIST | scientist specializing in study of plants<br>*A* botanist *is a scientist who studies plants.* |

| WORD | DEFINITION, CONTEXT, SYNONYMS |
| --- | --- |
| BOUNTY | generosity in giving; reward<br>*The police offered a* bounty *for the capture of the criminal.*<br>Synonyms: **abundance, cornucopia, reward, loot** |
| BRAVADO | showy and pretentious display of courage<br>*The coward's* bravado *quickly vanished when his captors threatened to hit him; he began to whine for mercy.*<br>Synonyms: **bluster, bombast, swagger** |
| BREVITY | state of being brief, of not lasting a long time<br>*The* brevity *of your visit to my home implied that you did not enjoy my family's company.*<br>Synonyms: **shortness, fleetness, swiftness** |
| BRIG | ship's prison<br>*Captain Bligh had the rebellious sailor thrown into the* brig.<br>Synonyms: **jail, prison** |
| BURNISH | (n) to make shiny by rubbing, as with a cloth<br>*Mr. Jin loved to stand in the sun and* burnish *his luxury car until it gleamed.*<br>Synonyms: **shine, polish, buff, varnish**<br>(n) shininess produced by burnishing<br>*They all admired the* burnish *on the car.*<br>Synonyms: **shine, luster, gleam, brilliance** |
| CACHE | hiding place for treasures, etc.; anything in such a hiding place<br>*The secret panel hid a* cache *of jewels.*<br>Synonyms: **stash** |
| CAJOLE | to wheedle, persuade with promises or flattery, coax<br>*The spoiled girl could* cajole *her father into buying her anything.*<br>Synonyms: **coax, wheedle** |
| CAMOUFLAGE | (n) disguise worn in order to deceive an enemy; for instance, uniforms the color of trees and dirt<br>*The soldiers wore* camouflage *on their helmets.*<br>Synonyms: **disguise**<br>(v) to deceive by means of camouflage<br>*They have* camouflaged *the missile silo in order to deceive enemy bombers.*<br>Synonyms: **disguise, obscure, cloud, hide** |

| WORD | DEFINITION, CONTEXT, SYNONYMS |
|---|---|
| **CANDOR** | frankness and sincerity; fairness <br><br> *The candor of his confession impressed his parents, and they gave him a light punishment as a result.* <br><br> Synonyms: **honesty, sincerity** |
| **CANINE** | relating to dogs <br><br> Canine *relates to dogs in the same way as feline relates to cats.* |
| **CANTANKEROUS** | quarrelsome and grouchy <br><br> *The old grouch was always in a* cantankerous *mood.* <br><br> Synonyms: **grouchy, argumentative, ill-tempered** |
| **CAPRICE** | sudden, unpredictable change <br><br> *With the* caprice *of an irrational man, he often went from rage to laughter.* <br><br> Synonyms: **impulse, whim, fancy** |
| **CASCADE** | (n) waterfall, as in a type of fireworks resembling a waterfall <br><br> Synonyms: **waterfall, torrent** <br><br> *The* cascade *of sparks from the fireworks caused the crowd to ooh and aah.* <br><br> (v) to fall like a cascade <br><br> *The stream flowed over the cliff and* cascaded *into the valley below.* |
| **CATASTROPHE** | disastrous event <br><br> *The eruption was truly a* catastrophe; *lava and ash buried several towns on the slopes of the volcano.* <br><br> Synonyms: **disaster, ruin, devastation** |
| **CELESTIAL** | relating to the heavens <br><br> *Venus is a* celestial *body sometimes visible from Earth.* <br><br> Synonyms: **heavenly, divine, spiritual** |
| **CENSOR** | to remove material from books, plays, magazines, etc. for moral, political, or religious reasons <br><br> *After they* censored *the "dirty" parts out of the book, all that was left was the dedication and half of the cover.* <br><br> Synonyms: **suppress, delete** |
| **CHASM** | gorge or deep canyon <br><br> *If you look down from the top floor of a New York City skyscraper, it seems as though you're looking into a deep* chasm. <br><br> Synonyms: **ravine, canyon, abyss** |
| **CHILLY** | uncomfortably cold in temperature or demeanor <br><br> *The evil king swept through the room, receiving a* chilly *reception from the townspeople.* <br><br> Synonyms: **cool, crisp, fresh, unfriendly, unwelcoming, frosty** |

| WORD | DEFINITION, CONTEXT, SYNONYMS |
|---|---|
| CHOLERIC | bad-tempered<br><br>*The grumpy old man was* choleric *whenever he didn't get his morning coffee.*<br><br>Synonyms: **bad-tempered** |
| CHOREOGRAPHER | person creating and arranging dances for stage performances<br><br>*After being an innovative dancer, Martha Graham became a* choreographer *and arranged many innovative dance performances for her company.* |
| CHORUS | group acting together<br><br>*The* chorus *of over fifty people harmonized as one.*<br><br>Synonyms: **group, band** |
| CHRONIC | continuing over a long period of time, long-standing<br><br>*Joshua suffered from* chronic *tiredness; most days he slept straight through geometry class.*<br><br>Synonyms: **continuous, constant, persistent, confirmed, settled** |
| CIRCUMSCRIBE | to encircle with a line; to limit in any way<br><br>*The Howards' country estate is* circumscribed *by rolling hills.*<br><br>Synonyms: **limit, outline, bound, define, encompass** |
| COARSE | rough or loose in texture or speech<br><br>*My feet felt smooth after walking though the rough,* coarse *sand of the beach.*<br><br>Synonyms: **rough, scratchy, prickly, rude, impolite, uncivil** |
| COCOON | a protective case that envelops (usually an insect) during development<br><br>*Our sleeping bags felt like* cocoons; *we were snug and warm despite the cold storm that raged outside.*<br><br>Synonyms: **wrap, swaddle, cloak, envelop, cover** |
| COLLISION | crash, clash, or conflict<br><br>*The* collision *of the two cars made a terrible sound and tied up traffic for hours.*<br><br>Synonyms: **crash, clash, impact** |
| COMMUNICATIVE | talkative and likely to communicate<br><br>*Despite their limited knowledge of English, the foreigners were eager to be* communicative *with the host family.*<br><br>Synonyms: **talkative, articulate, vocal, expressive** |
| COMPASSION | deep feeling of pity or sympathy for others<br><br>*The jury decided that the cold-hearted killer felt no* compassion *for his victims.*<br><br>Synonyms: **pity, sympathy, mercy** |

| WORD | DEFINITION, CONTEXT, SYNONYMS |
|------|-------------------------------|
| COMPEL | to force someone or something to act<br><br>*Even torture couldn't* compel *the spy to reveal his secrets.*<br><br>Synonyms: **force, coerce, goad, motivate** |
| COMPETENT | having enough skill for some purpose; adequate but not exceptional<br><br>*He was not the most qualified candidate, but at least he was competent.*<br><br>Synonyms: **qualified, capable, fit** |
| CONCISE | brief and compact<br><br>*Barry gave a* concise *speech: he said everything he needed to and was finished in five minutes.*<br><br>Synonyms: **brief, terse, succinct, compact** |
| CONDONE | to pardon, to forgive, or overlook<br><br>*"We cannot* condone *your behavior," said Ben's parents after he missed his curfew. "You are grounded for two weeks."*<br><br>Synonyms: **pardon, excuse, forgive, absolve, overlook, accept, tolerate, allow, permit, suffer, endure, bear, stomach** |
| CONFIDENTIAL | done secretly or in confidence<br><br>*The* confidential *memorandum listed everyone's salary.*<br><br>Synonyms: **secret, covert, off-the-record** |
| CONSTRICT | to squeeze, make tighter<br><br>*As my chest became* constricted, *I found it difficult to breathe.*<br><br>Synonyms: **choke, stifle, contract, smother** |
| CONTEMPLATION | thoughtful observation<br><br>*When the philosopher studied complicated issues, he often became so lost in* contemplation *that he forget to eat or sleep.*<br><br>Synonyms: **thought, deliberation, meditation, reflection** |
| CONTEND | to fight or struggle against; to debate<br><br>*Some people* contend *that no boxer past or present would have been able to* contend *with Muhammad Ali for boxing's World Heavyweight Championship.*<br><br>Synonyms: **combat, compete, argue, assert** |
| CONTENTIOUS | eager to quarrel<br><br>*The* contentious *gentleman angrily ridiculed whatever anyone said.*<br><br>Synonyms: **quarrelsome, cantankerous, feisty, combative, irascible, pugnacious** |
| CONVENE | to assemble or meet<br><br>*The members of the board* convene *at least once a week.*<br><br>Synonyms: **gather, assemble, meet** |

| WORD | DEFINITION, CONTEXT, SYNONYMS |
|---|---|
| CONVENTIONAL | established or approved by general usage |
| | Conventional *wisdom today says that a good job requires a college education.* |
| | Synonyms: **customary, well-established, habitual** |
| COOPERATE | act together to work toward the same end |
| | *Those who refuse to* cooperate *with law enforcement could eventually be jailed.* |
| | Synonyms: **collaborate, unite, combine, liaise** |
| COPIOUS | abundant, large in number or quantity, plentiful |
| | *The hostess had prepared* copious *amounts of food.* |
| | Synonyms: **abundant, plentiful, profuse** |
| COUNTENANCE | (n) face or facial expression, or the general appearance or behavior of something or someone |
| | *Jeremy felt quite unsettled about the new Music Appreciation instructor; she seemed to have an evil* countenance. |
| | Synonyms: **face, aspect, appearance, bearing, demeanor, air, visage** |
| | (v) to approve or support |
| | *When Dorothy and Irene started their nightly pillow fight, the babysitter warned them, "I will not* countenance *such behavior."* |
| | Synonyms: **sanction, approve, endorse, bless, favor, encourage, condone** |
| COUPLET | unit of poetry with two rhyming lines |
| | *"Rub a dub, dub/Three men in a tub" is an example of a* couplet. |
| COURIER | person who carries messages, news, or information |
| | *The* courier *will deliver the document.* |
| | Synonyms: **messenger, runner, carrier** |
| CUE | hint or guiding suggestion |
| | *My mother cleared her throat loudly, which was my* cue *to be quiet and let her speak.* |
| | Synonyms: **hint, prompt, signal** |
| CURVATURE | state of being curved |
| | *Someone with* curvature *of the spine usually doesn't stand up straight.* |
| | Synonyms: **arc, arch, bow** |
| DAWDLE | to waste time with idle lingering |
| | *If you* dawdle *on your way to school, you'll be late.* |
| | Synonyms: **delay, linger, dally** |
| DEADLOCK | standoff caused by opposition of two conflicting forces |
| | *Despite days of debate, the legislature remained at a* deadlock *with 50 votes "yea" and 50 votes "nay."* |
| | Synonyms: **stalemate, standoff, standstill** |

| WORD | DEFINITION, CONTEXT, SYNONYMS |
|---|---|
| DEARTH | scarcity, lack<br>*The* dearth *of supplies in our city made it difficult to hold out for long against the attack of the aliens.*<br>Synonyms: **shortage, lack, scarcity** |
| DEBRIS | charred or spoiled remains of something that has been destroyed<br>*Scavengers searched for valuables amid the* debris.<br>Synonyms: **trash, rubbish, wreckage, remains** |
| DECADE | period of ten years<br>*The 1960s are known as the* decade *of protest.* |
| DECEIT | deception or tricky falseness<br>*Morgan Le Fay, the sorceress, used spells and* deceit *to lure Merlin away from Camelot.*<br>Synonyms: **dishonesty, fraudulence, deception, trickery** |
| DECEIVE | to delude or mislead<br>*A liar often will try to* deceive *you by not telling the truth.*<br>Synonyms: **mislead, delude, trick, dupe, lie** |
| DECLAMATION | exercise in speech giving; attack or protest<br>*The candidate made a* declamation *against the new tax law.*<br>Synonyms: **long speech, harangue** |
| DEFICIENT | defective, insufficient, or inadequate<br>*Failing to study will make you* deficient *in your readiness for the test.*<br>Synonyms: **inadequate, defective, insufficient, failing, lacking** |
| DEHYDRATE | to remove water from<br>*Too much time in the sun will* dehydrate *you.*<br>Synonyms: **dry out, parch** |
| DEJECTED | depressed, sad<br>*He was too ambitious to become* dejected *by a temporary setback.*<br>Synonyms: **saddened, depressed, discouraged, disheartened** |
| DELAY | (v) to make something or someone late<br>*The announcement at the station let us know that our train was delayed; it arrived 45 minutes late.*<br>Synonyms: **detain, retard, postpone, hinder**<br>(n) a period of time in which something is late<br>*There was a 3-hour* delay *at the airport, and we nearly missed our connecting flight.*<br>Synonyms: **holdup, wait, deferment** |

| WORD | DEFINITION, CONTEXT, SYNONYMS |
|---|---|
| DELUDE | to deceive, to mislead<br>*After three hours of pouring rain, we stopped* deluding *ourselves that the picnic could go on.*<br>Synonyms: **deceive, dupe, hoax, trick** |
| DELUGE | (n) flood, large overflowing of water; too much of anything<br>*The president's veto of the housing bill brought a* deluge *of angry calls and letters from people all over America.*<br>Synonyms: **flood, overflow, inundation, torrent**<br>(v) to overflow, to inundate, to flood<br>*The actor was* deluged *with fan mail.*<br>Synonyms: **inundate, engulf, flood, overwhelm** |
| DEMOTE | to reduce to a lower grade or class<br>*The army will* demote *any soldier who disobeys orders.*<br>Synonyms: **downgrade** |
| DEPLORE | to regard as deeply regrettable and hateful<br>*"I simply* deplore *your table manners," she told him, as he stuck his head into the bowl to lick the last of the oatmeal.*<br>Synonyms: **regret, lament, bemoan, bewail, mourn, denounce, condemn, protest, oppose, despise, loathe, abominate** |
| DESOLATION | condition of being deserted and destroyed<br>*The terrible flood, which destroyed all the buildings and caused everyone to flee, left only* desolation *in its path.*<br>Synonyms: **barrenness, desertion, bleakness** |
| DESPICABLE | deserving contempt<br>*Stealing from poor people is* despicable. *In fact, stealing from anyone is* despicable.<br>Synonyms: **hateful, contemptible, base, mean, vile, detestable, depraved** |
| DESPONDENT | in a state of depression<br>*Mrs. Baker was* despondent *after her husband's death.*<br>Synonyms: **depressed, morose, gloomy, sad, brooding, desolate, forlorn, woeful, mournful, dejected** |
| DESTITUTE | bereft (of something), without or left without (something); poor<br>*Destitute of friends, Charlotte wandered the streets alone.*<br>Synonyms: **bereft, devoid, lacking; poor, impoverished** |

| WORD | DEFINITION, CONTEXT, SYNONYMS |
|------|-------------------------------|
| DEVASTATE | to lay waste, make desolate; to overwhelm<br><br>*News of the death of his beloved wife will* devastate *him.*<br><br>Synonyms: **ruin, wreck** |
| DEVOTEE | someone passionately devoted<br><br>*The opera* devotee *didn't mind standing on line for hours to get a ticket.*<br><br>Synonym: **enthusiast, fan, admirer** |
| DEVOUT | deeply religious<br><br>*Priests and nuns are known to be* devout *people.*<br><br>Synonyms: **pious, religious, reverent** |
| DEXTERITY | skill in using the hands or body, agility; cleverness<br><br>*The gymnast who won the contest demonstrated the highest level of* dexterity *of all the competitors. She was the only one who didn't fall off the balance beam.*<br><br>Synonyms: **skill, agility** |
| DIMINISH | to become or to make smaller in size, number, or degree<br><br>*He was once such a beautiful actor, but now his beauty has greatly* diminished! *As has his bank account.*<br><br>Synonyms: **decrease, lessen, dwindle, shrink, contract, decline, subside, wane, fade, recede, weaken, moderate** |
| DIN | loud, confused noise<br><br>*The* din *in the cafeteria made conversation difficult.*<br><br>Synonyms: **noise, uproar, clamor** |
| DINGY | dark or drab in color; dirty, shabby, squalid<br><br>*He lived alone in a depressing,* dingy *apartment.*<br><br>Synonyms: **dirty, filthy, shabby, dark** |
| DIPLOMATIC | tactful; skilled in the art of conducting negotiations and other relations between nations<br><br>*Our host had a very* diplomatic *nature, which enabled her to bring together people who disagreed strongly on many points.*<br><br>Synonyms: **polite, tactful** |
| DISCLAIM | to deny ownership of or association with<br><br>*Francine's statement was so silly that she later* disclaimed *it, pretending that it had been made by someone who looked exactly like her.*<br><br>Synonyms: **repudiate, reject, disown, disavow, renounce** |

| WORD | DEFINITION, CONTEXT, SYNONYMS |
|---|---|
| **DISCURSIVE** | covering a wide area or digressing from a topic<br><br>*The professor, who was known for his* discursive *speaking style, covered everything from armadillos to zebras in his zoology lecture.*<br><br>Synonyms: **digressive, rambling** |
| **DISMAL** | causing gloom; cheerless<br><br>*Our team made a* dismal *showing in the play-offs; we lost every game.*<br><br>Synonyms: **miserable, dreary** |
| **DISPUTE** | (n) argument or quarrel<br><br>*The* dispute *between the United States and the Soviet Union arose in part as a result of disagreement over the occupation of Berlin.*<br><br>Synonyms: **argument, disagreement**<br><br>(v) to argue or quarrel<br><br>*There was no way to* dispute *the DNA evidence.*<br><br>Synonyms: **argue, disagree with** |
| **DISSEMINATE** | to scatter or spread widely<br><br>*The Internet* disseminates *information rapidly, so events get reported all over the world shortly after they happen.*<br><br>Synonyms: **spread (an idea or a message), broadcast, disperse** |
| **DIVERT** | (1) to change the course of<br><br>*Emergency crews tried to* divert *the flood waters by building a wall of sandbags across the road.*<br><br>Synonyms: **deflect, reroute, turn, detour**<br><br>(2) to draw someone's attention by amusing them<br><br>*While their mother napped, Dad* diverted *the twins by playing hide-and-seek.*<br><br>Synonyms: **amuse, entertain, distract** |
| **DOFF** | to remove or take off, as clothing<br><br>*Baseball players usually* doff *their hats during the National Anthem.* |
| **DOGGED** | persistent in effort; stubbornly tenacious<br><br>*He worked steadily with a* dogged *determination to finish the difficult task.*<br><br>Synonyms: **stubborn (as a bulldog), obstinate** |
| **DOGMATIC** | asserting without proof; stating opinion as if it were fact in a definite and forceful manner<br><br>*The* dogmatic *professor would not listen to the students' views; she did not allow debate in class.*<br><br>Synonyms: **absolute, opinionated, dictatorial, authoritative, arrogant** |

| WORD | DEFINITION, CONTEXT, SYNONYMS |
|---|---|
| DOZE | to nap or sleep lightly<br><br>*I was so tired from working all night that I kept dozing off during the next day.*<br><br>Synonyms: **nap, sleep** |
| DUNGEON | underground room in fortress often used to keep prisoners<br><br>*Henry VIII ordered that Anne Boleyn be kept in the dungeon of the Tower of London until she was beheaded.*<br><br>Synonyms: **vault, cellar** |
| EBULLIENT | overflowing with fervor, enthusiasm, or excitement; high-spirited<br><br>*The ebullient child exhausted the babysitter, who lacked the energy needed to keep up with her.*<br><br>Synonyms: **bubbling, enthusiastic, exuberant** |
| ECCENTRIC | (n) person who differs from the accepted norms in an odd way<br><br>*The old eccentric was given to burning hundred-dollar bills.*<br><br>Synonyms: **freak, oddball, weirdo, nonconformist**<br><br>(adj) *deviating from accepted conduct*<br><br>*Her eccentric behavior began to worry her close friends.*<br><br>Synonyms: **odd, unorthodox, unconventional, offbeat** |
| ECSTATIC | deliriously overjoyed<br><br>*Mortimer was ecstatic when he learned of his 2400 SAT scores.*<br><br>Synonyms: **delighted, overjoyed, euphoric** |
| EDDY | small whirlpool or any similar current<br><br>*Eddies can be in the air or water. When water gets pulled down a drain, it forms a small whirlpool, or an eddy.*<br><br>Synonyms: **swirling water, whirlpool** |
| EFFECT | (n) result, impression<br><br>*The effect of the new policy will not be known for some time, as it often takes several years for new programs to have a noticeable impact.*<br><br>Synonyms: **result, impression**<br><br>(v) *to produce, make or bring about*<br><br>*We are willing to make any sacrifice in order to effect lasting change for the better.*<br><br>Synonyms: **produce, cause, bring about** |
| ELUSIVE | hard to find or express<br><br>*The elusive nature of the platypus makes it difficult to spot platypus in the wild. Their ugliness makes it unpleasant.*<br><br>Synonyms: **slippery, evasive** |

| WORD | DEFINITION, CONTEXT, SYNONYMS |
|------|-------------------------------|
| **EMBELLISH** | to add detail, make more complicated<br><br>*Sanjev's short story is too short: it needs to be* embellished *with more details about life among penguins.*<br><br>Synonyms: **elaborate, expand, ornament** |
| **EMINENT** | distinguished, high in rank or station<br><br>*They were amazed that such an* eminent *scholar could have made such an obvious error.*<br><br>Synonyms: **prominent, well-known, famous, distinguished, noteworthy** |
| **EMULATE** | to imitate or copy<br><br>*Hundreds of writers have* emulated *Stephen King, but the result is usually a poor imitation.*<br><br>Synonyms: **imitate, simulate, copy, follow** |
| **ENACT** | to make into law<br><br>*The government wishes to* enact *the new law in January.*<br><br>Synonyms: **pass (a law), decree, act out** |
| **ENCOMPASS** | to form a circle or a ring around<br><br>*In New York City, Manhattan is an island, so it is completely* encompassed *by water.*<br><br>Synonyms: **encircle, circumscribe** |
| **ENDORSE** | to approve, sustain, support<br><br>*The principal refused to* endorse *the plan to put a video arcade in the cafeteria.*<br><br>Synonyms: **accept, approve, authorize, accredit, encourage, advocate, favor, support** |
| **ENIGMA** | mystery or riddle<br><br>*The source of the mysterious hole remained an* enigma.<br><br>Synonyms: **mystery, riddle, puzzle** |
| **ENIGMATIC** | unexplainable, mysterious<br><br>*The students found the new history teacher to be* enigmatic; *none of them could figure out what he was thinking.*<br><br>Synonyms: **mysterious, unexplainable, inexplicable, incomprehensible, strange, puzzling, baffling, bewildering, perplexing, cryptic** |
| **ENSNARE** | to capture in, or involve, as in a snare<br><br>*The investigators managed to* ensnare *the corrupt official when they offered him a bribe that he accepted.*<br><br>Synonyms: **trap** |

| WORD | DEFINITION, CONTEXT, SYNONYMS |
|---|---|
| **ENTICE** | to lure or attract by feeding desires<br><br>*Millions of dollars couldn't* entice *Michael Jordan to play basketball in Europe.*<br><br>Synonyms: **tempt, lure, attract** |
| **ENTOURAGE** | group of followers, attendants, or assistants<br><br>*The movie star was always followed around by an* entourage *of flunkies and assistants.*<br><br>Synonyms: **group, retinue, coterie** |
| **ERA** | period of time<br><br>*The invention of the atomic bomb marked the beginning of a new* era *in warfare.*<br><br>Synonyms: **period (of time), age, epoch** |
| **ERR** | to make a mistake (as in error)<br><br>*To* err *is human; we have all made mistakes.*<br><br>Synonyms: **sin** |
| **ERUDITE** | knowledgeable and learned<br><br>*We were not surprised to read the praises of Mario's history of ancient Greece, for we had expected an* erudite *work from him.*<br><br>Synonyms: **wise, learned, knowledgeable, informed** |
| **ESSENTIAL** | of the innermost nature of something; basic, fundamental; of great importance<br><br>*Eating vegetables is* essential *to your well-being.*<br><br>Synonyms: **basic, central, fundamental, important, crucial, necessary, urgent** |
| **ETIQUETTE** | code of social behavior<br><br>*Some people think that* etiquette *forbids eating with your elbows on the table.*<br><br>Synonyms: **manners, propriety, decorum** |
| **EVACUATE** | to empty out, remove, or withdraw<br><br>*The National Guard had to* evacuate *thousands of people following the catastrophe.*<br><br>Synonyms: **expel, empty, vacate, remove** |
| **EXHIBIT** | (v) to publicly present for inspection<br><br>*The Car Exposition* exhibits *the latest model of sports cars.*<br><br>Synonyms: **show, reveal, display**<br><br>(n) an object or collection on public display<br><br>*The* exhibits *at the Metropolitan Museum of Art include a Roman sarcophagus and an Egyptian temple.*<br><br>Synonyms: **object, item, showpiece** |

| WORD | DEFINITION, CONTEXT, SYNONYMS |
|---|---|
| EXOTIC | of foreign origin or character; strange, exciting |
| | *The atmosphere of the restaurant was* exotic, *but the food was pedestrian.* |
| | Synonyms: **foreign, alien, unfamiliar** |
| EXPAND | to make greater, broader, larger, or more detailed |
| | *Friedrich now sells only scary plastic fangs, but he plans to* expand *his business to include rubber vampire bats with glowing eyes.* |
| | Synonyms: **enlarge, increase, augment, extend, broaden, widen, stretch, spread, swell, inflate, dilate, bloat** |
| EXPUNGE | to delete or omit completely |
| | *The censor wanted to* expunge *all parts of Joyce's Ulysses he thought were obscene.* |
| | Synonyms: **erase, obliterate, strike out** |
| EXTRACTION | process of removal or something removed |
| | *My toothache meant I had to undergo the* extraction *of my wisdom teeth.* |
| | Synonyms: **removal** |
| EXTRICATE | to release from difficulty or an entanglement |
| | *The fly was unable to* extricate *itself from the flypaper.* |
| | Synonyms: **disengage, release, withdraw** |
| EXTROVERTED | outgoing or interested in people |
| | *An* extrovert *wouldn't think twice about going to a party of strangers.* |
| | Synonyms: **outgoing, gregarious** |
| FANATIC | someone with excessive enthusiasm, especially in politics or religion |
| | *Unable to listen to differing opinions, the* fanatic *politician screamed at his opponent and ran out of the debate.* |
| | Synonyms: **zealous** |
| FATAL | causing, or capable of causing, death or ruin |
| | *The race car driver suffered a* fatal *accident when his car hit a patch of oil on the roadway.* |
| | Synonyms: **lethal, deadly, killing, mortal, malignant** |
| FATIGUE | (v) to exhaust the strength of |
| | *The energetic baby* fatigued *me.* |
| | Synonyms: **tire out, weary, enervate** |
| | (n) weariness, tiredness from exertion |
| | *The recruits suffered from* fatigue *after the twenty-mile march.* |
| | Synonyms: **exhaustion, weariness** |
| FAUNA | animals of a given area |
| | *Darwin studied the* fauna *of the Galapagos Islands.* |
| | Synonyms: **animals, creatures, beasts** |

| WORD | DEFINITION, CONTEXT, SYNONYMS |
|------|-------------------------------|
| **FELICITY** | happiness, bliss<br>*She was so good, she deserved nothing but* felicity *her whole life.*<br>Synonyms: **happiness, contentment, bliss** |
| **FEROCIOUS** | savage and fierce<br>Ferocious *Arctic wolves will hunt and kill much larger animals in pursuit of food.*<br>Synonyms: **fierce** |
| **FERVENT** | showing great warmth, intensity, feeling, enthusiasm; hot, burning, glowing<br>*I am a* fervent *admirer of that author's works; I think she is a genius.*<br>Synonyms: **warm, eager, enthusiastic** |
| **FICKLE** | easily changeable, especially in emotions<br>*She earned a reputation for being a* fickle *customer; she always changed her order at least twice.*<br>Synonyms: **inconstant** |
| **FIDELITY** | faithfulness to duties; truthfulness<br>*A traitor is someone whose* fidelity *is questioned.*<br>Synonyms: **loyalty, allegiance, faithfulness, devotion, truthfulness, accuracy** |
| **FINALE** | the final part of some entertainment, often music<br>*The* finale *of the 1812 Overture is often accompanied by fireworks.*<br>Synonyms: **end, finish, conclusion, wind-up** |
| **FLAGRANT** | outrageously glaring, noticeable, or evident; notorious, scandalous<br>*His* flagrant *disregard for the rules has resulted in his dismissal from the job.*<br>Synonyms: **obvious, glaring** |
| **FLIPPANT** | not serious, playful; irreverent<br>*John was* flippant *to the teacher, so she sent him to the principal's office*<br>Synonyms: **frivolous, flip, playful** |
| **FLOW** | to move along in a stream or like a stream; to proceed continuously (as in a computer flowchart, which shows how a program flows)<br>*People* flowed *out of the crowded department store through the main doors.*<br>Synonyms: **run, stream** (like water) |
| **FORETELL** | to predict the future<br>*Some prophets claim to* foretell *the future.*<br>Synonyms: **forecast, prophesy, auger** |

| WORD | DEFINITION, CONTEXT, SYNONYMS |
|---|---|
| FORMIDABLE | able to inspire awe or wonder because of outstanding power, size, etc. <br> *The steep face of rock we were directed to climb was indeed formidable.* <br> Synonyms: **impressive, awe-inspiring, impregnable, invincible** |
| FOUNDATION | basis or groundwork of anything, whether a building or idea <br> *The claim that the sun revolves around the earth has no foundation, because scientific evidence disproves this claim.* <br> Synonyms: **bottom, groundwork, basis** |
| FRAGILE | easily broken, or damaged <br> *The Ming dynasty porcelain vase was* fragile *and needed to be handled carefully* <br> Synonyms: **breakable, frail, brittle, delicate** |
| FRENZY | a spell of violent, wild behavior; temporary madness <br> *As she watched her basketball team lose the game, Susan gradually worked herself into a* frenzy. <br> Synonyms: **mania, hysteria, craze, furor, mania, turmoil** |
| FREQUENT | (adj) happening or occurring at short intervals <br> *He travels so much he's a member of five* frequent *flyer plans.* <br> Synonyms: **repeated, regular, habitual, common** <br> (v) to visit often <br> *My friend loves antique hunting and frequents the local antique shops.* |
| FUTILE | ineffective, useless; unimportant <br> *Our attempt to reach the shore before the storm was* futile; *the wind blew us back into the middle of the lake.* <br> Synonyms: **useless, hopeless, pointless** |
| GARRULOUS | talkative and likely to chatter <br> *My* garrulous *friend often talks on the telephone for hours at a time.* <br> Synonyms: **talkative, loquacious** |
| GERMINATE | to bud or sprout <br> *Three weeks after planting, the seeds will* germinate. <br> Synonyms: **sprout, grow** |
| GLEE | joy, pleasure, happiness <br> *The child was filled with* glee *at the sight of so many presents.* <br> Synonyms: **joy, elation** |
| GLIB | able to speak profusely; having a ready flow of words (It often implies lying or deceit.) <br> *The politician was a* glib *speaker.* <br> Synonyms: **flip, fluent, verbose, smooth, smug** |

| WORD | DEFINITION, CONTEXT, SYNONYMS |
|---|---|
| **GORGEOUS** | beautiful; splendid in appearance<br>*The Pacific Coast is well-known for its* gorgeous *beach sunsets.*<br>Synonyms: **spectacular, wonderful, impressive, stunning, incredible** |
| **GREGARIOUS** | fond of company<br>*For the* gregarious *person, dormitory life is a pleasure.*<br>Synonyms: **sociable, companionable, amiable, convivial** |
| **GROTESQUE** | odd or unnatural in some way<br>*The minotaur is a* grotesque *creature out of mythology: part man and part bull.*<br>Synonyms: **bizarre, outlandish, ugly** |
| **GROVEL** | to humble oneself, to beg<br>*The dog* groveled *at his owner's feet.*<br>Synonyms: **crawl, beg** |
| **GRUESOME** | grisly, horrible<br>*The horror film was filled with* gruesome *scenes.*<br>Synonyms: **frightful, shocking, ghastly** |
| **HALLOWED** | regarded as holy; sacred<br>*The Constitution is a* hallowed *document in the United States.*<br>Synonyms: **holy, sacred** |
| **HARBINGER** | omen, precursor, forerunner<br>*The groundhog's appearance on February 2 is a* harbinger *of spring.*<br>Synonyms: **precursor, forerunner, omen, messenger** |
| **HARSH** | stern or cruel; physically uncomfortable; unpleasant to the ear<br>Harsh *words were exchanged during their argument.*<br>Synonyms: **rough, strict, severe** |
| **HASTY** | done quickly (often too quickly); rushed, sloppy<br>*Henry was too* hasty *in completing his research paper, and forgot to put his name on it.*<br>Synonyms: **rushed, sloppy, shoddy, careless** |
| **HEED** | (n) careful attention, notice, observation<br>*Pay* heed *to his warnings about that place; he's been there enough times to know the dangers.*<br>Synonyms: **attention**<br>(v) to listen to and obey<br>*The naughty children did not* heed *their mothers rules.*<br>Synonyms: **listen to, obey** |

| WORD | DEFINITION, CONTEXT, SYNONYMS |
| --- | --- |
| HERBIVOROUS | feeding on plants<br><br>*A cow is an* herbivorous *animal.*<br><br>Synonyms: **plant eating** |
| HETEROGENEOUS | not uniform; made up of different parts that remain separate. (Its opposite is *homogeneous*.)<br><br>*The United Nations is a* heterogeneous *body.*<br><br>Synonyms: **mixed, unlike, diverse, dissimilar, various** |
| HEXAGON | polygon having six sides<br><br>*A hexagon* has six sides, and an octagon has eight. |
| HIBERNATE | to spend the winter in a sleeplike, dormant state<br><br>*During winter, bears* hibernate *in caves.*<br><br>Synonyms: **sleep** |
| HIVE | structure where bees live<br><br>*My friend Les is so interested in bees that he'll watch them going into and out of one of their* hives *for hours.* |
| HORRID | something that causes horror, or is at least pretty bad<br><br>*The weather has been just* horrid; *we've had three storms in a week.*<br><br>Synonyms: **dreadful, horrible, shocking** |
| HOVEL | small, miserable shack<br><br>*In Charles Dickens's novels poor people often live in terrible, dirty* hovels.<br><br>Synonyms: **shack, shanty** |
| HUMID | moist or damp<br><br>*It is so* humid *in the jungle that it is advisable to wear light, loose clothing.*<br><br>Synonyms: **moist, damp, sultry** |
| IGNITE | (literally) to set on fire; (figuratively) to stir emotionally (light a fire under someone)<br><br>(1) *If you* ignite *that match, you might burn the whole house down.*<br><br>(2) *Through his speaking ability, the speaker was able to* ignite *the people who attended his speeches.*<br><br>Synonyms: **light, kindle, inflame, rouse, excite, agitate, stir, provoke, prod, inspire** |
| ILLITERACY | inability to read and write<br><br>*If everyone learned how to read and write,* illiteracy *wouldn't be a problem.* |

| WORD | DEFINITION, CONTEXT, SYNONYMS |
|---|---|
| IMMACULATE | spotless; free from error<br><br>*After I cleaned my apartment for hours, it was finally* immaculate.<br><br>Synonyms: **errorless, faultless, unblemished, impeccable** |
| IMMINENT | about to happen, on the verge of occurring<br><br>*Joan was becoming nervous about her* imminent *wedding.*<br><br>Synonyms: **impending, approaching, near** |
| IMMORTAL | undying<br><br>*Someone who never grows old and never dies is* immortal.<br><br>Synonyms: **undying, eternal** |
| IMPASSE | (1) road having no exit<br><br>*A rock slide produced an* impasse, *so we could proceed no further on the road.*<br><br>(2) a dilemma with no solution<br><br>*The meeting was at an* impasse *because neither side was willing to compromise.*<br><br>Synonyms: **deadlock, standoff, stalemate, standstill** |
| IMPERVIOUS | incapable of being penetrated; unable to be influenced<br><br>*Superman is* impervious *to bullets.*<br><br>Synonyms: **impenetrable** |
| IMPIOUS | lacking piety or respect for religion<br><br>Synonyms: **irreverent, sacrilegious** |
| IMPLY | to suggest without stating directly<br><br>*Although Jane did not state that she loved Mr. Rochester, it was clearly* implied *in her look.*<br><br>Synonyms: **hint, suggest, intimate** |
| INADVERTENT | unintentional<br><br>*I wrote my paper in such a hurry that I made many* inadvertent *errors.*<br><br>Synonyms: **accidental, unintentional** |
| INCENTIVE | motivation or drive to do a particular task or to go in a given direction<br><br>*His father's encouragement gave him the* incentive *to try again.*<br><br>Synonyms: **motive, inducement, stimulus** |
| INCREDULOUS | not believing<br><br>*I was* incredulous *about Ismael's wild fishing story about "the one that got away."*<br><br>Synonyms: **skeptical, disbelieving** |
| INDICATE | to point out or make known with a good degree of certainty<br><br>*Recent polls* indicate *that the Democrats will probably be victorious.*<br><br>Synonyms: **disclose, show, reveal, imply, signify** |

| WORD | DEFINITION, CONTEXT, SYNONYMS |
|---|---|
| **INERT** | having no power to move or act; resisting motion or action<br><br>*In the heat of the desert afternoon, lizards are* inert.<br><br>Synonyms: **sluggish, passive, inactive, dormant, lethargic, lifeless** |
| **INFECTIOUS** | able to be passed from one person to another (such as an infection); contagious<br><br>*Her laughter was* infectious, *and soon we were all laughing.*<br><br>Synonyms: **catching, contagious** |
| **INGENIOUS** | possessing or displaying great creativity and resourcefulness<br><br>*Luther found an* ingenious *way to solve the math problem.*<br><br>Synonyms: **brilliant, inspired, imaginative, shrewd, crafty, cunning, resourceful** |
| **INGENUITY** | inventive skill or cleverness<br><br>*Use your* ingenuity *to come up with a new solution to the problem.*<br><br>Synonyms: **creativity, cleverness, inventiveness** |
| **INHABIT** | to reside or live in<br><br>*Arboreal creatures, such as monkeys,* inhabit *the trees.*<br><br>Synonyms: **live, occupy, reside, dwell, stay** |
| **INNATE** | present at birth<br><br>*The plan was doomed from the start; there was an* innate *problem with it.*<br><br>Synonyms: **natural, inborn, inherent, instinctive** |
| **INNOCENT** | pure, not guilty; someone with the simplicity of a baby<br><br>*Those accused of practicing witchcraft in Salem were clearly* innocent *of any such act.*<br><br>Synonyms: **pure, harmless, guiltless, naïve, chaste** |
| **INSINUATION** | devious hint or sly suggestion made to cause suspicion or doubts<br><br>*During the last election, the* insinuation *that the congressman had taken kickbacks cost him thousands of votes.*<br><br>Synonyms: **hint, suggestion, reference, implication** |
| **INSOMNIA** | inability to fall sleep<br><br>*No matter how tired I am, I continue to suffer from* insomnia.<br><br>Synonyms: **sleeplessness** |
| **INSURGENT** | (n) rebel<br><br>*When secrets were being leaked to the enemy, we realized we had an* insurgent *among our ranks.*<br><br>Synonyms: **rebel, mole**<br><br>(adj) rising in revolt, starting a revolution<br><br>*The* insurgent *crew staged a mutiny and threw the captain overboard.*<br><br>Synonyms: **rebellious, mutinous** |

| WORD | DEFINITION, CONTEXT, SYNONYMS |
|---|---|
| IRATE | full of anger, wrathful, incensed<br><br>*He was* irate *at being wrongly accused of the crime.*<br><br>Synonyms: **angry, indignant, infuriated, enraged** |
| JEER | (n) taunting remark<br><br>*The jeers of the crowd were enough to make the performers run off stage crying.*<br><br>Synonyms: **gibe, taunt**<br><br>(v) to mock in an abusive way<br><br>*My brother loved to jeer at me because he knew how much it hurt my feelings.*<br><br>Synonyms: **ridicule, mock, scoff** |
| JUBILANT | feeling joy or happiness<br><br>*We were* jubilant *after our victory in the state championships.*<br><br>Synonyms: **exultant, gleeful, joyful, ecstatic** |
| JUDICIOUS | having wise judgment<br><br>*The wise and distinguished judge was well-known for having a* judicious *temperament.*<br><br>Synonyms: **wise, sage, sagacious** |
| KINETIC | relating to motion<br><br>*A* kinetic *sculpture is one that moves.*<br><br>Synonyms: **animated, energetic, spirited, moving** |
| LAGOON | shallow body of water connected to a much larger one, as a lake or sea<br><br>*The pirates anchored their ship offshore and rowed into the* lagoon, *where they went ashore.*<br><br>Synonyms: **inlet, pool** |
| LENIENT | merciful, not strict<br><br>*When the commissioner only fined the pitcher fifty dollars for throwing a baseball at a batter, many fans thought the punishment was too* lenient.<br><br>Synonyms: **merciful, indulgent** |
| LETHARGY | drowsiness, tiredness, inability to do anything much<br><br>*A feeling of* lethargy *came over me, and I wanted nothing more than a nice long nap.*<br><br>Synonyms: **sluggishness, fatigue** |

| WORD | DEFINITION, CONTEXT, SYNONYMS |
|---|---|
| LIMBER | bending and moving easily<br>*The gymnast warmed up for thirty minutes so that she would be* limber *before her routine.*<br>Synonyms: **agile, supple** |
| LUNGE | to thrust something forward<br>*The toboggan* lunged *forward at the point where the slope became quite steep.*<br>Synonyms: **thrust, plunge** |
| MAGNANIMOUS | having a great or noble spirit, acting generously, patiently, or kindly<br>*Although at first he seemed cold, Uncle Frank turned out to be a very* magnanimous *fellow.*<br>Synonyms: **big-hearted, generous, noble, princely, forgiving, patient, tolerant, indulgent, ungrudging, unresentful** |
| MALFUNCTION | (n) an instance of failing to function<br>*The engine* malfunction *prevented the racer from making it to the finish line.*<br>Synonyms: **failure**<br>(v) to fail to function<br>*When my cell phone* malfunctioned, *I had to make all my calls from the land line.*<br>Synonyms: **fail** |
| MALLEABLE | can be molded or shaped<br>*Gold is so* malleable *that it can be beaten into a thin foil.*<br>Synonyms: **soft, flexible, yielding** |
| MAR | to damage something and make it imperfect<br>*Telephone poles* mar *the beauty of the countryside.*<br>Synonyms: **deform, impair, spoil, disfigure, damage** |
| MARVEL | (n) amazing thing; something astonishing or marvelous<br>*It was a* marvel *that they survived the crash.*<br>Synonyms: **miracle, prodigy, wonder**<br>(v) to be surprised or full of wonder<br>*I* marvel *at your ability to remain calm.*<br>Synonyms: **wonder** |
| MEAGER | very small or insufficient<br>*He rented an expensive apartment and dined at fine restaurants, but he earned a* meager *wage and soon ran out of money.*<br>Synonyms: **slight, trifling, skimpy, puny, scant, inadequate, insufficient, insubstantial** |

| WORD | DEFINITION, CONTEXT, SYNONYMS |
|---|---|
| MEEK | humble and submissive<br><br>*People who are too* meek *won't stand up for themselves.*<br><br>Synonyms: **passive, unassertive, docile, compliant** |
| MELANCHOLY | very sad or depressing<br><br>*The rainy weather made James feel* melancholy.<br><br>Synonyms: **gloomy, mournful, somber** |
| METAMORPHOSIS | the process of transformation in the appearance of something<br><br>*Jimmy Fallon has enjoyed his* metamorphosis *from comedian to talk-show host.*<br><br>Synonyms: **transformation, mutation, alteration, conversion** |
| METEOROLOGIST | scientist dealing with weather and weather conditions<br><br>*Although the* meteorologist *predicted a heat wave, the temperature remained below freezing.* |
| MIMIC | imitate, copy (not always in a complimentary way)<br><br>*Mary got in trouble for* mimicking *the teacher.*<br><br>Synonyms: **mock, impersonate, simulate, counterfeit** |
| MINUSCULE | tiny, miniature<br><br>*Dave needed a magnifying glass to read the* minuscule *print on the lease.*<br><br>Synonyms: **microscopic, minute** |
| MISBEGOTTEN | poorly conceived, poorly planned, based on false assumptions or false reasoning<br><br>*It came as no surprise when Fred's* misbegotten *scheme proved an utter failure.*<br><br>Synonyms: **illegitimate, ill-conceived** |
| MOLT | to shed old feather, hair, or skin to make way for new growth<br><br>*As the baby bird became a swan, its dull, gray feathers* molted *and it grew white ones.*<br><br>Synonyms: **lose, shed, cast** |
| MOURN | feel sad for, regret<br><br>*The family gathered to* mourn *for the dead.*<br><br>Synonyms: **lament, grieve** |
| MURKY | dark, dim<br><br>*Jill groped her way down the* murky *hallway.*<br><br>Synonyms: **obscure, gloomy** |

| WORD | DEFINITION, CONTEXT, SYNONYMS |
|------|-------------------------------|
| NAUSEOUS | sickening, makes you feel sick, or turns your stomach |
| | *The cook mixed skim milk with green eels and produced a concoction that was truly* nauseous. |
| | Synonyms: **revolting, disgusting, nauseating** |
| NEBULOUS | hazy, not well-defined |
| | *During the campaign, the candidate promised to fight crime. But when reporters asked for details, his plan was* nebulous—*he could not say whether he would hire more police or support longer jail sentences.* |
| | Synonyms: **hazy, cloudy, ill-defined, unclear, shapeless, vague, unspecific** |
| NIMBLE | quick and agile in movement or thought |
| | *A* nimble *athlete is a well-coordinated one.* |
| | Synonyms: **agile, active, quick, clever, cunning** |
| NOMAD | someone who has no permanent home and wanders |
| | *The Berbers are a tribe of* nomads *who travel from place to place searching for grassland for their herds.* |
| | Synonyms: **wanderer, vagrant** |
| NOTIFY | to tell, let know, give notice |
| | *The landlord failed to* notify *the tenants of the planned demolition of the building.* |
| | Synonyms: **tell, inform, apprise** |
| OBESE | very fat |
| | *Some* obese *people suffer from anxiety-induced overeating.* |
| | Synonyms: **fat, corpulent, portly** |
| OBNOXIOUS | offensive and very disagreeable |
| | *The last time I went to the movies, an* obnoxious *person sitting beside me talked loudly during the entire movie.* |
| | Synonyms: **offensive, repugnant, repellant** |
| OBSCURE | (adj) hard to see; unknown, uncertain |
| | *The references the author made were so* obscure, *I don't think half the readers knew what he was talking about.* |
| | Synonyms: **vague, unclear, dubious** |
| | (v) to hide or make difficult to find |
| | *Because he didn't want to go to jail, he tried to* obscure *the fact that he had been embezzling money for years.* |
| | Synonyms: **confuse, becloud** |

| WORD | DEFINITION, CONTEXT, SYNONYMS |
|---|---|
| OBSERVATION | (1) examination<br>*Close* observation *of Arnold led Anne to believe that he was hiding something.*<br>Synonyms: **attention, watching**<br>(2) remark, comment<br>*Damon amused the class with his witty* observation *about the teacher's methods.*<br>Synonyms: **pronouncement, opinion** |
| OBSOLETE | no longer in use; discarded or outmoded<br>*It's as* obsolete *as a telephone modem.*<br>Synonyms: **outdated, passé, old-fashioned** |
| OBSTINATE | stubborn<br>*Hal's mother tried to get him to eat his spinach, but he remained* obstinate.<br>Synonyms: **mulish, dogged** |
| OBSTRUCT | to get in the way of; to block; to hamper<br>*He removed his hat so as not to* obstruct *another's view of the stage.*<br>Synonyms: **block, check, clog, impede** |
| OBTUSE | not acute; someone who is not smart; thick, dull<br>*Alfred was too* obtuse *to realize that the sum of the angles of a triangle is 180 degrees.*<br>Synonyms: **slow, stupid** |
| OLFACTORY | relating to the sense of smell<br>*In human beings,* olfactory *sensations are perceived with the nose.* |
| OMINOUS | threatening, menacing, having the character of an evil omen<br>*The sky filled with* ominous *dark clouds before the storm.*<br>Synonyms: **foreboding** |
| OPPORTUNE | appropriate to time or circumstances: timely, lucky<br>*Dalbert's investment in plastics, made just before the demand for plastics began to rise, was* opportune.<br>Synonyms: **timely, appropriate, lucky** |
| OPTION | choice, selection, preference<br>*Donna carefully considered every* option *before making her final decision.*<br>Synonyms: **alternative, election** |

| WORD | DEFINITION, CONTEXT, SYNONYMS |
|---|---|
| **ORBIT** | (v) to move around some object, as a planet; to circle<br>*The moon* orbits *the earth, which in turn* orbits *the sun.*<br>Synonyms: **circle, revolve, circuit**<br>(n) the actual route the thing takes when it goes around the other thing, as in the orbit of the moon around the earth<br>*The German shepherd dog approached the intruder cautiously, circled him and sniffed, made two more* orbits, *and then walked away.*<br>Synonyms: **circuit, revolution** |
| **ORCHID** | purple (as in the flower)<br>*The vice principal turned* orchid *with rage.*<br>Synonyms: **lavender** |
| **OSTENTATIOUS** | pretentious and flashy<br>*Some think Donald Trump's Taj Mahal casino, which he proudly calls the Eighth Wonder of the World, is really an* ostentatious *display of wealth and poor taste.*<br>Synonyms: **conspicuous, flashy, flamboyant, showy** |
| **PALATABLE** | good tasting<br>*Her cooking is quite* palatable.<br>Synonyms: **savory, agreeable, appetizing, delicious, acceptable** |
| **PARADOX** | contradiction, something that doesn't fit; something that shouldn't be true because it seems to offend common sense, yet is true anyway<br>*The* paradox *of government is that the person who most desires power is the person who least deserves it.*<br>Synonyms: **contradiction** |
| **PASSIVE** | not active; someone who lets things happen rather than himself taking action<br>*Ned portrayed himself as the* passive *victim of external forces.*<br>Synonyms: **submissive** |
| **PEDDLE** | sell (although usually used in a somewhat bad way)<br>*Bill got a job going door to door to* peddle *vacuum cleaners.*<br>Synonyms: **hawk, vend** |

| WORD | DEFINITION, CONTEXT, SYNONYMS |
|---|---|
| **PEDESTRIAN** | (adj) common, everyday, usual<br><br>*The critics called the new restaurant's food* pedestrian; *it never had many customers and eventually closed.*<br><br>Synonyms: **plodding, prosaic, commonplace, ordinary, plain, mundane, humdrum, trite, banal, drab, colorless, boring, barren, unimaginative, uninspired, undistinguished, unremarkable, unexceptional**<br><br>(n) one who does not ride but walks<br><br>*With the way the taxis speed, it can be dangerous to be a* pedestrian *in New York. Of course, it's dangerous to be in the cab too, which leaves little choice but to stay home in bed.*<br><br>Synonyms: **walker, hiker, stroller** |
| **PERJURY** | making deliberately false statements when under oath<br><br>*Mr. Mason accused the witness of* perjury.<br><br>Synonyms: **falsehood, fraud, lies** |
| **PERSEVERE** | to continue in some course of action despite setbacks and opposition<br><br>*Although at first the problems looked difficult,* Wendy persevered *and found that she could answer almost all of them.*<br><br>Synonyms: **continue, struggle, endure, persist** |
| **PETRIFY** | (literally) to turn to stone; (figuratively) to paralyze with fear or with surprise<br><br>*The movie is so frightening that it would* petrify *even the bravest viewer.*<br><br>Synonyms: **shock, stun, stiffen, paralyze, fossilize** |
| **PIOUS** | religiously devout or moral<br><br>*Saul, a* pious *man, walks, to the synagogue on the Sabbath and prays daily.*<br><br>Synonyms: **devout, religious, God-fearing, reverent, moral, upstanding, scrupulous** |
| **PLAGIARISM** | copying of someone else's work and claiming it as your own<br><br>*The notable scientist lost his job when his* plagiarism *was revealed; years before, he had copied a research paper from a magazine.*<br><br>Synonyms: **copying, stealing** |
| **PLAUSIBLE** | seeming to be true<br><br>*Joachim's excuse for lateness to class sounded* plausible *at the time, but I later learned that it had been a lie.*<br><br>Synonyms: **credible, believable, likely, probable, conceivable** |

| WORD | DEFINITION, CONTEXT, SYNONYMS |
|---|---|
| **POMPOUS** | characterized by stiff, unnatural formality<br><br>*Gerald began his speech to the class with a* pompous *quote from Julius Caesar.*<br><br>Synonyms: **stuffy, stiff, affected, mannered, unnatural, pretentious, self-important, conceited** |
| **PROCRASTINATE** | to postpone; to put something off to a later time<br><br>*Don't* procrastinate; *do your homework now.*<br><br>Synonyms: **delay, postpone, defer** |
| **PROFOUND** | deep, wise, serious<br><br>*Both the* Book of Ecclesiastes *and the* Tao Te Ching *contain* profound *observations about human life.*<br><br>Synonyms: **wise, deep, sagacious** |
| **PROLIFIC** | producing great amounts; fertile<br><br>*Stephen King, a* prolific *writer, seems to write new books as fast as they are published.*<br><br>Synonyms: **productive, fertile** |
| **PROPEL** | to move, make something go forward<br><br>*An ill-timed push on the gas pedal* propelled *the car through the plate glass window of the dealership.*<br><br>Synonyms: **compel, project, drive** |
| **PROPHESY** | to predict the future using divine guidance<br><br>*The ancient Greek oracles at Delphi were supposed to be able to* prophesy *the future.*<br><br>Synonyms: **predict, foretell, forecast, auger** |
| **PUNGENT** | sharp, flavorful (sometimes too flavorful)<br><br>*The soup was so* pungent *that it brought tears to Alice's eyes.*<br><br>Synonyms: **peppery, hot, piquant, biting, acrid** |
| **PURSUE** | to chase, go after<br><br>*The cat* pursued *the squirrel up the tree.*<br><br>Synonyms: **trail, tail, dog, follow** |
| **QUELL** | to quiet something raucous (often a rebellion); crush, defeat, conquer<br><br>*The dictator dispatched troops to* quell *the rebellion.*<br><br>Synonyms: **quash, overpower, overcome, quench, suppress** |
| **QUENCH** | to satisfy a need or desire<br><br>*After coming in from the desert, Ezra needed gallons of water to* quench *his thirst.*<br><br>Synonyms: **satisfy, extinguish, subdue, sate** |

| WORD | DEFINITION, CONTEXT, SYNONYMS |
|------|-------------------------------|
| RABBLE | large, disorderly, and easily excited mob<br><br>*The* rabble *waited anxiously below the king's window for news of the tax decree.*<br><br>Synonyms: **crowd, mob, multitude, horde** |
| RABID | (literally) afflicted with rabies, a disease of the nervous system that causes convulsions and wildly irrational behavior<br><br>Rabid *animals can sometimes be identified by saliva dripping from their jaws and by frantic behavior.*<br><br>(figuratively) acting fanatically or madly, as if afflicted by rabies<br><br>*The first speaker was calm, but the second—a wild-eyed man advocating the destruction of all tractors—was positively* rabid.<br><br>Synonyms: **fanatical, mad, crazy, irrational, wild-eyed, maniacal, lunatic, incoherent** |
| RANCOR | bad feeling, bitterness<br><br>*Herbert was so filled with* rancor *that he could think of nothing but taking revenge on those who had humiliated him.*<br><br>Synonyms: **animosity, resentment, hatred, malice, spite** |
| RANDOM | lacking order, free from order or bias<br><br>*She conducted a* random *survey of garage mechanics by drawing their names from a hat.*<br><br>Synonyms: **chance, haphazard, unordered, unbiased** |
| RANSACK | to search thoroughly and messily<br><br>*Did the burglars* ransack *your entire house?*<br><br>Synonyms: **plunder, pillage, search, loot, pilfer, steal** |
| RATIFY | to approve formally<br><br>*The Senate* ratified *the treaty after only a brief debate.*<br><br>Synonyms: **confirm, affirm, endorse, approve, sanction** |
| RAVENOUS | (literally) wildly eager to eat<br><br>*The homeless man had not had a bite of food in two days and was* ravenous.<br><br>(figuratively) hungry for anything<br><br>*The abandoned puppy was* ravenous *for affection and tenderness.*<br><br>Synonyms: **hungry, famished, voracious, starved** |
| RAZE | to destroy (a building, city, etc.) utterly<br><br>*The house had been* razed: *Where once it had stood there was nothing but splinters and bricks.*<br><br>Synonyms: **demolish, destroy, wreck, level, flatten** |

| WORD | DEFINITION, CONTEXT, SYNONYMS |
| --- | --- |
| RECLUSE | someone who lives far away from other people<br><br>*Anthony left the city and lived as a* recluse *in the desert.*<br><br>Synonyms: **hermit, loner** |
| RECUR | to return; to occur again<br><br>*The problem is bound to* recur *if you don't solve it now.*<br><br>Synonyms: **return, repeat** |
| REEK | (literally) giving off a strong, offensive odor; strong smell<br><br>*Boy! Something really* reeks *in here. Did you bring a dead skunk with you or something?*<br><br>Synonyms: **stink**<br><br>(figuratively) to be pervaded by something unpleasant<br><br>*The legislature, with its history of bribery and cronyism,* reeked *of corruption.* |
| REFRAIN | to stop or avoid doing something, quit<br><br>*The librarian insisted that everyone* refrain *from making any noise.*<br><br>Synonyms: **abstain, cease, desist** |
| REGAL | royal, splendid<br><br>*Prince Charles was married with full* regal *ceremony.*<br><br>Synonyms: **kingly, majestic** |
| REIGN | rule over, govern, dominate<br><br>*The British monarch used to* reign *over the entire British Empire.*<br><br>Synonyms: **rule, prevail** |
| REIMBURSE | to repay someone for their expenses<br><br>*If you buy me lunch today, I'll* reimburse *you tomorrow.*<br><br>Synonyms: **repay, compensate** |
| REINFORCE | strengthen, add to<br><br>*The purpose of the homework is to* reinforce *what's taught in class.*<br><br>Synonyms: **support** |
| REMINISCENCE | memory or act of recalling the past<br><br>*The old timer's* reminiscence *of his childhood was of a time when there were no cars.*<br><br>Synonyms: **collection, recall, memory, nostalgia** |
| RENOWNED | well-known, famous, celebrated<br><br>*Having spent her whole childhood banging on things, Jane grew up to be a* renowned *drummer.*<br><br>Synonyms: **famed, distinguished, notable** |

| WORD | DEFINITION, CONTEXT, SYNONYMS |
|------|-------------------------------|
| REPARTEE | witty conversation, retort<br><br>*As a master of* repartee, *Bob was the hit of every party he attended.*<br><br>Synonyms: **banter** |
| REPUDIATE | to reject what one was once associated with<br><br>*After Grace discovered that her friends had been spreading false rumors about her, she* repudiated *them and made new friends.*<br><br>Synonyms: **disown, reject, renounce** |
| REPUGNANT | something gross, repulsive, or revolting<br><br>*Bill liked his macaroni and cheese with jelly, a combination that many of his friends found* repugnant.<br><br>Synonyms: **distasteful, objectionable, offensive** |
| RESIDUE | something that remains after a part is taken<br><br>*The fire burned everything, leaving only a* residue *of ash and charred debris.*<br><br>Synonyms: **remainder, remnant, leftover** |
| REVEAL | show, divulge, expose<br><br>*Wendy cut through the frog's abdominal wall to* reveal *the internal organs.*<br><br>Synonyms: **unveil, disclose** |
| REVEL | celebrate noisily, have a party<br><br>*The whole school got together to* revel *in the football team's victory.*<br><br>Synonyms: **celebrate, indulge, enjoy** |
| ROUT | conquer, defeat, and chase off<br><br>*The renewed onslaught* routed *the enemy.*<br><br>Synonyms: **overwhelm, overcome, subdue, scatter** |
| SATELLITE | moon, a small thing going around a bigger thing<br><br>*A spy* satellite *can take pictures of the people and things that it passes above as it circles the globe.*<br><br>Synonyms: **moon** |
| SATURATE | to fill something to the point where it can hold no more<br><br>*Reading the entire encyclopedia will* saturate *your mind with facts.*<br><br>Synonyms: **soak, fill, drench, permeate** |
| SAUCY | impudent, impertinent, flippant<br><br>*She always got in trouble with her parents for her* saucy *remarks.*<br><br>Synonyms: **pert, lively, rude, insolent** |

| WORD | DEFINITION, CONTEXT, SYNONYMS |
| --- | --- |
| SAVOR | to enjoy something with relish or delight |
| | *I* savored *every bite of my father's chocolate cream pie.* |
| | Synonyms: **taste, relish, enjoy, appreciate** |
| SCALD | burn with hot liquid or steam |
| | *Sharon was* scalded *when she bumped into a pot of boiling water.* |
| | Synonyms: **burn, scorch, boil** |
| SCARCE | rare, uncommon |
| | *Water is* scarce *in the Sahara Desert.* |
| | Synonyms: **sparse, infrequent** |
| SCATHING | overly critical |
| | *Walter was depressed by the* scathing *reviews that his play received.* |
| | Synonyms: **searing, crushing, harmful** |
| SCHISM | division or separation between groups of members within an organization |
| | *Because half of the student council wanted the jukebox in the cafeteria, and the other half wanted it in the library, the council suffered a* schism. |
| | Synonyms: **disunity, break, division, conflict, clash** |
| SCRUPULOUS | (1) acting in accordance with a strict moral code |
| | *David could not have stolen Sheila's money; he was too* scrupulous. |
| | Synonyms: **moral, upstanding, virtuous, principled, ethical** |
| | (2) thorough in the performance of a task |
| | *Roger is a* scrupulous *editor who checks every word his reporters write.* |
| | Synonyms: **careful, conscientious, thorough, diligent** |
| SECURE | (v) to fasten, make secure |
| | *I had* secured *my suitcase in the overhead luggage rack at the beginning of the journey.* |
| | Synonyms: **fasten, bind, clamp** |
| | (adj) well-fastened, not likely to fall or come loose |
| | *My suitcase seemed* secure *in the luggage rack. But then it fell on me.* |
| | Synonyms: **fastened, fixed, bound, safe, stable** |
| SEETHE | to heave or bubble from great inner turmoil, as a volcano; to boil |
| | *Immediately after learning of Roger's gossip about me, I began to boil with anger, and by the time I reached his house, I was* seething. |
| | Synonyms: **boil, bubble, steam, foam, surge, heave, swell** |

| WORD | DEFINITION, CONTEXT, SYNONYMS |
| --- | --- |
| SENTRY | guard, sentinel, watchman<br>*Mitchell stood as* sentry *while the others were in the boys' room goofing off.*<br>Synonyms: **watch, lookout** |
| SEQUEL | addition or result; story that continues a previous one<br>*I hear they're making another* sequel *to the* Friday the 13th *movies.*<br>Synonyms: **aftermath, outcome, continuation, consequence** |
| SHREWD | clever, keen-witted, cunning, sharp in practical affairs<br>*He was a* shrewd *businessman and soon parlayed his meager savings into a fortune.*<br>Synonyms: **clever, keen, astute, cunning, wily, sharp, discerning** |
| SIGNIFICANT | meaningful, important, relevant<br>*A good detective knows that something that hardly seems worth noticing may be highly* significant.<br>Synonyms: **consequential, momentous, weighty** |
| SINISTER | threatening, evil, menacing<br>*His friendly manner concealed* sinister *designs.*<br>Synonyms: **ominous, wicked** |
| SLACK | (n) lack of tautness or tension; a time of little activity or dullness<br>*There was no wind; the sails hung* slack, *and the boat was motionless.*<br>Synonyms: **lull, relaxation**<br>(adj) sluggish, idle, barely moving, loose, relaxed<br>*The* slack *atmosphere made it unlikely that anyone would work efficiently.*<br>Synonyms: **lax, negligent, remiss, careless, inactive, slow, loose, relaxed** |
| SOCIABLE | friendly, companionable<br>*Although they maintain their independence, cats are* sociable *creatures.*<br>Synonyms: **gregarious, companionable, friendly, affable, amiable** |
| SOLICIT | (1) to seek (something) from another<br>*The tennis player disagreed with the first judge's decision, so he* solicited *the opinion of a second judge.*<br>Synonyms: **seek**<br>(2) to make a request of someone<br>*I* solicited *my parents for money, but they said no.*<br>Synonyms: **request, petition, beg** |

| WORD | DEFINITION, CONTEXT, SYNONYMS |
|---|---|
| SPECIFY | to mention, name, or require specifically or exactly<br>*The report* specified *the steps to be taken in an emergency.*<br>Synonyms: **detail, identify, stipulate, itemize, define, state** |
| SPLICE | to join, bind, attach; in film editing, to join two pieces of film<br>*The editor removed all the scenes with the troublesome actress and* spliced *the remainder together.*<br>Synonyms: **join, bind, connect, attach, link, unite** |
| SPURN | reject with scorn, turn away<br>*When Harvey proposed to Harriet, she* spurned *him; she loved another man.*<br>Synonyms: **refuse, snub** |
| SQUALID | very dirty or foul; wretched<br>*The* squalid *living conditions in the tenement building outraged the new tenants.*<br>Synonyms: **filthy, sordid, poor, foul** |
| SQUANDER | to waste (often money) on some worthless purchase or practice<br>*While I have carefully saved money to buy the piano I have always wanted, my friend Sean has* squandered *his earnings on thousands of lottery tickets.*<br>Synonyms: **waste, fritter away, consume, exhaust** |
| STAUNCH | steady, loyal<br>*A dog is a* staunch *friend.*<br>Synonyms: **firm, sturdy, stable, solid, established, substantial, steadfast, faithful, unfailing** |
| STEALTHY | sneaky, secret<br>*The children made a* stealthy *raid on the refrigerator during the night.*<br>Synonyms: **sneaky, furtive, clandestine** |
| STRESS | emphasize, point out<br>*Vanessa wrote on the blackboard the main points that she was going to* stress *in her lecture.*<br>Synonyms: **highlight** |
| SUAVE | smooth, graceful, and confident in speech and behavior (sometimes insincerely)<br>*Nina was a* suave *young woman who knew exactly how to act in any situation.*<br>Synonyms: **smooth, gracious, courtly, worldly, sophisticated, urbane, cosmopolitan, cultivated, cultured, refined** |

| WORD | DEFINITION, CONTEXT, SYNONYMS |
|------|-------------------------------|
| **SUBDUE** | to bring under control; to decrease the intensity of (as in the adjective *subdued*)<br><br>*The king's army attempted to* subdue *the rebellious peasants, who were threatening to storm the castle.*<br><br>Synonyms: **control, vanquish, suppress, repress, master, overcome, tame** |
| **SUCCEED** | (1) to follow, come after<br><br>*George Bush* succeeded *Ronald Reagan as president.*<br><br>Synonyms: **follow, replace**<br><br>(2) to prosper, do well<br><br>*Valerie was resolved to* succeed *in her new school.*<br><br>Synonyms: **flourish, thrive** |
| **SUCCUMB** | to give in, to submit<br><br>*Don't* succumb *to temptation.*<br><br>Synonyms: **yield, surrender, give in, submit, die, expire** |
| **SUFFICE** | to be adequate or enough<br><br>*"A light dinner should* suffice *the average person," said the thin man, eating his lettuce sandwich.*<br><br>Synonyms: **satisfy** |
| **SUMMIT** | highest level or point<br><br>*The first people to reach the* summit *of Mount Everest were Tenzing Norgay and Edmund Hillary.*<br><br>Synonyms: **apex, peak, top, pinnacle** |
| **SUPERB** | wonderful, superior, excellent<br><br>*The main course was merely adequate, but the dessert was* superb.<br><br>Synonyms: **splendid, magnificent, grand** |
| **SUPPRESS** | crush, hold in, hide<br><br>*The students could hardly* suppress *their excitement on the last day of school.*<br><br>Synonyms: **quell, contain** |
| **SURFEIT** | overly abundant supply, an excess<br><br>*There certainly is no* surfeit *of gasoline this year.*<br><br>Synonyms: **excess, glut, overabundance** |

| WORD | DEFINITION, CONTEXT, SYNONYMS |
|---|---|
| **SURMISE** | (v) to guess, to infer<br><br>*From his torn pants and bloody nose I* surmised *that he had been in a fight.*<br><br>Synonyms: **guess, conjecture, speculate, hypothesize, infer**<br><br>(n) instance of surmising<br><br>*My* surmise *was correct; he had been in a fight.* |
| **SURROGATE** | person or thing substituted for another<br><br>*When I was ill, my friend agreed to act as my* surrogate *and give my speech for me.*<br><br>Synonyms: **proxy, substitute, alternate** |
| **SUSCEPTIBLE** | vulnerable, liable to be affected by something<br><br>*Because of her weakened state, Valerie was* susceptible *to infection.*<br><br>Synonyms: **vulnerable, open, exposed** |
| **SUSPENSE** | fear or anticipation of waiting for something; something having to do with fear or mystery, as in a suspense novel<br><br>*Joe was in an agony of* suspense *waiting to find out if he'd gotten the lead part in the school play.*<br><br>Synonyms: **apprehension, anxiety** |
| **SYNOPSIS** | short summary, outline<br><br>*Oren wrote a 1-page* synopsis *of a 55-page book.*<br><br>Synonyms: **summary, outline** |
| **TACITURN** | quiet, tending not to speak<br><br>*Lyle is a* taciturn *boy who plays by himself and rarely says a word.*<br><br>Synonyms: **quiet, shy, reserved, guarded** |
| **TACTFUL** | acting with sensitivity to others' feelings<br><br>*I sent Eva to explain our sudden departure to our rude hosts, for she is the most* tactful *person I know.*<br><br>Synonyms: **diplomatic, discreet, judicious, sensitive, considerate, thoughtful, politic, delicate** |
| **TAINT** | to poison, as a drink; to corrupt, as a person<br><br>*"I have* tainted *the princess's wine with a potion that will age her horribly in a few short weeks!" the witch proclaimed gleefully.*<br><br>Synonyms: **poison, contaminate, infect, spoil; corrupt, debase, pervert, stain, blemish** |

| WORD | DEFINITION, CONTEXT, SYNONYMS |
|---|---|
| TAMPER | bother, interfere, meddle<br><br>*Dan tampered* with the thermostat and raised the temperature in the room to 85 degrees<br><br>Synonyms: **tinker, manipulate** |
| TANGIBLE | can be felt by touching; having actual substance<br><br>*The storming of the castle didn't bring the soldiers* tangible *rewards, but it brought them great honor. They would have preferred the rewards.*<br><br>Synonyms: **material, real, touchable, palpable, concrete, perceptible** |
| TAUT | stretched tightly; tense<br><br>*The tightrope was* taut.<br><br>Synonyms: **tight, stretched, tense, strained** |
| TEMPERATE | (1) denying oneself too much pleasure; avoiding extreme positions, moderate, sensible<br><br>*Lloyd is the most* temperate *student I have ever met; even on Friday nights he goes to bed early.*<br><br>Synonyms: **self-denying, sensible, level-headed, rational**<br><br>(2) a mild climate<br><br>*The* temperate *weather of California is a welcome change from the harsh winters and muggy summers or New York City.*<br><br>Synonyms: **mild, moderate** |
| TENACIOUS | steadily pursuing a goal, unwilling to give up; stubborn<br><br>*For years, against all odds, women* tenaciously *fought for the right to vote.*<br><br>Synonyms: **persistent, persevering, untiring, tireless** |
| TEPID | (1) neither hot nor cold; lukewarm<br><br>*Roxanne refused to take a bath in the* tepid *water, fearing that she would catch a cold.*<br><br>Synonyms: **lukewarm, mild, temperate**<br><br>(2) lacking character or spirit, bland<br><br>*Neither liking nor disliking Finnegan's film, the critics gave it* tepid *reviews.*<br><br>Synonyms: **unenthusiastic, halfhearted, indifferent** |
| TERMINATE | to stop, end<br><br>*Amy and Zoe* terminated *their friendship and never spoke to each other again.*<br><br>Synonyms: **cease, finish, conclude** |

| WORD | DEFINITION, CONTEXT, SYNONYMS |
|---|---|
| TERSE | concise, brief, using few words<br><br>*Kate was noted for her* terse *replies, rarely going beyond "yes" or "no."*<br><br>Synonyms: **concise, succinct, compact** |
| TETHER | (n) chain or rope tied to an animal to keep it within specific bounds<br><br>*The cheetah chewed through its* tether *and wandered off.*<br><br>Synonyms: **rope, chain**<br><br>(v) to fasten or confine<br><br>*I have to* tether *my dog to the fence to keep it out of the neighbor's yard.*<br><br>Synonyms: **tie, fasten** |
| TOKEN | (n) sign or symbol<br><br>*I offered him a chocolate bar as a* token *of my gratitude for his help.*<br><br>Synonyms: **symbol, expression, representation**<br><br>(adj) existing in name or appearance only, without depth, or significance<br><br>*He offered me a* token *handshake, but I knew that we were in fact still enemies.*<br><br>Synonyms: **nominal, superficial, meaningless** |
| TORRID | extremely hot, scorching<br><br>*The* torrid *weather destroyed the crops.*<br><br>Synonyms: **hot, parched, sizzling** |
| TREPIDATION | fear, apprehension<br><br>*Mike approached the door of the principal's office with* trepidation.<br><br>Synonyms: **fright, anxiety, trembling, hesitation** |
| TRITE | lacking originality, inspiration, and interest<br><br>*Lindsay's graduation speech was the same* trite *nonsense we've heard a hundred times in the past.*<br><br>Synonyms: **tired, banal, unoriginal, common, stale, stock** |
| TUMULT | noise and confusion<br><br>*The* tumult *of the "no nukes" demonstrators drowned out the president's speech.*<br><br>Synonyms: **racket, disorder** |
| TYRANNY | harsh exercise of absolute power<br><br>*The students accused Ms. Morgenstern of* tyranny *when she assigned them seats instead of letting them choose their own.*<br><br>Synonyms: **oppression, repression** |

| WORD | DEFINITION, CONTEXT, SYNONYMS |
| --- | --- |
| ULTIMATE | marking the highest point; cannot be improved upon; final<br>*The new fashions from Paris are the* ultimate *in chic.*<br>Synonyms: **maximum, remotest, final, conclusive, last, elemental, primary, fundamental** |
| UNANIMOUS | approved by everyone concerned<br>*The student council voted* unanimously; *not one person opposed the plan.*<br>Synonyms: **unchallenged, uncontested, unopposed, united, harmonious** |
| UNKEMPT | messy, sloppily maintained<br>*Sam's long hair and wrinkled shirt seemed* unkempt *to his grandmother; she told him he looked like a bum.*<br>Synonyms: **sloppy, slovenly, ruffled, disheveled, messy, untidy, ragged** |
| UNUSUAL | not habitually occurring<br>*The sky was* unusually *orange during the beautiful sunset.*<br>Synonyms: **rare, uncommon, atypical** |
| USURP | to seize, take by force (most often used of abstract nouns like "power" rather than concrete nouns like "bathrobe").<br>*The vice principal was power hungry and tended to* usurp *the principal's power.*<br>Synonyms: **seize, grab, steal, snatch** |
| VACATE | leave<br>*The police ordered the demonstrators to* vacate *the park.*<br>Synonyms: **depart, go** |
| VACUOUS | silly, empty-headed, not serious<br>*The book that Victor loved when he was six struck him as utterly* vacuous *when he was twenty. But he still liked the pictures.*<br>Synonyms: **shallow, vapid** |
| VAGUE | not clear or certain<br>*It took us a while to find John's house because the directions were* vague.<br>Synonyms: **nebulous, imprecise** |
| VEHEMENT | with deep feeling<br>*Susanne responded to the accusation of cheating with a* vehement *denial.*<br>Synonyms: **passionate, earnest, fervent** |

| WORD | DEFINITION, CONTEXT, SYNONYMS |
|---|---|
| VEND | to sell goods<br><br>*Every Saturday in the summer, crafts people* vend *their products in the park.*<br><br>Synonyms: **sell, peddle, merchandise** |
| VEX | to irritate to a great degree, to annoy<br><br>*Your constant sniveling is beginning to* vex *me.*<br><br>Synonyms: **tease, irritate, provoke, torment, pester, harass, bother, annoy** |
| VITALIZE | make something come alive<br><br>*The government's flagrant acts of injustice* vitalized *the opposition.*<br><br>Synonyms: **animate, vivify** |
| VIVACIOUS | lively, full of spirit<br><br>*Quiet and withdrawn at first, Joan became increasingly* vivacious.<br><br>Synonyms: **animated, sprightly, spirited** |
| WAN | unnaturally pale, lacking color<br><br>*The sick child had a* wan *face.*<br><br>Synonyms: **pale, ashen, bloodless** |
| WANTONLY | without a reason<br><br>*Instead of singling out appropriate targets for his anger, the crazed robot struck out* wantonly.<br><br>Synonyms: **randomly, indiscriminately** |
| WRATH | extreme anger<br><br>*He denounced the criminals in a speech filled with righteous* wrath.<br><br>Synonyms: **ire, fury, rage** |
| WRETCHED | miserable, pathetic<br><br>*Steve felt* wretched *when he failed the test.*<br><br>Synonyms: **dejected, woebegone, forlorn** |
| WRITHE | to squirm or twist as if in pain<br><br>*After the being hit by a car, the pedestrian was* writhing *in pain.*<br><br>Synonyms: **squirm, twitch, twist** |
| ZEALOUS | enthusiastic, eager<br><br>*Serge was a* zealous *supporter of the cause and never missed a rally.*<br><br>Synonyms: **fervent, fervid, intense, passionate** |

# CHAPTER 25: 100 ESSENTIAL MATH CONCEPTS

The math on the SSAT and ISEE covers a lot of ground—from arithmetic to algebra to geometry.

Don't let yourself be intimidated. We've highlighted the 100 most important concepts that you'll need and listed them in this chapter.

Use this list to remind yourself of the key concepts you'll need to know. Do four concepts a day, and you'll be ready within a month. If a concept continually causes you trouble, circle it and refer back to it as you try to do the questions.

You've probably been taught most of these concepts in school already, so this list is a great way to refresh your memory.

## NUMBER PROPERTIES

### 1. Number Categories Signed

**Integers** are whole numbers; they include positive and negative numbers and zero, but not fractions or decimals.

A **rational number** is a number that can be expressed as a **ratio of two integers. Irrational numbers** are real numbers—they have locations on the number line—but they **can't be expressed precisely as a fraction or decimal.** For the purposes of the SSAT and ISEE, the most important **irrational numbers** are $\sqrt{2}$, $\sqrt{3}$, and $\pi$.

### 2. Adding/Subtracting Signed Numbers

To **add a positive and a negative,** first ignore the signs and find the positive difference between the number parts. Then attach the sign of the original number with the larger number part. For example, to add 23 and −34, first ignore the minus sign and find the positive difference between 23 and 34—that's 11. Then attach the sign of the number with the larger number part—in this case it's the minus sign from the −34. So, 23 + (−34) = −11.

Make **subtraction** situations simpler by turning them into addition. For example, you can think of $-17 - (-21)$ as $-17 + (+21)$.

To **add or subtract a string of positives and negatives,** first turn everything into addition. Then combine the positives and negatives so that the string is reduced to the sum of a single positive number and a single negative number.

### 3. Multiplying/Dividing Signed Numbers

To multiply and/or divide positives and negatives, treat the number parts as usual and **attach a minus sign if there were originally an odd number of negatives.** For example, to multiply $-2$, $-3$, and $-5$, first multiply the number parts: $2 \times 3 \times 5 = 30$. Then go back and note that there were **three**—an **odd** number—negatives, so the product is negative: $(-2) \times (-3) \times (-5) = -30$.

### 4. PEMDAS

When performing multiple operations, remember to perform them in the right order: **PEMDAS,** which means **Parentheses** first, then **Exponents,** then **Multiplication** and **Division** (left to right), and lastly **Addition** and **Subtraction** (left to right). In the expression $9 - 2 \times (5 - 3)^2 + 6 \div 3$, begin with the parentheses: $(5 - 3) = 2$. Then do the exponent: $2^2 = 4$. Now the expression is: $9 - 2 \times 4 + 6 \div 3$. Next do the multiplication and division to get: $9 - 8 + 2$, which equals 3. If you have difficulty remembering PEMDAS, use this sentence to recall it: **P**lease **E**xcuse **M**y **D**ear **A**unt **S**ally.

### 5. Counting Consecutive Integers

To count consecutive integers, **subtract the smallest from the largest and add 1.** To count the number of integers from 13 through 31, subtract: $31 - 13 = 18$. Then add 1: $18 + 1 = 19$.

## NUMBER OPERATIONS AND CONCEPTS

### 6. Exponential Growth

If $r$ is the ratio between consecutive terms, $a_1$ is the first term, $a_n$ is the $n$th term, and $S_n$ is the sum of the first $n$ terms, then $a_n = a_1 r^{n-1}$ and $S_n \dfrac{a_1 - a_1 r^n}{1 - r}$.

### 7. Union and Intersection of Sets

The things in a set are called elements or members. The union of Set $A$ and Set $B$, sometimes expressed as $A \cup B$, is the set of elements that are in either or both of Set $A$ and Set $B$. If Set $A = \{1, 2\}$ and Set $B = \{3, 4\}$, then $A \cup B = \{1, 2, 3, 4\}$. The intersection of Set $A$ and Set $B$, sometimes expressed as $A \cap B$, is the set of elements common to both Set $A$ and Set $B$. If Set $A = \{1, 2, 3\}$ and Set $B = \{3, 4, 5\}$, then $A \cap B = \{3\}$.

# DIVISIBILITY

### 8. Factor/Multiple

The **factors** of integer $n$ are the positive integers that divide into $n$ with no remainder. The **multiples** of $n$ are the integers that $n$ divides into with no remainder. For example, 6 is a factor of 12, and 24 is a multiple of 12. Therefore, 12 is both a factor and a multiple of itself, since $12 \times 1 = 12$ and $12 \div 1 = 12$.

### 9. Prime Factorization

To find the prime factorization of an integer, continue factoring until **all the factors are prime.** For example, to factor 36: $36 = 4 \times 9 = 2 \times 2 \times 3 \times 3$.

### 10. Relative Primes

Relative primes are integers that have no common factor other than 1. To determine whether two integers are relative primes, break them both down to their prime factorizations. For example: $35 = 5 \times 7$ and $54 = 2 \times 3 \times 3 \times 3$. They have **no prime factors in common,** so 35 and 54 are relative primes.

### 11. Common Multiple

A common multiple is a number that is a multiple of two or more integers. You can always get a common multiple of two integers by **multiplying** them, but unless the two numbers are relative primes, the product will not be the *least* common multiple. For example, to find a common multiple for 12 and 15, you could just multiply: $12 \times 15 = 180$.

To find the **least common multiple (LCM),** check out the **multiples of the larger integer** until you find one that's **also a multiple of the smaller.** To find the LCM of 12 and 15, begin by taking the multiples of 15: 15 is not divisible by 12, nor are 30 or 45. But the next multiple of 15, 60, *is* divisible by 12, so it's the LCM.

### 12. Greatest Common Factor (GCF)

To find the greatest common factor, break down the integers into their prime factorizations and multiply **all the prime factors they have in common.** For example, $36 = 2 \times 2 \times 3 \times 3$ and $48 = 2 \times 2 \times 2 \times 2 \times 3$. These integers have a $2 \times 2$ and a 3 in common, so the GCF is $2 \times 2 \times 3 = 12$.

### 13. Even/Odd

To predict whether a sum, difference, or product will be even or odd, just **take simple numbers such as 1 and 2 and see what happens.** There are rules—"odd times even is even," for example—but there's no need to memorize them. What happens with one set of numbers generally happens with all similar sets.

### 14. Multiples of 2, 4, and 8

An integer is divisible by 2 (even) if the **last digit is even.** An integer is divisible by 4 if the **last two digits form a multiple of 4.** An integer is divisible by 8 if the **last three digits form a multiple of 8.** The last digit of 562 is 2, which is even, so 562 is a multiple of 2. The last two digits form 62, which is *not* divisible by 4, so 562 is not a multiple of 4. The integer 512, however, is divisible by 4 because the last two digits form 12, which is a multiple of 4. The integer 1,136 is divisible by 8 because the last 3 digits form 136, which is $8 \times 17$.

### 15. Multiples of 3 and 9

An integer is divisible by 3 if the **sum of its digits is divisible by 3.** An integer is divisible by 9 if the **sum of its digits is divisible by 9.** The sum of the digits in 957 is 21, which is divisible by 3 but not by 9, so 957 is divisible by 3 but not by 9.

### 16. Multiples of 5 and 10

An integer is divisible by 5 if the **last digit is 5 or 0.** An integer is divisible by 10 if the **last digit is 0.** The last digit of 665 is 5, so 665 is a multiple of 5 but *not* a multiple of 10.

### 17. Remainders

The remainder is the **whole number left over after division.** For example, 487 is 2 more than 485, which is a multiple of 5, so when 487 is divided by 5, the remainder is 2.

## FRACTIONS AND DECIMALS

### 18. Reducing Fractions

To reduce a fraction to lowest terms, **factor out and cancel** all factors the numerator and denominator have in common.

$$\frac{28}{36} = \frac{4 \times 7}{4 \times 9} = \frac{7}{9}$$

### 19. Adding/Subtracting Fractions

To add or subtract fractions, first find a **common denominator,** then add or subtract the numerators.

$$\frac{2}{15} + \frac{3}{10} = \frac{4}{30} + \frac{9}{30} = \frac{4+9}{30} = \frac{13}{30}$$

### 20. Multiplying Fractions

To multiply fractions, **multiply** the numerators and **multiply** the denominators.

$$\frac{5}{7} \times \frac{3}{4} = \frac{5 \times 3}{7 \times 4} = \frac{15}{28}$$

### 21. Dividing Fractions

To divide fractions, **invert** the second one and **multiply.**

$$\frac{1}{2} \div \frac{3}{5} = \frac{1}{2} \times \frac{5}{3} = \frac{1 \times 5}{2 \times 3} = \frac{5}{6}$$

### 22. Mixed Numbers and Improper Fractions

To convert a mixed number to an improper fraction, **multiply** the whole number part by the denominator, then **add** the numerator. The result is the new numerator (over the same denominator). To convert $7\frac{1}{3}$, first multiply 7 by 3, then add 1, to get the new numerator of 22. Put that over the same denominator, 3, to get $\frac{22}{3}$.

To convert an improper fraction to a mixed number, divide the denominator into the numerator to get a **whole number quotient with a remainder.** The quotient becomes the whole number part of the mixed number, and the remainder becomes the new numerator—with the same denominator. For example, to convert $\frac{108}{5}$, first divide 5 into 108, which yields 21 with a remainder of 3. Therefore, $\frac{108}{5} = 21\frac{3}{5}$.

### 23. Reciprocal

To find the reciprocal of a fraction, **switch the numerator and the denominator.** The reciprocal of $\frac{3}{7}$ is $\frac{7}{3}$. The reciprocal of 5 is $\frac{1}{5}$. The product of reciprocals is 1.

### 24. Comparing Fractions

One way to compare fractions is to **reexpress them with a common denominator.** For example, $\frac{3}{4} = \frac{21}{28}$ and $\frac{5}{7} = \frac{20}{28}$. Now, $\frac{21}{28}$ is greater than $\frac{20}{28}$, so $\frac{3}{4}$ is greater than $\frac{5}{7}$. Another method is to **convert them both to decimals.** For example, $\frac{3}{4}$ converts to 0.75 , and $\frac{5}{7}$ converts to approximately 0.714.

### 25. Converting Fractions and Decimals

To convert a fraction to a decimal, **divide the bottom into the top.** To convert $\frac{5}{8}$, divide 8 into 5, yielding 0.625.

To convert a decimal to a fraction, set the decimal over 1 and **multiply the numerator and denominator by 10** raised to the number of digits which are to the right of the decimal point.

To convert 0.625 to a fraction, you would multiply $\frac{0.625}{1}$ by $\frac{10^3}{10^3}$ or $\frac{1,000}{1,000}$.

Then simplify: $\frac{625}{100} = \frac{5 \times 125}{8 \times 125} = \frac{5}{8}$.

## 26. Repeating Decimal

To find a particular digit in a repeating decimal, note the **number of digits in the cluster that repeats.** If there are 2 digits in that cluster, then every second digit is the same. If there are 3 digits in that cluster, then every third digit is the same. And so on.

For example, the decimal equivalent of $\frac{1}{27}$ is 0.037037037..., which is best written $0.\overline{037}$. There are 3 digits in the repeating cluster, so every 3rd digit is the same: 7. To find the 50th digit, look for the multiple of 3 just less than 50—that's 48. The 48th digit is 7, and with the 49th digit the pattern repeats with 0. The 50th digit is 3.

## 27. Identifying the Parts and the Whole

The key to solving most fraction and percent word problems is to identify the part and the whole. Usually you'll find the **part** associated with the verb *is/are* and the **whole** associated with the word *of.* In the sentence, "Half of the boys are blonds," the whole is the boys (*of* the boys), and the part is the blonds (*are* blonds).

# PERCENTS

## 28. Percent Formula

Whether you need to find the part, the whole, or the percent, use the same formula:

$$\textbf{Part} = \textbf{Percent} \times \textbf{Whole}$$

**Example:**  What is 12 percent of 25?
**Setup:**   Part $= 0.12 \times 25$

**Example:**  15 is 3 percent of what number?
**Setup:**   $15 = 0.03 \times$ Whole

**Example:**  45 is what percent of 9?
**Setup:**   $45 =$ Percent $\times 9$

## 29. Percent Increase and Decrease

To increase a number by a percent, **add the percent to 100 percent,** convert to a decimal, and multiply. To increase 40 by 25 percent, add 25 percent to 100 percent, convert 125 percent to 1.25, and multiply by 40:

$$1.25 \times 40 = 50$$

## 30. Finding the Original Whole

To find the **original whole before a percent increase or decrease,** set up an equation. Think of the result of a 15 percent increase over $x$ as $1.15x$.

**Example:**    After a 5 percent increase, the population was 59,346. What was the population before the increase?

**Setup:**    $1.05x = 59,346$

### 31.  Combined Percent Increase and Decrease

To determine the combined effect of multiple percent increases and/or decreases, **start with 100 and see what happens.**

**Example:**    A price went up 10 percent one year, and the new price went up 20 percent the next year. What was the combined percent increase?

**Setup:**    First year: 100 + (10 percent of 100) = 110. Second year: 110 + (20 percent of 110) = 132. That's a combined 32 percent increase.

## AVERAGES

### 32.  Average Formula

To find the average of a set of numbers, **add them and divide by the number of numbers.**

$$\text{Average} = \frac{\textbf{Sum of the terms}}{\textbf{Number of terms}}$$

To find the average of the five numbers 12, 15, 23, 40, and 40, first add them: 12 + 15 + 23 + 40 + 40 = 130. Then divide the sum by 5: 130 ÷ 5 = 26.

### 33.  Average of Evenly Spaced Numbers

To find the average of evenly spaced numbers, just **average the smallest and the largest.** The average of all the integers from 13 through 77 is the same as the average of 13 and 77:

$$\frac{13 + 77}{2} = \frac{90}{2} = 45$$

### 34.  Using the Average to Find the Sum

$$\textbf{Sum = (Average) × (Number of terms)}$$

If the average of ten numbers is 50, then they add up to $10 \times 50$, or 500.

### 35.  Finding the Missing Number

To find a missing number when you're given the average, **use the sum.** If the average of four numbers is 7, then the sum of those four numbers is $4 \times 7$, or 28. Suppose that three of the numbers are 3, 5, and 8. These three numbers add up to 16 of that 28, which leaves 12 for the fourth number.

### 36. Median and Mode

The median of a set of numbers is the **value that falls in the middle of the ordered set.** If you have five test scores, and they are 88, 86, 57, 94, and 73, you must first list the scores in increasing or decreasing order: 57, 73, 86, 88, 94.

The median is the **middle number,** or 86. If there is an even number of values in a set (six test scores, for instance), simply take the average of the two middle numbers.

The mode of a set of numbers is the **value that appears most often.** If your test scores were 88, 57, 68, 85, 99, 93, 93, 84, and 81, the mode of the scores would be 93 because it appears more often than any other score. If there is a tie for the most common value in a set, the set has more than one mode.

## RATIOS, PROPORTIONS, AND RATES

### 37. Setting Up a Ratio

To find a ratio, put the number associated with the word *of* **on top** and the quantity associated with the word *to* **on the bottom** and reduce. The ratio of 20 oranges to 12 apples is $\frac{20}{12}$, which reduces to $\frac{5}{3}$.

### 38. Part-to-Part Ratios and Part-to-Whole Ratios

If the parts add up to the whole, a part-to-part ratio can be turned into two part-to-whole ratios by putting **each number in the original ratio over the sum of the numbers.** If the ratio of males to females is 1 to 2, then the males-to-people ratio is $\frac{1}{1+2} = \frac{1}{3}$ and the females-to-people ratio is $\frac{2}{1+2} = \frac{2}{3}$. In other words, $\frac{2}{3}$ of all the people are female.

### 39. Solving a Proportion

To solve a proportion, **cross-multiply:**

$$\frac{x}{5} = \frac{3}{4}$$
$$4x = 3 \times 5$$
$$x = \frac{15}{4} = 3.75$$

### 40. Rate

To solve a rate problem, **use the units** to keep things straight.

**Example:** If snow is falling at the rate of one foot every four hours, how many inches of snow will fall in seven hours?

**Setup:**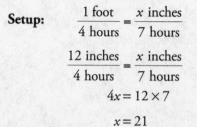

$$\frac{1 \text{ foot}}{4 \text{ hours}} = \frac{x \text{ inches}}{7 \text{ hours}}$$

$$\frac{12 \text{ inches}}{4 \text{ hours}} = \frac{x \text{ inches}}{7 \text{ hours}}$$

$$4x = 12 \times 7$$

$$x = 21$$

### 41. Average Rate

Average rate is *not* simply the average of the rates.

$$\text{Average } A \text{ per } B = \frac{\text{Total } A}{\text{Total } B}$$

$$\text{Average speed} = \frac{\text{Total distance}}{\text{Total time}}$$

To find the average speed for 120 miles at 40 mph and 120 miles at 60 mph, **don't just average the two speeds.** First figure out the total distance and the total time. The total distance is 120 + 120 = 240 miles. The times are three hours for the first leg and two hours for the second leg, or five hours total. The average speed, then, is $\frac{240}{5} = 48$ miles per hour.

## POSSIBILITIES AND PROBABILITY

### 42. Counting the Possibilities

The fundamental counting principle: if there are **m ways** one event can happen and **n ways** a second event can happen, then there are **m × n ways** for the two events to happen. For example, with five shirts and seven pairs of pants to choose from, you can have $5 \times 7 = 35$ different outfits.

### 43. Probability

$$\text{Probability} = \frac{\textbf{Favorable outcomes}}{\textbf{Total possible outcomes}}$$

For example, if you have 12 shirts in a drawer and 9 of them are white, the probability of picking a white shirt at random is $\frac{9}{12} = \frac{3}{4}$. This probability can also be expressed as 0.75 or 75%.

## POWERS AND ROOTS

### 44. Multiplying and Dividing Powers

To multiply powers with the same base, **add the exponents and keep the same base:**

$$x^3 \times x^4 = x^{3+4} = x^7$$

To divide powers with the same base, **subtract the exponents and keep the same base:**

$$y^{13} \div y^8 = y^{13-8} = y^5$$

### 45. Raising Powers to Powers

To raise a power to a power, **multiply the exponents:**

$$(x^3)^4 = x^{3 \times 4} = x^{12}$$

### 46. Simplifying Square Roots

To simplify a square root, **factor out the perfect squares** under the radical, unsquare them, and put the result in front.

$$\sqrt{12} = \sqrt{4 \times 3} = \sqrt{4} \times \sqrt{3} = 2\sqrt{3}$$

### 47. Adding and Subtracting Roots

You can add or subtract radical expressions **when the part under the radicals is the same:**

$$2\sqrt{3} + 3\sqrt{3} = 5\sqrt{3}$$

Don't try to add or subtract when the radical parts are different. There's not much you can do with an expression like:

$$3\sqrt{5} + 3\sqrt{7}$$

### 48. Multiplying and Dividing Roots

The product of square roots is equal to the **square root of the product:**

$$\sqrt{3} \times \sqrt{5} = \sqrt{3 \times 5} = \sqrt{15}$$

The quotient of square roots is equal to the **square root of the quotient:**

$$\frac{\sqrt{6}}{\sqrt{3}} = \sqrt{\frac{6}{3}} = \sqrt{2}$$

### 49. Negative Exponents and Rational Exponents

To find the value of a number raised to a negative exponent, simply rewrite the number, without the negative sign, as the bottom of a fraction with 1 as the numerator of the fraction: $3^{-2} = \frac{1}{3^2} = \frac{1}{9}$. If $x$ is a positive number and $a$ is a nonzero number, then $x^{\frac{1}{a}} = a\sqrt{x}$. So $4^{\frac{1}{2}} = 2\sqrt{4} = 2$. If $p$ and $q$ are integers, then $x^{\frac{p}{q}} = \sqrt[q]{x^p}$. So $4^{\frac{3}{2}} = \sqrt[2]{4^3} = \sqrt{64} = 8$.

# ABSOLUTE VALUE

### 50. Determining Absolute Value

The absolute value of a number is the distance of the number from zero on the number line. Because absolute value is a distance, it is always positive. The absolute value of 7 is 7; this is expressed $|7| = 7$. Similarly, the absolute value of $-7$ is 7: $|-7| = 7$. Every positive number is the absolute value of two numbers: itself and its negative.

# ALGEBRAIC EXPRESSIONS

### 51. Evaluating an Expression

To evaluate an algebraic expression, **plug in** the given values for the unknowns and calculate according to **PEMDAS.** To find the value of $x^2 + 5x - 6$ when $x = -2$, plug in $-2$ for $x$: $(-2)^2 + 5(-2) - 6 = -12$

### 52. Adding and Subtracting Monomials

To combine like terms, **keep the variable part unchanged while adding or subtracting the coefficients:**

$$2a + 3a = (2 + 3)a = 5a$$

### 53. Adding and Subtracting Polynomials

To add or subtract polynomials, **combine like terms:**

$$(3x^2 + 5x - 7) - (x^2 + 12) =$$
$$(3x^2 - x^2) + 5x + (-7 - 12) =$$
$$2x^2 + 5x - 19$$

### 54. Multiplying Monomials

To multiply monomials, **multiply the coefficients and the variables separately:**

$$2a \times 3a = (2 \times 3)(a \times a) = 6a^2$$

### 55. Multiplying Binomials—FOIL

To multiply binomials, use **FOIL.** To multiply $(x + 3)$ by $(x + 4)$, first multiply the **F**irst terms: $x \times x = x^2$. Next the **O**uter terms: $x \times 4 = 4x$. Then the **I**nner terms: $3 \times x = 3x$. And finally the **L**ast terms: $3 \times 4 = 12$. Then add and combine like terms:

$$x^2 + 4x + 3x + 12 = x^2 + 7x + 12$$

## 56. Multiplying Other Polynomials

FOIL works only when you want to multiply two binomials. If you want to multiply polynomials with more than two terms, make sure you **multiply each term in the first polynomial by each term in the second:**

$$(x^2 + 3x + 4)(x + 5) =$$
$$x^2(x + 5) + 3x(x + 5) + 4(x + 5) =$$
$$x^3 + 5x^2 + 3x^2 + 15x + 4x + 20 =$$
$$x^3 + 8x^2 + 19x + 20$$

After multiplying two polynomials together, the number of terms in your expression before simplifying should equal the number of terms in one polynomial multiplied by the number of terms in the second. In the example, you should have $3 \times 2 = 6$ terms in the product before you simplify like terms.

# FACTORING ALGEBRAIC EXPRESSIONS

## 57. Factoring Out a Common Divisor

A factor common to all terms of a polynomial can be **factored out.** All three terms in the polynomial $3x^3 + 12x^2 - 6x$ contain a factor of $3x$. Pulling out the common factor yields $3x(x^2 + 4x - 2)$.

## 58. Factoring the Difference of Squares

One of the test maker's favorite factorables is the **difference of squares.**

$$a^2 - b^2 = (a - b)\,(a + b)$$

$x^2 - 9$, for example, factors to $(x - 3)(x + 3)$.

## 59. Factoring the Square of a Binomial

Recognize polynomials that are squares of binomials:

$$a^2 + 2ab + b^2 = (a + b)^2$$
$$a^2 - 2ab + b^2 = (a - b)^2$$

For example, $4x^2 + 12x + 9$ factors to $(2x + 3)^2$, and $n^2 - 10n + 25$ factors to $(n - 5)^2$.

## 60. Factoring Other Polynomials—FOIL in Reverse

To factor a quadratic expression, **think about what binomials you could use FOIL on to get that quadratic expression.** To factor $x^2 - 5x + 6$, think about what First terms will produce $x^2$, what Last terms will produce $+6$, and what Outer and Inner terms will produce $-5x$. Some common sense—and a little trial and error—lead you to $(x - 2)(x - 3)$.

### 61. Simplifying an Algebraic Fraction

Simplifying an algebraic fraction is a lot like simplifying a numerical fraction. The general idea is to **find factors common to the numerator and denominator and cancel them.** Thus, simplifying an algebraic fraction begins with factoring.

For example, to simplify $\dfrac{x^2 - x - 12}{x^2 - 9}$, first factor the numerator and denominator:

$$\frac{x^2 - x - 12}{x^2 - 9} = \frac{(x-4)(x+3)}{(x-3)(x+3)}$$

Canceling $x + 3$ from the numerator and denominator leaves you with $\dfrac{x - 4}{x - 3}$.

## SOLVING EQUATIONS

### 62. Solving a Linear Equation

To solve an equation, do whatever is necessary to both sides to **isolate the variable.** To solve the equation $5x - 12 = -2x + 9$, first get all the $x$s on one side by adding $2x$ to both sides: $7x - 12 = 9$. Then add 12 to both sides: $7x = 21$. Then divide both sides by 7: $x = 3$.

### 63. Solving "in terms of"

To solve an equation for one variable **in terms of** another means to **isolate the one variable on one side of the equation,** leaving an expression containing the other variable on the other side of the equation. To solve the equation $3x - 10y = -5x + 6y$ for $x$ in terms of $y$, isolate $x$:

$$3x - 10y = -5x + 6y$$
$$3x + 5x = 6y + 10y$$
$$8x = 16y$$
$$x = 2y$$

### 64. Translating from English into Algebra

To translate from English into algebra, look for the key words and systematically turn phrases into algebraic expressions and sentences into equations. Be careful about order, especially with subtraction.

**Example:**    Celine and Remi play tennis. Last year, Celine won 3 more than twice the number of matches that Remi won. If Celine won 11 more matches than Remi, how many matches did Celine win?

**Setup:**    You are given two sets of information. One way to solve this is to write a system of equations—one equation for each set of information. Use variables that relate well with what they represent. For example, use $r$ to represent Remi's winning matches.

Use $c$ to represent Celine's winning matches. The phrase "Celine won 3 more than twice. . . Remi" can be written as:

$$c = 2r + 3$$

The phrase "Celine won 11 more matches than Remi" can be written as:

$$c = r + 11$$

### 65. Solving a Quadratic Equation

To solve a quadratic equation, put it in the "$ax^2 + bx + c = 0$" form, **factor** the left side (if you can), and set each factor equal to 0 separately to get the two solutions. To solve $x^2 + 12 = 7x$, first rewrite it as $x^2 - 7x + 12 = 0$. Then factor the left side:

$$(x - 3)(x - 4) = 0$$
$$x - 3 = 0 \text{ or } x - 4 = 0$$
$$x = 3 \text{ or } 4$$

### 66. Solving a System of Equations

You can solve for two variables only if you have two distinct equations. Two forms of the same equation will not be adequate. **Combine the equations** in such a way that **one of the variables cancels out.** To solve the two equations $4x + 3y = 8$ and $x + y = 3$, multiply both sides of the second equation by $-3$ to get: $-3x - 3y = -9$. Now add the two equations; the $3y$ and the $-3y$ cancel out, leaving: $x = -1$. Plug that back into either one of the original equations and you'll find that $y = 4$.

A second way to solve for two variables is to use substitution. This is especially useful if one of the variables has a coefficient of 1 or is already solved for. For example, to solve the two equations $5x + 2y = 12$ and $y = x ⊠ 1$, we can directly substitute from the second equation into the first one. This gives us $5x + 2(x ⊠ 1) = 12$, which becomes $5x + 2x ⊠ 2 = 12$. This is simplified to $7x = 14$, or $x = 2$. Now that we know $x$, we plug it back into the equations to find $y = 1$.

### 67. Solving an Inequality

To solve an inequality, do whatever is necessary to both sides to **isolate the variable.** Just remember that when you **multiply or divide both sides by a negative number,** you must **reverse the sign.** To solve $-5x + 7 < -3$, subtract 7 from both sides to get: $-5x < -10$. Now divide both sides by $-5$, remembering to reverse the sign: $x > 2$.

### 68. Radical Equations

A radical equation contains at least one radical expression. Solve radical equations by using standard rules of algebra. If $5\sqrt{x} - 2 = 13$, then $5\sqrt{x} = 15$ and $\sqrt{x} = 3$, so $x = 9$.

# FUNCTIONS

### 69. Function Notation and Evaluation

Standard function notation is written $f(x)$ and read "$f$ of 4." To evaluate the function $f(x) = 2x + 3$ for $f(4)$, replace $x$ with 4 and simplify: $f(4) = 2(4) + 3 = 11$.

### 70. Direct and Inverse Variation

In direct variation, $y = kx$, where $k$ is a nonzero constant. In direct variation, the variable $y$ changes directly as $x$ does. If a unit of Currency $A$ is worth 2 units of Currency $B$, then $A = 2B$. If the number of units of $B$ were to double, the number of units of $A$ would double, and so on for halving, tripling, etc. In inverse variation, $xy = k$, where $x$ and $y$ are variables and $k$ is a constant. A famous inverse relationship is *rate* $\times$ *time* $=$ *distance*, where distance is constant. Imagine having to cover a distance of 24 miles. If you were to travel at 12 miles per hour, you'd need two hours. But if you were to halve your rate, you would have to double your time. This is just another way of saying that rate and time vary inversely.

### 71. Domain and Range of a Function

The domain of a function is the set of values for which the function is defined. For example, the domain of $f(x) = \dfrac{1}{1 - x^2}$ is all values of $x$ except 1 and $-1$, because for those values the denominator has a value of 0 and is therefore undefined. The range of a function is the set of outputs or results of the function. For example, the range of $f(x) = x^2$ is all numbers greater than or equal to zero, because $x^2$ cannot be negative.

# COORDINATE GEOMETRY

### 72. Finding the Distance between Two Points

To find the distance between points, **use the Pythagorean theorem** or **special right triangles.** The difference between the $x$s is one leg and the difference between the $y$s is the other.

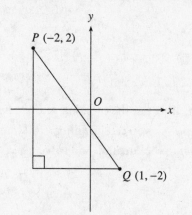

In the figure, $PQ$ is the hypotenuse of a 3-4-5 triangle, so $PQ = 5$.

You can also use the **distance formula:**

$$d = \sqrt{(x_1 - x_2)^2 + (y_1 - y_2)^2}$$

To find the distance between $R(3, 6)$ and $S(5, -2)$:

$$\begin{aligned} d &= \sqrt{(3-5)^2 + [6-(-2)]^2} \\ &= \sqrt{(-2)^2 + (8)^2} \\ &= \sqrt{68} = 2\sqrt{17} \end{aligned}$$

### 73. Using Two Points to Find the Slope

$$\text{Slope} = \frac{\text{Change in } y}{\text{Change in } x} = \frac{\text{Rise}}{\text{Run}}$$

The slope of the line that contains the points $A(2, 3)$ and $B(0, -1)$ is:

$$\frac{y_A - y_B}{x_A - x_B} = \frac{3-(-1)}{2-0} = \frac{4}{2} = 2$$

### 74. Using an Equation to Find the Slope

To find the slope of a line from an equation, put the equation into the **slope-intercept** form:

$$y = mx + b$$

The **slope is $m$.** To find the slope of the equation $3x + 2y = 4$, rearrange it:

$$3x + 2y = 4$$

$$2y = -3x + 4$$

$$y = -\frac{3}{2}x + 2$$

The slope is $-\frac{3}{2}$.

### 75. Using an Equation to Find an Intercept

To find the $y$-intercept, you can either put the equation into $y = mx + b$ (**slope-intercept**) form—in which case $b$ **is the $y$-intercept**—or you can just **plug $x = 0$** into the equation and **solve for $y$.** To find the $x$-intercept, **plug $y = 0$** into the equation and **solve for $x$.**

## LINES AND ANGLES

### 76. Intersecting Lines

When two lines intersect, **adjacent angles are supplementary and vertical angles are equal.**

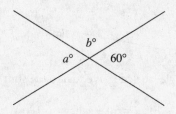

In the figure above, the angles marked $a°$ and $b°$ are adjacent and supplementary, so $a + b = 180$. Furthermore, the angles marked $a°$ and $60°$ are vertical and equal, so $a = 60$.

### 77. Parallel Lines and Transversals

A transversal across parallel lines forms **four equal acute angles and four equal obtuse angles.** If the transversal meets the lines at a right angle, then all eight angles are right angles.

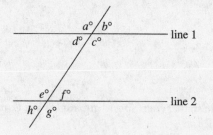

In the figure above, line 1 is parallel to line 2. Angles $a$, $c$, $e$, and $g$ are obtuse, so they are all equal. Angles $b$, $d$, $f$, and $h$ are acute, so they are all equal.

Furthermore, **any of the acute angles is supplementary to any of the obtuse angles.** Angles $a$ and $h$ are supplementary, as are $b$ and $e$; $c$ and $f$, and so on.

## TRIANGLES—GENERAL

### 78. Interior and Exterior Angles of a Triangle

The three angles of any triangle **add up to 180 degrees.**

In the figure above, $x + 50 + 100 = 180$, so $x = 30$.

An exterior angle of a triangle is equal to the **sum of the remote interior angles.**

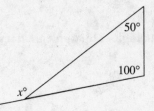

In the figure above, the exterior angle labeled $x°$ is equal to the sum of the remote angles:

$$x = 50 + 100 = 150$$

The three exterior angles of a triangle add up to 360 degrees.

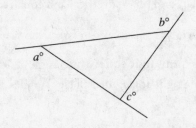

In the figure above, $a + b + c = 360$.

## 79. Similar Triangles

Similar triangles have the same shape: **corresponding angles are equal and corresponding sides are proportional.**

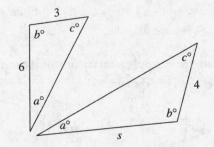

The triangles above are similar because they have the same angles. The 3 corresponds to the 4, and the 6 corresponds to the $s$.

$$\frac{3}{4} = \frac{6}{s}$$
$$3s = 24$$
$$s = 8$$

### 80. Area of a Triangle

$$\text{Area of Triangle} = \frac{1}{2}(\text{base})(\text{height})$$

The height is the perpendicular distance between the side that's chosen as the base and the opposite vertex.

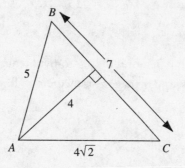

In the triangle above, 4 is the height when the 7 is chosen as the base.

$$\text{Area} = \frac{1}{2}bh = \frac{1}{2}(7)(4) = 14$$

### 81. Triangle Inequality Theorem

The length of one side of a triangle must be **greater than the difference and less than the sum** of the lengths of the other two sides. For example, if it is given that the length of one side is 3 and the length of another side is 7, then you know that the length of the third side must be greater than $7 - 3 = 4$ and less than $7 + 3 = 10$.

### 82. Isosceles and Equilateral Triangles

An isosceles triangle is a triangle that has **two equal sides.** Not only are two sides equal, but the angles opposite the equal sides, called **base angles,** are also equal.

Equilateral triangles are triangles in which **all three sides are equal.** Since all the sides are equal, all the angles are also equal. All three angles in an equilateral triangle measure 60 degrees, regardless of the lengths of sides.

# RIGHT TRIANGLES

### 83. Pythagorean Theorem

For all right triangles:

$$(\text{leg}_1)^2 + (\text{leg}_2)^2 = (\text{hypotenuse})^2$$

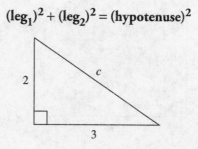

If one leg is 2 and the other leg is 3, then:

$$2^2 + 3^2 = c^2$$
$$c^2 = 4 + 9$$
$$c = \sqrt{13}$$

### 84. The 3-4-5 Triangle

If a right triangle's leg-to-leg ratio is 3:4, or if the leg-to-hypotenuse ratio is 3:5 or 4:5, it's a 3-4-5 triangle and you don't need to use the Pythagorean theorem to find the third side. Just figure out what multiple of 3-4-5 it is.

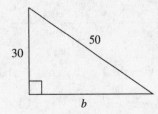

In the right triangle shown, one leg is 30 and the hypotenuse is 50. This is 10 times 3-4-5. The other leg is 40.

### 85. The 5-12-13 Triangle

If a right triangle's leg-to-leg ratio is 5:12, or if the leg-to-hypotenuse ratio is 5:13 or 12:13, then it's a 5-12-13 triangle and you don't need to use the Pythagorean theorem to find the third side. Just figure out what multiple of 5-12-13 it is.

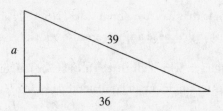

Here, one leg is 36 and the hypotenuse is 39. This is 3 times 5-12-13. The other leg is 15.

### 86. The 30-60-90 Triangle

The sides of a 30-60-90 triangle are in a ratio of $x:x\sqrt{3}:2x$. You don't need the Pythagorean theorem.

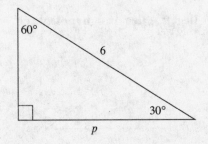

If the hypotenuse is 6, then the shorter leg is half that, or 3; and then the longer leg is equal to the short leg times $\sqrt{3}$, or $3\sqrt{3}$.

### 87. The 45-45-90 Triangle

The sides of a 45-45-90 triangle are in a ratio of $\boldsymbol{x : x : x\sqrt{2}}$.

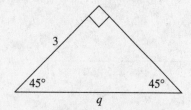

If one leg is 3, then the other leg is also 3, and the hypotenuse is equal to a leg times $\sqrt{2}$, or $3\sqrt{2}$.

# OTHER POLYGONS

### 88. Characteristics of a Rectangle

A rectangle is a **four-sided figure with four right angles.** Opposite sides are equal. Diagonals are equal.

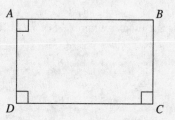

Quadrilateral *ABCD* above is shown to have three right angles. The fourth angle therefore also measures 90 degrees, and *ABCD* is a rectangle. The perimeter of a rectangle is equal to the sum of the lengths of the four sides, which is equivalent to 2(length + width).

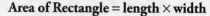

**Area of Rectangle = length × width**

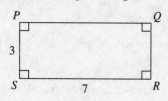

The area of a 7-by-3 rectangle is $7 \times 3 = 21$.

**89.  Characteristics of a Parallelogram**

A parallelogram has **two pairs of parallel sides.** Opposite sides are equal. Opposite angles are equal. Consecutive angles add up to 180 degrees.

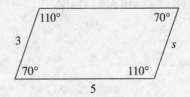

In the previous figure, $s$ is the length of the side opposite the 3, so $s = 3$.

**Area of Parallelogram = base × height**

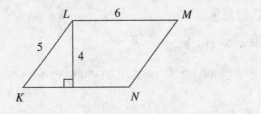

In parallelogram *KLMN* above, 4 is the height when *LM* or *KN* is used as the base. Base × height = $6 \times 4 = 24$.

**90.  Characteristics of a Square**

A square is a **rectangle with four equal sides.**

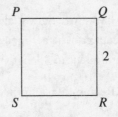

If *PQRS* is a square, all sides are the same length as *QR*. The perimeter of a square is equal to four times the length of one side.

**Area of Square = (side)$^2$**

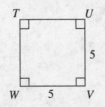

The square above, with sides of length 5, has an area of $5^2 = 25$.

### 91. Interior Angles of a Polygon

The **sum of the measures of the interior angles of a polygon** = $(n - 2) \times 180$, where $n$ is the number of sides.

$$\textbf{Sum of the Angles} = (n - 2) \times 180$$

The eight angles of an octagon, for example, add up to $(8 - 2) \times 180 = 1{,}080$.

## CIRCLES

### 92. Circumference of a Circle

$$\textbf{Circumference} = 2\pi r$$

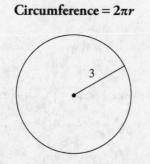

In the circle above, the radius is 3, and so the circumference is $2\pi(3) = 6\pi$.

### 93. Length of an Arc

An **arc** is a piece of the circumference. If $n$ is the degree measure of the arc's central angle, then the formula is:

$$\textbf{Length of an Arc} = \left(\frac{n}{360}\right)(2\pi r)$$

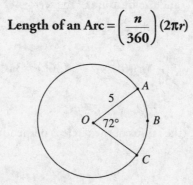

In the previous figure, the radius is 5 and the measure of the central angle is 72 degrees. The arc length is $\frac{72}{360}$ or $\frac{1}{5}$ of the circumference:

$$\frac{72}{360}\ (2\pi)(5) = \ \frac{1}{5}\ (10\pi) = 2\pi$$

### 94. Area of a Circle

**Area of a Circle = $\pi r^2$**

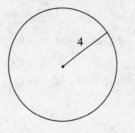

The area of the circle is $\pi(4)^2 = 16\pi$.

### 95. Area of a Sector

A **sector** is a piece of the area of a circle. If $n$ is the degree measure of the sector's central angle, then the formula is:

**Area of a Sector** $= \left(\dfrac{n}{360}\right)(\pi r^2)$

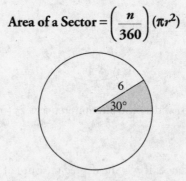

In the figure above, the radius is 6 and the measure of the sector's central angle is 30 degrees. The sector has $\dfrac{30}{360}$ or $\dfrac{1}{12}$ of the area of the circle:

$$\frac{30}{360}\,(\pi)(6^2) = \frac{1}{12}\,(36\pi) = 3\pi$$

### 96. Tangency

When a line is tangent to a circle, the radius of the circle is perpendicular to the line at the point of contact.

# SOLIDS

### 97. Surface Area of a Rectangular Solid

The surface of a rectangular solid consists of three pairs of identical faces. To find the surface area, find the area of each face and add them up. If the length is $l$, the width is $w$, and the height is $h$, the formula is:

$$\textbf{Surface Area} = 2lw + 2wh + 2lh$$

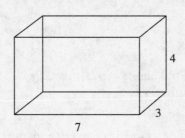

The surface area of the box above is: $2(7 \times 3) + 2(3 \times 4) + 2(7 \times 4) = 42 + 24 + 56 = 122$

### 98. Volume of a Rectangular Solid

$$\textbf{Volume of a Rectangular Solid} = lwh$$

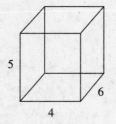

The volume of a 4-by-5-by-6 box is:

$$4 \times 5 \times 6 = 120$$

A cube is a rectangular solid with length, width, and height all equal. If $e$ is the length of an edge of a cube, the volume formula is:

$$\textbf{Volume of a Cube} = e^3$$

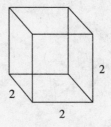

The volume of this cube is $2^3 = 8$.

### 99. Volume of a Cylinder

**Volume of a Cylinder = $\pi r^2 h$**

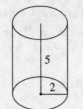

In the cylinder above, $r = 2$, $h = 5$, so:

$$\text{Volume} = \pi(2^2)(5) = 20\pi$$

### 100. Finding the Midpoint

The midpoint of two points on a line segment is the average of the $x$-coordinates of the endpoints and the average of the $y$-coordinates of the endpoints. If the endpoints are $(x_1, y_1)$ and $(x_2, y_2)$, the

midpoint is $\dfrac{x_1 + x_2}{2}, \dfrac{y_1 + y_2}{2}$ . The midpoint of (3, 5) and (9, 1) is $\dfrac{3+9}{2}, \dfrac{5+1}{2}$ .

# CHAPTER 26: WRITING SKILLS

As mentioned in Chapter 9, writing a strong, descriptive essay is a skill needed for admission to both private and boarding schools. Although your essay is not scored, it is a great way for schools to see how you express yourself.

## EXERCISE

Use the checklist that follows to evaluate the writing sample below.

> **Topic:** No good deed goes unpunished.
>
> **Assignment:** Do you agree or disagree with the topic statement? Support your position with one or two specific examples from personal experience, the experience of others, current events, history, or literature.

*People who believe this statement would apparently feel, as many people in our society seem to, that they should not help their nieghbors. Instead, they would ignore people in trouble because they would be afraid that they would get in trouble themselves. I do not agree with this belief. Many times people who do good deeds do get rewarded. Sometimes a reward of money or recognition. Even when they don't, this hardly seems like a "punishment." After all, just feeling good about something you've done can be a reward unto itself.*

*Just recently, for example, there was a story on television about a "Good Samaritan" who ran into a buring building to rescue a child. Because his bravery, the child was saved from a certain death. As a reward, this man got a lot of things. He was interviewed on the TV news, and a rich man who saw the news story gave the man a reward of $5,000. But this man had no way of knowing that any of this was going to happen when he saved the little girl, and I don't think he would have been sorry he'd done it, even if the TV news people and the rich man never heard about it. For the rest of his life, he will have the good feeling of knowing that he saved a little girl's life.*

*In conclusion, while it may be true that some deeds don't get rewarded or cause trouble for the person who did them, I think most times good deeds are rewarded, not punished. Sometimes the reward is just a good feeling for the person who did the deed, but that's enough. I also think we would have a better society if fewer people beleived in this statement that "No good deed goes unpunished."*

## Writing Sample Checklist

Does the writer answer the assignment question? ☐ Yes ☐ No

If so, where? _____

_____

Does the writing sample have an introduction? ☐ Yes ☐ No

Does the writing sample have a conclusion? ☐ Yes ☐ No

Does the writer provide a relevant example or examples? ☐ Yes ☐ No

If so, what example(s) did she provide? _____

_____

_____

Is/are the writer's example(s) well developed? ☐ Yes ☐ No

Does the writing sample have any errors? ☐ Yes ☐ No

If so, what are they? _____

_____

_____

Overall, do you think this is a good writing sample? ☐ Yes ☐ No

Why or why not? _____

_____

_____

# YOUR TURN

Use what you've learned to continue practicing writing, answering the question posed by the prompt below. Use the blank space on the next page for your plan; write your actual writing sample on the following page.

You'll have 25 minutes for SSAT; 30 minutes for ISEE; use the timing guidelines to help you budget your time.

**Directions:** Read the following topic carefully. Take a few minutes to think about the topic and organize your thoughts before you begin writing. Be sure that your handwriting is legible and that you stay within the lines and margins.

---

**Topic:** Which book do you wish you could read again and why?

**Assignment:** Support your position with one or two specific examples from personal experience, the experience of others, current events, history, or literature.

---

Use this space to plan your writing sample.

Continue to practice in this chapter by writing essays based on the following topics. Try to avoid brain freeze and remember to use the Kaplan Four-Step Method for Writing: brainstorm, make an outline, write the essay, and proofread!

**Directions:** Read the following topic carefully. Take a few minutes to think about the topic and organize your thoughts before you begin writing. Be sure that your handwriting is legible and that you stay within the lines and margins.

| |
|---|
| **Topic:** I peeked into the classroom and... |

Use this space to plan your writing sample.

Continue to practice in this chapter by writing essays based on the following topics. Try to avoid brain freeze and remember to use the Kaplan Four-Step Method for Writing: brainstorm, make an outline, write the essay, and proofread!

**Directions:** Read the following topic carefully. Take a few minutes to think about the topic and organize your thoughts before you begin writing. Be sure that your handwriting is legible and that you stay within the lines and margins.

---

**Topic:** Knowledge is power.

**Assignment:** Do you agree or disagree with the topic statement? Support your position with one or two specific examples from personal experience, the experience of others, current events, history, or literature.

---

Use this space to plan your writing sample.

Continue to practice in this chapter by writing essays based on the following topics. Try to avoid brain freeze and remember to use the Kaplan Four-Step Method for Writing: brainstorm, make an outline, write the essay, and proofread!

# PUNCTUATION REVIEW

## COMMAS

### 1. USE COMMAS TO SEPARATE ITEMS IN A SERIES

If more than two items are listed in a series, they should be separated by commas. The final comma—the one that precedes the word "and"—may be omitted. An omitted final comma would not be considered an error on the SSAT or ISEE.

>Example: My recipe for buttermilk biscuits includes flour, baking soda, salt, shortening, and buttermilk.

>ALSO RIGHT: My recipe for buttermilk biscuits includes flour, baking soda, salt, shortening and buttermilk.

Be watchful for commas placed **before** the first element of a series **or after** the last element.

>WRONG: My recipe for chocolate cake includes, flour, baking soda, sugar, eggs, milk and chocolate.

>WRONG: Flour, baking soda, sugar, eggs, milk and chocolate, are the ingredients in my chocolate cake.

### 2. USE COMMAS TO SEPARATE TWO OR MORE ADJECTIVES BEFORE A NOUN

>Example: I can't believe you sat through that long, dull movie three times in a row.

It is **incorrect** to place a comma **after** the last adjective in a series.

>WRONG: The manatee is a blubbery, bewhiskered, creature.

### 3. USE COMMAS TO SET OFF PARENTHETICAL CLAUSES AND PHRASES

If a phrase or clause is not necessary to the main idea expressed by a sentence, it should be set off by commas.

>Example: Phillip, who never had any formal chef's training, bakes excellent cheesecake.

The main idea here is that Phillip bakes an excellent cheesecake. The intervening clause merely serves to further describe Phillip; it should therefore be enclosed in commas.

### 4. USE COMMAS AFTER INTRODUCTORY PHRASES

>Example: Having watered his petunias every day during the drought, Harold was disappointed when his garden was destroyed by aphids.

>Example: After the banquet, Harold and Melissa went dancing.

### 5. USE COMMAS TO SEPARATE INDEPENDENT CLAUSES

Use a comma before a conjunction (*and, but, nor, yet,* etc.) that connects two independent clauses.

>Example: Marta is good at basketball, but she's better at soccer.

## SEMICOLONS

Like commas, semicolons can be used to separate independent clauses. As we saw above, two related independent clauses that are connected by a conjunction such as *and, but, nor,* or *yet* should be punctuated by a comma. If the words *and, but, nor,* or *yet* aren't used, the clauses should be separated by a semicolon.

Example: Whooping cranes are an endangered species; there are only 50 of them alive today.

Example: Whooping cranes are an endangered species, and they are unlikely to survive if we continue to pollute their habitat.

Semicolons may also be used between independent clauses connected by words like *therefore*, *nevertheless*, and *moreover*. For more on this topic, see the section on "Sentence Structure."

## COLONS

In Standard Written English, the colon is used only as a means of signaling that what follows is a list, definition, explanation, or restatement of what has gone before. A word or phrase such as *like the following*, *as follows*, *namely*, or *this* is often used along with the colon to make it clear that a list, summary, or explanation is coming up.

Example: This is what I found in her refrigerator: a moldy lime and a jar of peanut butter.

Example: Your instructions are as follows: Read the passage carefully, answer the questions, and turn over your answer sheet.

## THE DASH

The dash has two uses. One is to indicate an abrupt break in thought.

Example: The alligator, unlike the crocodile, will usually not attack humans—unless, that is, she feels that her young are in danger.

The dash can also be used to set off a parenthetical expression from the rest of the sentence.

Example: At 32° Fahrenheit—which is zero on the Celsius scale—water will freeze.

## THE APOSTROPHE

The apostrophe has two distinct functions. It is used with contracted verb forms to indicate that one or more letters have been eliminated:

Example: The **boy's** an expert at chess. (The boy is an expert at chess.)

Example: The **boy's** left for the day. (The boy has left for the day.)

The apostrophe is also used to indicate the possessive form of a noun.

Example: The **boy's** face was covered with mosquito bites after a day in the swamp.

# GRAMMAR REVIEW

## SUBJECT-VERB AGREEMENT

The form of a verb must match, or agree with, its subject in two ways: person and number.

### 1. AGREEMENT OF PERSON

When we talk about "person," we're talking about whether the subject and verb of a sentence show that the author is making a statement about himself (first person), the person he is speaking to (second person), or some other person, place, or thing (third person).

*First Person Subjects:* I, we.

Example: **I am** going to Paris. **We are** going to Rome.

*Second Person Subject:* you.

Example: **Are you** sure you weren't imagining that flying saucer?

*Third Person Subjects:* he, she, they, it, *and names of people, places, and things.*

Example: **He is driving** me crazy.

## 2. AGREEMENT OF NUMBER

When we talk about number, we're talking about whether the subject and verb show that one thing is being discussed (singular) or that more than one thing is being discussed (plural).

HINT: Subjects and verbs must agree in number.

WRONG: The **children catches** the school bus every morning.

RIGHT: The **children catch** the school bus every morning.

Be especially careful of subject-verb agreement when the subject and verb are separated by a long string of words.

WRONG: **Wild animals** in jungles all over the world **is endangered**.

RIGHT: **Wild animals** in jungles all over the world **are endangered**.

## PRONOUNS

A **pronoun** is a word that is used in place of a noun. The **antecedent** of a pronoun is the word to which the pronoun refers.

Example: <u>Mary</u> was late for work because <u>she</u>

    ANTECEDENT           PRONOUN

forgot to set the alarm.

Occasionally, an antecedent will appear in a sentence *after* the pronoun.

Example: Because <u>he</u> sneezes so often, <u>Arthur</u>

      PRONOUN      ANTECEDENT

always thinks <u>he</u> might have the flu.

PRONOUN

## 1. PRONOUNS AND AGREEMENT

In clear, grammatical writing, a pronoun must clearly refer to, and agree with, its antecedent.

## NUMBER AND PERSON

|  | <u>Singular</u> | <u>Plural</u> |
|---|---|---|
| **First Person** | I, me | we, us |
|  | my, mine | our, ours |
| **Second Person** | you | you |
|  | your, yours | your, yours |
| **Third Person** | he, him | they, them |
|  | she, her |  |
|  | it |  |
|  | one |  |
|  | his | their, theirs |
|  | her, hers |  |
|  | its |  |
|  | one's |  |

*Number Agreement*

Pronouns must agree in number with their antecedents. A singular pronoun should stand in for a singular antecedent. A plural pronoun should stand in for a plural antecedent.

WRONG: The bank turned Harry down when he applied for a loan because **their** credit department discovered that he didn't have a job.

What does the plural possessive *their* refer to? The singular noun *bank*. The singular possessive *its* is what we need here.

RIGHT: The bank turned Harry down for a loan because **its** credit department discovered that he didn't have a job.

*Person Agreement*

Pronouns must agree with their antecedents in person too. A first-person pronoun should stand in for a first-person antecedent, and so on. One more thing to remember about which pronoun to use with which antecedent: Never use the relative pronoun *which* to refer to a human being. Use *who* or *whom* or *that*.

WRONG: The woman **which** is standing at the piano is my sister.

RIGHT: The woman **who** is standing at the piano is my sister.

## 2. PRONOUNS AND CASE

A more subtle type of pronoun problem is one in which the pronoun is in the wrong case. Look at the following chart:

**CASE**

|  | Subjective | Objective |
| --- | --- | --- |
| **First Person** | I | me |
|  | we | us |
| **Second Person** | you | you |
| **Third Person** | he | him |
|  | she | her |
|  | it | it |
|  | they | them |
|  | one | one |
| **Relative Pronouns** | who | whom |
|  | that | that |
|  | which | which |

*When to Use Subjective Case Pronouns*

Use the subjective case for the subject of a sentence.

Example: **She** is falling asleep.

WRONG: Nancy, Claire, and **me** are going to the ballet.

RIGHT: Nancy, Claire, and **I** are going to the ballet.

Use the subjective case after a linking verb like *to be*.

Example: It is **I**.

Use the subjective case in comparisons between the subject of verbs that are not stated, but understood.

Example: Gary is taller than **they** (are).

*When to Use Objective Case Pronouns*

Use the objective case for the object of a verb.

Example: I called **her**.

Use the objective case for the object of a preposition.

Example: I laughed at **him**.

Use the objective case after infinitives and gerunds.

Example: Asking **him** to go was a big mistake.

Example: To give **him** the scare of his life, we all jumped out of his closet.

Use the objective case in comparisons between objects of verbs that are not stated but understood.

Example: She calls you more than (she calls) **me**.

### 3. WHO AND WHOM

Another thing you'll need to know is when to use the relative pronoun *who* (subjective case) and when to use the relative pronoun *whom* (objective case: *whom* goes with *him* and *them*). The following method is very helpful when you're deciding which one to use.

> Example: Sylvester, (*who* or *whom*?) is afraid of the dark, sleeps with a Donald Duck night-light on.

Look only at the relative pronoun in its clause. Ignore the rest of the sentence.

> (Who or whom?) is afraid of the dark.

Turn the clause into a question. Ask yourself:

> Who or whom is afraid of the dark?

Answer the question with an ordinary personal pronoun.

> **He** is.

If you've answered the question with a subjective case pronoun (as you have here), you need the subjective case *who* in the relative clause.

> Sylvester, **who** is afraid of the dark, sleeps with a Donald Duck night-light on.

If you answer the question with an objective case pronoun, you need the objective case *whom* in the relative clause.

> HINT: Try answering the question with *he* or *him*. *Who* goes with *he* (subjective case) and *whom* goes with *him* (objective case).

## SENTENCE STRUCTURE

A **sentence** is a group of words that can stand alone because it expresses a complete thought. To express a complete thought, it must contain a subject, about which something is said, and a verb, which says something about the subject.

> Example: Dogs bark.
>
> Example: The explorers slept in yak-hide tents.
>
> Example: Looking out of the window, John saw a flying saucer.

Every sentence consists of at least one clause. Many sentences contain more than one clause (and phrases, too).

A **clause** is a group of words that contains a subject and a verb. "Dogs bark," "The explorers slept in a yak-hide tent," and "John saw a flying saucer" are all clauses.

A **phrase** is a group of words that does not have both a subject and a verb. "Looking out of the window" is a phrase.

### 1. SENTENCE FRAGMENTS

A **sentence fragment** is a group of words that seems to be a sentence but which is *grammatically* incomplete because it lacks a subject or a verb, **or** which is *logically* incomplete because other elements necessary for it to express a complete thought are missing.

> WRONG: Eggs and fresh vegetables on sale at the farmers' market.

This is not a complete sentence because there's no verb to say something about the subject, *eggs and fresh vegetables*.

WRONG: Because Richard likes hippopotamuses.

Even though this contains a subject (Richard) and a verb (likes), it's not a complete sentence because it doesn't express a complete thought. We don't know what's true "*because* Richard likes hippopotamuses."

WRONG: Martha dreams about dinosaurs although.

This isn't a complete sentence because it doesn't express a complete thought. What makes Martha's dreaming about dinosaurs in need of qualification or explanation?

### 2. RUN-ON SENTENCES

Just as unacceptable as an incomplete sentence is a "too-complete" sentence, a run-on sentence.

A **run-on** sentence is actually two complete sentences stuck together either with just a comma or with no punctuation at all.

WRONG: The children had been playing in the park, they were covered with mud.

WRONG: The children had been playing in the park they were covered with mud.

There are a number of ways to fix this kind of problem. They all involve a punctuation mark or a connecting word that can properly connect two clauses.

Join the clauses with a semicolon.

RIGHT: The children had been playing in the park; they were covered with mud.

Join the clauses with a coordinating conjunction (*and, but, for, nor, or, so, yet*) and a comma.

RIGHT: The children had been playing in the park, and they were covered with mud.

Join the clauses with a subordinating conjunction (*after, although, if, since, while*).

RIGHT: Because the children had been playing in the park, they were covered with mud.

OR

RIGHT: The children were covered with mud because they had been playing in the park.

And, of course, the two halves of a run-on sentence can be written as two separate, complete sentences.

RIGHT: The children had been playing in the park. They were covered with mud.

## VERBS

English has six tenses, and each has a simple form and a progressive form.

|  | <u>Simple</u> | <u>Progressive</u> |
|---|---|---|
| **Present** | I work | I am working |
| **Past** | I worked | I was working |
| **Future** | I will work | I will be working |
| **Present Perfect** | I have worked | I have been working |
| **Past Perfect** | I had worked | I had been working |
| **Future Perfect** | I will have worked | I will have been working |

## 1. USING THE PRESENT TENSE

Use the present tense to describe a state or action occurring in the present time.

Example: I **am** a student.

Example: They **are studying** the Holy Roman Empire.

Use the present tense to describe habitual action.

Example: They **eat** at Joe's Diner every night.

Example: My father never **drinks** coffee.

Use the present tense to describe things that are always true.

Example: The earth **is** round.

Example: Grass **is** green.

## 2. USING THE PAST TENSE

Use the simple past tense to describe an event or state that took place at a specific time in the past and is now over and done with.

Example: Norman **broke** his toe when he tripped over his son's tricycle.

## 3. USING THE FUTURE TENSE

Use the future tense for actions expected in the future.

Example: I **will call** you on Wednesday.

We often express future actions with the expression *to be going to*.

Example: I **am going to move** to another apartment soon.

## 4. USING THE PRESENT PERFECT TENSE

Use the present perfect tense for actions and states that started in the past and continue up to and into the present time.

Example: I **have been living** here for the last two years.

Use the present perfect for actions and states that happened a number of times in the past and may happen again in the future.

Example: I **have heard** that song several times on the radio.

Use the present perfect for something that happened at an unspecified time in the past.

Example: Anna **has seen** that movie already.

## 5. USING THE PAST PERFECT TENSE

The past perfect tense is used to represent past actions or states that were completed before other past actions or states. The more recent past event is expressed in the simple past, and the earlier past event is expressed in the past perfect.

Example: When I turned my computer on this morning, I realized that I **had exited** the program yesterday without saving my work.

## 6. USING THE FUTURE PERFECT TENSE

Use the future perfect tense for a future state or event that will take place before another future event.

Example: By the end of the week, I **will have worked** four hours of overtime.

## 7. USING THE PROPER PAST PARTICIPLE FORM

If you use the present, past, or future perfect tense, make sure that you use the past participle and not the simple past tense.

> WRONG: I have **swam** in that pool every day this week.

> RIGHT: I have **swum** in that pool every day this week.

Irregular verbs have two different forms for simple past and past participle tenses. The following are some of the most common irregular verbs.

### IRREGULAR VERBS

| Infinitive | Simple Past | Past Participle |
| --- | --- | --- |
| arise | arose | arisen |
| become | became | become |
| begin | began | begun |
| blow | blew | blown |
| break | broke | broken |
| come | came | come |
| do | did | done |
| draw | drew | drawn |
| drink | drank | drunk |
| drive | drove | driven |
| eat | ate | eaten |
| fall | fell | fallen |
| fly | flew | flown |
| freeze | froze | frozen |
| give | gave | given |
| grow | grew | grown |
| know | knew | known |
| ride | rode | ridden |
| rise | rose | risen |
| run | ran | run |
| see | saw | seen |
| shake | shook | shaken |

| Infinitive | Simple Past | Past Participle |
| --- | --- | --- |
| shrink | shrank | shrunk |
| sing | sang | sung |
| speak | spoke | spoken |
| take | took | taken |
| throw | threw | thrown |

## ADJECTIVES AND ADVERBS

An **adjective** modifies, or describes, a noun or pronoun.

> Example: A woman in a **white** dress stood next to the **old** tree.

> Example: The boat, **leaky** and **dirty**, hadn't been used in years.

An adverb modifies a verb, an adjective, or another adverb. Most, but not all, adverbs end in -*ly*. (Don't forget that some **adjectives**—*friendly, lovely*—also end in -*ly*.)

> Example: The interviewer looked *approvingly* at the *neatly* dressed applicant.

## PARALLEL STRUCTURE

Matching constructions must be expressed in parallel form. Make sure that when a sentence contains a **list** or makes a **comparison**, the items being listed or compared exhibit parallel structure.

### 1. Items in a List

> WRONG: I love **skipping**, **jumping**, and **to play** tiddlywinks.

> WRONG: I love **to skip**, **jump**, and **to play** tiddlywinks.

> RIGHT: I love to **skip**, **jump**, and **play** tiddlywinks.

ALSO RIGHT: I love **to skip**, **to jump**, and **to play** tiddlywinks.

ALSO RIGHT: I love **skipping**, **jumping**, and **playing** tiddlywinks.

### 2.  *Items in a Comparison*

Comparisons must do more than just exhibit parallel structure. Most faulty comparisons relate to the notion that you can't compare apples and oranges. You don't merely want comparisons to be grammatically similar; they must be logically similar as well.

WRONG: **To visualize** success is not the same as **achieving** it.

RIGHT: **To visualize** success is not the same as **to achieve** it.

ALSO RIGHT: **Visualizing** success is not the same as **achieving** it.

WRONG: **The rules of chess** are more complex than **checkers**.

RIGHT: **The rules of chess** are more complex than **those of checkers**.

ALSO RIGHT: **Chess** is more complex than **checkers**.

# STYLE REVIEW

## PRONOUNS AND REFERENCE

When we talk about pronouns and their antecedents, we say pronouns refer to or refer back to their antecedents. We noted earlier that pronouns must agree in person and number with their antecedents. But a different kind of pronoun reference problem exists when a pronoun either doesn't refer to any antecedent at all or doesn't refer clearly to one, and only one, antecedent.

Sometimes an incorrectly used pronoun has no antecedent.

POOR: Joe doesn't like what **they play** on this radio station.

Who are *they*? We can't tell, because there is no antecedent for *they*.

RIGHT: Joe doesn't like what **the disc jockeys play** on this radio station.

Don't use pronouns without antecedents when doing so makes a sentence unclear. Sometimes a pronoun seems to have an antecedent until you look closely and see that the word that appears to be the antecedent is not a noun, but an adjective, a possessive form, or a verb. The antecedent of a pronoun must be a noun.

WRONG: When you are painting, make sure you don't get **it** on the floor.

RIGHT: When you are painting, make sure you don't get **paint** on the floor.

Other examples of pronoun reference problems:

WRONG: I've always been interested in astronomy and finally have decided to become **one**.

RIGHT: I've always been interested in astronomy and finally have decided to become an **astronomer**.

Don't use pronouns with remote references. A pronoun that is too far away from what it refers to is said to have a **remote antecedent**.

WRONG: Jane quit smoking and, as a result, temporarily put on a lot of weight. **It** was very bad for her health.

RIGHT: Jane quit smoking because **it** was very bad for her health, and, as a result, she temporarily gained a lot of weight.

Don't use pronouns with faulty broad reference. A pronoun with broad reference is one that refers to a whole idea instead of to a single noun.

WRONG: He built a fence to stop people from looking into his backyard. **That's** not easy.

RIGHT: He built a fence to stop people from looking into his backyard. **The fence was not easy to build**.

## REDUNDANCY

Words or phrases are **redundant** when they have basically the same meaning as something already stated in the sentence. Don't use two phrases when one is sufficient.

WRONG: The school was **established and founded** in 1906.

RIGHT: The school was **established** in 1906.

## RELEVANCE

Everything in the sentence should serve to get across the point in question. Something unrelated to that point should be cut.

POOR: No one can say for sure just how successful the new law will be in the fight against crime (just as no one can be sure whether he or she will ever be a victim of a crime).

BETTER: No one can say for sure just how successful the new law will be in the fight against crime.

## VERBOSITY

Sometimes having extra words in a sentence results in a style problem.

WORDY: The supply of **musical instruments that are antique** is limited, so they become more valuable each year.

BETTER: The supply of **antique musical instruments** is limited, so they become more valuable each year.

WORDY: We **were in agreement with each other** that Max was an unsuspecting old fool.

BETTER: We **agreed** that Max was an unsuspecting old fool.

## COMMONLY MISUSED WORDS

### accept/except

Don't confuse the two. To *accept* means to receive or agree to something, whereas *except* is usually a preposition meaning excluding, although it can also mean to leave out.

WRONG: Can you **except** my apology?

RIGHT: Can you **accept** my apology?

### affect/effect

These are easy to confuse. To *affect* means to have an *effect* on something. When the word is being used as a verb, the proper word to use is almost always *affect*; when it's being used as a noun, the proper word to use is almost always *effect*. (It should be noted that *effect* can also be a verb, meaning to bring about or cause to happen.)

WRONG: His affectations **effected** me to no good **affect**.

RIGHT: His affectations **affected** me to no good **effect**.

### among/between

In most cases, you should use *between* for two items and *among* for more than two.

Example: The competition **between** Anne and Michael has grown more intense.

Example: He is always at his best **among** strangers.

But use common sense. Sometimes *among* is not appropriate.

Example: Plant the trees in the area **between** the road, the wall, and the fence.

### amount/number

*Amount* should be used to refer to an uncountable quantity. *Number* should refer to a countable quantity.

Example: The **amount** of food he threw away would feed a substantial **number** of people.

### as/like

*Like* is a preposition; it takes a noun object. *As*, when functioning as a conjunction, introduces a subordinate clause. Remember, a clause is a part of a sentence containing a subject and verb.

Example: He sings **like** an angel.

Example: He sings **as** an angel sings.

### as . . . as . . .

The idiom is *as . . . as . . .* , **not** *as . . . than . . .*

WRONG: That suit is as expensive than this one.

RIGHT: That suit is as expensive as this one.

### fewer/less

Use *fewer* before a plural noun; use *less* before a singular one.

Example: There are **fewer** apples on this tree than there were last year.

Example: He makes **less** money than she does.

### neither . . . nor . . .

The correlative conjunction is *neither . . . nor . . .* , **not** *neither . . . or . . .*

Example: He is **neither** strong **nor** flexible.

Avoid the redundancy caused by using *nor* following a negative.

WRONG: Alice's departure was **not** noticed by Debby **nor** Sue.

RIGHT: Alice's departure was **not** noticed by Debby **or** Sue.

### its/it's

Many people confuse *its* and *it's*. *Its* is possessive; *it's* is a contraction of *it is* or *it has*.

Example: The cat licked **its** paws.

Example: **It's** raining cats and dogs.

### their/they're/there

Many people confuse *their*, *there*, and *they're*. *Their* is possessive; *they're* is a contraction of *they are*.

Example: The girls rode **their** bikes home.

Example: **They're** training for the big race.

*There* has two uses: It can indicate place and it can be used as an expletive—a word that doesn't do anything in a sentence except delay the subject.

Example: Put the book over **there**.

Example: **There** will be fifteen runners competing for the prize.

## IDIOMS

Some phrases are wrong simply because that's just not the way we say it in English. This is especially true of preposition-verb word combinations. For instance,

WRONG: The fashion police **frowns at** wearing hats adorned with flowers.

RIGHT: The fashion police **frowns upon** wearing hats adorned with flowers.

The first sentence is only wrong because *frowns at* is not the correct idiomatic expression. Either your ear will recognize the correct idiom or it won't.

**Idioms**

| | |
|---|---|
| associate *with* | different *from* |
| accuse *of* | discriminate *against* |
| apologize *for* | distinguish *from* |
| arrive *at* | dream *about/of* |
| believe *in* | forbid *to* |
| believe *to be* | frown *upon* |
| apologize *for* | object *to* |
| attribute *to* | prohibit *from* |
| continue *to* | substitute *for* |
| contrast *with* | target *at* |
| credit *with* | use *as* |
| decide *to* | view *as* |
| define *as* | worry *about* |